# Organizational Behavior

## TENTH EDITION

**Don Hellriegel**
Texas A & M University

**John W. Slocum, Jr.**
Southern Methodist University

THOMSON

SOUTH-WESTERN

Australia · Canada · Mexico · Singapore · Spain · United Kingdom · United States

## THOMSON
## SOUTH-WESTERN

**Organizational Behavior, 10/e**

Don Hellriegel and John W. Slocum, Jr.

**Editor-in-Chief:**
Jack W. Calhoun

**Team Director:**
Michael P. Roche

**Acquisitions Editor:**
Joseph A. Sabatino

**Developmental Editor:**
Leslie Kauffman, Litten Editing and Productions, Inc.

**Marketing Manager:**
Rob Bloom

**Production Editor:**
Margaret M. Bril

**Manufacturing Coordinator:**
Rhonda Utley

**Production House:**
Cover to Cover Publishing, Inc.

**Compositor:**
Janet Sprowls, Cover to Cover Publishing, Inc.

**Printer:**
Transcontinental Interglobe
Beauceville-Quebec,
Canada G5X 3P3

**Internal and Cover Designer:**
Michael H. Stratton

**Cover Image:**
PhotoDisc

Library of Congress Control
Number:

2002108753

ISBN: 0-324-15684-7

To Jill, Kim, and Lori (DH)

Christopher, Bradley, and Jonathan (JWS)

# Brief Contents

# CONTENTS

**Chapter 6**  **Motivating Individuals for High Performance**   **144**

## Part 3:  The Organization   317

# PREFACE

This edition, our tenth, represents a milestone. When the first edition was published in 1976, we never dreamed of a tenth edition. With each edition, we have pursued the enduring goal of presenting the fundamentals of organizational behavior along with contemporary concepts, issues, and practices in the field. A second, more specific, goal for this edition is to engage students fully as active learners; to help them develop the competencies they will need to become successful employees, professionals, managers, and/or leaders—a lifelong endeavor. A third goal is to present timely real-life examples to encourage and support student learning.

As with previous editions, achieving these goals for the tenth edition required a number of revisions. For example, in response to suggestions from users, each chapter has been carefully revised to become more focused and concise, resulting in a more learner-friendly presentation for those studying organizational behavior. Two chapters, Power and Political Behavior and Job Design, not considered to be essential in a foundation course, were dropped. For interested adopters, these two chapters are available to students on the CD-ROM that accompanies this textbook and through the authors' Web site at http://hellriegel.swlearning.com. Other revisions in this edition are noted throughout this Preface.

The effective management and leadership of organizations requires the thoughtful application of competencies related to the behavior of people at work. Few, if any, of the dramatic challenges facing organizations can be handled effectively without a good understanding of human behavior—both of oneself and others. Highly motivated and committed employees and managers are central to organizational success and effectiveness. Organizations fail or succeed, decline or prosper because of people—what people do or fail to do every day on the job. Effective organizational behavior is the bedrock on which effective organizational action rests. Long-term competitive advantage comes from the rich portfolio of individual and team-based competencies of an organization's employees, managers, and leaders.

## OUR MAP TO YOUR LEARNING

Our map to guide your active learning of the fundamental concepts of and competencies in organizational behavior is outlined in this section and revealed in greater detail in Chapter 1.

### FOUNDATION COMPETENCIES

Throughout the book, we develop seven foundation competencies that are essential to your future effectiveness as an employee, a professional, a manager, and/or a leader. In Chapter 1 we develop these seven foundation competencies in some detail, setting the stage for continuously weaving them into the various topics discussed in the book and the applications that support them. Here we briefly identify and describe them.

- The *managing self competency* involves the overall ability to assess your own strengths and weaknesses, set and pursue professional and personal goals, balance work and personal life, and engage in new learning—including new or modified knowledge, skills, behaviors, and attitudes.
- The *managing communication competency* involves the overall ability to use all the modes of transmitting, understanding, and receiving ideas, thoughts, and feelings—verbal listening, nonverbal, written, electronic, and the like—for accurately transferring and exchanging information and emotions.

- The *managing diversity competency* involves the overall ability to value unique individual and group characteristics, embrace such characteristics as potential sources of organizational strength, and appreciate the uniqueness of each individual.
- The *managing ethics competency* involves the overall ability to incorporate values and principles that distinguish right from wrong in making decisions and taking action.
- The *managing across cultures competency* involves the overall ability to recognize and embrace similarities and differences among nations and cultures and then approach relevant organizational and strategic issues with an open and curious mind.
- The *managing teams competency* involves the overall ability to develop, support, facilitate, and lead groups to achieve organizational goals.
- The *managing change competency* involves the overall ability to recognize and implement needed adaptations or entirely new transformations in people and the tasks, strategies, structures, or technologies in their areas of responsibility.

We provide a wide range of action learning opportunities for you to develop your competencies. These opportunities include self-assessment instruments, exercises, cases, and discussion questions. Self-assessment instruments provide benchmarks against which you can gauge your competencies independently and to compare your competency levels with those of other students and even practicing managers. The Professional Competencies Self-Assessment Inventory in the *Developing Competencies* section at the end of Chapter 1 is one such application. You must be able to assess accurately your levels of proficiency in each of the seven foundation competencies and then begin to develop action plans for improving your potential as an effective employee, professional, manager, and/or leader. In this book, we provide action learning features to help you in your journey.

## CHAPTER-OPENING PREVIEW CASES

Each chapter opens with a Preview Case with the focus on a person, team, or organization. Their purpose is to engage you in the focus of the chapter. Typically, they illustrate effective or ineffective applications of one or several of the foundation competencies. Within the chapter, there are references to how the Preview Case illustrates particular concepts or practices. Fifteen of the 16 Preview Cases are new to this edition.

## IN-CHAPTER COMPETENCY BOXES

Each chapter typically includes four boxed features that relate to one of the seven competencies, paralleling the chapter's themes and topics. They provide insights, examples, and applications to help you develop your competencies. For a quick insight into how these competency-based features are used, see Chapter 1. We have retained and updated some, but most of the features are new to this edition.

- *Competency: Managing Self*—Of the 11 boxed features, 10 are new to this edition. In addition, much of Chapter 2, Understanding Individual Differences, and Chapter 3, Understanding Perceptions and Attributions, are devoted to the development of this competency.
- *Competency: Managing Communication*—Of the 13 boxed features, 10 are new to this edition. In addition, Chapter 12, Fostering Interpersonal Communication, is devoted to the development of this competency.
- *Competency: Managing Diversity*—Of the 4 boxed features, 2 are new to this edition. We incorporated the diversity dimension into a number of the other boxed features, Preview Cases, and end-of-chapter Developing Competencies feature. In addition, several chapters have major sections on diversity.

- *Competency: Managing Ethics*—Of the 7 boxed features, 6 are new to this edition. In addition, several chapters have sections on ethical concepts and issues. For example, Chapter 13, Making Decisions in Organizations, stresses ethical foundations for the decision-making process.
- *Competency: Managing Across Cultures*—Of the 12 boxed features, 9 are new to this edition. In addition, across culture issues are woven into the text of several chapters. For example, Chapter 12, Fostering Interpersonal Communication, has sections on cultural barriers and cultural differences that hinder effective communication.
- *Competency: Managing Teams*—Of the 10 boxed features, 6 are new to this edition. In addition, Chapter 8, Managing Teams, is devoted to the development of this competency.
- *Competency: Managing Change*—Of the 7 boxed features, 6 are new to this edition. In addition, Chapter 16, Guiding Organizational Change, is devoted to the development of this competency.

## END-OF-CHAPTER DEVELOPING COMPETENCIES

In addition to the competency features within each chapter, we end each chapter with *Developing Competencies* exercises, questionnaires, or cases—31 in all, 14 of which are new to this edition. Those retained and revised, as appropriate, were favorites that worked well for students and faculty in the past. Thirty of the 31 exercises, questionnaires, or cases focus on a particular competency. The comprehensiveness of the Professional Competencies Self-Assessment Inventory in the *Developing Competencies* section of Chapter 1 resulted in our decision to include only this one inventory. The end-of-chapter *Developing Competencies* features provide an additional means for your active engagement in the development of your professional competencies and to deepen your understanding of the many facets of each competency.

## SELF-ASSESSMENT INSTRUMENTS

We present self-assessment instruments that typically focus on one or more of the foundation competencies throughout the book. They are aimed at helping you gain self-insights, readily learn concepts, identify issues, and effectively lead others. These instruments provide insights for further sharpening your strengths, overcoming your weaknesses, and, in general, developing your competencies in order to become more effective. Examples of these self-assessment instruments presented in each chapter and in the end-of-chapter *Developing Competencies* section include the following.

- Ethical Practices Questionnaire (Chapter 1)
- Professional Competencies Self-Assessment Inventory (Chapter 1)
- Big Five Personality Questionnaire (Chapter 2)
- Women as Managers (Chapter 3)
- What Is Your Self-Efficacy? (Chapter 4)
- What Do You Want from Your Job? (Chapter 5)
- Goal-Setting Questionnaire (Chapter 6)
- Determining Your Stress Level (Chapter 7)
- A Self-Assessment of Type A Personality (Chapter 7)
- Team Assessment (Chapter 8)
- Team Empowerment Questionnaire (Chapter 8)
- Conflict Handling Styles (Chapter 9)
- What Is Your Leadership Style? (Chapter 10)
- Transformational Leadership (Chapter 11)
- Interpersonal Communication Practices (Chapter 12)
- The Polychronic Attitude Index (Chapter 12)
- Ethical Intensity of Selected Behaviors (Chapter 13)

- Ethical Assessment of a Decision (Chapter 13)
- Inventory of Effective Design (Chapter 14)
- Assessing Ethical Behaviors in an Organization (Chapter 15)
- What Do You Value at Work? (Chapter 15)
- Are You Ready to Change? (Chapter 16)

## END-OF-CHAPTER DISCUSSION QUESTIONS

We again present *Discussion Questions*, typically 8 to 10 in number, at the end of each chapter. They are designed to prompt you to learn and relate concepts, models, and competencies to your own experiences or to the competency features presented in the chapter. Many questions also trigger self-insight and reflection, thus further promoting the learning of chapter content.

## END-OF-BOOK INTEGRATING CASES

Ten integrative cases appear at the end of the book, of which six are new to this edition. Each case requires students to develop their ability to draw from a variety of concepts presented throughout the book. We have used the cases in a variety of classroom settings and found them to challenge students understanding of the materials. The cases can be easily linked to the seven basic foundation competencies that are woven into the text throughout the book or used to assess students understanding of a specific chapter.

## ENRICHING WEB SITE

A Web site at http://hellriegel.swlearning.com complements and enriches the text, providing many extras for both you and your instructor. Resources include interactive quizzes, cases, downloadable ancillaries, and links to useful sites, online publications, and databases.

## ENRICHING CD-ROM

The CD-ROM packaged with every copy of the book provides a detailed self-assessment tool for you to use and to reuse as your competencies mature. Individual ratings can be compared with those of practicing professionals as well as with those of other students, leading to additional insights and the spurring of targeted development. Video, glossaries, and links to online resources complete this collection of technology-based tools and content.

# LEARNING FRAMEWORK

The framework for learning about organizational behavior and developing competencies is fully presented in a major section entitled *Learning Framework* in Chapter 1. Here we briefly outline this framework.

- Chapter 1 introduces and develops each of the seven foundation competencies and our learning framework.
- Part I, Individuals in Organizations, includes Chapters 2–7 and focuses on the behavior of individuals, especially in organizations.
- Part II, Team and Leadership Behaviors, includes Chapters 8–12 and focuses on how individuals, managers, and leaders influence others as well as how they can develop their competencies.
- Part III, The Organization, includes Chapters 13–16 and focuses on both internal and external factors that influence individual, team, and organizational decisions and behaviors.

Our learning framework for introducing students to organizational behavior is to move from the individual level to the team level to the organizational level. However, the chapters are written to stand alone, which allows material to be covered in any order desired by the instructor. At the end of the book, we include the usual Author Index, and Subject and Organization Index. Throughout the book, we present Internet addresses of featured organizations. By visiting these Web sites, students can develop a deeper understanding of the challenges now facing organizations in a highly competitive, global economy.

## SUPPLEMENTS

A full range of teaching and learning supplements is available for use with the tenth edition of *Organizational Behavior*.

### INSTRUCTOR'S MANUAL (ISBN 0-324-15687-1)

Written by Michael K. McCuddy of Valparaiso University, the Instructor's Manual contains comprehensive resource materials for lectures, including enrichment modules for enhancing and extending relevant chapter concepts. It presents suggested answers for all end-of-chapter discussion questions. It includes notes on using end-of-chapter *Developing Competencies* exercises, questionnaires, and cases, including suggested answers to case questions, and notes for the integrating cases. Finally, it contains a guide to the videos available for use with the text.

### TEST BANK (ISBN 0-324-15670-7)

Written by Bert Morrow of Birmingham-Southern College, the Test Bank contains almost 4,000 questions from which to choose. A selection of true/false, multiple choice, short essay, and critical-thinking essay questions are provided for each chapter. Questions are categorized by difficulty level, by learning objective, and according to Bloom's taxonomy. Cross-references to material in the textbook, where answers can be found, are also included. Explanations are provided for why statements are false in the true/false sections.

A computerized version of the Test Bank is available upon request. **Exam View® Pro (ISBN 0-324-17675-9)**, an easy-to-use test-generating program, enables instructors to quickly create printed tests, Internet tests, and online (LAN-based) tests. Instructors can enter their own questions, using the word processor provided, and customize the appearance of the tests they create. The QuickTest wizard permits test generators to use an existing bank of questions to create a test in minutes, using a step-by-step selection process.

### STUDY GUIDE (ISBN 0-324-15671-5)

Written by Roger D. Roderick of University of Arkansas-Fort Smith and Georgia M. Hale of Iowa State University, the Study Guide contains learning objectives, chapter outlines with ample room for student note taking, practice questions (both directed and applied), and answers to all practice questions.

### INFOTRAC COLLEGE EDITION

With InfoTrac College Edition, students can receive anytime, anywhere online access to a database of full-text articles from hundreds of popular and scholarly periodicals, such as *Newsweek*, *Fortune*, *Entrepreneur*, *Journal of Management*, and *Nation's Business*, among others. Students can use its fast and easy search tools to find relevant news and analytical information among the tens of thousands of articles in the database—updated daily and going back as far as 4 years—all at a single Web site. InfoTrac is a great way to expose students to online research techniques, with the security that the content is academically based and reliable. An InfoTrac College Edition subscription card is packaged free with new copies of *Organizational Behavior*, tenth edition. For more information, visit http://www.infotrac-college.com.

## VIDEOS

A video library is available to users of the tenth edition to show how real organizations and leaders deal with real organizational behavior issues. A tape of *Video Cases* (ISBN 0-324-17676-7) illustrates how various companies cope with a range of issues. A *Video Cohesion Case* is included on the CD-ROM that accompanies this book and features Horizons Companies, a provider of multimedia, video, Web development, branding, and marketing services, with three locations (Columbus, Ohio; San Diego; and Nashville) and eight divisions, including its own record label. A comprehensive video guide appears in the Instructor's Manual, with supporting case material and notes for each video segment. *CNN Video: Management and Organizations* (ISBN 0-324-13495-9) features 45 minutes of short segments from CNN, the world's first 24-hour all-news network, available on VHS cassette to use as lecture launchers, discussion starters, topical introductions, or directed inquiries.

## POWERPOINT™ PRESENTATION SLIDES (AVAILABLE ONLINE AT HTTP://HELLRIEGEL.SWLEARNING.COM)

Developed by Michael K. McCuddy, of Valparaiso University, and prepared in conjunction with the Instructor's Manual, more than 225 PowerPoint slides are available to supplement course content, adding structure and visual dimension to lectures.

## MANAGEMENT POWER! POWERPOINT SLIDES (ISBN 0-324-13380-4)

Management Power! is a CD-ROM of PowerPoint slides covering 14 major management and organizational behavior topics: communication, control, decision making, designing organizations, ethics and social responsibility, foundations of management, global management, human resources, innovation and change, leadership, motivation, planning, strategy, and teams. These easy-to-use, multimedia slides can easily be modified and customized to suit individual preferences.

## INSTRUCTOR'S RESOURCE CD-ROM (ISBN 0-324-15686-3)

Key instructor ancillaries (Instructor's Manual, Test Bank, Exam View, and PowerPoint slides) are provided on CD-ROM, giving instructors the ultimate tool for customizing lectures and presentations.

## EXPERIENCING ORGANIZATIONAL BEHAVIOR (ISBN 0-324-07352-6)

An innovative new product, *Experiencing Organizational Behavior*, is a totally online collection of Web-based modules that uses the latest Flash technology in its animated scenarios, graphs, and models. Designed to reinforce key organizational behavior principles in a dynamic learning environment, *Experiencing Organizational Behavior* maintains high motivation through the use of challenging problems. Try it by visiting http://www.experiencingob.com. *Experiencing Organizational Behavior* is available for purchase online by each individual module, or as a collection of all 13 modules.

All of these supplements are available from South-Western Publishing or from your Thomson Learning representative.

## TEXTCHOICE: MANAGEMENT EXERCISES AND CASES

TextChoice is the home of Thomson Learning's online digital content. TextChoice provides the fastest, easiest way for you to create your own learning materials. South-Western's Management Exercises and Cases database includes a variety of experiential exercises, classroom activities, management in film exercises, and cases to enhance any management course. Choose as many exercises as you like and even add your own material to create a supplement tailor fitted to your course. Contact your South-Western/Thomson Learning sales representative for more information.

## ACKNOWLEDGEMENTS

We express our sincere and grateful appreciation to the following individuals who provided thoughtful reviews and useful suggestions for improving this edition of our book. Their insights were crucial in guiding a number of the revisions.

Carole K. Barnett
*University of New Hampshire*

Steve Brown
*University of Houston*

D. Anthony Butterfield
*University of Massachusetts Amherst*

Ken Butterfield
*Washington State University*

Willam Cron
*Texas Christian University*

Ron A. DiBattista
*Bryant College*

Eric B. Dent
*University of Maryland University College*

David Elloy
*Gonzaga University*

Larry Garner
*Tarleton State University*

William Joyce
*Dartmouth College*

Dong I. Jung
*San Diego State University*

Andrew (A.J.) Lutz II
*Park University & Avila College*

Sidney A. Mohsberg, III
*The Catholic University of America*

Kevin Mossholder
*Louisiana State University-Baton Rouge*

Theodore H. Rosen
*George Washington University*

Stephen P. Schappe
*Penn State University at Harrisburg*

Ralph Sorrentino
*Deloitte Consulting*

Michael Trulson
*Amberton University*

Roger Volkema
*American University*

Edward Ward
*St. Cloud State University*

For their invaluable professional guidance and collegial support, we sincerely and deeply thank the following individuals who served on the team responsible for this edition.

- John Szilagyi, our initial editor on this edition who worked with us on formulating the revisions, and Joe Sabatino, who worked with us in the various stages of implementing the revisions.
- Leslie Kauffman, our developmental editor, who worked with us on all facets of this edition as well as providing a key interface with the authors of the various supplements.
- Jerrold Moore, our copyeditor.

- Marge Bril, our production editor.
- Billie Boyd at Southern Methodist University for her superb support with manuscript preparation.
- Argie Butler at Texas A&M University for her superb support with manuscript preparation.

Don Hellriegel expresses appreciation to his colleagues at Texas A&M University who collectively create a work environment that nurtures his continued learning and professional development. In particular, the learning environment fostered by Jerry Strawser, Dean, and Angelo DeNisi, Head of the Department of Management, is gratefully acknowledged.

John Slocum, Jr., acknowledges his SMU colleagues, Al Casey, David Lei, and Don VandeWalle, for their constructive inputs and reviews of his work. Also, special thanks are extended to Al Niemi, Dean of the Cox School of Business, who has made it fun to work hard and play hard. John also thanks his golfing group at Stonebriar Country Club (Cecil Ewell, Jon Wheeler, Joe Holmes, and Phil Ramsey) for delaying tee-times so that he could work on this project.

John and Don acknowledge the collegiality and professionalism of Dick Woodman of Texas A&M University who served as a coauthor on a number of previous editions. We respect Dick's decision not to participate in this edition due to his writing of a major book on organizational change and development.

Finally, we celebrate this tenth edition, some 27 years after publication of the first edition in 1976. We thank the many hundreds of reviewers, adopters, students, and professionals who supported the development of these 10 editions over the past three decades. Moreover, John and Don gratefully thank each other for their deep and mutual friendship that took root in a master-level industrial relations course at Kent State University in 1962. Being colleagues for more than 40 years has been very, very special to each of us.

Don Hellriegel, Texas A&M University

John W. Slocum, Jr., Southern Methodist University

# ABOUT THE AUTHORS

## DON HELLRIEGEL

Don Hellriegel is Professor of Management and holds the Bennett Chair in Business within the Lowry Mays College and Graduate School of Business at Texas A&M University. He received his B.S. and M.B.A. from Kent State University and his Ph.D. from the University of Washington. Dr. Hellriegel has been a member of the faculty at Texas since 1975 and has served on the faculties of the Pennsylvania State University and the University of Colorado.

His research interests include corporate venturing, effect of organizational environments, managerial cognitive styles, and organizational innovation and strategic management processes. His research has been published in a number of leading journals.

Professor Hellriegel served as Vice President and Program Chair of the Academy of Management (1986), President Elect (1987), President (1988), and Past President (1989). In September 1999, he was elected to a three-year term as Dean of the Fellows Group of the Academy of Management. He served a term as Editor of the *Academy of Management Review* and served as a member of the Board of Governors of the Academy of Management (1979–1981 and 1982–1989). Dr. Hellriegel has performed many other leadership roles, among which include President, Eastern Academy of Management; Division Chair, Organization and Management Theory Division; President, Brazos County United Way; Co-Consulting Editor, West Series in Management; Head (1976–1980 and 1989–1994), Department of Management (TAMU); Interim Dean, Executive Associate Dean (1995–2000), Mays School of Business (TAMU); and Interim Executive Vice Chancellor (TAMUS).

He has consulted with a variety of groups and organizations, including—among others—3DI, Sun Ship Building, Penn Mutual Life Insurance, Texas A&M University System, Ministry of Industry and Commerce (Nation of Kuwait), Ministry of Agriculture (Nation of Dominican Republic), American Assembly of Collegiate School of Business, and Texas Innovation Group.

## JOHN W. SLOCUM, JR.

John Slocum, Jr., holds the O. Paul Corley Professorship in Organizational Behavior at the Edwin L. Cox School of Business, Southern Methodist University. He has also taught on the faculties of the University of Washington, the Ohio State University, the Pennsylvania State University, the International University of Japan, and Dartmouth's Amos Tuck School. He holds a B.B.A. from Westminster College, an M.B.A. from Kent State University, and a Ph.D. in organizational behavior from the University of Washington.

Professor Slocum has held a number of positions in professional societies. He was elected as a Fellow to the Academy of Management in 1976 for his outstanding contributions to the profession of management and as a Fellow to the Decision Sciences Institute in 1984 for his research in behavioral decision theory. He was awarded the Alumni Citation for Professional Accomplishment by Westminster College and both the Nicolas Salgo and the Rotunda Outstanding Teaching Awards from SMU. He served as President of the Eastern Academy of Management in 1973. From 1975–1976, he served as a member of the Board of Governors, Academy of Management. From 1979–1981, he served as Editor of the *Academy of Management Journal*. In 1983–1984, he served as 39th President of the 8,500-member Academy and as

About the Authors

Chairman of the Board of Governors of that organization. Currently, he serves as Associate Editor of Organizational Dynamics and Co-Editor of the *Journal of World Business* and *Journal of Leadership and Organizational Studies*.

Professor Slocum has served as a consultant to such organizations as OxyChem, ARAMARK, The Associates First Capital Corporation, Fort Worth Museum of Science and History, Pier 1, Mack Trucks, Celanese, NASA, Lockheed Martin Corporation, and Key Span Energy. He is currently on the Board of Directors of Kisco Senior Living Communities of Carlsbad, CA, The Winston School of Dallas, GoToLearn (a non-profit corporation) and Applied Management Sciences Institute of Houston, TX.

# Organizational Behavior

## TENTH EDITION

# Learning About Organizational Behavior

1

## PIKE PLACE FISH

In 1985, John Yokoyama, the owner of Pike Place Fish, a retail fish market in Seattle's historic Farmer's Market, and his employees committed themselves to becoming *World Famous* Pike Place Fish. With his business at a crisis point, Yokoyama had contacted Jim Bergquist, founder of Biz-Futures Consulting Company, for advice. The two of them decided to create an extraordinary future for Pike Place Fish. To do so they asked and answered some significant questions: What's beyond successful survival and prosperity in business? Can the people in a company intentionally create their own future? What happens if you truly empower your employees? Can a company make a difference in the quality of life for people?

Much has happened since those initial meetings. Pike Place Fish became *World Famous* Pike Place Fish, a dynamic, fast-paced place that's fun for both its customers and its 17 employees. The antics of the fish-flinging staff have become the highlight of the Pike Place Market, and have been featured in Spike Lee's Levi commercial on NBC's *Frasier*, MTV's *Real World*, and ABC's *Good Morning America*. The "low-flying fish" have been captured on film and immortalized in print by filmmakers and journalists from all over the world. John Yokoyama and Jim Bergquist believe that human beings are powerful and creative. They further believe that starting and running an organization is fundamentally a creative endeavor, probably more akin to conducting an orchestra or coaching a sports team than it is to operating a machine. From this basic insight, they developed some underlying principles. Four of them are central to Pike Place Fish.

- The principle of personal power—empowering our associates that allows them to take personal responsibility for the whole job.
- The principle of being-in-alignment—based on a common purpose that honors diversity of thought, creates enormous synergy, and leads to ongoing breakthroughs.
- The principle of vision-in-action—being guided by a vision of possibility; having a powerful purpose that gives meaning to people's lives and work; the soul of our organization.
- The principle of transformation—our situations and circumstances may not be nearly as solid as we think they are. They may in fact be far more malleable than we ever realized.

These and the other principles that John Yokoyama and Jim Bergquist derived and the practices they instituted at Pike Place Fish may be applied in many organizations, both small and large.

The company is very profitable. Its sales volume has increased by a factor of 4, and its employees are working in the same 1,200 square feet they've always occupied. In terms of sales per square foot, finding a comparable retail operation *anywhere* would be difficult. Since John Yokoyama committed to empowering his employees and including them in the running of Pike Place Fish, his cost of doing business has dropped from 77 percent to 54 percent of sales. Each individual in the company has taken personal responsibility for company profitability, and they share in it. They like to win. They take it personally.[1]

For more information on Pike Place Fish, visit the organization's home page at *http://www.pikeplacefish.com*.

Pike Place Fish is a unique organization. We point out in this chapter and throughout the book that its principles and practices reflect the latest thinking and perspectives in organizational behavior. John Yokoyama has a mosaic of competencies that enabled him to create Pike Place Fish. A **competency** is an interrelated set of abilities, behaviors, attitudes, and knowledge needed by an individual to be effective in most professional and managerial positions. A number of competencies can be identified as important to most organizations.[2] From among them, we identified seven foundation competencies that we believe significantly affect behavior in organizations. These particular competencies are increasingly important to the effectiveness of most professionals, not just those in managerial and leadership roles, as in the case of John Yokoyama. One of the themes of this book is to define, describe, and illustrate how the seven foundation competencies can be used in organizations. We weave these ideas into the discussion of organizational behavior throughout.

One of our goals is to help you further develop these competencies, which are identified and illustrated in Figure 1.1. The double-headed arrows indicate that these competencies are interrelated and that drawing rigid boundaries between them isn't feasible. We discuss them in considerable depth in specific chapters. For example, most of Chapter 12, Fostering Interpersonal Communication, focuses on developing the managing communication competency. In addition, in other chapters, we discuss capabilities that build on the foundation competencies and address specific issues. For example, in Chapters 10 and 11, we discuss their importance and that of other capabilities in relation to being an effective leader.

A second theme of this book is to emphasize that there are no easy or complete answers as to why people and organizations function smoothly or fail to do so. Thus

**Figure 1.1**        **Foundation Competencies for Individual and Managerial Effectiveness**

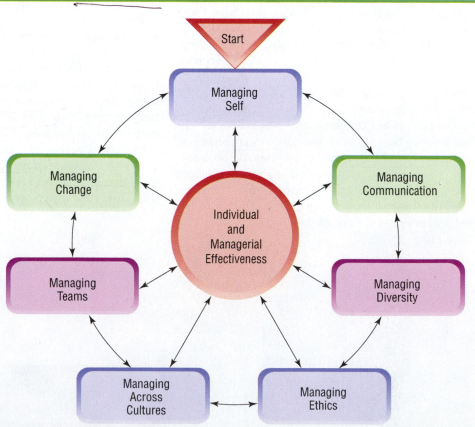

another of our goals is to give you the basic ability to look at and understand the behavior of people in organizations to help you address organizational and behavioral issues and develop ways to resolve them. **Organizational behavior** is the study of human behavior, attitudes, and performance in organizations. It is interdisciplinary—drawing on concepts from social and clinical psychology, sociology, cultural anthropology, industrial engineering, and organizational psychology.

A third theme of this book stresses the importance of organizational behavior to you. You are or probably will be an employee of an organization—and perhaps of several during your career. You may eventually become a team leader, a manager, or an executive. Studying organizational behavior should help you attain the competencies needed to be an effective employee, team leader, manager, and/or executive. The competencies that you acquire should help you diagnose, understand, explain, and act on what is happening around you in your job.

**Learning Objective:**

1. Describe the managing self competency.

# COMPETENCY: MANAGING SELF

The **managing self competency** involves the overall ability to assess your own strengths and weaknesses, set and pursue professional and personal goals, balance work and personal life, and engage in new learning—including new or modified skills, behaviors, and attitudes.[3]

## CORE ABILITIES

The managing self competency includes the core abilities to do the following.

- Understand your own and others' personality and attitudes (see especially Chapter 2, Understanding Individual Differences).

- Perceive, appraise, and interpret accurately yourself, others, and the immediate environment (see especially Chapter 3, Understanding Perceptions and Attributions).

- Understand and act on your own and others' work-related motivations and emotions (see especially Chapter 5, Achieving Motivation in the Workplace).

- Assess and establish your own developmental, personal (life-related), and work-related goals (see especially Chapter 6, Motivating Individuals for High Performance).

- Take responsibility for managing yourself and your career over time and through stressful circumstances (see especially Chapter 7, Managing Individual Stress).

In our view, managing self is the most basic of the seven competencies. Its achievement creates the underlying personal attributes needed for successfully developing the other six competencies. For example, you can't develop the managing diversity competency if you are unable to perceive, appraise, and interpret accurately your own values, reactions, and behaviors with respect to cultural beliefs, practices, and behaviors that differ from your own. This competency is a cornerstone, for example, of leading and working at Pike Place Fish. The managing self competency includes the concept of **emotional intelligence**—the capacity for recognizing one's own and others' emotions; including self-awareness, self-motivation, being empathetic, and having social skills.[4]

## CAREER DEVELOPMENT

A **career** is a sequence of work-related positions occupied by a person during a lifetime.[5] It embraces attitudes and behaviors that are part of ongoing work-related tasks and experiences. The popular view of a career usually is restricted to the idea of moving up the ladder in an organization. At times, this opportunity no longer is available to many people because of downsizing, mergers, and the increasing tendency of management to place the responsibility on employees to develop their own competencies. A person may remain at the same level, acquiring and developing new competencies, and have a successful career without ever being promoted. A person also can build a career by moving among various jobs in different fields, such as accounting, management information systems, and marketing, or among organizations such as Hewlett-Packard, Dell, and McDonald's. Thus a career encompasses not only traditional work experiences but also the opportunity of career alternatives, individual choices, and individual experiences. Let's briefly consider five aspects of a career.

- The nature of a career in itself doesn't imply success or failure or fast or slow advancement. Career success or failure is best determined by the individual, rather than by others.
- No absolute standards exist for evaluating a career. Career success or failure is related to a person's self-concept, goals, and competencies. Individuals should evaluate their own career goals and progress in terms of what is personally meaningful and satisfying.
- An individual should examine a career both subjectively and objectively. Subjective elements of a career include values, attitudes, personality, and motivations, which may change over time. Objective elements of a career include job choices, positions held, and specific competencies developed.
- **Career development** involves making decisions about an occupation and engaging in activities to attain career goals. The central idea in the career development process is time. The shape and direction of a person's career over time are influenced by many factors (e.g., the economy, availability of jobs, skill acquisition, personal characteristics, family status, and job history).
- Cultural factors play a role in careers. Cultural norms in countries such as Japan, the Philippines, and Mexico also influence the direction of a person's career. By U.S. standards, women are discriminated against as managers in these cultures. In India and South Korea, social status and educational background largely determine an individual's career paths.

Ralph Waldo Emerson's classic essay "Self-reliance" offers good advice for a person's career: "Trust thyself." To be successful, people need to commit themselves to a lifetime of learning, including the development of a career plan. A **career plan** is the individual's choice of occupation, organization, and career path.

Johnson & Johnson (J&J) has developed a strong career development program that reflects these five aspects of a career. J&J is a global health-care organization that comprises 190 operating companies. The following Managing Self Competency feature briefly describes several aspects of the interplay between the managing self competency and career development at the company.

## COMPETENCY: MANAGING SELF

### CAREER DEVELOPMENT AT JOHNSON & JOHNSON

Navigating a business landscape where change is constant requires leaders at every level. Our philosophy for developing leaders throughout our company is encompassed by our Standards of Leadership. These standards combine our Credo values, business results and leadership competencies into a comprehensive, objective set of principles and behaviors that individuals and autonomous operating units can use to guide their ongoing development of leadership skills. These leadership skills are

- customer/marketplace focus,
- innovation,
- interdependent partnering,
- mastering complexity, and
- organizational and people development.

The employees play a key role in driving their own development at Johnson & Johnson. The i-Lead process helps by providing a model through which individuals work with their managers to establish a development plan that is highly personalized and self-directed. The model illustrates the combined roles of the individual, the manager and the organization in the development of a person's leadership competencies. In the i-Lead process

- the *individual* drives the development process by seeking feedback and by demonstrating commitment to ongoing improvement;
- the *manager* supports the commitment of the individual, leads by example, and establishes an effective communication process; and
- the *organization* provides a culture that is supportive of leadership development at every level, while providing the systems, processes, tools and resources necessary to develop leadership skills.[6]

*For more information on Johnson & Johnson, visit the organization's home page at http://www.jnj.com.*

**Learning Objective:**

2. Describe the managing communication competency.

## COMPETENCY: MANAGING COMMUNICATION

The **managing communication competency** involves the overall ability to use all the modes of transmitting, understanding, and receiving ideas, thoughts, and feelings—verbal, listening, nonverbal, written, electronic, and the like—for accurately transferring and exchanging information and emotions.[7] This competency may be thought of as the *circulatory system* that nourishes the other competencies. Just as arteries and veins provide for the movement of blood in a person, communication allows the exchange of information, thoughts, ideas, and feelings. One of John Yokoyama's strengths is the managing communication competency, as suggested by his comments:

> In one of our early Pike Place Fish meetings with BizFutures, we asked, "Who do we want to be?" One of the young kids working for me said, "Hey! Let's be world famous!" I thought, "World famous? What a stupid thing to say!" But the more we talked about it, the more we became excited about being world famous. So we printed "World Famous" on our boxes.[8]

### CORE ABILITIES

The managing communication competency includes the core abilities to do the following.

- Convey information, ideas, and emotions to others in such a way that they are received as intended. This ability is strongly influenced by the **describing skill**—identifying concrete, specific examples of behavior and its effects. This skill also includes recognizing that too often individuals don't realize that they are not being clear and accurate in what they say, resulting from a tendency to jump quickly to generalizations and judgments (see especially Chapter 12, Fostering Interpersonal Communication).
- Provide constructive feedback to others (see especially Chapter 9, Managing Interpersonal Conflict and Negotiation, and Chapter 12).

- Engage in **active listening**—the process of integrating information and emotions in a search for shared meaning and understanding. Active listening requires the use of the **questioning skill**—the ability to ask for information and opinions in a way that gets relevant, honest, and appropriate responses. This skill helps to bring relevant information and emotions into the dialogue and reduce misunderstandings, regardless of whether the parties agree (see especially Chapters 9 and 12).

- Use and interpret **nonverbal communication**—facial expressions, body movements, and physical contact are often used to send messages. The **empathizing skill** refers to detecting and understanding another person's values, motives, and emotions. It is especially important in nonverbal communication and active listening. The empathizing skill helps to reduce tension and increase trust and sharing (see especially Chapter 3, Understanding Perceptions and Attributions, and Chapter 12).

- Engage in **verbal communication** effectively—presenting ideas, information, and emotions to others, either one-to-one or in groups. We provide the opportunity for you to apply this skill in the Developing Competencies section at the end of many chapters.

- Engage in **written communication** effectively—the ability to transfer data, information, ideas, and emotions by means of reports, letters, memos, notes, e-mail messages, and the like.

- Use a variety of computer-based (electronic) resources, such as e-mail and the Internet. The **Internet** is a worldwide collection of interconnected computer networks. Through an array of computer-based information technologies, the Internet directly links organizations and their employees to customers, suppliers, information sources, the public, and millions of individuals worldwide. We help you develop this skill throughout the book by presenting numerous Internet addresses and encouraging you to learn more about the organizations, issues, and people discussed.

The following Managing Communication feature vividly illustrates the failure to apply a number of the core abilities in the managing communication competency. This presentation is based on an actual incident, but the names are disguised.

## COMPETENCY: MANAGING COMMUNICATION

### GLEN MILLER AND MEGAN EVAN'S DIFFICULT CONVERSATION

Glen Miller and Megan Evan were two managers working at the same level at an IT firm. Evan was leading a presentation to a client, and the information was weak and disorganized. She and the team weren't able to answer even basic questions. The client had been patient, then quiet, then clearly exasperated. When the presentation really started to fall apart, the client put the team on the spot with questions that made them look increasingly inadequate.

On this particular day, Glen Miller wasn't part of the presenting team; he was simply observing. He was as surprised as the client was at Evan's poor performance. After the client left, he asked Evan what happened. She lashed out at him. "You're not my boss, so don't start patronizing me. You always undercut me no matter what I do." Evan continued to shout at Miller, her antagonism clear. Each time he spoke, she interrupted him with accusations and threats. "I can't wait to see how you like it when people leave you flailing in the wind." Miller tried to remain reasonable, but Evan didn't wind down. "Megan," he said, "pull yourself together. You are twisting every word I say."

Miller's problem was that all her tactics—accusation, distortion, and digression—were aggressive. Most people don't like to be on the receiving end of aggressive tactics because they don't know whether, or how far, the aggression will escalate. Miller wanted to avoid Evan's aggression, but his insistence on rationality in the face of her emotional state wasn't working. His cool approach was overcome by her aggressive one. As a result, Miller found himself in an uneasy situation. Evan's threats that she would pay him back with the client rattled him. He couldn't tell whether she was just bluffing or meant it. He finally turned to the managing director, who grew frustrated with, and later angry at, Miller and Evan for their inability to resolve their communication problems.

In the end, their lack of competency in handling their difficult communications cost them dearly. Both were passed over for promotion after the company lost the client.[9]

**Learning Objective:**

3. Describe the managing diversity competency.

## COMPETENCY: MANAGING DIVERSITY

The **managing diversity competency** involves the overall ability to value unique individual and group characteristics, embrace such characteristics as potential sources of organizational strength, and appreciate the uniqueness of each individual.[10] This competency also involves the ability to help people work effectively together even though their interests and backgrounds may be quite diverse. Recall the "principle of being in alignment" at Pike Place Fish, which is based on a common purpose that honors diversity of thought.

### CORE ABILITIES

The managing diversity competency includes the core abilities to do the following.

- Foster an environment of inclusion with people who possess characteristics different from your own (see especially Chapter 2, Understanding Individual Differences, and Chapter 3, Understanding Perceptions and Attributions).
- Learn from those with different characteristics, experiences, perspectives, and backgrounds. Diversity of thought and behavior is vital to stimulating creativity and innovation (see especially Chapter 13, Making Decisions in Organizations, and Chapter 16, Guiding Organizational Change).
- Embrace and develop personal tendencies—such as *intellectual openness* and attitudes that demonstrate respect for people of other cultures and races—that support diversity in the workplace and elsewhere (see especially Chapter 2).
- Communicate and personally practice a commitment to work with individuals and team members because of their talents and contributions, regardless of their personal attributes (see especially Chapter 8, Managing Teams).
- Provide leadership—*walk the talk*—in confronting obvious bias, promoting inclusion, and seeking win–win or compromise solutions to power struggles and conflicts that appear to be based on diversity issues (see especially Chapter 9, Managing Interpersonal Conflict and Negotiation).
- Apply governmental laws and regulations as well as organizational policies and regulations concerning diversity as they relate to a person's position.

The case for the managing diversity competency is well stated by Elizabeth Pathy Salett, president of the National Multicultural Institute. She comments:

As our nation becomes more culturally diverse, we are presented with a series of opportunities and challenges for the future. Can we capitalize on the strength that begins from our differences? Can we create a work environment that draws upon the talents of all our workers? Can we attract a diverse market, serving a variety of tastes and interests? Our ability to meet these challenges will have an enormous impact on worker productivity, management strategies, and organizational success.[11]

## CATEGORIES OF DIVERSITY

As suggested in Figure 1.2, diversity includes many categories and characteristics. Even a single aspect of diversity, such as physical abilities and qualities, contains various characteristics that may affect individual or team behaviors. One challenge for managers is to determine whether those effects deny opportunity and are wasteful and counterproductive, simply reflect a tolerance of differences, or lead to embracing diversity as a value-added organizational resource. A second challenge is to assist in developing individual, team, and organizational competencies—including learning new knowledge, attitudes, skills, and methods of intervention—to value and embrace diversity as a source of creativity and strength.

Figure 1.2 identifies the more common categories of diversity dealt with in organizations. They are subdivided into *primary categories*—genetic characteristics that affect a person's self-image and socialization—and *secondary categories*—learned characteristics that a person acquires and modifies throughout life. As suggested by the arrows, these categories aren't independent. For example, a woman (gender) with children (parental status) is likely to be directly affected by an organization with

**Figure 1.2**          **Selected Categories of Diversity**

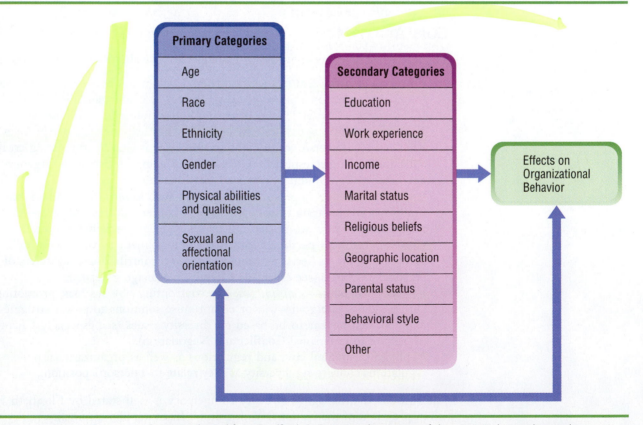

Source: Adapted from Bradford, S. Fourteen dimensions of diversity: Understanding and appreciating differences in the workplace. In J. W. Pfeiffer (ed.), 1996 *Annual: Volume 2, Consulting.* San Diego: Pfeiffer and Associates, 1996, 9–17.

*family-friendly* or *family-unfriendly* policies and attitudes. An example of a family-unfriendly attitude would be: Your job must always come first if you are to get ahead in this organization.

The following are brief explanations of the primary categories of diversity. Individuals have relatively little influence over these characteristics.

- *Age:* the number of years a person has been alive and the generation into which she was born (e.g., depression era, baby boomers, or generation X in the United States).
- *Race:* the biological groupings within humankind, representing superficial physical differences, such as eye form and skin color. Race accounts for less than 1 percent of the difference in a person's genetic heredity.
- *Ethnicity:* identification with a cultural group that has shared traditions and heritage, including national origin, language, religion, food, and customs. Some people identify strongly with these cultural roots; others do not.
- *Gender:* biological sex as determined by XX (female) or XY (male) chromosomes.
- *Physical abilities and qualities:* a variety of characteristics, including body type, physical size, facial features, specific abilities or disabilities, and visible and invisible physical and mental talents or limitations.
- *Sexual orientation:* feelings of sexual attraction toward members of the same or opposite gender, such as heterosexual, homosexual, or bisexual.

The following are brief explanations of the secondary categories of diversity. Individuals have relatively more influence over them during their lifetimes by making choices.

- *Education:* the individual's formal and informal learning and training.
- *Work experience:* the employment and volunteer positions the person has held and the variety of organizations for which the person has worked.
- *Income:* the economic conditions in which the person grew up and his current economic status.
- *Marital status:* the person's situation as never married, married, widowed, or divorced.
- *Religious beliefs:* fundamental teachings received about deities and values acquired from formal or informal religious practices.
- *Geographic location:* the location(s) in which the person was raised or spent a significant part of her life, including types of communities and urban areas versus rural areas.
- *Parental status:* having or not having children and the circumstances in which the children are raised, such as single parenting and two-adult parenting.
- *Personal style:* tendency of the individual to think, feel, or act in a particular way.

We discuss many of these categories of diversity throughout the book. In addition, many of the chapters contain a Managing Diversity Competency feature that relates one or more categories of diversity to a specific organizational topic. In the remainder of this section, we present a brief overview of the organizational implications for some of the primary categories of diversity. As you consider them, think about their potential impact on your career.

## CHANGING WORKFORCE

The makeup of the workforce in the United States, Canada, and many other countries will continue to change rapidly. The majority of new employees will be women, members of non-Caucasian races, and from ethnically diverse groups (virtually every country in the world is represented in the U.S. population and workforce). In addition, an increasing number of global organizations, such as Coca-Cola and IBM, have many employees, customers, and suppliers in locations throughout the world.

Workforces in Asia, Western Europe, Latin America, and North America are growing more complex and diverse. Managers and employees need to recognize and embrace differences resulting from this diversity, particularly in terms of what employees want from their jobs. Organizations face three challenges of a diverse workforce: language differences, formation of natural ethnic groupings, and attitudinal and cultural differences.[12]

**Language Differences.**   Unless employees can understand each other, communication is difficult or even impossible. Employees can't train each other or work together if they can't communicate. Translators may be used for hiring, but—for the day-to-day communication that fosters a friendly, informal, and productive work setting—language barriers pose real and often serious problems. Such problems may lead to misunderstandings regarding performance goals, work methods, safety measures, and other essential working conditions.

**Formation of Natural Ethnic Groupings.**   The formation of natural ethnic groupings within an organization is a tendency that needs to be constructively managed. Employees, especially if they don't speak English, may seek out others of the same ethnic group for assistance. At the Marriott's Quorum Hotel in Addison, Texas, a large percentage of its housekeeping staff is from Vietnam. With English as a second language, these employees often seek out other Vietnamese rather than a supervisor for help. They don't want to embarrass themselves because of their inability to speak English fluently. Although natural ethnic groupings may create a strong sense of togetherness, they may not promote working with others who don't share the same language and cultural heritage. At J. C. Penney's corporate headquarters in Plano, Texas, once a month the cafeteria staff prepares meals, hangs flags, and displays other items from countries in which the company does business. This type of observance is one way for employees to get some feeling for living and working in different cultures.

**Attitudes and Cultural Differences.**   Most people have developed attitudes and beliefs about others by the time they seek a job. However, some attitudes and beliefs create frustration, anger, and bitterness in those at whom they're aimed. Managers and others who want to foster employee tolerance recognize that major changes are required. In some organizations, women and minorities are bypassed when important, formal decisions are made. Informally, these people often are left out when others go to lunch or a sporting event. These informal get-togethers often give older employees a chance to counsel younger employees about coping with problems—an advantage not shared by those left out.

## GENDER

Women now represent nearly half (47 percent) of the workforce in the United States. They also account for about 11 percent of officers at large corporations, up from about 8.5 percent in 1995.[13] One reason for the limited number of executive women is the glass ceiling.

The **glass ceiling** is a barrier so subtle that it is transparent, yet so strong that it prevents women and minorities from moving up in management. There appear to be three primary causes of the glass ceiling. First, many executives and managers aren't held accountable for results in the areas of equal employment opportunity and affirmative action. Second, women and minorities aren't encouraged to apply for or even made aware of job openings at higher levels. At times, these openings are discussed at golf outings, card games, and other activities to which women and minority employees are not invited. Third, these groups lack training and development opportunities that would allow them to improve their competencies and chances for promotion.

Let's consider one of the programs at Aetna—the global provider of health, retirement, and financial services products—intended to help shatter the glass ceiling. The Aetna Emerging Leaders Program is designed to groom the next generation of leaders by guiding participants through a rigorous multiyear development plan. One of the goals is to build wide-ranging diversity into Aetna's talent base. Candidates must have 5 to 7 years of work experience either within Aetna or outside the company. The program guides participants through a series of 12- to 24-month assignments in different areas of the business. According to Orlene Weyland, program director, this program is different because it's highly individualized, and it reaches people early in their careers. Each candidate receives coaching, education, mentoring, and career path guidance.[14]

Many women with children hold full-time jobs and still bear primary responsibility for family care. An estimated 75 percent of working women are in their childbearing years. DuPont, Eli Lilly, and Marriott International are among the firms having family-friendly policies and strategies. Such firms often offer child care, flextime (ability to arrive and leave work at varied hours), job-sharing (two individuals, often women, who want to work part-time and share a job), telecommuting (opportunity for certain groups of employees to work at home some or most of the time), and other types of flexibility in accommodating employees with urgent family needs.[15]

## RACE AND ETHNICITY

Each year, one-third of the newcomers to the U.S. workforce are minority group members. The U.S. workforce has approximately 17 million African Americans, up almost 20 percent from 1990; Hispanics, Asians, and other minorities comprise 15 percent of the workforce, up 4 percent from 1980.[16] In addition to the glass ceiling, minority group members also face **racism**, the notion that a person's genetic group is superior to all others. As suggested in Figure 1.3, racism takes three interrelated basic forms: (1) *individual racism*—the extent to which a person holds attitudes, values, feelings, and/or engages in behaviors that promote the person's own racial group as superior; (2) *cultural racism*—the arrogant elevation of the cultural features and achievements of one race as superior while actively ignoring or denigrating those of other races; and (3) *institutional racism*—organizational and/or social rules, regulations, laws, policies, and customs that serve to maintain the dominant status of and control by one racial group. Each form of racism may operate openly or secretly and intentionally or unintentionally.

**Figure 1.3**　　　　　　　　**Interrelated Forms of Racism**

## AGE

The U.S. and Canadian workforces are aging along with the baby boomers. From 1990 to 2000, the number of people aged 35 to 47 increased by 38 percent, whereas the number between 48 and 53 increased by 67 percent.[17] The increase in the number of middle-aged employees has collided with the efforts of many companies, such as Kodak, Sanyo Electric, and British Petroleum, to reduce layers of middle management in order to remain competitive. Over time, the competencies that many of these employees have gained are valuable only to the firms they work for. Displaced, older employees who lose their jobs often have great difficulty matching previous levels of responsibility and salaries, even when they are able to find new jobs. Moreover, older workers often are less likely than younger workers to relocate or train for new occupations.

Fannie Mae, formally known as the Federal National Mortgage Association, is an organization that continues to receive major awards for embracing many forms of diversity—including gender, race, ethnicity, and age. Headquartered in Washington, D.C., Fannie Mae is one of the largest sources of financing for home mortgages. The firm has approximately 4,500 employees. Forty-six percent of employees in management are women, and 23 percent are minorities. In 1999, Frank Rains assumed the position of chairman and CEO, making him the first African American to lead a Fortune 500 company. The following Managing Diversity Competency feature highlights Fannie Mae's commitment and initiatives that develop and support this competency among all its employees.

# COMPETENCY:  MANAGING DIVERSITY

## FANNIE MAE'S DIVERSITY LEADERSHIP

Ten commitments govern every business decision made at Fannie Mae. They represent the values that define the spirit of the company. Diversity is one of these commitments, and the organization's diversity commitment states:

> We are committed to foster a diverse work force and recognize and value every individual's unique skills and perspectives.

Fannie Mae is dedicated to providing all employees an equal opportunity to achieve their full potential. The cornerstones of its diversity philosophy are clearly communicated to each employee, with a promise that the organization is committed to providing an environment in which

- employees are treated fairly;
- employees are recognized and rewarded based on ability and merit for their contributions;
- employees have equal access to opportunity for growth and advancement;
- employees respect each other and are free from harassment, discrimination, and intolerance;
- the diversity of society is represented at all levels throughout the organization; and
- the management and development of employees is recognized as crucial to the success of the organization.

To lead the organization's efforts to achieve its diversity goals, Fannie Mae created a dedicated department, the office of diversity. Working closely with the human resources division, the office develops, manages, and evaluates the organization's policies, plans, programs, and practices with regard to equal employment opportunity (EEO), affirmative action, dispute resolution, and workforce diversity.

Fannie Mae aims to foster a culture in which employees recognize and appreciate the diversity of their coworkers. Within this environment, many employees who share a common interest in race, ethnicity, gender, sexual orientation, age, religion, national origin, or cultural heritage have chosen to form or join an existing employee support group. These grassroots organizations provide a voice for its members and enable them to communicate diversity issues and concerns to senior management. Representatives from these groups serve on the company's diversity advisory council.[18]

*For more information on Fannie Mae, visit the organization's home page at http://www.fanniemae.com.*

**Learning Objective:**

4. Describe the managing ethics competency.

# COMPETENCY: MANAGING ETHICS

The **managing ethics competency** involves the overall ability to incorporate values and principles that distinguish right from wrong in making decisions and choosing behaviors. **Ethics** are the values and principles that distinguish right from wrong.[19]

## CORE ABILITIES

The managing ethics competency includes the core abilities to do the following.

- Identify and describe the principles of ethical decision making and behavior (see especially Chapter 13, Making Decisions in Organizations).
- Assess the importance of ethical issues in considering alternative courses of action. The decision to shop at Wal-Mart versus Target is not related to any ethical issue of consequence.
- Apply governmental laws and regulations, as well as the employer's rules of conduct, in making decisions and taking action within a person's level of responsibilities and authority. In general, the greater a person's level of responsibilities and authority, the more the person is likely to face increasingly complex and ambiguous ethical issues and dilemmas. For example, decisions having ethical demands and importance are likely to be far less for an associate at a Home Depot store than for the store manager (see especially Chapter 10, Leading Effectively: Foundations).
- Demonstrate dignity and respect for others in working relationships—such as taking action against discriminatory practices as individually feasible and in terms of a person's position. The manager at a Sears store is more able to stop an employee from showing disrespect to members of a minority group than is a checkout associate in the store (see especially Chapter 11, Leading Effectively: Contemporary Developments).
- Demonstrate honesty and openness in communication, limited only by legal, privacy, and competitive considerations (i.e., Do what you say and say what you do). (See especially Chapter 9, Managing Interpersonal Conflict and Negotiation, and Chapter 12, Fostering Interpersonal Communication.)

## ETHICAL DILEMMAS

The ethical issues facing managers and other employees have grown in significance in recent years, fueled by public concern about how business is conducted. In Chapters 12 and 15, we develop this point with Ethics Competency features on Enron. Ethical behavior sometimes is difficult to define, especially in a global economy with its varied beliefs and practices. Although ethical behavior in business clearly has a legal component, it involves more than that, and absolutes in one country aren't always applicable in another country.

Managers and employees alike face situations in which there are no clear right or wrong answers. The burden is on individuals to make ethical decisions. An **ethical dilemma** occurs when an individual or team must make a decision that involves multiple values. An ethical dilemma doesn't simply involve choosing right over wrong because there may be several competing values. Some ethical dilemmas arise from competitive and time pressures, among other factors.[20] Consider these three real-to-life examples of ethical dilemmas:

- A customer asked for a product from us today. After telling him our price, he said he couldn't afford it. I know he could get it cheaper from a competitor. Should I tell him about the competitor—or let him go without getting what he needs? What should I do?
- A fellow employee told me that he plans to quit the company in two months and start a new job that has been guaranteed to him. Meanwhile, my boss told me that she wasn't going to give me a new opportunity in our company because she was going to give it to my fellow employee now. What should I do?
- My boss told me that one of my employees is among several to be laid off soon and that I'm not to tell my employee yet or he might tell the whole organization, which would soon be in an uproar. Meanwhile, I heard from my employee that he plans to buy braces for his daughter and a new carpet for his house. What should I do?[21]

Top-management leadership, policies and rules, and the prevailing organizational culture can do much to reduce, guide, and help the individual confront and resolve ethical dilemmas. Table 1.1 provides a brief questionnaire that asks you to assess an organization or manager that you have worked for with respect to its commitment to various ethical behaviors, practices, and policies.

The following Managing Ethics Competency feature on Johnson & Johnson's (J&J's) Credo is a natural follow-up to the competency feature on career development at J&J. Not just a plaque on the wall, the principles stated in J&J's Credo drive ethical behavior at all levels of the organization.

## COMPETENCY:  MANAGING ETHICS

### JOHNSON & JOHNSON CREDO

We believe our first responsibility is to the doctors, nurses, and patients, to mothers and fathers and all others who use our products and services. In meeting their needs everything we do must be of high quality. We must constantly strive to reduce our costs in order to maintain reasonable prices. Customers' orders must be serviced promptly and accurately. Our suppliers and distributors must have an opportunity to make a fair profit.

We are responsible to our employees, the men and women who work with us throughout the world. Everyone must be considered as an individual. We must respect their dignity and recognize their merit. They must have a sense of security in their jobs. Compensation must be fair and adequate, and working conditions clean, orderly, and safe. We must be mindful of ways to help our employees fulfill their family responsibilities. Employees must feel free to make suggestions and complaints. There must be equal opportunity for employment, development, and advancement for those qualified. We must provide competent management, and their actions must be just and ethical.

*For more information on Johnson & Johnson, visit the organization's home page at http://www.jnj.com.*

We are responsible to the communities where we live and work and to the world community as well. We must be good citizens—support good works and charities and bear our fair share of taxes. We must encourage civic improvements and better health and education. We must maintain in good order the property we are privileged to use, protecting the environment and natural resources.

Our final responsibility is to our stockholders. Business must make a sound profit. We must experiment with new ideas. Research must be carried on, innovative programs developed, and mistakes paid for. New equipment must be purchased, new facilities provided, and new products launched. Reserves must be created for adverse times. When we operate according to these principles, the stockholders should realize a fair return.[22]

## Table 1.1

### Ethical Practices Questionnaire

**Instructions.** Think of an organization for which you have worked or currently work. Respond to the 10 statements that follow the scale in terms of the degree to which you think the organization reflects the behavior, policy, and/or practice in each statement. Use the following 10-point scale, which ranges from 10 (highly descriptive of the organization) to 1 (not at all descriptive). The middle point in the scale, 5, indicates that you are neutral or undecided.

| Not at all Descriptive | | | | Neutral | | | | | Highly Descriptive |
|---|---|---|---|---|---|---|---|---|---|
| 1 | 2 | 3 | 4 | 5 | 6 | 7 | 8 | 9 | 10 |

Record your number next to each statement.

_____ 1. I did not fear retaliation from higher management for reporting misconduct by others.

_____ 2. Management was trusted to do the right thing by me and other employees.

_____ 3. When making important decisions, managers and other employees considered the ethical implications of the alternatives being considered.

_____ 4. There were well-established policies and practices by higher management for dealing honestly with customers.

_____ 5. The core abilities in the managing ethics competency were seen as important and applied consistently by higher management.

_____ 6. I and my coworkers never felt pressured to engage in practices that we found to be questionable or unethical.

_____ 7. My organization had a practice of doing what was right, not just what brought quick profits or other benefits.

_____ 8. The organization's ethics policies and expected behaviors were effectively communicated to all employees.

_____ 9. There were clearly communicated consequences for deviations from or violations of ethics policies and expected behaviors—which were backed up by action in the case of such violations.

_____ 10. High levels of individual performance that were achieved by violating or distorting the organization's ethics policies and expected behaviors were not tolerated.

**Results and Interpretation.** Sum the point values for items 1 through 10. Totals of 80 to 100 provide indicators of a highly ethical organization. Totals of 61 to 79 suggest needed improvements. Totals of 40 to 60 may suggest confusing and inconsistent ethical signals and practices. Scores of 10 to 40 suggest a highly unethical organization that requires a major transformation.

**Learning Objective:**

5. Describe the managing across cultures competency.

# COMPETENCY: MANAGING ACROSS CULTURES

The **managing across cultures competency** involves the overall ability to recognize and embrace similarities and differences among nations and cultures and then approach key organizational and strategic issues with an open and curious mind. **Culture** is the dominant pattern of living, thinking, and believing that is developed and transmitted by people, consciously or unconsciously, to subsequent generations.[23] For a *culture* to exist, it must

- be shared by the vast majority of the members of a major group or entire society;
- be passed on from generation to generation; and
- shape behavior, decisions, and perceptions of the world.[24]

A key feature of a culture is its **cultural values**—those consciously and subconsciously deeply held beliefs that specify general preferences, behaviors, and define what is right and wrong. Cultural values are reflected in a society's morals, customs, and established practices.

## CORE ABILITIES

The managing across cultures competency includes the core abilities to do the following.

- Understand, appreciate, and use the characteristics that make a particular culture unique and recognize which are likely to influence a person's behaviors.
- Identify and understand how work-related values, such as individualism and collectivism, influence the choices of individuals and groups in making decisions.
- Understand and motivate employees with different values and attitudes. These may range from the more individualistic, Western style of work to paternalistic, non-Western attitudes to the extreme "the-state-will-take-care-of-me" collectivist mindset.
- Communicate in the language of the country with which the individual has working relationships. This ability is crucial for employees that have ongoing communication with those who have a different native language.
- Deal with extreme conditions, especially for those with assignments in foreign countries. This need applies even if the assignment is short term or the person has international responsibilities from the home office. Some extreme conditions include economic instability, political unrest, cultural conflicts, governmental bureaucratic obstacles, lack of laws or constantly shifting laws governing and protecting business interests, public anger or resentment of outsiders, armed insurrections or even full-blown military coups, and so on.
- Address managerial and other issues through a **global mindset**. That means scanning the environment with a worldwide perspective, always looking for unexpected trends that may create threats or opportunities for a unit or an entire organization. Some call this the ability to *think globally, act locally.*

## WORK-RELATED CULTURAL VALUES

There are a number of classifications of cultural values. We briefly introduce you to a portion of one that is particularly helpful in understanding individual and societal differences in three work-related values.[25] As suggested in Figure 1.4, these and other cultural values in combination influence the behaviors and decisions of employees.

**Individualism–Collectivism.** Individualism and collectivism are two of the fundamental work-related values that must be thoroughly understood and used to develop the managing across cultures competency. **Individualism** is the tendency of people to look after themselves and their immediate families, which implies a loosely integrated

**Figure 1.4**             **Influence of Culturally Based Work-Related Values**

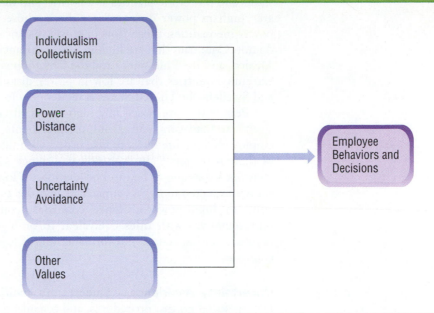

society. The individual is emotionally detached from organizations and institutions. The culture emphasizes individual initiative, decision making, and achievement. Everybody is believed to have the right to privacy and personal freedom of expression. Countries characterized by an emphasis on individualism include the United States, Canada, New Zealand, the United Kingdom, and Australia.

In contrast, **collectivism** is the tendency of people to emphasize their belonging to groups and to look after each other in exchange for loyalty. The social framework tends to be tight, and in-groups (relatives, communities, and organizations) focus on their common welfare and distinguish themselves from out-groups. Collectivism usually involves emotional dependence of the individual on groups, organizations, and institutions. The sense of belonging and "we" versus "I" in relationships is fundamental. Individuals' private lives are open to the groups and organizations to which they belong. In-group goals are generally thought to be more important than the individual's personal goals. When conflict arises between individual goals and in-group goals, the general expectation is that in-group goals and decision making should prevail. Countries characterized by an emphasis on collectivism include Japan, China, Venezuela, and Indonesia.

Harmony is another feature of cultures that emphasize collectivism. People in the same group are supposed to have similar views. Individuals in China, Japan, Taiwan, and South Korea care about whether their behavior would be considered shameful by the other members of their groups. They also avoid pointing out other people's mistakes in public so that the others won't lose face. Face-saving is important in these cultures because it allows people to maintain their dignity and status. Because individuals are tightly integrated, they feel that they have a common fate.

In contrast, the people in countries that emphasize individualism, such as Canada, the United States, and the United Kingdom, do not often form such tight-knit groups. Individuals in these countries generally do not believe that they have a common fate with others. They view themselves as independent, unique, and special. They are less likely to conform to the expectations of others. When group goals conflict with personal goals, individuals commonly pursue their own goals. In addition, seeking personal identity is highly valued in individualistic cultures. Confrontation with others within an in-group is acceptable. Personal achievement, pleasure, and competition are all highly valued.

**Power Distance.**    **Power distance** is the extent to which people in a society accept status and power inequalities as a normal and functional aspect of life. Countries that are "high in power distance" are those whose citizens generally accept status and power inequalities; those "low in power distance" are those whose citizens generally do not. Countries that are high in power distance include Argentina, India, Malaysia, Mexico, and the Philippines and the Commonwealth of Puerto Rico. At the opposite extreme, countries that are low in power distance include Finland, Israel, Norway, and Sweden (the United States is moderately low).

People that are raised in a high power distance culture tend to behave submissively to managers and avoid disagreements with them. High power distance employees are more likely to take orders without question and follow the instructions of their managers.[26] In high power distance societies, managers and subordinates consider bypassing to be insubordination. In low power distance countries, employees are expected to bypass a manager in order to get their work done. When negotiating in high power distance countries, companies find it necessary to send representatives with titles equivalent to or higher than those of their bargaining partners. Titles, status, and formality are of less importance in low power distance countries.

**Uncertainty Avoidance.**    **Uncertainty avoidance** is the extent to which people rely on social norms, procedures, and organizations (including government) to avoid ambiguity, unpredictability, and risk. With "high" uncertainty avoidance, individuals seek orderliness, consistency, structure, formalized procedures, and laws to cover situations in their daily lives. Societies that are high on uncertainty avoidance, such as Japan, Sweden, and Germany, have a strong tendency toward orderliness and consistency, structured lifestyles, clear specification of social expectations, and many rules and laws. In contrast, in countries such as the United States and Canada and in Hong Kong, there is strong tolerance of ambiguity and uncertainty. More secure and long-term employment is common in "high" uncertainty avoidance countries. In contrast, job mobility and layoffs are more commonly accepted in "low" uncertainty avoidance countries.[27]

**Avoiding Stereotypes.**    In future chapters, we introduce additional value concepts that are important in managing across cultures. The three cross-culture value dimensions presented here and others to be developed in later chapters are a useful beginning point for explaining, predicting, and relating to individuals or groups with cultural values different than your own. However, we caution that there are often wide variations of behavior and values by various individuals and groups within a given society.

You need to be wary of stereotyping cultures in simple terms and thus glossing over nuances and complexities in a particular culture. Further, the specific issues and situations—such as work, family, friends, and recreation—can play a significant role in understanding the impact of different cultural values on behaviors. For example, when Japanese businesspeople make contracts, they seek ambiguous contracts. The dominant value underlying this approach is collectivism (cultural value). In this context, collectivism is revealed as a belief that those entering into agreement are joined together and share something in common; thus they should rely on and trust one another. Collectivism is more important than high uncertainty avoidance (cultural value of Japanese) in this context, but uncertainty avoidance is not completely absent. Some of the uncertainty surrounding the contract is dealt with in the process by carefully choosing and getting to know business partners and by using third parties. An additional consideration is that many Japanese like flexible contracts, because they have a greater recognition of the limits of contracts and the difficulties of foreseeing all contingencies (context of cultural history of business practices). Even though Americans are typically more tolerant of uncertainty (low uncertainty avoidance), they value pragmatism and don't like to take unnecessary risks (context of market economy). If a deal falls through, they rely on the legal system for a resolution (context of cultural history of institutions).[28]

The following Managing Across Cultures feature presents the perspectives of June Delano, director of executive and management education for Eastman Kodak Company. She discusses the nuances and complexities in managing across cultures. Delano works with Kodak managers around the world and has lived in several countries. Kodak is headquartered in Rochester, New York, and has operations or offices in 32 countries in the Americas, Europe, and Asia/Pacific regions.

## COMPETENCY:    MANAGING ACROSS CULTURES

### JUNE DELANO OF EASTMAN KODAK

I doubt that anyone with cross-cultural experience can't remember a moment when careful cross-cultural preparation had to be jettisoned. The moment that came to my mind was meeting a Japanese colleague on a visit to the United States. Instead of the formality and reserve I expected, he kicked off his shoes, tucked his feet under him in a chair, and leaned close to me, saying: "So what is it really like here at corporate headquarters?" His behavior made no sense within my "sophisticated stereotype" of Japanese culture, but we nonetheless found common ground and developed a good working relationship. Over time, I came to realize that he was a free spirit whose exuberant personality overrode his cultural group norms.

Kodak has fewer and fewer true expatriates. Instead, we have people of many nationalities who lead multicultural teams, work on multicountry projects, and travel monthly outside their home countries. In any year, they may work in Paris, Shanghai, Istanbul, Moscow, or Buenos Aires with colleagues from a different set of countries. It is impossible for these global travelers to remember a stereotype for each culture they encounter, much less develop a deep understanding of each.

Kodak has also gone beyond traditional cultural training by addressing multiculturalism from a team perspective. In this regard, we developed a workbook for leaders managing global teams. The workbook explains in simple terms the roles of team members and team leaders in different cultures using cultural value dimensions such as individualism/collectivism, power distance, and uncertainty avoidance, among others. Our workbook also offers the following advice:

> Because a team member comes from a country where a particular orientation exists does not mean that she will necessarily embody that orientation. Cross-cultural tools are not flawlessly predictive, so be prepared for individual surprises and contradictions.

I give great emphasis to avoiding "black-and-white thinkers" for cross-cultural assignments. When a manager asks for the "rules" for operating in a given culture and then accepts them as gospel, I am suspect of his ability to succeed in that culture or any other culture than his own. I do not believe everyone is cut out for cross-cultural work. Kodak screens managers for cross-cultural assignments based on their ability to deal with paradox, conflicting realities, ambiguity, and contradiction. Kodak is pessimistic that managers will be able to work effectively in a cross-cultural environment if they do not have these abilities.[29]

*For more information on Eastman Kodak Company, visit the organization's home page at http://www.kodak.com.*

# COMPETENCY: MANAGING TEAMS

The **managing teams competency** involves the overall ability to develop, support, facilitate, and lead groups to achieve organizational goals.[30] The components of this competency are developed in several chapters, especially Chapter 8, Managing Teams, and Chapter 9, Managing Interpersonal Conflict and Negotiation. In addition, the other competencies reviewed in this chapter contribute to the variety of abilities needed to be effective as a team member or leader (as suggested previously in Figure 1.1).

John Yokoyama of Pike Place Fish places great emphasis on the managing teams competency. Always mindful of the commitment that each person has made to the company's vision, the employees at Pike Place Fish coach each other. As one fish seller explains, you act differently when you're "being" world famous; you coach each other differently. Any action that's inconsistent with the vision—being grouchy or pessimistic, leaving a knife on the counter, becoming distracted, or throwing a fish improperly—is reviewed in light of the vision and coached accordingly. Everyone coaches and everyone, including the owner, can be coached, even by the newest employee. It's not just about making Pike Place Fish a better place; it's also about becoming people of integrity. The employees respect and care about each other enough to remind each other continually of the possibilities and purpose they've declared for themselves.[31]

## CORE ABILITIES

The managing teams competency includes the core abilities to do the following.

*   Determine the circumstances in which a team approach is appropriate and, if using it is appropriate, the type of team to use.
*   Engage in and/or lead the process of setting clear performance goals for the team.
*   Participate in and/or provide the leadership in defining responsibilities and tasks for the team as a whole, as well as its individual members.
*   Demonstrate a sense of mutual and personal accountability for the achievement of team goals, not just an individual's own goals. That is, the individual doesn't approach problems and issues with a mindset of: That's not my responsibility or concern.
*   Apply decision-making methods and technologies that are appropriate to the goals, issues, and tasks confronting the team.
*   Resolve personal and task-related conflicts among team members before they become too disruptive.
*   Assess a person's own performance and that of the team in relation to goals, including the ability to take corrective action as needed.

## TEAMS AND INDIVIDUALISM

Again, in some countries, people strongly believe in the importance and centrality of the individual. In the United States, the United Kingdom, and Canada, educational, governmental, and business institutions frequently state that they exist to serve individual goals. Two cultural values that strongly affect decisions about whether to use teams and groups in organizations are individualism and collectivism.

The cultural belief in individualism creates uneasiness over the influence that teams or groups have in organizations. Employees in individualistic cultures are expected to act on the basis of their personal goals and self-interest. In collectivistic countries, such as China and South Korea, the use of teams by organizations is a natural extension of the nations' cultural values. Uneasiness revolves around the relative influence of individuals in teams. Thus we might characterize the basic difference as "fitting into the team" versus "standing out from the team." Even in societies that value individualism, the use of teams is substantial in such firms as Hewlett-Packard, Ford, General Electric, and MONY.

The potential for teams and individuals to have incompatible goals clearly exists, but these goals need not always conflict and in fact often are compatible. The potential for conflict and commonality is suggested by the following observations.

- Teams do exist, and employees need to take them into account.
- Teams mobilize powerful forces that create important effects for individuals.
- Teams may create both good and bad results.
- Teams can be managed to increase the benefits from them.

The circumstances under which teams should be used versus sole reliance on the individual—that is, a single employee or manager taking primary control and personal accountability for performing a task, resolving an issue, or solving a problem—should be assessed continually.

The following Managing Teams Competency feature provides insights on the use of teams at Pillsbury's Green Giant vegetable food processing plant in Belvedere, Illinois.

## COMPETENCY: MANAGING TEAMS

### PILLSBURY'S GREEN GIANT TEAMS

The structure of Pillsbury's Green Giant Belvedere plant comprises 48 business teams and additional ongoing improvement teams. The results of the Green Giant plant teams are impressive. The twin tube team has managed to reduce average changeover time significantly in going from the processing of one vegetable to another, thereby reducing vegetable inventories. The bulk freeze improvement team reengineered a tunnel freezer to freeze rice and pasta. In so doing, it reduced ergonomic, waste, repair, training, and annual labor costs.

Green Giant Plant Manager Vince Castle recalls that, when management first implemented teams at the Belvedere facility, "the focus was on getting the teams to direct or manage themselves." That remained the case until relatively recently, when it became apparent that the plant could further improve its performance by providing each team with a leader. Castle comments: "It's a real balancing act. If you put all of your effort into developing teams, you find that you sometimes don't really have an end goal in sight." Providing the Belvedere teams with leaders was part of an effort to focus more pointedly on developing—and meeting—specific, measurable goals. Castle says: "We'd reached a plateau, and it was time for leaders to step in and take a more prominent role so that teams could keep moving forward." The team leaders also provide the continuity necessary for teams to build on past achievements, given the inevitability of employee turnover. "If workforces never changed, we might not be going down the team leader path," Castle said.

Distribution team leader Russ Kitsemble matter-of-factly relates how he and his teams of forklift operators recently integrated frozen and dry distribution into a single, centralized distribution center supported by cross-functional work teams. "We had our forklift operators in training for six months, going back and forth between dry and frozen, but now we're seeing significant cost savings. And we're making better utilization of our people. Less overtime." Kitsemble notes that cases per wage hour are currently running better than the plan, and it has been 27 months since any recordable accidents have occurred in distribution.

For more information on Pillsbury, visit the organization's home page at *http://www.pillsbury. com.*

At the Belvedere plant, management has implemented a gain-sharing program in which 50 percent of plant favorability (cost performance versus fiscal operating plan) is allocated to a pool that is shared among all team members. The plant has also initiated a safety reward program based on the number of months that employees log without injury. At 3 months, employees receive a $15 Media Play gift certificate, at 6 months a catered dinner, and at 12 months a day off.[32]

**Learning Objective:**

7.   Describe the managing change competency.

# COMPETENCY: MANAGING CHANGE

The **managing change competency** involves the overall ability to recognize and implement needed adaptations or entirely new transformations in the people, tasks, strategies, structures, or technologies in a person's area of responsibility.

## CORE ABILITIES

The managing change competency includes the core abilities to do the following.

* Apply the six previously discussed competencies in the diagnosis, development, and implementation of needed changes.
* Provide leadership in the process of planned change (see especially Chapter 10, Leading Effectively: Foundations, and Chapter 11, Leading Effectively: Contemporary Developments). As we describe them in those chapters, leadership styles and approaches may need to vary under conditions of crisis and the need for major changes. Consider the case of Jack Welch, GE's recently retired CEO. At one time, he was nicknamed "Neutron Jack" because of his autocratic approach and style of leadership. He was faced with the need to make transformational and difficult decisions, including the elimination of tens of thousands of employees, entire levels of management, and several divisions. After completing this overhaul, Welch shifted his leadership approach and made it known that there was no place for autocrats at GE. Not many leaders can change their behaviors as dramatically as Welch did. In many instances, the directive autocrat needs to be replaced by a more democratic or permissive leader when a crisis has passed.[33]
* Diagnose pressure for and resistance to change in specific situations. These pressures may be internal—such as the organizational culture—or external—such as new technologies or competitors (see especially Chapter 15, Cultivating Organizational Culture, and Chapter 16, Guiding Organizational Change).
* Apply the systems model of change and other processes to introduce and achieve organizational change. Individuals with this ability are able to identify key issues and diagnose them by examining the basic factors of *who, what, why, when, where,* and *how.* We provide insights for developing this ability in most of the chapters of this book.
* Seek, gain, share, and apply new knowledge in the pursuit of constant improvement, creativity, and entirely new approaches or goals. These behaviors require **risk taking**, or the willingness to take reasonable chances by recognizing and capitalizing on opportunities while also recognizing their potential negative outcomes and monitoring progress toward goals.

## TECHNOLOGICAL FORCES

Technological forces, especially computer-based information technologies, continue to revolutionize how customers are served; employees communicate and network with one another and external stakeholders, such as customers, suppliers, competitors, and governmental agencies; tasks are performed; organizations are structured; human resources are led and managed; and so on.

Technological change may have positive effects, including products and services of higher quality and lower costs. But it also may have negative effects, including erosion of personal privacy, work-related stress, and health problems (e.g., eyestrain, carpal tunnel syndrome, and exposure to toxic substances).

New technologies are increasing the need for constant learning, adaptation, and innovation by individuals, teams, and entire organizations. In *Blur: The Speed of Change in the Connected Economy*, S. Davis and C. Meyer proposed a formula to represent the rapidly accelerating rate of technological and other changes:

$$\text{Speed} \times \text{connectivity} \times \text{intangibles} = \text{blur}.$$

| | |
|---|---|
| *Speed* | Every aspect of organizations operate and change in real time. |
| *Connectivity* | Everything is becoming electronically connected to everything else: products, people, companies, countries—everything. |
| *Intangibles* | Every transaction has both tangible and intangible economic value. The intangible is growing faster; it is the increasing role of personal services for many organizations and the economy as a whole. |
| *Blur* | The new world in which we will come to live and work.[34] |

The revolution in technologies is a driving force in creating the state of *blur* and the need to actively manage change. Throughout this book, we discuss topics that are related to the introduction and use of technology and which, in turn, are affected by it.

The rapid rise in use of the Internet in the United States is the most obvious expression of an economy and a culture that focus on speed. The Internet is a technology that seems to bring the entire world to a person's desktop instantaneously and to satisfy quickly any query or curiosity. The ever-expanding online World Wide Web is but the most recent indication of a trend over the past few decades that has brought businesses, customers, and others continually closer in real time. Technologies ranging from PCs to television to automated teller machines to 1-hour photo processing have shaped our expectations about acceptable time frames for seeing results.

The following Managing Change Competency feature reveals how Drew Santin and his firm, Santin Engineering, Inc., of Peabody, Massachusetts, increased speed to meet the needs of their clients.

## COMPETENCY: MANAGING CHANGE

### SANTIN ENGINEERING EMBRACES SPEED

Drew Santin's company, Santin Engineering, Inc., makes quick prototypes for manufacturers who want to see how their newest products will look, feel, and perform—and they want to know now, not tomorrow. Compounding the pressure is the fact that Santin's biggest markets—computer-component manufacturers and makers of clothing accessories and costume jewelry—are among the most demanding. His customers count on him to help them cope with ever-accelerating customer demand for quick turnaround.

Santin states, "I'm dealing with an industry, in PC components, where the two-year time frame for developing a new product, which was the case not long ago, now has become six months or less. And in some cases, we have to be able to help our customers turn around in a window that may be as short as a month. The fashion industry is the same way: They can see things get knocked off by competitors even before they go to market. So our ability to get a customized solution in front of the customer is crucial. The pressure is constant to reduce their time frames and to help them get a performing product in the shortest possible period of time." Instead of carrying around the need for speed like an albatross, he and his 60 employees are embracing it—and making Santin Engineering a speed merchant. Employees routinely work nights and weekends to help customers trim precious hours and days from the developmental process.

Santin cross-trains its employees to ensure maximum flexibility for customers. With computer-based software, engineers can produce quick plastic representations of production components on the spot—even while a meeting with a client is taking place.[35]

*For more information on Santin Engineering, Inc., visit the organization's home page at http://www.santineng.com.*

**Learning Objective:**

8. Explain the framework for learning about organizational behavior.

# LEARNING FRAMEWORK

The long-term effectiveness of an organization is determined by its ability to anticipate, manage, and respond to changes in the environment. Shareholders, unions, employees, financial institutions, government agencies, among others, exert numerous and ever-changing pressures, demands, and expectations on the organization. The competencies that we have identified highlight the connection between environmental forces and the actions of managers and employees. Throughout this book, therefore, we discuss the relationships among various environmental influences, competencies, and organizational behavior in general.

The framework for learning about organizational behavior and improving the competencies of employees in organizations consists of three basic components: (1) individuals in organizations; (2) team and leadership behaviors; and (3) the organization itself. Figure 1.5 shows the relationships among these components, as well as the

**Figure 1.5**                    **Framework for Learning**

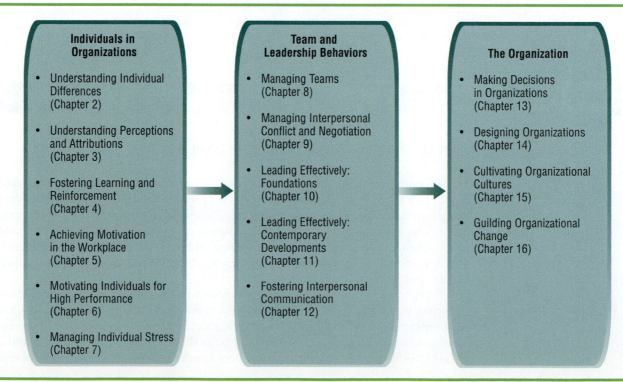

| Individuals in Organizations | Team and Leadership Behaviors | The Organization |
|---|---|---|
| • Understanding Individual Differences (Chapter 2) | • Managing Teams (Chapter 8) | • Making Decisions in Organizations (Chapter 13) |
| • Understanding Perceptions and Attributions (Chapter 3) | • Managing Interpersonal Conflict and Negotiation (Chapter 9) | • Designing Organizations (Chapter 14) |
| • Fostering Learning and Reinforcement (Chapter 4) | • Leading Effectively: Foundations (Chapter 10) | • Cultivating Organizational Cultures (Chapter 15) |
| • Achieving Motivation in the Workplace (Chapter 5) | • Leading Effectively: Contemporary Developments (Chapter 11) | • Guilding Organizational Change (Chapter 16) |
| • Motivating Individuals for High Performance (Chapter 6) | • Fostering Interpersonal Communication (Chapter 12) | |
| • Managing Individual Stress (Chapter 7) | | |

principal aspects of each. These relationships are much too dynamic—in terms of variety and change—to define them as laws or rules. As we discuss each component, the dynamics and complexities of organizational behavior will become clear.

## INDIVIDUALS IN ORGANIZATIONS

People make assumptions about those with whom they work or spend time in leisure activities. To some extent, these assumptions influence a person's behavior toward others. Effective employees understand what affects their own behaviors before attempting to influence the behaviors of others. In Part I, Chapters 2–7, we focus on the behavior of individuals, especially in organizations.

Individual behavior is the foundation of organizational performance. Understanding individual behavior, therefore, is crucial for effective management. Each person is a physiological system composed of various subsystems—digestive, nervous, circulatory, and reproductive—and a psychological system composed of various subsystems—attitudes, perceptions, learning capabilities, personality, needs, feelings, and values. In Part I, we concentrate on the individual's psychological system. Both internal and external factors shape a person's behavior on the job. Internal factors include learning ability, motivation, perception, attitudes, personality, and values. Among the external factors that affect a person's behavior are the organization's reward system, organizational politics, group behavior, managerial leadership styles, and the organization's design. We examine these factors in Parts II and III.

## TEAM AND LEADERSHIP BEHAVIORS

Being inherently social, people generally don't choose to live or work alone. Most of their time is spent interacting with others: People are born into a family group, worship in groups, work in teams, and play in groups. Much of a person's identity is based on the ways that other individuals and groups perceive and treat that person. For these reasons—and because many managers and employees spend considerable amounts of time interacting with other people—competencies in communication, interpersonal, and team dynamics are vital to everyone in an organization.

Organizations need leaders who can integrate customer, employee, and organizational goals. The ability of organizations to achieve their goals depends on the degree to which leadership abilities and styles enable managers and team leaders to control, influence, and act effectively. In Part II, Chapters 8–12, we examine how leaders influence others and how individuals can develop leadership competencies. Effective leadership involves management of conflict, which may arise over any number of issues. How employees communicate with superiors, peers, subordinates, and others can help make them effective team members or lead to low morale and lack of commitment. For that reason and because most managers and professionals spend considerable amounts of time dealing with others, we stress interpersonal communication in this part.

## THE ORGANIZATION ITSELF

Decision making in organizations isn't particularly orderly or totally within the control of the decision makers. In Part III, Chapters 13–16, we consider the factors, both internal and external, that influence individual, team, and organizational decisions. We identify and explore the phases of decision making and some ethical concepts and ethical dilemmas encountered.

To work effectively, all employees must clearly understand their jobs and the organization's design. We identify factors that influence organization design and present some typical organization designs.

Individuals enter organizations to work, earn money, and pursue career goals. We discuss how employees learn what is expected of them. Basically, they do so by exposure to the organization's culture. It is the set of shared assumptions and understandings about how things really work—that is, policies, practices, and norms—in the organization that are important.

The management of change involves adapting an organization to the demands of the environment and modifying the actual behaviors of employees. We explore the dynamics of organizational change and present several basic strategies for achieving change.

## CHAPTER SUMMARY

**1.** Describe the managing self competency.

The managing self competency involves the overall ability to assess a person's own strengths and weaknesses; set and pursue professional and personal goals; balance work and personal life; and engage in new learning—including new or modified skills, behaviors, and attitudes. This competency underlies the other six foundation competencies. Mastering it requires a lifelong process of learning and career management.

**2.** Describe the managing communication competency.

The managing communication competency involves the overall ability to transmit, receive, and understand data, information, thoughts, and emotions—nonverbal, verbal, written, listening, electronic, and the like. Core abilities included in this competency are describing, active listening, questioning, nonverbal communication, empathizing, verbal communication, and written communication. This competency is like the body's circulatory system, nourishing and carrying the other competencies.

**3.** Describe the managing diversity competency.

The managing diversity competency involves the overall ability to value unique individual and group characteristics, embrace such characteristics as potential sources of organizational strength, and respect the uniqueness of each individual. The core abilities in this competency are related to a framework of six primary categories of diversity: age, race, ethnicity, gender, physical abilities and qualities, and sexual orientation. Eight secondary categories of diversity include education, work background, and religious beliefs. Several types of diversity—changing workforce and customers, gender, race, and ethnicity, and age—affect most employees, managers, teams, departments, and organizations. These types of diversity are important because they often reflect differences in perspectives, lifestyles, attitudes, values, and behaviors. How managers and employees embrace and respond to diversity greatly influence an organization's effectiveness.

**4.** Describe the managing ethics competency.

The managing ethics competency involves the overall ability to incorporate values and principles that distinguish right from wrong into decision making and behaviors. Ethics are the values and principles that distinguish right from wrong. Managers and employees often experience ethical dilemmas—situations in which the individual or team must make a decision that involves multiple values.

**5.** Describe the managing across cultures competency.

The managing across cultures competency involves the overall ability to recognize and embrace similarities and differences among nations and cultures—even within the same organization—and then to approach key organizational and strategic issues with an open and inquisitive mind. Individualism, collectivism, uncertainty avoidance, and power distance are several of the fundamental work-related values that need to be understood in order to develop this competency. These and other values affect people's perceptions, communication, decisions, and behaviors.

**6.** Describe the managing teams competency.

The managing teams competency involves the overall ability to develop, support, facilitate, and lead groups to achieve organizational goals. Important also is recognition of the potential for individual and team differences and commonalities in goals.

**7.** Describe the managing change competency.

The managing change competency involves the overall ability to recognize and implement needed adaptations or entirely new transformations in the people, tasks, strategies, structures, or technologies in a person's area of responsibility. Technological forces are one of the primary sources of change. The ever-increasing pace of change, or *blur*, was defined as a function of *speed* times *connectivity* times *intangibles*. The Internet is one of the primary enablers of increasing speed and the state of blur.

**8.** Explain the framework for learning about organizational behavior.

Organizational behavior involves the dynamic interplay among individuals in organizations, team and leadership behaviors, and the organization itself. The seven fundamental competencies introduced are developed through the dynamic interplay among the parts of this framework, which are addressed throughout this book.

## KEY TERMS AND CONCEPTS

Active listening
Career
Career development
Career plan
Collectivism
Competency
Cultural values
Culture
Describing skill
Emotional intelligence
Empathizing skill
Ethical dilemma
Ethics
Glass ceiling
Global mindset
Individualism
Internet

Managing across cultures competency
Managing change competency
Managing communication competency
Managing diversity competency
Managing ethics competency
Managing self competency
Managing teams competency
Nonverbal communication
Organizational behavior
Power distance
Questioning skill
Racism
Risk taking
Uncertainty avoidance
Verbal communication
Written communication

## DISCUSSION QUESTIONS

1. Identify two strengths and two weaknesses in your own competencies. What specific steps might you take over the next 2 years to reduce the weaknesses?

2. What competencies are illustrated in the Preview Case about Pike Place Fish?

3. Identify three categories of diversity that represent significant issues in a team or an organization of which you are currently a member. How is this team or organization—and its members—addressing these issues?

4. The most successful teams and organizations are those that recognize the challenge and opportunity of embracing a diverse workforce. What obstacles stand in the way of doing so in a team or an organization of which you are or have been a member? Select a team or organization different from the one you used to respond to Question 3.

5. Identify two ethical dilemmas that you have faced during the past year. How did you resolve them?

6. How would you describe your society's work-related cultural values? What impact have they had on your education?

7. What is your dominant personal value orientation—individualism or collectivism? What is the basis for your answer?

8. Think of a team on which you are currently or have been a member. How would you evaluate its members—in general—with respect to the core abilities of the managing teams competency? Which members stand out, as either especially strong or especially weak, in terms of these abilities? Briefly describe their characteristics.

9. For the most challenging job you now have or have had in the past, list the technologies you are using or have used to help you do the job. How would your performance of the tasks involved change if any two of the technologies were no longer available?

10. What aspect of your life or role that you play reflects some or all of the variables that go into creating the state of blur? Explain.

# DEVELOPING COMPETENCIES

## Competency: Managing Self

## Professional Competencies Self-Assessment Inventory

*Instructions:* The statements in this inventory describe specific abilities and behaviors representative of outstanding and experienced managers and professionals. For each specific ability or behavior, you are to assess yourself on a scale from 1 to 10, according to the descriptive statements provided on the scale shown here.

10  I am outstanding on this ability/behavior.
9  I am very good on this ability/behavior.
8  I am good on this ability/behavior.
7  I am average on this ability/behavior.
6  I am barely adequate on this ability/behavior.
5  I am lacking on this ability/behavior.
4  I am weak on this ability/behavior.
3  I am very weak on this ability/behavior.
2  I have little relevant experience on this ability/ behavior, but the experiences I have had are poor.
1  I have no relevant experience. I have not yet begun to develop this ability/behavior.

Fill in the blank next to each listed specific ability/behavior with a number from the preceding scale that you think is most descriptive of yourself. You should choose a number that is most descriptive of what you are actually like rather than what you would prefer to be like.

### Specific Abilities/Behaviors

_____  1. Maintains an awareness of own behavior and how it affects others.
_____  2. Is able to set priorities and manage time.
_____  3. Knows own limitations and asks for help when necessary.
_____  4. Assesses and establishes own life- and work-related goals.
_____  5. Takes responsibility for decisions and managing self.
_____  6. Perseveres in the face of obstacles or criticism.
_____  7. Is not self-promoting or arrogant.
_____  8. Recovers quickly from failure, including learning from mistakes.
_____  9. Tries to learn continuously.
_____ 10. Pursues feedback openly and nondefensively.
_____ 11. Organizes and presents ideas effectively.
_____ 12. Detects and understands others' values, motives, and emotions.
_____ 13. Presents written materials clearly and concisely.
_____ 14. Listens actively and nonjudgmentally.
_____ 15. Responds appropriately to positive and negative feedback.
_____ 16. Is aware of and sensitive to nonverbal messages.
_____ 17. Holds people's attention when communicating.
_____ 18. Shares information willingly.

_____ 19. Expresses own needs, opinions, and preferences without offending others.
_____ 20. Uses a variety of computer-based (electronic) resources to communicate.
_____ 21. Encourages the inclusion of those who are different from self.
_____ 22. Seeks to learn from those with different characteristics and perspectives.
_____ 23. Embraces and demonstrates respect for people of other cultures and races.
_____ 24. Shows sensitivity to the needs and concerns of others.
_____ 25. Seeks positive win–win or appropriate compromise solutions to conflicts based on diversity issues.
_____ 26. Embraces unique individual and group characteristics as potential sources of organizational strength.
_____ 27. Is sensitive to differences among people and seeks ways to work with them.
_____ 28. Respects ideas, values, and traditions of others.
_____ 29. Identifies opportunities to promote diversity.
_____ 30. Invests personal effort in helping people with attributes different from self to succeed.
_____ 31. Demonstrates dignity and respect for others in working relationships.
_____ 32. Is honest and open in communication, limited only by privacy, legal, and competitive considerations.
_____ 33. Assesses the right or wrong in own decisions and behaviors.
_____ 34. Adheres to professional and organizational codes of conduct.
_____ 35. Avoids consistently pressures from others to engage in unethical conduct.
_____ 36. Understands ethical principles and rules.
_____ 37. Is seen by others as a person of integrity.
_____ 38. Sets clear expectations of ethical behavior and regularly reinforces this expectation with others.
_____ 39. Is sensitive to the rights of others.
_____ 40. Takes responsibility for own decisions and actions—doesn't place blame on others to escape responsibility.
_____ 41. Seeks to understand and appreciate the characteristics that make a particular culture unique.
_____ 42. Treats people from different cultures with respect.
_____ 43. Considers managerial and other issues from a worldwide perspective, that is, the ability to think globally, act locally.
_____ 44. Works effectively with members from different cultures.
_____ 45. Likes to experience different cultures.
_____ 46. Learns from those with different cultural backgrounds.

_____ 47. Knows which cultures have the expectation that individuals are to take care of themselves.

_____ 48. Possesses firsthand knowledge that different cultures are risk adverse and use rules to minimize trying to deal with uncertainty.

_____ 49. Knows how masculinity and femininity in different societies affect interpersonal relationships.

_____ 50. Works effectively with people from different cultures who value unequal distribution of power in society.

_____ 51. Works effectively in team situations.

_____ 52. Encourages teams to celebrate accomplishments.

_____ 53. Demonstrates mutual and personal responsibility for achieving team goals.

_____ 54. Observes dynamics when working with groups and raises relevant issues for discussion.

_____ 55. Promotes teamwork among groups, discourages "we versus they" thinking.

_____ 56. Supports and praises others for reaching goals and accomplishing tasks.

_____ 57. Encourages and supports creativity in teams.

_____ 58. Shares credit with others.

_____ 59. Motivates team members to work toward common goals.

_____ 60. Is able to use groupware and related information technologies to achieve team goals.

_____ 61. Demonstrates the leadership skills to implement planned change.

_____ 62. Understands how to diagnose pressures for and resistances to change.

_____ 63. Prepares people to manage change.

_____ 64. Learns, shares, and applies new knowledge to improve a team, department, or whole organization.

_____ 65. Knows how to diagnose a firm's culture.

_____ 66. Uses a variety of technologies to achieve successful change.

_____ 67. Understands how various organizational designs can be used to bring about successful organizational change.

_____ 68. Possesses a positive attitude toward considering changes and new ideas.

_____ 69. Is able to negotiate and resolve conflicts that are often part of any significant change.

_____ 70. Understands how organizational cultures influence organizational change.

## Scoring and Interpretation

The Professional Competencies Self-Assessment Inventory seeks your self-perceptions on characteristics and dimensions that are representative of seven foundation competencies. A competency is an interrelated set of abilities, behaviors, attitudes, and knowledge needed to be effective in most professional and managerial positions.

Total your responses for each competency as instructed. The sum of your responses is your score. The maximum score is 100 points.

*Managing Self Competency:* Involves the overall ability to assess your own strengths and weaknesses; set and pursue professional and personal goals; balance work and personal life;

and engage in new learning—including new or changed skills, behaviors, and attitudes.

- Add your responses for items 1 through 10 = _____, which is your self-assessment on the managing self competency.

*Managing Communication Competency:* Involves the overall ability to transmit, receive, and understand ideas, thoughts, and feelings—nonverbal, verbal, written, listening, electronic, and the like—for transferring and exchanging information and emotion.

- Add your responses for items 11 through 20 = _____, which is your self-assessment on the managing communication competency.

*Managing Diversity Competency:* Involves the overall ability to value unique individual and group characteristics, embrace such characteristics as potential sources of organizational strength, and respect the uniqueness of each individual.

- Add your responses for items 21 through 30 = _____, which is your self-assessment on the managing diversity competency.

*Managing Ethics Competency:* Involves the overall ability to incorporate values and principles that distinguish right from wrong in decision making and behavior.

- Add your responses for items 31 through 40 = _____, which is your self-assessment on the managing ethics competency.

*Managing Across Cultures Competency:* Involves the overall ability to recognize and embrace similarities and differences among nations and cultures and then to approach key organizational and strategic issues with an open and curious mind.

- Add your responses for items 41 through 50 = _____, which is your self-assessment on the managing across cultures competency.

*Managing Teams Competency:* Involves the overall ability to develop, support, facilitate, or lead teams to achieve organizational goals.

- Add your responses for items 51 through 60 = _____, which is your self-assessment on the managing teams competency.

*Managing Change Competency:* Involves the overall ability to recognize and implement needed adaptations or entirely new transformations in the people, tasks, strategies, structures, or technologies in the person's area of responsibility.

- Add your responses for items 61 through 70 = _____, which is your self-assessment on the managing change competency.

## Your Overall Profile

Plot your overall profile of competencies on the following grid by using the summary (total) score for each competency.

## Comparative Populations

Compare and contrast your scores with those of two sample populations: (1) experienced managerial professionals and (2) undergraduate students of organizational behavior at colleges

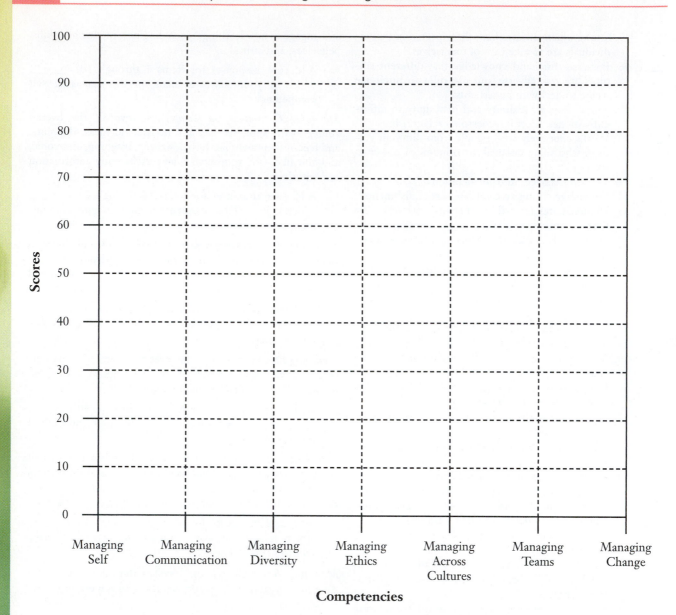

**Competencies**

and universities. (See pages 33 and 34.) Mean scores and standard deviations are based on a sample of more than 300 individuals. One standard deviation from the mean covers 68% of the sample population; that is, if your score falls within one standard deviation of the mean score of either the managerial or the student population, your score is similar to the scores of 68% of that population.

## Overall Interpretations

| Scores | Meaning |
| --- | --- |
| 20–39 | You see yourself as having little relevant experience and are deficient on this competency. |
| 40–59 | You see yourself as generally lacking on this competency but may be performing satisfactorily or better on a few of the abilities/behaviors. |
| 60–74 | You see yourself as average on this competency—probably below average on some abilities/behaviors and above average on others. |
| 75–89 | You see yourself as generally above average on this competency and very good on a number of abilities/behaviors. |
| 90–100 | You see yourself as generally outstanding on this competency. |

## Questions

1. What does your overall profile suggest in relation to your needs for personal and professional development?
2. Based on the competency most in need of development, identify three possible actions that you might take to reduce the gap between your current and desired level for that competency.
3. Would others who work with you closely or know you well agree with your self-assessment profile? In what dimensions might their assessments of you be similar to your own? Why? In what dimensions might they differ? Why?

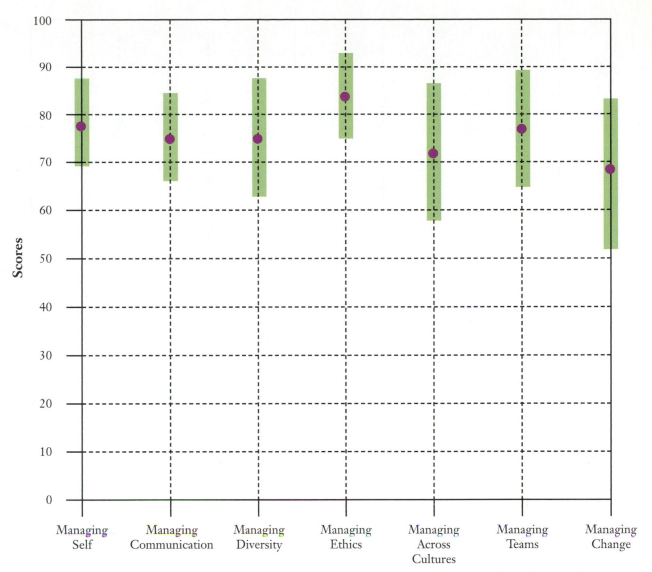

**Competencies, as rated by experienced managers and managerial professionals**

● = Mean          ▮ = 68% of scores fall within this range

## Managerial Population

| Competency | Mean | One Standard Deviation From Mean | Numerical Range for 68% of Population (High & Low) |
|---|---|---|---|
| Self | 78 | 9 | 87–69 |
| Communication | 75 | 9 | 84–66 |
| Diversity | 75 | 11 | 87–63 |
| Ethics | 84 | 9 | 93–75 |
| Across Cultures | 72 | 14 | 86–58 |
| Teams | 77 | 12 | 89–65 |
| Change | 69 | 14 | 83–52 |

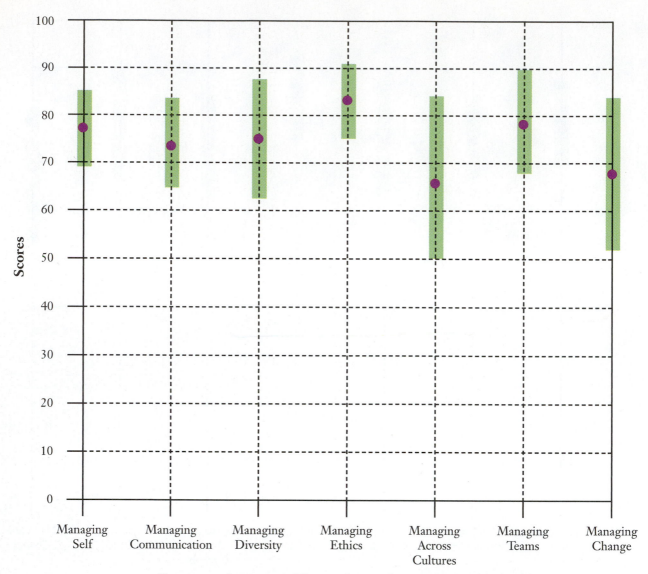

**Competencies, as rated by students of organizational behavior**

● = Mean     ▉ = 68% of scores fall within this range

## Student Population

| Competency | Mean | One Standard Deviation From Mean | Numerical Range for 68% of Population (High & Low) |
|---|---|---|---|
| Self | 77 | 8 | 85–69 |
| Communication | 74 | 9 | 84–65 |
| Diversity | 75 | 12 | 88–63 |
| Ethics | 83 | 8 | 91–75 |
| Across Cultures | 66 | 16 | 84–50 |
| Teams | 79 | 11 | 90–68 |
| Change | 67 | 16 | 84–52 |

# 1

# Individuals in Organizations

# Understanding Individual Differences

When you have finished studying the chapter, you should be able to:

1. Explain the basic sources of personality determinants.
2. Identify some personality traits that affect behavior.
3. State how attitudes affect behavior.
4. Indicate how job satisfaction and organizational commitment affect performance.
5. Describe the relationship between individual differences and ethical behavior.

2

## LARRY ELLISON AT ORACLE COMPUTER

Larry Ellison, founder and CEO of the software company Oracle Computer, has seen his company's stock price nosedive by 53 percent recently. Oracle has just turned in its worst quarterly results in 10 years. Addressing stockholders in Oracle's auditorium in Redwood Shores, California, he delivered a 30-minute, profanity-riddled speech in which he attacked his partners, his competitors, the government, and almost everyone in the room. He attacked IBM's new Unix-based DB2 as a real piece of crap that only Canadian programmers know how to operate, and he reamed Microsoft for breaking the law and designing a "stupid-ass" architecture for its SQL Server database. Although many in the audience applauded, to achieve Ellison's vision of shoving aside Microsoft as the biggest software company, Oracle must succeed where it has repeatedly failed: in applications software.

For the first time in more than 10 years, Ellison is running Oracle without much input from others. He is famous for firing people because he doesn't like them. He lost Oracle's President Raymond Lane and senior executive Gary Bloom recently and refuses to name successors. "It's a dumb idea," he says.

Ellison's outlandish behavior doesn't foster a lot of loyalty. In fact, many of Silicon Valley's new CEOs started their career at Oracle and were fired by Ellison. People stay at Oracle because they are paid well and fear recrimination. According to

Thomas Siebel, founder of Siebel Systems, "Larry is a control freak. He has a knack for taking the best and the brightest—and then he tries to destroy them." Ellison's defectors often end up competing against him, and he likes the challenge. "Larry Ellison is a silver-backed gorilla alpha male," says his friend and former Oracle employee, David Roux. "He will respond to a direct challenge, but only to a direct challenge." Ellison likes to compete, rather than collaborate. Oracle is a bully and is proud of it says another competitor. He has always rewarded ruthless behavior. For example, he gave sales bonuses in gold coins when Oracle drove Ingres, Sybase, and others out of business. "When you alienate everybody, you become someone no one wants to play with." Ellison's favorite quote is from a Zen proverb: "Your garden is never complete until there is nothing left to take out of it." To his competitors, this sends a cryptic message: Ellison will not be satisfied until there is no more business to take away from his competitors.

Ellison might be a nightmare to work for, but his methods have created unimaginable wealth for the company's shareholders, managers, and employees. Since its initial public offering (IPO) in early 1986, Oracle's share price has risen by more than 1,000 percent. Oracle began with a staff of 3; today, it has more than 40,000 employees throughout the world.[1]

For more information on Oracle, visit the organization's home page at http://www.oracle.com.

As the Preview Case indicates, people react to how they are treated by others. You might ask yourself whether you would be willing to work for Ellison. Depending on your personality, preferences, and goals, you might answer either *yes* or *no*. As an employee and future manager, you must recognize and appreciate individual differences in order to understand and respond appropriately to the behavior of people in organizations.[2]

In Part I of this book we cover individual processes in organizations. We focus first on the individual to help you develop an understanding of organizational behavior. The term **individual differences** refers to the fact that people vary in many ways. In this chapter, we discuss individual differences in personality and attitudes. We begin by addressing the concept of personality. Later in the chapter, we explore the role of attitudes in organizational behavior.

## PERSONALITY DETERMINANTS

**Learning Objective:**

1. Explain the basic sources of personality determinants.

Behavior always involves a complex interaction of the person and the situation. Events in the surrounding environment (including the presence and behavior of others) strongly influence the way people behave at any particular time; yet people always bring something of themselves to the situation. This "something," which represents the unique qualities of the individual, is *personality*.[3] No single definition of personality is accepted universally. However, one key idea is that personality represents personal characteristics that lead to consistent patterns of behavior. People quite naturally seek to understand these behavioral patterns in interactions with others. **Personality** represents the overall profile or combination of stable characteristics that capture the unique nature of a person. Therefore personality combines a set of physical and mental characteristics that reflect how a person looks, thinks, acts, and feels. This definition contains two important ideas.

First, theories of personality often describe what people have in common and what sets them apart. To understand the personality of an individual, then, is to understand both what that individual has in common with others and what makes that particular individual unique. Thus each employee in an organization is unique and may or may not act differently in a similar situation. This uniqueness makes managing and working with people extremely challenging.

Second, our definition refers to personality as being "stable" and having "continuity in time." Most people intuitively recognize this stability. If your entire personality could change suddenly and dramatically, your family and friends would confront a stranger. Although significant changes normally don't occur suddenly, an individual's personality may change over time. Personality development occurs to a certain extent throughout life, but the greatest changes occur in early childhood.

How is an individual's personality determined? Is personality inherited or genetically determined, or it is formed after years of experience? There are no simple answers because too many variables contribute to the development of each individual's personality. As Figure 2.1 shows, two primary sources shape personality differences: heredity and environment. An examination of these sources helps explain why individuals are different.

### HEREDITY

Deeply ingrained in many people's notions of personality is a belief in its genetic basis. Expressions such as "She is just like her father" or "He gets those irritating qualities from your side of the family, dear" reflect such beliefs. Some people believe that personality is inherited; others believe that a person's experiences determine personality. Our thinking is balanced—both heredity (genes) and environment (experiences) are important, although some personality characteristics may be influenced

**Figure 2.1**                    **Sources of Personality Differences**

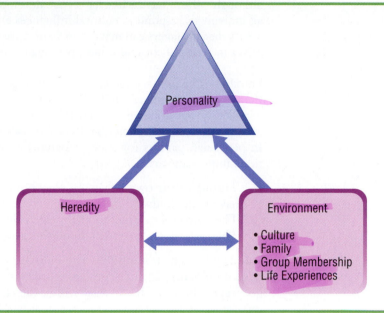

more by one factor than the other. Some personality traits seem to have a strong genetic component, whereas other traits seem to be largely learned (based on experiences).[4]

Some people argue that heredity sets limits on the range of development of characteristics and that within this range environmental forces determine personality characteristics. However, recent research on the personalities of twins who have been raised apart indicates that genetic determinants may play a larger role than many experts had believed. Some studies of twins suggest that as much as 50 to 55 percent of personality traits may be inherited. Further, inherited personality traits seem to explain about 50 percent of the variance in occupational choice. In other words, you probably inherited some traits that will influence your career choices.

## ENVIRONMENT

Many people believe that the environment plays a large role in shaping personality; in fact, the environment plays a more important role than do inherited characteristics. Aspects of the environment that influence personality formation include culture, family, group membership, and life experiences.

**Culture.**    The term **culture** refers to the distinctive ways that people in different societies organize and live their lives. Anthropologists have clearly demonstrated the important role that culture plays in personality development.[5] Individuals born into a particular society are exposed to family and societal values and to norms of acceptable behavior—the culture of that society. Culture also defines how various roles in that society are to be performed. For example, U.S. culture generally rewards people for being independent and competitive, whereas Japanese culture generally rewards individuals for being cooperative and group-oriented.

Culture helps determine broad patterns of behavioral similarity among people, but differences in behavior—which at times can be extreme—usually exist among individuals within a society. Most societies aren't homogeneous (although some are more homogeneous than others). For example, the work ethic (hard work is valued; an unwillingness to work is sinful) usually is associated with Western cultures. But this value doesn't influence everyone within Western cultures to the same degree. Thus, although culture has an impact on the development of employees' personalities, not all individuals respond to cultural influences equally. Indeed, one of the most serious errors that managers can make is to assume that their subordinates are just like themselves in terms of societal values, personality, or any other individual characteristic.

**Family.**   The primary vehicle for socializing an individual into a particular culture is the person's immediate family. Both parents and siblings play important roles in the personality development of most individuals. Members of an extended family—grandparents, aunts, uncles, and cousins—also can influence personality formation. In particular, parents (or a single parent) influence their children's development in three important ways:

- Through their own behaviors, they present situations that bring out certain behaviors in children.
- They serve as role models with which children often strongly identify.
- They selectively reward and punish certain behaviors.[6]

The family's situation also is an important source of personality differences. Situational influences include the family's size, socioeconomic level, race, religion, and geographic location; birth order within the family; parents' educational level; and so on. For example, a person raised in a poor family simply has different experiences and opportunities than does a person raised in a wealthy family. Being an only child is different in some important respects from being raised with several brothers and sisters.

**Group Membership.**   The first group to which most individuals belong is the family. People also participate in various groups during their lives, beginning with their childhood playmates and continuing through teenaged schoolmates, sports teams, and social groups to adult work and social groups. The numerous roles and experiences that people have as members of groups represent another important source of personality differences. Although playmates and school groups early in life may have the strongest influences on personality formation, social and group experiences in later life continue to influence and shape personality. Understanding someone's personality requires understanding the groups to which that person belongs or has belonged in the past.

**Life Experiences.**   Each person's life also is unique in terms of specific events and experiences, which can serve as important determinants of personality. For example, the development of self-esteem (a personality dimension that we discuss shortly) depends on a series of experiences that include the opportunity to achieve goals and meet expectations, evidence of the ability to influence others, and a clear sense of being valued by others. Thus a complex series of events and interactions with other people helps shape the adult's level of self-esteem. For example, employees at Oracle have noticed a remarkable change in their company as a result of Ellison's leadership.

**Learning Objective:**

2. Identify some personality traits that affect behavior.

## PERSONALITY AND BEHAVIOR

The vast number and variety of specific personality traits or dimensions are bewildering. The term **personality trait** typically refers to the basic components of personality. Researchers of personality have identified literally *thousands* of traits over the years. Trait names simply represent the terms that people use to describe each other. However, a list containing hundreds or thousands of terms isn't very useful either in understanding the structure of personality in a scientific sense or in describing individual differences in a practical sense. To be useful, these terms need to be organized into a small set of concepts or descriptions. Recent research has done just that, identifying several general factors that can be used to describe a personality.

### BIG FIVE PERSONALITY FACTORS

The **"Big Five" personality factors**, as they often are referred to, describe the individual's adjustment, sociability, conscientiousness, agreeableness, and intellectual openness.[7] As shown in Figure 2.2, each factor includes a potentially large number and range of specific traits. That is, each factor is both a collection of related traits and a continuum.

The main reason that we are interested in individual personality in the study of organizational behavior is the linkage between personality and behavior. Researchers have investigated extensively the relationships between the Big Five personality factors and job performance. Their findings indicate that employees who are responsible, dependable, persistent, and achievement-oriented perform better than those who lack these traits (the extremes of the *conscientiousness* continuum in Figure 2.2). An individual with a personality at one extreme of the *agreeableness* factor continuum might be described as warm and considerate. But with a personality at this factor's other

| Figure 2.2 | The "Big Five" Personality Factors |
|---|---|

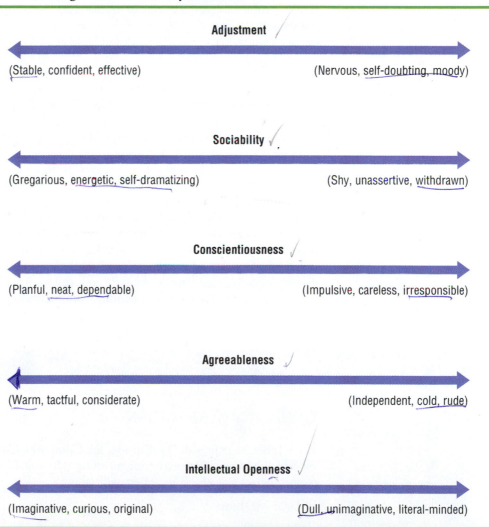

**Adjustment**

(Stable, confident, effective)                    (Nervous, self-doubting, moody)

**Sociability**

(Gregarious, energetic, self-dramatizing)                    (Shy, unassertive, withdrawn)

**Conscientiousness**

(Planful, neat, dependable)                    (Impulsive, careless, irresponsible)

**Agreeableness**

(Warm, tactful, considerate)                    (Independent, cold, rude)

**Intellectual Openness**

(Imaginative, curious, original)                    (Dull, unimaginative, literal-minded)

Source: Developed from Hogan, R. T. Personality and personality measurement. In M. D. Dunnette and L. M. Hough (eds.), *Handbook of Industrial and Organizational Psychology*, vol. 2, 2nd ed. Palo Alto, Calif.: Consulting Psychologists Press, 1991, 878–879; McCrae, R. R., and Costa, P. T. A five-factor theory of personality. In L. A. Pervin and O. P. John (eds.), *Handbook of Personality*, 2nd ed. New York: Guilford, 1999, 139–153.

extreme, the person would be considered cold or rude. The first Developing Competencies section at the end of this chapter contains a questionnaire that you can use to assess yourself in terms of these five personality factors. We invite you to complete it now to help you better understand your own personality.

Although each personality factor represents a collection of related traits, the link between personality and specific behaviors often is most clear when we focus on a single trait rather than all five factors at once. Here we examine several *specific* personality traits that are particularly important for understanding aspects of organizational behavior. Then, throughout the book, we explain additional personality traits as they relate to topics under discussion—for example, in relation to perception (Chapter 3), work stress (Chapter 7), political behavior (Chapter 9), and leadership (Chapter 11).

As we weave an understanding of personality and other individual differences into our exploration of a variety of topics in organizational behavior, we hope that you come to understand the crucial role that personality plays in explaining behavior. People clearly pay a great deal of attention to attributes of the personalities of the coworkers with whom they interact. The following Managing Across Cultures Competency feature shows how Peter Jones, a vice president of Computex, was faced with serious problems created by one of his managers who apparently had a less than pleasing personality.

### SELF-ESTEEM

**Self-esteem** results from an individual's continuing self-evaluation.[8] In other words, people develop, hold, and sometimes modify opinions of their own behaviors, abilities, appearance, and worth. These general assessments reflect responses to people and situations, successes and failures, and the opinions of others. Such evaluations are sufficiently accurate and stable to be widely regarded as a basic personality trait or dimension. In terms of the Big Five personality factors, self-esteem most likely would be part of the *adjustment* factor (see Figure 2.2).

Self-esteem affects behavior in organizations and other social settings in several important ways. It is related to initial vocational choice. For example, individuals with high self-esteem take risks in job selection, are attracted to high-status occupations (e.g., medicine or law), and are more likely to choose unconventional or nontraditional jobs (e.g., forest ranger or jet pilot) than are individuals with low self-esteem. A study of college students looking for jobs reported that those with high self-esteem (1) received more favorable evaluations from recruiters, (2) were more satisfied with

## COMPETENCY:    MANAGING ACROSS CULTURES

### COMPUTEX CORPORATION

Peter Jones, vice president—Europe, for Computex Corporation, opened a letter at his San Francisco office early one morning. He was dismayed at the letter's contents (some portions of which have been edited out).

Dear Mr. Jones:

The writers of this letter represent the sales force from Computex Sweden with the exception of our sales manager. We have decided to bring to your attention a rather serious matter, which if left unresolved, will result in resignations from the majority of us in the near future. We don't want to be in this situation, and we recognize that we are going outside of the chain-of-command with this letter, but we are approaching you in an attempt to save our sales team for the benefit of Computex Corporation and ourselves.

We consider ourselves to be an experienced, professional, and competent group of people. We have always been proud to work for Computex. We are well known in many areas of business in Sweden—many of our customers are friends and they view us as representatives of Computex. It is our feeling that the business will be significantly harmed if most of us were to leave. We provide this background because none of us have ever personally met you.

Our problems seem, to us, fairly straightforward. They arise solely as the result of the personality, character traits, and behavior of our general manager, Mr. Miller. He loses his temper almost daily, and most of these outbursts are an overreaction to small things. His mood and opinions seem to change almost on an hourly basis. He treats us with disrespect, and seldom delivers on his promises to "value our opinions" and "involve us more deeply in the business." Most of the fine slogans that he states publicly in meetings and individual discussions have proven to be only words. Interpersonal relationships between Mr. Miller and us have deteriorated to the point where most of us spend as little time as possible in the office. None of us have ever before experienced working with an individual who has such a mercurial personality and treats the people around him in such a fashion.

If this sales team was not composed of mature individuals who continue to be interested in working for Computex, most of us would have left by now. As it is, so far only one salesperson has left the company because of Mr. Miller. However, we are not willing to put up with this situation indefinitely. As we stated earlier, unless some positive changes are made, most of us will soon be working for your competitors.

It is not our objective to cost Mr. Miller his job. We recognize that he has done some good things in terms of generating new business. He presents himself well to the outside world. The problem, rather, is internal to our office and our day-to-day working relationships with him, which have become intolerable. If he could control his mood, treat us with more respect, and deliver on his promises, we think the office could succeed under his leadership.

We are fully aware of the seriousness of contacting you in this way. However, we believe that one person is ruining the entire organization and immediate action is required. Because the problem is so personal, we don't see how it can be resolved without some sort of action from you.

We are hoping for a positive solution.

*Signed:* "Nine of your sales representatives in Sweden"

Jones sighed heavily as he finished reading the letter. He was unsure whether this was strictly a "personality" conflict or a "cross-cultural" problem. He didn't particularly like Miller personally and thought that he had a rather abrasive personality, but nothing like this had ever happened in his previous assignments, one of which had been international. He began to wish that he hadn't sent Miller to Sweden in the first place. I wish I'd sent Gonzalez or Taylor, he thought to himself. "What do I do now?" he wondered. Jones knew that this problem would be a real test of his management skills.[9]

*For more information on Computex Corporation, visit the organization's home page at http://www.computexas.com.*

the job search, (3) received more job offers, and (4) were more likely to accept jobs before graduation than were students with low self-esteem.

Self-esteem is also related to numerous behaviors. Employees with low self-esteem are more easily influenced by the opinions of other workers than are employees with high self-esteem. Employees with low self-esteem set lower goals for themselves than do employees with high self-esteem. Furthermore, employees with high self-esteem place more value on actually attaining those goals than do employees with low self-esteem. Employees with low self-esteem are more susceptible than employees with high self-esteem to adverse job conditions such as stress, conflict, ambiguity, poor supervision, poor working conditions, and the like. In a general sense, self-esteem is positively related to achievement and a willingness to expend effort to accomplish tasks. Clearly, self-esteem is an important individual difference in terms of work behavior.[10]

## LOCUS OF CONTROL

**Locus of control** refers to the extent to which individuals believe that they can control events affecting them. On the one hand, individuals who have a high **internal locus of control** (internals) believe that their own behavior and actions primarily, but not necessarily totally, determine many of the events in their lives. On the other hand, individuals who have a high **external locus of control** (externals) believe that chance, fate, or other people primarily determine what happens to them. Locus of control typically is considered to be a part of the *conscientiousness* factor (see Figure 2.2). What is your locus of control? Table 2.1 contains a measure that you can use to assess your own locus of control beliefs.

Many differences between internals and externals are significant in explaining aspects of behavior in organizations and other social settings.[11] Internals control their own behavior better, are more active politically and socially, and seek information about their situations more actively than do externals. Compared to externals, internals are more likely to try to influence or persuade others and are less likely to be influenced by others. Internals often are more achievement-oriented than are externals. Compared to internals, externals appear to prefer a more structured, directive style of supervision. As we pointed out in Chapter 1, the ability to manage effectively in the global environment is an important competency. Managers with a high internal locus of control often adjust more readily to international assignments than do managers with a high external locus of control. The letter from the Swedish sales force of Computex Corporation may reflect an internal locus of control orientation and an effort, by attempting to influence Peter Jones, to gain greater control over the events in their working lives.

Again, we are particularly interested in the relationship between these personality dimensions and specific behaviors. Figure 2.3 (page 46) shows some of the important relationships between locus of control and job performance.

## GOAL ORIENTATION

Another individual difference of importance for behavior in work settings is *goal orientation*.[12] Specifically, two orientations are considered important in terms of understanding an individual's performance. A person with a **learning goal orientation** develops by continually acquiring new competencies and mastering new situations. A person with a **performance goal orientation** demonstrates and validates competencies by seeking favorable judgments from others (e.g., a manager) and avoiding negative judgments. Table 2.2 (page 47) contains a questionnaire that you can use to assess your own learning and performance goal orientations with regard to your academic studies.

**Table 2.1**

### A Locus of Control Measure

For each of these 10 questions, indicate the extent to which you agree or disagree, using the following scale.

| | |
|---|---|
| 1 = strongly disagree | 5 = slightly agree |
| 2 = disagree | 6 = agree |
| 3 = slightly disagree | 7 = strongly agree |
| 4 = neither disagree nor agree | |

_____ 1. When I get what I want it's usually because I worked hard for it.

_____ 2. When I make plans I am almost certain to make them work.

_____ 3. I prefer games involving some luck over games requiring pure skill.

_____ 4. I can learn almost anything if I set my mind to it.

_____ 5. My major accomplishments are entirely due to my hard work and ability.

_____ 6. I usually don't set goals, because I have a hard time following through on them.

_____ 7. Competition discourages excellence.

_____ 8. Often people get ahead just by being lucky.

_____ 9. On any sort of exam or competition I like to know how well I do relative to everyone else.

_____ 10. It's pointless to keep working on something that's too difficult for me.

To determine your score, reverse the values you selected for questions 3, 6, 7, 8, and 10 (1 = 7, 2 = 6, 3 = 5, 4 = 4, 5 = 3, 6 = 2, 7 = 1). For example, if you strongly disagreed with the statement in question 3, you would have given it a value of "1." Change this value to a "7." Reverse the scores in a similar manner for questions 6, 7, 8, and 10. Now add the 10 point values together.

Your score: _____

A study of college students found a mean of 51.8 for men and 52.2 for women using this questionnaire. The higher your score, the higher your internal locus of control. Low scores are associated with external locus of control.

Source: Adapted from Burger, J. M. *Personality: Theory and Research*. Belmont, Calif.: Wadsworth, 1986, pp. 400–401.

The implications of these goal orientations at work are dramatic. A performance goal orientation can lead to a "helpless" response pattern in behavior. Employees with a strong performance goal orientation may avoid challenges at work and perform poorly when they encounter obstacles that are difficult to overcome. When faced with failure, such individuals are likely to become unhappy and dissatisfied and seek to withdraw from the situations in which they find themselves. By contrast, individuals with a strong learning goal orientation are more likely to exhibit "mastery-oriented" responses to work challenges. Employees with a strong learning goal orientation strive to overcome failure and setbacks by increasing their efforts and seeking new solutions to a problem. They treat failure as a form of useful feedback, typically maintain their composure when challenged, and sustain or increase performance even when they face obstacles that are difficult to overcome. A strong learning goal orientation may be summed up by the slogan often placed by coaches on the walls of locker rooms: When the going gets tough, the tough get going.

A study of salespeople employed by a medical supplies distributor investigated the relationship between goal orientation and job performance. As expected, superior sales performance was associated with a learning goal orientation. The consultants concluded that salespeople who simply "wanted to look good" (a performance goal orientation) would not succeed in their jobs. These salespeople needed to have the

**Figure 2.3**                    **The Effects of Locus of Control on Performance**

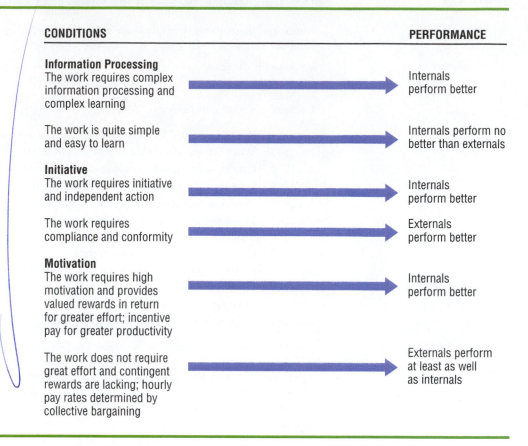

| CONDITIONS | | PERFORMANCE |
|---|---|---|
| **Information Processing**<br>The work requires complex information processing and complex learning | → | Internals perform better |
| The work is quite simple and easy to learn | → | Internals perform no better than externals |
| **Initiative**<br>The work requires initiative and independent action | → | Internals perform better |
| The work requires compliance and conformity | → | Externals perform better |
| **Motivation**<br>The work requires high motivation and provides valued rewards in return for greater effort; incentive pay for greater productivity | → | Internals perform better |
| The work does not require great effort and contingent rewards are lacking; hourly pay rates determined by collective bargaining | → | Externals perform at least as well as internals |

Source: Miner, J. B. *Industrial–Organizational Psychology*. New York: McGraw-Hill, 1992, 151. Reprinted with permission of McGraw-Hill.

desire to develop the skills needed for success (a learning goal orientation). One of the consultants' recommendations to the organization was to seek evidence of a learning goal orientation when selecting new employees for its sales force.[13]

## INTROVERSION AND EXTROVERSION

In everyday usage, the words *introvert* and *extrovert* describe a person's congeniality. **Introversion** is a tendency to be directed inward and have a greater affinity for abstract ideas and sensitivity to personal feelings. Introverts are quiet, introspective, and emotionally unexpressive. **Extroversion** is an orientation toward other people, events, and objects. Extroverts are sociable, lively, impulsive, and emotionally expressive. Gordon Ellison at Oracle is an extrovert. Introversion and extroversion are part of the collection of traits that comprise the *sociability* factor (see Figure 2.2). Many experts consider introversion and extroversion to be a personality dimension with a relatively high genetically determined component.

Although some people exhibit the extremes of introversion and extroversion, most are only moderately introverted or extroverted, or are even relatively balanced between the extremes. Introverts and extroverts appear in all educational, gender, and occupational groups. As might be expected, extroverts are well represented in managerial occupations because the manager's role often involves working with others and influencing them to attain organizational goals. Some people suggest that some extroversion may be essential to managerial success. However, either extreme extrover-

## Table 2.2

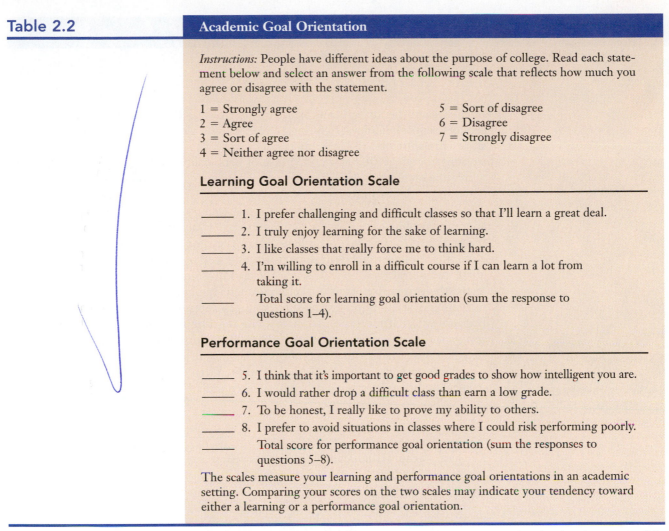

### Academic Goal Orientation

*Instructions:* People have different ideas about the purpose of college. Read each statement below and select an answer from the following scale that reflects how much you agree or disagree with the statement.

1 = Strongly agree                    5 = Sort of disagree
2 = Agree                             6 = Disagree
3 = Sort of agree                     7 = Strongly disagree
4 = Neither agree nor disagree

#### Learning Goal Orientation Scale

_____  1. I prefer challenging and difficult classes so that I'll learn a great deal.

_____  2. I truly enjoy learning for the sake of learning.

_____  3. I like classes that really force me to think hard.

_____  4. I'm willing to enroll in a difficult course if I can learn a lot from taking it.

_____     Total score for learning goal orientation (sum the response to questions 1–4).

#### Performance Goal Orientation Scale

_____  5. I think that it's important to get good grades to show how intelligent you are.

_____  6. I would rather drop a difficult class than earn a low grade.

_____  7. To be honest, I really like to prove my ability to others.

_____  8. I prefer to avoid situations in classes where I could risk performing poorly.

_____     Total score for performance goal orientation (sum the responses to questions 5–8).

The scales measure your learning and performance goal orientations in an academic setting. Comparing your scores on the two scales may indicate your tendency toward either a learning or a performance goal orientation.

Source: Adapted from VandeWalle, D., Cron, W., and Slocum, J. W. The role of goal orientation following performance feedback. *Journal of Applied Psychology*, 2001, 86, 629–640.

sion or extreme introversion can interfere with an individual's effectiveness in an organization.[14]

One of the most striking implications of the introversion–extroversion personality dimension involves task performance under different working conditions. The evidence suggests that introverts perform better alone and in a quiet environment, whereas extroverts perform better in an environment with greater sensory stimulation, such as a noisy office with many people and a high level of activity.

## ORGANIZATIONAL USES

It should be evident by now that the personality dimensions have important implications for understanding behavior. However, managers or groups should not try to change or otherwise directly control employee personality because being able to do so is generally impossible. Even if such control were possible, it would be highly unethical. Rather, the challenge for managers and employees is to understand the crucial role played by personality in explaining some aspects of human behavior in the workplace. Knowledge of important individual differences provides managers, employees, and students of organizational behavior with valuable insights and a framework that they can use to diagnose events and situations. The following

## COMPETENCY:    MANAGING TEAMS

### TEAMS AT HEWLETT-PACKARD

Reed Breland became a team facilitator at Hewlett-Packard's 180-person financial services center in Colorado Springs 2 years ago. After several months in his new position, Breland noticed that members of one of his teams were having a difficult time working together. "It was a classic case of personality conflict," he says. "They just didn't like each other. But when two people on an eight-person team don't get along, believe me, it's disruptive."

Breland gave the team time to try to work things out. "Of course, I spoke to them about the problems, but I was mainly interested in making sure they understood that the work had to get done, regardless of how they got along," he says. However, after 9 months team members still weren't working well together. Productivity was inadequate and morale was poor. "I knew I had to do something then, because it had affected their work," explains Breland. He then simply dissolved the team and placed its members in other jobs rather than trying to determine who was right and wrong. Breland says that the team members are doing fine in their other assignments. He compares their team dynamics with those of a sports team: "If the chemistry isn't right, it doesn't matter how good or bad the players are. It's not going to work. As a team leader you have to know when it's reached that point. It's more of an art than a science, but that's what makes the job so interesting."[15]

*For more information on Hewlett-Packard, visit the organization's home page at http://www.hp.com.*

Managing Teams Competency feature above describes such a situation—an attempt at Hewlett-Packard to create effective work teams.

### THE PERSON AND THE SITUATION

Although understanding differences in personality is important, behavior always involves an interaction of the person and the situation. Sometimes the demands of the situation may be so overwhelming that individual differences are relatively unimportant. For example, if an office building is burning, everyone in it will try to flee. However, the fact that all employees behaved the same way says nothing about the personalities of those individuals. In other situations, individual differences may explain more about behavior.

The relative importance of situational versus personal determinants of behavior continues to be debated, but considerable evidence exists for roles by both. We believe that considering both determinants will help you to understand behavior in organizations. For that reason, our perspective is consistently used throughout this book. You will discover that many of the topics covered, such as leadership, political behavior, power differences, stress, and resistance to change, examine both *personal* and *situational causes* for the organizational behavior discussed. Both *interact* to determine behavior.

## ATTITUDES AND BEHAVIOR

Attitudes are another type of *individual difference* that affects behavior. **Attitudes** are relatively lasting feelings, beliefs, and behavioral tendencies aimed at specific people, groups, ideas, issues, or objects.[16] Attitudes reflect an individual's background and experiences. As with personality development, significant people in a person's life—

parents, friends, and members of social and work groups—strongly influence attitude formation. Also, some evidence points to genetic influences on the attitudes that people develop.

## COMPONENTS OF ATTITUDES

People often think of attitudes as a simple concept, but in reality attitudes and their effects on behavior can be extremely complex. An attitude consists of

- an *affective* component—the feelings, sentiments, moods, and emotions about some person, idea, event, or object;
- a *cognitive* component—the thoughts, opinions, knowledge, or information held by the individual; and
- a *behavioral* component—the predisposition to act on a favorable or unfavorable evaluation of something.[17]

These components don't exist or function separately. An attitude represents the *interplay* of a person's affective, cognitive, and behavioral tendencies with regard to something—another person or group, an event, or an issue. For example, suppose that a college student holds a negative attitude about the use of tobacco. During a job interview with the representative of Skippy Peanut Butter, she discovers that Skippy is owned by Kraft Foods, which is a major division of Phillip Morris, a major supplier of cigarettes. She might feel a sudden intense dislike for the company's interviewer (the affective component). She might form a negative opinion of the interviewer based on beliefs and opinions about the type of person who would work for such a company (the cognitive component). She might even be tempted to make an unkind remark to the interviewer or suddenly terminate the interview (the behavioral component). However, the person's *actual* behavior may or may not be easy to predict and will depend on several factors that we discuss shortly.

## LINKS TO BEHAVIOR

To what extent do attitudes predict or cause behavior? A simple, direct link between attitudes and behavior usually doesn't exist. In the preceding interview example, the college student might have a negative attitude but choose not to behave negatively toward the interviewer. She might not act on her attitude because (1) she needs a job, (2) the norms of courteous behavior outweigh her desire to express her negative attitude, (3) she decides that the interviewer is an inappropriate target for negative behavior, and/or (4) she acknowledges the possibility of having incomplete information.

Pollsters and others often measure attitudes and attempt to predict subsequent behavior. Often, doing so is difficult; however, observing three principles can improve the accuracy of predicting behavior from attitudes.

- General attitudes best predict general behaviors.
- Specific attitudes best predict specific behaviors.
- The less time that elapses between attitude measurement and behavior, the more consistent will be the relationship between attitude and behavior.

For example, attitudes toward women in management in general aren't as good a predictor of whether someone will work well for a female manager as are specific attitudes toward a particular manager. General attitudes toward religion aren't good predictors of specific behavior, such as giving to a certain church-related charity or observing a specific religious holiday. However, these general attitudes may accurately predict general religious behavior, such as the overall level of involvement in church activities. Moreover, attitudes may change over time. Generally, the longer the elapsed time between the measurement of an attitude and a behavior, the less likely it is that the relationship between them will be strong. This third principle is well known to political pollsters (after some earlier embarrassments), and they typically are careful not to predict voting behavior too far ahead of an actual election. (Or they may be careful to add certain qualifiers to published polls, such as: If the election were held today. . . .)

You should recognize that the link between attitudes and actual behaviors is tentative. Attitudes result in *intended* behaviors; this intention may or may not be carried out in a particular situation. It is not uncommon to hear people say, "He has a bad attitude." One of the things that has been found to affect the link between an attitude and behavior is hope.

**Hope.**   **Hope** involves a person's mental willpower (determination) and waypower (road map) to achieve goals.[18] Simply wishing for something isn't enough; a person must have the means to make it happen. However, all the knowledge and skills needed to solve a problem won't help if the person doesn't have the willpower to do so. Therefore a simple definition of hope is

Hope = mental willpower + waypower to achieve goals.

Answering the questions in Table 2.3 will help you understand this definition of *hope*. The value of this concept is that it applies to a variety of work-related attitudes. For example, optimism, internal locus of control, and achievement motivation are closely and strongly related. Managers who are hopeful spend more time with employees, establish open lines of communication with employees and others, and help employees set difficult, but achievable, goals. High-hope individuals tend to be more certain of their goals, value progress toward achieving those goals, enjoy interacting with people, readily adapt to new relationships, and are less anxious in stressful situations than are low-hope individuals.

**Table 2.3**

**Hope Scale**

Read each item carefully. For each item, what number best describes you?

1 = definitely false          3 = mostly true
2 = mostly false              4 = definitely true

_____  1. I energetically pursue my work (academic) goals.
_____  2. I can think of many ways to get out of a jam.
_____  3. My past experiences have prepared me well for my future.
_____  4. There are lots of ways around any problem.
_____  5. I've been pretty successful in life.
_____  6. I can think of many ways to get things in life that are most important to me.
_____  7. I meet the goals (work/academic) that I set for myself.
_____  8. Even when others get discouraged, I know I can find a way to solve the problem.

**Scoring**

Total the eight numbers. If you score higher than 24, you are a hopeful person. If you score less than 24, you probably aren't hopeful. Items 1, 3, 5, and 7 relate to willpower, and items 2, 4, 6, and 8 relate to waypower.

Source: Adapted from Snyder, C. R. Managing for high hope. *R & D Innovator*, 1995, 4(6), 6–7; Snyder, C. R., LaPointe, A. B., Crowson, J. J., and Early, S. Preferences of high- and low-hope people for self-referential input. *Cognition and Emotion*, 1998, 12, 807–823.

Managers can help employees increase their level of hope in at least three ways. First, they can help employees set clear *goals* that have benchmarks so that the employees can track their progress toward the goal; vague goals may actually lessen hope because the result sought is unclear and tracking progress therefore is difficult, if not impossible. Employees who set goals that are slightly higher than previous levels of performance learn to expand their range of hope. They also learn a great deal about which goals are best for them. Second, managers can help employees break overall, long-term goals into *small subgoals* or *steps*. Remember how you learned to ride a bike? Through many falls and wobbles, you learned that each consecutive subgoal (moving the pedals, balancing, going a block without falling) is a stretch. These small steps provided you with positive mental maps about how to reach your goal—riding a bike. Third, managers can help employees figure out how to *motivate* themselves to reach their goals. At Don Herring dealership, the largest Mitsubishi dealership in the United States, the names of all salespersons are posted on a chart in the break room.[19] The typical new-car salesperson sells 8 to 10 cars a month. At Herring, a salesperson sells 20 to 25 a month. How has Herring achieved such results? When a salesperson sells a car, a gold star is placed beside that person's name. The purpose of the chart and gold star is to illustrate positive movement toward achieving a realistic sales goal. The perception of positive movement is crucial for hope.

## WORK ATTITUDES

**Learning Objective:**

4. Indicate how job satisfaction and organizational commitment affect performance.

The importance of attitude–behavior relationships can best be demonstrated by examining two key work attitudes—job satisfaction and organizational commitment. Of interest also are the complex relationships between job satisfaction and job performance.

### JOB SATISFACTION

Perhaps the attitude of greatest interest to managers and team leaders is job satisfaction.[20] Do people generally like their jobs? Despite what you may hear in the news about dissatisfied workers going on strike or even acting violently toward their coworkers and/or manager, people are generally quite satisfied with their jobs. These feelings, reflecting attitudes toward a job, are known as **job satisfaction**. Low job satisfaction can result in costly turnover, absenteeism, tardiness, and even poor mental health. Because job satisfaction is important to organizations, we need to look at the factors that contribute to it.

**Sources of Job Satisfaction.**    A popular measure of job satisfaction is shown in Table 2.4. Take a minute and complete it. Obviously, you may be satisfied with some aspects of your job (e.g., job security) and, at the same time, be dissatisfied with others (e.g., pay).

The sources of job satisfaction and dissatisfaction vary from person to person. Sources important for many employees include the challenge of the job, interest that the work holds for the employee, physical activity required, working conditions, rewards available from the organization, nature of coworkers, and the like. Table 2.5 lists work factors that often are related to levels of employee job satisfaction. An important implication suggested is that job satisfaction be considered an outcome of an individual's work experience. Thus high levels of dissatisfaction should indicate to managers that problems exist, say, with working conditions, the reward system, or the employee's role in the organization.

**Relation to Job Behavior.**    Of special interest to managers and employees are the possible relationships between job satisfaction and various job behaviors and other outcomes in the workplace. A common sense notion is that job satisfaction leads

**Table 2.4**

## Measure of Job Satisfaction

Please indicate the extent of your satisfaction on the scale to each of the following statements.

A = Very dissatisfied            D = Satisfied
B = Dissatisfied               E = Very satisfied
C = Can't decide whether satisfied or not

On my present job, this is how I feel about. . . .

_____ 1. Being able to keep busy all the time.
_____ 2. The chance to be somebody in this organization.
_____ 3. The way my job provides for steady employment.
_____ 4. My pay and the amount of work I do.
_____ 5. The freedom to use my own judgment about how to work.
_____ 6. The chance to work by myself.
_____ 7. The chance to develop close friendships with others.
_____ 8. The way I get full credit for the work I do.
_____ 9. The chance to help others.
_____10. My job security.

Source: Adapted from Weiss, D. J. *Manual for the Minnesota Satisfaction Questionnaire.* Minneapolis, MN: Minnesota Studies in Vocational Rehabilitation, University of Minnesota, 1967.

**Table 2.5**

## Effects of Various Work Factors on Job Satisfaction

| WORK FACTORS | EFFECTS |
|---|---|
| Work itself | |
|   Challenge | Mentally challenging work that the individual can successfully accomplish is satisfying. |
|   Physical demands | Tiring work is dissatisfying. |
|   Personal interest | Personally interesting work is satisfying. |
| Reward structure | Rewards that are equitable and that provide accurate feedback for performance are satisfying. |
| Working conditions | |
|   Physical | Satisfaction depends on the match between working conditions and physical needs. |
|   Goal attainment | Working conditions that promote goal attainment are satisfying. |
| Self | High self-esteem is conducive to job satisfaction. |
| Others in the organization | Individuals will be satisfied with supervisors, coworkers, or subordinates who help them attain rewards. Also, individuals will be more satisfied with colleagues who see things the same way they do. |
| Organization and management | Individuals will be satisfied with organizations that have policies and procedures designed to help them attain rewards. Individuals will be dissatisfied with conflicting roles and/or ambiguous roles imposed by the organization. |
| Fringe benefits | Benefits do not have a strong influence on job satisfaction for most workers. |

Source: Adapted from Landy, F. J. *Psychology of Work Behavior,* 4th ed. Pacific Grove, Calif.: Brooks/Cole, 1989, 470.

directly to effective performance. (A happy worker is a good worker.) Yet, numerous studies have shown that a simple, direct linkage between job satisfaction and job performance often doesn't exist.[21] The difficulty of relating attitudes to behavior is pertinent here. Earlier, we noted that general attitudes best predict general behaviors and that specific attitudes are related most strongly to specific behaviors. These principles explain, at least in part, why the expected relationships often don't exist. As indicated previously, job satisfaction is a collection of numerous attitudes toward various aspects of the job and represents a general attitude. Performance of a specific task, such as preparing a particular monthly report, can't necessarily be predicted on the basis of a general attitude. However, studies have shown that the level of overall workforce job satisfaction and organizational performance are linked. That is, organizations with satisfied employees tend to be more effective than organizations with unsatisfied employees. Further, management in many organizations recognize the important linkage between customer satisfaction and the satisfaction of employees who interact with their customers. Examples of this linkage are apparent in the following Managing Communication Competency feature.

## COMPETENCY: MANAGING COMMUNICATION

### THE CONTAINER STORE

With employee turnover greater than 100 percent in most retail stores but only at 15 to 25 percent at the Container Store, how do its managers attract new employees and retain employees?

The Container Store recently was named by *Fortune* magazine as America's best place to work for a second year in a row. In 2001, sales exceeded $273 million for its 22 stores. How did it get this ranking? First, it practices what it preaches. Every first-year full-time employee gets about 235 hours of training. It is provided both formally and informally by ongoing communication with managers, who not only ask what their people need to do their jobs well, but also regularly assess how to provide necessary assistance. Each store has a back room where new products are housed prior to display. Employees receive formal training on how to display these new products and how to communicate their benefits. According to Garrett Boone and Kip Tindell, the Container Store's CEOs, "Nothing goes out on the sales floor until our people are ready for it." This program is coupled with extensive training programs designed to meet individual skills and job functions and team-based incentive programs. Moreover, a "super sales trainer" serves each store. These trainers are top sales performers who know how to sell the hard stuff and who have an aptitude for leadership and strong communication and presentation skills. These people give on-the-spot help to employees who ask, but employees are encouraged to take responsibility for their own development.

The Container Store pays above-industry salaries to employees. Part-time employees earn between $9 to $10 per hour and full-time employees average $15 to $17 per hour, as well as benefits. Employees do not sell on a commission basis. The company is attractive to employees because it offers flexible shifts, allowing college students to earn some cash between classes and mothers to work while their kids are in school (9 A.M. to 2 P.M.).

Guided by what Boone and Tindell call a "do-unto-others," philosophy, the Container Store's more than 2,000 employees, of which 27 percent are minority and 60 percent are women, work in an environment that ensures open communication throughout the company, including regular discussions of store sales, company goals, and expansion plans. Another guiding principle is to offer the best selection, the

*For more information on The Container Store, visit the organization's home page at http://www.containerstore.com.*

best service plus the best price. All employees are encouraged to treat customers like they would treat visitors in their homes. Boone and Tindell empathize with those who must cope with multiple demands on their time and energy and need to bring some order to their lives. Balancing both work and motherhood symbolizes their clientele—90 percent of whom are professional women earning more than $75,000.[22]

Job satisfaction is important for many reasons. Because satisfaction represents an outcome of the work experience, high levels of dissatisfaction help to identify organizational problems that need attention. In addition, job dissatisfaction is strongly linked to absenteeism, turnover, and physical and mental health problems.[23] High levels of absenteeism and turnover are costly for organizations. According to John Semyan, an executive at TNS Partners, Inc., it typically costs firms about 20 percent of a person's salary to recruit a replacement. Thus, when Deloitte & Touche, one of the Big Five accounting firms, loses a $50,000 per year staff accountant, it may have to spend $10,000 to hire a comparable employee. Many management experts suggest that the strong relationship between dissatisfaction and absenteeism and turnover is a compelling reason for paying careful attention to employee job satisfaction.

## ORGANIZATIONAL COMMITMENT

Another important work attitude that has a bearing on organizational behavior is commitment to the organization. **Organizational commitment** refers to the strength of an employee's involvement in the organization and identification with it. Strong organizational commitment is characterized by

- a support of and acceptance of the organization's goals and values;
- a willingness to exert considerable effort on behalf of the organization; and
- a desire to remain with the organization.[24]

Organizational commitment goes beyond loyalty to include an active contribution to accomplishing organizational goals. Organizational commitment represents a broader work attitude than job satisfaction because it applies to the entire organization rather than just to the job. Further, commitment typically is more stable than satisfaction because day-to-day events are less likely to change it.

**Sources of Commitment.**   As with job satisfaction, the sources of organizational commitment may vary from person to person. Employees' initial commitment to an organization is determined largely by their individual characteristics (e.g., personality and attitudes) and how well their early job experiences match their expectations. Later, organizational commitment continues to be influenced by job experiences, with many of the same factors that lead to job satisfaction also contributing to organizational commitment or lack of commitment: pay, relationships with supervisors and coworkers, working conditions, opportunities for advancement, and so on. Over time, organizational commitment tends to become stronger because (1) individuals develop deeper ties to the organization and their coworkers as they spend more time with them; (2) seniority often brings advantages that tend to develop more positive work attitudes; and (3) opportunities in the job market may decrease with age, causing workers to become more strongly attached to their current job.

**Relation to Job Behavior.**   Managers are interested in the relationships between organizational commitment and job behavior because the lack of commitment often leads to turnover. The stronger an employee's commitment is to the organization, the less likely the person is to quit. Strong commitment also is often correlated with low absenteeism and relatively high productivity. Attendance at work (being on time and taking little time off) is usually higher for employees with strong organizational commitment. Moreover, committed individuals tend to be more goal directed and waste

## COMPETENCY: MANAGING SELF

### DIANE HOOK AT MERCK–MEDCO

Diane Hook was hit by a crime that is every parent's nightmare. She and her husband did their best to hire a good nanny for their baby daughter. They used an agency that did criminal and personal background checks. She personally checked references and had friends actually help interview candidates to get multiple opinions. The person they hired had glowing references, which spoke of their newly hired nanny "as if she was Mother Teresa," Hook recalls.

Yet, despite their care in the hiring process, the new nanny seriously abused their baby. A secretly installed videotape actually caught her slapping the 9-month old baby, twisting the baby's leg, and angrily stuffing a blanket into her mouth. Diane Hook and her husband were afraid of the public exposure that prosecuting the nanny would bring, but they filed charges anyway in order to protect other parents from having to go through the same experience.

The case dragged on for 2 years before the nanny agreed to a plea bargain that put her in prison for 4 years. The experience was extremely trying for the Hooks as it included difficult publicity, threatening phone calls, and a great deal of expense. However, crucial support emerged from an unlikely source: Diane Hook's employer, Merck–Medco.

Shortly after the videotaping, Hook walked into the office of her manager, Margie McGlynn, prepared to resign. At the time, she felt like she could never again entrust her child to anyone but family. Instead of allowing her to quit, however, McGlynn said, "Now isn't the time to make a decision that has such a tremendous bearing on your life." McGlynn urged her to take time off to help her family recover. She offered to keep Hook on the payroll and allow her to work from home as she felt able to. Per Lofberg, the president of Merck–Medco, approved the arrangement.

Fortunately, the baby suffered no lasting harm. Diane Hook believes that the respite from job worries speeded her own recovery from the ordeal. For a time, she worked only when the baby slept or when her husband stayed home from work one day a week to keep the child. Now, she is back at work on a permanent part-time schedule. The baby (now 3 years old) stays with a trusted friend, and a second child is in a high-quality childcare center.

Needless to say, Diane Hook is deeply committed to Merck–Medco. Recently, when a distressed coworker decided to quit after her child was diagnosed with developmental difficulties, Hook told her "exactly what Margie said to me—now is not the time." Hook strongly believes that all firms should provide the same kinds of support that she received from her employer. She holds that "employers who help their employees work through significant personal traumas end up being better for it."[25]

*For more information on Merck–Medco, visit the organization's home page at http://www.merck-medco.com.*

less time while at work, which has a positive impact on productivity. Effective management can foster increased commitment and loyalty to the organization as the above Managing Self Competency feature indicates.

**Learning Objective:**

5. Describe the relationship between individual differences and ethical behavior.

## INDIVIDUAL DIFFERENCES AND ETHICAL BEHAVIOR

Ethical behavior in organizations has received great attention lately. The tire separation problem that has plagued both Ford and Firestone, smokers' lawsuits against tobacco manufacturers, and Enron's implosion (including Arthur Andersen's involvement) are recent examples. In each case, media attention has focused on the ethical behavior of top management. Although assigning blame to specific executives may or may not be appropriate in any particular case, consideration of their cognitive moral development may help explain whether managers in these and other organizations behaved ethically or unethically.[26] **Cognitive moral development** refers to an individual's level of moral judgment. People seem to pass through stages of moral reasoning and judgment as they mature. Judgment with regard to right and wrong becomes less dependent on outside influences (e.g., parents) and less self-centered (It's right because it's right for me.). At higher levels of cognitive moral development, individuals develop a deeper understanding of the principles of justice, ethical behavior, and balancing individual and social rights.

Research has demonstrated that individuals with high internal locus of control exhibit more ethical behavior when making organizational decisions than do individuals with high external locus of control. Moreover, individuals with higher levels of cognitive moral development are more likely to behave ethically than are others.

## TYPES OF MANAGEMENT ETHICS

The terms *immoral*, *amoral*, and *moral* management identify important ethical differences among managers.[27]

**Immoral Management.**    Managerial behaviors devoid of any ethical principles represent **immoral management**. Those practicing immoral management believe in the maximum exploitation of opportunities for corporate or personal gain to the exclusion of other considerations. Corners will be cut if doing so appears useful. Legal standards are viewed as barriers to be overcome rather than guidelines for appropriate behavior.

The Frigitemp Corporation provides an example of immoral management at the highest levels of the firm. According to testimony provided during federal investigations and criminal trials, corporate officials (including the chairman of the board of directors and the president) admitted making illegal payoffs of millions of dollars. In addition, corporate officers embezzled funds, exaggerated earnings in reports to shareholders, took kickbacks from suppliers, and even provided prostitutes for customers. Frigitemp eventually went bankrupt because of the misconduct of some of its top-level managers.

**Moral Management.**    The opposite extreme from immoral management is **moral management**. Managerial and employee behaviors focus on and follow ethical norms, professional standards of conduct, and compliance with applicable regulations and laws. Moral management doesn't mean lack of interest in profits. But moral managers will not pursue profits outside the boundaries of the law and sound ethical principles.

McCulloch Corporation, a manufacturer of chain saws, provides a good example of moral management. Chain saws can be dangerous to use, and studies have consistently shown large numbers of injuries from saws not equipped with chain brakes and other safety features. The Chain Saw Manufacturers Association fought hard against mandatory federal safety standards, preferring to rely on voluntary standards even in the face of evidence that voluntary standards were neither high enough nor working. However, McCulloch consistently supported and practiced higher safety standards; in fact, chain brakes have been standard on McCulloch saws since 1975. McCulloch made numerous attempts to persuade the Chain Saw Manufacturers Association to adopt higher standards when research results indicated that they could greatly reduce injuries. When McCulloch failed to persuade the association to support these higher standards, it withdrew from the association.

**Amoral Management.**    Managerial behaviors that are indifferent to ethical considerations—as though different standards of conduct apply to business than to other aspects of life—characterize **amoral management**. Amoral managers and employees seem to lack awareness of ethical or moral issues and act with no thought for the impact that their actions might have on others.

An example of amoral management was Nestlé's decision to market infant formula in Third World countries. Nestlé received massive amounts of negative publicity for this marketing strategy, and governments in several countries launched investigations. These investigations indicated that the company apparently gave no thought to the possible disastrous health consequences of selling the formula to illiterate and impoverished people in areas where it would likely be mixed with impure, disease-ridden water.[28]

## ESTABLISHING ETHICAL ATTITUDES

An organization cannot directly manage personality dimensions (e.g., locus of control) or cognitive individual differences (e.g., cognitive moral development). Still, top executives and managers at all levels can take steps such as the following to instill moral management by fostering ethical attitudes in the workforce.

- Identify ethical attitudes crucial for the organization's operations. For example, a security firm might stress honesty, whereas a drug manufacturer may identify responsibility as most important to ensure product quality. After executives have identified desired ethical attitudes, training programs can focus on developing such attitudes among employees.
- Select employees with desired attitudes. At Southwest Airlines, interviewers use standard interview questions that assess an applicant's attitudes toward work, employees, and customers—and their ethical values.
- Incorporate ethics in the performance evaluation process. Criteria used to evaluate individuals influence work-related attitudes that managers and employees develop. Executives and managers at all levels should be sure that ethical concerns are part of job descriptions and evaluations.
- Establish a work culture that reinforces ethical attitudes. Executives and managers at all levels can take many actions to influence organizational culture. This culture, in turn, greatly influences ethical behavior throughout an organization.

Citicorp, the huge multinational financial services organization, stresses development of ethical attitudes and behaviors among its employees. Its concerns about ethical behavior resulted in the development and use of an ethics game, or exercise, entitled "The Work Ethic—An Exercise in Integrity."[29] The game can be played by individuals in a small group or by large groups divided into several teams. Individuals or teams are presented with ethical dilemmas based on the company's actual experiences. Employees can compare their proposed solutions to what Citicorp management considers to be the correct, ethical course of action. Managers use the game in training programs, staff meetings, and departmental retreats and to orient new employees. The goals of the game are to help employees recognize ethical dilemmas in decision making, to teach employees how Citicorp responds to misconduct, and to increase understanding of its rules and policies regarding ethical behavior. The ethics game isn't the only ethics training that Citicorp uses, but it is an excellent example of how an organization can foster ethical attitudes and behaviors among managers and employees.

# CHAPTER SUMMARY

**1.** Explain the basic sources of personality determinants.

Personality is a person's set of relatively stable characteristics and traits that account for consistent patterns of behavior in various situations. Each individual in some ways is like other people and in some ways is unique. An individual's personality is determined by inherited traits, or tendencies, and life experiences. Experiences occur within the framework of the individual's biological, physical, and social environment—all of which are modified by the culture, family, and other groups to which the person belongs.

**2.** Identify some personality traits that affect behavior.

An individual's personality may be described by a set of factors known as the Big Five. Specifically, these personality factors describe an individual's degree of adjustment, sociability, conscientiousness, agreeableness, and intellectual openness. Remember that, if you didn't do so earlier, you can assess your own profile in terms of the Big Five by using this questionnaire at the end of this chapter. Many specific personality dimensions, including self-esteem, locus of control, goal orientation, and introversion/extroversion have important relationships to work behavior and outcomes. In addition, an understanding of interactions between the person and the situation is important for comprehending organizational behavior.

**3.** State how attitudes affect behavior.

Attitudes are patterns of feelings, beliefs, and behavioral tendencies directed toward specific people, groups, ideas, issues, or objects. Attitudes have affective (feelings, emotions), cognitive (beliefs, knowledge), and behavioral (a predisposition to act in a particular way) components. The relationship between attitudes and behavior isn't always clear, although important relationships exist. The prediction of behavior from attitudes can be improved by remembering that general attitudes best predict general behaviors and that specific attitudes most accurately predict specific behaviors.

**4.** Indicate how job satisfaction and organizational commitment affect performance.

Job satisfaction—the general collection of attitudes that an employee holds toward the job—is of great interest to managers. The simple notion that job satisfaction directly causes an individual to perform all tasks well all the time doesn't stand up to careful scrutiny. Nevertheless, the overall level of satisfaction among employees does have an important relationship to the effectiveness of the organization. Among other things, dissatisfied employees are more likely to be absent, more likely to quit, more likely to treat customers poorly, and so on, than are satisfied employees.

Another work attitude of interest is commitment to the organization. As an attitude, organizational commitment represents the strength of an employee's involvement in an organization and identification with it. As does job satisfaction, commitment has a strong relationship to turnover. High levels of organizational commitment among a workforce are associated with many positive outcomes, including strong loyalty, high productivity, and low absenteeism.

**5.** Describe the relationship between individual differences and ethical behavior.

Individual differences such as locus of control and cognitive moral development are related to ethical behavior. The terms *immoral management*, *moral management*, and *amoral management* capture further, important ethical differences among managers. Top-level executives and managers at all levels can and should constructively foster ethical attitudes and moral management among their managers and employees.

## KEY TERMS AND CONCEPTS

Amoral management  
Attitudes  
"Big Five" personality factors  
Cognitive moral development  
Culture  
Emotional intelligence  

External locus of control  
Extroversion  
Hope  
Immoral management  
Individual differences  
Internal locus of control

Introversion ✓                                          Organizational commitment
Job satisfaction                                        Performance goal orientation
Learning goal orientation                               Personality ✓
Locus of control ✓                                      Personality trait ✓
Moral management                                        Self-esteem

## DISCUSSION QUESTIONS

1. How would you describe Larry Ellison's personality? What effect did his personality have on decision making at Oracle?
2. Describe the basic sources of personality differences between yourself and a person you know well.
3. What influences on personality development seem most important to you. Why?
4. Using the Big Five personality factors, describe the personality of (a) a close family member and (b) a person for whom you have worked. How did these factors affect your behavior toward them?
5. Identify a specific personality factor that seems particularly interesting to you. Provide an example from your own work or other experience of an instance when this factor seemed strongly related to behavior.

6. Select a strong attitude that you hold and describe it in terms of the three components of an attitude.
7. Describe the levels of (a) job satisfaction and (b) organizational commitment that seemed to exist in some organization with which you have first-hand experience.
8. From the popular business press (e.g., *Wall Street Journal*, *Fortune*, *Forbes*, or *Business Week*) or similar publications identify and describe instances of immoral management, moral management, and amoral management in the Enron controversy.
9. Describe an incident in which a coworker or your manager demonstrated moral, immoral, or amoral behavior with a customer.

## DEVELOPING COMPETENCIES

### Competency: Managing Self

### Assessing the Big Five

#### The Big Five Locator Questionnaire

*Instructions:* On each numerical scale that follows, indicate which point is generally more descriptive of you. If the two terms are equally descriptive, mark the midpoint.

| | | | |
|---|---|---|---|
| 1. | Eager | 5 4 3 2 1 | Calm |
| 2. | Prefer Being with Other People | 5 4 3 2 1 | Prefer Being Alone |
| 3. | A Dreamer | 5 4 3 2 1 | No-Nonsense |
| 4. | Courteous | 5 4 3 2 1 | Abrupt |
| 5. | Neat | 5 4 3 2 1 | Messy |
| 6. | Cautious | 5 4 3 2 1 | Confident |
| 7. | Optimistic | 5 4 3 2 1 | Pessimistic |
| 8. | Theoretical | 5 4 3 2 1 | Practical |
| 9. | Generous | 5 4 3 2 1 | Selfish |
| 10. | Decisive | 5 4 3 2 1 | Open-Ended |
| 11. | Discouraged | 5 4 3 2 1 | Upbeat |
| 12. | Exhibitionist | 5 4 3 2 1 | Private |
| 13. | Follow Imagination | 5 4 3 2 1 | Follow Authority |
| 14. | Warm | 5 4 3 2 1 | Cold |
| 15. | Stay Focused | 5 4 3 2 1 | Easily Distracted |
| 16. | Easily Embarrassed | 5 4 3 2 1 | Don't Give a Darn |
| 17. | Outgoing | 5 4 3 2 1 | Cool |
| 18. | Seek Novelty | 5 4 3 2 1 | Seek Routine |
| 19. | Team Player | 5 4 3 2 1 | Independent |
| 20. | A Preference for Order | 5 4 3 2 1 | Comfortable with Chaos |
| 21. | Distractible | 5 4 3 2 1 | Unflappable |
| 22. | Conversational | 5 4 3 2 1 | Thoughtful |
| 23. | Comfortable with Ambiguity | 5 4 3 2 1 | Prefer Things Clear-Cut |
| 24. | Trusting | 5 4 3 2 1 | Skeptical |
| 25. | On Time | 5 4 3 2 1 | Procrastinate |

## Big Five Locator Score Conversion Sheet

| Norm Score | Adjustment | Sociability | Openness | Agreeableness | Conscientiousness | Norm Score |
|---|---|---|---|---|---|---|
| 80 | | | | | | 80 |
| 79 | | | 25 | | | 79 |
| 78 | | | | | | 78 |
| 77 | 22 | | | | | 77 |
| 76 | | | 24 | | | 76 |
| 75 | | | | | | 75 |
| 74 | | | | | | 74 |
| 73 | 21 | | 23 | | | 73 |
| 72 | | 25 | | | | 72 |
| 71 | | | | 25 | | 71 |
| 70 | 20 | 24 | 22 | | | 70 |
| 69 | | | | | 25 | 69 |
| 68 | | | | 24 | | 68 |
| 67 | | 23 | 21 | | 24 | 67 |
| 66 | 19 | | | | | 66 |
| 65 | | 22 | | 23 | 23 | 65 |
| 64 | | | 20 | | | 64 |
| 63 | | | | | 22 | 63 |
| 62 | 18 | 21 | 19 | 22 | | 62 |
| 61 | | | | | 21 | 61 |
| 60 | | 20 | | | | 60 |
| 59 | 17 | | 18 | 21 | 20 | 59 |
| 58 | | | | | | 58 |
| 57 | | 19 | | | | 57 |
| 56 | | | 17 | | | 56 |
| 55 | 16 | 18 | | 20 | 19 | 55 |
| 54 | | | 16 | 19 | | 54 |
| 53 | | | | | | 53 |
| 52 | | 17 | | | 18 | 52 |
| 51 | 15 | | | | | 51 |
| 50 | | 16 | 15 | 18 | 17 | 50 |
| 49 | | | | | | 49 |
| 48 | 14 | 15 | | | 16 | 48 |
| 47 | | | 14 | 17 | | 47 |
| 46 | | 14 | | | 15 | 46 |
| 45 | | | 13 | | | 45 |
| 44 | 13 | | | 16 | 14 | 44 |
| 43 | | 13 | | | | 43 |
| 42 | | | 12 | | | 42 |
| 41 | | | | 15 | 13 | 41 |
| 40 | 12 | 12 | 11 | | | 40 |
| 39 | | | | | | 39 |
| 38 | | | | 14 | 12 | 38 |
| 37 | | 11 | 10 | | | 37 |
| 36 | 11 | | | | | 36 |
| 35 | | 10 | | 13 | 11 | 35 |
| 34 | | | 9 | | | 34 |
| 33 | 10 | 9 | | | 10 | 33 |
| 32 | | | | 12 | | 32 |
| 31 | | | 8 | | | 31 |
| 30 | | 8 | | | 9 | 30 |
| 29 | 9 | | | 11 | | 29 |

| Norm Score | Adjustment | Sociability | Openness | Agreeableness | Conscientiousness | Norm Score |
|---|---|---|---|---|---|---|
| 28 |   | 7 | 7 |   | 8 | 28 |
| 27 |   |   |   | 10 |   | 27 |
| 26 |   | 6 |   |   | 7 | 26 |
| 25 | 8 |   | 6 |   |   | 25 |
| 24 |   |   |   | 9 | 6 | 24 |
| 23 |   |   |   |   |   | 23 |
| 22 |   |   | 5 |   | 22 | 22 |
| 21 | 7 | 5 |   |   |   | 21 |
| 20 |   |   |   | 8 |   | 20 |
| Enter Norm Scores Here | Adj = | S = | O = | A = | C = |   |

*Instructions:*

1. Find the sum of the circled numbers on the *first* row of each of the five-line groupings (Row 1 + Row 6 + Row 11 + Row 16 + Row 21 = _____). This is your raw score for "adjustment." Circle the number in the ADJUSTMENT column of the Score Conversion Sheet that corresponds to this raw score.

2. Find the sum of the circled numbers on the *second* row of each of the five-line groupings (Row 2 + Row 7 + Row 12 + Row 17 + Row 22 = _____). This is your raw score for "sociability." Circle the number in the SOCIABILITY column of the Score Conversion Sheet that corresponds to this raw score.

3. Find the sum of the circled numbers on the *third* row of each of the five-line groupings (Row 3 + Row 8 + Row 13 + Row 18 + Row 23 = _____). This is your raw score for "openness." Circle the number in the OPENNESS column of the Score Conversion Sheet that corresponds to this raw score.

4. Find the sum of the circled numbers on the *fourth* row of each of the five-line groupings (Row 4 + Row 9 + Row 14 + Row 19 + Row 24 = _____). This is your raw score for "agreeableness." Circle the number in the AGREEABLENESS column of the Score Conversion Sheet that corresponds to this raw score.

5. Find the sum of the circled numbers on the *fifth* row of each of the five-line groupings (Row 5 + Row 10 + Row 15 + Row 20 + Row 25 = _____). This is your raw score for "conscientiousness." Circle the number in the CONSCIENTIOUSNESS column of the Score Conversion Sheet that corresponds to this raw score.

6. Find the number in the far right or far left column that is parallel to your circled raw score. Enter this norm score in the box at the bottom of the appropriate column.

7. Transfer your norm score to the appropriate scale on the Big Five Locator Interpretation Sheet.

## Big Five Locator Interpretation Sheet

| | | | | | |
|---|---|---|---|---|---|
| STRONG ADJUSTMENT: secure, unflappable, rational, unresponsive, guilt free | Resilient 35 | Responsive 45 | Reactive 55 | 65 | WEAK ADJUSTMENT: excitable, worrying, reactive, high-strung, alert |
| LOW SOCIABILITY: private, independent, works alone, reserved, hard to read | Introvert 35 | Ambivert 45 | Extrovert 55 | 65 | HIGH SOCIABILITY: assertive, sociable, warm, optimistic, talkative |
| LOW OPENNESS: practical, conservative, depth of knowledge, efficient, expert | Preserver 35 | Moderate 45 | Explorer 55 | 65 | HIGH OPENNESS: broad interests, curious, liberal, impractical, likes novelty |
| LOW AGREEABLENESS: skeptical, questioning, tough, aggressive, self-interest | Challenger 35 | Negotiator 45 | Adapter 55 | 65 | HIGH AGREEABLENESS: trusting, humble, altruistic, team player, conflict averse, frank |
| LOW CONSCIENTIOUSNESS: spontaneous, fun loving, experimental, unorganized | Flexible 35 | Balanced 45 | Focused 55 | 65 | HIGH CONSCIENTIOUSNESS: dependable, organized, disciplined, cautious, stubborn |

Note: The Big Five Locator is intended for use only as a quick assessment for teaching purposes.[30]

## Competency: Managing Self

## Emotional IQ

An individual difference that has recently received a great deal of interest is *emotional intelligence*. You can assess your EQ by using the following scale.

*Instructions:* Using a scale of 1 through 4, where 1 = strongly disagree, 2 = somewhat disagree, 3 = somewhat agree, and 4 = strongly agree, respond to the 32 statements.

_____ 1. I know when to speak about my personal problems to others.

_____ 2. When I'm faced with obstacles, I remember times I faced similar obstacles and overcame them.

_____ 3. I expect that I will do well on most things.

_____ 4. Other people find it easy to confide in me.

_____ 5. I find it easy to understand the nonverbal messages of other people.

_____ 6. Some of the major events of my life have led me to reevaluate what is important and not important.

_____ 7. When my mood changes, I see new possibilities.

_____ 8. Emotions are one of the things that make life worth living.

_____ 9. I am aware of my emotions as I experience them.

_____ 10. I expect good things to happen.

_____ 11. I like to share my emotions with other people.

_____ 12. When I experience a positive emotion, I know how to make it last.

_____ 13. I arrange events others enjoy.

_____ 14. I seek out activities that make me happy.

_____ 15. I am aware of the nonverbal messages I send to others.

_____ 16. I present myself in a way that makes a good impression on others.

_____ 17. When I am in a positive mood, solving problems is easy for me.

_____ 18. By looking at facial expressions, I can recognize the emotions that others are feeling.

_____ 19. I know why my emotions change.

_____ 20. When I am in a positive mood, I am able to come up with new ideas.

_____ 21. I have control over my emotions.

_____ 22. I easily recognize my emotions as I experience them.

_____ 23. I motivate myself by imagining a good outcome to the tasks I do.

_____ 24. I compliment others when they have done something well.

_____ 25. I am aware of the nonverbal message other people send.

_____ 26. When another person tells me about an important event in their life, I almost feel as though I have experienced this event myself.

_____ 27. When I feel a change in emotions, I tend to come up with new ideas.

_____ 28. When I am faced with a challenge, I usually rise to the occasion.

_____ 29. I know what other people are feeling just by looking at them.

_____ 30. I help other people feel better when they are down.

_____ 31. I use good moods to help myself keep trying in the face of obstacles.

_____ 32. I can tell how people are feeling by listening to the tone of their voices.

## Scoring:

Add your responses to questions 1, 6, 7, 8, 12, 14, 17, 19, 20, 22, 23, and 27. Put this total here_____. This is your *self-awareness* score.

Add your responses to questions 4, 15, 18, 25, 29, and 32. Put this total here_____. This is your *social awareness* score.

Add your responses to questions 2, 3, 9, 10, 16, 21, 28, and 31. Put this total here_____. This is your *self-management* score.

Add your responses to questions 5, 11, 13, 24, 26, and 30. Put this total here_____. This is your *social skills* score.

## Discussion and Interpretation:

Psychologist Daniel Goleman states that emotional intelligence (EQ) is actually more crucial than general intelligence (IQ) in terms of career success. **Emotional intelligence** refers to how well an individual handles herself and others rather than how smart she is or how capable she is in terms of technical skills.[31] Emotional intelligence includes the attributes of self-awareness, impulse control, persistence, confidence, self-motivation, empathy, and social deftness. Think of EQ as being the social equivalent of IQ. In organizations undergoing rapid change, emotional intelligence may determine who gets promoted and who gets passed over or who gets laid off and who stays, according to Goleman. Studies have consistently shown, for example, that the competencies associated with emotional intelligence (e.g., the ability to persuade others, the ability to understand others, and so on) are twice as important for career success as intelligence (IQ) or technical competencies.

According to Goleman, the higher your score is in each of these four areas, the more emotionally intelligent you are. People who score high (greater than 36) in *self-awareness* recognize their emotions and their effects on others, accurately assess their strengths and limitations, and have a strong sense of their self-worth and capabilities. People who score high (greater than 18) in *social awareness* are good at understanding others, taking an active interest in their concerns, and empathizing with them, and recognize the needs others have at work. People who score high (greater than 24) in *self-management* can keep their disruptive emotions and impulses under control, maintain standards of integrity and honesty, are conscientious, adapt their behaviors to changing situations, and have internal standards of excellence that guide their behaviors. People who have high (greater than 18) *social skills* sense others' developmental needs, inspire and lead groups, send clear and convincing messages, build effective interpersonal relationships, and work well with others to achieve shared goals.[32]

## Questions

1. Do you find EQ a useful personality characteristic? Is it genetic or shaped by experience?
2. What's Gordon Ellison's emotional intelligence?

# C H A P T E R

# Understanding Perceptions and Attributions

## LEARNING OBJECTIVES

When you have finished studying the chapter, you should be able to:

1. Describe the major elements in the perceptual process.
2. Identify the main factors that influence what individuals perceive.
3. Identify the factors that determine how one person perceives another.
4. Describe the primary errors in perception that people make.
5. Explain how attributions influence behavior.

3

# NAVEEN JAIN AT INFOSPACE

Naveen Jain, founder of InfoSpace, had seen his company's share price triple in less than a year as his dot-com company grew. Based in Bellevue, Washington, InfoSpace sells applications to users that permit them to access online phone directories, maps, games, and stock quotes. In less than a year, the company had established relationships with more than 1,500 Internet portal sites, such as America Online, Yahoo!, 60 content providers, and more than 20 wireless carriers. As his company grew, he needed someone to fill the position of CEO. He chose Arun Sarin, the number-two person at Vodafone AirTouch. Jain finally persuaded Sarin to take the job. According to Jain, "Most people think of me as arrogant, and that's the perception I want. It says: "Don't mess with me or you'll get crushed."

"Aggressive," "relentless," and "dynamic" is how Allyson Rogers, an analyst with Wells Fargo, describes Jain. And these qualities rub off on those around him. "People inside the company are absolutely dedicated to him. He's always in the hallways," says Rogers. Jain is a strong-willed leader who thinks nothing of putting in very long workdays and doesn't believe in vacations. Jain's charisma and energy turned many of his employees into wealthy people. Why? On paper, many InfoSpace employees were millionaires as its stock rose from less than $2 per share to more than $138 per share in less than a year. Using stock options to lure people to work for him, Jain made lavish promises to them if they stayed with InfoSpace for at least a year. When Mark Kaleem was hired as vice president of strategic development, Jain offered him options to buy 500,000 shares of InfoSpace and told him he could stay in Campbell, California. But when Kaleem sought to exercise his options, Jain said "Mark, you don't need to exercise. You can exercise it anytime . . . why are you worried about that? Kaleem said that he had a heart condition and wanted to take some of the stock and put it into trust accounts for his children. Shortly after that, Jain fired Kaleem. The reason was "We have to move, move along. We can't afford to have two offices." Kaleem's monthly office rent was $250. When Kaleem asked Jain about his stock options, Jain said: "You don't understand. You have nothing."

Sarin, who lasted 8 months, recently resigned. According to stock analysts, when senior managers leave the company, it sends signals that the company is in trouble. Indeed, recently the company's stock was trading for less than $1.70 a share.[1]

For more information on InfoSpace, visit the organization's home page at http://www.infospace.com.

The Preview Case illustrates the importance of perceptions. People perceived Info-Space as a successful dot-com company and were attracted to Jain, who often said "I believe willpower can get you through anything." Behavior is a function of perceptions. People base their behaviors on what they *perceive*, not necessarily on what reality *is*. People joined InfoSpace because they perceived it as a place where they could make a lot of money. Recognizing the difference between the perceptual worlds of employees and managers and the reality of the organization is important in understanding behavior.

In this chapter, we explore the importance of *perception* and *attribution*. First, we describe the perceptual process. Then, we examine the external and internal factors that influence perception, the ways that people organize perceptions, the process of *person perception*, and various errors in the perceptual process. Finally, we explore the attributions that people make to explain the behaviors of themselves and others.

## THE PERCEPTUAL PROCESS

**Perception** is the process by which people select, organize, interpret, and respond to information from the world around them. This information is gathered from the five senses—sight, hearing, touch, taste, and smell. It represents the psychological process whereby people take information from the environment and make sense of their worlds.[2]

The key words in the definition of perception are *selection* and *organization*. Different people often perceive a situation differently, both in terms of what they selectively perceive and how they organize and interpret the things perceived. Figure 3.1 (on page 68) summarizes the basic elements in the perceptual process from initial observation to final response.

Everyone selectively pays attention to some aspects of the environment and selectively ignores other aspects. For example, when Jain was recruiting employees to InfoSpace, what messages were they paying attention to and what messages were they ignoring? A person's selection process involves both external and internal factors. In other words, a complex set of factors, some internal to the person and some in the external environment, combine to determine what the person perceives. We discuss this important process in more detail shortly.

The individual then organizes the stimuli selected into meaningful patterns. How people interpret what they perceive also varies considerably. A wave of the hand may be interpreted as a friendly gesture or as a threat, depending on the circumstances and the state of mind of those involved. Certainly, in organizations managers and employees need to recognize that perceptions of events and behaviors may vary among individuals and be inaccurate.

As shown in Figure 3.1, people's interpretations of their environments affect their responses. Everyone selects and organizes things differently, which is one reason why people behave differently in the same situation. In other words, people often perceive the same things in different ways, and their behaviors depend, in part, on their perceptions.

The ways that individuals select, organize, and interpret their perceptions to make sense of their environments isn't something that managers should ignore. The following Managing Communication Competency feature explores the impact that feng shui has on employee behavior at Nortel Networks. What is being communicated may be subtle, yet of great importance.

## COMPETENCY: MANAGING COMMUNICATION

### FENG SHUI AT NORTEL NETWORKS

When Nortel Networks, a Canadian telecommunications firm, moved its global headquarters from downtown Toronto to suburban Brampton, it based its building design on the layout of ancient Rome and the Chinese science of art called *feng shui*. Literally, **feng shui** means wind (feng) and water (shui). In office design, it refers to creating harmony between people and their environment. A feng shui consultant was hired to help Nortel design its new office. Employees were asked to fill out surveys focusing on their needs and to review the organization's communication needs. The consultant talked with people about the location of entrances, evaluated air pollution levels, reviewed where people and teams gathered to make decisions, and studied places to maximize sales of new products and minimize theft. After gathering these data, the consultant prepared a geomantic (landscape design) chart for management.

The chart provides a personnel energy blueprint of the building that reveals problem areas and areas that might be underserved. Enhancements to ensure greater utilization could include better use of light, space, color, natural landscape, position of office and furniture, office ergonomics, and aesthetics. For example, the building has only two main entrances, which form its main focus. Extending from them are pathways providing access to Nortel's neighborhoods (departments). Nortel's CEO Frank A. Dunn doesn't occupy a formal office. He sits at a desk attached to his assistant's cubicle. If he has to do paperwork, he works at that spot. If he has a meeting, he connects his laptop in a convenient place somewhere in the building and has a meeting. In its new building Nortel provided seven indoor "parks," a Zen garden, a full-service branch of a bank, basketball and volleyball courts, a physiotherapy area, a dry cleaning service, and a café. The Docklands—the shipping and receiving area—features an imposing 20-foot-tall graffiti mural created by 12 local street artists. There is even a spirituality room so that employees of various religious beliefs can pray and meditate—and even wash their feet if they're Muslim.[3]

*For more information on Nortel's headquarters, visit the organization's home page at http://www.nortel.com.*

**Learning Objective:**

2. Identify the main factors that influence what individuals perceive.

## PERCEPTUAL SELECTION

The phone is ringing, your TV is blaring, a dog is barking outside, your PC is making a strange noise, and you smell coffee brewing. Which of these events will you ignore? Which will you pay attention to? Can you predict or explain why one of these events grabs your attention at a particular time?

**Selective screening** is the process by which people filter out most information so that they can deal with the most important matters. Perceptual selection depends on several factors, some of which are in the external environment and some of which are internal to the perceiver.[4]

### EXTERNAL FACTORS

External factors are characteristics that influence whether the event will be noticed. The following external factors may be stated as *principles* of perception. In each case we present an example to illustrate the principle.

- *Size.* The larger the object, the more likely it is to be perceived. A hiker is far more likely to notice a fully grown fir tree than a seedling.
- *Intensity.* The more intense an external factor (bright lights, loud noises, and the like), the more likely it is to be perceived. The language in an e-mail message from a manager to an employee can reflect the intensity principle. For example, an e-mail message that reads, Please stop by my office at your convenience, wouldn't fill you with the same sense of urgency as an e-mail message that reads, Report to my office immediately!
- *Contrast.* External factors that stand out against the background or that aren't what people expect are the most likely to be noticed. In addition, the contrast of

**Figure 3.1**                    **Basic Elements in the Perceptual Process**

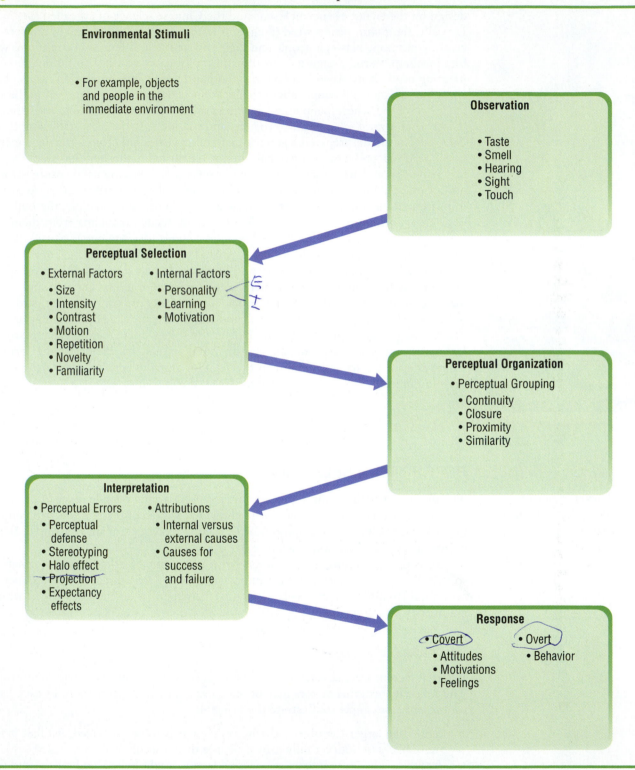

objects with others or with their backgrounds may influence how they are perceived. Figure 3.2 illustrates this aspect of the contrast principle. Which of the
solid center circles is larger? The one on the right appears to be larger, but it
isn't: The two circles are the same size. The solid circle on the right appears to
be larger because its background, or frame of reference, is composed of much

**Figure 3.2**                          **Contrast Principle of Perception**

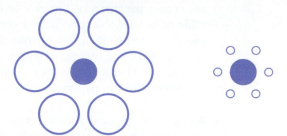

smaller circles. The solid circle on the left appears to be smaller because its background consists of larger surrounding circles.

- *Motion.* A moving factor is more likely to be perceived than a stationary factor. Soldiers in combat learn this principle very quickly. Video games also demonstrate that motion is quickly detected.
- *Repetition.* A repeated factor is more likely to be noticed than a single factor. Marketing managers use this principle in trying to get the attention of prospective customers. An advertisement may repeat key ideas, and the ad itself may be presented many times for greater effectiveness. Marketing managers at Nike have developed the Nike "swoosh" symbol that is consistently used worldwide on all its products.
- *Novelty and familiarity.* Either a familiar or a novel factor in the environment can attract attention, depending on the circumstances. People would quickly notice an elephant walking along a city street. (Both novelty and size increase the probability of perception.) Someone is likely to notice the face of a close friend first among a group of approaching people.[5]

A combination of these or similar factors may be operating at any time to affect perception. Along with a person's internal factors, they determine whether any particular stimulus is more or less likely to be noticed.

## INTERNAL FACTORS

Internal factors are aspects of the perceiver that influence their selection. The powerful role that internal factors play in perception shows itself in many ways. Some of the more important internal factors include personality (Chapter 2), learning (Chapter 4), and motivation (Chapters 5 and 6).

**Personality.**    Personality has an interesting influence on what and how people perceive. Any of the several personality dimensions that we discussed in Chapter 2, along with numerous other traits, may influence the perceptual process.[6] Under many circumstances, personality appears to affect strongly how an individual perceives other people.

In Chapter 2, we introduced you to the Big Five personality factors. To illustrate how personality can influence perception, let's examine one of the Big Five—conscientiousness. A conscientious person tends to pay more attention to external environmental cues than does a less conscientious person. On the one hand, less conscientious people are impulsive, careless, and irresponsible. They see their environment as hectic and unstable, which affects the way in which they make perceptual selections. On the other hand, more conscientious people organize their perceptions into neat categories, allowing themselves to retrieve data quickly and in an organized manner. In other words they are careful, methodical, and disciplined in making perceptual selections.

**Learning.**   Another internal factor affecting perceptual selection is learning. Among other things, learning determines the development of perceptual sets. A **perceptual set** is an expectation of a particular interpretation based on past experience with the same or similar object. What do you see in Figure 3.3? If you see an attractive, elegantly dressed woman, your perception concurs with the majority of first-time viewers. However, you may agree with a sizable minority and see an ugly, old woman. The woman you first see depends, in large part, on your perceptual set.

In organizations, managers' and employees' past experiences and learning strongly influence their perceptions. Managers are influenced by their functional backgrounds (e.g., accounting, engineering, marketing, or production) when making decisions. Thus, under some circumstances, they are likely to interpret problems in terms of their own experiences and values. Roa Telidevara, president of Qatalys, Inc., thinks that his firm has a cash flow problem. The firm's accounting manager perceives the problem to be one of extending credit to slow-paying customers, whereas the marketing manager sees the problem as trying to bring in different customers who are used to paying within 60, not 30, days.  Successful managers need to "rise above" their own experiences and limitations, accurately recognizing and effectively solving problems in areas other than those with which they are most familiar.[7] Indeed, essential decision-making skills include the ability to recognize the types of knowledge and expertise needed with regard to a particular problem and to avoid framing issues only in terms of the person's own expertise.

The effects of learning on perception have important implications for organizational behavior. First, managers should avoid overly simplistic assumptions about the abilities of people to process information and make decisions. Individual differences clearly bias which information managers and employees might pay the most attention to. At the same time, through education and experience, people can overcome perceptual biases. Second, the existence of biases presents another type of management challenge. That is, employees from different areas of the organization may have trouble working together on task forces and teams because each will tend to see problems and issues from the perspectives of their own departments or functions. Thus, to be effective in group efforts, managers and employees must learn how to deal with such diversity.

The culture into which a person is born determines many life experiences, and learned cultural differences influence the perceptual process. Differences in perceptions of punctuality among managers in Japan, Mexico, Taiwan, and the United States

**Figure 3.3**                    **Test of Perceptual Set**

is often a problem in running meetings.[8] On average, U.S., Swiss, and German managers would consider a colleague late for an important business meeting after about 5 minutes. Managers in the other three countries are somewhat more tolerant of tardiness and would perceive a colleague as late only after about 10 or 11 minutes. The following Managing Across Cultures Competency feature briefly examines how the meanings of some commonly used hand gestures vary across cultures.

**Motivation.**    Motivation also plays an important role in determining what a person perceives. A person's most urgent needs and desires at any particular time can influence perception. For example, imagine that, while taking a shower, you faintly hear what sounds like the telephone ringing. Do you get out of the shower, dripping wet, to answer it? Or do you conclude that it is only your imagination? Your behavior in this situation may depend on factors other than the loudness of the ringing. If you are

## COMPETENCY:   MANAGING ACROSS CULTURES

### HAND GESTURES: DIFFERENT MEANINGS IN DIFFERENT COUNTRIES[9]

**The A-OK Sign**

In the United States, this is just a friendly sign for "All right!" or "Good going." In Australia and Islamic countries, it is equivalent to what generations of high school students know as "flipping the bird."

**The "Hook 'em Horns" Sign**

This sign encourages University of Texas athletes, and it's a good luck gesture in Brazil and Venezuela. In parts of Africa it is a curse. In Italy, it is signaling to another that "your spouse is being unfaithful."

**"V" for Victory Sign**

In many parts of the world, this means "victory" or "peace." In England, if the palm and fingers face inward, it means "Up yours!" especially if executed with an upward jerk of the fingers.

**Finger-Beckoning Sign**

This sign means "come here" in the United States. In Malaysia, it is used only for calling animals. In Indonesia and Australia, it is used for beckoning "ladies of the night."

expecting an important call, you're likely to leap from the shower. If you aren't expecting a call, you're more likely to attribute the ringing sound to shower noises. Your decision, then, has been influenced by your expectations and motivations.

This example illustrates a significant aspect of perception: Internal factors such as motivation influence the interpretation of information. Perhaps many people left their jobs at Microsoft, IBM, and other companies to join Jain at InfoSpace because of his promises of wealth.

In general, people perceive things that promise to help satisfy their needs and that they have found rewarding in the past. They tend to ignore mildly disturbing events (a barking dog) but will react to dangerous events (the house being on fire). Summarizing an important aspect of the relationship between motivation and perception is the **Pollyanna principle**, which states that people process pleasant events more efficiently and accurately than they do unpleasant events. For example, an employee who receives both positive and negative feedback during a performance appraisal session may more easily and clearly remember the positive statements than the negative statements.[10]

## PERSON PERCEPTION

**Learning Objective:**

3.  Identify the factors that determine how one person perceives another.

**Person perception** is the process by which individuals attribute characteristics or traits to other people. It is closely related to the attribution process, which we discuss later in this chapter. The person perception process relies on the same general process of perception shown in Figure 3.1. That is, the process follows the same sequence of observation, selection, organization, interpretation, and response. However, the object being perceived is another person. Perceptions of situations, events, and objects are important, but individual differences in perceptions of other people are crucial at work. For example, suppose that you meet a new employee. To get acquainted and make him feel at ease, you invite him to lunch. During lunch, he begins to tell you his life history and focuses on his accomplishments. Because he talks only about himself (he asks you no questions about yourself), you may form the impression that he is very self-centered. Later, you may come to see other aspects of his personality, but your perceptions may always be strongly affected by this first impression, called the **primacy effect**.

In general, the factors influencing person perception are the same as those that influence perceptual selection: Both external and internal factors affect person perception. However, we may usefully categorize factors that influence how a person perceives another as

- characteristics of the perceived,
- characteristics of the perceiver, and
- the situation or context within which the perception takes place.

### THE PERCEIVED

When perceiving someone else, you need to be aware of various cues given by that person: facial expressions, general appearance, skin color, posture, age, gender, voice quality, personality traits, behaviors, and the like. Such cues usually provide important information about the person. People seem to have **implicit personality theories** about the relationships among physical characteristics, personality traits, and specific behaviors.[11] Table 3.1 illustrates implicit personality theory in action. People often seem to believe that some voice-quality characteristics indicate that the speaker has certain personality traits. However, the relationships presented in Table 3.1 have no scientific basis. Think about your first contact with someone in a chat room on the Internet. Later, upon meeting, did that person look and act as you expected?

**Table 3.1**

| VOICE QUALITY: HIGH IN | MALE VOICE | FEMALE VOICE |
|---|---|---|
| **Personality Judgments on the Basis of Voice Quality** | | |
| Breathiness | Younger, artistic | Feminine, pretty, petite, shallow |
| Flatness | Similar results for both sexes: Masculine, cold, withdrawn | |
| Nasality | Similar results for both sexes: Having many socially undesirable characteristics | |
| Tenseness | Cantankerous (old, unyielding) | Young, emotional, high-strung, not highly intelligent |

Source: Adapted from Hinton, P. R. *The Psychology of Interpersonal Perception*, London: Routledge, 1993, 16.

## THE PERCEIVER

Listening to an employee describe the personality of a coworker may tell you as much about the employee's personality as it does about that of the person being described. That shouldn't surprise you if you recall that factors internal to the perceiver, including personality, learning, and motivation, influence perception. A person's own personality traits, values, attitudes, current mood, past experiences, and so on, determine, in part, how that person perceives someone else.

Accurately perceiving the personality of an individual raised in another culture often is difficult.[12] For example, Japanese managers in the United States and U.S. managers in Japan may face disorienting experiences as they try to learn how to deal with business associates from the other culture. One reason is that the perceiver interprets the other person's traits and behavior in light of his own cultural experiences, attitudes, and values. Often these factors are inadequate for making accurate judgments about the personality and behavior of people from a different culture. Cross-cultural negotiations are an important part of every global manager's job. The dynamics of negotiating, however, reflects each culture's value and beliefs. In Mexico, personal qualities and social connections influence the selection of a negotiator, whereas in the United States, many companies select negotiators on the basis of position and competence. In U.S.–Japanese negotiations, U.S. companies often prefer to send a small team or only a single person to represent them, whereas the Japanese prefer to send a large group. The large group allows them to have representatives from different areas of the organization.

## THE SITUATION

The situation, or setting, also influences how one person perceives another. The situation may be particularly important in understanding first impressions. For example, if you meet someone for the first time and she is with another person that you respect and admire, that association may positively influence your assessment of the new acquaintance. But, if she is with someone you dislike intensely, you may form a negative first impression. Of course, these initial perceptions may change over time if you continue to interact with her and get to know her better. Nevertheless, the first impression may continue to color your later perception of the individual.

## IMPRESSION MANAGEMENT

**Impression management** is an attempt by an individual to manipulate or control the impressions that others form about them. People in organizations use several impression management tactics to affect how others perceive them.[13] They are especially likely to use these tactics when talking with people who have power over them or on whom they are dependent for raises, promotions, and good job assignments. Impression management is used by individuals at all organizational levels as they talk with suppliers, coworkers, managers, and others—and vice versa. Table 3.2 describes five common impression management tactics: behavioral matching, self-promotion, conforming to norms, flattering others, and being consistent.

Impression management provides another example of an *individual difference*. Some people seem preoccupied with impression management; others are less concerned about how they might be perceived. However, most people care about the impressions they make on others, at least part of the time. Certainly, in organizations the impressions made on others may have significant implications for employees' careers. That consideration is illustrated in the following Managing Self Competency feature.

## COMPETENCY:  MANAGING SELF

### ALAN PAGE AT MOTT'S

Alan Page loved electronics as far back as he can remember. As a child, he was more interested in how the Christmas tree lights worked than he was in opening presents. He took his first course in computer programming in the seventh grade. Looking back, he figures that it was inevitable that he would become an electronic "techie" of one type or another.

In his first job, he repaired computer systems. Then he got a position designing databases for a consumer-research company. Finally, he landed a position at Mott's, Inc., the Stamford, Connecticut, food company, as a database analyst. He hoped that his new position, which was to find new ways to use technology to advance the business, would carry him beyond simply performing technological "fix-up" projects. He discovered, however, that he had to manage the impressions that others had of his role.

Page explained: "I had to learn the business, navigate tricky office politics, and figure out how to influence nontechnical people who were sometimes suspicious of a techie. Most of all, I had to transform my image from that of a support person to that of a strategic thinker. This took time."

At first, it was an uphill battle for Page. By default, he often became the technological fix-it person on projects because of his background. Page says that sometimes he was his own worst enemy. "I would drift back to fixing things, because I was comfortable with that," he says, "I thought, 'if I fix this, that person will be happy.'"

He soon developed a more effective approach. He learned to seek the viewpoints of others and to work with colleagues to develop an understanding of what they wanted to accomplish. He learned how to compromise and how to listen. Page developed the capacity to see the bigger picture and to avoid quick-fix "techie" solutions that ignored the people side of the business. As a result, he was able to begin designing solutions and systems to move the business forward.

Page thinks that his colleagues' perceptions of him have changed dramatically for the better. "Now I'm not just seen as someone who can fix tech problems; they see me as someone who can help solve business problems." For Alan Page, this change in his image has stirred hopes of advancement. "You can't go anywhere in this company if you're just seen as the techie guy."[14]

*For more information on Mott's, Inc., visit the organization's home page at www.motts.com.*

**Table 3.2**

| Impression Management Tactics | | |
| --- | --- | --- |
| **TACTIC** | **DESCRIPTION** | **EXAMPLE** |
| Behavioral matching | Person matches his behavior to that of the perceiver. | Employee tries to imitate her manager's behavior by being aggressive and fast-paced. |
| Self-promotion | The person tries to present herself in as positive a light as possible. | Employee reminds his boss about his past accomplishments and associates with coworkers who are evaluated highly. |
| Conforming to norms | Person follows agreed-upon norms for behavior in the organization. | Employee stays late at night even if she has completed all her assignments because staying late is one of the norms of her organization. |
| Flattering others | Person compliments others. This tactic works best when flattery is not extreme and when it involves a dimension important to the other person. | Employee compliments manager on his excellent handling of a customer who constantly complains about poor service. |
| Being consistent | Person's beliefs and behaviors are consistent. | Subordinate whose views on diversity are well known flatters her boss for her handling of a conflict between two coworkers of different ethnic backgrounds. When speaking to her boss, the person looks her boss straight in the eye and has a sincere expression on her face. |

**Learning Objective:**

4. Describe the primary errors in perception that people make.

# PERCEPTUAL ERRORS

The perceptual process may result in errors in judgment or understanding. An important part of understanding individual differences in perception is knowing the source of these errors. First, we examine the notion of accuracy of judgment in person perception. Then, we explore five of the most common types of perceptual errors: perceptual defense, stereotyping, the halo effect, projection, and expectancy effects.

## ACCURACY OF JUDGMENT

How accurate are people in their perceptions of others? This question is important in organizational behavior.[15] For example, misjudging the characteristics, abilities, or behaviors of an employee during a performance appraisal review could result in an inaccurate assessment of the employee's current and future value to the firm. Another example of the importance of accurate person perception comes from the employment interview. Considerable evidence suggests that interviewers can easily make errors in judgment and perceptions when basing employment decisions on information gathered in face-to-face interviews.[16] The following types of interview errors are the most common.

- *Similarity error.* Interviewers are positively predisposed toward job candidates who are similar to them (in terms of background, interests, hobbies, and the like) and negatively biased against job candidates who are unlike them.
- *Contrast error.* Interviewers have a tendency to compare job candidates to other candidates interviewed at about the same time, rather than to some absolute standard. For example, an average candidate might be rated too highly if preceded by several mediocre candidates; however, an average candidate might be scored too low if preceded by an outstanding applicant.
- *Overweighting of negative information.* Interviewers tend to overreact to negative information as though looking for an excuse to disqualify a job candidate.
- *Race, gender, and age bias.* Interviewers may be more or less positive about a candidate on the basis of the candidate's race, gender, or age.
- *First-impression error.* The primacy effect previously discussed may play a role in the job interview, as some interviewers are quick to form impressions that are resistant to change.

There are no easy answers to the general problem of ensuring accuracy. Some people accurately judge and assess others, and some people do so poorly. People can learn to make more accurate judgments if they follow some basic guidelines: (1) avoid generalizing from an observation of a single trait (e.g., tactful) to other traits (e.g. stable, confident, energetic, dependable); (2) avoid assuming that a behavior will be repeated in all situations; and (3) avoid placing too much reliance on physical appearance. Accuracy in person perception can be improved when the perceiver understands these potential biases.

## PERCEPTUAL DEFENSE

**Perceptual defense** is the tendency for people to protect themselves against ideas, objects, or situations that are threatening. A well-known folk song suggests that people "hear what they want to hear and disregard the rest." Once established, an individual's way of viewing the world may become highly resistant to change. Sometimes perceptual defense may have negative consequences. This perceptual error can result in a manager's inability to perceive the need to be creative in solving problems. As a result, the individual simply proceeds as in the past even in the face of evidence that "business as usual" isn't accomplishing anything.

## STEREOTYPING

**Stereotyping** is the belief that all members of specific groups share similar traits and behaviors. The use of stereotypes can have powerful effects on the decisions that managers make. If a human resource manager believes that members of certain groups, such a Gen Xers or disabled people, are lazy, he purposely may avoid hiring people from those groups. The human resource manager may believe that he is using sound judgment—gathering all the necessary information and listening carefully to candidates. Still, without being aware of it, the stereotype he holds may influence the way he judges people. A study conducted at DuPont over a 30-year period, for example, found that the job performance levels of the disabled were equal to or better than the performance levels of other employees. Over 90 percent of disabled workers had above-average performance records, as well as excellent attendance and safety records. Does that fit your stereotype of a disabled worker?[17]

Stereotypes of women continue to hamper their advancement in some organizations.[18] This issue is explored in the first Developing Competencies section at the end of this chapter. It contains a questionnaire that you can use to assess your own perceptions with regard to women as managers. Women face a big obstacle when it comes to overseas assignments: They can't get them. Although women comprise almost half the global workforce, they account for less than 12 percent of the expatriate population. Why is this happening (or failing to happen, as the case may be)?

A number of male managers still think that women aren't interested in overseas jobs or won't be effective in them. These managers typically cite dual career issues, a presumed heightened risk of sexual harassment, and gender prejudices in many countries as reasons why their female employees often aren't seriously considered for international assignments. In contrast, a recent survey of female expatriates and their managers revealed that women, on average, are just as interested in foreign assignments and every bit as effective once there. Indeed, some of the traits considered crucial for success overseas—such as knowing when to keep your mouth shut, being a strong team player, and soliciting a variety of opinions and perspectives when solving problems—are more often associated with women's management styles than with men's.

An interesting challenge for organizations is to determine whether women managers essentially are like their male counterparts. If they are, gender differences should be only a marginal concern. However, a debate is raging in scientific and management circles around the world with regard to gender differences in thought, emotions, and information processing styles. Some evidence from the research being conducted suggests that women are, on average, superior to men in many organizational roles. Such roles include interacting with customers or clients, facilitating discussions, and smoothing conflicts. With regard to the latter two roles, one study indicated that female project team leaders were more effective, on average, than males in leading cross-functional teams designed to foster high rates of innovation.

For many years, conventional wisdom seemed to be that, to be successful, female managers needed to become more like the typical male manager. However, now the question seems to be: Will tomorrow's businesswomen succeed by becoming more like men or less like them? The jury is still out, but the evidence indicates that gender differences are real, and that, for many organizational roles in the years ahead, women will have a competitive advantage.

One company that has tried hard to eliminate stereotyping people in their hiring practices is Home Depot. As the world's largest home improvement chain, the company operates more than 1,200 stores in the United States, as well as stores in Canada, Argentina, Chile, and Puerto Rico. With more than 227,000 employees, Home Depot is constantly hiring new employees. The following Managing Diversity Competency feature highlights how Home Depot uses a computer system to eliminate stereotyping in hiring decisions.

## COMPETENCY:   MANAGING DIVERSITY

### HOME DEPOT

Home Depot settled a class-action lawsuit on behalf of women who claimed they were hired for low-paying cashier positions instead of higher paying positions for which they were qualified and were not getting promoted because of their gender. Part of the settlement required Home Depot to install a computer system for use in hiring and promoting. The system, called Job Preference Program (JPP), works like this: A Home Depot manager who needs to fill a certain position in the garden section, for example, enters the position description into JPP; JPP then gives the manager a list of prescreened, qualified individuals for the position, along with advice on how to conduct an interview. Managers like JPP because, rather than having to search for qualified people, JPP does the work for them. Employees seeking promotions register with JPP and are given advice concerning management of their careers. They also are able to update their profiles as they gain more knowledge and experience. Promotions are given only to employees who have registered with JPP.

*For more information on Home Depot, visit the organization's home page at www.homedepot.com.*

JPP seems to be helping overcome the effects of stereotyping that lead managers to perceive women inaccurately as not qualified for managerial positions or for certain positions historically considered to be for men only, such as selling building materials. After Home Depot starting using JPP, the number of female managers increased by 30 percent and the number of minority managers increased by 28 percent.[19]

### HALO EFFECT

Evaluation of another person solely on the basis of one attribute, either favorable or unfavorable, is called the **halo effect**. In other words, a halo blinds the perceiver to other attributes that also should be evaluated to obtain a complete, accurate impression of the other person. Managers have to guard against the halo effect in rating employee performance. A manager may single out one trait and use it as the basis for judging all other performance measures. For example, an excellent attendance record may produce judgments of high productivity, quality work, and industriousness, whether they are accurate or not.

### PROJECTION

**Projection** is the tendency for people to see their own traits in other people. That is, they project their own feelings, personality characteristics, attitudes, or motives onto others. For example, AT&T's decision to lay off employees in New Jersey may cause employees in Texas not only to judge others as more frightened than they are but also to assess various job changes to be more threatening than need be. Projection may be especially strong for undesirable traits that perceivers possess but fail to recognize in themselves. People whose personality traits include stinginess, obstinacy, and disorderliness tend to rate others higher on these traits than do people who don't have these personality traits.

### EXPECTANCY EFFECTS

**Expectancy effects** are the extent to which prior expectations bias perceptions of events, objects, and people.[20] Sometimes people simply perceive what they anticipate perceiving.

Expectancy effects may also bias perception even in less ambiguous situations. For example, your perception of a team to which you have been assigned recently may be positive if your supervisor told you that the team's work is important and that it will be staffed by talented people from several departments. However, your perception may be negative if she told you that the team exists solely for political reasons and contains some real "deadwood" from other departments. You might also perceive identical behavior by other members of the team quite differently under each set of expectations.

An important aspect of expectancy effects is the self-fulfilling prophecy. The **self-fulfilling prophecy** is the tendency for someone's expectations about another to cause that individual to behave in a manner consistent with those expectations.[21] Expecting certain things to happen shapes the behavior of the perceiver in such a way that the expected is more likely to happen. Self-fulfilling prophecies can take both positive and negative forms. In the positive case, holding high expectations of another tends to improve the individual's performance, which is known as the **Pygmalion effect**. Subordinates whose managers expect them to perform well do perform well.[22] The reverse is also true. Subordinates whose managers expect them to perform poorly do in fact perform poorly. Obviously, this effect can be quite devastating.

To increase the likelihood of being positive Pygmalions managers need to remember three things.

1. *Individuals behave toward others consistent with their expectations of them.* Managers who have high expectations of their employees are supportive and generally give employees more training and challenging jobs. By contrast, managers who have low expectations of their employees aren't supportive and generally won't give employees training and challenging jobs.
2. *A person's behavior affects others.* Not only will those treated positively benefit from special opportunities, but these opportunities will also bolster their self-esteem.
3. *People behave in ways following from how they are treated.* People who have benefited from special treatment and who have confidence in their abilities are likely to be high performers.

Gordon Bethune, CEO of Continental Airlines, has taken steps to promote the Pygmalion effect. When he took over this airline in 1994, it was on the brink of bankruptcy. He encouraged the unionized workforce to suggest how to make things better. His staff and the employees together created "Our Working Together" program, stressing that people must work as a team and that every person on the team has to know what's going on. So every Friday, all the employees are told how the company performed during the week on key airline indicators, including cost of fuel, baggage handling, on-time performance, etc. He praises good performance and is open to ways of making further improvements. Every month in Houston, he holds open house to which employees—along with spouses, friends, kids, etc.—are invited to learn about the Continental's successes. Videotapes of employees doing their jobs well are available for all to see. According to Bethune, "It's not just rewards that matter, but it's how you are treated. If you recognize people's contribution and their value and treat them as part of the team, the organization will succeed." As a result of its performance, Continental was recently recognized as one of *Fortune's* best places to work and Bethune was ranked sixth among the 50 best CEOs to work for by *Business Week*.[23]

**Learning Objective:**

5. Explain how attributions influence behavior.

## ATTRIBUTIONS: WHY PEOPLE BEHAVE AS THEY DO

A question often asked about others is "why?" Why did this engineer use these data in his report? or Why did Howard Schultz, CEO and founder of Starbucks, start his Partner Connection Program of employee benefits? or Why did Naveen Jain deceive people about their opportunities at InfoSpace? Such questions are an attempt to get at why a person behaved in a particular way. The **attribution process** refers to the ways in which people come to understand the causes of their own and others' behaviors.[24] In essence, the attribution process reflects people's need to explain events through the deliberate actions of others rather than viewing them as random events. To maintain the illusion of control, people need to create causal attributions for events. Attributions also play an important role in perceptions. Attributions made about the reasons for someone's behavior may affect judgments about that individual's basic characteristics (what that person is really like).

The attributions that employees and managers make concerning the causes of behavior are important for understanding behavior. For example, managers who attribute poor performance directly to their subordinates tend to behave more punitively than do managers who attribute poor performance to circumstances beyond their subordinates' control. A manager who believes that an employee failed to perform a task correctly because he lacked proper training might be understanding and give the employee better instructions or more training. The same manager might be quite angry if he believes that the subordinate made mistakes simply because he didn't try very hard.

Responses to the same outcome can be dramatically different, depending on the attributions made about the reasons for that outcome. Table 3.3 lists some of the possible differences in managerial behavior when employees are perceived positively versus when they are perceived negatively. The relationships between attributions and behavior will become clearer as we examine the attribution process.

## THE ATTRIBUTION PROCESS

People make attributions in an attempt to understand why people behave as they do and to make better sense of their situations. Individuals don't consciously make attributions all the time (although they may do so unconsciously much of the time).[25] However, under certain circumstances, people are likely to make causal attributions consciously. For example, causal attributions are common in the following situations.

- The perceiver has been asked an explicit question about another's behavior. (Why did she do that?)
- An unexpected event occurs. (I've never seen him behave that way. I wonder what's going on?)
- The perceiver depends on another person for a desired outcome. (I wonder why my boss made that comment about my expense account?)
- The perceiver experiences feelings of failure or loss of control. (I can't believe I failed my midterm exam!)

Figure 3.4 presents a schematic model of the attribution process. People infer "causes" to behaviors that they observe in others, and these interpretations often largely determine their reactions to those behaviors. The perceived causes of behavior reflect several antecedents: (1) the amount of information the perceiver has about the people and the situation and how that information is organized by the perceiver; (2) the perceiver's beliefs (implicit personality theories, what other people might do in a similar situation, and so on); and (3) the motivation of the perceiver (e.g., the importance to the perceiver of making an accurate assessment). Recall our discussion of internal factors that influence perception—learning, personality, and motivation. These same internal factors influence the attribution process. The perceiver's information and beliefs depend on previous experience and are influenced by the perceiver's personality.

## Table 3.3

| Possible Results Stemming from Differences in Perceptions of Performance | |
|---|---|
| **BOSS'S BEHAVIOR TOWARD PERCEIVED STRONG PERFORMERS** | **BOSS'S BEHAVIOR TOWARD PERCEIVED WEAK PERFORMERS** |
| Discusses project objectives. Gives subordinate the freedom to choose own approach to solving problems or reaching goals. | Gives specific directives when discussing tasks and goals. |
| Treats mistakes or incorrect judgments as learning opportunities. | Pays close attention to mistakes and incorrect judgments. Quick to emphasize what subordinate is doing wrong. |
| Is open to subordinate's suggestions. Solicits opinions from subordinate. | Pays little attention to subordinate's suggestions. Rarely asks subordinate for input. |
| Gives subordinate interesting and challenging assignments. | Gives subordinate routine assignments. |
| May frequently defer to subordinate's opinions in disagreements. | Usually imposes own views in disagreements. |

**Figure 3.4**                          **The Attribution Process**

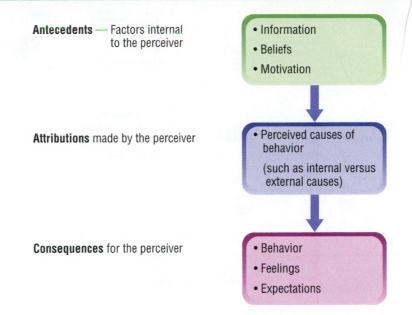

Antecedents — Factors internal to the perceiver
- Information
- Beliefs
- Motivation

Attributions made by the perceiver
- Perceived causes of behavior
  (such as internal versus external causes)

Consequences for the perceiver
- Behavior
- Feelings
- Expectations

## INTERNAL VERSUS EXTERNAL CAUSES OF BEHAVIOR

In applying attribution theory, you should be especially concerned with whether a person's behavior has been internally or externally caused. Internal causes are believed to be under an individual's control—you believe that your Web site designer's performance is poor because she's often late to work. External causes are believed to be beyond a person's control—you believe that her performance is poor because her Windows operating system is old. According to attribution theory, three factors influence the determination of internal or external cause:

- *consistency*—the extent to which the person perceived behaves in the same manner on other occasions when faced with the same situation. If your Web site designer's behavior has been poor for several months, you would tend to attribute it to an internal cause. If her performance is an isolated incident, you would tend to attribute it to an external cause.
- *distinctiveness*—the extent to which the person perceived acts in the same manner in different situations. If your Web site designer's performance is poor, regardless of the computer program with which she's working, you would tend to make an internal attribution; if her poor performance is unusual, you would tend to make an external attribution.
- *consensus*—the extent to which others, faced with the same situation, behave in a manner similar to the person perceived. If all the employees in your Web site designer's team perform poorly, you would tend to make an external attribution. If other members of her team are performing well, you would tend to make an internal attribution.

As Figure 3.5 suggests, under conditions of high consistency, high distinctiveness, and high consensus, the perceiver will tend to attribute the behavior of the perceived to external causes. When distinctiveness and consensus are low, the perceiver will tend to attribute the behavior of the perceived to internal causes. Other combinations of high and low consistency, distinctiveness, and consensus are possible. Some combinations may not provide the perceiver with a clear choice between internal and external causes.

**Figure 3.5**                      **Kelley's Theory of Causal Attributions**

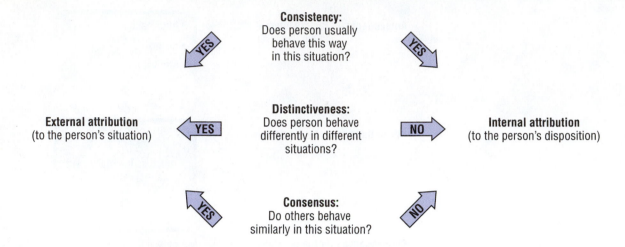

Source: Myers, D. G. *Social Psychology*, 4th ed. New York: McGraw-Hill, 1993, 77. Reprinted with permission from McGraw-Hill.

Note that consistency is high under both attribution outcomes. When consistency is low, the perceiver may attribute the behavior to either internal or external causes, or both. For example, imagine that a candidate running for the U.S. Senate gives a speech in favor of gun control while campaigning in his home state and then speaks in opposition to gun control when addressing a convention of the National Rifle Association in another state. In this case, an observer might make either an internal attribution (e.g., a character flaw "causes" the politician to tell these people what he thinks they want to hear) or an external attribution (e.g., the audience "causes" the politician to change his speech), or both.

With regard to internal versus external causes of behavior, people often make what is known as the fundamental attribution error. The **fundamental attribution error** is the tendency to underestimate the influence of situational factors and to overestimate the influence of personal factors in evaluating someone else's behavior. In organizations, employees often tend to assign blame to other departments or individuals and fail to recognize the effect of the situation. For example, a CEO might attribute a high level of political behavior on the part of her vice presidents to aspects of their personalities, not recognizing that competition for scarce resources is causing much of the political behavior.

Some cultural differences exist in the fundamental attribution error. For example, in North America, this type of error would be as just described (underestimating external causes and overestimating internal causes). In India, however, the more common attribution error is for people to overestimate situational or external causes for the observed behavior.[26] This difference in attributions may reflect the way that people view personal responsibility or perhaps differences in "average" locus of control beliefs in the different societies.

The fundamental attribution error isn't the only bias that can influence judgments concerning internal versus external causes of behavior. A study of supervisors showed that they were more likely to attribute effective performance to internal causes for high-status employees and less likely to attribute success to internal causes for low-status employees. Similarly, supervisors were more likely to attribute ineffective performance to internal causes for low-status employees and less likely to attribute failure to internal causes for high-status employees.[27]

## ATTRIBUTIONS OF SUCCESS AND FAILURE

The attributions that employees and managers make regarding success or failure are very important. Managers may base decisions about rewards and punishments on their perceptions of why subordinates have succeeded or failed at some task. In general, individuals often attribute there own and others' success or failure to four causal factors: ability, effort, task difficulty, and luck.[28]

- I succeeded (or failed) because I had the competencies to do the task (or because I did not have the competencies to do the task). Such statements are ability attributions.
- I succeeded (or failed) because I worked hard at the task (or because I did not work hard at the task). Such statements are effort attributions.
- I succeeded (or failed) because the task was easy (or because the task was too hard). Such statements are attributions about task difficulty.
- I succeeded (or failed) at the task because I was lucky (or unlucky). Such statements are attributions about luck or the circumstances surrounding the task.

Causal attributions of ability and effort are internal, and causal attributions of task difficulty and luck are external. These attributions about success or failure reflect differences in self-esteem and locus of control—personality dimensions discussed in Chapter 2. For example, individuals with high self-esteem and high internal locus of control are likely to assess their own performance positively and to attribute their good performance to internal causes.

Not surprisingly, many people tend to attribute their successes to internal factors (ability or effort) and attribute their failures to external factors (task difficulty or luck), which is known as a **self-serving bias**. The tendency of employees to accept responsibility for good performance but to deny responsibility for poor performance often presents a serious challenge for managers during performance appraisals. A self-serving bias may also create other types of problems. For example, it prevents individuals from accurately assessing their own performance and abilities and makes more difficult determining why a course of action has failed. The general tendency to blame others for a person's own failures often is associated with poor performance and an inability to establish satisfying interpersonal relationships at work and in other social settings. In general, a version of the self-serving bias seems to operate when people are asked to compare themselves to others in the work setting. That is, managers and employees often view themselves to be more ethical, more effective, better performing, and so on, than the "average" other person.

One of the more traumatic events that can occur to anyone is being fired.[29] Today losing a job doesn't carry the stigma that it once did. But—it still hurts!  Inevitably the person asks himself: What went wrong? What could I have done differently? And, perhaps most important: What am I going to do now?

For most people, undertaking a job search at any time is always stressful. It has been described as a combination of the worst aspects of a blind date and a fraternity rush party. Undertaking a job search after suffering the psychological blow of being fired can be a formidable challenge for anyone. Suppose that you have just been fired. You can take certain constructive actions to increase your chances of success and even end up with a more satisfying job.

1. *Work through the firing psychologically.* Emotionally, you might feel like hiding or taking a sabbatical. But, experts suggest that beginning the search for a new job immediately is crucial. The first contact or two may be hard, but the sooner you get started and the more people you talk to, the quicker you will find another position. Of course, reestablishing your normal good spirits may be either a long or slow process, depending on your ability to bounce back. Maintaining a sense of humor helps. Hal Lancaster, of the *Wall Street Journal*, suggests that

"getting fired is nature's way of telling you that you had the wrong job in the first place."

2. *Figure out what went wrong.* This step is an important part of coming to grips, psychologically, with the situation. Experts suggest that if you don't understand what led to your being fired, you're likely to repeat the same mistakes in the future. Moreover, they suggest that you need to talk to your former employer, coworkers, and friends and seek honest feedback to help you understand your strengths and weaknesses. Doing so may well be difficult, as many firms' human resource professionals prefer to say as little as possible at the time of dismissal in order to minimize lawsuits. If you can't get insights from your former employer, experts suggest utilizing a career counselor to help you make the same evaluation.

3. *Work with your former employer to develop an exit statement.* Experts almost always recommend that you have something in writing from your former employer that will be an asset in your job search. Specific suggestions include having a paragraph that describes what you accomplished in your former job followed by a paragraph that explains why you are no longer with the firm. There are lots of "socially acceptable" reasons that can be given in such a document: a change in management style, a change in strategy, the desire to pursue interests that no longer fit what the employer wants, and so on. Surprisingly, the fired employee can often get a former boss or other officials to sign such a document. People often want to be helpful, and if such a request is approached in a constructive, problem-solving manner, many times the former employer is willing to help create a letter or other document that condemns neither the company nor yourself. This approach has the advantage of creating a situation where prospective future employers hear the same "story" from both the former employer and the job applicant.

4. *Avoid negative attributions as part of your explanation.* Experts say that you should never say anything bad about your former employer. Don't make excuses; don't trash the people you used to work for; and don't blame everything on other people. Focus on the positive aspects of any written understanding that you have obtained. Accept responsibility for both your failures and successes. Quickly move the discussion to the future, stressing what you've learned from previous jobs and focus on what you can do for a new employer.

## CHAPTER SUMMARY

**1.** Describe the major elements in the perceptual process.

Perception is the psychological process whereby people select information from the environment and organize it to make sense of their worlds. Environmental stimuli are observed, selected, organized, interpreted, and responded to as a result of the perceptual process. Understanding the two major components of this process—selection and organization—is particularly important.

**2.** Identify the main factors that influence what individuals perceive.

People use perceptual selection to filter out less important information in order to focus on more important environmental cues. Both external factors in the environment and factors internal to the perceiver influence perceptual selection. External factors can be thought of as characteristics of the event perceived that influence whether it is likely to be noticed. Internal factors include personality, learning, and motivation.

**3.** Identify the factors that determine how one person perceives another.

How people perceive each other is particularly important for organizational behavior. Person perception is a function of the characteristics of the person perceived, the characteristics of the perceiver, and the situation within which the perception takes place. People may go to great lengths to manage the impressions that others form about them. Understanding the dynamics of impression management is also useful for understanding the behavior of people at work.

**4.** Describe the primary errors in perception that people make.

The perceptual process may result in errors of judgment or understanding in various ways. The more important and common perceptual errors include perceptual defense, stereotyping, halo effect, projection, and expectancy effects. However, through training and experience, individuals can learn to judge or perceive others more accurately.

**5.** Explain how attributions influence behavior.

Attribution deals with the perceived causes of behavior. People infer causes for the behavior of others, and their perceptions of why certain behaviors occur influence their own subsequent behavioral responses and feelings. Whether behavior is internally caused by the nature of the person or is externally caused by circumstances is an important attribution that people make about the behaviors of others. Individuals also make attributions concerning task success and failure, which have important implications for organizational behavior.

## KEY TERMS AND CONCEPTS

Attribution process
Expectancy effects
Feng shui
Fundamental attribution error
Halo effect
Implicit personality theories
Impression management
Perception
Perceptual defense
Perceptual set

Person perception
Pollyanna principle
Primacy effect
Projection
Pygmalion effect
Selective screening
Self-fulfilling prophecy
Self-serving bias
Stereotyping

## DISCUSSION QUESTIONS

1. Describe a time when the *situation* played a key role in your perception of another person. How might that perception have been different if the situation had been different?
2. Using the concepts of feng shui, diagnose a department store or company that you are familiar with. What did you learn from this exercise?
3. Provide two examples of impression management based on your own experience. Why do people try to manage impressions?
4. From your own experience, provide other examples of gestures that have different meanings in different countries.
5. Give three examples of the halo effect that you have personally observed.
6. How do you perceive Naveen Jain as a manager? What factors influenced your perception?
7. Describe an important task at which you failed. Describe a second important task at which you succeeded. Identify the attributions that you made to explain your failure and your success.
8. Provide two real examples of the Pygmalion effect.

## DEVELOPING COMPETENCIES

### Competency: Managing Diversity

### Women as Managers

Gender role stereotypes limit the opportunity for women to advance to managerial positions in many firms. Although these stereotypes are slowly changing, widely held attitudes about the inadequacies of women as managers represent a barrier to greater career opportunities for many women.

Because specific attitudes and stereotypes can be pervasive and powerful influences on behavior, considering their role in the treatment—by both men and women—of women in managerial positions is important. Attitudes about the managerial abilities of women may affect how a manager or executive judges a woman's performance in a managerial role. In addition, such attitudes may influence the granting or withholding of developmental opportunities. The following questionnaire is designed to help you explore your attitudes toward women as managers.

*Instructions:* From each set (of three) statements, select the one with which you *most agree* and place an M (for "most agree") in the blank to the right of that statement. For each set, also select the statement with which you *least agree* and place an L (for "least agree") in the blank to the right of that statement. Note that one statement in each set will not be chosen.

1. A. Men are more concerned with the cars they drive than with the clothes their wives wear.
   B. Any man worth his salt should not be blamed for putting his career above his family. _____
   C. A person's job is the best single indicator of the sort of person he is. _____

2. A. Parental authority and responsibility for discipline of the children should be divided equally between the husband and the wife. _____
   B. It is less desirable for women than for men to have jobs that require responsibility. _____
   C. Men should not continue to show courtesies to women, such as holding doors open for them and helping them with their coats. _____

3. A. It is acceptable for women to assume leadership roles as often as men. _____
   B. In a demanding situation, a female manager would be no more likely to break down than would a male manager. _____
   C. Some professions and types of businesses are more suitable for men than for women. _____

4. A. Recognition for a job well done is less important to women than it is to men. _____
   B. A woman should demand money for household and personal expenses as a right rather than a gift. _____
   C. Women are temperamentally fit for leadership positions. _____

5. A. Women tend to allow their emotions to influence their managerial behavior more than men do. _____
   B. The husband and the wife should be equal partners in planning the family budget. _____
   C. If both husband and wife agree that sexual fidelity is not important, there is no

reason why both should not have extramarital affairs. _____

6. A. A man's first responsibility is to his wife, not to his mother. _____
   B. A man who is able and willing to work hard has a good chance of succeeding in whatever he wants to do. _____
   C. Only after a man has achieved what he wants from life should he concern himself with the injustices in the world. _____

7. A. A wife should make every effort to minimize irritations and inconveniences for the male head of the household. _____
   B. Women can cope with stressful situations as effectively as men can. _____
   C. Women should be encouraged not to become sexually intimate with anyone, even their fiancés, before marriage. _____

8. A. The "obey" clause in the marriage service is insulting to women. _____
   B. Divorced men should help to support their children but should not be required to pay alimony if their former wives are capable of working. _____
   C. Women have the capacity to acquire the necessary skills to be successful managers. _____

9. A. Women can be aggressive in business situations that demand it. _____
   B. Women have an obligation to be faithful to their husbands. _____
   C. It is childish for a woman to assert herself by retaining her maiden name after marriage. _____

10. A. Men should continue to show courtesies to women, such as holding doors open for them or helping them with their coats. _____
    B. In job appointments and promotions, women should be given equal consideration with men. _____
    C. It is all right for a wife to have an occasional casual, extramarital affair. _____

11. A. The satisfaction of her husband's sexual desires is a fundamental obligation of every wife. _____
    B. Most women should not want the kind of support that men traditionally have given them. _____
    C. Women possess the dominance to be successful leaders. _____

12. A. Most women need and want the kind of protection and support that men traditionally have given them. _____
    B. Women are capable of separating their emotions from their ideas. _____
    C. A husband has no obligation to inform his wife of his financial plans. _____

Score your responses by using the form and following the instructions given. Your total score indicates your feelings about women managers. The higher your score, the more prone you are to hold negative gender role stereotypes about women in management. Possible total scores range from 10 to 70; a "neutral" score (one that indicates neither positive nor negative attitudes about women as managers) is in the range of 30 to 40.

*Instructions:*

1. Record your response for the indicated items in the spaces provided.

2. On the basis of the information provided, determine the points for each item and enter these points in the space provided to the right. For example, if in item 3 you chose alternative A as the one with which you *most agree* and alternative B as the one with which you *least agree*, you should receive three points for item 3. Note that items 1 and 6 are "buffer items" and are not scored.

3. When you have scored all 10 scorable items, add the points and record the total at the bottom of this page in the space provided. That is your total score.[30]

| Your Response | Item No. | POINTS PER ITEM RESPONSE* | | | | | | Points |
|---|---|---|---|---|---|---|---|---|
| | | 1 | 3 | | 5 | | 7 | |
| | 1 | Not Scored | | | | | | |
| M ____ | 2 | C(M) | A(M) | C(M) | A(M) | B(M) | B(M) | |
| L ____ | | B(L) | B(L) | A(L) | C(L) | A(L) | C(L) | |
| M ____ | 3 | A(M) | A(M) | B(M) | C(M) | B(M) | C(M) | |
| L ____ | | C(L) | B(L) | C(L) | B(L) | A(L) | A(L) | |
| M ____ | 4 | C(M) | C(M) | A(M) | B(M) | A(M) | B(M) | |
| L ____ | | B(L) | A(L) | B(L) | A(L) | C(L) | C(L) | |
| M ____ | 5 | C(M) | C(M) | B(M) | A(M) | B(M) | A(M) | |
| L ____ | | A(L) | B(L) | A(L) | B(L) | C(L) | C(L) | |
| M ____ | 6 | Not Scored | | | | | | |
| L ____ | | | | | | | | |
| M ____ | 7 | B(M) | B(M) | C(M) | A(M) | C(M) | A(M) | |
| L ____ | | A(L) | C(L) | A(L) | C(L) | B(L) | B(L) | |
| M ____ | 8 | C(M) | C(M) | A(M) | B(M) | A(M) | B(M) | |
| L ____ | | B(L) | A(L) | B(L) | A(L) | C(L) | C(L) | |
| M ____ | 9 | A(M) | A(M) | C(M) | B(M) | C(M) | B(M) | |
| L ____ | | B(L) | C(L) | B(L) | C(L) | A(L) | A(L) | |
| M ____ | 10 | B(M) | B(M) | C(M) | A(M) | C(M) | A(M) | |
| L ____ | | A(L) | C(L) | A(L) | C(L) | B(L) | B(L) | |
| M ____ | 11 | C(M) | C(M) | B(M) | A(M) | B(M) | A(M) | |
| L ____ | | A(L) | B(L) | A(L) | B(L) | C(L) | C(L) | |
| M ____ | 12 | B(M) | B(M) | C(M) | A(M) | C(M) | A(M) | |
| L ____ | | A(L) | C(L) | A(L) | C(L) | B(L) | B(L) | |
| | | | | | | | Total | ____ |

*M indicates item chosen as "most"; L indicates item chosen as "least."

## Competency: Managing Ethics

### Fudge the Numbers or Leave

Sara Page joined MicroPhone—a large telecommunications company with headquarters in Denver—almost 2 months ago to take over the implementation of a massive customer service training project. The program, lodged in human resources, was rumored to be a favorite of the CEO and had been created by Kristin Jurgen. Industry competition was heating up and the strategies of the company called for being the very best at customer service. That translated into having the most highly trained people in the industry, especially those who would work directly with customers.

Two months earlier, Jurgen had formed a crash team in human resources to develop a new training program that could address those needs. It called for an average of 1 full week of intense, highly effective training for each of 3,000 people, and it had a price tag in the neighborhood of $40 million. Jurgen's team—made up of several staffers who already felt overwhelmed with their day-to-day workload—rushed to put the proposal together. It was scheduled to go to the company's board of directors in December.

Jurgen needed someone well qualified and dedicated just to manage and implement the project. Page had 8 years of experience, a list of significant accomplishments, and advanced business degrees in finance and organizational behavior. But perhaps what Jurgen failed to see in Page was the quiet moral compass that she invariably followed, even at the risk of her own welfare.

When Page agreed to come aboard, Jurgen expressed her relief and confidence in Page's ability to make the program work. And those closest to Jurgen believed that she was hoping this project alone would give her the "star quality" needed to earn a promotion from Jack Davies, a charismatic chief executive who had told her he was pleased with her plans thus far.

But 6 weeks ago, Jurgen had asked Page to look over the plan. "I don't think you'll find any major problems," she said. "Just tidy it up for submission to the guys over at strategic planning. They'll take a look at it before it goes to the board." Page's first cursory review turned up a few inconsistencies. Jurgen's unspoken reaction to Sara's findings seemed odd, as if she were secretly harboring the thought, "You located some mistakes. I hate you for finding them."

When Page conducted a second and more thorough review, she found some assumptions built into the formulas of the proposal that raised red flags. She asked Dan Sotal, the project's team coordinator, about her concerns. The more he tried to explain how the financial projections were derived, the more Page realized Jurgen's proposal was seriously flawed.

But no matter how she tried to work them out, the most that could be squeezed out of the $40 million budget was 20 hours of training per person, not 40, as everyone had expected for such a high price tag.

Today was the day that Page was to discuss her review with Jurgen, a consultant, and one other human resources staff member. She knew that despite the fact that this proposal had been developed largely before she came on board, it would bear her signature. She carefully walked everyone through what she described as significant problems with the program and its potentially devastating consequences. Jurgen tapped her pencil on the tabletop for a few minutes before she stood up, leaned forward, and interrupted Page, quietly saying, "Sara, make the numbers work so that it adds up to 40 hours for each employee and stays within the $40 million figure."

Page looked up at her and said, "It can't be done unless we either change the number of employees who are to be trained or the cost figure...." Jurgen's smile moved into place and the crows feet around the corners of her eyes deepened as she again interrupted: "I don't think you understand what I'm saying: Make the previous numbers work!"

Stunned, Page belatedly realized what was being asked of her. Jurgen adjusted her glasses and continued to stare coldly at Page. The other two people at the meeting sat frozen in their chairs, while Page considered what she should do.[31]

### Questions

1. Make a list of the possible differences in perceptions between Sara Page and Kristin Jurgen.
2. What attributions would you expect Page to make about Jurgen's behavior? What attributions would you expect Jurgen to make about Page's behavior?
3. If you were Sara Page, what would you do?

# Fostering Learning and Reinforcement

## LEARNING OBJECTIVES

When you have finished studying the chapter, you should be able to:
1. Explain the differences between classical and operant conditioning.
2. Describe the contingencies of reinforcement.
3. List the four schedules of reinforcement and explain when each is effective.
4. Describe social learning theory.

# PIONEER TELEPHONE COOPERATIVE

Located in Kingfisher, Oklahoma, Pioneer Telephone Cooperative was founded in 1953, currently employs more than 600 people, and has no formal sales department. This phone company serves 50,000 people in some 11,000 square miles and 30 suburban and rural areas in Oklahoma. It provides subscribers with services such as caller ID, call forwarding, call waiting, speed dialing, and last call return and various phone products.

How does Pioneer get new subscribers? All employees at Pioneer are salespeople. Employees refer qualified leads to the company via Pioneer's intranet. A lead is qualified when employees, on their own time, recommend or explain products or services to potential customers and ask them to contact the employees at work. Employees are rewarded for each successful lead; bonuses are deposited in their company accounts and paid each quarter. Pioneer periodically offers double points for leads. To ensure that all employees are aware of the company's products and services, each month they receive a computer-based learning module. Each topic is designed to be an interactive adult learning experience. Employees read the information and answer 10 questions. Those who successfully answer at least 90% of the questions receive $5.

Pioneer recently launched an e-billing service and uses its computer-based learning module program to inform employees about its e-billing services and benefits. Recognizing the expense of advertising, Pioneer offered a free T-shirt to the first 100 employees who enrolled in the program. The expense of a T-shirt was minimal, and now Pioneer has 100 employees who are familiar with this new service and can inform customers about it.

Pioneer recently used the same type of program to get customers involved with new services offered by Pioneer. Called Take 5—Win $25, this program requires customers to read the information in the company's newsletter, answer five questions, and mail the questionnaire back to Pioneer for a chance to win $25. Each month, one winner is drawn from each of Pioneer's 13 districts. Two hundred ninety-three customers entered the first contest. More than 700 customers entered the next contest. Most recently, several thousand participated in a chance to win $25.

Johnnie Ruhl, Pioneer's CEO, believes that rewarding employees to promote Pioneer accomplishes four things: (1) educates employees about products and services, (2) increases sales through good leads, (3) reduces sales expenses, and (4) makes employees ambassadors for the company.[1]

*For more information on Pioneer Telephone Cooperative, visit the organization's home page at http://www.ptci.com.*

Pioneer's motivational tactics are based on specific principles drawn from an area of psychology called *learning*. **Learning** is a relatively permanent change in knowledge or observable behavior that results from practice or experience.[2] Desirable work behaviors contribute to achieving organizational goals; conversely, undesirable work behaviors hinder achieving these goals. Labeling behavior as *desirable* or *undesirable* may be somewhat subjective and depend on the value systems of the organization (most often represented by an employee's manager) and the employee exhibiting the behavior. For example, a team member at Pioneer who returns late from a coffee break exhibits undesirable behavior from the manager's viewpoint, desirable behavior from the viewpoint of friends with whom the worker chats during the break, and desirable behavior from the worker's viewpoint because of the satisfaction of social needs. Employees quickly learn the difference from the manager's reaction to the behavior and how to change an undesirable to a desirable (from the manager's viewpoint) behavior.

Usually, however, the work setting and organizational norms provide objective bases for determining whether a behavior is desirable or undesirable. The more a behavior deviates from organizational expectations, the more undesirable it is. At Southwest Airlines, undesirable behavior includes anything that results in lost baggage and late departures and arrivals. Expectations vary considerably from one organization to another. For example, at Microsoft's research and development laboratory, engineers and scientists are encouraged to question top-management's directives because innovation and professional judgment are crucial to the organization's success in the telecommunications market. In contrast, in a military unit such questioning may be considered insubordination and justification for severe disciplinary action.

Effective managers do not try to change employees' personalities or basic beliefs. As we pointed out in Chapters 2 and 3, an individual's personality and perceptual processes influence behavior and directly influencing them is often difficult, if not impossible. Rather, effective managers focus on identifying observable employee behaviors and the environmental conditions that affect these behaviors. They then attempt to influence external events in order to guide employee behaviors—to help employees learn and exhibit desirable behaviors. In this chapter, we explore three major theories of learning: classical conditioning, operant conditioning, and social learning theory. Each theory proposes a different way by which people learn, but focusing on observable behaviors is common to all three.

**Learning Objective:**

1. Explain the differences between classical and operant conditioning.

# LEARNING THROUGH REWARDS AND PUNISHMENTS

In an organization, employees need to learn and practice productive work behaviors.[3] Learning new work often depends on many factors. The manager's task, then, is to provide learning experiences in an environment that will simplify the learning process and promote employee behaviors desired by the organization. For learning to occur, some types of behavioral change are required. Just as students learn basic educational skills in the classroom, when Pioneer wanted to change the behavior of its salespeople, it used a computer-based training program as its classroom. This training not only prepared employees to meet the challenges of the job, but also provided them with incentives to learn and practice these newly learned behaviors.

## CLASSICAL CONDITIONING

**Classical conditioning** is the process by which individuals learn to link the information from a neutral stimulus to a stimulus that causes a response. This response may not be under an individual's conscious control.[4] In the classical conditioning process, an unconditioned stimulus (environmental event) brings out a natural response. Then a neutral environmental event, called a *conditioned stimulus*, is paired with the unconditioned stimulus that brings out the behavior. Eventually, the conditioned stimulus alone brings out the behavior, which is called a *conditional response*.

The name most frequently associated with classical conditioning is Ivan Pavlov, the Russian physiologist whose experiments with dogs led to the early formulations of classical conditioning theory. In Pavlov's famous experiment, the sound of a metronome (the conditioned stimulus) was paired with food (the unconditioned stimulus). The dogs eventually exhibited a salivation response (conditioned response) to the sound of the metronome alone. The classical conditioning process is illustrated in Figure 4.1.

The classical conditioning process helps explain a variety of behaviors that occur in everyday organizational life. At Presbyterian Hospital's emergency room, special lights in the hallway indicate that a patient who needs treatment has just arrived. Nurses and other hospital staff report that they feel nervous when the lights go on. In contrast, at a recent luncheon in the dining room at Stonebriar Country Club, Ralph Sorrentino, a partner at Deloitte & Touche, was thanked by his friend Jon Wheeler, vice president of Centex Homes, for introducing a new work system. Now, whenever Sorrentino sees the dining room, he feels good.

Organizations spend billions of dollars on advertising campaigns designed to link the information value of a stimulus to customer purchase behavior. In a TV ad, AFLAC has successfully created a link between its duck and supplemental insurance. The duck is the unconditioned stimulus, and insurance is the conditioned stimulus. The positive feelings that buyers have toward the duck are associated with insurance, which AFLAC hopes will lead people to buy its products. Similarly, Blue Bell Creameries has linked its cow, Belle, in an award winning TV ad. When people see Belle (unconditioned stimulus) singing in a pasture of purple flowers, they associate her with Blue Bell ice cream (the conditioned stimulus). Associating the upbeat mood and dairy freshness created by the cow, Blue Bell hopes to lead customers to eat its ice cream. Both organizations have successfully used the concepts of classical conditioning to increase sales of their products.

Classical conditioning isn't widely used in work settings. The reason is that desired employee behaviors usually don't include responses that can be changed with classical conditioning techniques. There is greater interest in the voluntary behaviors of employees and how they can be changed via operant conditioning.

## OPERANT CONDITIONING

The person most closely linked with this type of learning is B.F. Skinner.[5] He coined the term **operant conditioning** to refer to a process by which individuals learn

**Figure 4.1**                          **Classical Conditioning**

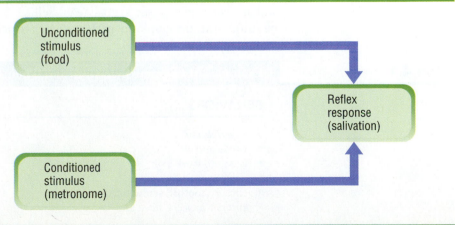

voluntary behavior. Voluntary behaviors are called *operants* because they operate, or have some influence, on the environment. Learning occurs from the consequences of behaviors, and many employee work behaviors are operant behaviors. In fact, most behaviors in everyday life (e.g., talking, walking, reading, or working) are forms of operant behavior. Table 4.1 shows some examples of operant behaviors and their consequences. Managers are interested in operant behaviors because they can influence the results of such behaviors. For example, the frequency of an employee behavior can be increased or decreased by changing the results of that behavior. The crucial aspect of operant conditioning is what happens as a consequence of the behavior. The strength and frequency of operantly conditioned behaviors are determined mainly by consequences. Thus managers and team members must understand the effects of different types of consequences on the task behaviors of employees.

In operant conditioning, a response is learned because it leads to a particular consequence (reinforcement), and it is strengthened each time it is reinforced. The success of Pioneer Telephone Cooperative's sales program is based on operant conditioning principles. Employees learn to operate on their environment by engaging in specific behaviors (e.g., signing up new customers) in order to achieve certain consequences (money). At school, you've probably learned that if you study hard, you will receive good grades, and if you keep up with your reading throughout the semester, you can cope with the stress of finals week. Thus you've learned to operate on your environment to achieve your desired goals.

## CONTINGENCIES OF REINFORCEMENT

A **contingency of reinforcement** is the relationship between a behavior and the preceding and following environmental events that influence that behavior. A contingency of reinforcement consists of an antecedent, a behavior, and a consequence.[6]

An **antecedent** precedes and is a stimulus to a behavior. Antecedents are instructions, rules, goals, and advice from others that help individuals to know which behaviors are acceptable and which are not and to let them know the consequences of such behaviors. At Pioneer, antecedents were the instructions that management sent to all employees about how to sell its services to subscribers. Antecedents play an essential educational role by letting employees know in advance the consequences (extra money) of different behaviors (signing up new subscribers).

A **consequence** is the result of a behavior, which can be either positive or negative in terms of goal or task accomplishment. A manager's response to an employee is contingent on the consequence of the behavior (and sometimes on the behavior itself, regardless of consequence). The consequence for the employees at Pioneer is meeting their goals and those of the organization.

Figure 4.2 shows an example of contingent reinforcement. First, the employee and manager jointly set a goal (e.g., selling $100,000 worth of equipment next month). Next, the employee performs tasks to achieve this goal (e.g., calling on four

**Table 4.1**

| Examples of Operant Behaviors and Their Consequences | |
|---|---|
| **BEHAVIORS** | **CONSEQUENCES** |
| *The Individual* | |
| • works and | is paid. |
| • is late to work and | is docked pay. |
| • enters a restaurant and | eats. |
| • enters a football stadium and | watches a football game. |
| • enters a grocery store and | buys food. |

**Figure 4.2**                          **Example of Contingent Reinforcement**

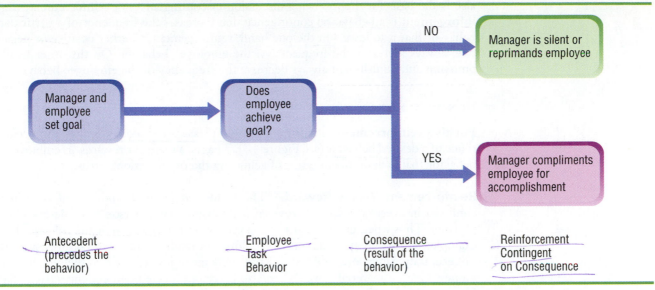

| Antecedent (precedes the behavior) | Employee Task Behavior | Consequence (result of the behavior) | Reinforcement Contingent on Consequence |

new customers a week, having regular lunches with current buyers, and attending a 2-day training program on new methods of selling). If the employee reaches the sales goal, the manager praises the employee—an action contingent on achievement of the goal. If the employee fails to reach the goal, the manager doesn't say anything or reprimands the employee.

The contingency of reinforcement concept involves three main types of contingency. First, an event can be presented (applied) or withdrawn (removed), contingent on employee behavior. The event also may be positive or aversive. **Positive events** are desirable, or pleasing, to the employee. **Aversive events** are undesirable, or displeasing, to the employee. Figure 4.3 shows how these events can be combined to produce four types of contingencies of reinforcement. It shows whether a particular

**Figure 4.3**                          **Types of Contingencies of Reinforcement**

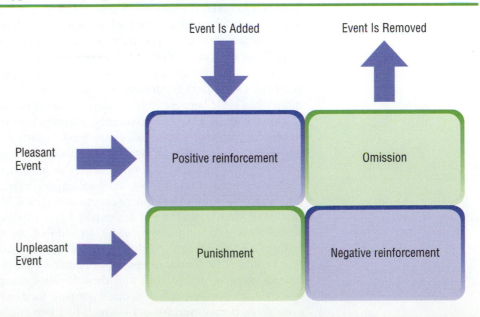

type of contingency is likely to increase or decrease the frequency of the behavior. It also is the basis for the following discussion of contingencies of reinforcement. **Reinforcement** is a behavioral contingency that increases the frequency of a particular behavior that it follows. On the one hand, reinforcement, whether positive or negative, always increases the frequency of the employee behavior. On the other hand, omission and punishment always decrease the frequency of the employee behavior.

## POSITIVE REINFORCEMENT

**Positive reinforcement** entails presenting a pleasant consequence after the occurrence of a desired behavior (see Figure 4.3). That is, a manager rewards an employee's behavior that is desirable in terms of achieving the organization's goals.

### Reinforcement Versus Reward.

The terms *reinforcement* and *reward* are often confused in everyday usage. A **reward** is an event that a person finds desirable or pleasing. Thus whether a reward acts as a reinforcer is influenced by the culture.[7] For example, praise and appreciation of employee in family-dominated cultures such as Greece, Italy, Singapore, and South Korea may mean just as much to the recipient as money. Certain material rewards can also carry unexpected consequences. In India, for example, the reward of a cowhide leather wallet or key case with a corporate logo would be extremely offensive because the cow is a sacred animal for Hindus, the major religion of India. The same reactions may occur with nonmaterial rewards. A manager who singled out and praised a Japanese employee in front of coworkers for finding an error in the team's report believed that she was reinforcing the desired behavior. Later, however, she learned that the employee was given the silent treatment by other team members and had stopped looking for errors.

Thus, to qualify as a reinforcer, a reward must increase the frequency of the behavior it follows. Recall that, at Pioneer Telephone Cooperative, employees earn commissions only if they bring in new qualified subscribers. Money can be regarded as a positive reinforcer for a particular individual only if the frequency of desired behavior (in this case, high performance) increases. A reward doesn't act as a reinforcer if the frequency of the behavior decreases or remains unchanged.

### Primary and Secondary Reinforcers.

A **primary reinforcer** is an event for which the individual already knows the value. Food, shelter, and water are primary reinforcers. However, primary reinforcers don't always reinforce. For example, food may not be a reinforcer to someone who has just completed a five-course meal.

In organizations, secondary reinforcers influence most behaviors. A **secondary reinforcer** is an event that once had neutral value but has taken on some value (positive or negative) for an individual because of past experience. Money is an obvious example of a secondary reinforcer. Although it can't directly satisfy a basic human need, money has value because an individual can use it to purchase both necessities and discretionary items. Calvert, a Bethesda, Maryland, financial firm, groups its secondary reinforcers into three categories: *core benefits*, such as life insurance, sick leave, holiday pay, and a retirement savings plan; *optional benefits*, such as dental and eye-care coverage, and spending accounts for health and dependent care; and *other benefits*, such as tuition reimbursement, car pooling, and career planning.[8]

The following Managing Communication Competency feature details how Rockford Memorial Hospital designed a reward system to minimize unscheduled absences among its 2,400 employees. Unscheduled absences were a big problem for this hospital. They affected productivity and morale because last-minute replacements often couldn't be found, forcing coworkers to do their own work and that of the absentees. As a result, patients and their families complained about poor service. To make things worse, employees often got paid for not being at work, taking sick leave even though they weren't sick—which had become a common practice. Many employees felt that they simply were entitled to such leave and took advantage of it.

## COMPETENCY: MANAGING COMMUNICATION

### ROCKFORD MEMORIAL HOSPITAL

Employees at Rockford had enjoyed paid sick leave for years. It was originally intended to provide sick employees with a salary until they could return to work. A survey of employees, however, showed that 45 percent of personal illness days were taken when the employees weren't actually sick; 27 percent were for family reasons, 13 percent for personal needs, 13 percent for entitlement, and 6 percent for stress. These absences were costing the hospital more than $1 million a year. The average number of legitimate sick days was determined to be only five per year.

Before taking corrective action, managers held a series of brown-bag lunches with employees to clarify the organization's objectives. The employees were told that previous time-off policies had become too costly and didn't encourage good attendance. The managers indicated that the hospital must lower its costs of unscheduled absences, reward good attendance, and provide employees with greater flexibility for meeting their personal needs.

To control the cost of such absences, Rockford's Steve Eckberg, manager of the human resources department, devised a paid leave bank. The concept is simple: Employees receive a bank of time to be used for various types of absence (sick, vacation, and personal time). Legal holidays are excluded, as well as other time-off benefits, such as jury duty, death in the family, or military leave. Every time employees need time off, they dip into their reserve day bank. The number of days in each employee's bank is determined by seniority—new employees get 18 days; fifth year employees get 23 days. If employees have 23 days of paid time off in the bank (comprising 15 vacation days, 4 personal days, and 4 sick days), they are entitled to use those days however they want (all employees also have a catastrophic account, which is 6 days regardless of seniority). If employees take more than their banked days, they are to be terminated. The plan also enables employees to accrue up to 60 days of leave. Senior employees with more than 60 days in the bank would be asked to convert these extra days to paid vacation time. Upon termination, for whatever reason, employees are to receive compensation for their unused bank days.

Once the plan was devised, Eckberg and his human resource team met with non-management people who had "influence" in all departments in the hospital. These opinion leaders gave Eckberg's team feedback on the plan. After these meetings, the plan was presented to the employees. Employees' ideas and suggestions were addressed before the plan was finalized and announced. Rockford prided itself on being a good employer, so it decided that the plan would only affect new employees. Long-time employees would continue under the original leave program and not be covered by the plan. Hypothetical examples were used to illustrate the financial savings to the hospital.

What have been the results? Over 3 years, Rockford saved more than $2,723,000 in salaries and $391,660 in overtime pay and realized a $1,982,783 increase in productivity because of a 36 percent decline in unscheduled absenteeism.[9]

*For more information on Rockford Memorial Hospital, visit the organization's home page at http://www.rhsnet.org.*

**Principles of Positive Reinforcement.**   Several factors influence the effectiveness of positive reinforcement. These factors can be thought of loosely as principles because they help explain optimum reinforcement conditions.[10]

The **principle of contingent reinforcement** states that the reinforcer must be administered only if the desired behavior is performed. A reinforcer administered when the desired behavior has not been performed is ineffective. At Rockford Memorial, perfect attendance was rewarded.

The **principle of immediate reinforcement** states that the reinforcer will be most effective if administered immediately after the desired behavior has occurred. The more time that elapses after the behavior occurs, the less effective will be the reinforcer.

The **principal of reinforcement size** states that the larger the amount of reinforcer delivered after the desired behavior, the more effect the reinforcer will have on the frequency of the desired behavior. The amount, or size, of the reinforcer is relative. A reinforcer that may be significant to one person may be insignificant to another person. Thus the size of the reinforcer must be determined in relation both to the behavior and the individual. ARAMARK, a supplier of food services to college campuses, gives T-shirts to workers with perfect attendance for a month and a $50 gift certificate to those with perfect attendance for a semester.

The **principal of reinforcement deprivation** states that the more a person is deprived of the reinforcer, the greater effect it will have on the future occurrence of the desired behavior. However, if an individual recently has had enough of a reinforcer and is satisfied, the reinforcer will have less effect.

## ORGANIZATIONAL REWARDS

Although the material rewards—salary, bonuses, fringe benefits, and the like—that organizations commonly use are obvious, most organizations also offer a wide range of other rewards, many of which aren't immediately apparent. They include verbal approval, assignment to desired tasks, improved working conditions, and extra time off. At Toyota's Camry assembly plant in Georgetown, Kentucky, management rewards employees for *kaizens*. A **kaizen** is a suggestion that results in safety, cost, or quality improvements.[11] The awards are distributed equally among all members of a team. The awards aren't cash payments; rather, they are gift certificates redeemable at local retail stores. Toyota learned that an award that could be shared by the employees' families was valued more than extra money in the paycheck. These awards instill pride and encourage other employees to scramble for new ideas and products in the hope that they, too, will receive them. In addition, self-administered rewards are important. For example, self-congratulation for accomplishing a particularly difficult assignment can be an important personal reinforcer. Table 4.2 contains an extensive list of organizational rewards. Remember, however, that such rewards will act as reinforcers only if the individuals receiving them find them desirable or pleasing.

## NEGATIVE REINFORCEMENT

In **negative reinforcement** (see Figure 4.3), an unpleasant event that precedes the employee behavior is removed when the desired behavior occurs. This procedure increases the likelihood that the desired behavior will occur. Negative reinforcement is sometimes confused with punishment because both use unpleasant events to influence behavior. However, negative reinforcement is used to increase the frequency of a desired behavior, whereas punishment is used to decrease the frequency of an undesired behavior.

Managers and team members frequently use negative reinforcement when an employee hasn't done something that is necessary or desired. For example, air-traffic controllers want the capability to activate a blinking light and a loud buzzer in the cockpits of planes that come too close to each other. The air-traffic controllers wouldn't shut these devices off until the planes moved farther apart. This type of procedure is called **escape learning** because the pilots quickly learn to move their planes away from each other to escape the light and buzzer. In escape learning, an unpleasant event occurs until an employee performs a behavior, or escape response, to terminate it.

**Table 4.2**

| MATERIAL REWARDS | SUPPLEMENTAL BENEFITS | STATUS SYMBOLS |
|---|---|---|
| Pay | Company automobiles | Corner offices |
| Pay raises | Health insurance plans | Offices with windows |
| Stock options | Pension contributions | Carpeting |
| Profit sharing | Vacation and sick leave | Drapes |
| Deferred compensation | Recreation facilities | Paintings |
| Bonuses/bonus plans | Child-care support | Watches |
| Incentive plans | Club privileges | Rings |
| Expense accounts | Parental leave | Private restrooms |
| **SOCIAL/ INTERPERSONAL REWARDS** | **REWARDS FROM THE TASK** | **SELF-ADMINISTERED REWARDS** |
| Praise | Sense of achievement | Self-congratulation |
| Developmental feedback | Jobs with more responsibility | Self-recognition |
| Smiles, pats on the back, and other nonverbal signals | Job autonomy/self-direction | Self-praise |
| Requests for suggestions | Performing important tasks | Self-development through expanded knowledge/skills |
| Invitations to coffee or lunch | | Greater sense of self-worth |
| Wall plaques | | |

## OMISSION

**Omission** is the removal of all reinforcing events. Whereas reinforcement increases the frequency of a desirable behavior, omission decreases the frequency and eventually extinguishes an undesirable behavior (see Figure 4.3). Managers use omission to reduce undesirable employee behaviors that prevent achievement of organizational goals. The omission procedure consists of three steps:

1.  identifying the behavior to be reduced or eliminated,
2.  identifying the reinforcer that maintains the behavior, and
3.  stopping the reinforcer.

Omission is a useful technique for reducing and eventually eliminating behaviors that disrupt normal workflow. For example, a team reinforces the disruptive behavior of a member by laughing at the behavior. When the team stops laughing (the reinforcer), the disruptive behavior will diminish and ultimately stop.

Omission can also be regarded as a failure to reinforce a behavior positively. In this regard, the omission of behaviors may be accidental. If managers fail to reinforce desirable behaviors, they may be using omission without recognizing it. As a result, the frequency of desirable behaviors may inadvertently decrease.

Omission may effectively decrease undesirable employee behavior, but it doesn't automatically replace the undesirable behavior with desirable behavior. Often when omission is stopped, the undesirable behavior will return if alternative behaviors haven't been developed. Therefore, when omission is used, it should be combined with other methods of reinforcement to develop the desired behaviors.

## PUNISHMENT

**Punishment** (see Figure 4.3) is an unpleasant event that follows a behavior and decreases its frequency. As in positive reinforcement, a punishment may include a specific antecedent that cues the employee that a consequence (punisher) will follow a specific behavior. Whereas a positive contingency of reinforcement encourages the frequency of a desired behavior, a contingency of punishment decreases the frequency of an undesired behavior.

To qualify as a punisher, an event must decrease the undesirable behavior. Just because an event is thought of as unpleasant, it isn't necessarily a punisher. The event must actually reduce or stop the undesired behavior before it can be defined as a punisher.

Organizations typically use several types of unpleasant events to punish individuals.[12] Material consequences for failure to perform adequately include a cut in pay, a disciplinary suspension without pay, a demotion, or a transfer to a dead-end job. The final punishment is the firing of an employee for failure to perform. In general, organizations reserve the use of unpleasant material events for cases of serious behavior problems.

Interpersonal punishers are used extensively. They include a manager's oral reprimand of an employee for unacceptable behavior and nonverbal punishers such as frowns, grunts, and aggressive body language. Certain tasks themselves can be unpleasant. The fatigue that follows hard physical labor can be considered a punisher, as can harsh or dirty working conditions. However, care must be exercised in labeling a punisher. In some fields and to some employees, harsh or dirty working conditions may be considered as just something that goes with the job.

The principles of positive reinforcement discussed earlier have equivalents in punishment. For maximum effectiveness, a punisher should be directly linked to the undesirable behavior (principle of contingent punishment); the punisher should be administered immediately (principle of immediate punishment); and, in general, the greater the size of the punisher, the stronger will be the effect on the undesirable behavior (principle of punishment size).

**Negative Effects of Punishment.**    An argument against the use of punishment is the chance that it will have negative effects, especially over long or sustained periods of time. Even though punishment may stop an undesirable employee behavior, the potential negative consequences may be greater than the original undesirable behavior. Figure 4.4 illustrates some potential negative effects of punishment.

Punishment may cause undesirable emotional reactions.[13] An employee who has been reprimanded for staying on break too long may react with anger toward the manager and the organization. Such reactions may lead to behavior detrimental to the organization. Sabotage, for example, typically is a result of a punishment-oriented management system.

Punishment frequently leads only to short-term suppression of the undesirable behavior, rather than to its elimination. Thus suppression of an undesirable behavior over a long period of time usually requires continued and, perhaps, increasingly severe punishment. Another problem is that control of the undesirable behavior becomes contingent on the manager's presence. When the manager isn't around, the undesirable employee behavior is likely to recur.

In addition, the punished individual may try to avoid or escape the situation. From an organizational viewpoint, this reaction may be unacceptable if an employee avoids a particular, essential task. High absenteeism is a form of avoidance that is likely to occur when punishment is used frequently. Quitting is the employee's final form of escape, and organizations that depend on punishment are likely to have high rates of employee turnover. Some turnover is desirable, but excessive turnover is damaging to an organization. Recruitment and training are costly, and competent, high-performing employees are more likely to become frustrated and leave.

**Figure 4.4**                    **Potential Negative Effects of Punishment**

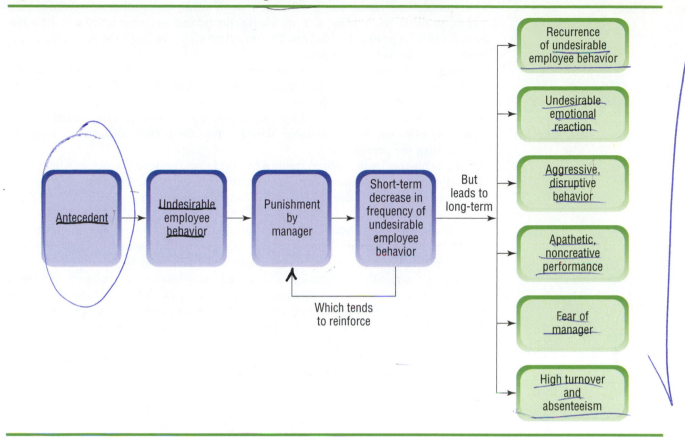

Punishment suppresses employee initiative and flexibility. Reacting to punishment, many an employee has said: "I'm going to do just what I'm told and nothing more." Such an attitude is undesirable because organizations depend on the personal initiative and creativity that individual employees bring to their jobs. Overusing punishment produces apathetic employees, who are not an asset to an organization. Sustained punishment can also lead to low self-esteem. Low self-esteem, in turn, undermines the employee's self-confidence, which is necessary for performing most jobs (see Chapter 2).

Punishment produces a conditioned fear of management. That is, employees develop a general fear of punishment-oriented managers. Such managers become an environmental cue, indicating to employees the probability that an aversive event will occur. If operations require frequent, normal, and positive interaction between employee and manager, the situation can quickly become intolerable. Responses to fear, such as "hiding" or reluctance to communicate with a manager, may well hinder employee performance.

A manager may rely on punishment because it often produces fast results in the short run. In essence, the manager is reinforced for using punishment because the approach produces an immediate change in an employee's behavior. That may cause the manager to ignore punishment's long-term detrimental effects, which can be cumulative. Although a few incidents of punishment may not produce negative effects, its long-term, sustained use most often results in negative outcomes for the organization.

**Effective Use of Punishment.**    Positive reinforcement is more effective than punishment over the long run. Effectively used, however, punishment does have an appropriate place in management. The most common form of punishment in organizations is the oral reprimand. It is intended to diminish or stop an undesirable employee behavior. An old rule of thumb is: Praise in public; punish in private. Private punishment establishes a different type of contingency of reinforcement than public punishment. In general, a private reprimand can be constructive and informative. A public reprimand is likely to have negative effects because the person has been embarrassed in front of her peers.

Oral reprimands should never be given about behavior in general and especially never about a so-called bad attitude. An effective reprimand pinpoints and specifically describes the undesirable behavior to be avoided in the future. It focuses on the target behavior and avoids threatening the employee's self-image. The effective reprimand punishes specific undesirable behavior, not the person. Behavior is easier to change than the person.

Punishment (by definition) trains a person in what not to do, not in what to do. Therefore a manager must specify an alternative behavior to the employee. When the employee performs the desired alternative behavior, the manager must then reinforce that behavior positively.

Finally, managers should strike an appropriate balance between the use of pleasant and unpleasant events. The absolute number of unpleasant events isn't important, but the ratio of pleasant to unpleasant events is. When a manager uses positive reinforcement frequently, an occasional deserved punishment can be quite effective. However, if a manager never uses positive reinforcement and relies entirely on punishment, the long-run negative effects are likely to counteract any short-term benefits. Positive management procedures should dominate in any well-run organization.

John Huberman, a Canadian psychologist, began promoting the idea of positive discipline in the mid 1960s, but it wasn't until the 1970s when Richard Grote introduced positive discipline at Frito-Lay that the idea took hold. Grote began searching for a better management technique after a customer discovered a vulgar message written by a disgruntled employee on a corn chip. Grote gave the employee a day off with pay and called it "positive discipline." **Positive discipline** emphasizes changing employee behaviors by reasoning rather than by imposing increasingly severe punishments.[14] Management's primary duty is to help employees understand that the needs of the organization require certain standards of behavior and performance. A manager's task is to coach employees, issuing oral and then written reminders only when they fail to maintain behavioral and performance standards. It is the employee's responsibility to exercise self-discipline in achieving those standards. More than 200 companies, including AT&T, General Electric's plant in Vermont, and Union Carbide, have used positive discipline to deal with problem employees and change undesirable employee behaviors. On the face of it, this approach sounds like a contradiction in terms. However, as illustrated in the following Managing Change Competency feature about General Electric's approach, positive discipline places the responsibility for behavioral change with the one person who can best change that behavior—the employee.

## USING CONTINGENCIES OF REINFORCEMENT

For a positive reinforcer to cause an employee to repeat a desired behavior, it must have value to that employee. If the employee is consistently on time, the manager or team leader positively reinforces this behavior by complimenting the employee. But, if the employee has been reprimanded in the past for coming to work late and then reports to work on time, the manager or team leader uses negative reinforcement and refrains from saying anything to embarrass the employee. The employee is expected to learn to avoid these unpleasant comments by coming to work on time.

If the employee continues to come to work late, the manager or team leader can use either omission or punishment to try to stop this undesirable behavior. The team leader who chooses omission doesn't praise the tardy employee but simply ignores the employee. The use of punishment may include reprimanding, fining, or suspending—and ultimately firing—the employee if the behavior persists.

## COMPETENCY: MANAGING CHANGE

### DISCIPLINE WITHOUT PUNISHMENT

General Electric's program at its Vermont plant works as follows. An employee who comes to work late, does a sloppy job, or mistreats another employee gets an oral reminder about the behavior rather than a written reprimand. If the undesirable behavior persists, the employee is issued a written reminder. If the behavior still persists, the employee is then suspended with pay for a day, called a "decision-making day." The purpose of the day is for the employee to decide whether to conform to the standards. The company pays the employee for this day to demonstrate its sincere effort to help him change. Paying the employee accomplishes two important things. First, doing so gives GE the opportunity to tell the employee that it is serious about the problem and wants the individual to use time to think through whether GE is the right place for them.  One boss said: "But if you decide to remain with us, another disciplinary problem will result in your termination." Second, paying the employee often eliminates the anger that commonly results from a person's ultimately being fired. The purpose of the day off with pay is to send a wake-up call.

This procedure accomplishes several things. First, it communicates to the employee that the organization is serious about the matter. The specific gap between the employee's performance and the performance GE expects is highlighted. It reminds the employee of his responsibility to meet GE's standards and gains the employee's agreement to solve this problem. Second, it sends a clear message to other employees who have been thinking about challenging the standards that the organization doesn't put up with unacceptable behavior—that GE's values and standards will not be compromised. Finally, the suspension provides tangible evidence that the employee's job is at risk.

General Electric's approach has been very successful. More than 85 percent of the employees going through the positive discipline program have changed their behaviors and stayed with the organization. Since the program started, reported written warnings and reminders dropped from 39 to 23 to 12 during a recent 2-year period. Employees that don't change their behaviors are fired.

*For more information on General Electric, visit the organization's home page at http://www.ge.com.*

The following guidelines are recommended for using contingencies of reinforcement in the work setting.

- Do not reward all employees in the same way.
- Carefully examine the consequences of nonactions as well as actions.
- Let employees know which behaviors will be reinforced.
- Let employees know what they are doing wrong.
- Don't punish employees in front of others.
- Make the response equal to the behavior by not cheating workers out of their just rewards.[15]

**Learning Objective:**

3. List the four schedules of reinforcement and explain when each is effective.

## SCHEDULES OF REINFORCEMENT

Managers using reinforcement to encourage the learning and performance of desired behaviors must choose a schedule for applying reinforcers. Although the schedule of reinforcement often depends on practical considerations (e.g., the nature of the person's job and the type of reinforcer being used, deliberately or not), reinforcement is always delivered according to some schedule.

## CONTINUOUS AND INTERMITTENT REINFORCEMENT

**Continuous reinforcement** means that the behavior is reinforced each time it occurs and is the simplest schedule of reinforcement. An example of continuous reinforcement is dropping coins in a soft-drink vending machine. The behavior of inserting coins is reinforced (on a continuous schedule) by the machine delivering a can of soda (most of the time!). Verbal recognition and material rewards generally are not delivered on a continuous schedule in organizations. In organizations such as Mary Kay Cosmetics, Tupperware, and Amway, salespeople are paid a commission for each sale, usually earning commissions of 25 to 50 percent of sales. Although the reinforcer (money) isn't paid immediately, as it is at Pioneer Telephone Cooperative, people track their sales immediately and quickly convert sales into amounts owed them by the organization. However, most managers who supervise employees other than salespeople seldom have the opportunity to deliver a reinforcer every time their employees demonstrate a desired behavior. Therefore behavior typically is reinforced intermittently.

**Intermittent reinforcement** refers to a reinforcer being delivered after some, but not every, occurrence of the desired behavior. Intermittent reinforcement can be subdivided into (1) interval and ratio schedules and (2) fixed and variable schedules. In an **interval schedule**, reinforcers are delivered after a certain amount of time has passed. In a **ratio schedule**, reinforcers are delivered after a certain number of behaviors have been performed. These two schedules can be further subdivided into fixed (not changing) or variable (constantly changing) schedules. Figure 4.5 shows these four primary types of intermittent schedules: fixed interval, variable interval, fixed ratio, and variable ratio.[16]

## FIXED INTERVAL SCHEDULE

In a **fixed interval schedule**, a constant amount of time must pass before a reinforcer is provided. The first desired behavior to occur after the interval has elapsed is reinforced. For example, in a fixed interval, 1-hour schedule, the first desired behavior that occurs after an hour has elapsed is reinforced.

Administering rewards according to this type of schedule tends to produce an uneven pattern of behavior. Prior to the reinforcement, the behavior is frequent and en-

**Figure 4.5**  **Four Types of Reinforcement Schedules**

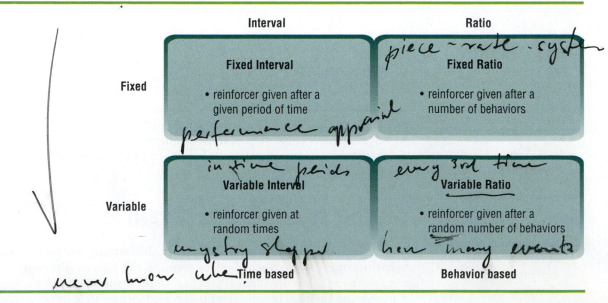

ergetic. Immediately following the reinforcement, the behavior becomes less frequent and energetic. Why? Because the individual rather quickly figures out that another reward won't immediately follow the last one—a certain amount of time must pass before it is given again. A common example of administering rewards on a fixed interval schedule is the payment of employees weekly, biweekly, or monthly. That is, monetary reinforcement comes regularly at the end of a specific period of time. Such time intervals, unfortunately, are generally too long to be an effective form of reinforcement for newly acquired work-related behavior.

## VARIABLE INTERVAL SCHEDULE

A **variable interval schedule** represents changes in the amount of time between reinforcers. Jack Gustin, COO for University Hospitals in Cleveland, Ohio, uses a variable interval schedule to observe and reinforce the behaviors of housekeeping personnel. A person would receive $100 for a perfect attendance and a score above 92 percent on 23 performance indicators (e.g., floor swept, trash baskets emptied, room dusted, etc.) To observe their behavior, Gustin announced to all housekeeping employees that, during the month, he would make seven inspections at random times. During the first week, he observed and recorded the performance of employees on Tuesday between 3:00 and 4:00 P.M. and Wednesday from 6:00 to 7:30 A.M. The following week, he made no observations. During the third week, he observed employees on Monday between 10:00 and 11:00 A.M. and Friday from 12:00 to 1:45 P.M. During the fourth week, he observed employees on Monday between 8:00 and 9:00 P.M. and from 11:00 P.M. to 12:00 A.M. and on Thursday from 2:00 to 3:30 P.M. If he didn't change his schedule, the employees would anticipate his tours and adjust their behaviors to get a reward.

## FIXED RATIO SCHEDULE

In a **fixed ratio schedule**, the desired behavior must occur a specified number of times before it is reinforced. Administering rewards under a fixed ratio schedule tends to produce a high response rate when the time for reinforcement is close, followed by periods of steady behavior. The employee soon determines that reinforcement is based on the number of responses and performs the responses as quickly as possible in order to receive the reward. The individual piece-rate system used in many manufacturing plants is an example of such a schedule. Great North American, Answer First, and other telemarketers use this schedule of reinforcement to pay their salespeople.

## VARIABLE RATIO SCHEDULE

In a **variable ratio schedule**, a certain number of desired behaviors must occur before the reinforcer is delivered, but the number of behaviors varies around some average. Managers frequently use a variable ratio schedule with praise and recognition. For example, team leaders at Sprint vary the frequency of reinforcement when they give employees verbal approval for desired behaviors. Gambling casinos, such as Bally's and Harrah's, among others, and state lotteries use this schedule of reinforcement to lure patrons to shoot craps, play poker, feed slot machines, and buy lottery tickets. Patrons win, but not on any regular basis. The reason why variable ratio schedules are effective is that they create uncertainty about when the consequence will occur. Using this schedule makes sense for giving praise or auditing the behavior of people. People know that a consequence will be delivered, but not when. To avoid consequences of either punishment or omission, the person keeps demonstrating the desired behaviors.

## COMPARISON OF INTERMITTENT REINFORCEMENT SCHEDULES

Table 4.3 summarizes the four types of intermittent reinforcement schedules. The ratio schedules—fixed or variable—usually lead to better performance than do interval schedules. The reason is that ratio schedules are more closely related to the occurrence of desired behaviors than are interval schedules, which are based on the passage of time. The particular schedule of reinforcement is not as critical as the fact that reinforcement is based on the performance of desired behaviors.[17]

**Table 4.3**

### Comparison of Reinforcement Schedules

| SCHEDULE | INFLUENCE ON PERFORMANCE | EXAMPLE |
|---|---|---|
| Fixed interval | Leads to average performance | Monthly paycheck |
| Fixed ratio | Leads quickly to high and stable performance | Piece rate pay |
| Variable interval | Leads to moderately high and stable performance | Occasional praise by team members |
| Variable ratio | Leads to very high performance | Random quality checks with praise for zero defects |

## SOCIAL LEARNING THEORY

Although operant conditioning accurately describes some of the major factors that influence learning, certain aspects are not covered by this theory. For example, a person's feelings and thoughts aren't considered. Albert Bandura and others have extended and expanded Skinner's work by demonstrating that people can learn new behavior by watching others in a social situation and then imitating their behavior.[18] According to the **social learning theory**, learning is viewed as knowledge acquisition through the mental processing of information. In other words, the social part acknowledges that individuals learn by being part of a society and the learning part recognizes that individuals use thought processes to make decisions. People actively process information when they learn. By watching others perform a task, people develop mental pictures of how to perform the task. Bandura suggested that observers often learn faster than those who do not observe the behaviors of others because they don't need to unlearn behaviors and can avoid needless and costly errors.

Social learning theory has five dimensions—symbolizing, forethought, vicarious learning, self-control, and self-efficacy—as shown in Figure 4.6. These five dimensions can help you understand why different employees may behave differently when facing the same situation.

### SYMBOLIZING

Individuals have an ability to use *symbols* that enable them to react to their environment. By using symbols, people process visual experiences and use the memories of them to guide their behavior. People imitate parents, friends, teachers, heroes, and others because they can identify with them. The symbolic process yields guidelines for behavior. If a golfer observes the swings of Tiger Woods (at http://www.tigerwoods.com) or Anika Sorenstam (at members.aol.com/ripey/annika/anni.htm) on their Web pages, this observation creates an image (symbol) in that person's mind of what a good golf swing looks like. Such images or symbols help the per-

**Figure 4.6**                    **Five Dimensions of Social Cognitive Theory**

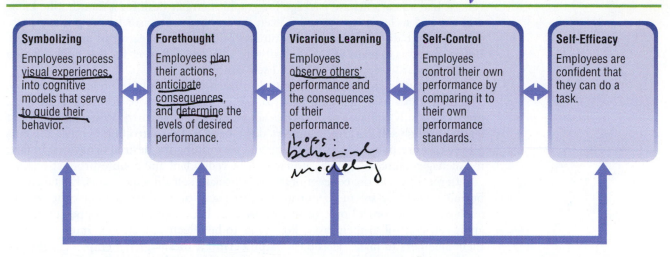

Source: Adapted from Stajkovic, A. D., and Luthans, F. Social cognitive theory and self-efficacy. *Organizational Dynamics*, Spring 1998, 65. Reprinted with permission.

son swing a golf club the next time she plays golf. In a social situation, when those at the head of the table at a formal dinner begin to eat, their actions let the other diners know that starting to eat now is appropriate.

## FORETHOUGHT

People use *forethought* to anticipate, plan, and guide their behaviors and actions. For example, as the golfer who has watched the video of Woods or Sorenstam approaches a shot from a sand trap, she recalls the clips in the video where the pro was getting out of a trap. As a result, she adjusts her hands, feet, and body posture to the correct playing position to hit the shot. She anticipates where the ball will land and mentally plans her next shot.

## VICARIOUS LEARNING

Almost all forms of learning can occur *vicariously* by observing the behavior of others and the consequences of that behavior. Employees' capacity to learn by observation enables them to obtain accurate information without having to perform these behaviors through trial and error. All self-help videos rely on vicarious learning. For **vicarious learning** to occur, several conditions must be met.

- The learner must observe the other person—the model—when the behavior is being performed.
- The learner must accurately perceive the model's behavior.
- The learner must remember the behavior.
- The learner must have the skills and abilities necessary to perform the behavior.
- The learner must observe that the model receives rewards for the behavior.[19]

## SELF-CONTROL

Not everyone is cut out to work as a flight attendant, salesperson, or construction worker or to become a manager. Many people never apply for particular jobs because what they see isn't consistent with their own ideas of the type of job they want. **Self-control** leads to the learning of a new behavior even though there is no external pressure to do so. Billie Boyd, an administrative assistant at Southern Methodist University, had a new software package for graphics on her desk for a month. She knew that she had to learn how to use it even though her supervisor hadn't put any pressure on her to do so. She worked Saturdays on her own to learn this new technique. Boyd's goal was to learn to use the software to produce figures for this book—which she achieved. Her approach exhibited self-control.

Most people engage in self-control to learn behaviors both on and off the job. Mundane tasks (e.g., learning how to use e-mail) and more complex tasks (e.g., preparing a subordinate's performance appraisal) can be learned. When an employee learns through self-control, managers don't need to be controlling because the employee takes responsibility for learning and performing the desired behaviors. In fact, if a manager exercises control, it may well be redundant and counterproductive.

In recent years, the concept of teams, especially self-directed teams, has taken the business world by storm. Unfortunately, in many cases, management continues to exert too much control over teams, whose members then have few opportunities to apply self-control to their tasks. For teams to be effective, managers must empower their members to make decisions. **Empowerment** means giving employees the authority, skills, and self-control to perform their tasks.[20] The following Managing Teams Competency feature highlights how Steelcase, Incorporated, a Minnesota manufacturer of business furniture, empowers teams to improve productivity.

## Self-Efficacy

**Self-efficacy** refers to the individual's estimate of his or her own ability to perform a specific task in a particular situation.[21] The greater the employee's perceived ability to perform the task, the higher will be the employee's self-efficacy. Employees with high self-efficacy believe that (1) they have the ability needed, (2) they are capable of the effort required, and (3) no outside events will keep them from performing at a

## COMPETENCY:    MANAGING TEAMS

### STEELCASE, INCORPORATED

For 18 years, Jerry Hammond had been a spot welder, making parts of business furniture without even knowing the people in nearby departments by name. Now, he knows his fellow workers because they are a team responsible for deciding how to manufacture a part and for running as many as six different pieces of equipment. Team members are cross-trained, as time permits, during regular working hours.

When Steelcase's management decided to create teams and empower them, it realized that barriers between workers and managers would have to be removed. As a result, only customers now have reserved parking spaces, a common cafeteria is provided, and only a few walls remain in the plant. Whenever new equipment is needed, a team of employees who will be responsible for operating it makes the decision about what to buy and how it should be positioned on the shop floor. Forty-one self-directed production teams and four support teams tackle day-to-day problems, such as safety, scrap and waste, paint quality, shipping, and the like. As a result, Steelcase has only 1 supervisor for every 33 workers, compared to its competitors' ratio of 1 to 12. Steelcase's workers are 45 percent more productive than its competitors', turning a customer's order into a finished product in 3 days instead of the 3 weeks formerly needed and slashing costs. Teams of employees working with suppliers also have been able to cut raw material inventory by half.

*For more information on Steelcase, visit the organization's home page at http://www.steelcase.com.*

high level. If employees have low self-efficacy, they believe that no matter how hard they try, something will happen to prevent them from reaching the desired level of performance. Self-efficacy influences people's choices of tasks and how long they will spend trying to reach their goals.[22] For example, a novice golfer who has taken only a few lessons might shoot a good round. Under such circumstances, the golfer might attribute the score to "beginner's luck" and not to ability. But, after many lessons and hours of practice, a person with low self-efficacy who still can't break 100 may decide that the demands of the game are too great to justify spending any more time on it. However, a high self-efficacy individual will try even harder to improve her game. This effort might include taking more lessons, watching videotapes of the individual's own swing, and practicing even harder and longer.

Self-efficacy has an impact on learning in three ways.

1. *It influences the activities and goals that individuals choose for themselves.* In a sales contest at Pioneer Telephone Cooperative, employees with low self-efficacy didn't set challenging, or "stretch" goals. These people weren't lazy; they simply thought that they would fail to achieve a lofty goal. The high self-efficacy employees thought that they were capable of achieving high-performance goals—and did so.
2. *It influences the effort that individuals exert on the job.* Individuals with high self-efficacy work hard to learn new tasks and are confident that their efforts will be rewarded. Low self-efficacy individuals lack confidence in their ability to succeed and see their extra effort as futile because they are likely to fail anyway.
3. *It affects the persistence with which a person stays with a complex task.* Because high self-efficacy people are confident that they will perform well, they are likely to persist in spite of obstacles or in the face of temporary setbacks. At IBM, low-performing employees were more likely than high-performing employees to dwell on obstacles hindering their ability to do assigned tasks. When people believe that they aren't capable of doing the required work, their motivation to do a task will be low.

## ORGANIZATIONAL USES

Managers (and fellow team members) can use social learning theory to help employees learn to believe in themselves. Past experience is the most powerful influence on behavior. At work, the challenge is to create situations in which the employee may respond successfully to the task(s) required. A manager's expectations for a subordinate's performance—as well as the expectations of peers—also can affect a person's self-efficacy. If a manager holds high expectations for an employee and provides proper training and suggestions, the person's self-efficacy is likely to increase. Small successes boost self-efficacy and lead to more substantial accomplishments later. If a manager holds low expectations for an employee and gives little constructive advice, the employee is likely to form an impression that he can't achieve the goal and, as a result, perform poorly.

Guidelines for using social learning theory to improve behavior in organizations are just starting to emerge. They include the following.

- Identify the behaviors that will lead to improved performance.
- Select the appropriate model for employees to observe.
- Be sure that employees are capable of meeting the technical skills required by the new behaviors.
- Structure a positive learning situation to increase the likelihood that employees will learn the new behaviors and act accordingly.
- Provide positive consequences (praise, raises, or bonuses) to employees who perform as desired.
- Develop organizational practices that maintain the newly learned behaviors.

The effective use of self-control in learning requires that several conditions be met. First, the person must engage in behaviors that he wouldn't normally want to perform. This distinguishes performing activities that the person enjoys from those involving self-control. At Pioneer, not all employees wanted to be involved with selling services for the phone company. They had to take the initiative to learn about the new products, pass a test, establish good leads, and the like. Of the 75 percent of the phone company's employees involved in these activities, many had to exhibit self-control to do so. Second, the person must be able to use self-reinforcers, which are rewards that individuals give themselves. Some self-reinforcers include buying oneself a present, going out to a "great" restaurant, playing a round of golf at a nice course, and the like. Self-reinforcers come simply from a feeling of accomplishment or achievement. Third, the person must set goals that determine when self-reinforcers are to be applied. A person high in self-control doesn't randomly reward himself, but sets goals that determine when to self-reinforce. In doing so, the person relies on his own past performance, the performance of others on similar kinds of tasks, or some standard set by others. For example, one of the authors of this book is an accomplished golfer with a single-digit handicap. After playing a round in the 70s, he frequently buys himself a golf shirt as a self-reinforcer for a good round. Finally, the person must administer the self-reinforcer when the goal is achieved. The author buys himself a golf shirt only when he shoots a round in the 70s.

Employees who manage their own behavior through self-control are often referred to as *self-managing*. At times, even these workers need some coaching and guidance to become self-managing. Managers can provide the training and support that workers need to become truly self-managing. Many organizations, such as Texas Instruments, Exxon Mobil, and IBM, recognize this need and have programs specifically designed to teach self-management. As more and more people work from their homes instead of offices, it is important that they learn how to become self-managers.[23]

## CHAPTER SUMMARY

**1.** Explain the differences between classical and operant conditioning.

Classical conditioning began with Pavlov's work. He started a metronome (conditioned stimulus) at the same time food was placed in the dog's mouth (unconditioned stimulus). Quickly the sound of the metronome alone evoked salivation. Operant conditioning focuses on the effects of reinforcement on desirable and undesirable behaviors. Changes in behavior result from the consequences of previous behavior. People tend to repeat a behavior that leads to a pleasant result and not to repeat a behavior that leads to an unpleasant result. In short, when a behavior is reinforced, it is repeated; when it is punished or not reinforced, it is not repeated.

**2.** Describe the contingencies of reinforcement.

There are two types of reinforcement: (1) positive reinforcement, which increases a desirable behavior because the person is provided with a pleasurable outcome after the behavior has occurred; and (2) negative reinforcement, which also maintains the desirable behavior by presenting an unpleasant event before the behavior occurs and stopping the event when the behavior occurs. Both positive and negative reinforcement increase the frequency of a desirable behavior. Conversely, omission and punishment reduce the frequency of an undesirable behavior. Omission involves stopping everything that reinforces the behavior. A punisher is an unpleasant event that follows the behavior and reduces the probability that the behavior will be repeated.

**3.** List the four schedules of reinforcement and explain when each is effective.

There are four schedules of reinforcement. In the fixed interval schedule, the reward is given on a fixed time basis (e.g., a weekly or monthly paycheck). It is effective for maintaining a level of behavior. In the variable interval schedule, the reward is given around some average time during a specific period of time (e.g., the plant manager walking through the plant an average of five times every week). This schedule of reinforcement can maintain a high level of performance because employees don't know when the reinforcer will be delivered. The fixed ratio schedule ties rewards to certain outputs (e.g., a piece-rate system). This schedule maintains a steady level of behavior once the person has earned the reinforcer. In the variable ratio schedule, the reward is given around some mean, but the number of behaviors varies (e.g., a payoff from a slot machine). This schedule is the most powerful because both the number of desired behaviors and their frequency change.

**4.** Describe social learning theory.

Social learning theory focuses on people learning new behaviors by observing others and then modeling their own behaviors on those observed. The five factors emphasized in social learning theory are symbolizing, forethought, vicarious learning, self-control, and self-efficacy.

## KEY TERMS AND CONCEPTS

Antecedent

Aversive events

Classical conditioning

Consequence

Contingency of reinforcement

Continuous reinforcement

Empowerment

Escape learning

Fixed interval schedule

Fixed ratio schedule

Intermittent reinforcement

Interval schedule

Kaizen

Learning

Negative reinforcement

Omission

Operant conditioning

Positive discipline

Positive events

Positive reinforcement

Primary reinforcer

Principle of contingent reinforcement

Principle of immediate reinforcement

Principle of reinforcement deprivation

Principle of reinforcement size

Punishment

Ratio schedule

Reinforcement

Reward

Secondary reinforcer

Self-control

Self-efficacy

Social learning theory

Variable interval schedule

Variable ratio schedule

Vicarious learning

## DISCUSSION QUESTIONS

1. What principles of reinforcement did Pioneer Telephone Cooperative use?
2. Describe the basic differences between classical conditioning and operant conditioning. Which type is most important for managers? Why?
3. Visit either a local health club or diet center and schedule an interview with the manager. What types of rewards does it give its members who achieve targeted goals? Does it use punishment?
4. Steven Kerr wrote an article entitled "On the Folly of Rewarding A While Hoping for B." The essence of the article is that organizations often unintentionally reward behaviors that they don't want to occur. Based on this premise, what behavior(s) does Rockford Memorial Hospital reward that may have a negative impact on its patients?
5. How can a team leader use punishment effectively?
6. What schedule(s) of reinforcement can a manager use to stop employees from fighting with each other?
7. How do producers of self-help videos use social learning theory to change a person's behavior?
8. How can a manager or a team raise an employee's level of self-efficacy?
9. When are employees likely to engage in self-control?
10. How can managers use social learning theory to achieve desired employee behaviors?

# DEVELOPING COMPETENCIES

## Competency: Managing Self

### What Is Your Self-Efficacy?

The following questionnaire gives you a chance to gain insights into your self-efficacy in terms of achieving academic excellence. Please answer the following seven questions in the spaces provided, using the following five-point scale. An interpretation of your score follows.

5 = Strongly agree
4 = Agree
3 = Moderate
2 = Disagree
1 = Strongly disagree

1. I am a good student.                                      5  4  3  2  1
2. It is difficult to maintain a study
   schedule.                                                 5  4  3  2  1
3. I know the right things to do to
   improve my academic performance.                          5  4  3  2  1
4. I find it difficult to convince my
   friends who have different viewpoints
   on studying than mine.                                    5  4  3  2  1
5. My temperament is not well suited
   to studying.                                              5  4  3  2  1
6. I am good at finding out what
   teachers want.                                            5  4  3  2  1
7. It is easy for me to get others to see
   my point of view.                                         5  4  3  2  1

Add your scores to questions 1, 3, 6, and 7. Enter that score here _____. For questions, 2, 4, and 5, reverse the scoring key. That is, if you answered question 2 as strongly agree, give yourself 1 point, agree is worth 2 points, and so on. Enter your score here for questions 2, 4, and 5 _____. Enter your combined score here _____. This is your *self-efficacy* score for academic achievement. If you scored between 28 and 35, you believe that you can achieve academic excellence. Scores lower than 18 indicate that you believe no matter how hard you try to achieve academic excellence, something may prevent you from reaching your desired level of performance. Scores between 19 and 27 indicate a moderate degree of self-efficacy. Your self-efficacy may vary with the course you are taking. In courses in your major, you may have greater self-efficacy than in those outside of your major.[24]

## Competency: Managing Ethics

### Prescription Drugs

A joint venture of Abbott Laboratories and Takeda Chemical Industries (TAP) has agreed to pay $875 million to settle criminal and civil charges that it had illegally manipulated the Medicare and Medicaid Programs. Prosecutors contend that TAP sales representatives gave doctors free samples of Lupron, a drug used to treat prostate cancer and infertility and then helped doctors get government reimbursement at hundreds of dollars for each dose. Medicare covers only a limited number of drugs, most of which must be administered directly by a physician. Drug companies routinely supply doctors with drugs to administer to Medicare patients, and Medicare then repays the doctors based on a price provided by the companies, called the "average wholesale price."

TAP admitted that it provided free samples of Lupron to a number of physicians, knowing that the doctors would seek reimbursement from the federal government. The doctors were encouraged to give these drugs rather than lower priced drugs or those of competitors to Medicare and Medicaid patients and bill the government for them. If the doctors purchased the drug, TAP would inflate the price so that the doctors could be reimbursed more than TAP actually charged them for the drug. The doctors would keep the profits in ei-

ther case. In addition, the government pays the doctors only 80 percent of the price of the drug, and patients pay the rest. Thus TAP and certain doctors apparently had also defrauded hundreds of elderly Medicare patients, mostly men suffering from prostrate cancer, by inflating Lupron's average wholesale price. At least one lawsuit is pending to recover excessive payments by patients.

The government also charged five doctors with health-care fraud in the case. The government said that those doctors had conspired with the company to receive excessive Medicare reimbursements. The investigation began when Douglas Durand, a former vice president for sales at TAP, and Dr. Joseph Gerstein, a urologist employed by a health maintenance organization (HMO) told the government about what they believed to be illegal practices. Dr. Gerstein met with TAP sales representatives who offered him $65,000 in kickbacks that he could use for any purpose (including trips to resorts, purchase of medical equipment, and "educational grants") if he would reverse his decision to have his HMO use only Zoladex, a less expensive drug than Lupron.

As part of the settlement, TAP also agreed to train its employees in the proper methods of promoting and marketing drugs covered by all federal health programs. The agreement also requires TAP to report its true average sales price for Lupron and all other drugs. TAP would be forced to pay a fine of $2,500 for each day it fails to comply with the agreement, which is effective for 7 years.[25]

## Questions

1. Why would salespeople at TAP engage in such behaviors? What behaviors are being reinforced?
2. What contingency of reinforcement is being used by the government? Will it be effective in controlling abuses?

# CHAPTER

# Achieving Motivation in the Workplace

## LEARNING OBJECTIVES

When you have finished studying the chapter, you should be able to:

1. Define motivation and describe the motivational process.
2. Describe two basic human needs approaches to motivation.
3. Explain how the design of jobs affects motivation.
4. Describe the expectancy model of motivation.
5. Explain how feelings of equity affect motivation.

5

## HOW STARBUCKS MOTIVATES EMPLOYEES

The Starbucks Support Center is located at Starbucks Coffee Company's headquarters in Seattle. As one of *Fortune* magazine's "100 Best Companies to Work for in America," not to mention one of the world's fastest growing chain of coffee houses, Starbucks has been treating its employees well since it started in 1971. Woven into the company's mission statement is the objective to "Provide a great work environment and treat each other with respect and dignity." It takes more than company declarations to motivate and inspire people. So how does this company on an aggressive growth track motivate more than 47,000 people and inspire balance and a team spirit?

The answer is what Starbucks refers to as "a special blend of employee benefits" and a work/life program that focuses on the physical, mental, emotional, and creative aspects of each person. Starbucks developed an innovative work/life program to create a committed coffee culture—and a long-term partnership. In fact employees at Starbucks are called *partners*.

Joan Moffat, the Starbucks manager of partner relations and work/life, is responsible for the company's work/life program. It includes on-site fitness services, referral and educational support to help employees meet child-care and elder-care needs, an Info-line for convenient information, and the Partner Connection—a program that links employees with shared interests and hobbies. Starbucks has comparatively low health-care costs, low absenteeism, and one of the strongest retention rates in the industry. "Our turnover rate is 60 percent, which is excellent as compared to the restaurant and retail industry," says Moffat. Moreover, employees reap the benefits of the company's ongoing success.

Starbucks is committed to providing an atmosphere that fosters respect and values the contributions that people make each day, regardless of who or where they are within the company. All partners who work a minimum 20 hours a week receive full medical and dental coverage, vacation days, and stock options as part of the Starbucks Bean Stock program. Eligible partners can choose health cov-

erage from two managed care plans or a catastrophic plan. They also can select one of two dental plans or a vision plan. Because its workforce is young and healthy, Starbucks has low health-benefit costs. According to Annette King, the human resources (HR) benefits manager, the company's health-care costs are approximately 20 percent lower than the national average.

The company also provides disability and life insurance, a discounted stock purchase plan, and a retirement savings plan with company matching contributions. These benefits provide a powerful incentive for partners, particularly those working part time, to stay with the company, thus reducing Starbucks' recruiting and training costs. "We have historically had low turnover, most of which can be attributed to the culture and a sense of community," says Moffat.

Several years ago, the HR staff began examining how the company could become more attuned to employees' wants and needs. For instance, some employees who started with the company when they were in college are now buying homes and dealing with the realities of child care and elder care. Starbucks responded by providing flexible work schedules as part of its work/life program. "Our environment lends itself to meet multiple life demands. By virtue of our strong sales and accelerated growth, flex schedules have not hurt productivity in the least," says Moffat. "Flexibility is particularly inherent in our stores because of our extended hours of operation and the diversity of our workforce—from students to parents—who need to work alternative hours."

Recent studies have shown that 60 percent of U.S. workers have child- or elder-care responsibilities. Starbucks recognized—as many other companies have—that partners less encumbered by personal stress and obligations are more innovative and productive. Starbucks implemented several

*For more information on Starbucks, visit the organization's home page at http://www.starbucks.com.*

programs that specifically address the life stages and personal needs of its workforce. To help deal with the fast-paced and demanding environment at Starbucks, it also provides referral services for partners and eligible dependents enrolled in the medical plan. It connects them with information that helps make extraordinary life demands more manageable. Moffat recently put the program to use when she needed elder-care advice for her grandmother. In another case, a partner needed emergency child care for his ill son. Starbuck's Working Solutions program made prompt arrangements for a certified in-home caretaker, no work was missed, and Starbucks covered half the cost.[1]

Howard Schultz, chairman and CEO of Starbucks, says that his greatest challenge is to attract, develop, and manage a worldwide workforce. He believes that Starbucks must provide motivational systems that will cut costs while maintaining high quality. Permitting employees to participate in the incentive programs described in the Preview Case, among others, has led to greater productivity. Since going public in 1992, the company's stock has risen by more than 800 percent; its retail sales exceeded $2.6 billion in 2002. Starbucks can be found in restaurants, hotels, offices, on airline flights, and in more than 3,300 stores in Australia, Germany, Japan, China, the United States, and the United Kingdom.[2]

**Learning Objective:**

1. Define motivation and describe the motivational process.

## THE BASIC MOTIVATIONAL PROCESS

The question of exactly what it takes to motivate people to work has received a great deal of attention. In addressing this question, we focus on four different approaches: (1) meeting basic human needs, (2) designing jobs that motivate people, (3) enhancing the belief that desired rewards can be achieved, and (4) treating people equitably. The interrelated nature of these approaches is illustrated in Figure 5.1. Before turning our attention to these approaches, we need to define motivation.

**Figure 5.1**               **Basics of Workplace Motivation**

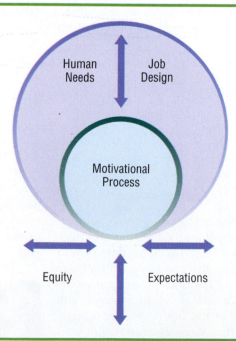

**Motivation** represents the forces acting on or within a person that cause the person to behave in a specific, goal-directed manner.[3] Because motives of employees affect their productivity, one of management's jobs is to channel employee motivation effectively toward achieving organizational goals. However, motivation isn't the same as performance. Even the most highly motivated employees may not be successful in their jobs, especially if they don't have the competencies needed to perform the jobs or work under unfavorable job conditions. Although job performance involves more than motivation, motivation is an important factor in achieving high performance.[4]

Experts might not agree about everything that motivates employees—and the effects of working conditions on their careers—but they do agree that an organization must:

- attract people to the organization and encourage them to remain with it,
- allow people to perform the tasks for which they were hired, and
- stimulate people to go beyond routine performance and become creative and innovative in their work.

Thus, for an organization to be effective, it must tackle the motivational challenges involved in arousing people's desires to be productive members of the organization.

## CORE PHASES OF THE PROCESS

A key motivational principle states that performance is a function of a person's level of ability and motivation. This principle is often expressed by the formula

$$Performance = f(ability \times motivation)$$

According to this principle, no task can be performed successfully unless the person who is to carry it out has the ability to do so. **Ability** is the person's talent for performing goal-related tasks. However, regardless of a person's competence, ability alone isn't enough to ensure performance at a high level. The person must also want to achieve a high level of performance. Thus discussions of motivation generally are concerned with (1) what drives behavior, (2) what direction behavior takes, and (3) how to maintain that behavior.

The motivational process begins with identifying a person's needs, shown as phase 1 in Figure 5.2. **Needs** are deficiencies that a person experiences at a particular time (phase 1). These deficiencies may be psychological (e.g., the need for recognition), physiological (e.g., the need for water, air, or food), or social (e.g., the need for friendship). Needs often act as energizers. That is, needs create tensions within the individual, who finds them uncomfortable and therefore is likely to make an effort (phase 2) to reduce or eliminate them.

Motivation is goal directed (phase 3). A **goal** is a specific result that an individual wants to achieve. An employee's goals often are driving forces, and accomplishing those goals can significantly reduce needs. For example, some employees have strong drives for advancement and expectations that working long hours on highly visible projects will lead to promotions, raises, and greater influence. Such needs and expectations often create uncomfortable tension within such individuals. Believing that certain specific behaviors can overcome this tension, these employees act to reduce it. Employees striving to advance may seek to work on major problems facing the organization in order to gain visibility and influence with senior managers (phase 4). Promotions and raises are two of the ways that organizations attempt to maintain desirable behaviors. They are signals (feedback) to employees that their needs for advancement and recognition and their behaviors are appropriate (phase 5). Once the employees have received either rewards or punishments, they reassess their needs (phase 6).

**Figure 5.2**          **Core Phases of the Motivational Process**

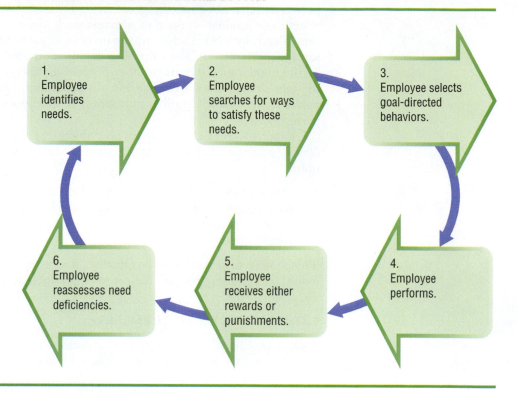

## MOTIVATIONAL CHALLENGES

In concept the basic motivational process just described is simple and straightforward. In the real world, of course, the process isn't so clear-cut. The first challenge is that motives can only be inferred; they cannot be seen. Gert Christen, head of project and systems management at Nokia, observed two employees in his department who were debugging software programs that estimate service requirements for Nokia's mobile phones. He knows that both employees are responsible for the same type of work, have received similar training, have similar competencies, and have been with the organization for about 5 years. One employee is able to spot problems more easily and quickly than the other, so the difference in their output strongly suggests that they have different levels of motivation. Christen recognized that he would have to investigate further to determine what motivates each person.

A second challenge centers on the dynamic nature of needs. As we pointed out in the Preview Case, Starbucks has developed numerous programs in its attempt to meet employee needs. Doing so is always difficult because, at any one time, everyone has various needs, desires, and expectations. Moreover, these factors change over time and may also conflict with each other. Employees who put in many extra hours at work to fulfill their needs for accomplishment may find that these extra work hours conflict directly with needs for affiliation and their desires to be with their families.

A third challenge involves the considerable differences in people's motivations and in the energy with which people respond to them. Just as different organizations produce a variety of products and offer a variety of services, different people have a variety of motivations. Paul Ginn, a sales manager for Telstra in Australia, took a 1-year job assignment in his firm's Hong Kong office. Ginn joined a group of Australian managers there so that he could satisfy his needs to belong to such a group and to learn quickly about Chinese business customs. He learned that Chinese managers are taught to be indirect in conversation, carefully editing remarks to reflect both good manners and the status of their listeners. He also discovered that many Chinese managers think that Australians are impatient, noisy, disruptive, and confrontational, often saying things that are better left unsaid.[5]

All of these challenges are things that managers can do something about. They can determine what motivates employees and use this knowledge to channel employees' energies toward the achievement of the organization's goals. With this opportunity in mind, we devote the rest of the chapter to various approaches to motivation that managers can apply.

**Learning Objective:**

2. Describe two basic human needs approaches to motivation.

# MOTIVATING EMPLOYEES THROUGH MEETING HUMAN NEEDS

## NEEDS HIERARCHY MODEL

The most widely recognized model of motivation is the **needs hierarchy model**. Abraham H. Maslow suggested that people have a complex set of exceptionally strong needs, which can be arranged in a hierarchy.[6] Underlying this hierarchy are the following basic assumptions.

- Once a need has been satisfied, its motivational role declines in importance. However, as one need is satisfied, another need gradually emerges to take its place, so people are always striving to satisfy some need.
- The needs network for most people is very complex, with several needs affecting behavior at any one time. Clearly, when someone faces an emergency, such as desperate thirst, that need dominates until it is gratified.
- Lower level needs must be satisfied, in general, before higher level needs are activated sufficiently to drive behavior.
- There are more ways of satisfying higher level than lower level needs.

This model states that a person has five types of needs: physiological, security, affiliation, esteem, and self-actualization. Figure 5.3 shows these five needs categories, arranged in Maslow's hierarchy.

**Figure 5.3**                    **Maslow's Needs Hierarchy**

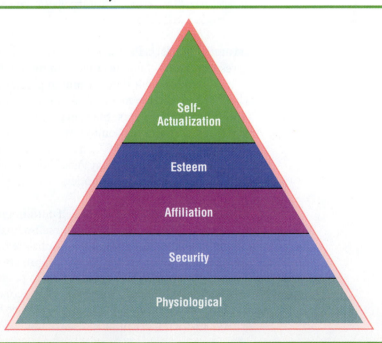

**Physiological Needs.**    The needs for food, water, air, and shelter are all **physiological needs** and are the lowest level in Maslow's hierarchy. People concentrate on satisfying these needs before turning to higher order needs. Managers should understand that, to the extent employees are motivated by physiological needs, their concerns do not center on the work they are doing. They will accept any job that meets those needs. Managers who focus on physiological needs in trying to motivate subordinates assume that people work primarily for money. Hershey Foods, for example, offers insurance rebates to employees who live healthy lifestyles (e.g., physically fit nonsmokers) and raise premiums for those at greater risk. In this way, they offer incentives to encourage wellness activities.

**Security Needs.**    The needs for safety, stability, and absence of pain, threat, or illness are all **security needs**. Like physiological needs, unsatisfied security needs cause people to be preoccupied with satisfying them. People who are motivated primarily by security needs value their jobs mainly as defenses against the loss of basic needs satisfaction. Managers who feel that security needs are important focus on protecting workers from hazards in their environment by providing them with hard hats, goggles, and ergonomic keyboards (which prevent carpal tunnel syndrome). Psychological safety is also important. By offering health, life, and disability insurance, organizations promote their employees' sense of security and well-being.

**Affiliation Needs.**    The needs for friendship, love, and a feeling of belonging are all **affiliation needs**. When physiological and security needs have been satisfied, affiliation needs emerge. Managers should realize that, when affiliation needs are the primary source of motivation, people value their work as an opportunity for finding and establishing warm and friendly interpersonal relationships. To help satisfy their affiliation needs while stationed in Singapore for Celanese Chemical, John Lichtenthal and his wife, Mica, joined a group of U.S. managers and their spouses. This group attended plays, toured other countries, celebrated U.S. holidays, enjoyed each others' friendship, and helped each other cope with the trials and enjoy the adventures of living in a foreign country. Managers and team leaders who believe that employees are striving primarily to satisfy these needs are likely to act supportively. They emphasize employee acceptance by coworkers, extracurricular activities (e.g., organized sports programs, cultural events, and company celebrations), and team-based norms.

**Esteem Needs.**    Personal feelings of achievement and self-worth and recognition or respect from others meet **esteem needs**. People with esteem needs want others to accept them for what they are and to perceive them as competent and able. Managers who focus on esteem needs try to motivate employees with public rewards and recognition for achievements. Such managers may use lapel pins, articles in the company paper, achievement lists on the bulletin board, and the like to foster employees' pride in their work. Mary Kay Cosmetics rewards top performers with a pink Cadillac. According to the late Mary Kay Ash, the founder of her company, people want recognition and praise more than money.

**Self-Actualization Needs.**    Self-fulfillment comes from meeting **self-actualization needs**. People who strive for self-actualization seek to increase their problem-solving abilities. Managers who emphasize self-actualization may involve employees in designing jobs, make special assignments that capitalize on employees' unique skills, or give employee teams leeway in planning and implementing their work. The self-employed often have strong self-actualization needs. When Mary Kay Ash founded her firm in 1963, she acted on her belief that, when a woman puts her priorities in order, she can indeed have it all.

**Using Maslow's Need Hierarchy.**   Maslow's needs hierarchy model also suggests the types of behaviors that will help fulfill various needs. The three lowest categories of needs—physiological, safety, and social—are also known as **deficiency needs**. According to Maslow, unless these needs are satisfied, an individual will fail to develop into a healthy person, both physically and psychologically. In contrast, esteem and self-actualization needs are known as **growth needs**. Satisfaction of these needs helps a person grow and develop as a human being.

This model provides incomplete information about the origin of needs. However, it implies that higher level needs are present in most people, even if they don't recognize or act to meet those needs. These higher level needs will motivate most people if nothing occurs to block their emergence.

The needs hierarchy is based on U.S. cultural values. In cultures that value uncertainty avoidance, such as Japan and Greece, job security and lifelong employment are stronger motivators than self-actualization. Moreover, in Denmark, Sweden, and Norway the value and rewards of a high quality of life are more important than productivity. Thus social needs are stronger than self-actualization and self-esteem needs. In countries such as China, Japan, and Korea that value collectivist and community practices over individual achievements, belonging and security are considerably more important than meeting growth needs. Therefore, although the needs that Maslow identified may be universal, the logic or sequence of the hierarchy differs from culture to culture.[7]

Maslow's work has received much attention from managers, as well as psychologists.[8] Research has found that top managers are better able to satisfy their esteem and self-actualization needs than are lower level managers; part of the reason is that top managers have more challenging jobs and opportunities for self-actualization. Employees who work on a team have been able to satisfy their higher level needs by making decisions that affect their team and organization. At the Miller Brewing Company's plant in Trenton, Ohio, groups of employees are trained to perform multiple tasks, including hiring and training team members—and even firing those who fail to perform adequately. As team members learn new tasks, they start satisfying their higher level needs. Employees who have little or no control over their work (e.g., assembly-line workers) may not even experience higher level needs in relation to their jobs. Studies have also shown that the fulfillment of needs differs according to the job a person performs, a person's age and background, and the size of the company. "Not everyone is motivated in the same way. You shouldn't assume that it's a one-size-fits-all solution. You have to understand people's needs," says Susan Dallas, a manager for business development at Gartner, an information technology consulting firm, in San Diego.

The Managing Communication feature on the following page illustrates how information technology managers are trying to keep their employees motivated during periods of corporate layoffs, global unrest, and volatile stock markets. According to Allan McLaughlin, chief technology officer at LexisNexis, communicating with employees is the key. He believes that disconnected workers aren't motivated to work to their fullest potential and that finding a way to avoid this situation requires insight into the needs of workers. What employee needs is McLaughlin satisfying at LexisNexis with his communication program?

## ACHIEVEMENT MOTIVATION MODEL

David McClelland proposed a learned needs model of motivation that he believed to be rooted in culture.[9] He argued that everyone has three particularly important needs: for achievement, affiliation, and power. Individuals who possess a *strong power motive* take action that affects the behaviors of others and has a strong emotional appeal. These individuals are concerned with providing status rewards to their

## COMPETENCY:  MANAGING COMMUNICATION

### TAILORING REWARDS AT LEXISNEXIS

Allan McLaughlin believes that managers need to address employee needs through open, straightforward communication. McLaughlin holds "skip-level" meetings, where he meets and talks informally with 10 or 15 employees randomly picked from his staff of 830. "The only rule is that there are no rules to these meetings," he explains. During these meetings, employees have a chance to talk with the boss, to discuss their opinions on a variety of matters, and to meet employees from other departments. At one meeting, employees suggested ways to speed up a project time line. After studying their proposal, management approved and implemented it. Employees were supportive of the changes because of their involvement. McLaughlin also shares news about what's going on in the company. At another skip-level meeting, he shared news that the company was in the process of downsizing cubicles to fit more employees in less space. Employees took offense at the proposal, stating that taking their workspace away from them was very demoralizing. McLaughlin says that he "bet his career" on the fact that, by acquiring more office space and leaving cubicles as they were, turnover and morale would improve. He was right: Fewer people quit and morale improved dramatically.

McLaughlin also learned that many information technology (IT) employees don't want advancement that required long hours of work and managing others. Some employees are more interested in quality time with their families than in advancement. By providing flexible work schedules, LexisNexis allows these employees to participate in many family activities that they might otherwise miss and increases their motivation to do a good job. Employees also are encouraged to broaden their competencies beyond technical areas. They are encouraged to work on boards (e.g., school and charitable) and in other associations to acquire different learning experiences. For example, employees suggested and McLaughlin approved two LexisNexis IT employees to work at a local technical association for a year. According to him, "They learned things they wouldn't get in corporate IT."

McLaughlin also found out that recognition and appreciation of employee efforts can be very motivating. By thanking employees and acknowledging their exceptional contributions, he tries to foster a strong sense of loyalty and promote a greater interest in employees' work activities. Using low-cost expressions of appreciation, such as thank-you notes, verbal compliments, staff awards, and noting accomplishments in LexisNexis's internal newspapers, he shows employees that their contributions are appreciated.[10]

*For more information on LexisNexis, visit the organization's home page at* **http://www. LexisNexis.com**.

followers. Individuals who have a *strong affiliation motive* tend to establish, maintain, and restore close personal relationships with others. Individuals who have a *strong achievement motive* compete against some standard of excellence or unique contribution against which they judge their behaviors and achievements.

McClelland has studied achievement motivation extensively, especially with regard to entrepreneurship. His **achievement motivation model** states that people are motivated according to the strength of their desire either to perform in terms of a standard of excellence or to succeed in competitive situations. According to McClelland, almost all people believe that they have an "achievement motive," but probably only about 10 percent of the U.S. population are strongly motivated to achieve. The amount of achievement motivation that people have depends on their childhood, their personal and occupational experiences, and the type of organization for which they work. Table 5.1 shows an application of McClelland's model to presidents of the United States. Presidents' motives can be documented by the legislation they have proposed and the policies they have pursued during their tenures. Do your choices match ours?

According to McClelland's model, motives are "stored" in the preconscious mind just below the level of full awareness. They lie between the conscious and the unconscious, in the area of daydreams, where people talk to themselves without quite being aware of it. A basic premise of the model is that the pattern of these daydreams can be tested and that people can be taught to change their motivation by changing these daydreams.

**Measuring Achievement Motivation.**    McClelland measured the strength of a person's achievement motivation with the **Thematic Apperception Test (TAT)**. The TAT uses unstructured pictures that may arouse many kinds of reactions in the person being tested. Examples include an inkblot that a person can perceive as many different objects or a picture that can generate a variety of stories. There are no right or wrong answers, and the person isn't given a limited set of alternatives from which to choose. A major goal of the TAT is to obtain the individual's own perception of the world. The TAT is called a projective method because it emphasizes individual perceptions of stimuli, the meaning each individual gives to them, and how each individual organizes them (recall the discussion of perception in Chapter 3).

One projective test involves looking at the picture shown in Figure 5.4 for 10 to 15 seconds and then writing a short story about it that answers the following questions.

- What is going on in this picture?
- What is the woman thinking?
- What has led up to this situation?

Write your own story about the picture. Then compare it with the following story written by a manager exhibiting strong achievement motivation, whom McClelland would describe as a high achiever.

The individual is an officer in a small entrepreneurial organization that wants to get a contract for her company. She knows that the competition will be tough, because all the big firms are bidding on this contract. She is taking a moment to think how happy she will be if her company is awarded the large contract. It will

**Table 5.1**

| PRESIDENT | NEEDS | | |
| --- | --- | --- | --- |
| | Power | Achievement | Affiliation |
| Bush, G. W. | Moderate | High | Low |
| Clinton, B. | Moderate | High | High |
| Reagan, R. | High | Moderate | Low |
| Kennedy, J. F. | High | Low | High |
| Roosevelt, F. D. | High | Moderate | Low |
| Lincoln, A. | Moderate | Low | Moderate |
| Washington, G. | Low | Low | Moderate |

Presidents' Needs for Power, Achievement, and Affiliation

**Figure 5.4**    **Sample picture used in a projective test**

Source: ©Tom McCarthy/Photo Edit

mean stability for the company and probably a large raise for her. She is satisfied because she has just thought of a way to manufacture a critical part that will enable her company to bring in a low bid and complete the job with time to spare.

What motivational profile did you identify? Does it match the executive's?

**Characteristics of High Achievers.**   Self-motivated high achievers have three main characteristics.[11] First, they like to set their own *goals*. Seldom content to drift aimlessly and let life happen to them, they nearly always are trying to accomplish something. High achievers seek the challenge of making tough decisions. They are selective about the goals to which they commit themselves. Hence they are unlikely to automatically accept goals that other people, including their superiors, attempt to select for them. They exercise self-control over their behaviors, especially the ways they pursue the goals they select. They tend to seek advice or help only from experts who can provide needed knowledge or skills. High achievers prefer to be as fully responsible for attaining their goals as possible. If they win, they want the credit; if they lose, they accept the blame. For example, assume that you are given a choice between rolling dice with one chance in three of winning or working on a problem with one chance in three of solving the problem in the time allotted. Which would you choose? A high achiever would choose to work on the problem, even though rolling the dice is obviously less work and the odds of winning are the same. High achievers prefer to work at a problem rather than leave the outcome to chance or to other people.

Second, high achievers avoid selecting extremely difficult goals. They prefer *moderate goals* that are neither so easy that attaining them provides no satisfaction nor so difficult that attaining them is more a matter of luck than ability. They gauge what is possible and then select as difficult a goal as they think they can attain. The game of ringtoss illustrates this point. Most carnivals have ringtoss games that require participants to throw rings over a peg from some minimum distance but specify no maximum distance. Imagine the same game but with people allowed to stand at any distance they want from the peg. Some will throw more or less randomly, standing close and then far away. Those with high-achievement motivation will seem to calculate carefully where they should stand to have the greatest chance of winning a prize and still feel challenged. These individuals seem to stand at a distance that isn't so close as to make the task ridiculously easy and isn't so far away as to make it impossible. They set a distance moderately far away from which they can potentially ring a peg. Thus they set personal challenges and enjoy tasks that will stretch their abilities.

Third, high achievers prefer tasks that provide *immediate feedback*. Because of the goal's importance to them, they like to know how well they're doing. That's one reason why the high achiever often chooses a professional career, a sales career, or entrepreneurial activities. Golf appeals to most high achievers: Golfers can compare their scores to par for the course, to their own previous performance on the course, and to their opponents' score; performance is related to both feedback (score) and goal (par).

**Financial Incentives.**   Money has a complex effect on high achievers. They usually value highly their services and place a high price tag on them. High achievers are usually self-confident. They are aware of their abilities and limitations and thus are confident when they choose to do a particular job. They are unlikely to remain very long in an organization that doesn't pay them well. Whether an incentive plan actually increases their performance is an open question because they normally work at peak efficiency. They value money as a strong symbol of their achievement and adequacy. A financial incentive may create dissatisfaction if they feel that it inadequately reflects their contributions.

When achievement motivation is operating, outstanding performance on a challenging task is likely. However, achievement motivation doesn't operate when high achievers are performing routine or boring tasks or when there is no competition against goals. An example of a high achiever is John Schnatter, CEO and founder of Papa John's. Schnatter's drive to become number 1 in the pizza industry has made Papa John's a major competitor in this $28 billion a year industry. While holding just under a 27 percent share of the take-out pizza market, Schnatter's goal is to take market share away from Pizza Hut (which has about 38 percent) by having better ingredients and making a better pizza. He has achieved remarkable results by being singularly obsessive about high quality and performance. He preaches to his employees about pizza in very passionate terms. He requires all employees to memorize the company's Six Core Values, including stay focused, customer satisfaction must be superior, and people are priority No. 1 *always*—and calls on employees during meetings to stand up and shout them out. He created a Ten Point Perfect Pizza Scale that measures the quality of pizzas. For example, pieces of the toppings should not touch, there should be no "peaks or valleys" along the pizza's border, all mushrooms should be sliced to 0.25 inch, and no splotchy coloring should appear on the crust. The employee newsletter carries articles such as "The Papa John's Black Olive Story" or "The Papa John's Tomato Story." Such articles inform employees about how special ingredients are used to make Papa John's pizza.

At its headquarters in Louisville, Kentucky, most employees (including Schnatter) wear Papa John's teal-blue polo shirts, with Pizza Wars embroidered across them. Employees even have their own clothing embroidered with Papa John's logo. By 2003, Schnatter wants Papa John's to be the number 1 pizza brand in the world in terms of name recognition and by 2008, the leader in sales.[12]

**Using McClelland's Achievement Motivation Model.**    McClelland and his associates at McBer and Company have conducted most of the research supporting the achievement motivation model. Based on this research, they recommend the following approach.

- Arrange tasks so that employees receive periodic feedback on their performance. Feedback enables employees to modify their behaviors as necessary.
- Provide good role models of achievement. Employees should be encouraged to have heroes to emulate.
- Help employees modify their self-images. High-achievement individuals accept themselves and seek job challenges and responsibilities.
- Guide employee aspirations. Employees should think about setting realistic goals and the ways that they can attain them.
- Make it known that managers who have been successful are those that are higher in power motivation than in affiliation motivation.

One of the main problems with the achievement motivation model is also its greatest strength. The TAT method is valuable because it allows the researcher to tap the preconscious motives of people. This method has some advantages over questionnaires, but the interpretation of a story is more of an art than a science. As a result, the method's reliability is open to question. The permanency of the model's three needs has also been questioned.  Further research is needed to explore the model's validity.

**Learning Objective:**

3.  Explain how the design of jobs affects motivation.

# MOTIVATING EMPLOYEES THROUGH JOB DESIGN

Frederick Herzberg and his associates took a different approach to examining what motivates people. He and his staff simply asked people to tell them when they felt exceptionally good about their jobs and when they felt exceptionally bad about their job. As shown in Table 5.2, people identified somewhat different things when they felt good or bad about their jobs. From this study they developed the *two-factor theory*, better known as the **motivator–hygiene model**, which proposes that two sets of factors—motivators and hygienes—are the primary causes of job satisfaction and job dissatisfaction.[13]

## MOTIVATOR FACTORS

The first set of factors, **motivator factors**, includes the work itself, recognition, advancement, and responsibility. These factors are related to an individual's positive feelings about the job and to the content of the job itself. These positive feelings, in turn, are associated with the individual's experiences of achievement, recognition, and responsibility. They reflect lasting rather than temporary achievement in the work setting. In other words, motivators are **intrinsic factors**, which are directly related to the job and are largely internal to the individual. The organization's policies may have only an indirect impact on them. But, by defining exceptional performance, for ex-

**Table 5.2**

| Sources of Job Satisfaction and Job Dissatisfaction | |
| --- | --- |
| **MOTIVATOR FACTORS THAT AFFECT JOB SATISFACTION** | **HYGIENE FACTORS THAT AFFECT JOB DISSATISFACTION** |
| • Achievement | • Organizational rules and policies |
| • Advancement | • Relationships with coworkers |
| • Autonomy | • Relationships with supervisors |
| • Challenge | • Salary |
| • Feedback | • Security |
| • Responsibility | • Working conditions |

ample, an organization may enable individuals to feel that they have performed their tasks exceptionally well. Can you identify some motivators that Starbucks uses to motivate its employees (see the Preview Case)?

## HYGIENE FACTORS

The second set of factors, **hygiene factors**, includes company policy and administration, technical supervision, salary, fringe benefits, working conditions, and interpersonal relations. These factors are associated with an individual's negative feelings about the job and are related to the environment in which the job is performed. Hygienes are **extrinsic factors**, or factors external to the job. They serve as rewards for high performance only if the organization recognizes high performance. Can you identify the hygiene factors used by Starbucks to attract new employees?

**Cultural Influences.**   One of the important themes of this book is recognizing and addressing cultural diversity in the workforce. As U.S. organizations continue to expand overseas and foreign organizations establish manufacturing operations in Canada, Mexico, and the United States, managers must be aware of cultural differences and how these differences can affect the motivation of employees.[14] Herzberg believes that, despite cultural differences, motivators and hygienes affect workers similarly throughout the world. For U.S. workers about 80 percent of the factors that lead to job satisfaction can be traced to motivators. For workers in the other countries listed, motivators accounted for 60 to 90 percent of the reason for job satisfaction. Hygienes accounted for most of the reasons that workers were dissatisfied with their jobs. In Finland, 80 percent of the workers indicated that hygiene factors contributed mainly to job dissatisfaction, whereas only 10 percent said that hygiene factors contributed to their job satisfaction.

With the passage of the North American Free Trade Agreement (NAFTA), managers and employees in North America began working more closely with others who don't necessarily share similar work motivation. It doesn't take U.S. managers very long to realize that employees in Mexico have different attitudes toward work. In the United States workers generally favor taking the initiative, having individual responsibility, and taking failure personally. They are competitive, have high goals, and live for the future. Workers are comfortable operating in a group, with the group sharing both success and failure. They tend to be cooperative, flexible, and enjoy life as it is now.

In Mexico, employees' priorities are family, religion, and work—in that order. During the year, plant managers host family dinners to celebrate anniversaries of employees who have worked there 5, 10, 15, and 20 years. Employees may use the company clubhouse for weddings, baptisms, anniversary parties, and other family celebrations. Organizations also host a family day during which employees' families can tour the plant, enjoy entertainment and food, and participate in sports.

The typical workday in Mexico is 8 A.M. to 5:30 P.M. Employees are picked up by a company bus at various locations throughout the city. Employees like to eat their main meal in the middle of the day, the cost of which is heavily subsidized (as much as 70 percent) by the company. Interestingly, managers serve the employees this meal.[15]

In every culture, certain factors act as motivators and others act as demotivators. Specific motivators and their relative importance are unique to each culture and, all too frequently, to each situation. The tale of two water plants in Romania illustrated in the Managing Across Cultures feature highlights these differences. What motivator factors are present in each plant? What hygiene factors are present in each plant?

**Using Motivators and Hygienes.**   The motivator–hygiene model appeals to managers because it offers straightforward advice on how to motivate people. For

## COMPETENCY: MANAGING ACROSS CULTURES

### PERLA HARGITA

Perla Hargita is a mineral water bottling firm in the Transylvania Alps of northwestern Romania. It is a family-owned company that has been in business for more than two generations. Its two plants employ 285 people, 60 percent of whom live in the town. The two plants combined bottle a minimum of 30,000 liters of water a day, which increases to 45,000 liters in the summer. The water is shipped all over Romania and exported to other Eastern European countries, as well as to Canada and Australia.

In the glass-bottling plant, most of the equipment is antiquated. The oldest equipment was manufactured in Germany and is very reliable, but the newer equipment made in Romania has frequent breakdowns. The Romanian equipment can't be replaced with better equipment from manufacturers in other countries because all firms are now required to "buy Romanian." Safety standards in the factory are virtually nonexistent. Steam rises in clouds from the open bottle washer as hot water splashes on the concrete floor. The machinery screeches and grinds as bottles progress through the system. Recycled glass bottles are washed, filled, capped, and labeled on an open conveyor belt line. One group of workers, mainly young women, visually inspects the empty bottles for defects while others make certain that the bottles are filled to the proper level. Bottle caps frequently blow off the filled bottles, sounding like shotgun blasts. There are no safety guards to keep workers' fingers from being caught in the conveyor and no yellow lines to mark off safe areas for walking, and the lighting in many areas of the plant is poor. Accidents are frequent, but workers don't report them to the plant manager for fear of being dismissed. The machinery makes such a deafening noise that the workers can't be heard without shouting. The workers are not provided with ear plugs or eye protection. Micu Korton, the plant manager, acknowledges that most workers suffer severe hearing loss but states that it is just an occupational hazard.

In stark contrast, the plastic-bottling plant is modern, all white, brightly lit, clean, dry, and quiet enough for workers to talk with each other in a normal voice. Three white-coated technicians monitor digital control panels. Only a soft hum can be heard from the computerized machinery. The bottling line is completely enclosed in a clear acrylic tunnel that provides a safe, sanitary, and efficient environment for the operation. In a seamless process, heated plastic pellets are formed into bottles. The bottles are filled with water, capped, labeled, and banded into 12-packs for boxing and shipping.

During the summer, workers in both plants eagerly work 4 hours overtime a day. They make at least 10 percent more than they could by farming potatoes or working in the declining textile industry. Wages at Perla Hargita average 1,235,537 lieu, or about $124, per month, which in the summer increases to $186 for a 12-hour workday. In addition, both plants provide bottled water, beer, and other bottled drinks to all employees at a discount. Workers at both plants get several paid holidays per year and a small bonus at Christmas. Women make up most of the workforce in the glass-bottling plant, whereas men are employed in the plastic-bottling plant. In Romania, women typically earn 25 percent less than men.[16]

example, instead of having several people perform separate parts of a job, having one person perform the entire job would be better. Doing so would help provide greater motivators for that person. Corning Glass, Sea-Land, and American Greeting Cards, among others, have redesigned jobs to make them more motivating for employees. Jobs designed with motivators enhance employee teamwork, managing self, and communication competencies because people take their jobs more seriously. Also, motivators give employees as much feedback as possible. As we stated in Chapter 4, if people know how they are doing, they are more motivated to perform well. Because the motivator–hygiene model holds that satisfaction and dissatisfaction do not form a single continuum, a person can be both satisfied and dissatisfied at the same time. These separate continuums are illustrated in Figure 5.5

Despite its attractive features, several significant criticisms have been leveled at the motivator–hygiene model.[17] One is that Herzberg used a method-bound procedure; that is, the method he used to measure the factors determined the results. He asked two key questions: "Can you describe, in detail, when you felt exceptionally good about your job?" and "Can you describe, in detail, when you felt exceptionally bad about your job?" In response to such questions, people tend to give socially desirable answers, that is, answers that they think the researcher wants to hear or that sound "reasonable." Also, people tend to attribute good job results to their own efforts and to attribute reasons for poor results to others (recall the discussion of the self-serving bias attribution in Chapter 3).

Another serious question about the motivator–hygiene model is whether satisfaction and dissatisfaction really are two separate dimensions, as Figure 5.5 indicates. Research results are mixed. Some researchers have found factors that can contribute to both satisfaction and dissatisfaction, whereas others have found that motivator factors can contribute to dissatisfaction and hygiene factors can contribute to satisfaction. For example, at Starbucks, employees reported that hygiene factors are strongly related to their job satisfactions. These findings, however, haven't disproved the concept that satisfaction and dissatisfaction are two different continuums.

**Learning Objective:**

4. Describe the expectancy model of motivation.

## MOTIVATING EMPLOYEES THROUGH PERFORMANCE EXPECTATIONS

Besides creating jobs that people find challenging and rewarding, people are also motivated by the belief that they can expect to achieve certain rewards by working hard to attain them. Believing that you can get an "A" in this class by expending enough effort can be a very effective motivator. If you can clearly see a link between your

**Figure 5.5**                              **Motivator–Hygiene Situations**

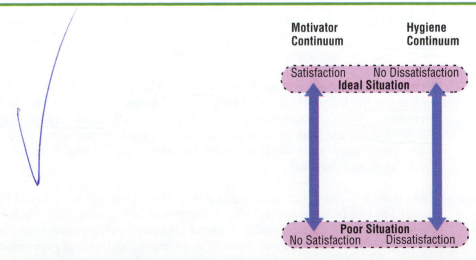

Motivator Continuum    Hygiene Continuum

Satisfaction    No Dissatisfaction
**Ideal Situation**

**Poor Situation**
No Satisfaction    Dissatisfaction

study behaviors (effort) and your grade, you will be motivated to study. If you see no link, why study at all? To understand better this approach to motivation, let's take a look at the expectancy model.

## EXPECTANCY MODEL

The **expectancy model** states that people are motivated to work when they expect to achieve things they want from their jobs. These things might include satisfaction of safety needs, the excitement of doing a challenging task, or the ability to set and achieve difficult goals. A basic premise of the expectancy model is that employees are rational people. They think about what they have to do to be rewarded and how much the rewards mean to them before they perform their jobs. Four assumptions about the causes of behavior in organizations provide the basis for this model.

First, a combination of forces in the individual and the environment determines behavior. Neither the individual nor the environment alone determines behavior. People go to work for organizations with expectations about their jobs that are based on their needs, motivations, and past experiences. These factors influence how people respond to an organization, but they can and do change over time.

Second, individuals decide their own behaviors in organizations, even though many constraints are placed on individual behavior (e.g., through rules, technology, and work-group norms). Most individuals make two kinds of conscious decisions: (1) decisions about coming to work, staying with the same organization, and joining other organizations (membership decisions); and (2) decisions about how much to produce, how hard to work, and the quality of workmanship (job-performance decisions).

Third, different individuals have different needs and goals. Employees want different rewards from their work, depending on their gender, race, age, and other characteristics. Of the many rewards that Starbucks offers to its employees, which do you find attractive? Why? In 5 years, are these same rewards likely to be attractive to you?

Fourth, individuals decide among alternatives based on their perceptions of whether a specific behavior will lead to a desired outcome. Individuals do what they perceive will lead to desired outcomes and avoid doing what they perceive will lead to undesirable outcomes.[18]

In general, the expectancy model holds that individuals have their own needs and ideas about what they desire from their work (rewards). They act on these needs and ideas when making decisions about what organization to join and how hard to work. This model also holds that individuals are not inherently motivated or unmotivated but rather that motivation depends on the situations that individuals face and how their responses to these situations fit their needs.

To help you understand the expectancy model, we must define its most important variables and explain how they operate. They are first-level and second-level outcomes, expectancy, valence, and instrumentality.

**First-Level and Second-Level Outcomes.**   The results of behaviors associated with doing the job itself are called **first-level outcomes**. They include level of performance, amount of absenteeism, and quality of work. **Second-level outcomes** are the rewards (either positive or negative) that first-level outcomes are likely to produce. They include a pay increase, promotion, acceptance by coworkers, job security, reprimands, and dismissal.

**Expectancy.**   The belief that a particular level of effort will be followed by a particular level of performance is called **expectancy**. It can vary from the belief that there is absolutely no relationship between effort and performance to the certainty that a given level of effort will result in a corresponding level of performance. Expectancy has a value ranging from 0, indicating no chance that a first-level outcome will occur after the behavior, to +1, indicating certainty that a particular first-level outcome will follow a behavior. For example, if you believe that you have no chance of getting a good grade on the next exam by studying this chapter, your expectancy value would be 0. Having this expectancy, you shouldn't study this chapter. Good teachers will do things that help their students believe that hard work will lead students to achieve to better grades.

**Instrumentality.**    The relationship between first-level outcomes and second-level outcomes is called **instrumentality**. It can have values ranging from –1 to +1. A –1 indicates that attainment of a second-level outcome is inversely related to the achievement of a first-level outcome. For example, Sharron Coon, a staff manager at AT&T, wants to be accepted as a member of her work group, but it has a norm for an acceptable level of performance. If she violates this norm, her work group won't accept her. Therefore Coon limits her performance so as not to violate the group's norm. A +1 indicates that the first-level outcome is positively related to the second-level outcome. For example, if you received an A on all your exams, the probability that you would achieve your desired second-level outcome (passing this course) approaches +1. If there were no relationship between your performance on a test and either passing or failing this course, your instrumentality would be 0.

**Valence.**    An individual's preference for a particular second-level outcome is called **valence**. Outcomes having a positive valence include being respected by friends and coworkers, performing meaningful work, having job security, and earning enough money to support a family. Valence is just not the amount of the reward received, but what is means to the person receiving it. Outcomes having a negative valence are things that you want to avoid, such as being laid off, being passed over for a promotion, or being discharged for sexual harassment. An outcome is positive when it is preferred and negative when it is not preferred or is to be avoided. An outcome has a valence of 0 when the individual is indifferent about receiving it.

**Putting It All Together.**    In brief, the expectancy model holds that work motivation is determined by individual beliefs regarding effort–performance relationships and the desirability of various work outcomes associated with different performance levels. Simply put, you can remember the model's important features by the saying:

> People exert work effort to achieve performance that leads to valued work-related outcomes.

**The Expectancy Model in Action.**    The five key variables just defined and discussed lead to a general expectancy model of motivation, as shown in Figure 5.6. Motivation is the force that causes individuals to expend effort, but effort alone isn't enough. Unless an individual believes that effort will lead to some desired performance level (first-level outcome), he won't make much of an effort. The effort–performance relationship is based on a perception of the difficulty of achieving a particular behavior (say, working for an A in this course) and the probability of achieving that behavior. On the one hand, you may have a high expectancy that, if you attend class, study the book, take good notes, and prepare for exams, you can achieve an A in this class. That expectancy is likely to translate into making the effort required on those activities to get an A. On the other hand, you may believe that, even if you attend class, study the book, take good notes, and prepare for exams, your chances of getting an A are only 20 percent. That expectancy is likely to keep you from expending the effort required on these activities to achieve an A.

Performance level is important in obtaining desired second-level outcomes. Figure 5.6 shows six desirable second-level outcomes: self-confidence, self-esteem, personal happiness, overall GPA this semester, approval of other people, and respect of other people. In general, if you believe that a particular level of performance (A, B,

**Figure 5.6**                    **Expectancy Model in Action**

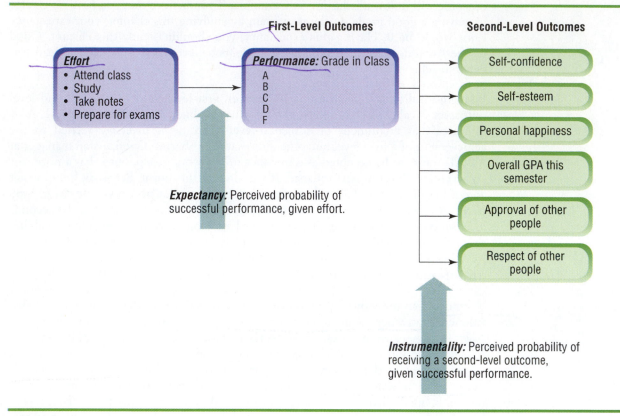

Source: VandeWalle, D., Cron, W. L., and Slocum, J. W. The rule of goal orientation following performance feedback. *Journal of Applied Psychology*, 2001, 86, 629–640.

C, D, or F) will lead to these desired outcomes, you are more likely to try to perform at that level. If you really desire these six second-level outcomes and you can achieve them only if you get an A in this course, the instrumentality between receiving an A and these six outcomes will be positive. But, if you believe that getting an A in this course means that you won't gain personal happiness and the approval and respect of other people, the instrumentality between an A and these outcomes will be negative. That is, if the higher the grade, the less likely you are to experience personal happiness, you might choose not to get an A in this course. Once you have made this choice, you will lessen your effort and start cutting class, not studying for exams, and so on.

Researchers are still working on ways to test this model, which has presented some problems.[19]

1.  The model tries to predict choice or the amount of effort an individual will expend on one or more tasks. However, there is little agreement about what constitutes choice or effort for different individuals. Therefore this important variable is difficult to measure accurately.

2.  The model doesn't specify which second-level outcomes are important to a particular individual in a given situation. Although researchers are addressing this issue, comparison of the limited results to date is often difficult because each study is unique. Take another look at the second-level outcomes in Figure 5.6. Would you choose them? What others might you choose?

3.  The model contains an implicit assumption that motivation is a conscious choice process. That is, the individual consciously calculates the pain or pleasure that she expects to attain or avoid when making a choice. The expectancy model says

nothing about unconscious motivation or personality characteristics. In fact, people often do not make conscious choices about which outcomes to seek. Can you recall going through this process concerning your grade while taking this course?

4.  The model works best in cultures that emphasize internal attribution. When people in a culture believe that they can control their work environment and their own behavior, such as in the United States, Canada, and the United Kingdom, the expectancy model can explain behavior. In cultures where people believe the work environment and their own behavior aren't completely under their control, such as in Brazil, Saudi Arabia, Iran, Japan, and China, the assumptions of the model might not be valid. For example, a Canadian manager in Japan decided to promote one of her young female Japanese sales representatives to manager (a status and monetary reward). To her surprise, the promotion diminished the new Japanese manager's performance. Why? Japanese have a high need for harmony—to fit in with their colleagues. The promotion, an individualistic reward, separated the new manager from her colleagues, embarrassed her, and therefore diminished her work motivation.[20]

**Organizational Uses.**    Although some research problems remain, the expectancy model has some important implications for motivating employees. These implications can be grouped into seven suggestions for action.[21]

1.  Managers should try to determine the outcomes that each employee values. Two ways of doing so are observing employee reactions to different rewards and asking employees about the types of rewards they want from their jobs. However, managers must recognize that employees can and do change their minds about desired outcomes over time.

2.  Managers should define good, adequate, and poor performance in terms that are observable and measurable. Employees need to understand what is expected of them and how these expectations affect performance. When the Baxter Pharmaceutical Company announced a new examination table for doctors, its salespeople wanted to know what behaviors, such as cold-calling on new accounts or trying to sell the new tables to their existing accounts, would lead to more sales. To the extent that Baxter was able to train its salespeople in selling its new product, it was able to link salespeople's efforts with performance.

3.  Managers should be sure that desired levels of performance set for employees can be attained. If employees feel that the level of performance necessary to get a reward is higher than they can reasonably achieve, their motivation to perform will be low. For example, Nordstrom tells its employees: "Respond to Unreasonable Customer Requests." Employees are urged to keep scrapbooks with "heroic" acts, such as hand delivering items purchased by phone to the airport for a customer leaving on a last-minute business trip, changing a customer's flat tire, or paying a customer's parking ticket when in-store gift wrapping has taken longer than expected. It is hardly surprising that Nordstrom pays its employees much more than they could earn at a rival's store. For those who love to sell and can meet its demanding standards, Nordstrom is nirvana.

4.  Managers should directly link the specific performance they desire to the outcomes desired by employees. Recall the discussion in Chapter 4 of how operant conditioning principles can be applied to improve performance. If an employee has achieved the desired level of performance for a promotion, the employee should be promoted as soon as possible. If a high level of motivation is to be created and maintained, it is extremely important for employees to see clearly and quickly the reward process at work. Concrete acts must accompany statements of intent in linking performance to rewards.

5.  Managers should never forget that perceptions, not reality, determine motivation. Too often, managers misunderstand the behavior of employees because

they tend to rely on their own perceptions of the situation and forget that employees' perceptions may be different.

6. Managers should analyze situations for conflicts. Having set up positive expectancies for employees, managers must look at an entire situation to determine whether other factors conflict with the desired behaviors (e.g., the informal work group or the organization's formal reward system). Motivation will be high only when employees perceive many rewards and few negative outcomes associated with good performance.

7. Managers should be sure that changes in outcomes or rewards are large enough to motivate significant efforts. Trivial rewards may result in minimal efforts, if any, to improve performance. Rewards must be large enough to motivate individuals to make the effort required to substantially change performance.

Managers at Dean Foods have been using most of these seven suggestions in their 58 dairy plants. As in most organizations, managers at Dean Foods were concerned about making improvements that would affect quality, cost, and customer service. Since the arrival of Gary Flickinger, vice president for manufacturing, all employees have been included in an Employee Involvement program that has generated more than 4,700 ideas in less than 18 months and pushed plant efficiency to higher levels. The following Managing Teams Competency feature illustrates how these results were accomplished. You should be able to identify many of the seven principles based on the expectancy model in this account.

## COMPETENCY: MANAGING TEAMS

### DEAN FOODS

Dean Foods' management had long been aware of the potential profit buried in operations and supply chain inefficiency. When Gary Flickinger joined the company, he indicated that one of his goals would be to build a program whereby employees would take on more responsibility for eliminating production bottlenecks, making maintenance schedules and procedures more effective, and eliminating unnecessary work.

At each of the company's 58 plants, employees and managers were asked to evaluate their plant with regards to safety, cost, delivery, and quality. The results were shared, and cross-functional teams were formed. Each team was trained in the basics of running effective meetings. Each group was led by a facilitator and included a recorder or "scribe." All areas of the plant were represented. A supervisor sat in on most meetings but wasn't a facilitator. The meetings lasted only 10 minutes and focused on one of the four areas of concern.

Because the meetings last only 10 minutes, they have to be direct and to the point. Members of each group ask themselves and each other a simple question: What in the process caused us to meet or miss our goals for the day? One simple response was that employees needed new cleanup goggles. A more complicated response occurred when a foreman slipped and broke a rib in a plant. A team immediately began looking for answers and soon recommended that all employees be given new rubber boots. Now a rubber over-boot given to all plant employees provides them with better footing, even on slick surfaces. Quick decisions by management to such responses from the groups got the employees' attention.

Goals and performance are posted on charts, poster boards, and the like for everyone to see. The purpose of the 10-minute meeting is to improve two-way communication and in doing so to identify an issue or a problem, find its cause, and fix it. Someone on the team that raised the issue or problem then takes responsibility to address or correct it within 30 days. If the issue or problem hasn't been addressed or

*For more information on Dean Foods, visit the organization's home page at http://www.deanfoods. com.*

corrected within that time, the team asks the person why. High-ticket, unbudgeted purchases or expenditures resulting from a team response have to be approved by the plant manager.

One of the benefits of using teams is that employees are learning the business. They see how the work of their department fits with and affects the work of other departments in the plant. For example, at the company's Buena Park, California plant, teams recommended energy savings of more than $10,000 a year and a trash-saving idea that generated $20,000 worth of recyclables. Plant efficiency rose by more than 15 percent because the teams suggested ways to save energy and also do preventative maintenance.[22]

**Learning Objective:**

5. Explain how feelings of equity affect motivation.

# MOTIVATING EMPLOYEES THROUGH EQUITY

Feelings of unfairness were among the most frequent sources of job dissatisfaction reported to Herzberg and his associates. Some researchers have made this desire for fairness, justice, or equity a central focus of their models. Assume that you just received a 7 percent raise. Will this raise lead to higher performance, lower performance, or no change in performance? Are you satisfied with this increase? Would your satisfaction with this pay increase vary with the consumer price index, with what you expected to get, or with what others in the organization performing the same job and at the same performance level received?

## EQUITY MODEL: BALANCING INPUTS AND OUTCOMES

The **equity model** focuses on an individual's feelings of how fairly she is treated in comparison with others.[23] It is based on the belief that people are motivated to maintain a fair, or equitable, relationship between themselves and others and to avoid relationships that are unfair or inequitable. It contains two major assumptions. The first is that individuals evaluate their interpersonal relationships just as they would evaluate the buying or selling of a home, shares of stock, or a car. The model views relationships as exchange processes in which individuals make contributions and expect certain results. The second assumption is that individuals don't operate in a vacuum. They compare their situations to those of the others in exchanges to determine fairness. In other words, what happens to individuals is important when they compare themselves to similar others (e.g., coworkers, relatives, and neighbors).

**General Equity Model.**   The equity model is based on the comparison of two variables: inputs and outcomes. **Inputs** represent what an individual contributes to an exchange; **outcomes** are what an individual receives from the exchange. Some typical inputs and outcomes are shown in Table 5.3. A word of caution: The items in the two lists aren't paired and don't represent specific exchanges.

According to the equity model, individuals assign weights to various inputs and outcomes according to their perceptions of the situation. Because most situations involve multiple inputs and outcomes, the weighting process isn't precise. However, people generally can distinguish between important and less important inputs and outcomes. After they arrive at a ratio of inputs and outcomes for themselves, they compare it with their perceived ratios of inputs and outcomes of others who are in the same or a similar situation. These relevant others become the objects of comparison for individuals in determining whether they feel equitably treated.[24]

Equity exists whenever the perceived ratio of a person's outcomes to inputs equals that for relevant others. For example, an individual may feel properly paid in terms of what he puts into a job compared to what other workers are getting for their inputs.

**Table 5.3**

| INPUTS | OUTCOMES |
|---|---|
| Age | Challenging job assignments |
| Attendance | Fringe benefits |
| Interpersonal skills, communication skills | Job perquisites (parking space or office location) |
| Job effort (long hours) | Job security |
| Level of education | Monotony |
| Past experience | Promotion |
| Performance | Recognition |
| Personal appearance | Responsibility |
| Seniority | Salary |
| Social status | Seniority benefits |
| Technical skills | Status symbols |
| Training | Working conditions |

**Examples of Inputs and Outcomes in Organizations**

Inequity exists when the perceived ratios of outcomes to inputs are unequal. Greg Hyslop, a director of program engineering at Boeing, works harder than his coworkers, completes all his tasks on time even though others don't, and puts in longer hours than others, but receives the same pay raise as the others. What happens? Hyslop believes that his inputs are greater than those of his coworkers and therefore should merit a greater pay raise. Inequity can also occur when people are overpaid. In this case, the overpaid employees might be motivated by guilt or social pressure to work harder to reduce the imbalance between their inputs and outcomes and those of their coworkers.

**Consequences of Inequity.**    **Inequity** causes tension within and among individuals. Tension isn't pleasurable, so people are motivated to reduce it to a tolerable level, as illustrated in Figure 5.7. To reduce a perceived inequity and the corresponding level of tension, people may choose to act in one or more of the following ways.

- People may either increase or decrease their inputs to what they feel to be an equitable level. For example, underpaid people may reduce the quantity of their production, work shorter hours, be absent more frequently, and so on.
- People may change their outcomes to restore equity. Many union organizers try to attract nonmembers by pledging to improve working conditions, hours, and pay without an increase in employee effort (input).
- People may distort their own inputs and outcomes. As opposed to actually changing inputs or outcomes, people may mentally distort them to achieve a more favorable balance. For example, people who feel inequitably treated may distort how hard they work (This job is a piece of cake.) or attempt to increase the importance of the job to the organization (This really is an important job!).

**Figure 5.7**     **Inequity as a Motivational Process**

- People may leave the organization or request a transfer to another department. In doing so, they hope to find an equitable balance.
- People may shift to a new reference group to reduce the source of the inequity. The star high school athlete who doesn't get a scholarship to a major university might decide that a smaller school has more advantages, thereby justifying a need to look at smaller schools when making a selection.
- People may distort the inputs or outcomes of others. They may come to believe that others in a comparison group actually work harder than they do and therefore deserve greater rewards.

Keeping these six actions in mind, let's take a look at employee theft as a reaction to inequity. Employee theft is one of the most serious problems facing organizations. Each day they lose an average of $9 per employee. One of every 28 employees is stealing from his organization. Cashier dishonesty accounts for 48 percent of theft in supermarkets, and the average theft of people working in restaurants is $1,500 per year. The American Management Association estimates that employee theft costs U.S. organizations more than $400 billion a year. Of that amount, about $250 billion is stolen from retail department stores and over the Internet. Theft is up almost 22.2 percent a year for the past 5 years. After reading both accounts in the following Managing Ethics Competency feature, how would you explain such behaviors?

## COMPETENCY:    MANAGING ETHICS

### EMPLOYEE THEFT

#### Account 1

An employee is working out of town for several days. One evening, he has dinner and returns to the hotel room. Flipping through the TV channels, he finds a movie that he wants to watch and does so. When he checks out the next day a $5 item appears on the hotel bill. For what? A pay-per-view movie. The employee submits his expense account for the week. The hotel bill is $500. The accounts payable clerk crosses off the $5 movie charge and reimburses the employee $495 for the hotel bill. Why? Because movies are a personal expense and their reimbursement is against company policy.

#### Account 2

A young couple purchased a home in an exclusive area of Dallas and applied for membership in Stonebriar Country Club, which has an entrance fee of $38,500. On the application the wife indicated that she worked as a clerk for a local bank. The country club manager called her manager to verify employment. The husband was a local high school math teacher. The club manager called the local school district to verify his employment. The bank manager was aware of the high entrance fee at Stonebriar and the costs of homes in the area that the couple had purchased. On a hunch, the bank manager initiated an internal investigation, which uncovered an embezzlement of $1.8 million by the wife.

#### Explanations

In account 1, the person reasoned that he had been away from home, working 10 to 12 hours a day. He's earning his company three times his salary of $65,000. He's missing his kids' soccer games and parent–teacher meetings. He feels justified in charging this small amount to the company for relaxation.

In account 2, the wife was motivated to steal from her bank because she and her husband needed money to support a lifestyle that their friends enjoyed. She believed that the bank owed her more money because she was more highly qualified (she had a college degree, was older, and had worked at the bank for more than 15 years before accepting this position) for her job than any of the other clerks (all of whom were only high school graduates, 19 years old, and were working at their first jobs).[25]

## PROCEDURAL JUSTICE: MAKING DECISIONS FAIRLY

Equity theory focuses on the outcomes people receive after they have expended effort, time, or other inputs. It doesn't deal with how decisions leading to outcomes were made in the first place. Procedural justice examines the impact of the *process* used to make a decision. The perceived fairness of rules and procedures is referred to as **procedural justice**.[26] Procedural justice holds that employees are going to be more motivated to perform at a high level when they perceive as fair the procedures used to make decisions about the distribution of outcomes. In organizations procedural justice is very important to most employees, who are motivated to attain fairness in how decisions are made, as well as in the decisions themselves.

Reactions to pay raises, for example, are greatly affected by employees' perceptions about the fairness of the raises. If in the minds of the employees the pay raises were administered fairly, the employees were more satisfied with their increases than if the employees judged the procedures used to make these increases to be unfair. The perceived fairness of the procedures used to allocate pay raises is a better predictor of satisfaction than the absolute amount of pay received. Similarly, students base their faculty member evaluations on perceptions of fair grading decisions.

In both the pay and evaluation situations, the individual can't directly control the decision but can react to the procedures used to make it. Even when a particular decision has negative outcomes for the individual, fair procedures help ensure that the individual feels that her interests are being protected.

Employees' assessments of procedural justice have also been related to their trust in management, intention to leave the organization, evaluation of their supervisor, employee theft, and job satisfaction. Consider some of the relatively trivial day-to-day issues in an organization that are affected by procedural justice: decisions about who will cover the phones during lunch while others are away from their desks, the choice of the site of the company picnic, or who gets the latest software for a personal computer.

Procedural justice has also been found to affect the attitudes of workers who survive a layoff. When workers are laid off, survivors (those who remain on the job) are often in a good position to judge the fairness of the layoff in terms of how it was handled. When a layoff is handled fairly, survivors feel more committed to the organization than when they believe that the laid-off workers were treated unfairly.[27]

### Organizational Citizenship Behavior: Going Beyond the Call of Duty.   In many organizations, employees perform tasks that are not formally required.[28] **Organizational citizenship behavior** exceeds formal job duties but is necessary for the organization's survival or important to its image and acceptance. Examples of organizational citizenship behavior include helping coworkers solve problems, making constructive suggestions, volunteering to perform community service work (e.g., blood drives, United Way campaigns, and charity work). Although not formally required by employers, these behaviors are important in all organizations. Helping coworkers is an especially important form of organizational citizenship behavior when it comes to computers. Every organization has some computer gurus, but often it's the secretary who doesn't go to lunch who can fix a problem easier and without putting down the

struggling user. Managers often underestimate the amount of this informal helping that takes place in organizations.

Employees have considerable discretion over whether to engage in organizational citizenship behaviors. Employees who have been treated fairly and are satisfied are more likely to do so than employees who feel unfairly treated. Fairly treated employees engage in citizenship behaviors because they want to give something back to the organization. Most people desire to have fair exchanges with coworkers and others in their organization.

Ray Hertz, a marketing consultant for the Internet & New Media division of EDS, developed a simple yet innovative method to acknowledge organizational citizenship behaviors at his Dallas office. At the beginning of the year, Hertz gives each of his 10 employees a jar containing 12 marbles. Throughout the year, employees may give marbles to others who have helped them in some way or who have provided an extraordinary service. Employees are recognized throughout the year and are proud of the number of marbles they accumulate, even though they receive no monetary reward from Hertz.

**Organizational Uses.**   Managers often use the equity model in making a variety of decisions, such as taking disciplinary actions, giving pay raises, allocating office and parking space, and dispensing other perquisites (perks). The equity model leads to two primary conclusions. First, employees should be treated fairly. When individuals believe that they are not being treated fairly, they will try to correct the situation and reduce tension by means of one or more of the types of actions identified previously in this section. A sizable inequity increases the probability that individuals will choose more than one type of action to reduce it. For example, individuals may partially withdraw from the organization by being absent more often, arriving at work late, not completing assignments on time, or stealing. The organization may try to reduce the inputs of such employees by assigning them to monotonous jobs, taking away some perks, and giving them only small pay increases.

Second, people make decisions concerning equity only after they compare their inputs and outcomes with those of comparable employees.[29] These relevant others may be employees of the same organization or of other organizations. The latter present a major problem for managers, who cannot control what other organizations pay their employees. For example, Ralph Sorrentino, a partner at Deloitte Consulting, hired a recent business school undergraduate for $43,500, the maximum the company could pay for the job. The new employee thought that this salary was very good until she compared it to the $48,250 that fellow graduates were getting at Accenture, McKinsey, and Bain. She felt that she was being underpaid in comparison with her former classmates, causing an inequity problem for her (and the company).[30]

The idea that fairness in organizations is determined by more than just money has received a great deal of attention from managers. Organizational fairness is influenced by how rules and procedures are used and how much employees are consulted in decisions that affect them.

# CHAPTER SUMMARY

**1.** Define motivation and describe the motivational process.

A six-stage motivational model indicates that individuals behave in certain ways to satisfy their needs. Managers have three motivational challenges—motives can only be inferred, needs are dynamic, and there are considerable differences in people's motivations.

**2.** Describe two basic human needs approaches to motivation.

Two human needs models of motivation are widely recognized. Maslow proposed that people have five types of needs: physiological, security, affiliation, esteem, and self-actualization and that when a need is satisfied it no longer motivates a person.

McClelland believed that people have three learned needs (achievement, affiliation, and power) that are rooted in the culture of a society. We focused on the role of the achievement need and indicated the characteristics associated with high achievers, including that they like to set their own moderate goals and perform tasks that give them immediate feedback.

**3.** Explain how the design of jobs affects motivation.

Herzberg claimed that two types of factors affect a person's motivation: motivators and hygienes. Motivators, such as job challenge, lead to job satisfaction but not to job dissatisfaction. Hygiene factors, such as working conditions, prevent job dissatisfaction but can't lead to job satisfaction. Managers need to structure jobs that focus on motivators because they lead to high job satisfaction and performance.

**4.** Describe the expectancy model of motivation.

The expectancy model holds that individuals know what they desire from work. They choose activities only after they decide that the activities will satisfy their needs. The primary components of this model are first- and second-level outcomes, expectancy, instrumentality, and valence. An individual must believe that effort expended will lead (expectancy) to some desired level of performance (first-level outcome) and that this level of performance will lead (instrumentality) to desired rewards (second-level outcomes and valences). Otherwise, the individual won't be motivated to expend the effort necessary to perform at the desired level.

**5.** Explain how feelings of equity affect motivation.

The equity model focuses on the individual's perception of how fairly he is treated in comparison to others in similar situations. To make this judgment, an individual compares his inputs (experience, age) and outcomes (salary) to those of relevant others. If equity exists, the person isn't motivated to act. If inequity exists, the person may engage in any one of six behaviors to reduce this inequity. Both procedural justice and organizational citizenship behavior are based on the equity model and have significant implications for employees' perceptions of equity. Procedural justice examines the impact of the process (rules and procedures) used to make a decision. Organizational citizenship behaviors are employee behaviors that go above and beyond their job requirements.

# KEY TERMS AND CONCEPTS

Ability
Achievement motivation model
Affiliation needs
Deficiency needs
Equity model
Esteem needs
Expectancy
Expectancy model
Extrinsic factors
First-level outcomes
Goal
Growth needs
Hygiene factors
Inequity
Inputs
Instrumentality

Intrinsic factors
Motivation
Motivator–hygiene model
Motivator factors
Needs
Needs hierarchy model
Organizational citizenship behavior
Outcomes
Physiological needs
Procedural justice
Second-level outcomes
Security needs
Self-actualization needs
Thematic Apperception Test (TAT)
Valence

## DISCUSSION QUESTIONS

1. "I'm bored," says Sam Wesson, a clerk at Home Depot. What would you recommend to make Wesson's job more interesting?
2. Think about the worst job you've had. What motivational approach was used in that organization? Now think about the best job you've had. What motivational approach was used in that organization?
3. Identify the hygiene factors in the Starbucks Preview Case. According to Herzberg, what role do they play? Do hygiene factors attract people to jobs? Explain.
4. What are your own assumptions about motivation? How do they reflect the culture in which you were raised?
5. Why is job satisfaction not strongly related to job performance?
6. How could someone like John Schnatter, CEO of Papa John's, apply McClelland's model of motivation to motivate his employees?
7. Why might an employee with a low level of motivation be a top performer?
8. Why were managers at Dean Foods successful in motivating employees?
9. Imagine that you have just been selected to become a new sales manager for Dell Computers in Romania. What would you do to motivate employees to become high producers?
10. What steps can an organization take to encourage procedural justice by its managers?
11. If treating employees fairly and establishing equitable relationships at work are important, what steps can managers take to be sure that people are being treated fairly?

## DEVELOPING COMPETENCIES

### Competency: Managing Self

### What Do You Want from Your Job?

We have listed the 16 most often mentioned characteristics that employees want from their jobs in random order. Please rank them in order of both their importance to you and then in terms of satisfaction for you. Rank these characteristics 1 (most important), 2 (next most important), 3 (next most important), and so on, through 16 (least important). Use the same procedure to rank satisfaction. Then compare your answers to those of managers working in a wide variety of jobs and industries provided at the end of this exercise.

| Job Characteristics | Importance Rank | Satisfaction Rank |
|---|---|---|
| 1. Working independently | _____ | _____ |
| 2. Chances for promotion | _____ | _____ |
| 3. Contact with people | _____ | _____ |
| 4. Flexible hours | _____ | _____ |
| 5. Health insurance and other benefits | _____ | _____ |
| 6. Interesting work | _____ | _____ |
| 7. Work important to society | _____ | _____ |
| 8. Job security | _____ | _____ |
| 9. Opportunity to learn new skills | _____ | _____ |
| 10. High income | _____ | _____ |
| 11. Recognition from team members | _____ | _____ |
| 12. Vacation time | _____ | _____ |

| Job Characteristics | Importance Rank | Satisfaction Rank |
|---|---|---|
| 13. Regular hours | _____ | _____ |
| 14. Working close to home | _____ | _____ |
| 15. Little job stress | _____ | _____ |
| 16. A job in which I can help others | _____ | _____ |

### Answers Given by Managers

For job importance, the rank order of characteristics is 1-6; 2-14; 3-15; 4-16; 5-1; 6-2; 7-13; 8-3; 9-4; 10-11; 12-5; 13-8; 14-12; 15-10; 16-9.

For job satisfaction, the rank order of characteristics is 1-3; 2-14; 3-2; 4-6; 5-13; 6-4; 7-9; 8-7; 9-11; 10-12; 11-15; 12-8; 13-5; 14-1; 15-16; 16-10.[31]

### Questions

1. Choose any model of motivation and think about your answers. What situational factors (e.g., being in school, looking for a new job, desiring more responsibility, desiring to work for a foreign organization, and the like) influenced your ranking of importance?
2. What characteristics gave most of the respondents their greatest job satisfaction? What model of motivation helps you understand these rankings?

## Competency: Managing Change

# Carol Bernick, President of Alberto-Culver, North America

In 1994 when Carol Bernick and her husband took over the reins of a company that her father and mother had built, they faced flat sales and poor profitability on Culver's best-known brands—Alberto VO5, St. Ives, and Mrs. Dash. Retailer consolidation was under way, and the competitive nature of the industry was tough. Colgate-Palmolive, L'Oreal, and Unilever all had superior marketing and manufacturing. Total sales of all Alberto-Culver products were under $350 million. The Bernicks looked around and realized that the organization wasn't equal to the challenge. In an effort not to hurt people, her parents had sheltered employees from the details of the operation and the business realities facing the firm (losing market share, high costs, etc.).

In an effort to change employee motivation, Carol Bernick engaged a consulting firm to study the level of job satisfaction of the company's employees. The results devastated her. Even the company's best performers complained about noncompetitive benefits, hard to understand policies, the lack of family-friendly policies, infrequent performance evaluations, lack of team spirit, and the like. As soon as she received the survey, she decided to make changes. She started the process by scattering pennies on the floor before her "state of the company" address. As she waited for people to be seated, she noticed that no one picked up any pennies. After her speech, she asked the group: "Can anyone name our best-selling product?" The response came back VO5 shampoo. She then asked: "What are the profits from VO5?" The group didn't answer, but then she said "Look on the floor, and if you spot a penny, pick it up. That penny represents our total profit on one bottle of VO5 shampoo." The process of turning employees into businesspeople had begun.

She created a new position called growth development leader (GDL). There are now about 70 of these positions in the company. The people who occupy them are involved in the careers and lives of their subordinates, helping them set goals that contribute to Culver's profitability, participating in their performance review processes, and being sure that they understand and take advantage of Culver's benefits and human resource policies. Annually, the GDLs and their employees split into four teams and are given 15 minutes to agree on the four biggest challenges facing the business and the four most irritating aspects of their job. After the teams come up with their lists, they are told: "Okay, you're the CEO. You have only so many resources, and you can't do it all. Which four deserve attention?" At a recent meeting, the top irritation was that there weren't enough laptops for each person who is traveling to have one. Bernick immediately ordered laptops for everyone who had to travel. She also noticed that lots of irritations, such as Culver's lack of personal days and no direct deposits of paychecks, needed to be taken care of before employees could really think about strategic issues.

She is a firm believer that you need to measure change. Therefore once a year all employees are asked a series of questions, such as "How often does your GDL meet with you?" and "During the last year, has the GDL made you feel better, the same, or worse about working for Alberto-Culver?" Once the results have been tabulated, she recognizes all GDLs who scored well in key categories and the overall best-scoring GDLs are given company stock. She personally sits down and talks with all GDLs about their results and what drives them.

Bernick and her staff celebrate successes that teams and individuals achieve during the year. Recently, the company threw a surprise thank-you party to celebrate an exceptional year (sales exceeded $600 million). Alberto-Culver has a Business Builder Award, given to individuals who make a real impact on its growth and profitability. Employees also have a chance to vote in People's Choice Awards. Employees vote for the person they'd most like to have on their team, the person who blends in commitment to a local community with high performance at Alberto-Culver, and even the person with the best hair. All these reward programs are designed to reinforce the central point: Individuals make a difference, and companies don't succeed—people do.[32]

## Questions

1. What's Carol Bernick's philosophy for motivating employees at Alberto-Culver?
2. What employee needs is she reaching by her reward programs?
3. What do you think motivates people to be a GDL?

# CHAPTER

# Motivating Individuals for High Performance

## LEARNING OBJECTIVES

When you have finished studying the chapter, you should be able to:

1. Explain how performance is affected by goal setting.
2. Describe reward systems for fostering high performance.

6

## ENTERPRISE RENT-A-CAR

Enterprise Rent-A-Car was founded by Jack Crawford in 1957 and is now run by his son. This privately held company started out as a small auto-leasing business and moved into car rentals in the late 1960s with a very different strategy from that of Hertz, Avis, and Budget. Only 5 percent of its $6.3 billion in revenue comes from airport locations; 95 percent is generated through its 4,800 outlets in suburban markets. The company opens, on average, one new office every business day somewhere in the world. Enterprise currently has contracts with 63 percent of the body shops and insurance replacement businesses in North America. It provides body shops with a Web site tracking device, an appealing feature for small auto-repair shops. Instead of spending time on the phone giving customers an estimate of when their vehicles will be ready, mechanics can post estimates on the Web site. In this way, Enterprise knows when to expect its vehicles back and can notify customers about theirs. This approach saves an estimated eight to nine phone calls per customer.

Enterprise's success can be traced to how it manages its employees. It recruits heavily at colleges and promotes from within. Today's chief financial officer started out washing cars just like everybody else and moved up through the ranks based on his performance. Graduates are lured by the prospect of earning a substantial salary. Enterprise teaches recruits how to find leads, uses role-playing to simulate customers, and generously rewards high performance. If a customer forgets her driver's license at home, an agent will drive her back to pick it up. If the license has expired, he'll take her to obtain a new one. Everyone, from management assistant to branch manager, gets a base salary of about $30,000, plus a sliding percentage of profits generated by their branch. Thus employees are highly motivated to push extra services. Some branches offer incentives based on the number of collision-damage waivers they sell (an extra $9 a day); others reward employees for steering customers to Enterprise outlets that sell preowned cars (Enterprise buys and sells more than 400,000 autos a year). Employee turnover is crucial in the car-rental industry, averaging 31 percent a year, because of the long hours; at Enterprise, though, turnover is less than 25 percent. One reason for the lower turnover is that employees work in teams of less than 10 people. In these teams, individuals think about building relationships with the people with whom they work.

Enterprise is basically an organization of independent profit centers. Once a branch grows to 200 cars, the company usually opens a new branch, sometimes less than 2 miles away. All employees are ranked, and pay is based on monthly reports of customer satisfaction. Employees who rank in the bottom half for their outlet aren't eligible for promotion. In an effort to improve their ranking, however, some employees have deliberately changed digits in an unhappy customer's phone number. That way, the outside firm that does monthly follow-up phone interviews can't reach the unhappy customer.[1]

For more information on Enterprise Rent-A-Car, visit the organization's home page at http://www.enterprise.com.

To survive in today's global competitive market, setting challenging goals that take into account the crucial factors of time and quality and providing feedback to employees is no longer an option. It must happen!

The motivational practices that produce the achievements in Enterprise Rent-A-Car are based on setting goals, developing feedback systems, and providing reward systems that get individuals to strive to reach those goals. Goals play an important part in motivating individuals to strive for high performance. The basic concepts in goal setting remain an important source for motivating employees. At PPG Industries, a Pittsburgh-based paint and glass manufacturer that employs more than 36,000 worldwide, employee objectives are called "SMART" goals, an acronym for "Specific, Measurable, Agreed-upon by the employee and manager, Realistic, and Timebound," says George Kock, director of human resource and planning. Before the SMART goal system was implemented, a sales manager would be told by her boss to increase sales over the next year. Now she might be asked to develop, by September 30, three new customers in the Southeast region with annual sales volumes of $100,000 each. Under the SMART system, performance has increased by more than 25 percent.[2]

In this chapter, we begin by presenting a model of goal setting and performance based on the individual. Then we focus on four commonly used reward systems that reinforce desired behaviors of employees.

Learning Objective:

1. Explain how performance is affected by goal setting.

# MODEL OF GOAL SETTING AND PERFORMANCE

**Goals** are future outcomes (results) that individuals and groups desire and strive to achieve.[3] An example of an individual goal is: I intend to graduate with a 3.0 grade point average by the end of the spring semester, 2006. **Goal setting** is the process of specifying desired outcomes toward which individuals, teams, departments, and organizations will strive and is intended to increase organizational efficiency and effectiveness.

## IMPORTANCE OF GOAL SETTING

The goal-setting process is no easy task, but the effort is not only worthwhile, it is also becoming essential in the current highly competitive global business and institutional environments. The most important reasons for having goals include the following.

- Goals guide and direct behavior. They increase role clarity by focusing effort and attention in specific directions, thereby reducing uncertainty in day-to-day decision making.
- Goals provide challenges and indicators against which individual, team, departmental, or organizational performance can be assessed.
- Goals justify the performance of various tasks and the use of resources to pursue them.
- Goals define the basis for the organization's design. They determine, in part, communication patterns, authority relationships, power relationships, and division of labor.
- Goals serve an organizing function.
- Goals reflect what employees and managers alike consider important and thus provide a framework for planning and control activities.[4]

Just as organizations strive to achieve certain goals, individuals also are motivated to strive for and attain goals. In fact, the goal-setting process is one of the most important motivational tools for affecting the performance of employees in organizations. In this section we consider one of the most widely accepted models of goal setting and indicate how goal-setting techniques can be applied to motivate individuals and teams.

Ed Locke and Gary Latham developed a sophisticated model of individual goal setting and performance. Figure 6.1 presents a simplified version of their model.[5] It shows the key variables and the general relationships that can lead to high individual performance, some of which we have discussed in previous chapters. The basic idea behind this model is that a goal serves as a motivator because it allows people to compare their present performance with that required to achieve the goal. To the extent that people believe they will fall short of a goal, they will feel dissatisfied and work harder to attain it so long as they believe that it can be achieved. Having a goal also may improve performance because the goal makes clear the type and level of performance expected. John Schnatter's goals for Papa John's are very clear: Expand the business by 10 percent a year, hire drivers who maintain safe-driving records, and deliver a hot pizza to every customer within 30 minutes. Such goals clearly communicate performance expectations to all the company's employees. By reviewing performance against the goals each year, Schnatter also shows employees how well they're doing in terms of these agreed upon targets. With this background in mind, let's consider the basic features of the Locke–Latham goal-setting model.

## CHALLENGE

Stated another way, goal setting is the process of developing, negotiating, and establishing targets that challenge the individual. Employees with unclear goals or no goals are prone to work slowly, perform poorly, exhibit a lack of interest, and accomplish less than employees whose goals are clear and challenging. In addition, employees with clearly defined goals appear to be more energetic and productive. They get things done on time and then move on to other activities (and goals).

Goals may be implicit or explicit, vague or clearly defined, and self-imposed or externally imposed. Whatever their form, goals serve to structure the individual's time and effort. Two key attributes of goals are particularly important: goal difficulty and goal clarity.

- **Goal difficulty.** A goal should be challenging but not impossible to achieve. If it is too easy, the individual may delay or approach the goal lackadaisically. If it is too difficult, the individual may not really accept the goal and thus not try to meet it.

**Figure 6.1**                    **Model of Goal Setting**

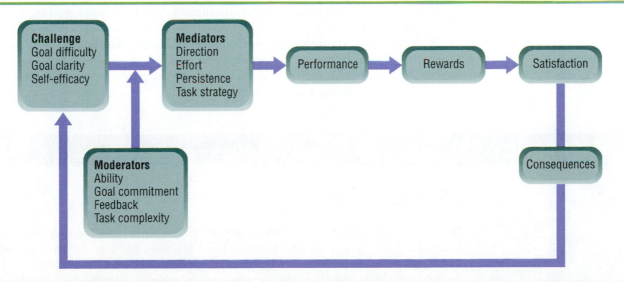

Source: Adapted from Locke, E. A., and Latham, G. P. *A Theory of Goal Setting and Task Performance.* Englewood Cliffs, N.J.: Prentice-Hall, 1990, 253.

- **Goal clarity.** A goal must be clear and specific if it is to be useful in directing effort. The individual thus will know what is expected and not have to guess. FedEx's customer service agents are expected to answer customers' questions within 140 seconds.

Clear and challenging goals lead to higher performance than do vague or general goals. **Management by Objectives** (MBO) is a management system that uses goal difficulty and goal clarity as its foundation for motivating employees. In essence this management system involves managers and employees jointly setting goals for performance and personal development, periodically evaluating the employee's progress toward achieving these goals, and then rewarding the employee. One company that has made extensive use of management by objectives is Texas Industries (TXI) of Dallas, which sells more than $1.3 billion worth of concrete, steel, and dirt a year. Robert Rogers, TXI's president, installed a goal-setting program that pays employees as much as 20 percent of their salaries if product innovations they come up with are implemented. Barnett Reese, a TXI sales manager in Houston, developed a way to mix red clay and slag. This mixture absorbs wetness and is now used in the infields at many major league baseball parks. Selling for more than $100 a ton, or 10 times the ingredients' worth, Reese's innovation is extremely profitable and he was well rewarded for it. Rogers and his top management team have set a company goal of earning 15 percent of the company's total revenues from innovative products each year. Rogers believes that setting the goal at a specific amount (e.g., 15 percent) is better than setting a goal of "trying to be innovative" or "doing your best."[6] Goals that are difficult but not impossible lead to higher performance than do easy goals. However, unrealistically high goals may not be accepted or may lead to high performance only in the short run. Individuals eventually get discouraged and stop trying, as predicted by the expectancy model (see Chapter 5).

Along with goal difficulty and clarity, a third key factor that influences the establishment of challenging goals is self-efficacy. In Chapter 4, we defined self-efficacy as the individual's belief that he can perform at a certain level in a given situation. As might be expected, individuals who set high goals perform at a high level when they also have high self-efficacy. A person's self-efficacy is dependent on the task. For example, a golfer with a low handicap has high self-efficacy on the golf course. But the same person might have low self-efficacy when meeting sales quotas for a new piece of equipment that her company has just introduced.[7]

With clear and challenging goals, employee behaviors are more likely to be focused on job-related tasks, high levels of performance, and goal achievement. Table 6.1 on page 150, provides a summary of the key links between goal setting and individual performance.

The following Managing Teams Competency feature illustrates how people in teams use the basic concepts of goal challenge, goal clarity, and self-efficacy to instill teamwork. In NASCAR racing, it is often how well the pit crew performs that determines whether the driver wins the race.

## COMPETENCY: MANAGING TEAMS

### NASCAR RACING

Ray Evernham is considered by many NASCAR people to be a premier crew chief. Over the past 5 years, he and Jeff Gordon have won more races than any other NASCAR team. Evernham and Gordon give much of the credit to their pit crew, known as the Rainbow Warriors, because crew members wear rainbow-striped jumpsuits.

When the Rainbow Warriors crew was assembled more than 5 years ago, its members decided to do things differently. In the past, mechanics that had worked on a race car all week also suited up on Sunday to work as the pit crew. The car was the number one priority, and the crew relied on horsepower and the driver to win the race. Pit crews didn't practice and set goals. Evernham and Gordon knew that all drivers have essentially the same equipment. The ingredient that would separate winning from losing drivers was their ability to create a team. They decided to have two crews: The first crew was responsible for the mechanics of the car (e.g., engine and suspension components); the second—the pit crew—was responsible for the car during the race.

Under Evernham and Gordon's leadership, the Rainbow Warriors hired a coach to develop specifically the teamwork competency of the pit crew. Training included rope climbing, scaling walls, wind sprints, guys carrying each other on their backs, and the like. All members of the pit crew also needed to be trained to perform all necessary tasks so that they could rotate tasks among themselves, depending on race conditions. By analyzing other NASCAR drivers, Evernham determined that, if Gordon's car could leave the pit 1 second faster than the competition, Gordon would gain 300 feet on the competition (a car going 200 mph travels nearly 300 feet a second). The pit crew set a goal of having the car exit the pit in 17 seconds or less. During a race, all crew members listen to each other on their scanners. They use special code words to signal whether they are changing two or four tires when Gordon pulls into the pit. The crew also determines whether to gas the car fully or just to put in enough gas to finish the race. Evernham and his crew also determine when Gordon should come in for a pit stop. Before the race, all the Rainbow Warriors sit in a circle to discuss race strategy. The circle symbolizes that the team is stronger than any individual. When Gordon wins a race, signs a personal services contract, or is paid to sign autographs, all the members of both crews receive a percentage of that money.[8]

*For more information on NASCAR, visit the organization's home page at http://www.nascar.com.*

## MODERATORS

Figure 6.1 also shows four of the factors that moderate the strength of the relationship between goals and performance: ability, goal commitment, feedback, and task complexity. We begin with ability because it limits an individual's capacity to respond to a challenge.

**Ability.**    The relation of goal difficulty to performance is curvilinear, not linear. That is, performance levels off as the limits of a person's ability are approached. In Chapter 2, we discussed the two types of goal orientation—performance and learning—that can affect a person's ability to perform. Individuals with a learning goal orientation believe that they have the ability to acquire new competencies and master new situations. They seek challenging new assignments that open their eyes to new ways of doing tasks. Those with a performance goal orientation believe that their ability to complete a task is relatively stable and avoid placing themselves in situations in which they might receive a negative evaluation.[9]

**Goal Commitment.**    The second factor, **goal commitment**, refers to an individual's determination to reach a goal, regardless of whether the goal was set by that person or someone else.[10] What is your goal commitment in this class? Take a minute and complete the questionnaire in Table 6.2. Your commitment to achieve a goal is likely to be stronger if you make it publicly, if you have a strong need for achievement, and if you believe that you can control the activities that will help you reach that goal.

**Table 6.1**

| WHEN GOALS ARE | PERFORMANCE WILL TEND TO BE |
|---|---|
| Specific and clear | Higher |
| Vague | Lower |
| Difficult and challenging | Higher |
| Easy and boring | Lower |
| Set participatively | Higher |
| Set by management (top down) | Lower |
| Accepted by employees | Higher |
| Rejected by employees | Lower |
| Accompanied by rewards | Higher |
| Unrelated to rewards | Lower |

*Impact of Goals on Performance*

The effect of participation on goal commitment is complex. Positive goal commitment is more likely if employees participate in setting their goals, which often leads to a sense of ownership. Not expecting or wanting to be involved in goal setting reduces the importance of employee participation in terms of goal commitment. Even when a manager has to assign goals without employee participation, doing so leads to more focused efforts and better performance than if no goals were set.

The expected rewards for achieving goals play an important role in the degree of goal commitment. The greater the extent to which employees believe that positive re-

**Table 6.2**

**Goal Commitment Questionnaire**

| ITEM | RESPONSE CATEGORY | | | | |
|---|---|---|---|---|---|
| | Strongly Agree | Agree | Undecided | Disagree | Strongly Disagree |
| 1. I am strongly committed to achieving a grade of _____ . | _____ | _____ | _____ | _____ | _____ |
| 2. I am willing to expend the effort needed to achieve this goal. | _____ | _____ | _____ | _____ | _____ |
| 3. I really care about achieving this grade. | _____ | _____ | _____ | _____ | _____ |
| 4. Much personal satisfaction can be gained if I achieve this grade. | _____ | _____ | _____ | _____ | _____ |
| 5. Revising my goal, depending on how other classes go, isn't likely. | _____ | _____ | _____ | _____ | _____ |
| 6. A lot would have to happen to abandon my grade goal. | _____ | _____ | _____ | _____ | _____ |
| 7. Expecting to reach my grade goal in this class is realistic for me. | _____ | _____ | _____ | _____ | _____ |

**Scoring:** Give yourself 5 points for each Strongly Agree response; 4 points for each Agree response; 3 points for each Undecided response; 2 points for each Disagree response; and 1 point for each Strongly Disagree response. The higher your total score, the greater is your commitment to achieve your grade goal in this class.

Source: Adapted from VandeWalle, D., Cron, W. L., and Slocum, J. W., Jr. Effects of feedback on goal setting. Unpublished paper, SMU, Cox School of Business, Dallas, Texas, 2000; Hollenbeck, J. R., Williams, C. R., and Klein, H. J. An empirical examination of the antecedents of commitment to goals. *Journal of Applied Psychology*, 1989, 74, 18–23.

wards (merit pay raises, bonuses, promotions, opportunities to perform interesting tasks, and the like) are contingent on achieving goals, the greater is their commitment to the goals. These notions are similar to the ideas contained in the expectancy model of motivation. Similarly, if employees expect to be punished for not achieving goals, the probability of goal commitment also is higher. However, recall that punishment and the fear of punishment as the primary means of guiding behavior may create long-term problems (see Chapter 4).

Employees compare expected rewards against rewards actually received. If received rewards are consistent with expected rewards, the reward system is likely to continue to support goal commitment. If employees think that the rewards they receive are much less than the rewards they expected, they may perceive inequity. If perceived or actual inequity exists, employees eventually lessen their goal commitment. Teamwork and peer pressures are other factors that affect a person's commitment to a goal. IBM recently launched a Web site for its 9,000 salespeople. The initial prompt asks a salesperson for his title, job description, and base salary. Following the representative's response, another window opens, showing information on that person's progress toward meeting goals that had been set. Getting such personalized information to each salesperson was a complex and challenging task. Now that the task has been accomplished, each salesperson can use the data to calculate the difference between hitting, say, 105 percent and 115 percent of a quota. IBM spends millions of dollars annually on incentives, so employees are anxious to know how their performance at any particular time compares to their goals. The more than 3,500 people who regularly check their personal data reflect the advantages of receiving timely and accurate feedback. The Web site averages 500 hits a day, and hits usually peak at the end of each quarter.[11]

**Feedback.**    Feedback makes goal setting and individual responses to goal achievement (performance) a dynamic process. It provides information to the employee and others about outcomes and the degree of employee performance.[12] Feedback enables the individual to relate received rewards to those expected in terms of actual performance. This comparison, in turn, can influence changes in the degree of goal commitment.

**Task Complexity.**    Task complexity is the last moderator of the strength of the relationship between goals and performance that we consider. For simple tasks (e.g., answering telephones at Marriott's reservation center), the effort encouraged by challenging goals leads directly to high task performance. For more complex tasks (e.g., studying to achieve a high grade), effort doesn't lead directly to effective performance. The individual must also decide where and how to allocate effort.

## MEDIATORS

Let's assume that an individual has challenging goals and that the moderating factors support achievement of these goals. How do the four mediators—direction, effort, persistence, and task strategy—affect performance? *Direction of attention* focuses behaviors on activities expected to result in goal achievement and steers the individual away from activities irrelevant to achieving the goals. The *effort* a person exerts usually depends on the difficulty of the goal. That is, the greater the challenge, the greater will be the effort expended, assuming that the person is committed to reaching the goal. *Persistence* involves a person's willingness to work at the task over an extended period of time until the results are achieved. Most sports require participants to practice long and hard to hone their competencies and maintain them at a high level. Finally, *task strategy* is the way in which an individual—often through experience and instruction—decides to tackle a task.

## PERFORMANCE

Performance is likely to be high when (1) challenging goals have been set, (2) the moderators (ability, goal commitment, feedback, and task complexity) are present, and (3) the mediators (direction, effort, persistence, and task strategy) are operating. Columbia Energy Service Corporation, a Columbus, Ohio-based organization, recently won a Wellness Council of America award for encouraging healthful lifestyles among its employees. Yearly cash incentives for six healthful behaviors or conditions were jointly set by all employees: not smoking or chewing tobacco ($100); wearing a seat belt at all times ($25); a cholesterol level below 150 ($100); blood pressure below 135/85 ($50); a waist-to-hip ratio of 0.8 or less for women and 0.95 for men ($50); and getting 30 minutes of exercise three times a week. In addition, spouses can earn half that amount by achieving these goals. Recently, the company distributed more than $20,000 and saved more than 654 percent on its health insurance premiums. Absenteeism is down and morale is up.[13]

Three basic types of quantitative indicators can be used to assess performance: units of production or quality (amount produced or number of errors); dollars (profits, costs, income, or sales); and time (attendance and promptness in meeting deadlines). When such measures are unavailable or inappropriate, qualitative goals and indicators may be used. In addition, many organizations have developed a code of ethics to support employees in setting ethical goals and making ethical decisions. Creating ethics guidelines has several advantages that Lockheed Martin, GE, and Johnson & Johnson, among others, consider important. Some of the advantages for setting ethical goals are:

- to help employees identify what their organization recognizes as acceptable behaviors;
- to legitimize the consideration of ethics as part of decision making;
- to avoid uncertainties among employees about what is right and wrong; and
- to avoid inconsistencies in decision making caused by an organizational reward system that appears to reward unethical behavior.[14]

The vast amount of information and resources available on the Internet has actually increased the need for organizations to create a code of ethics. On the one hand, employees can access Web sites to find all kinds of information that may actually help them perform their jobs and solve problems. On the other hand, they can also plan vacations, visit pornographic Web sites, shop for clothes, and trade stocks over the Internet on the organization's time. Such behaviors have raised ethical dilemmas for organizations as the following Managing Ethics Competency feature illustrates.

## COMPETENCY:   MANAGING ETHICS

### SURFING THE WEB AT WORK

A growing problem for more and more organizations is employee Web surfing at work. A recent survey indicated that 90 percent of employees said they surfed for nonwork-related sites during the day. What are they surfing for? Look at the list:

- 72% read the news;
- 45% make travel arrangements;
- 40% make purchases;

- 37% do job searches;
- 34% check stock prices;
- 28% coordinate social events; and
- 4% visit pornographic sites.

This behavior creates an ethical dilemma for many organizations. On the one hand, employees value their privacy, and access to the Internet has become almost a perk. Charles Schwab and Company estimates that the majority of stock trades made using its online broker are made from organizations' offices during working hours. When an employee surfs the Web on his employer's time, not only is his job performance likely to suffer, but he also is stealing time and thus money from the organization. Xerox recently fired 40 of its employees for visiting pornographic Web sites on the job, which is prohibited by Xerox's code of ethics. Associates First Capital, a division of Citigroup, fired managers who left pornographic materials on their computer screens while at lunch—for sexual harassment—when female employees took offense at this behavior and complained. Other organizations have found employees coming in on weekends to surf sexually explicit Web sites while being paid overtime.

Many organizations have Web traffic monitoring systems, but the real issue is how to create a code of ethics by which Web surfing doesn't hurt performance nor violate a person's rights. Simply blocking access to Web sites can make good employees angry if they have been Web surfing on their own time (lunch hour and break times). Hoping to keep employees focused on their jobs by punishing wrongdoers might have the unintended effect of decreasing productivity. Employees may come to feel that they have no freedom to go online and find other ways to "goof off" or use their free time—some perhaps detrimental to the organization.

In organizations that utilize Web monitoring systems, employees retain some personal freedom and, at the same time, the organization can ensure that visits to Web sites are infrequent, short, and appropriate. Before an organization begins monitoring Web traffic, though, its management needs to set standards and make a commitment to their enforcement. For example, if an organization has zero tolerance for downloading sexually explicit Web pages—and management knows that employees are doing so but doesn't do anything about it—under the sexual-harassment law, it becomes liable for such behavior.[15]

## REWARDS

When an employee attains a high level of performance, rewards can become important inducements for the employee to continue to perform at that level. Rewards can be external (bonuses, paid vacations, and the like) or internal (a sense of achievement, pride in accomplishment, and feelings of success). Enterprise Rent-A-Car, IBM, and Jeff Gordon's NASCAR organization all reward people for high performance. However, what is viewed as a reward in one culture may not be viewed as a reward in another. For example, doing business in Vietnam requires the exchange of gifts during the first day of a business meeting. Although they may be small and relatively inexpensive, gifts with a company logo are highly valued. The gifts should be wrapped, but white or black paper should not be used because these colors are associated with death. In contrast, exchanging gifts at a business meeting in the United States generally is not expected. Praising an individual in public for achievement in Vietnam will embarrass the individual; rewards are not to be given in public. Conversely, public acclaim for achievement in the United States is highly valued.[16]

## SATISFACTION

Many factors—including challenging work, interesting coworkers, salary, the opportunity to learn, and good working conditions—influence a person's satisfaction with the job (see Chapter 2). However, in the Locke–Latham model, the primary focus is on the employee's degree of satisfaction with performance. Employees who set extremely high, difficult goals may experience less job satisfaction than employees who set lower, more easily achievable goals. Difficult goals are less frequently achieved, and satisfaction with performance is associated with success. Thus some compromise on goal difficulty may be necessary in order to maximize both satisfaction and performance. However, some level of satisfaction is associated with simply striving for difficult goals, such as responding to a challenge, making some progress toward reaching the goals, and the belief that benefits may still be derived from the experience regardless of the outcome.

## THE EFFECT OF GOAL SETTING ON MOTIVATION AND PERFORMANCE

Goal setting motivates individuals to achieve high performance for several reasons. First, difficult but achievable goals prompt people to concentrate on achievement of the goals. At Enterprise, agents focus on customer satisfaction goals because they know that results are measured monthly and ranked and that these rankings affect their chances for advancement. Second, difficult goals motivate people to spend lots of time and effort on developing methods for achieving them. At Enterprise, agents communicate with customers, sometimes at length, so that the agents understand their needs and provide the most suitable vehicles to them, whether it be a sedan, convertible, pickup, or SUV. Customer satisfaction and loyalty are critical to the success of the business. Third, difficult goals increase people's persistence in trying to achieve them. If people perceive that goals can be reached by luck or with little effort, they tend to dismiss the goals as irrelevant and not follow through with the actions needed to reach them.

To sum up, specific, difficult goals affect motivation and performance by

- encouraging people to develop action plans to reach these goals,
- focusing people's attention on these goal-relevant actions,
- causing people to exert the effort necessary to achieve the goals, and
- spurring people to persist in the face of obstacles.

The following Managing Self Competency feature describes how the Chemical Group at Monsanto uses goal setting to reach its objectives by linking its performance appraisal processes with its business strategy. Using the components of the goal-setting model, the Monsanto group has created a unique performance appraisal system.

## COMPETENCY:  MANAGING SELF

### PERFORMANCE APPRAISAL AT MONSANTO

The human resource department at Monsanto was charged with redesigning the Chemical Group's performance management system to improve employee and organizational effectiveness. Interviews were conducted with more than 1,500 employees to identify the behaviors that had an impact on performance. Based on these data and a review of best practices used at other organizations, the HR department recommended the following principles.

- Focus on development rather than judgment.
- Focus employee effort on continuous improvement.
- Simplify goal setting.
- Shift the supervisory role from judgment to coaching.
- Clarify roles and increase the amount of feedback.

The following process was undertaken to carry out these recommendations. Supervisors and employees meet to establish job accountabilities and goals. Job accountabilities are the actual behaviors that directly contribute to achieving the organization's overall goals. The individuals' goals are specific accomplishments to be achieved during the year. In each case no more than five goals are set, and one must be related to the employee's personal development. The manager and subordinate try to avoid setting low goals that aren't challenging, using fuzzy language that allows for different interpretations of results, or specifying a long list of assumptions about what might go wrong. Together, the manager and subordinate develop and agree on a competency expectation profile (like the one we presented in Chapter 1). Each competency is clearly defined, and the employee's expected progress toward mastering it in her current job during the coming year is spelled out.

After a year has passed, the employee evaluates her performance according to the stated accountabilities, goals, and competency expectations. The supervisor is not allowed to edit this appraisal, and the appraisal becomes part of the employee's permanent record. At the initial goal-setting meeting, the supervisor and employee had also agreed on a list of peers and others to provide feedback from multiple viewpoints about the employee's performance. This feedback is summarized and given to the employee during a "coaching dialogue" session that the manager has with the employee. The supervisor facilitates the process and helps the employee make sense of this information, which doesn't go in the employee's permanent file. The employee and supervisor then repeat the performance appraisal cycle.[17]

*For more information on Monsanto, visit the organization's home page at http://www.monsanto.com.*

## LIMITATIONS TO GOAL SETTING

Although goal setting has been shown to increase performance in a variety of settings, you should be aware of three limitations.[18] First, when employees lack the skills and abilities needed to perform at a high level, goal setting doesn't work. Giving an employee a goal of writing a computer program will not lead to high performance if the worker doesn't know how to write such a program. To overcome this limitation, new hires at Enterprise are required to attend training sessions at which they are taught how to process requests and complaints, build customer loyalty, establish relationships with auto-body shops, and the like.

Second, when employees are given complicated tasks that require a considerable amount of learning, successful goal setting takes longer. Good performance on complicated tasks also requires that employees be able to direct all their attention to the tasks and not be interrupted by side issues. Ray Evernham's Rainbow Warriors pit crew is able to perform complicated tasks quickly because they are the only tasks that the crew is focusing on while the car is in the pit.

Third, when the goal-setting system rewards the wrong behavior, it can lead to major problems. Rod Rodin is the CEO of Marshall Industries, a billion dollar electronics distributor in Los Angeles that serves more than 30,000 customers who order more than 700,000 parts a month. He quickly recognized that the company's reward system was encouraging behaviors that led to poor service, dissatisfied customers, and, ultimately, lower profits. Rodin found that over 20 percent of each month's sales were shipped to clients during the last 3 days of the month. Managers were hiding customer returns or opening bad credit accounts just to make their monthly sales goals. Divisions were hiding products from each other or saying that products had been shipped when they really had none on hand. Salespeople fought over how to split commissions on revenue from a customer who did design work in Boston but made purchases in Dallas. Employee and team performance was reviewed and ranked on the basis of numerical criteria, such as receivables outstanding and gross sales dollars. Rodin's solution was to scrap the incentive compensation system. He declared that there would be no more contests, prizes, or bonuses for individual achievements. Everyone at Marshall was put on a salary and shared in a companywide bonus pool if the organization as a whole met its goals.[19]

## ORGANIZATIONAL USE

Individuals who are both satisfied with and committed to an organization are more likely to stay with it and to accept the challenges that it presents than are individuals who are less satisfied and committed. Turnover and absenteeism rates for satisfied individuals are low. This link brings us full circle to the beginning of the Locke–Latham goal-setting model. What might happen if things go badly and an individual who had been satisfied becomes dissatisfied? Individual responses fall into at least six categories: (1) job avoidance (quitting); (2) work avoidance (absenteeism, arriving late, and leaving early); (3) psychological defenses (alcohol and/or drug abuse); (4) constructive protest (complaining); (5) defiance (refusing to do what is asked); and (6) aggression (theft or assault). Quitting is the most common outcome of severe dissatisfaction.[20]

The goal-setting model has important implications for employees, managers, and teams alike. First, it provides an excellent framework to assist the manager or team in diagnosing the potential problems with low- or average-performing employees. Diagnostic questions might include: (1) How were the goals set? (2) Are the goals challenging? (3) What is affecting goal commitment? and (4) Does the employee know when he has done a good job? Second, it provides concrete advice to the manager on how to create a high-performance work environment. Third, it portrays the system of relationships and interplay among key factors, such as goal difficulty, goal commitment, feedback, and rewards, to achieve high performance.

**Learning Objective:**

2. Describe reward systems for fostering high performance.

# REWARD SYSTEMS FOR HIGH PERFORMANCE

In Chapters 4 and 5 we discussed types of rewards that organizations make available to employees. From the concepts discussed in those chapters, along with the concepts presented so far in this chapter, you should by now recognize that one of the basic goals of managers should be to motivate employees to perform at their highest levels. The term **high-performance work system** is often used to describe the integration of well-established methods of motivation with new technologies that link pay and performance. Managers agree that tying pay to job performance is essential. However, the actual implementation of programs designed to bring about such a relationship is often quite difficult. Questions that arise include: Should pay increases be tied to the performance of an individual or team? Recall that Rod Rodin, CEO of Marshall Industries, found that rewarding individuals created unhealthy competition among employees and destroyed morale. Deciding to reward all employees in the organization raises another question: Should the reward be based on cost savings or profits and be distributed annually or when people retire or otherwise leave the organization? The accounting procedures required by cost savings plans is enormous and complex, but if efficient they allow rewards to be distributed relatively quickly. Moreover, many employees view fringe benefits, salaries, opportunities to engage in challenging assignments, and the achievement of difficult goals as rewards.

Considerable research has been done on how rewards affect individual and team performance. From this research, the ability of rewards to motivate individuals or a team to high performance depends on six factors.

1. *Availability.* For rewards to reinforce desired performance, they must be available. Too little of a desired reward is no reward at all. For example, pay increases are often highly desired but unavailable. Moreover, pay increases that are below minimally accepted standards may actually produce negative consequences, including theft, falsifying records, and the like.
2. *Timeliness.* Like performance feedback, rewards should be given in a timely manner. A reward's motivating potential is reduced to the extent that it is separated in time from the performance it is intended to reinforce.
3. *Performance contingency.* Rewards should be closely linked with particular performances. If a goal is met, the reward is given. The clearer the linkage between performance and rewards, the better able rewards are to motivate desired behavior. Forty percent of employees nationwide believe that there is no linkage between their performance and pay.
4. *Durability.* Some rewards last longer than others. Intrinsic rewards, such as increased autonomy, challenge, and accountability, tend to last longer than extrinsic rewards, such as pay increases.
5. *Equity.* Employees' motivation to perform is improved when they believe that the pay policies of their organization are fair and equitable.
6. *Visibility.* To promote a reward system, management must ensure that rewards are visible throughout an organization. Visible rewards, such as assignments to important committees or promotion to a new job, send signals to employees that rewards are available, timely, and based on performance.

To the extent that reward systems are used to motivate employees to achieve high performance, we discuss four popular reward systems: gain-sharing, profit sharing, skill-based pay, and flexible benefit plans. The strengths and limitations of each are summarized in Table 6.3.

## GAIN-SHARING PROGRAMS

**Gain-sharing programs** are designed to share with employees the savings from productivity improvements. The underlying assumption of gain-sharing is that employees and the employer have similar goals and thus should share in economic gains. Regular cash bonuses are provided to employees for increasing productivity, reducing

**Table 6.3**

### Reward Systems in High-Performance Work Settings

| REWARD SYSTEM | STRENGTHS | LIMITATONS |
|---|---|---|
| Gain-sharing programs | Rewards employees who reach specified production levels and control costs. | Formula can be complex; employees must trust management. |
| Profit-sharing programs | Rewards organizational performance. | Individuals and teams are not likely to have an impact on overall organizational performance. |
| Skill-based pay | Rewards employee with higher pay for acquiring new skills. | Labor costs increase as employees master more skills. Employee can "top out" at the highest wage rate. |
| Flexible benefits | Tailored to fit individual needs. | Administrative costs are high and the program is difficult to use with teams. |

costs, or improving quality. According to Buck Cons, a compensation consulting organization, over 21 percent of all U.S. companies had some type of gain-sharing pay plan for their employees. The average payout for employees was 7.6 percent, up from 5.9 percent just a few years ago. Many organizations, such as Georgia-Pacific, Huffy Bicycle Company, TRW, Inland Container Corporation, and General Electric, are discovering that, when designed correctly, gain-sharing plans can contribute to employee motivation and involvement. Specific formulas tailor-made for each organization are used to calculate both performance contributions and gain-sharing awards. Many gain-sharing plans encourage employees to become involved in making decisions that will affect their rewards. Gain-sharing plans are tied to a plant, division, or department's improvement.[21]

A popular version of gain-sharing is the Scanlon plan, named after Joe Scanlon, a union leader in the 1930s.[22] The **Scanlon plan** is a system of rewards for improvements in productivity. This plan is designed to save labor costs, and incentives are calculated as a function of labor costs relative to the sales value of production. Working together, employees and managers develop a formula that bases the distribution of rewards on a ratio of total labor costs to total sales volume. If actual labor costs are less than expected, the surplus goes into a bonus pool. For example, Baltimore County workers calculated that they needed $100,000 worth of labor to generate $500,000 worth of services to residents of that county. In the following year, the same services were provided for $80,000 worth of labor. Forty percent of the $20,000 saved was then distributed to the employees, with the county keeping the balance. Employee bonuses were based on a percentage of salary.[23] In many cases, the bonus pool is equally split between organization and employees.

Gain-sharing programs are better suited to certain situations than to others. Table 6.4 illustrates a list of conditions favoring this plan. In general, gain-sharing programs seem suited to small organizations with a good market, simple measures of performance, and production costs controllable by employees. Top management should support the plan and the employees should be interested in and knowledgeable about gain sharing.

**Table 6.4**

| Conditions Favoring Gain-Sharing Plans | |
| --- | --- |
| **ORGANIZATIONAL CHARACTERISTIC** | **FAVORABLE CONDITION** |
| Size of organization | Usually less than 500 employees |
| Product costs | Controllable by employees |
| Organizational climate | Open, high level of trust |
| Style of management | Participative |
| Union status | No union, or one that is favorable to a cooperative effort |
| Communication policy | Open, willing to share financial results |
| Plant manager | Trusted, committed to plan, able to articulate goals and ideals of plan |
| Management | Technically competent, supportive of participative management style, good communication skills, able to deal with suggestions and new ideas |
| Workforce | Technically knowledgeable, interested in participation and higher pay, financially knowledgeable and interested |

Source: Adapted from Cummings, T. G., and Worley, C. G. *Organization Development and Change,* 7th ed. Cincinnati: South-Western, 2001, 403.

Although gain-sharing plans sound good, there have been notable failures. The Fleet Financial Group recently abandoned its gain-sharing program. As a part of a 2-year cost-cutting effort, management had created a gain-sharing program tied to the company's ratio of expenses to revenue and its stock prices. The more costs were cut and the higher the stock rose, the more employees were supposed to be rewarded. But when Fleet's stock price remained depressed even after cost cutting, workers got the minimum payout—averaging $615 per employee. Many employees stated that, considering the blood, sweat, and tears that went into getting the bonus, it turned out to be meaningless. What further enraged employees was that top management received big bonuses that weren't tied to the same measures.[24]

## PROFIT-SHARING PROGRAMS

In contrast, **profit-sharing programs** give employees a portion of the company's profits. As the name suggests, profit-sharing plans distribute profits to all employees. Average profit-sharing figures are difficult to calculate, but according to some experts they typically range between 4 and 6 percent of a person's salary. According to Steve Watson, managing director at Stanton Chase, an executive-recruiting firm, profit sharing may have a limited impact because employees may feel that they can do little to influence the organization's overall profitability. That is, company profits are influenced by many factors (e.g., competitor's products, state of the economy, and inflation rate) that are well beyond the employees' control. However, profit-sharing plans are very popular in Japan. For example, at Seiko Instruments many managers and workers receive bonuses twice a year that equal 4 or 5 months' salary. These bonuses are based on the company's overall performance.[25]

## SKILL-BASED PAY

Paying people according to their value in the labor market makes a great deal of sense. After all, employees having highly developed skills—and especially those who develop multiple skills—are valuable assets to the organization. As we have emphasized earlier, competencies such as managing communication, team building, and change are often based on mastering a number of individual skills, such as verbal, written, and media presentations. **Skill-based pay** depends on the number and level of job-related skills that an employee has learned.[26] The underlying assumption is that by focusing on the individual rather than the job, skill-based reward systems recognize learning and growth. Employees are paid according to the number of different skills they can perform. Over 16 percent of the Fortune 1000 companies use skill-based pay systems to motivate employees. For example, in General Mills' Squeeze-It plant, new employees are paid a starting wage at the low end of the skilled worker wage rate for premium employees in the community. They are then assigned to one of four skill blocks corresponding to a particular set of activities in the production process. Each skill block has three levels of skill requirements. Pay is based on the level of skill achieved in each block; the more proficient the skill in each block and the more blocks the employee is proficient at, the higher is the pay. After an employee has mastered all the skill blocks, the top rate is paid. The progression in skills typically takes 2 years to complete, and employees are given support and training to help them learn the skills required for each job.[27]

There is a major drawback of skill-based pay: the tendency to "top out." Topping-out occurs when employees learn all the skills there are to learn and then run up against the top end of the pay scale, with no higher levels to attain. Some organizations, such as GE and United Technologies, have resolved the topping-out effect by installing a gain-sharing program after most employees have learned all the skills required. Other organizations have resolved this problem by making skills obsolete, eliminating them, and adding new ones, thus raising the standards of employee competence. Skill-based pay systems also require a heavy investment in training, as well as a measurement system capable of telling when employees have learned the new skills.

## FLEXIBLE BENEFIT PLANS

**Flexible benefit plans** allow employees to choose the benefits they want, rather than having management choose for them. Flexible benefit plans often are called **cafeteria-style benefits plans**. According to David Norwood, president of Denwood Corporation, a compensation consulting firm, a typical corporation's benefits plan currently is about 36 percent of its total employee compensation package.[28] That represents a huge cost, considering that only 5 percent or less is set aside for merit pay increases in most organizations. Under flexible benefit plans, employees decide—beyond a base program—which additional benefits they want, tailoring the benefits package to their needs. The idea is that employees can make important and intelligent decisions about their benefits. Some employees take all their discretionary benefits in cash; others choose additional life insurance, child or elder care, dental insurance, or retirement plans. Extensive benefits options may be highly attractive to an employee with a family. However, many benefits might be only minimally attractive to a young, single employee. Older employees value retirement plans more than younger employees and are willing to put more money into them. Employees with elderly parents may desire financial assistance in providing care for them. At Traveler's Insurance Company employees can choose benefits of up to $5,000 a year for the care of dependent elderly parents.

Thousands of organizations now offer flexible benefits plans. They have become very popular because they offer three distinct advantages. First, they allow employees to make important decisions about their personal finances and to match employees' needs with their benefits plans. Second, such plans help organizations control their costs, especially for health care. Employers can set the maximum amount of benefit dollars they will spend on employees' benefits and avoid automatically absorbing cost increases. Third, such plans highlight the economic value of many benefits to employees. Most employees have little idea of the cost of benefits because the organization is willing to pay for them even though employees might not want some of them or might prefer alternatives.

Moreover, the changing workforce is causing employers to consider flexible benefits as a tool to recruit and retain employees. Starbucks Coffee Company believes that its use of flexible benefits plans has cut employee turnover from 150 to 60 percent (see Chapter 5). Starbucks calculates that hiring an employee costs $550. If so, a competitor with 300 percent turnover would have to hire three people at a cost of $3 \times \$550 = \$1,650$ per job per year, whereas Starbucks would need to spend only $0.6 \times \$550 = \$330$ per job per year.

Some limitations are associated with flexible benefits plans. First, because different employees choose different benefits packages, record keeping becomes more complicated. Sophisticated computer systems are essential for keeping straight the details of employees' records. Second, accurately predicting the number of employees that might choose each benefit is difficult. That may affect the firm's group rates for life and medical insurance, as the costs of such plans are based on the number of employees covered.

## ORGANIZATIONAL USE

Management must make certain trade-offs when choosing among these four reward systems. Figure 6.2 provides some guidance for choosing a suitable reward system. It shows under what circumstances an individual or team plan is appropriate and under what situations specific individual or team plans are most effective. If you answer the first five diagnostic questions yes, reward systems that permit individuals to calculate

**Figure 6.2**                              **Deciding Among Alternative Reward Systems**

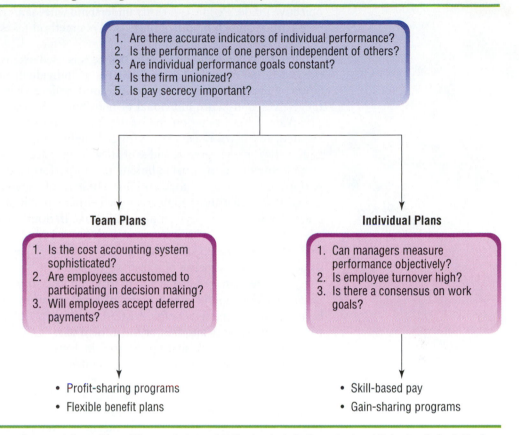

Source: Adapted from Wagner, J. A., and Hollenbeck, J. R. *Organizational Behavior,* 3rd ed. Englewood Cliffs, N.J.: Simon and Schuster, 1998, 100.

their own rewards might be of value. If you answer the first five diagnostic questions no, team, department, or organizationwide reward systems might be more appropriate. If you want to reward individuals' performance, you should then ask three additional questions. If the answers to all these questions are yes, a skill-based or gain-sharing system is appropriate. Similarly, if a group or team reward system seems appropriate, you should ask three additional questions. If the answers to all these questions are yes, profit-sharing and flexible benefit programs are appropriate.

Organizations in various countries utilize different reward systems. Cultural values learned in childhood are passed down from one generation to the next and serve to differentiate one country from another. The following Managing Across Cultures Competency feature highlights how reward practices differ by country.

## COMPETENCY:  MANAGING ACROSS CULTURES

### REWARD PRACTICES IN DIFFERENT COUNTRIES

The information displayed in Table 6.5 was taken from a large international study. Using data gathered from IBM, Towers Perrin, and Price Waterhouse, the researchers examined the pay and fringe benefit practices of companies in 24 countries. Here, we have used 3 countries as examples for each reward system. In societies where unpredictability and risky situations are to be avoided (e.g., Japan, Korea, and France), basing pay on seniority was used frequently because seniority provides an objective guide. People can easily understand what seniority is and can calculate their own without much help from others. This method takes the uncertainty out of pay decisions.

Pay based on individual performance was used extensively in countries that value the individual more highly than the team. Individualistic cultures (e.g., the United States, Canada, and the United Kingdom) believe that people should take care of themselves, and hence individual responsibility for results is important. In countries that place a high value on the quality of life and caring for others (e.g., Denmark, Sweden, and Norway), extensive fringe benefits (e.g., workplace child-care programs, maternity-leave programs, and sabbatical leaves) are stressed. Finally, companies operating in cultures that value linking pay to performance—either individual or team performance—favored stock options. These results are supported by the fact that, in the United States, most companies used either a profit-sharing or a gain-sharing program to reward high-performing individuals. In South Korea, Japan, and other countries where "fitting in" is important, such reward systems do not support and advance the culture's values. Gain-sharing and skill-based pay systems reward individuals, sometimes at the expense of a team or department.

Japanese managers place a high value on seniority and fringe benefits, including discounts for employees at company-owned vacation resorts, stipends for funerals, housing, and medical benefits. Instead of firing people, managers move employees from one division to another, or force them to take a cut in pay. There has been some discussion about work sharing. Started in Europe, this concept is simple: split the workday into more shifts and cut the number of working hours. In Japan, at NSK, a ball-bearing manufacturer, and Toto, a toilet producer, managers have divided the day into three 6-hour shifts—a cut of 4 hours per worker. Overtime pay can be reduced, if not eliminated. And, if part-time workers are hired for the third shift, they'd receive less pay and benefits. Work sharing means shorter shifts and smaller paychecks.[29]

**Table 6.5**

| Reward Practices in Different Countries | |
|---|---|
| **TYPE OF REWARD PRACTICE** | **COUNTRY** |
| Pay based on seniority | Greece, Portugal, Belgium |
| Pay based on individual/team performance | Australia, United Kingdom, United States |
| Extensive fringe-benefit plans | Sweden, Norway, the Netherlands |
| Stock options and bonus plans linked to individual/team/firm performance | Austria, United Kingdom, United States |

Source: Adapted from Schuler, R. S., and Rogovsky, N. Understanding compensation practices variation across firms: The impact of national culture. *Journal of International Business Studies*, 1998, 29, 159–177.

## CHAPTER SUMMARY

**1.** Explain how performance is affected by goal setting.

Goal setting is a process intended to increase efficiency and effectiveness by specifying the desired outcomes toward which individuals, departments, teams, and organizations should work. The goal-setting model developed by Locke and Latham emphasizes the challenges provided for the individual: goal difficulty, goal clarity, and self-efficacy. Setting difficult but clear and achievable goals for individuals who believe that they have the ability to complete their tasks leads to high performance. Four moderators—ability, goal commitment, feedback, and task complexity—influence the strength of the relationship between challenging goals and performance. If the individual has the ability, is committed to the goal, and is given feedback on progress toward achievement of the goal—and if the task is complex—high performance will result. All four moderators must be present to motivate a person to achieve goals. Four mediators—direction, effort, persistence, and task strategy—facilitate goal attainment. That is, these four characteristics channel or focus the person's motivational efforts. Performance, rewards, satisfaction, and consequences complete the model.

**2.** Describe reward systems for fostering high performance.

Reward systems represent a powerful means for motivating high levels of individual and team performance. Four reward systems, in particular, are designed to enhance performance: gain sharing, profit sharing, skilled-based pay, and flexible benefits. Gain-sharing programs are regular cash bonuses for employees who increase their productivity, reduce costs, or improve quality. A similar program is profit sharing, which gives employees a portion of the organization's profits. Skilled-based pay systems pay a person according to the number and level of job-related skills that the employee masters. The value of these skills is determined by the organization. Flexible benefit plans allow employees to choose the benefits that are important to them.

## KEY TERMS AND CONCEPTS

Cafeteria-style benefit plans

Flexible benefit plans

Gain-sharing programs

Goal clarity

Goal commitment

Goal difficulty

Goal setting

Goals

High-performance work system

Management by Objectives (MBO)

Profit-sharing programs

Scanlon plan

Skill-based pay

## DISCUSSION QUESTIONS

1. Explain Enterprise Rent-A-Car's program according to the concepts presented in the goal-setting model. Why is it so successful?

2. List your five most important personal goals. Evaluate the difficulty and clarity of each goal. What are the implications, if any, of this assessment for your future?

3. Think of this course. Evaluate your level of goal commitment. What factors influenced your level of goal commitment? Did your level of commitment influence your performance? Explain.

4. Use the goal-setting model to analyze Jeff Gordon's NASCAR team. Why is it so effective?

5. Why do people sometimes falsify records to achieve goals?

6. Nancy Arnold, CEO of CardioMetrics in Austin, Texas, said: "If you cannot define it and measure it, you are not going to get it." What implications does this statement have for setting goals? For measuring them?

7. What are the similarities and differences between gain-sharing and profit-sharing plans? Which system would motivate you to achieve greater performance? Why?

8. What are some problems that employees might face in an organization that has adopted a skill-based pay program?

9. Can a flexible benefits plan be tied to employee performance? If so, what are the advantages of doing so? The disadvantages?

10. How does a country's culture affect the type of rewards that high-performing employees are offered?

# DEVELOPING COMPETENCIES

## Competency: Managing Self

### Goal-Setting Questionnaire

*Instructions:* The following statements refer to a job you currently hold or have held. Read each statement and then select a response from the following scale that best describes your view. You may want to use a separate sheet of paper to record your responses and compare them with the responses of others.

### Scale

Almost Never    1    2    3    4    5    Almost Always

_____ 1. I understand exactly what I am supposed to do on my job.

_____ 2. I have specific, clear goals to aim for on my job.

_____ 3. The goals I have on this job are challenging.

_____ 4. I understand how my performance is measured on this job.

_____ 5. I have deadlines for accomplishing my goals on this job.

_____ 6. If I have more than one goal to accomplish, I know which are most important and which are least important.

_____ 7. My goals require my full effort.

_____ 8. My manager tells me the reasons for giving me the goals I have.

_____ 9. My manager is supportive with respect to encouraging me to reach my goals.

_____ 10. My manager lets me participate in the setting of my goals.

_____ 11. My manager lets me have some say in deciding how I will go about implementing my goals.

_____ 12. If I reach my goals, I know that my manager will be pleased.

_____ 13. I get credit and recognition when I attain my goals.

_____ 14. Trying for goals makes my job more fun than it would be without goals.

_____ 15. I feel proud when I get feedback indicating that I have reached my goals.

_____ 16. The other people I work with encourage me to attain my goals.

_____ 17. I sometimes compete with my coworkers to see who can do the best job in reaching our goals.

_____ 18. If I reach my goals, my job security will be improved.

_____ 19. If I reach my goals, my chances for a pay raise are increased.

_____ 20. If I reach my goals, my chances for a promotion are increased.

_____ 21. I usually feel that I have a suitable action plan(s) for reaching my goals.

_____ 22. I get regular feedback indicating how I am performing in relation to my goals.

_____ 23. I feel that my training was good enough so that I am capable of reaching my goals.

_____ 24. Organization policies help rather than hurt goal attainment.

_____ 25. Teams work together in this company to attain goals.

_____ 26. This organization provides sufficient resources (e.g., time, money, and equipment) to make goal setting effective.

_____ 27. In performance appraisal sessions, my supervisor stresses problem solving rather than criticism.

_____ 28. Goals in this organization are used more to help you do your job well rather than punish you.

_____ 29. The pressure to achieve goals here fosters honesty as opposed to cheating and dishonesty.

_____ 30. If my manager makes a mistake that affects my ability to attain my goals, he or she admits it.

### Scoring and Interpretation

Add the points shown for items 1 through 30. Scores of 120 to 150 may indicate a high-performing, highly satisfying work situation. Your goals are challenging and you are committed to reaching them. When you achieve your goals, you are rewarded for your accomplishments. Scores of 80 to 119 may suggest a highly varied work situation with some motivating and satisfying features and some frustrating and dissatisfying features. Scores of 30 to 79 may suggest a low-performing, dissatisfying work situation.[30]

## Competency: Managing Change

### Sola Optical

When Sola Optical, a global designer of optical lenses, failed to return to profitability despite increased demand for its products, management decided to conduct an in-depth analysis of the company's financial performance. The analysis revealed that, in the process of growing, the company had added equipment, recruited and trained more employees to do specialized jobs, and added shifts.

Sola's manufacturing process consisted of three main stages, with each stage handled by a different section of the company. During the first stage, employees in the "base curve" section shaped the curve of the lens that fits against the eye. During the second stage, employees in the "front curve" section shaped the customer's prescribed amount of optical correction on the front of the lens. During the third stage, employees in the "finishing" section polished and buffed the edge and surfaces of the lens to make it microscopically smooth. In all, between 25 and 30 different jobs had to be completed to manufacture a lens ready for packaging.

Management concluded that high manufacturing costs, lack of accountability, and other manufacturing problems could be corrected by reorganizing the manufacturing process. Manufacturing "modules" were created and given responsibility for producing lenses from start to finish. Under this new organizational design, a typical module consists of approximately 25 employees including workers from each of the former manufacturing sections, as well as a supervisor and two work coordinators. Each module is responsible for completing the 25 to 30 jobs that result in a finished contact lens.

Sola's compensation system gave employees no incentive to grow and learn new jobs or even to be willing to perform a variety of tasks. The system assigned manufacturing employees to one of three job grades, based on the sophistication or difficulty of the particular jobs they performed. Unfortunately, an employee who knew a variety of lower rated jobs and who therefore was extremely valuable to a work module might have a job grade of only 2, whereas an employee who knew only one, more difficult job might have a job grade of 3. Employees perceived this system of compensation to be unfair, and management recognized its unfairness. Richard Bunning, director of human resources, convened a task force of manufacturing supervisors and employees to develop a proposal to correct this problem. That proposal not only underscored the need to reward employees for the number of jobs in the manufacturing process that they knew, but also identified several other problems with the company's existing compensation system.

"One problem identified by the task force concerned the disincentive for employees to cross-train into jobs that were not rated at a higher level," said Bunning. "Employees received no financial incentive or reward for such cross-training, yet they faced the possibility of learning a new job that they might not be able to do as successfully as they could their current job. Moreover, cross-trained employees who were assigned to a lower level job perceived that job assignment as demeaning, while management perceived it as a waste of money."

Still another problem with Sola's compensation system, as many people were quick to point out, was the amount of time and money lost because of the "domino" hiring effect it created. When a work coordinator's position became available, for instance, many grade 3 employees would apply for it. If one were selected, then grade 2 employees would apply for the promoted employee's position and so on until only a grade 1 position was left open. A job at that level generally had to be filled by an untrained job applicant from outside the company.

According to Bunning, "Devising a reward system that would be consistent and fair and that would meet the needs of the business was the most complex aspect of designing the new compensation system." That job was made even more difficult because the new reward system had to be consistent with the quality assurance department's goals for quality.

Bunning decided to use a two-phase approach in designing the new rating system. During the first phase, senior managers, technical experts, and employees from all product lines met to comparatively rank all jobs. That ranking was based on three criteria: difficulty of learning the job, importance of the job, and impact of the job on the cost of the product. Thus two jobs that were equally difficult to learn might have different ratings because one job was near the end of the manufacturing process and therefore had a greater impact on cost if done incorrectly.

Once the pay grades had been established, the task force and management still had to address a wide variety of implementation and management details. The following are some of the more important procedures and policies that were developed.

- Employees who initially qualified for an increase in pay grade would receive a bonus instead of a promotional increase to avoid immediately raising the labor-cost base. A one-grade increase would merit 40 hours' pay; a two-grade increase, 60 hours' pay; and a three-grade increase, 80 hours' pay.
- After the implementation period, employees would receive a 5% increase per grade whenever they were promoted to a higher grade level.
- Employees would have to pass a semiannual audit of attained skills to maintain both their grade level and rate of pay.
- Cross-training would be guided by "skill-depth" plans. Each job would have only two or three employees trained in a backup capacity to limit and direct the amount of cross-training. Thus cross-training for the sake of promotion would be avoided.
- No employee would initially drop to a lower pay grade if assigned to that level under the new rating system. Instead the employee would be given time to cross-train in extra jobs to maintain his grade level.

When the skill-based pay system was implemented, employees and managers almost universally supported it. Although a few concerns were expressed about the feasibility of the system in terms of costs, most results over time indicate that the system has been a success.

Although employees initially greeted the new compensation system with much enthusiasm, over time the advantages of the system began to be taken for granted and some complaints surfaced. According to Bunning, "The most common complaint was the lack of enough training opportunities, which made getting promotions more difficult. Employees also perceived that some supervisors acted arbitrarily in choosing workers for cross-training. Nevertheless, employees—and supervisors, for that matter—quickly learned the nuances of the new system and worked it effectively. For instance, they discovered that significantly more dollars could be earned if promotional increases were earned after the annual merit-pay increase rather than before."[31]

## Questions

1. What features of the Sola Optical plan illustrate the goal-setting model shown in Figure 6.1?
2. Why was this plan successful?
3. Could management have chosen another reward system? If so, which one?

# Managing Individual Stress

**LEARNING OBJECTIVES**

**LEARNING OBJECTIVES**

When you have finished studying the chapter, you should be able to:

1. Explain the concept of stress and stressors and a person's response to stress.
2. Discuss the relationship between personality and stress.
3. State the primary sources of stress in organizations.
4. Describe the effects of stress on health and job performance.
5. Identify individual and organizational practices for managing stress.

## DAVID STERNS AND THERESA WRIGHT

The longer he waited, the more David Sterns worried. For weeks he had been plagued by aching muscles, loss of appetite, restless sleep, and a complete sense of exhaustion. At first he tried to ignore these problems, but eventually he became so short-tempered and irritable that his wife insisted he get a checkup. Now, sitting in the doctor's office and wondering what the verdict would be, he didn't even notice when Theresa Wright took the seat beside him. They had been good friends when she worked in the front office at the plant, but he hadn't seen her since she left 3 years ago to take a job as a customer service representative in another firm. Her gentle poke in the ribs brought him around, and within minutes they were talking and gossiping as if she had never left.

"You got out just in time," he told her. "Since the reorganization, nobody feels safe. It used to be that as long as you did your work, you had a job. That's not for sure anymore. They expect the same product rates even though two guys are now doing the work of three. We're so backed up I'm working twelve-hour shifts six days a week. I swear I hear those machines humming in my sleep. Guys are calling in sick just to get a break. Morale is so bad they're talking about bringing in some consultants to figure out a better way to get the job done."

"Well, I really miss you guys," she said. "I'm afraid I jumped from the frying pan into the fire. In my new job, the computer routes the calls and they never stop. I even have to schedule my bathroom breaks. All I hear the whole day are complaints from unhappy customers. I try to be helpful and sympathetic, but I can't promise anything without getting my boss's approval. Most of the time I'm caught between what the customer wants and company policy. I'm not sure who I'm supposed to keep happy. The other reps are so uptight and tense they don't even talk to one another. We all go to our own little cubicles and stay there until quitting time. To make matters worse, my mother's health is deteriorating. If only I could use some of my sick time to look after her. No wonder I'm in here with migraine headaches and high blood pressure. A lot of the reps are seeing the employee assistance counselor and taking stress management classes, which seem to help. But sooner or later, someone will have to make some changes in the way the place is run."[1]

David Sterns' and Theresa Wright's stories are unusual but not rare. Job stress has become a common and costly problem in the workplace, leaving few workers untouched. For example, studies of workplace stress report the following.

- One-fourth of employees view their jobs as the number one stressor in their lives.
- Three-fourths of employees believe that the worker has more on-the-job stress than a generation ago.
- Problems at work are more strongly associated with health complaints than are any other life stressors—more so than even financial or family problems.
- The estimated financial costs of stress vary widely. One estimate by the U.S. Bureau of Labor Statistics indicates that stress costs employers $10,000 per worker per year. Also, the U.S. National Institute for Occupational Safety and Health estimates that 40 percent of the workforce is affected by stress, making it the number one cause of worker disability.[2]

Organizations that ignore stress management, or assign it a low priority, are likely to suffer declines in productivity and morale and increased legal costs. The negative consequences of stress are so dramatic that managers need to (1) work hard to reduce excessive stress in the workplace and (2) assist employees in developing stress-coping skills. David Sterns and Theresa Wright are experiencing both physical and emotional consequences of high levels of stress.

In this chapter, we explain the nature of stress, the role of personality differences in handling stress, sources of stress, and the effects of stress. We conclude with a discussion of actions that can be taken by organizations and individuals to manage stress.

## NATURE OF STRESS

**Learning Objective:**

1. Explain the concept of stress, stressors, and a person's response to stress.

**Stress** is the excitement, feeling of anxiety, and/or physical tension that occurs when the demands placed on an individual are thought to exceed his ability to cope.[3] This most common view of stress is often called *distress* or negative stress. The physical or psychological demands from the environment that cause this condition are called **stressors**. Stressors can take various forms, but all stressors have one thing in common: They create stress or the potential for stress when an individual perceives them as representing a demand that may exceed that person's ability to respond.

### FIGHT-OR-FLIGHT RESPONSE

Numerous changes occur in the human body during a stress reaction. Breathing and heart rates change so that the body can operate with maximum capacity for physical action. Brain wave activity goes up to allow the brain to function maximally. Hearing and sight become momentarily more acute, and muscles ready themselves for action. These biochemical and bodily changes represent a natural reaction to an environmental stressor: the **fight-or-flight response**.[4] An animal attacked by a predator in the wild basically has two choices: to fight or to flee. The animal's bodily responses to the stressor (the predator) increase its chances of survival. Similarly, our cave-dwelling ancestors benefited from this biological response mechanism. People gathering food away from their caves would have experienced a great deal of stress upon meeting a saber-toothed tiger. In dealing with the tiger, they could have run away or stayed and fought. The biochemical changes in their bodies prepared them for either alternative and contributed to their ability to survive.

The human nervous system still responds the same way to environmental stressors. This response continues to have survival value in a true emergency. However, for most people most of the time, the "tigers" are imaginary rather than real. In work situations, for example, a fight-or-flight response usually isn't appropriate. If an employee receives an unpleasant work assignment from a manager, physically assaulting the manager or storming angrily out of the office obviously is inappropriate. Instead, the employee is expected to accept the assignment calmly and do the best job possible. Remaining calm and performing effectively may be especially difficult when the employee perceives an assignment as threatening and the body is prepared to act accordingly.

Medical researcher Hans Selye first used the word stress to describe the body's biological response mechanisms. Selye considered stress to be the nonspecific response of the human body to any demand made on it.[5] However, the body has only a limited capacity to respond to stressors. The workplace makes a variety of demands on people, and too much stress over too long a period of time will exhaust their ability to cope with those stressors.

## EXPERIENCING STRESS

A variety of factors influence how an individual experiences stress. Figure 7.1 identifies four of the primary factors: (1) the person's perception of the situation, (2) the person's past experience, (3) the presence or absence of social support, and (4) individual differences in reacting to stress.

**Perception.**   In Chapter 3 we defined *perception* as a process whereby a person selects and organizes environmental information into a concept of reality. Employee perceptions of a situation can influence how (or whether) they experience stress. For example, two Microsoft employees have their job duties substantially changed—a situation likely to be stressful for many people. The first employee views the new duties as an opportunity to learn new competencies and thinks that the change is a vote of confidence from management in her ability to be flexible and take on new challenges. In contrast, the second employee perceives the same situation to be extremely threatening and concludes that management is unhappy with his performance.

**Past Experience.**   A person may perceive a situation as more or less stressful, depending on how familiar that person is with the situation and his prior experience with the particular stressors involved. Past practice or training may allow some employees to deal calmly and competently with stressors that would greatly intimidate less experienced or inadequately trained employees. The relationship between experience and stress is based on reinforcement (see Chapter 4). Positive reinforcement or

**Figure 7.1**                    **Relationship Between Stressors and Experienced Stress**

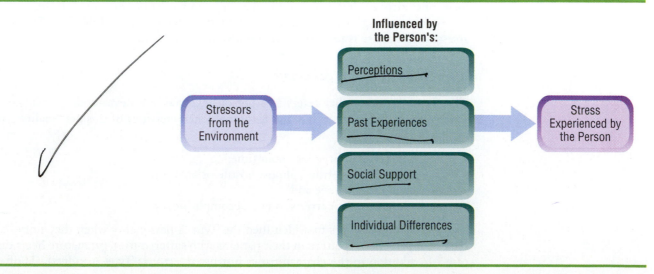

previous success in a similar situation can reduce the level of stress that a person experiences under certain circumstances; punishment or past failure under similar conditions can increase stress under the same circumstances.

**Social Support.**     The presence or absence of other people influences how individuals in the workplace experience stress and respond to stressors.[6] The presence of coworkers may increase an individual's confidence, allowing that person to cope more effectively with stress. For example, working alongside someone who performs confidently and competently in a stressful situation may help an employee behave similarly. Conversely, the presence of fellow workers may irritate some people or make them anxious, reducing their ability to cope with stress.

**Individual Differences.**     Individual differences in motivation, attitudes, personality, and abilities also influence whether employees experience work stress and, if they do, how they respond to it.[7] Simply stated, people are different, as we pointed out in Chapters 2 and 3. What one person considers a major source of stress, another may hardly notice. Personality characteristics, in particular, may explain some of the differences in the ways that employees experience and respond to stress. For example, the Big Five personality factor that we labeled *adjustment* in Chapter 2 seems to be important in individual responses to various stressors in the work setting. Individuals at one extreme of adjustment (described as stable and confident) are more likely to cope well with a wide variety of work stressors; individuals at the other extreme (described as nervous and self-doubting) typically have greater difficulty in coping with the same stressors. We further discuss relationships between personality and stress in the following section.

## PERSONALITY AND STRESS

**Learning Objective:**

2. Discuss the relationship between personality and stress.

Many personality traits are related to stress, including self-esteem and locus of control (personality traits discussed in Chapter 2). A personality trait may affect how a person will perceive and react to a situation or an event as a stressor.[8] For example, an individual with low self-esteem is more likely to experience stress in demanding work situations than is a person with high self-esteem. Individuals high in self-esteem typically have more confidence in their ability to meet job demands than do those with low self-esteem. Employees with high internal locus of control may take more effective action, more quickly, in coping with a sudden emergency (a stressor) than might employees with high external locus of control. Individuals high in internal locus of control are likely to believe that they can moderate the stressful situation.

Before reading further, please respond to the statements in Table 7.1. This self-assessment exercise is related to the discussion that follows.

### THE TYPE A PERSONALITY

The **Type A personality** refers to a person involved in a never-ending struggle to achieve more and more in less and less time. Characteristics of this personality type include

- a chronic sense of urgency about time;
- an extremely competitive, almost hostile orientation;
- an aversion to idleness; and
- an impatience with barriers to task accomplishment.

Two medical researchers first identified the Type A personality when they noticed a recurrent personality pattern in their patients who suffered from premature heart disease.[9] In addition to the characteristics just listed, *extreme* Type A individuals often

| Table 7.1 | A Self-Assessment of Type A Personality |
|---|---|

Choose from the following responses to answer the questions below:

A.  Almost always true        C.  Seldom true
B.  Usually true            D.  Never true

_____ 1. I do not like to wait for other people to complete their work before I can proceed with my own.

_____ 2. I hate to wait in most lines.

_____ 3. People tell me that I tend to get irritated too easily.

_____ 4. Whenever possible, I try to make activities competitive.

_____ 5. I have a tendency to rush into work that needs to be done before knowing the procedure I will use to complete the job.

_____ 6. Even when I go on vacation, I usually take some work along.

_____ 7. Even when I make a mistake, it is usually due to the fact that I have rushed into the job before completely planning it through.

_____ 8. I feel guilty for taking time off from work.

_____ 9. People tell me I have a bad temper when it comes to competitive situations.

_____ 10. I tend to lose my temper when I am under a lot of pressure at work.

_____ 11. Whenever possible, I will attempt to complete two or more tasks at once.

_____ 12. I tend to race against the clock.

_____ 13. I have no patience for lateness.

_____ 14. I catch myself rushing when there is no need.

Score your responses according to the following key:

- *An intense sense of time urgency* is a tendency to race against the clock, even when there is little reason to. The person feels a need to hurry for hurry's sake alone, and this tendency has appropriately been called "hurry sickness." Time urgency is measured by items 1, 2, 8, 12, 13, and 14. Every A or B answer to these six questions scores one point.

  Your score = _____

- *Inappropriate aggression and hostility* reveals itself in a person who is excessively competitive and who cannot do anything for fun. This inappropriately aggressive behavior easily evolves into frequent displays of hostility, usually at the slightest provocation or frustration. Competitiveness and hostility is measured by items 3, 4, 9, and 10. Every A or B answer scores one point.

  Your score = _____

- *Polyphasic behavior* refers to the tendency to undertake two or more tasks simultaneously at inappropriate times. It usually results in wasted time due to an inability to complete the tasks. This behavior is measured by items 6 and 11. Every A or B answer scores one point.

  Your score = _____

- *Goal directedness without proper planning* refers to the tendency of an individual to rush into work without really knowing how to accomplish the desired result. This usually results in incomplete work or work with many errors, which in turn leads to wasted time, energy, and money. Lack of planning is measured by items 5 and 7. Every A or B response scores one point.

  Your score = _____

  TOTAL SCORE = _____

If your score is 5 or greater, you may possess some basic components of the Type A personality.

Source: Reproduced with permission of the Robert J. Brady Co., Bowie, Maryland, 20715, from its copyrighted work *The Stress Mess Solution: The Causes and Cures of Stress on the Job*, by G. S. Everly and D. A. Girdano, 1980, 55.

speak rapidly, are preoccupied with themselves, and are dissatisfied with life. They tend to give quick replies to questions with no pause to deliberate before answering the questions. Type A personalities often give sarcastic, rude, and hostile responses. They may try to appear to be humorous, but with the underlying intent to be hurtful.

The questionnaire in Table 7.1 measures four sets of behaviors and tendencies associated with the Type A personality: (1) time urgency, (2) competitiveness and hostility, (3) polyphasic behavior (trying to do several things at once), and (4) a lack of planning. Medical researchers have discovered that these behaviors and tendencies often relate to life and work stress. They tend to cause stress or make stressful situations worse than they otherwise might be.

Evidence links Type A behavior with a vulnerability to heart attacks. Current research, however, suggests that the Type A personality description is too broad to predict coronary heart disease accurately. Rather, research now indicates that only those individuals with certain aspects of the Type A personality—particularly anger, hostility, and aggression—are strongly related to stress reactions and heart disease.[10] Type A individuals with these specific attributes appear to be two to three times more likely to develop heart disease than are Type B individuals. Type B individuals tend to be more easygoing and relaxed, less concerned about time pressures, and less likely to overreact to situations in hostile or aggressive ways. In sum, the **Type B personality** is considered to be the opposite of the Type A personality.

The following Managing Self Competency feature illustrates the behaviors of an extreme Type A personality lacking in this competency. Note the effect that he had on other managers.

## THE HARDY PERSONALITY

What aspects of personality might protect individuals from the negative health consequences of stress? Personality traits that seem to counter the effects of stress are known collectively as the **hardy personality**. As a personality type, **hardiness** is de-

## COMPETENCY: MANAGING SELF

### AL DUNLAP'S FAILURE TO MANAGE SELF

Al Dunlap failed miserably in his attempt to rescue Sunbeam and was fired by the board of directors. Although his termination eventually occurred because he soft-pedaled and tried to disguise a string of serious quarterly losses, his loud, gruff, and demeaning style were reported to have alienated those around him. Richard Boynton, president of the household products division of Sunbeam, described Dunlap's first series of meetings with his senior staff: "It was like a dog barking at you for hours. He just yelled, ranted, and raved. He was condescending, belligerent, and disrespectful." Dunlap browbeat those around him by telling them in a very loud voice over and over again that they were responsible for the demise of Sunbeam. He blamed individuals in front of others, threatened people with termination and, in fact, fired a large number of senior executives.

Because of the stressful organizational environment, others simply left Sunbeam on their own. David Fanin, Sunbeam's general counsel, told the board of directors: "I cannot work for that man another day. I just cannot do it. The day-to-day atmosphere at the company has really deteriorated. Al is no longer in touch with the business and what's going on at the company. Al isn't talking to people. He has cut himself off."[11]

fined as "a cluster of characteristics that includes feeling a sense of commitment, responding to each difficulty as representing a challenge and an opportunity, and perceiving that one has control over one's own life."[12] The hardy personality is characterized by

- a sense of positive involvement with others in social situations;
- a tendency to attribute one's own behavior to internal causes (recall the discussion of attribution in Chapter 3); and
- a tendency to perceive or welcome significant changes in life with interest, curiosity, and optimism.[13]

A high degree of hardiness reduces the negative effects of stressful events. Hardiness seems to reduce stress by altering the way that people perceive stressors. The concept of the hardy personality provides a useful insight into the role of individual differences in reactions to environmental stressors. An individual having a low level of hardiness perceives many events as stressful; an individual having a high level of hardiness perceives fewer events as stressful. A person with a high level of hardiness isn't overwhelmed by challenging or difficult situations. Rather, faced with a stressor, the hardy personality copes or responds constructively by trying to find a solution—to control or influence events. This behavioral response typically reduces stress reactions, lowers blood pressure, and reduces the probability of illness.

Through development of the *managing self competency*, we contend that a person may come to reflect the attributes of the hardy personality. Recall from Chapter 1 that the managing self competency involves the ability to assess your own strengths and weaknesses, set and pursue professional and personal goals, balance work and personal life, and engage in new learning—including new or changed skills, behaviors, and attitudes.

## SOURCES OF STRESS

Employees often experience stress in both their personal and work lives. Understanding these sources of stress and their possible interaction is important. To consider either source in isolation may give an incomplete picture of the stress that an employee is experiencing.

### ORGANIZATIONAL SOURCES

As indicated in the Preview Case and early in this chapter, stress in the workplace is a problem of considerable significance. Surveys typically show that about 25 percent of all employees suffer from a variety of stress-induced problems. A survey of more than 400,000 employees conducted by International Survey Research of Chicago reported that about 40 percent of these people say that their workloads are excessive and that they have too much "pressure" at work.[14] Organizational sources of stress take a variety of forms. Thus managers and employees need a framework for thinking about and diagnosing organizational sources of work stress. Figure 7.2 presents such a framework, identifying seven principal work stressors and showing that internal factors influence the ways in which employees experience these stressors.

**Workload.**   For many employees, having too much work to do and not enough time or resources to do it can be stressful. **Role overload** exists when demands exceed the capacity of a manager or employee to meet all of them adequately. Many stressful jobs may be in a continuous condition of role overload. Surveys commonly identify work overload or "having to work too hard" as a major source of stress. Recall the Preview Case. David Sterns feels that he is working to the point of exhaustion. Theresa Wright feels that she is tied to the phone and computer, allowing little room for rest, flexibility, or self-initiative.

**Figure 7.2**    **Sources of Work Stressors and Experienced Stress**

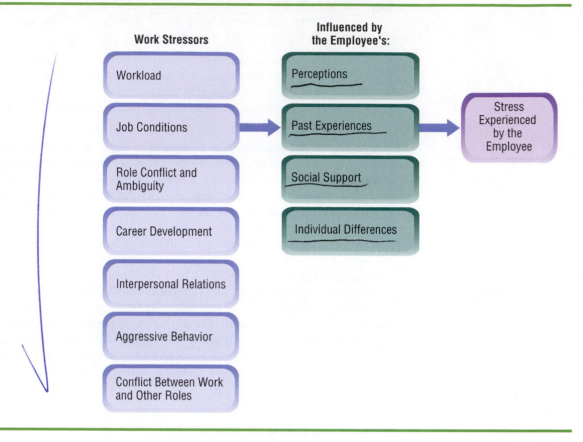

Having too little work to do also may create stress.[15] Have you ever had a job with so little to do that the workday seemed never to end? If so, you can understand why many people find too little work stressful. Managers sometimes are guilty of trying to do their subordinates' work, or *micromanage*, when their jobs aren't challenging enough. Micromanaging might reduce the manager's stress caused by boredom, but it is likely to increase subordinates' stress because the superior constantly watches them or second-guesses their decisions.

**Job Conditions.**    Poor working conditions represent another important set of job stressors. Temperature extremes, loud noise, too much or too little lighting, radiation, and air pollution are but a few examples of working conditions that can cause stress in employees.

Recall David Sterns' distress in the Preview Case regarding the constant loud noise at work. Job performance deteriorates, sometimes markedly, when these environmental stressors are present. Moreover, their effects are cumulative over time. Heavy travel demands or long-distance commuting are other aspects of jobs that employees may find stressful. Poor working conditions, excessive travel, and long hours all add up to increased stress and decreased performance. In addition, cutting-edge technology, while clearly of great benefit to society in general and many individuals in particular, nevertheless has created job conditions that may be quite stressful. Recall from the Preview Case Theresa Wright's physical isolation that reduces her opportunities to interact with other employees or receive help from them. Another example of this observation is made clear in the following Managing Communication Competency feature that addresses the relationship of communication technology to stress.

## COMPETENCY:   MANAGING COMMUNICATION

### COMMUNICATION TECHNOLOGY AND STRESS

A number of technology-assisted jobs have both maximum flexibility and maximum stress. Computers have lowered the entry barriers to many high-stress jobs, from accounting to programming, by making it possible to perform them anytime, anywhere. Abigail Roitman, an electronic day-trader of stocks, provides a good example of the maximum flexibility–maximum stress combination that often comes with high-tech occupations. Roitman's job gives her the flexibility needed to cut her hours short, to be home during the day if she chooses (she can trade stocks either from home or her office in Manhattan), or to take time off to be with her family. However, the job also gives her the opportunity to work and to stay stressed-out around the clock. She is trying to survive as both a stock trader and a devoted mother, but doing so requires her to draw mental boundaries between work and home. Often that is difficult, as work and home can be the same place.

The stress of day-trading can be endless because markets are open somewhere in the world 24 hours a day. Sometimes, Roitman stays up long after her family has gone to bed, checking international exchanges and studying price patterns on stocks from the previous day. She has successfully made a living at day-trading for almost 4 years, although most day-traders wash out quickly, in part due to high stress. Despite her obvious success, she says, "It's easy to take it very, very seriously and get stressed-out."[16]

**Role Conflict and Ambiguity.**   Differing expectations of or demands on a person at work produce **role conflict**. (We discuss role conflict in detail in Chapter 9.) **Role ambiguity** occurs when an employee is uncertain about assigned job duties and responsibilities. Role conflict and role ambiguity are particularly significant sources of job-related stress. Many employees suffer from role conflict and ambiguity, but conflicting expectations and uncertainty particularly affect managers. Having responsibility for the behavior of others and a lack of opportunity to participate in important decisions affecting their job are other aspects of employees' roles that may be stressful. Recall in the Preview Case that Theresa Wright often feels being caught in the difficult situation of trying to resolve the conflicting pressures between customer's needs and the company's expectations.

**Career Development.**   Major stressors related to career planning and development involve job security, promotions, transfers, and developmental opportunities. An employee can feel stress by underpromotion (failure to advance as rapidly as desired) or overpromotion (promotion to a job that exceeds the individual's competencies).

The current wave of reorganization and downsizing may seriously threaten careers and cause stress as indicated in the Preview Case. Since the reorganization at David Sterns' plant, everyone is worried about the future and what will happen next. When jobs, teams, departments, or entire organizations are restructured, employees often have numerous career-related concerns: Can I perform competently in the new situation? Can I advance? Is my new job secure? Typically, employees find these concerns stressful.

**Interpersonal Relations.**   Teams and groups have a great impact on the behavior of employees. (We explore these dynamics in Chapter 8.) Good working relationships and interactions with peers, subordinates, and superiors are crucial aspects of organizational life, helping employees achieve personal and organizational goals. When relationships are poor, they can become sources of stress. In a recent national poll, 90 percent of respondents believed that incivility at work and elsewhere has become a major problem. **Incivility** implies rudeness and disregard of others. It includes the violation of workplace norms for mutual respect. Consider two anonymous employee reports of workplace incivility and their feelings of distress.

> *Female employee:* "During a presentation that I was making to all of the company's international country managers and vice presidents, the division president stood up and shouted, 'No one is interested in this stuff.' His comment made me so nervous and upset that I could barely go on. I had been with this company for many years, you'd think he could have offered me a little respect for that alone."

> *Male employee:* "I was pulling off a payroll cycle for a month during December, and I entered '12' (the calendar month) when I should have entered '6' (the fiscal month). The cycle was garbage accordingly. The accountant called me insulting names with my new boss sitting right there next to me. It was humiliating and unfair. It was my first payroll with the company. I was new—it was an honest mistake."[17]

A high level of political behavior, or "office politics," also may create stress for managers and employees. The nature of relationships with others may influence how employees react to other stressors. In other words, interpersonal relationships can be either a source of stress or the social support that helps employees cope with stressors.

**Aggressive Behavior.**   A frightening category of work stressors is overly aggressive behavior in the workplace, often taking the form of violence or sexual harassment. Aggressive behavior that intentionally threatens or causes physical harm to an employee is classified as **workplace violence**. A recent survey asked executives to rank the top security threats to their organizations. Workplace violence topped the list.[18] Homicide is second only to transportation accidents as the most common cause of workplace fatalities.

Although homicide is the most extreme example of workplace violence, more than a million employees a year in the United States are subjected to violence of one form or another, ranging from actual physical assaults to threats or other forms of unwanted harassment. Individuals subject to violence or the threat of violence in the workplace are more likely to experience negative stress reactions, including lower productivity and higher absenteeism. Lost productivity and legal expenses related to workplace violence cost employers throughout the world billions of dollars annually.[19] The current level of violence in organizations is a major source of work stress that needs to be understood and managed.

A second form of overly aggressive behavior in the workplace is sexual harassment. **Sexual harassment** is unwanted contact or communication of a sexual nature.[20] In a *New York Times/CBS News* poll, fully 30 percent of female employees reported that they had been the object of unwanted sexual advances, propositions, or discussions at work. As with workplace violence, sexual harassment is a serious problem. Management clearly has a strong responsibility to do everything in its power to prevent sexual harassment from occurring. When it does occur, it needs to be dealt with quickly and firmly. Some practical suggestions for managers who have to deal with this disruptive issue include the following.

- Take all complaints about sexual harassment seriously.
- Publish a policy strongly condemning sexual harassment and conduct training sessions on it.
- Inform all employees of their rights and responsibilities under the policy.

- Develop a complaint procedure that provides alternative means for filing a complaint.
- Immediately respond to any complaint and investigate it with objectivity, confidentiality, and due process. Keep thorough records of complaints, investigations, and actions taken.
- Discipline managers and employees involved in sexual harassment.[21]

Policies need to clearly identify what constitutes sexual harassment, procedures for dealing with it, and penalties for engaging in this unacceptable behavior. Policies are not sufficient, however, if managers don't back them up with serious and prompt action.

**Conflict Between Work and Other Roles.**    A person has many roles in life (e.g., breadwinner, family member, little league coach, and/or church volunteer, to name a few), only one of which is typically associated with work (although some individuals may hold more than one job at a time). These roles may present conflicting demands that become sources of stress. Furthermore, work typically meets only some of a person's goals and needs. Recall the Preview Case. Theresa Wright needs to get her manager's approval for everything, and the company is insensitive to her family needs. Other goals and needs may conflict with career goals, presenting an additional source of stress. For example, employees' personal desires to spend time with their families may conflict with the extra hours they must work to advance their careers. Current demographic trends, such as the increasingly large number of dual-career couples, have brought work and family role conflicts into sharp focus.

## LIFE STRESSORS

The distinction between work and nonwork stressors isn't always clear, although a primary source of stress for many people clearly is conflict between work and family demands.[22] As Figure 7.3 illustrates, both work and family stressors may contribute to work–family conflict because stress in one area can reduce a person's ability to cope with stress in the other. This conflict represents a further source of stress that in turn can lead to problems, such as dissatisfaction, frustration, and even depression.

Much of the stress felt by managers and employees may stem from stressors in their personal lives, or **life stressors**. People must cope with a variety of life stressors; they deal with these stressors differently because of personality, age, gender, experience, and other characteristics. Events that cause stress for one person may not do so for another person. However, life stressors that affect almost everyone are those

**Figure 7.3**                              **Stressors and Work–Family Conflict**

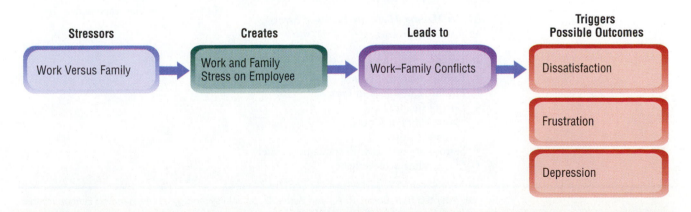

caused by significant changes: divorce, marriage, death of a family member, and the like. The human body has a limited capacity to respond to stressors. Too much change too quickly can exhaust the body's ability to respond, with negative consequences for a person's physical and mental health.

Table 7.2 contains some stressful events that college students typically face. These events are rated on a 100-point scale, with 1 indicating the least stressful event and 100 the most stressful. Events labeled "high levels of stress" might be assigned 71 to 100 points, depending on the specific circumstances of the student being evaluated. "Moderate levels of stress" might be scored from 31 to 70 points, and "low levels of stress" assigned scores from 1 to 30 points. During the course of a year, if a student faces events that total 150 points or more, the student has a 50–50 chance of getting sick as a result of excessive stress.[23]

Recall that stress is the body's general response to any demand made on it. Note that the list of stressful events in Table 7.2 contains both unpleasant events, such as failing a course, and pleasant events, such as finding a new love interest. This dual nature of life stressors demonstrates that they involve both negative and positive experiences. For example, vacations and holidays actually may be quite stressful for some people but very relaxing and refreshing for others. In addition, viewing unpleasant life events as having only negative effects is incorrect. People often can both cope with and grow from experiencing unpleasant events. They can also enjoy the positive effects and stimulation of pleasurable events, such as significant accomplishments, vacations, or gaining a new family member.

**Learning Objective:**

4. Describe the effects of stress on health and job performance.

# EFFECTS OF STRESS

All forms of stress can have both positive and negative effects. Our concern with work stress in this chapter focuses on its negative effects because of its adverse impacts on health and organizational effectiveness.

The effects of work stress occur in three main areas: physiological, emotional, and behavioral. Examples of the effects of distress in these areas are as follows.

**Table 7.2**

## Stressful Events for College Students

*Events Having High Levels of Stress*
- Death of parent
- Death of spouse
- Divorce
- Flunking out
- Unwed pregnancy

*Events Having Moderate Levels of Stress*
- Academic probation
- Change of major
- Death of close friend
- Failing important course
- Finding a new love interest
- Loss of financial aid
- Major injury or illness
- Parents' divorce
- Serious arguments with romantic partner
- Outstanding achievement

*Events Having Relatively Low Levels of Stress*
- Change in eating habits
- Change in sleeping habits
- Change in social activities
- Conflict with instructor
- Lower grades than expected

Source: Adapted from Baron, R. A., and Byrne, D. *Social Psychology: Understanding Human Interaction*, 6th ed. Boston: Allyn & Bacon, 1991, 573.

- **Physiological effects of stress** include increased blood pressure, increased heart rate, sweating, hot and cold spells, breathing difficulties, muscular tension, and gastrointestinal disorders.
- **Emotional effects of stress** include anger, anxiety, depression, low self-esteem, poor intellectual functioning (including an inability to concentrate and make decisions), nervousness, irritability, resentment of supervision, and job dissatisfaction.
- **Behavioral effects of stress** include poor performance, absenteeism, high accident rates, high turnover rates, high alcohol and substance abuse, impulsive behavior, and difficulties in communication.

These effects of work stress have important implications for organizational behavior and organizational effectiveness. We examine some of these effects in terms of health and performance, including job burnout.

### IMPACTS ON HEALTH

Stress and coronary heart disease are strongly linked. Other serious health problems commonly associated with stress include back pain, headaches, stomach and intestinal problems, upper respiratory infections, and various mental problems. Medical researchers recently have discovered possible links between stress and cancer. Although determining the precise role that stress plays in individual cases is difficult, many illnesses appear to be stress-related.[24]

Stress-related illnesses place a considerable burden on people and organizations. The costs to individuals seem more obvious than the costs to organizations. However, at least some of the organizational costs associated with stress-related disease can be identified. First, costs to employers include increased premiums for health insurance, as well as lost workdays from serious illnesses (e.g., heart disease) and less-serious illnesses (e.g., headaches). Estimates are that each employee who suffers from a stress-related illness loses an average of 16 days of work a year. Second, more than three-fourths of all industrial accidents are caused by a worker's inability to cope with emotional problems worsened by stress. Third, legal problems for employers are growing. The number of stress-related worker compensation claims is increasing. The link between the levels of stress in the workplace and worker compensation claims is clear. When employees experience higher amounts of stress, more worker compensation claims are filed. Studies have shown similar patterns in many different industries.[25]

Courts are recognizing **post-traumatic stress disorder** as a condition that may justify a damage claim against an employer. Post-traumatic stress disorder is normally thought of as a psychological disorder brought on, for example, by horrible experiences in combat during wartime, acts of violence and terrorism, and the like. Employees have successfully claimed suffering from this stress disorder as a result of sexual harassment, violence, and other traumatic circumstances in the workplace. Awards of damages in the millions of dollars have resulted from court cases involving workplace post-traumatic stress disorder claims.

### IMPACTS ON PERFORMANCE

The positive and negative effects of stress are most apparent in the relationship between stress and performance. Figure 7.4 depicts the general stress–performance relationship in the shape of an arch. At low levels of stress, employees may not be sufficiently alert, challenged, or involved to perform at their best. As the curve indicates, increasing a low amount of stress may improve performance—but only up to a point. An optimal level of stress probably exists for most tasks. Beyond that point, performance begins to deteriorate.[26] At excessive levels of stress, employees are too agitated, aroused, or threatened to perform well.

**Figure 7.4**                   **Typical Relationship Between Performance and Stress**

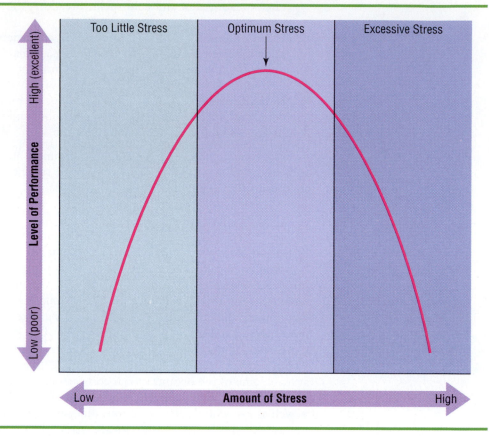

Managers often want to know the optimum stress points for both themselves and their subordinates. This information, however, is difficult to pin down. For example, an employee may be absent from work frequently because of boredom (too little stress) or because of overwork (excessive stress). Also, the curve shown in Figure 7.4 changes with the situation; that is, it varies for different people and different tasks. Too little stress for one employee may be just right for another on a particular task. Similarly, the optimal amount of stress for a specific individual for one task may be too much or too little for that person's effective performance of other tasks.

As a practical matter, managers should be more concerned about excessive stress than with how to add to stress. Motivating individuals to perform better is always important, but attempting to do so by increasing the level of stress is shortsighted.

Studies of the stress–performance relationship in organizations often show a strong negative correlation between the amount of stress in a team or department and its overall performance. This is, the greater the stress that employees are experiencing, the lower will be their productivity. This negative relationship indicates that these work settings are operating on the right-hand side (excessive stress) of the curve shown in Figure 7.4. Managers and employees in these situations need to find ways to reduce the number and magnitude of stressors. The following Managing Teams Competency feature shows how a new manager effectively diagnosed and helped to resolve the stresses and performances problems being experienced by his employees.

## IMPACTS ON JOB BURNOUT

**Job burnout** refers to the adverse effects of working conditions under which stressors seem unavoidable and sources of job satisfaction and relief from stress seem unavailable. The burnout phenomenon typically contains three components:

## COMPETENCY:   MANAGING TEAMS

### ANDREW SCOTT'S TEAM LEADERSHIP

When Andrew Scott started as technology director at AeroGroup International, Inc., the tension in the IT department was spreading throughout the entire company. The Edison, N.J.-based maker of AeroSoles shoes had already given up on one failed initiative. Its second attempt at this initiative had been put on hold when the U.K.-based vendor, JBA Holdings PLC, was bought by Toronto-based Geac Computer Corp.

The vice president of IT had just been fired, and the IT director quit. The entire IT department was taking a beating from employees throughout the company. They were divided along two lines: those who thought the old system was fine and were mad at IT for messing things up, and those who saw the benefits of the new system but thought IT didn't have the expertise to carry out the implementation.

Scott knew he had to do something about the stress his employees were experiencing. He had one-on-one meetings with every person in the IT department to discuss their concerns. He also spent a lot of time in team meetings with his staff to address common concerns, develop team goals, and reach agreed upon actions to take. Scott got the company's executive leadership to show support publicly for the department. Implementation of the major initiative was delayed, giving Scott the time he needed to get the department back on track.

Scott comments: "We're pretty much stable now. We've jelled great. The biggest thing we get stressed out on is deadlines. If you allocate enough time for projects, it can make a huge difference."[27]

*For more information on AeroGroup International, Inc., visit the organization's home page at http://www.aerosoles.com.*

- a state of emotional exhaustion,
- depersonalization of individuals, and
- feelings of low personal accomplishment.[28]

**Depersonalization** refers to the treatment of people as objects. For example, a nurse might refer to the "broken knee" in room 306, rather than use the patient's name. Doing so allows the nurse to disassociate with the patient as a person. The patient becomes seen and treated according to rules and procedures.

Most job burnout research has focused on the human services sector of the economy—sometimes called the "helping professions." Burnout is thought to be most prevalent in occupations characterized by continuous direct contact with people in need of aid. The highest probability of burnout occurs among those individuals who have both a high frequency and a high intensity of interpersonal contact. This level of interpersonal contact may lead to emotional exhaustion, a key component of job burnout.[29] Those who may be most vulnerable to job burnout include social workers, police officers, and teachers. Burnout also may affect managers or shop owners who are under increasing pressure to reduce costs, increase profits, and better serve customers.

Individuals who experience job burnout seem to have some common characteristics. Three characteristics in particular are associated with a high probability of burnout.

1. Burnout candidates experience a great deal of stress as a result of job-related stressors.
2. Burnout candidates tend to be idealistic and self-motivating achievers.
3. Burnout candidates often seek unattainable goals.[30]

Individuals who suffer from burnout often have unrealistically high expectations concerning their work and their ability to accomplish their goals because of the nature of the situation in which they find themselves. Unrelieved stressful working conditions, coupled with an individual's unrealistic expectations or ambitions, may lead to physical, mental, and emotional exhaustion. In experiencing burnout, the individual can no longer cope with job demands, and willingness even to try drops dramatically.

Traditionally, some managers treated the potential for burnout as an "acceptable" risk that goes along with serving clients or customers. However, more and more organizations are recognizing just how counterproductive overwork and burnout can be. The steps being taken by some organizations to dispel the management "myths" that lead to burnout are reported in the following Managing Communication Competency feature.

## COMPETENCY:  MANAGING COMMUNICATION

### MYTHS AND BURNOUT

Sue Shellenbarger, of the *Wall Street Journal*, interviewed dozens of managers in an attempt to understand managerial behavior that seems to push employees over the edge into job burnout. In the process, she identified three myths that organizations need to dispel if they are to reduce incidents of burnout among their staffs.

*Myth One:  When a client says jump, the only answer is: "How high?"*
Lawyers, accountants, and management consultants are particularly vulnerable to believing in this myth even when it appears to result in high levels of burnout and turnover on their staffs. However, Shellenbarger reports that a few professional firms are taking steps to integrate personal needs and concerns with the work lives of their employees. For example, Deloitte & Touche has implemented a policy that limits its employees' travel time. It is no longer company policy for employees to spend all 5 working days of the week at clients' offices. At a maximum, employees are to spend only 3 nights (4 working days) away from home and work the fifth day in their own offices each week, even when on lengthy assignments.

*Myth Two:  Reining in employees' workloads will turn them into slackers.*
Managers often behave as though a reduction in work overload will cause productivity to drop. Yet, studies often show the opposite result. Ernst & Young has a committee that monitors its staff accountants' workloads to head off burnout. The company says that its policies are raising retention rates and improving client service.

*Myth Three:  If employees are working themselves into the ground, it's their own fault.*
Although this myth may sometimes be true for some people, it is far from true for most. At the International Food Policy Research Institute, a nonprofit research organization in Washington, D.C., consultants discovered that a "crisis mentality" was driving scientists and support staff to work incredibly long hours. Management of the institute assumed that either (1) employees wanted to work these hours or (2) employees were managing their time poorly. Management learned that neither of these assumptions were valid and made major changes in workplace practices.[31]

*For more information on Deloitte & Touche, Ernst & Young, and the International Food Policy Institute, visit the organizations' home pages at http://www.deloitte.com/, http://www.ey.com/, and http://www.ifpri.org/.*

**Learning Objective:**

5. Identify individual and organizational practices for managing stress.

## MANAGING STRESS

Individual and organizational practices to help managers and employees cope with stress have become increasingly popular as stress has become more widely recognized as a problem. A variety of initiatives are available to individuals and organizations for managing stress and reducing its harmful effects. **Stress management** refers to any initiative that reduces stress by helping people understand the stress response, recognize stressors, and use coping techniques to minimize the negative impact of stress.[32]

## INDIVIDUAL INITIATIVES

Managing stress by individuals includes activities and behaviors designed to (1) eliminate or control the sources of stress and (2) make the individual more resistant to or better able to cope with stress. The first step in individual stress management involves recognizing the stressors that are affecting the person's life. Next, the individual needs to decide what to do about them. Figure 7.5 shows how personal goals and values, coupled with practical stress management skills, can help individuals cope with stressors and reduce negative stress reactions.

Practical initiatives for managing stress by individuals include the following.

- Plan ahead and practice good time management.
- Get plenty of exercise, eat a balanced diet, get adequate rest, and generally take care of yourself.
- Develop a sound philosophy of life and maintain a positive attitude as well as sense of humor.

**Figure 7.5**                    **Individual Strategy for Stress Management**

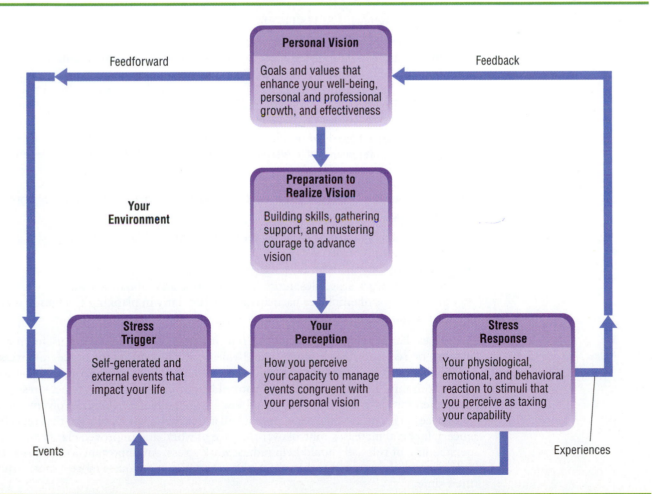

Source: Kindler, H. S., and Ginsburg, M. *Stress Training for Life*. Nichols Publishing Company. Reprinted with permission.

- Concentrate on balancing your work and personal life. Always take time to have fun.
- Learn a relaxation technique.[33]

Individuals can use relaxation techniques during the workday to cope with job demands. For example, a common "relaxation response" to stress is to (1) choose a comfortable position, (2) close your eyes, (3) relax your muscles, (4) become aware of your breathing, (5) maintain a passive attitude when thoughts surface, and (6) continue for a set period of time (e.g., 20 minutes).[34]

An in-depth study of successful top executives revealed that they used similar methods of coping with stress.[35] These executives came from a variety of industries and included the president of an oilfield service company, the founder of a residential real estate firm, the CEO of a large commercial bank, and a U.S. Navy admiral. First, they worked hard at balancing work and family concerns. Work was central to their lives, but it wasn't their sole focus. These executives also made effective use of leisure time to reduce stress. In addition, they were skilled time managers and goal setters. Important components of their effective use of time were identifying crucial goals and constructively planning how to reach them. Finally, these executives cited the essential role of social support in coping with stress. They didn't operate as loners; rather they received emotional support and important information from a diverse network of family, friends, coworkers, and industry colleagues. Additionally, these executives worked hard at maintaining fair exchanges in these relationships. That is, they both received support from and gave support to others in their networks.

## ORGANIZATIONAL INITIATIVES

Organizational initiatives for managing stress are typically designed to reduce the harmful effects of stress in three ways: (1) identify and then modify or eliminate work stressors, (2) help employees modify their perception and understanding of work stress, and (3) help employees cope more effectively with the consequences of stress.[36] As suggested in Figure 7.6, organizational stress management programs are often designed to reduce the harm effects of stress (distress) in one or more of the following ways: (1) identify and reduce or eliminate the work stressors, (2) assist employees in changing their perceptions of the stressors and experienced stress, and (3) assist employees in coping more effectively with the outcomes from stress.

### Reducing Work Stressors.
Initiatives aimed at eliminating or modifying work stressors include:

- improvements in the physical work environment;
- job redesign;
- changes in workloads and deadlines;
- changes in work schedules, more flexible hours, and sabbaticals; and
- greater levels of employee participation, particularly in planning changes that affect them.

Initiatives that promote role clarity and role analysis can be particularly useful in removing or reducing role ambiguity and role conflict—two main sources of stress. When diagnosing stressors in the workplace, managers should be particularly aware that uncertainty and perceived lack of control heighten stress. The greatest stress occurs when jobs are high in stressors and low in controllability. Thus involvement of employees in organizational changes that will affect them, work redesign that reduces uncertainty and increases control over the pace of work, and improved clarity and understanding of roles all should help reduce work stress. An important way to provide employees with more control and less stress is to give individuals more control over their time.

Sam Noble, a heath-care analyst who works for Value Management Group in Dallas, perhaps typifies the type of employee who attaches great importance to time.

**Figure 7.6**                    **Targets of Organizational Stress Management Programs**

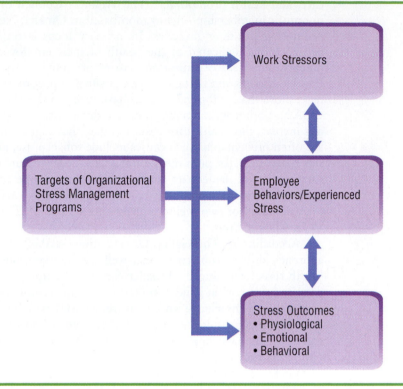

Noble says, "There's a point where money doesn't matter anymore after I have a certain amount of disposable income. It's more important to have reduced stress, a relaxed work style, and the time I need to be with my children and family." He was attracted to Value Management by its avowed corporate philosophy: "Make sure you get the job done and done well. Then, take what time you need as long as you don't abuse it."[37]

**Modifying Behaviors.**   Initiatives targeted at behaviors and experiences of stress and outcomes of stress include:

- team building,
- career counseling and other employee assistance programs,
- workshops on time management,
- workshops on job burnout to help employees understand its nature and symptoms, and
- training in relaxation techniques.

Dividing stress management initiatives into these categories doesn't mean that they are necessarily unrelated in practice. In addition, such programs might overlap in terms of their impact on the three target areas mentioned previously. For example, a workshop dealing with role problems might clarify job descriptions and duties, reducing the magnitude of these potential stressors. At the same time, through greater knowledge and insight into roles and role problems, employees might be able to cope more effectively with this source of stress. Similarly, career counseling might reduce career concerns as a source of stress while improving the ability of employees to cope with career problems.

**Creating Wellness Programs.**   One comprehensive method of improving the ability of individuals to cope with stress is a **wellness program**—a health management initiative that incorporates the components of disease prevention, medical care, self-care, and health promotion.[38] The Wellness Council of America (WELCOA) is a nonprofit membership organization based in Omaha, Nebraska, that is dedicated to promoting healthier lifestyles. Its primary focus is on building *Well Workplaces*—organizations dedicated to the health of their employees. The council provides a blueprint to help organizations create programs to help employees make better lifestyle choices and that can have a positive impact on the organizations' profits. To date, more than 500 organizations have received the Well Workplace Award. WELCOA and other wellness programs are driven by, among other factors, the continuous increases in health-care costs and data that suggest that leading causes of illness are often preventable. Such causes include tobacco use, alcohol and substance abuse, sedentary lifestyles, poor nutritional habits, excessive and unnecessary stressors in the workplace, and inadequate employee abilities to cope with stress.[39] The scope and features of wellness programs among organizations vary widely. Let's consider the main features of two wellness programs—those of The Gallup Organization and W.D. Class & Sons.

According to The Gallup Organization—a Well Workplace Award winner—its approach differs from traditional wellness interventions that attempt to minimize health risks by adding the broader concept of employee engagement with the company and the work at hand. Jim Harter, Gallup's senior research director, states: "The cost of losing knowledge workers is tremendous, worth millions to most large organizations. To get employees engaged, they need to know what is expected of them, feel cared about, have opportunities to do what they do best and feel connected to coworkers they respect."

Gallup promotes good health with traditional self-care literature, a 24-hour nurse hotline, and online health management services. It attends to the broader considerations of employee well-being with a concerted effort to match the knowledge worker's individual strengths with job requirements. Gallup's main tool is its Strength Finder survey, a personnel assessment instrument. The survey explores 34 different "life themes"—recurrent patterns of thought, feeling, and behavior—to determine which five constitute the individual's greatest personal and professional strengths. The themes are divided into four groups that deal with how a person relates to others, has an impact on the workplace, gets things done, and comprehends the job at hand.

Matching talents to jobs makes it far more likely that people will enjoy their work, an acknowledged factor in personal health and well being. It also engages the knowledge worker in tasks that need to be performed day in and day out, improving performance. Says Harter: "The engagement of knowledge workers results in productivity, profitability, customer loyalty and retention."[40]

Ralph Dudek is director of human resources for W.D. Class & Sons, Inc., a wholesale produce distributor in Jessup, Maryland. He notes that the company established its program, called *Wellness Incentive Now*, in 1993. Once each year, Class & Sons has its wellness provider hold for its 280 employees free health screenings that evaluate factors such as cholesterol levels, blood pressures, and levels of aerobic activity. The results of these assessments, which are voluntary, ultimately affect the amount of premium employees pay for their medical insurance.

An employee can get a refund of as much as $41 per monthly paycheck on her insurance premium for being labeled "low risk," though employees who are classified as "high risk" do not pay more than the 20 percent deductible. Dudek comments: "It means something to the employees if they can get healthy scores. Nearly all the company's employees willingly submit to the evaluations. It's a win–win situation. It's a win for the employees, because if they have some health problems, the screening can help identify that. From the company point of view, you tend to have fewer health-care claims if your employees have identified problem areas. These screenings are contributing to reduced medical claims, so it saves the company money."[41]

# CHAPTER SUMMARY

**1.** Explain the concept of stress and stressors and a person's response to stress.

Stress is the excitement, feeling of anxiety, and/or physical tension that occur when the demands placed on an individual exceed his ability to cope. This view of stress is often called *distress* or negative stress. The body's general biological response to stressors prepares the individual to fight or flee—behaviors generally inappropriate in the workplace. Many factors determine how employees experience work stress, including their perception of the situation, past experiences, the presence or absence of social support, and a variety of individual differences.

**2.** Discuss the relationship between personality and stress.

A variety of personality differences are related to differences in how individuals cope with stress. Individuals having a Type A personality are prone to stress and have an increased chance of heart disease. Some specific dimensions of the Type A personality, such as hostility, are particularly important in terms of stress-related illness. In contrast, the collection of personality traits known as hardiness seems to reduce the effects of stress.

**3.** State the primary sources of stress in organizations.

Organizational sources of stress at work include (1) workload, (2) job conditions, (3) role conflict and ambiguity, (4) career development, (5) interpersonal relations, (6) aggressive behavior, including violence and sexual harassment, and (7) conflict between work and other roles. In addition, significant changes or other events in an individual's personal life may also be sources of stress.

**4.** Describe the effects of stress on health and job performance.

Stress affects individuals physiologically, emotionally, and behaviorally. Stress has been linked to serious health problems, particularly coronary heart disease. An arch-shaped relationship exists between stress and performance. In other words, an optimal level of stress probably exists for any particular task, and less or more stress than that level may lead to reduced performance. Job burnout is a major result of unrelieved job-related stress.

**5.** Identify individual and organizational practices for managing stress.

Stress is a real issue for both individuals and organizations. Fortunately, various initiatives, both organizational and individual, can help managers and employees manage stress in the workplace. These initiatives often focus on identifying and removing workplace stressors as well as helping employees cope with stress. Wellness programs are particularly promising in helping employees cope with stress.

# KEY TERMS AND CONCEPTS

Behavioral effects of stress
Depersonalization
Emotional effects of stress
Fight-or-flight response
Hardiness
Hardy personality
Incivility
Job burnout
Life stressors
Physiological effects of stress
Post-traumatic stress disorder

Role ambiguity
Role conflict
Role overload
Sexual harassment
Stress
Stress management
Stressors
Type A personality
Type B personality
Wellness program
Workplace violence

## DISCUSSION QUESTIONS

1. Based on your own experience, describe a work situation that you found stressful. Use Figures 7.1 and 7.2 to identify the factors causing the stress and explain their impact.
2. Give examples of times when the fight-or-flight response seemed particularly inappropriate for (a) your own behavior and (b) the behavior of another person.
3. How do your individual differences (e.g., age, gender, past experience, and personality) contribute to your stress? Explain.
4. Identify and list some of the stressors in a job that you have held. Which were the most difficult to deal with? Why?
5. Provide an example from your own experience (at work, in sports activities, etc.) that illustrates the arch-shaped relationship between stress and performance.
6. Either from your own experience or from something you have read or seen in the business media, describe a real-world example of job burnout. What was its likely cause?
7. How would you describe yourself in comparison to (a) the Type A personality, (b) the hardy personality?
8. Describe a situation in which you coped well with stress. Describe another situation in which you didn't cope well with stress. How did your perception of the two situations differ?
9. What techniques, approaches, and competencies do you use to cope with stress? Which seem to work best for you?

## DEVELOPING COMPETENCIES

### Competency: Managing Self

### Determining Your Stress Level

The following questionnaire[42] has been widely used to measure stress levels. As you answer the questions, think only of the past month. After selecting an answer for each question, add your points to obtain a total.

_____ 1. How often have you been upset because of something that happened unexpectedly?

0 = never　1 = almost　2 = sometimes　3 = fairly　4 = very
　　　　　　　never　　　　　　　　　　　　often　　　often

_____ 2. How often have you felt that you were unable to control the important things in your life?

0 = never　1 = almost　2 = sometimes　3 = fairly　4 = very
　　　　　　　never　　　　　　　　　　　　often　　　often

_____ 3. How often have you felt nervous and "stressed"?

0 = never　1 = almost　2 = sometimes　3 = fairly　4 = very
　　　　　　　never　　　　　　　　　　　　often　　　often

_____ 4. How often have you felt confident about your ability to handle your personal problems?

4 = never　3 = almost　2 = sometimes　1 = fairly　0 = very
　　　　　　　never　　　　　　　　　　　　often　　　often

_____ 5. How often have you felt that things were going your way?

4 = never　3 = almost　2 = sometimes　1 = fairly　0 = very
　　　　　　　never　　　　　　　　　　　　often　　　often

_____ 6. How often have you been able to control irritations in your life?

4 = never　3 = almost　2 = sometimes　1 = fairly　0 = very
　　　　　　　never　　　　　　　　　　　　often　　　often

_____ 7. How often have you found that you could not cope with all the things that you had to do?

0 = never　1 = almost　2 = sometimes　3 = fairly　4 = very
　　　　　　　never　　　　　　　　　　　　often　　　often

_____ 8. How often have you felt that you were on top of things?

4 = never　3 = almost　2 = sometimes　1 = fairly　0 = very
　　　　　　　never　　　　　　　　　　　　often　　　often

_____ 9. How often have you been angered because of things that were outside your control?

0 = never　1 = almost　2 = sometimes　3 = fairly　4 = very
　　　　　　　never　　　　　　　　　　　　often　　　often

_____ 10. How often have you felt difficulties were piling up so high that you could not overcome them?

0 = never　1 = almost　2 = sometimes　3 = fairly　4 = very
　　　　　　　never　　　　　　　　　　　　often　　　often

_____ TOTAL POINTS

Stress levels vary among individuals. Compare your total score to the following averages.

| AGE | GENDER | MARITAL STATUS |
|---|---|---|
| 18–29 . . . . . 14.2 | Men . . . . . 12.1 | Widowed . . . . . 12.6 |
| 30–44 . . . . . . 13.0 | Women . . . 13.7 | Married or |
| 45–54 . . . . . . 12.6 | | living with . . . . 12.4 |
| 55–64 . . . . . . 11.9 | | Single or |
| 65 and over . 12.0 | | never wed . . . . . 14.1 |
| | | Divorced . . . . . 14.7 |
| | | Separated . . . . . 16.6 |

## Questions

1.  If it is excessive, what actions can you take to lower your stress level?

2.  What three competencies are likely to be most effective and important to you in managing your stress level?

## Competency: Managing Change

### The Stress of Shift Work

Marilyn Baker sat at her kitchen table and leafed through the entertainment section of the local paper, slowly sipping her second cup of coffee. An Academy Award–winning movie was playing at one of the theaters in town, and she hoped that it would stay for several weeks so that she and her husband, Carl, could fit it into their hectic schedules. Carl Baker had changed jobs recently and was now working for St. Regis Aluminum, a manufacturer of lightweight metal products. St. Regis worked shifts, and he was about to start a two-week stint on the night shift (midnight to 8 A.M.). Neither of the Bakers had had previous experience with shift work.

Carl worked cycles that included 2 weeks of day shift (8 A.M. to 4 P.M.), 2 weeks of swing shift (4 P.M. to midnight), and 2 weeks of night shift. Then, the whole cycle began again. The couple had to plan their family life around this changing schedule, but Marilyn couldn't seem to get the hang of it. Little things that would have been minor irritants before now seemed to become major problems. For example, the boy next door was taking trumpet lessons and practiced after school. When Carl needed to sleep in the afternoon, the noise of the trumpet often woke him. The couple had already had two arguments about whether to call the boy's mother to request that he practice at another time.

Marilyn Baker was an excellent cook and particularly enjoyed preparing foods that her family liked. Yesterday, roast beef, one of Carl's favorite foods, had been on sale. However, with Carl starting the night shift, Marilyn decided to freeze the roast and wait for a time when the entire family could enjoy it. Even though Carl could sit down to a full meal after coming off the night shift, that early morning time wasn't very appealing to the rest of the family. So, Marilyn was learning that "special" meals were pretty much restricted to the times when Carl worked the day shift.

Shift work was also proving awkward for their social life. The Bakers were members of a poker club that met twice a month on Friday nights. Couples in the club usually met at 8 P.M. and played for four hours. When Carl was on the swing shift, there was no way they could play. When he worked the night shift, they could stay for only part of the evening, as Carl would have to leave in time to get ready for work. Only when he was on the day shift could they participate fully. So, now they were playing with their club only once or twice every 2 months. Their friends had gotten another couple to substitute for them, but the Bakers were afraid they might have to drop out of the club because the substitute couple was playing more frequently than they were.

Marilyn Baker had started to feel a bit sorry for herself. Still, she admitted to herself that this shift work must be more stressful to Carl than it was to her. She remembered that he was working the swing shift on the weekend when the Custom Boat and Trailer Show came to town. He had been looking forward to seeing the new bass boats for weeks but got to visit the show for only about an hour before having to leave for work. Weekends seemed particularly hard on Carl. On Saturdays and Sundays, just when he found something he liked to do, it often was time to go to work.

Their 10-year-old son, Tom, wandered into the kitchen holding a Little League schedule in his hand. "Mom," Tom said, "the regional tournament is in three weeks. Will you and Dad be able to see my games?" Marilyn got up to look at Carl's work schedule, which was taped to the refrigerator door. "Dad will be working the swing shift that week, but I can come. I'll work some extra hours and can trade days off with someone on my work team. So, I'll be able to take off enough time to see all your games," Marilyn said. Tom loved to have his mother at his baseball games, but still his face fell. "Dad sure doesn't see many of my games any more," he said, as he slowly walked from the kitchen.[43]

## Questions

1.  Identify the stressors that exist in this situation. Which do you think are the most important?
2.  Can you predict other possible disruptions in the Bakers' family life that might stem from shift work?
3.  Suggest some things that St. Regis Aluminum might do to reduce stress for shift workers.
4.  Suggest some stress-coping strategies that Marilyn and Carl Baker could use.

# 2

# Team and Leadership Behaviors

# CHAPTER

# Managing Teams

## LEARNING OBJECTIVES

When you have finished studying the chapter, you should be able to:

1. State the basic characteristics of groups, including informal groups.
2. Describe the distinguishing features of five types of teams.
3. Explain the five-stage model of team development.
4. Describe seven key factors that influence team effectiveness.
5. Relate how the use of the nominal group technique, traditional brainstorming, and electronic brainstorming can foster team creativity.

8

## ROCHE'S GO TEAM

Most the time, cancer researcher Barry Goggin does his best work either at his desk or inside one of Roche's laboratories. The Roche Company is involved in the discovery, development, manufacture, and marketing of drugs. A couple of years ago, Goggin noticed a change in work practices. "We started having corridor meetings. We would just start talking. It might be a couple of us from oncology and then a person from genomics. Back then, there wasn't any official way for us to work together. So we'd just get together in the corridors and design all sorts of small projects."

A bureaucratic boss might have told the researchers to stop gossiping and get back to the lab. But Roche's head of preclinical research, Lee Babiss, liked what he saw. In fact, he wanted to cut across traditional departmental boundaries and create interdisciplinary teams. That way, Roche could harness the energy of those corridor meetings and try to direct it toward breakthrough science.

Roche formed the Genomics Oncology (GO) team—a combination of seven researchers from the genetics and oncology departments. It was one of the most diverse teams Roche had ever assembled. Team members had backgrounds ranging from immunology to statistics. They were born in countries as varied and distant as China and Germany. But they were united by a desire to identify new targets for cancer drugs using genomics tools.

Leading the GO team was Juergen Hammer, a German-born genomics expert. He had been irritated by the fact that his department was producing a lot of exciting data, but no one else at Roche had been able to look at it. Now he had his chance. The team's charge: to focus on colon cancer, a disease that was common and well understood on a molecular level but that still wasn't being treated very effectively with existing drugs.

Eventually, two genes were selected by the team and endorsed by management for further research. Both genes had been among the 50 most promising prospects in early gene experiments. But neither had been among the top 10 at the time. By combining genomics and oncology techniques, researchers had isolated new drug targets that would have been overlooked by either set of specialists working alone.[1]

*For more information on the Roche Company, visit the organization's home page at http://www.roche.com.*

The Preview Case illustrates two important points about outstanding organizations: (1) individual performance by committed individuals is crucial, and (2) individuals working together as a team can often achieve more than if they work in isolation.

In this chapter, we focus on one of the seven core competencies introduced in Chapter 1. Recall that the *managing teams competency* involves the ability to develop, support, facilitate, and lead groups to achieve organizational goals. Throughout the chapter, we present ways to understand and increase the effectiveness of groups and teams. We focus on (1) the fundamentals of groups in organizations, (2) the types of teams frequently used in organizations, (3) the ways in which team members develop and learn, (4) the principal factors that influence team effectiveness, and (5) two of the many methods that can be used to encourage team creativity.

**Learning Objective:**

1. State the basic characteristics of groups, including informal groups.

# FUNDAMENTALS OF GROUPS

For our purposes, a **group** is any number of people who share goals, often communicate with one another over a period of time, and are few enough so that each individual may communicate with all the others, person-to-person.[2]

## GROUP CLASSIFICATION

Most individuals belong to various types of groups, which can be classified in many ways. For example, a person concerned with obtaining membership in a group or gaining acceptance as a group member might classify groups as open or closed to new members. A person evaluating groups in an organization according to their primary goals might classify them as friendship groups or task groups. A **friendship group** evolves informally to meet its members' personal security, esteem, and belonging needs. A **task group** is created by management to accomplish certain organizational goals. However, a single group in an organization may serve both friendship and task purposes. The primary focus of this chapter is on types of task groups, commonly known today as teams.

## INFORMAL GROUPS

An **informal group** is one that develops out of the day-to-day activities, interactions, and sentiments that the members have for each other. Informal groups typically meet their members' security and social needs. In the work setting, the purpose of informal groups isn't necessarily related to organizational goals. The organization, however, often has considerable influence on the development of informal groups through the physical layout of work, the leadership practices of managers, and the types of technology used.[3] For example, EDS found that moving its professionals from one building to another had an impact on the membership of informal groups. The distance between members may make face-to-face communication difficult and cause groups to wither or reconstitute themselves. In contrast, a new manager taking over a department and telling its employees to "shape up or ship out" may cause an informal group to form, with its members uniting against the manager. Some managers believe that close-knit informal groups have undesirable effects on an organization. They view groups as a potential source of anti-establishment power, as a way of holding back information when the group doesn't identify with organizational goals, or as a means of pressuring individuals to slow production.

Informal groups can provide their members with desirable benefits (e.g., security and protection). Some informal groups set production limits for their members, fearing that management might use an outstanding worker as a standard for output and that increased production might lead to some workers being laid off. An informal group can provide positive feedback to other members. The all-too-common belief that higher productivity will work against the interests of workers is kept alive and enforced by some informal groups within organizations.[4]

Informal groups can also exercise undesirable power over individual members. Such power usually falls into two categories. First, a group may be able to manipulate rewards and punishments and thus pressure members to conform to its standards of behavior. Second, a group may restrict a member's freedom and the ways by which the social needs of its members can be satisfied on the job. Informal groups have been known to ridicule certain members or give them the silent treatment for not conforming to group standards of "acceptable" production. Such treatment may threaten the individual's safety, social, and esteem needs. Managers probably should try to minimize the undesirable effects of informal groups rather than try to eliminate them.[5]

Informal groups in organizations can't always be classified simply as positive or negative because many exhibit both characteristics from time to time, depending on the circumstances or issues facing the organization. The following Managing Diversity Competency feature illustrates the potential negative impacts of informal groups and practices on the career progress and roles of African-American managers in organizations with predominantly white, male managers. These incidents reflect what can happen when the managing diversity competency is inadequate in the eyes of black managers.

## COMPETENCY: MANAGING DIVERSITY

### INFORMAL GROUPS AND BLACK MANAGERS

Bob Tassie, an African American and former vice president of communications for CBS Sports, comments on this situation: A group of managers—all white—go out regularly once a week for refreshments after work and blacks aren't invited. "If you don't reach out, you'll never be a part of that group," says Tassie, now president of Unity Media, a media buying company. "And the chitchat that goes on there is as important as what goes on at work. Once you're part of the informal group, colleagues will start seeing you not as an icon, but as someone who pays a mortgage, has children in school, just like them."

Black managers often walk a fine line between accommodating the white corporate culture and maintaining their identity. "Maybe that means displaying African-American art in my office," says Robert Phillips, director of affirmative action for the City of Portland and Multnomah County, Oregon. But, he adds, "I can't come in wearing dashikis and beads or the organization will push me to the side."

Black managers sometimes have to contend with the informal group view that they got there because of being black. Jim Kennedy, president of Management Team Consultants of San Rafael, California, advises companies on how to hire a diverse workforce. He recommends a staff meeting to discuss the criteria used to fill the position and the qualifications of the new black manager. Kennedy suggests that management acknowledge that adding a minority candidate may have been a consideration but that if the person isn't competent, he'll be fired in a few weeks and management will be embarrassed. The meeting may not change minds, but it at least brings the issue into the open. Phillips contends: "In organizations where there were only white managers for a long time, the best thing is to put it on the table up front. If you don't, you get an undercurrent of people talking."[6]

## EFFECTIVE GROUPS

To make groups, especially teams, more effective, a manager must know how to recognize effective and ineffective groups. In brief, an effective group has the following basic characteristics. Its members

- know why the group exists and have shared goals;
- support agreed upon guidelines or procedures for making decisions;
- communicate freely among themselves;
- receive help from one another and to give help to one another;
- deal with conflict within the group; and
- diagnose individual and group processes and improve their own and the group's functioning.[7]

The degree to which a group lacks one or more of these characteristics determines whether—and to what extent—it is ineffective. These basic characteristics apply both to formal groups (e.g., the cross-functional GO team at Roche discussed in the Preview Case) and to informal groups (e.g., the white managers who go out for refreshments once a week noted in the Managing Diversity Competency feature).

**Learning Objective:**

2. Describe the distinguishing features of five types of teams.

## TYPES OF TEAMS

A **team** is a small number of employees with complementary competencies (abilities, skills, and knowledge) who are committed to common performance goals and working relationships for which they hold themselves mutually accountable.[8] The heart of any team is a shared commitment by its members for their joint performance. Team goals could be as basic as responding to all customers' calls within 24 hours or as involved as reducing defects by 20 percent over the next 6 months. The key point is that such goals can't be achieved without the cooperation and communication of team members. When a team is formed, its members must have (or quickly develop) the right mix of competencies to achieve the team's goals. Also, its members need to be able to influence how they will work together to accomplish those goals. The GO team at Roche has the goal and shared commitment to find the genes underlying colon cancer and develop new ways to treat this disease. The team is relatively small—seven members—and brought together complementary competencies in the fields of genetics oncology, immunology, statistics, and other specialties.

Of the many basic types of teams, we consider five of the most common: functional teams, problem-solving teams, cross-functional teams, self-managed teams, and virtual teams.

### FUNCTIONAL TEAMS

**Functional teams** usually include individuals who work together daily on similar tasks. Functional teams often exist within functional departments—marketing, production, finance, auditing, human resource, and the like. Within a human resource department, one or more functional teams could perform recruiting, compensation, benefits, safety, training and development, affirmative action, industrial relations, and similar functions. Several years ago, Macy's implemented a team system at its Herald Square flagship store in New York City. Macy's team system included functional teams for receiving and delivery, placement, fill-in, recovery, and administration. The administrative team handles all damaged goods, merchandise returns to vendors, markdowns and other price changes, and hanger and security tag pickup at the cash register and wrapping areas.[9]

## PROBLEM-SOLVING TEAMS

**Problem-solving teams** focus on specific issues in their areas of responsibility, develop potential solutions, and often are empowered to take action within defined limits. Such teams frequently address quality or cost problems. Their members usually are employees from a specific department who meet at least once or twice a week for an hour or two. Teams may have the authority to implement their own solutions if they don't require major procedural changes that might adversely affect other operations or require substantial new resources. Problem-solving teams do not fundamentally reorganize work or change the role of managers. In effect, managers delegate certain problems and decision-making responsibilities to a team.

As indicated in Table 8.1, Ford Motor Company's 8D team problem-solving process provides guidelines to be followed by its problem-solving teams. The process steps and suggested actions are representative of the guidelines for problem-solving teams in many organizations.

The many different types of goals, problems, and tasks confronting an organization require varying degrees of interdependency among individuals and teams. Some require both individual and team problem solving. Organizations can incur excessive costs if either individual or team decision making is used improperly. The unnecessary use of team problem solving is wasteful because the participants' time could have been used more effectively on other tasks; it creates boredom, resulting in a feeling that time is being wasted, and reduces motivation. Conversely, the improper use of individual problem solving can result in poor coordination, little creativity, and numerous errors. In brief, team problem solving is likely to be superior to individual problem solving when

- the greater diversity of information, experience, and approaches to be found in a team is important to the task at hand;
- acceptance of the decisions arrived at is crucial for effective implementation by team members;
- participation is important for reinforcing the values of representation versus authoritarianism and demonstrating respect for individual members through team processes; and
- team members rely on each other in performing their jobs.

## CROSS-FUNCTIONAL TEAMS

**Cross-functional teams** bring together people from various work areas to identify and solve mutual problems. Cross-functional teams draw members from several specialties or functions and deal with problems that cut across departmental and functional lines to achieve their goals. Some cross-functional teams operate on an extended basis, as is the case with the cross-functional GO team at Roche. Other cross-functional teams may be disbanded after the problems they addressed have been solved and their goals achieved.

Cross-functional teams are often most effective in situations that require innovation, speed, and a focus on responding to customer needs.[10] They may design and introduce quality improvement programs and new technology, meet with customers and suppliers to improve inputs or outputs, and link separate functions (e.g., marketing, finance, manufacturing, and human resource) to increase product or service innovations.

Seeking efficiency and better alignment with major retail customers, Nestlé USA changed its decentralized functional organization in its chocolate and confections division to cross-functional teams. One aim of the reorganization is to give the company a focal point for communicating and implementing its strategy, allaying a frequent gripe of its retail customers. "There was no one coordinating the whole

**Table 8.1**                **Ford Motor Company's 8D Team Problem-Solving Process**

| STEP NO. | PROCESS STEP | WHAT TO DO |
|---|---|---|
| 1 | Become aware of the problem. | Make each problem-solving team member aware of bad parts, processes, nonconformances, and customer concerns. |
| 2 | Use team approach. | Establish a small group of people with the process of product knowledge, allocated time, authority, and skill in the technical discipline to solve the problem and implement corrective actions. This team is to have a designated leader. |
| 3 | Describe the problem. | Specify the customer problem by identifying in specific terms the who, what, when, where, why, how, and how many of the problem.<br>• Analyze existing data.<br>• Establish operational definition. |
| 4 | Implement and verify interim (containment) actions. | Define and implement containment actions to isolate the problem from any customer until permanent corrective action is available. Verify effectiveness of actions. |
| 5 | Define and verify root cause. | Check team composition and process. Identify potential causes.<br>• Review and improve the problem description.<br>• Evaluate each potential cause by comparison to the problem description.<br>Select likely causes.<br>• Test each potential cause through experimentation and statistical analysis.<br>• Identify alternative corrective actions to eliminate root cause. |
| 6 | Choose and verify corrective actions. | Check team composition and process. Evaluate solutions for improved interim actions. Evaluate the degree of problem reduction or elimination using preproduction tests. |
| 7 | Implement permanent corrective actions. | Check team composition and process. Identify prevention and protection actions. Monitor effectiveness of problem reduction or elimination. |
| 8 | Prevent recurrence. | Modify the management systems, operating systems, practices, and procedures to prevent recurrence of this and all similar problems. |
| 9 | Congratulate the team. | Use various recognition and reward techniques. |

Source: Adapted from Chaudhry, A. M. To be a problem solver, be a classicist. *Quality Progress*, June 1999, 47–51.

thing: said a drugstore buyer. "I've been at Nestlé meetings where there's 32 people in the room, and they couldn't figure out how to order lunch." Retailers had long complained that, when they have questions about shipments, off-invoice trade allowances, shippers, and promotions, they have to contact several Nestlé people for answers.[11]

## SELF-MANAGED TEAMS

**Self-managed teams** normally consist of employees who must work together effectively daily to manufacture an entire product (or major identifiable component) or provide an entire service to a set of customers. A major characteristic of such teams is that they are empowered. The term **team empowerment** refers to the degree to which its members perceive the group as (1) being effective (potency), (2) performing important and valuable tasks (meaningfulness), (3) having independence and discretion (autonomy) in performing the work, and (4) experiencing a sense of importance and significance (impact) in the work performed and goals achieved.[12] You may relate the key dimensions of empowerment—*potency, meaningfulness, autonomy*, and *impact*—to your own experience with a task-related team by responding to the brief questionnaire in Table 8.2 on page 200. To obtain your team empowerment score, follow the directions in the table.

Self-managed teams are often empowered to perform a variety of managerial tasks, such as (1) scheduling work and vacations by members, (2) rotating tasks and assignments among members, (3) ordering materials, (4) deciding on team leadership (which can rotate among team members), (5) setting key team goals, (6) budgeting, (7) hiring replacements for departing team members, and (8) sometimes even evaluating one another's performance.[13] Each member may even learn all the tasks that have to be performed by the team.

The impact of self-managed teams on productivity may be enormous. They have raised productivity 30 percent or more and have substantially raised quality in organizations that have used them. They fundamentally change how work is organized and leadership is practiced.[14] The introduction of self-managed teams typically eliminates one or more managerial levels, thereby creating a flatter organization.

The Whole Foods Market natural foods grocery store chain, with more than 21,000 employees and 126 stores, is very successful. Its key organizing approach and management philosophy is the use of empowered self-managing teams, as clearly illustrated in the Managing Teams Competency feature on page 201.

**Organizational Use.**   Empowered self-managed teams aren't necessarily right for every situation or organization. Both costs and benefits accrue in implementing such a system. A number of questions need to be addressed in considering the introduction of empowered self-managed teams, including the following.

1. Is the organization fully committed to aligning all management systems with empowered work teams, including selection of leaders, team-based rewards, and open access to information?
2. Are organizational goals and the expected results from the teams clearly specified?
3. Will the teams have access to the resources they need for high performance?
4. Will team members carry out interdependent tasks (i.e., tasks that require a high degree of coordination and communication)?
5. Do employees have the necessary maturity levels to effectively carry out peer evaluations, selection and discipline decisions, conflict management, and other administrative tasks?
6. Are employee ability levels sufficient for handling increased responsibility and, if not, will increased training result in appropriate ability levels?[15]

We discuss additional aspects of the conditions and actions necessary for creative effective teams throughout this chapter and book.

## VIRTUAL TEAMS

Functional, problem-solving, cross-functional, and even self-managed teams increasingly operate as virtual teams. A **virtual team** is a group of individuals who

**Table 8.2**

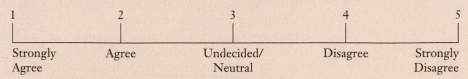

### Team Empowerment Questionnaire

**Instructions:** Think of a team that you have been (or are) a member of in a work setting. Respond to each statement below by indicating the degree to which you agree or disagree with it in terms of the team identified. The scale is as follows.

| 1 | 2 | 3 | 4 | 5 |
|---|---|---|---|---|
| Strongly Agree | Agree | Undecided/ Neutral | Disagree | Strongly Disagree |

Place the appropriate number value next to each item.

*Potency Items*

_____ 1. The team had confidence in itself.
_____ 2. The team believed that it could be very good at producing high-quality work.
_____ 3. The team expected to be seen by others as high performing.
_____ 4. The team was confident that it could solve its own problems.
_____ 5. The team viewed no job as too tough.

*Meaningfulness Items*

_____ 6. The team cared about what it did.
_____ 7. The team thought that its work was valuable.
_____ 8. The team viewed its group goals as important.
_____ 9. The team believed that its projects were significant.
_____10. The team considered its group tasks to be worthwhile.

*Autonomy Items*

_____11. The team could select different ways to do its work.
_____12. The team determined how things were done.
_____13. The team had a lot of choice in what it did without being told by management.
_____14. The team had significant influence in setting its goals.
_____15. The team could rotate tasks and assignments among team members.

*Impact Items*

_____16. The team assessed the extent to which it made progress on projects.
_____17. The team had a positive impact on other employees.
_____18. The team had a positive impact on customers.
_____19. The team accomplished its goals.
_____20. The team made a difference in the organization.

_____ **Total:** Add points for items 1 through 20. This total is your perceived team empowerment score. Scores may range from 20 to 100. Scores of 20 through 45 suggest low team empowerment. Scores of 46 through 74 indicate moderate levels of team empowerment. Scores of 75 through 100 reveal a state of significant to very high team empowerment.

Source: Adapted from Kirkman, B. I., and Rosen, B. Beyond self-management: Antecedents and consequences of team empowerment. *Academy of Management Journal*, 1999, 42, 58–74; Kirkman, B. L., and Rosen, B. Powering up teams. *Organizational Dynamics*, Winter 2000, 48–65.

collaborate through various information technologies on one or more projects while being at two or more locations.[16] Unlike teams that operate primarily through person-to-person meetings by members of the same organization, virtual teams work primarily across distance (any place), across time (any time), and increasingly across organizational boundaries (members from two or more organizations).

**Core Features.**    The core features of a virtual team are goals, people, and links. Goals are important to any team, but especially so to a virtual team. Clear, precise,

## COMPETENCY:    MANAGING TEAMS

### SELF-MANAGED TEAMS AT WHOLE FOODS MARKET

The Whole Foods Market culture is based on decentralized teamwork. Each of the stores is a profit center that typically has 10 self-managed teams—produce, grocery, prepared foods, and so on—with designated leaders and clear performance targets. The team leaders in each store are a team, store leaders in each region are a team, and the company's six regional presidents are a team. Three principles define how the company operates.

The first principle is *all work is teamwork*. Everyone who joins Whole Foods quickly grasps the importance of teamwork. That's because teams—and only teams—have the power to approve new hires for full-time jobs. Store leaders screen candidates and recommend them for a job on a specific team. But it takes a two-thirds vote of the team, after what is usually a 30-day trial period, for the candidate to become a full-time employee. Team members are tough on new hires for another reason: money. The company's gain-sharing program ties bonuses directly to team performance—specifically, to sales per labor hour, the most important productivity measurement at Whole Foods.

The second principle is *anything worth doing is worth measuring*. Whole Foods takes that simple principle to extremes—and then shares what it measures with everyone in the company. John Mackey, the CEO, calls it a "no-secrets" management philosophy. He states, "In most companies, management controls information and therefore controls people. By sharing information, we stay aligned to the vision of shared fate." The reports are indispensable to the teams, which make the decisions about labor spending, ordering, and pricing—the factors that determine profitability.

The third principle is *be your own toughest competitor*. "All-for-one" doesn't imply complacency. Whole Foods is serious about accountability. Teams are expected to set ambitious goals and achieve them. Teams compete against their own goals for sales, growth, and productivity.[17]

*For more information on Whole Foods Market, visit the organization's home page at http://www.wholefoodsmarket.com.*

and mutually agreed upon goals are the glue that holds a virtual team together. The ability to hire and fire by a superior and reliance on rules and regulations are minimized in effective virtual teams.

As in all teams, people are at the core of effective virtual teams, but with some unique twists. Everyone in a virtual team needs to be autonomous and self-reliant while simultaneously working collaboratively with others. This duality requires a certain type of person and a foundation of trust among team members. The most apparent feature of a virtual team is the array of technology-based links used to connect members and enable them to carry out its tasks. Virtual teams are increasingly common because of rapid advances in computer and telecommunications technologies.[18]

**Technology Links.**    Three broad categories of technologies are often used in the operation of virtual teams: desktop videoconferencing systems, collaborative software systems, and Internet/intranet systems.[19] Virtual teams can function with only simple e-mail and telephone systems, including voice mail. However, desktop video conferencing systems (DVCSs) re-create some of the aspects of face-to-face interactions of conventional teams. This technology makes possible more complex levels of communication among team members. The DVCS is a relatively simple system for users to operate. A small camera mounted atop a computer monitor provides the video feed to the system; voice transmissions operate through an earpiece–

microphone combination or speakerphone. Connection to other team members is managed through software on the user's computer.

Collaborative software systems (group support systems) comprise the second category of technologies that enable the use of virtual teams. Collaborative software is designed for both independent and interactive use. For example, Lotus Notes, a dominant collaborative software product, is designed specifically for communication and data sharing when team members are working at different times, at the same time, independently, or interactively. It combines scheduling, electronic messaging, and document and data sharing. Although Lotus Notes and other such software may be used to support teamwork in a traditional work environment, they are vital to the operation of empowered virtual teams.

Internet and intranet technologies represent the third main enabler of virtual teams. Recall that intranets give organizations the advantage of using Internet technology to disseminate organizational information and enhance interemployee communication while maintaining system security. They allow virtual teams to archive text, visual, audio, and numerical data in a user-friendly format. The Internet and intranets also allow virtual teams to keep other organizational members and important external stakeholders, such as suppliers and customers, up-to-date on a team's progress.[20]

The following Managing Across Cultures Competency feature provides an example of the successful use of virtual teams in the United States and across national boundaries by BakBone Software, headquartered in San Diego, California. This firm develops and globally distributes software to network storage and open systems markets.

## COMPETENCY: MANAGING ACROSS CULTURES

### VIRTUAL TEAMS AT BAKBONE SOFTWARE

When Roger Rodriguez goes to work at BakBone Software, he may be dealing with customer support problems that were passed on to him by colleagues in Lanham, Maryland, or in the city of Poole in the United Kingdom. As his workday ends, Rodriguez, a client service senior engineer, may hand off other support problems to teammates in Tokyo. Rodriguez has never met most of these coworkers face-to-face, and he probably never will. But they work with him daily on a virtual team whose members are spread across three continents to provide "follow the sun" customer support.

Tim Miller, director of client services at BakBone Software comments: "One of the reasons we went to virtual teams in our support centers is that it's difficult to attract the caliber of people you want who are willing to work at 2:00 and 3:00 in the morning on Saturday and Sunday." Virtual teaming also is the alternative to having a massive staff in one location. Miller's staff of 13 technical support representatives is spread over four call centers in San Diego, Lanham, Poole, and Tokyo. Regular and accurate communication becomes overwhelmingly important for global virtual teams. For example, Rodriguez stays in touch with others via telephone (especially voice mail), e-mail, and a companywide database that tracks actions taken on specific customer problems. Rodriguez also has learned to express himself clearly and concisely, because a coworker thousands of miles away can't ask him in the middle of San Diego's night to clarify his last voice mail message. Rodriguez states: "Passing off information to another virtual team member requires a certain level of discipline. We have to summarize the issues in an analytical engineering fashion. We have to be clear."

*For more information on BakBone Software, visit the organization's home page at http://www. bakbone.com.*

Rodriguez says that being a virtual team member taught him how to phrase carefully his questions to Japanese coworkers. The reason for his care is that questions to his Japanese counterparts may elicit different answers than from his English-speaking colleagues. His state-side team members will usually say what they mean. In Japan, a yes-or-no question almost always results in a "yes" answer—even if it shouldn't. [21]

**Learning Objective:**

3. Explain the five-stage model of team development.

# STAGES OF TEAM DEVELOPMENT

The formation of effective teams is not automatic. Various conditions for success or failure occur throughout a team's development. To provide a sense of these conditions, we present a basic five-stage developmental sequence that teams may go through: forming, storming, norming, performing, and adjourning.[22] The types of work-related and socially related behaviors that may be observed differ from stage to stage. Figure 8.1 shows the five stages on the horizontal axis and the level of team maturity on the vertical axis. It also indicates that a team can fail and disband during a

**Figure 8.1**          **Stages of Team Development**

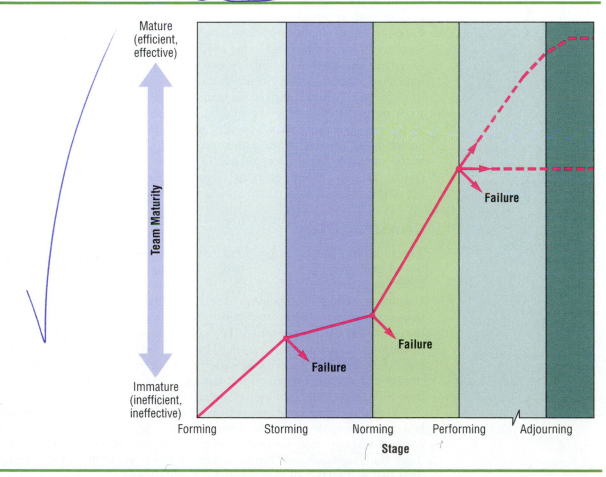

Source: Adapted from Tuckman, B. W., and Jensen, M. A. C. Stages of small-group development revisited. *Groups and Organization Studies*, 1977, 2, 419–442; Kormanski, C. Team interventions: Moving the team forward. In J. W. Pfeiffer (ed.). *The 1996 Annual: Volume 2 Consulting.* San Diego: Pfeiffer and Company, 1996, 19–26.

stage or when moving from one stage to another. Pinpointing the developmental stage of a team at any specific time is difficult. Nevertheless, managers and team members need to understand these developmental stages because each can influence a team's effectiveness. In the following discussion, we describe behaviors that might occur at each stage. Of course, teams and groups do not necessarily develop in the straightforward manner depicted in this model.[23] Team members with high levels of the seven core competencies presented throughout this book are likely to speed up and alter the stages of development presented here.

### FORMING STAGE

Team members often focus on defining or understanding goals and developing procedures for performing their tasks in the forming stage. Team development in this stage involves getting acquainted and understanding leadership and other member roles. In terms of social behaviors, it should also deal with members' feelings and the tendency of most members to depend too much on one or two of the team's members. Otherwise, individual members might (1) keep feelings to themselves until they know the situation, (2) act more secure than they actually feel, (3) experience confusion and uncertainty about what is expected of them, (4) be nice and polite, or at least certainly not hostile, and (5) try to size up the personal benefits relative to the personal costs of being involved with the team or group.

M. Caouette and B. O'Connor investigated the impact of a collaborative software system on the development and performance of two corporate teams.[24] One strength of their study involved investigation of actual corporate teams solving real problems. Caouette and O'Connor were fortunate in having access to an organization whose top managers were as interested in the results of the study as they were. This interest allowed the investigators to study the two teams in detail, using meeting transcripts and individual interviews. One team studied had used a collaborative software system from the start, whereas the second team used the system only after the team had met a few times. The investigators' findings indicated that the two teams developed and performed quite differently. The team that started with the collaborative system improved faster than the other team at each stage of development, but most noticeably at the storming stage. Caouette and O'Connor found that a collaborative software system can help a group get started (forming), but only when the group considers that use of the system is important to doing the task at hand.

### STORMING STAGE

The storming stage is characterized by conflicts over work behaviors, relative priorities of goals, who is to be responsible for what, and the task-related guidance and direction of the team leader. Social behaviors are a mixture of expressions of hostility and strong feelings. Competition over the leadership role and conflict over goals may dominate this stage. Some members may withdraw or try to isolate themselves from the emotional tension generated. The key is to manage conflict during this stage, not to suppress it or withdraw from it. The team can't effectively evolve into the third stage if its members go to either extreme. Suppressing conflict will likely create bitterness and resentment, which will last long after team members attempt to express their differences and emotions. Withdrawal may cause the team to fail.

This stage may be shortened or mostly avoided if the members use a team-building process from the beginning. This process involves the development of decision-making, interpersonal, and technical capabilities when they are lacking. Team-building facilitators can help team members work through the inevitable conflicts that will surface during this and the other stages.

Levi Strauss & Company implemented a team system in its factories several years ago and abandoned the individually based piecework incentive system for a team-based incentive system. In the new system, teams of 10 to 35 employees were formed. The team members rotated in performing the tasks needed to make pairs of jeans or slacks. The pay of team members was based on team outputs. For some teams with members of comparable skills and motivation, the team approach seemed to work. But, in most cases, the teams seemed to become stuck in the storming stage. The more skilled employees on many of the teams pitted themselves against slower team members, which damaged morale and triggered infighting. Threats and insults became common. Longtime friendships dissolved as faster workers tried to banish slower ones. "You heard so much shouting, lots of times you didn't even look up from your work," recalls seamstress Mary Farmer. Adds Deborah Mulvaney, a former team coach at the Dockers plant in Powell, Tennessee: "My girls were getting into it every day of the week." Moreover, in a number of cases, efficiency—defined as the quantity of quality pants produced per hour worked—initially went down to 77 percent of the preteam level and after several years returned only to 93 percent of the preteam individual piecework level.[25]

## NORMING STAGE

Work behaviors at the norming stage evolve into a sharing of information, acceptance of different options, and positive attempts to make decisions that may require compromise. During this stage, team members set rules by which the team will operate. Social behaviors focus on empathy, concern, and positive expressions of feelings that lead to a sense of cohesion. Cooperation and a sense of shared responsibility develop among team members.

Rich Claiborne is a vice president of APAC Teleservices, a sales and service company headquartered in Cedar Raids, Iowa. He recounts the negative norm of not speaking out at meetings for fear of killing a person's career. He comments: "Speaking either wasn't valued or it was quickly tabled and you got the feeling it was considered stupid. So the tendency becomes not to say anything at all." He recalls wasting hours in meetings about a new contract because the team leader didn't want to raise issues that might kill the deal. Claiborne states: "In the past, it was really easy to hide out at meetings for me. When anyone asked if there were any problems, I would say no."[26]

## PERFORMING STAGE

Team members show how effectively and efficiently they can achieve results together during the performing stage. The roles of individual members are accepted and understood. The members have learned when they should work independently and when they should help each other. The two dashed lines in Figure 8.1 suggest that teams may differ after the performing stage. Some teams continue to learn and develop from their experiences, becoming more efficient and effective. Other teams—especially those that developed norms not fully supportive of efficiency and effectiveness—may perform only at the level needed for their survival. Excessive self-oriented behaviors, development of norms that inhibit effective and efficient task completion, poor leadership, or other factors may hurt productivity. In contrast, the self-managed teams at Whole Foods Market are designed to have norms, members, leaders, information systems, and reward mechanisms that strongly support the performing stage.

As Caouette and O'Connor demonstrated, the team that began initially to use collaborative software systems found that the improvements in the first stages of team development paid off later in greater productivity. They concluded that when a team gets off to a good start, it tends to perform better—that good work begets more good work (performing).

## ADJOURNING STAGE

The termination of work behaviors and disengagement from social behaviors occurs during the adjourning stage. A problem-solving team or a cross-functional team created to investigate and report on a specific issue within 6 months, has well-defined points of adjournment. Other teams, such as the self-managed teams at Whole Foods Market and the virtual teams at BakBone Software, may go on indefinitely. These teams will "adjourn" only if top management decides to revise the current team system. In terms of relations-oriented behaviors, some degree of adjourning occurs when team members resign or are reassigned.

The developmental stages of teams—regardless of the framework used to describe and explain them—are not easy to move through. Failure can occur at any point in the sequence, as indicated in Figure 8.1. Several primary factors influence team behaviors and effectiveness. These influences help explain variations in outcomes between teams and within a specific team over time.

**Learning Objective:**

4.  Describe seven key factors that influence team effectiveness.

## IMPORTANT INFLUENCES ON TEAM EFFECTIVENESS

The factors that influence team and group effectiveness are interrelated. Figure 8.2 identifies seven of the main factors. They should be analyzed both separately and in relation to each other. This approach is necessary to gain an understanding of team dynamics and effectiveness—and to develop the competencies needed to be an effective team member and leader.

### CONTEXT

The **context** within which a team works can directly affect each of the six other factors because it comprises the external conditions that affect a team. Examples of a

**Figure 8.2**              **Some Influences on Team Effectiveness**

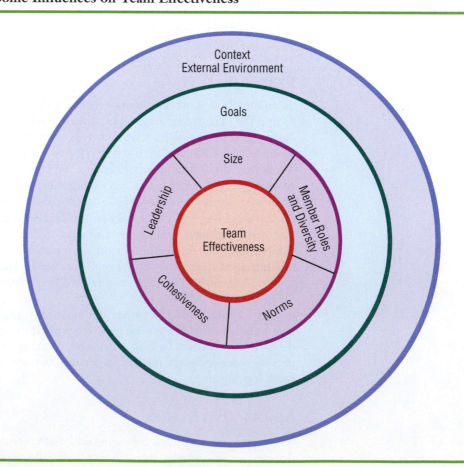

team's context include technology, physical working conditions, management practices, and organizational rewards and punishments. Our discussion of virtual teams illustrated the contextual influence of technology. Also, we noted the contextual influence of management's decision at Levi Strauss to change from an individual piecework incentive system to a team-based incentive compensation system. In that case, the influence was negative and certainly not anticipated.

If the members of a team or organization tend to be oriented much more to *individualism* than *collectivism* (contextual factor), perhaps the compensation system should be tailored so that individuals can see that their own interests are being served by being strong team contributors. This notion is based on three assumptions.

1.  Motivation primarily comes from the individual, not the team.
2.  The development of competencies and the application of behaviors are individual undertakings.
3.  Fairness in dealing with teams does not mean equal pay for all.

Introduction of the team system at Levi Strauss seemingly did not adequately consider these assumptions, which appeared to be valid for many of its factory employees. In contrast, Kendall-Futuro Inc. (K-F), of Newport, Kentucky, has had a great deal of success with teams, and management contends that credit is due to its compensation program. The company uses gain sharing, in which team members are financially rewarded for gains in productivity. It no longer bases pay on a salary plus piecework combination but rather on a salary plus team performance combination. As illustrated in Chapter 6, gain sharing has been around for decades, but increasingly it is being used to reward team performance. Gain sharing measures performance against a standard, and a bonus is awarded for meeting it. In gain sharing, team members normally aren't penalized for failing to meet the standard. Each team member receives a basic salary and, in addition, a gain-sharing bonus when it has been earned.[27]

Kendall-Futuro's approach is one way to compensate teamwork, but it's not for everyone. There are few hard-and-fast rules for fostering team performance, but there are several general guidelines. For example, companies that use teams most effectively in the United States generally still base a substantial portion of pay on the individual's contributions but with a significant difference. They make teamwork and the ability to work with others a key factor in determining an individual's annual adjustment in pay based on the person's performance review.

## GOALS

Many aspects of goals are discussed in Chapter 6. Throughout the book, we return repeatedly to the concept that goals influence individual, team, and organizational effectiveness. Obviously, individual and organizational goals are likely to influence team goals and behaviors in pursuit of these goals. **Team goals** are the outcomes desired for the team as a whole, not just goals of the individual members.

Both compatible and conflicting goals often exist within a team. Moreover, teams typically have both relations-oriented and task-oriented goals. Effective teams spend two-thirds or more of their time on task-oriented issues and roughly one-third or less of their time on relations-oriented issues. The pursuit of only one or the other type of goal over the long run can hurt performance, increase conflicts, and cause a team to disband. The influence of goals on group dynamics and outcomes becomes even more complex when the possible compatibilities and conflicts among member goals, broader team goals, and even broader organizational goals are considered.

One mechanism for dealing with these issues is the use of **superordinate goals**, which two or more individuals, teams, or groups might pursue but can't be achieved without their cooperation. These goals do not replace or eliminate individual or team goals and may be either qualitative or quantitative. An example of a qualitative goal is: We need to pull together for the good of the team. An example of a quantitative goal is: We need to work together if we are to reach the team goal of launching a new line within 9 months. Superordinate goals are likely to have a more powerful effect on the willingness of individuals or teams to cooperate if they are accompanied by superordinate rewards. Such rewards are given to the interacting and cooperating individuals or team members and are determined by the results of their joint efforts. Kendall-Futuro's gain-sharing compensation system is designed to link an individual's goals (higher individual pay and good merit reviews) with team goals (working together to earn bonuses awarded for meeting standards), which represent superordinate goals for each team member.

## TEAM SIZE

The effective size of a team can range from 2 members to a normal upper limit of about 16 members. However, collaborative software systems and the Internet are enabling larger teams to work effectively on some tasks. Twelve members probably is the largest size that allows each member to interact easily with every other member face-to-face. Table 8.3 shows six dimensions of teams in terms of leader behaviors, member behaviors, and team process. The likely effects of team size on each dimension are listed. Note that members of teams of 7 or less interact differently than do members of teams or groups of 13 to 16. A 16-member board of directors will operate differently from a 7-member board. Large boards of directors often form committees of 5 to 7 members to consider specific matters in greater depth than can the entire board.

As with all influences on teams, the effects identified in Table 8.3 need to be qualified. For example, adequate time and sufficient member commitment to a team's goals and tasks might lead to better results from a team of 9 or more members than from a hurried and less committed team of a smaller size. If a team's primary task is to tap the knowledge of the members and arrive at decisions based primarily on expertise rather than judgment, a larger team won't necessarily reflect the effects identified in Table 8.3.

In one recent survey of companies, the typical upper limit on team size was 15 members. Larger teams usually were associated with the performance of simpler tasks. Wilson Sporting Goods' surlyn cover injection golf-ball manufacturing teams, with 12 to 15 members each, are examples of simple work teams. Here, injection mold operators place golf ball cores in a mold having the appropriate dimple pattern. The surlyn cover material is injected around each core. Production of thousands of

**Table 8.3**

### Typical Effects of Size on Teams

| | TEAM SIZE | | |
| DIMENSION | 2–7 Members | 8–12 Members | 13–16 Members |
|---|---|---|---|
| 1. Demands on leader | Low | Moderate | High |
| 2. Direction by leader | Low | Moderate | Moderate to high |
| 3. Member tolerance of direction by leader | Low to moderate | Moderate | High |
| 4. Member inhibition | Low | Moderate | High |
| 5. Use of rules and procedures | Low | Moderate | Moderate to high |
| 6. Time taken to reach a decision | Low | Moderate | High |

golf balls each day requires the effective functioning of a team of operators, all doing similar tasks. For problem-solving teams, the survey found that the size used most often was generally 10 or less members. As a team becomes larger, the emotional identification and sense of deeply shared commitment becomes more difficult to establish and maintain.[28]

## TEAM MEMBER ROLES AND DIVERSITY

Similarities and differences among members and their roles influence team behaviors. Obviously, managers can't alter the basic personalities or attributes of team members (see Chapters 2 and 3). Therefore attempts to influence their roles in a team or group are more useful. These roles may be formally classified as task-oriented, relations-oriented, and self-oriented. Each member has the potential for performing each of these roles over time.

**Task-Oriented Role.**    The **task-oriented role** of a team member involves facilitating and coordinating work-related decision making. This role may include:

- *initiating* new ideas or different ways of considering team problems or goals and suggesting solutions to difficulties, including modification of team procedures;
- *seeking information* to clarify suggestions and obtain key facts;
- *giving information* that is relevant to the team's problem, issue, or task;
- *coordinating* and clarifying relationships among ideas and suggestions, pulling ideas and suggestions together, and coordinating members' activities; and
- *evaluating* the team's effectiveness, including questioning the logic, facts, or practicality of other members' suggestions.

**Relations-Oriented Role.**    The **relations-oriented role** of a team member involves building team-centered feelings and social interactions. This role may include:

- *encouraging* members through praise and acceptance of their ideas, as well as indicating warmth and solidarity;
- *harmonizing* and mediating intrateam conflicts and tensions;
- *encouraging* participation of others by saying: Let's hear from Susan, or Why not limit the length of contributions so all can react to the problem? or Juan, do you agree?
- *expressing* standards for the team to achieve or apply in evaluating the quality of team processes, raising questions about team goals, and assessing team progress in light of these goals; and
- *following* by going along passively or constructively and serving as a friendly member.

**Self-Oriented Role.**    The **self-oriented role** of a team member involves the person's self-centered behaviors that are at the expense of the team or group. This role may include:

- *blocking progress* by being negative, stubborn, and unreasoningly resistant—for example, the person may repeatedly try to bring back an issue that the team had considered carefully and rejected;
- *seeking recognition* by calling attention to oneself, including boasting, reporting on personal achievements, and in various ways avoiding being placed in a presumed inferior position;
- *dominating* by asserting authority, manipulating the team or certain individuals, using flattery or proclaiming superiority to gain attention, and interrupting the contributions of others; and
- *avoiding* involvement by maintaining distance from others and remaining insulated from interaction.

Effective teams often are composed of members who play both task-oriented and relations-oriented roles over time. A particularly adept individual who reveals behaviors valued by the team probably has relatively high *status*—the relative rank of an individual in a team. A team dominated by individuals who exhibit mainly self-oriented behaviors is likely to be ineffective because the individuals don't adequately address team goals and engage in needed collaboration.

Table 8.4 provides a questionnaire for evaluating some of your task-oriented, relations-oriented, and self-oriented behaviors as a team member. The questionnaire asks you to assess your tendency to engage in each role, on a scale of 1 to 5 (or almost never to almost always). Member composition and roles greatly influence team or group behaviors. Either too much or too little of certain member behaviors can adversely affect team performance and member satisfaction.[29]

**Team Diversity.**    The growing diversity of the workforce adds complexity—beyond individuals' personalities and team roles—to understanding team behavior and processes. As discussed in previous chapters, the composition of the workforce is undergoing continued change in terms of age, gender, race, cultural values, physical well-being, lifestyle preferences, ethnicity, educational background, religious prefer-

**Table 8.4**

| **Assessing Your Role-Oriented Behavior as a Team Member** |
|---|

**Instructions:** Assess your behavior on each item for the team that you selected by using the following scale.

| 1 | 2 | 3 | 4 | 5 |
|---|---|---|---|---|
| Almost Never | Rarely | Sometimes | Often | Almost Always |

Place the appropriate number value next to each item.

*Task-oriented behaviors: In this team, I . . .*
_____ 1. initiate ideas or actions.
_____ 2. facilitate the introduction of facts and information.
_____ 3. summarize and pull together various ideas.
_____ 4. keep the team working on the task.
_____ 5. ask whether the team is near a decision (determine consensus).

*Relation-oriented behaviors: In this team, I . . .*
_____ 6. support and encourage others.
_____ 7. harmonize (keep the peace).
_____ 8. try to find common ground.
_____ 9. encourage participation.
_____10. actively listen.

*Self-oriented behaviors: In this team, I . . .*
_____11. express hostility.
_____12. avoid involvement.
_____13. dominate the team.
_____14. free ride on others.
_____15. take personal credit for team results.

_____**Total:** Add points for items 1 through 15.

**Interpretation:** Scores of 20–25 on task-oriented behaviors, 20–25 on relations-oriented behaviors, and 5–10 on self-oriented behaviors probably indicates that you are an effective team member. This conclusion assumes that other team members perceive you as you see yourself.

ence, occupational background, and the like. Team effectiveness will be hampered if members hold false stereotypes about each other in terms of such differences.

Although attitudes are changing, diversity all too often still is viewed more negatively than positively. This negative reaction may be due, in large part, to four underlying attitudes involving stereotypical false assumptions.

1. Diversity poses a threat to the organization's effective functioning.
2. Expressed discomfort with the dominant group's values is perceived as oversensitivity by minority groups.
3. Members of all groups want to become and should be more like the dominant group.
4. Equal treatment means the same treatment.

The goal of achieving diversity creates unique challenges in making it work for rather than against the long-term interests of individuals, teams, and organizations. Once a we–they distinction is perceived, people tend to discriminate against others who are different. Moreover, they tend to perceive these others as inferior, adversarial, and competitive.[30]

The attitude expressed throughout this book about diversity is that of **positive multiculturalism**. This condition allows an individual to acquire new competencies, perspectives, and attitudes that improve the person's ability to relate effectively to others regardless of their backgrounds and characteristics. Positive multiculturalism is additive; that is, individuals can maintain their self-defining attributes while adding competencies and positive attitudes to help them form and maintain sound working relationships with others. Thus a person can become bilingual by learning English but retaining a native language.[31]

## NORMS

**Norms** are the rules and patterns of behavior that are accepted and expected by members of a team. They help define the behaviors that members believe to be necessary to help them reach their goals. Over time, every team establishes norms and enforces them on its members. Norms often are more rigidly defined and enforced in informal groups—by peer pressure—than in formally organized teams. Such norms may further or inhibit achievement of organizational goals.

**Norms Versus Organizational Rules.**   Norms differ from organizational rules. Managers may write and distribute formal organizational rules to employees in the form of manuals and memoranda. At times, employees refuse to accept such rules and ignore them. In contrast, norms are informal, often unwritten expectations that are enforced by team members. If a member consistently and excessively violates these norms, the other members sanction the individual in some way. Sanctions may range from physical abuse to threats to ostracism to positive inducements (rewards) for compliance. Those who consistently adhere to the team's norms typically receive praise, recognition, and acceptance from the other members.

Team members may be only vaguely aware of some of the norms that are operating, but they should be made aware of these norms for at least two reasons. First, awareness increases the potential for individual and team freedom and maturity. Second, norms can positively or negatively influence the effectiveness of individuals, teams, and organizations. For example, team norms of minimizing and correcting defects are likely to reinforce an organization's formal quality standards.

**Relation to Goals.**   Teams often adopt norms to help them attain their goals. Moreover, some organizational development efforts are aimed at helping members evaluate whether their team's norms are consistent with, neutral with respect to, or conflict with organizational goals. For example, a team may claim that one of its goals is to become more efficient to help it meet organizational goals. However, the team members' behaviors might be inconsistent with this stated goal; that is, the team's norms might actually inhibit production and attempts to make changes.

Even if team members are aware of such norms, they may think of them as being necessary in order to achieve their own goals. Members may claim that producing more than the norm will "burn them out" or reduce product or service quality, resulting in lower long-term effectiveness. If a team's goals include minimizing managerial influence and increasing the opportunity for social interaction, its members could perceive norms restricting employee output as desirable.

**Enforcing Norms.**   Teams don't establish norms for every conceivable situation. They generally form and enforce norms with respect to behaviors that they believe to be particularly important. Members are most likely to enforce norms under one or more of the following conditions.

- Norms aid in team survival and provide benefits. For instance, a team might develop a norm not to discuss individual salaries with other members in the organization to avoid calling attention to pay inequities.
- Norms simplify or make predictable the behaviors expected of members. When coworkers go out for lunch together, there can be some awkwardness about how to split the bill at the end of the meal. A group may develop a norm that results in some highly predictable way of behaving—split the bill evenly, take turns picking up the tab, or individually pay for what each ordered.
- Norms help avoid embarrassing interpersonal situations. Norms might develop about not discussing romantic involvements in or out of the office (so that differences in moral values don't become too obvious) or about not getting together socially in members' homes (so that differences in taste or income don't become too obvious).[32]

Norms express the central values and goals of the team and clarify what is distinctive about its identity. Employees of an advertising agency may wear unconventional but stylish clothing. Other professionals may view their doing so as deviant behavior. However, the advertising agency personnel may say: We think of ourselves, personally and professionally, as trendsetters, and being fashionably dressed conveys that to our clients and the public.

**Conforming to Norms.**   Conformity may result from the pressures to adhere to norms. The two basic types of conformity are compliance and personal acceptance. **Compliance conformity** occurs when a person's behavior reflects the team's desired behavior because of real or imagined pressure. In fact, some individuals may conform for a variety of reasons, even though they don't personally agree with the norms. They may think that the appearance of a united front is necessary for success in accomplishing team goals. On a more personal level, someone may comply in order to be liked and accepted by others. Meeting this need may apply especially to members of lower status in relation to those of higher status, such as a subordinate and a superior. Finally, someone may comply because the costs of conformity are much less than the costs of nonconformity, which could threaten the personal relationships in the team.

The second type of conformity is based on positive personal support of the norms. In **personal acceptance conformity**, the individual's behavior and attitudes are consistent with the team's norms and goals. This type of conformity is much stronger than compliance conformity because the person truly believes in the goals and norms.[33]

All of the preceding helps explain why some members of highly conforming teams may easily change their behavior (compliance type of conformity), whereas others may oppose changes and find them highly stressful (personal acceptance type of conformity). Without norms and reasonable conformity to them, teams would be chaotic and few tasks could be accomplished. Conversely, excessive and blind conformity may threaten expressions of individualism and a team's ability to change and learn.

## COHESIVENESS

**Cohesiveness** is the strength of the members' desire to remain in a team and their commitment to it. Cohesiveness is influenced by the degree of compatibility between team goals and individual members' goals. Members who have a strong desire to remain in a team and personally accept its goals form a highly cohesive team.

This relationship between cohesiveness and conformity isn't a simple one. Low cohesiveness usually is associated with low conformity. However, high cohesiveness doesn't exist only in the presence of high conformity. High-performing teams may have high member commitment and a desire to stick together while simultaneously respecting and encouraging individual differences. This situation is more likely to develop when cohesiveness arises from trusting relationships and a common commitment to performance goals.

In confronting problems, members of a cohesive team are likely to encourage and support nonconformity. For example, a **hot group** performs extremely well and is dedicated; it usually is small, and its members are turned on by an exciting and challenging goal. A hot group completely engages its members, capturing their attention to the exclusion of almost everything else. For its members, the characteristics of a hot group are the same: vital, absorbing, full of debate and laughter, and very hard working.[34] They may arise from the need for dealing with major challenges and changes, innovation, complex projects, or crises. For example, the development of the Boeing 777 jetliner spawned several hot groups.

**Relation to Groupthink.**   When decision-making teams are both conforming and cohesive, a phenomenon called groupthink can emerge. **Groupthink** is an agreement-at-any-cost mentality that results in ineffective team decision making and poor decisions. Irving L. Janis, who coined the term, focused his research on high-level government policy teams faced with difficult problems in a complex and dynamic environment. Team decision making is common in all types of organizations, so the possibility of groupthink exists in both private-sector and public-sector organizations.[35]

In a study of 23 top-management teams, the CEOs of 6 expressed concern about groupthink in their organizations' teams. The CEO of a global financial services firm commented:

> There's a lack of genuine debate. Sometimes there's a half-hearted "devil's advocate" gesture, but they really don't confront each other or me on the big issues. We're too comfortable, too self-congratulatory. It's gotten obvious to me in the past few months. I have to find a way to shake things up.[36]

Groupthink isn't inevitable, and several steps can be taken to avoid it. For example, a leader should try to remain neutral and encourage dialogue and new ideas. Small subgroups or outside consultants can be used to introduce new viewpoints. People holding diverse views can be encouraged to present them.

**Impact on Effectiveness.**   Team performance and productivity can be affected by cohesiveness. **Productivity** is the relationship between the inputs consumed (labor hours, raw materials, money, machines, and the like) and the outputs created (quantity and quality of goods and services). Cohesiveness and productivity can be related, particularly for teams having high performance goals. If the team is successful in reaching those goals, the positive feedback of its successes may heighten member commitment and satisfaction. For example, a winning basketball team is more likely to be cohesive than one with a poor record, everything else being equal. Also, a cohesive basketball team may be more likely to win games. Conversely, low cohesiveness may interfere with a team's ability to win games. The reason is that members aren't as likely to communicate and cooperate to the extent necessary to reach the team's goals. High team cohesiveness actually may be associated with low efficiency if team goals conflict with organizational goals. Team members might think that the boss holds them accountable rather than that they hold themselves accountable to achieve results. Therefore the relationships among cohesiveness, productivity, and performance can't be anticipated or understood unless the team's goals and norms are also known.

## LEADERSHIP

Studies of teams emphasize the importance of emergent, or informal, leadership in accomplishing goals. An **informal leader** is an individual whose influence in a team grows over time and usually reflects a unique ability to help the team reach its goals.

**Multiple Leaders.**   Team leadership is often thought of in terms of one person. Whole Foods Market teams have different leaders over time and for different tasks. Moreover, because a team often has both relations-oriented and task-oriented goals, it may have two or more leaders. These two types of goals may require different skills and leadership styles, creating a total set of demands that one person may have difficulty satisfying. Informal leaders of teams aren't likely to emerge unless the formal leader ignores task-related responsibilities or lacks the necessary skills to carry them out. In contrast, relations-oriented leaders of teams are likely to emerge informally.

**Effective Team Leaders.**   Leaders greatly influence virtually all aspects of team composition and behaviors (e.g., size, members and roles, norms, goals, and context). A leader often assumes a key role in the relations between the team and external groups, such as customers or suppliers, and often influences the selection of new members. Even when the team participates in the selection process, the team leader may screen potential members, thereby limiting the number and range of candidates, as at Whole Foods Market.

At Whole Foods Market top management, especially John Mackey (founder and current CEO), established and emphasizes a set of core values and principles to reflect what is truly important to the organization as a whole. Four of its core values and principles focus on the central role of teams.

1.   Our success is dependent upon the collective energy and intelligence of all our team members. We strive to create a work environment where motivated team members can flourish and succeed to their highest potential. We appreciate effort and reward results.
2.   The fundamental work unit of the company is the self-directed team. Teams meet regularly to discuss issues, solve problems, and appreciate each other's contributions.
3.   We believe knowledge is power and we support our team members' right to access information that impacts their jobs. Our books are open to our team members, including our annual individual compensation report. We also recognize everyone's right to be listened to and heard regardless of their point of view.
4.   Our company continually improves through unleashing the collective creativity and intelligence of all our team members. We recognize that everyone has a contribution to make. We keep getting better at what we do.[37]

The seven key factors that influence team effectiveness discussed so far (see Figure 8.2) make the creation and maintenance of effective teams no easy leadership task. We discuss leadership and the qualities and characteristics of effective leaders in detail in Chapters 10 and 11.

5.  Relate how the use of the nominal group technique, traditional brainstorming, and electronic brainstorming can foster team creativity.

# FOSTERING TEAM CREATIVITY

Before discussing three of the many approaches for fostering team creativity, we note that the broader issues of fostering organizational creativity are covered in Chapter 13. In any event, fostering creativity is in the hands of managers as they think about and establish the work environment. For example, poorly designed motivational and reward systems will likely result in ineffective team approaches. One creativity expert comments: "The thing about creativity is that you can't tell at the outset which ideas will succeed and which will fail. . . . Now, leaders pay a lot of lip service to the notion of rewarding failure. . . . Often, they have a forgive-and-forget policy. Forgiveness is crucial but it's not enough. In order to learn from mistakes, it's even more important to forgive and *remember*."[38]

The three approaches presented in this section—the nominal group technique, traditional brainstorming, and electronic brainstorming—can assist team members with the process of defining problems, generating possible solutions, and evaluating alternative solutions.

## NOMINAL GROUP TECHNIQUE

The **nominal group technique** (NGT) is a structured process designed to guide and stimulate creative team decision making where agreement is lacking or team members have incomplete knowledge about the nature of the problem or alternative solutions. This technique has a special purpose: to make individual judgments the essential inputs in arriving at a team decision. Team members must pool their judgments in order to determine a satisfactory course of action leading to solution of a problem or resolution of an issue.

The NGT is most beneficial for (1) identifying the critical variables in a specific situation; (2) identifying key elements of a plan designed to implement a particular solution to some problem; or (3) establishing priorities with regard to the problem to be addressed and goals to be attained. The NGT isn't particularly well suited for routine team meetings that focus primarily on task coordination or information exchange. Nor is it usually appropriate for negotiations that take place between incompatible groups (e.g., a union's representatives and a management committee). The NGT consists of four distinct stages: generating ideas, recording ideas, clarifying ideas, and voting on ideas.[39] Various suggestions have been made for modifying or tailoring these stages to specific situations. Collaborative software technology is now available to aid in doing the tasks called for in these stages. Some research suggests that computer-assisted implementation of the NGT can be more effective than the traditional face-to-face process. Effectiveness is defined as generating more and better ideas in less time. Also, the computer assisted-approach enables the participants to remain at their normal locations, thus saving on travel time and costs.[40]

**Generating Ideas.**   The first stage in the process is to have team members generate ideas. Each participant separately writes down ideas in response to a statement of the problem, a question, or some other central focus of the team. A question could be something as simple as What problems do you think we should consider over the next year? followed by Take 5 minutes to write down some of your own ideas on a piece of paper. The generation of ideas or solutions privately by team members avoids the direct pressures of status differences or competition among members to be heard. This procedure, however, retains some of the peer and creative tension in the individual generated by the presence of others. This stage and the subsequent stages provide time for thinking and reflection to avoid premature choices among ideas.

**Recording Ideas.**   The second stage is to record one idea (generated in the first stage) from each group member in turn on a flip chart, white board, or other device displayed for all team members to see. A variation is to have members submit their ideas anonymously on index cards. The process continues until the team members are satisfied that the list reflects all the ideas individually generated. This round-robin approach emphasizes equal participation by team members and avoids losing ideas that individuals consider significant. Listing them for everyone to see depersonalizes the ideas and reduces the potential for unnecessary conflict. Team members often are impressed and pleased with the list of ideas presented, which provides momentum and enthusiasm for continuing the process.

**Clarifying Ideas.**   Team members then discuss in turn each idea on the list during the third stage. The purpose of this discussion is to clarify the meaning of each idea and allow team members to agree or disagree with any item. The intent is to present the logic behind the ideas and minimize misunderstanding, not to win arguments concerning the relative merits of the ideas. Differences of opinion aren't resolved at this stage, but rather by the voting procedure in the fourth stage.

**Voting on Ideas.**   Using the list, which may contain 15 to 30 or more ideas, the team may proceed in one of several ways. Perhaps the most common voting procedure is to have team members individually select a specific number (say, 5) of the ideas that they believe are the most important. Each person writes these 5 ideas on index cards. The team leader then asks the members to rank their items from most to least important. The index cards are collected and the votes tabulated to produce a priority list. An alternative to this single vote is to feed back the results of a first vote, allow time for discussion of the results, and then vote again. Feedback and discussion are likely to result in a final decision that most closely reflects the members' actual preferences.

Regardless of format, the voting procedure determines the outcome of the meeting: a team decision that incorporates the individual judgments of the participants. The procedure is designed to document the collective decision and provide a sense of accomplishment and closure.

**Organizational Use.**   The advantages of the NGT over traditional team discussion include greater emphasis and attention to idea generation, increased attention to each idea, and greater likelihood of balanced participation by each member. Nominal groups may not be superior when people are aware of existing problems and willing to communicate them. The approach may be most effective when certain blockages or problems exist in a team, such as domination by a few team members. The NGT is being used by managers and team leaders in numerous organizations—ranging from Coca-Cola to General Motors to the U.S. Marines.

## TRADITIONAL BRAINSTORMING

**Traditional brainstorming** is a process whereby individuals state as many ideas as possible during a 20- to 60-minute period. It is usually done with 5 to 12 people. Guidelines for brainstorming include (1) the wilder the ideas the better, (2) don't be critical of any ideas, and (3) hitchhike on or combine previously stated ideas. The team setting for traditional brainstorming is supposed to generate many more and better ideas than if the same number of individuals worked alone.[41] Some research indicates that brainstorming may not be nearly as effective as once thought.

To brainstorm effectively is to think of an idea, express it, and get on with thinking of and expressing more new ideas. In face-to-face brainstorming, however, people may be prevented from doing so because someone else is talking. As a result, team members may get bogged down waiting for other people to finish talking. Team members also may be anxious about how others will view them if they express their ideas. This problem may be particularly acute when ideas can be interpreted as critical of current practice or when superiors or others who may affect team members' futures are present. Withholding ideas for these reasons defeats the purpose of brainstorming.[42]

The following Managing Communication Competency feature reveals how Play, a consulting firm, uses brainstorming, among other methods, to help its clients foster creativity. This firm helps create ideas that make products better, strategies smarter, brands richer, and cultures stronger. Play's definition of creativity is: "Look at more stuff, think about it harder."[43] The firm is located near Richmond, Virginia, and has about 35 employees.

# COMPETENCY:   MANAGING COMMUNICATION

## CREATIVE PROCESS AT PLAY

At Play, the crux of creativity is putting old ideas together in new ways or giving common concepts a twist that makes them uncommon. "You can get better at doing that if you practice," says Andy Stefanovich, Play's cofounder. For example, there's a chalkboard in one hallway that has daily random topics, such as "$H_2O$," "city," "marathon running," or "teens." People who pass by the board then jot down related words and thoughts, which go into a file and are used in brainstorming sessions on those topics. Stefanovich states: "We get some of our best ideas from 'recreational' thinking. Like the brainstorming you do while getting to work or exercising, when your mind is not completely task-focused."

You can't come up with new ideas if you approach each problem the same way. Play's creativity exercises are built around "forcing connections"—making yourself connect seemingly unrelated ideas. For instance, coaches in brainstorming sessions give clients lists of random quotes from kindergartners and ask them to relate those sayings to their business problem.

One way to lose your fear of looking foolish and to come up with great ideas is to offer the worst possible idea you can think of, and then riff off it. When Play was asked by the Woolmark Company to come up with an event that would promote summer-weight wool clothing, the brainstorming team started with a strange question: What's the worst way to promote wool? How about letting a bunch of sheep loose in New York City? From there, the team refined it. The final iteration was to have wool-clad models walk sheep on leashes on Madison Avenue. The stunt snared more than 8 million media impressions—the number of times individuals observed wool-clad models walking sheep on leashes.[44]

*For more information on Play, visit the organization's home page at http://www.lookatmorestuff.com.*

## ELECTRONIC BRAINSTORMING

**Electronic brainstorming** involves the use of collaborative software technology to enter and automatically disseminate ideas in real time to all team members, each of whom may be stimulated to generate other ideas. For example, Ventana Corporation of Tucson, Arizona, is one of the leading providers of collaborative software technology, including electronic brainstorming software. For this approach to work, each team member must have a computer terminal that is connected to all other members' terminals. The software allows individuals to enter their ideas as they think of them. Every time an individual enters an idea, a random set of the team's ideas is presented on each person's screen. The individual can continue to see new random sets of ideas by pressing the appropriate key.[45]

Research on electronic brainstorming is encouraging. It tends to produce more novel ideas than traditional brainstorming. It also removes the main barrier of traditional brainstorming: members seeing and hearing which ideas are whose; that is, it permits anonymity and thus lets team members contribute more freely to idea generation. They need not fear "sounding like a fool" to other employees and managers when spontaneously generating ideas. These advantages appear to be greater for teams of seven or more people.[46] Jay Nunamaker, CEO of Ventana Corporation and a professor at the University of Arizona's Karl Eller Graduate School of Management, is a leading expert on electronic meetings. He says, "Ventana initially added anonymity to its software to meet the needs of the U.S. military. Admirals can really dampen interaction at a meeting. But we didn't realize the impact it would have in corporate settings. Even with people who work together all the time, anonymity changes the social protocols. People say things differently."[47] Of course, if there is a high degree of trust and mutual support among the participants, negative outcomes are not so likely, as at Play.

# CHAPTER SUMMARY

**1.** State the basic characteristics of groups, including informal groups.

In this chapter, we focused on developing the *managing teams competency*—the ability to develop, support, facilitate, and lead groups to achieve team and organizational goals. Groups and teams are classified in numerous ways. In organizations, a basic classification is by the group's primary purpose, including informal groups and task groups (now commonly called teams). Informal groups develop out of the day-to-day activities, interactions, and sentiments of the members for the purpose of meeting their security or social needs. Informal groups may support, oppose, or be indifferent to formal organizational goals. Effective groups, formal or informal, have similar basic characteristics.

**2.** Describe the distinguishing features of five types of teams.

Functional teams include members from the same functional department, such as marketing, production, or finance. Problem-solving teams include individuals from a particular area of responsibility to address specific problems such as cost overruns or a decline in quality. Cross-functional teams include individuals from a number of specialties and departments to deal with problems that cut across areas. Self-managed teams include employees who must work together daily to manufacture an entire product (or major identifiable component) or provide an entire service to a set of customers. For maximum effectiveness, self-managed teams need to be empowered—that is have a strong sense of potency, meaningfulness, autonomy, and impact. A variety of organizational, team, and individual factors must be satisfied for introduction of self-managed teams. Any type of task group could function somewhat or primarily as a virtual team.

**3.** Explain the five-stage model of team development.

The five-stage developmental model focuses on forming, storming, norming, performing, and adjourning. The issues and challenges a team faces change with each stage. Teams do not necessarily develop in the straightforward manner presented in this model, especially when the members possess strong team management and related competencies. Several other models are available to aid in understanding the developmental sequence of teams.

**4.** Describe seven key factors that influence team effectiveness.

Team dynamics and effectiveness are influenced by the interplay of context, goals, size, member roles, norms, cohesiveness, and leadership. One type of changing contextual influence on how teams work, interact, and network with other teams is that of information technology, especially the rapid developments in collaborative software systems. Other contextual influences are the nature of the organization's reward system and how it fits the basic value orientations of team members, especially in terms of individualism and collectivism. Team members need to clearly understand and accept team goals as outcomes desired by each member for the team as a whole. Team size can substantially affect the dynamics among the members and the ability to create a sense of mutual accountability. Teams of about 16 or more members typically break into smaller task groups. Member roles may be task-oriented, relationship-oriented, or self-oriented. Norms differ from rules in important ways and can have a positive or negative impact on performance. The pressures to adhere to norms may result in either compliance conformity or personal acceptance conformity. Another factor having an impact on the effectiveness of teams is cohesiveness, which is related to conformity, groupthink, and productivity. Team leaders may be selected formally or emerge informally.

**5.** Relate how the use of the nominal group technique, traditional brainstorming, and electronic brainstorming can foster team creativity.

The nominal group technique (NGT) is a structured process designed to guide and stimulate creativity where agreement is lacking or there is incomplete knowledge about the problem or alternative solutions. It consists of four distinct stages: (1) generating ideas, (2) recording ideas, (3) clarifying ideas, and (4) voting on ideas. It is especially useful when agreement is lacking or team members have incomplete knowledge as to the nature of a problem. Traditional brainstorming involves using a set of guidelines for a face-to-face session in which the individuals state as many ideas as possible during a 20- to 60-minute period. Electronic brainstorming involves the use of collaborative software technology by each team member to enter into a computer and automatically disseminate ideas to all other members.

## KEY TERMS AND CONCEPTS

Cohesiveness
Compliance conformity
Context
Cross-functional teams
Electronic brainstorming
Friendship group
Functional teams
Group
Groupthink
Hot group
Informal group
Informal leader
Nominal group technique
Norms
Personal acceptance conformity

Positive multiculturalism
Problem-solving teams
Productivity
Relations-oriented role
Self-managed teams
Self-oriented role
Superordinate goals
Task group
Task-oriented role
Team
Team empowerment
Team goals
Traditional brainstorming
Virtual team

*p. 7 – 15 in handout*

## DISCUSSION QUESTIONS

1. Think of one informal and one task group of which you are or have been a member during the past 2 years. In terms of the types of groups and teams presented in this chapter, how would you classify each of them? Did either of them appear to be of more than one type? Explain.

2. For one of the groups you identified in Question 1, how would you evaluate it in terms of the basic characteristics of effective groups?

3. Based on your answers to the questions in Table 8.2, what actions are needed to increase the degree of empowerment for this team? Are those actions feasible?

4. If you were employed at Whole Foods Market, what would you tend to like or dislike about its self-managed teams?

5. Assume that you had to complete a class project as a member of a virtual team that could meet face-to-face

only twice. Identify at least four special challenges that your virtual team would face in undertaking the project.

6. Think of a new team or group in which you participated during the past 3 years. Describe and explain the degree to which the development of this team or group matched the five-stage model of team development.

7. For a team or group of which you have been a member, describe its environment (context) in terms of technology, organizational rules, and management's influence.

In what ways did the context appear to affect the team's or group's effectiveness?

8. What were the formal and informal goals of the team or group you identified in Question 7? Were the informal goals consistent and supportive of the formal goals? Explain.

9. What are the similarities and differences between the nominal group technique (NGT) and electronic brainstorming?

# DEVELOPING COMPETENCIES

## Competency: Managing Teams

### Team Assessment

*Instructions:* Think of a student or work-related team in which you have been a member and that was formed to achieve one or more goals. This team could be associated with a specific course, student organization, or job.

1. Evaluate the *success* of your team on each *item* in this instrument. Use the following scale and assign a value from 1 to 5 to each item. Record the number next to each numbered item. How successful do you think your team was on each of the items?

| 1 | 2 | 3 | 4 | 5 |
|---|---|---|---|---|
| Not at all successful (well below expectations) | Somewhat successful (though below expectations) | Moderately successful (meets expectations) | Fairly high level of success (exceeds expectations) | Very high level of success (far exceeds expectations) |

2. Based on the item assessments and any other related dimensions for each factor, evaluate the *overall success* of your team on each of the seven summary *factors*. Sum the item scores for each factor. Divide the sum (total) by the number of items in that factor.

## I. Goals Factor

_____ 1. Team members understood the goals and scope of the team.

_____ 2. Team members were committed to the team goals, and took ownership of them.

☐ *Overall Goals Factor:* Add the scores for items 1 through 2 and divide by 2 = _____.

## II. Team Performance Management Factor

_____ 3. Individual roles, responsibilities, goals, and performance expectations were specific, challenging, and accepted by team members.

_____ 4. Team goals and performance expectations were specific, challenging, and accepted by team members.

_____ 5. The workload of the team was shared more or less equally among team members.

_____ 6. Everyone on my team did his or her fair share of the work.

_____ 7. No one on my team depended on other team members to do his or her work.

_____ 8 Nearly all the members on my team contributed equally to the work.

☐ *Overall Team Performance Management Factor:* Add the scores for items 3 through 8 and divide by 6 = _____.

## III. Team Basics Factor

_____ 9. My team had enough members to handle the tasks assigned (i.e., small enough to meet and communicate frequently and easily, and yet not too small for the work required of the team).

_____ 10. The team as a whole possessed the competency levels required to achieve its goals.

_____ 11. The team members possessed the complementary competencies required to achieve the team's goals.

☐ *Overall Team Basics Factor:* Add the scores for items 9 through 11 and divide by 3 = _____.

## IV. Team Processes Factor

_____ 12. My team was able to solve problems and make decisions.

_____ 13. My team was able to encourage desirable but to discourage undesirable team conflict.

_____ 14. My team members were able to communicate, listen, and give constructive feedback.

_____ 15. Team meetings were conducted effectively.

_____ 16. Members of my team were very willing to share information with other team members about our work.

_____ 17. Members of my team cooperated to get the work done.

_____ 18. Being on my team gave me the opportunity to work on a team and to provide support for other team members.

_____ 19. My team increased my opportunities for positive social interaction.

_____ 20. Members of my team helped each other when necessary.

[ ] *Overall Team Processes Factor:* Add the scores for items 12 through 20 and divide by 9 = _____.

## V.  Team Spirit Factor

_____ 21. Members of my team had great confidence that the team could perform effectively.

_____ 22. My team took on the tasks assigned and completed them.

_____ 23. My team had a lot of team enthusiasm.

_____ 24. My team had high morale.

_____ 25. The team developed norms (i.e., expectations concerning team member behavior) that contributed to effective team functioning and performance.

_____ 26. Team members invested energy intensely on behalf of the team.

[ ] *Overall Team Spirit Factor:* Add the scores for items 21 through 26 and divide by 6 = _____.

## VI.  Team Outcomes Factor

_____ 27. The team attained measurable results (if objective or quantifiable measures were available).

_____ 28. The product or service delivered by the team met or exceeded the expectations of those receiving it.

_____ 29. My team carried out its work in such a way as to maintain or enhance its ability to work together on future team tasks.

_____ 30. Generally, the team experience served to satisfy, rather than frustrate, the personal needs of team members.

[ ] *Overall Team Outcomes Factor:* Add the scores for items 27 through 30 and divide by 4 = _____.

## VII.  Team Learning Factor

_____ 31. We took time to figure out ways to improve team processes.

_____ 32. Team members often spoke up to test assumptions about issues under discussion.

_____ 33. Team members got all the information they needed from others.

_____ 34. Someone always made sure that we stopped to reflect on the team's processes.

_____ 35. The team as a whole asked for feedback from others as it progressed.

_____ 36. The team actively reviewed its own progress and performance.

[ ] *Overall Team Learning Factor:* Add the scores for items 31 through 36 and divide by 6 = _____.

### Interpretation

An overall score of 4 or 5 on a factor suggests considerable success (exceeding expectations and success). An overall score of 3 on a factor suggests a satisfactory level of success and a feeling of just "okay." An overall score of 1 or 2 on a factor suggests that the team processes needed considerable improvement. You might consider all seven factors as a whole to arrive at a final summary assessment. Insights for action steps are likely to be learned through each factor and the specific items that are in it.[48]

## Competency: Managing Teams

### Great Majestic Company

Susan Hoffman, manager of the Great Majestic Lodge, was sitting at her desk and debating what she would say and what action she would take at a meeting with her bellmen, which was scheduled to begin in two hours. She has just weathered a stormy encounter with Bob Tomblin, the general manager of the Great Majestic Company's recreational and lodging facilities in the area.

The Great Majestic Lodge was located in a popular park in the western United States. It was rather remote, yet offered all the modern conveniences of a fine large-city hotel. Because of its size and accommodations, the lodge was a favorite spot for large, organized tours. Most of the tours stayed one night and none stayed more than 2 days. They were good moneymakers for the lodge because they always met their schedules, paid their bills promptly, and usually were gone early on checkout day.

Most of the employees hired by the Great Majestic Company were college students. This situation was ideal because the opening and closing dates of the lodge corresponded to most universities' summer vacations. The employees lived and ate at the company facilities and were paid about $800 a month.

### The Lodge Bellmen

The bellmen at the Great Majestic Lodge were directly responsible to Hoffman. They were college students who, before being chosen for a bellman position, had worked for the company at least three summers. Each year, Tomblin, rather than Hoffman, chose seven on the basis of their past performance, loyalty, efficiency, and ability to work with the public. Employees considered the position of being bellmen to be prestigious and important. In the eyes of the public, the bellmen represented every aspect of the Great Majestic Lodge. They were the first ones to greet the guests upon arrival, the people the guests called when anything was needed or went wrong, and the last ones to see the guests off upon their departure. Clad in their special cowboy apparel complete with personalized name tags and company insignia, the bellmen functioned as an effective public relations team for the lodge, as well as providing prompt and professional service for each guest.

The bellmen all lived together in the back area of the most secluded employees' dorm at the lodge. They shared this facility with other lodge employees who had been with the company for 2 years or more. The older student employees were especially close-knit, and all were looking forward to the time they would have the opportunity to be chosen as bellmen. The first-year employees usually occupied a dorm to themselves, adjacent to the senior dorm. For the most part, a warm team spirit existed among all the staff at the lodge. Traditionally, the bellmen had a comfortable relationship with Tomblin, so this latest incident was of great concern to Hoffman. She realized that Tomblin was dead serious about firing them. It was midsummer, and finding qualified replacements would be difficult. The bellmen this year had been especially productive. They received $5.00 per hour plus tips, which they pooled and divided equally at the end of each week; daily tips averaged $40 per person. Hoffman was particularly concerned about the situation because it involved employees for whom she was directly responsible.

## Organized Tours

The bellmen had the responsibility of placing the tour luggage in the guests' rooms as soon as the bus arrived. The front desk provided them with a list of guests' names and the assigned cottage numbers. Speed was particularly important because the guests wanted to freshen up and wanted their bags to be delivered promptly. On the morning of departure, the guests left their packed bags in their rooms while they went to breakfast. The bellmen picked up the bags, counted them, and then loaded them on the bus.

As payment for the service rendered by the bellmen, tour directors paid the standard gratuity of $1.00 per bag. It was considered a tip, but it was included in the tour expenses by each company. For large tours, the tip could be as high as $125, although the average was $75.

## Jones Transportation Agency

The Jones Transportation Agency had a reputation throughout the area of being fair and equitable with its tips. However, one of its tour directors, Don Sirkin, didn't live up to the company's reputation. On a visit to the Great Majestic Lodge, Sirkin had not given a tip. The bellmen knew that their service to Sirkin's group had been very good. They were upset about the situation but assumed that Sirkin had forgotten the tip in the rush before his tour departed. The tour was large and the tip would have amounted to $110. Sirkin's tour also stayed at several other nearby resorts. Several of the Great Majestic Lodge bellmen knew the bellmen at the other lodges and, in discussing the situation, discovered that Sirkin had neglected the tip at each of the other lodges. Sirkin apparently had pocketed almost $1,000 on his group's 4-day tour through the region.

## The Letter

Upon hearing of Sirkin's actions, the Majestic Lodge bellmen decided that some action had to be taken. They immediately ruled out telling Hoffman. On previous occasions when there had been a problem, Hoffman had done very little to alleviate the situation.

Roger Sikes, a first-year bellman and a business undergraduate, suggested that they write a letter directly to the president of Jones Transportation Agency. He felt that the agency would appreciate knowing that one of its tour directors had misused company funds. After some discussion, the other bellmen present agreed. Sikes prepared a detailed letter, which told the Jones Agency president the details of the Sirkin incident. The bellmen didn't expect to recover the money from the tour, but they felt that this was the appropriate action to take.

Five of the bellmen signed the letter as soon as it was completed. Two more opposed, but after more discussion and considerable peer pressure, agreed to sign the letter. They mailed it with the expectation of a speedy reply and justice for the offending Don Sirkin.

## Reaction to the Letter

Three weeks after the bellmen's letter had been mailed to the Jones Transportation Agency, Tomblin was thumbing through his morning mail. He noticed a letter from his good friend Grant Cole, the president of the Jones Transportation Agency. Tomblin opened this letter first. Cole had written that there was a problem at the Great Majestic Lodge and he thought that Tomblin should be made aware of it. He enclosed the letter from the bellmen and suggested that, if the bellmen had any problems with any Jones tour directors in the future, it might be wise for them to speak to Tomblin before taking any action. Cole informed Tomblin that Jones was investigating the Sirkin incident.

Tomblin was enraged. The bellmen had totally ignored their supervisor and had written a letter without first consulting the lodge manager or any of the other managers of the Great Majestic Company. This action not only was a breach of company policy, but also a personal humiliation for Tomblin. Tomblin, yelling with outrage, leaped to his feet and charged through the lobby to Hoffman's office. He spotted bellman George Fletcher and ordered him to get out of his sight. The bewildered Fletcher quickly obeyed. Hoffman's meeting with Tomblin was unpleasant. She had never seen Tomblin so upset at the actions of employees. Tomblin was a proud person, and, because his pride has been hurt, he wanted revenge. He showed Hoffman the bellmen's letter and the reply from Cole. Tomblin made it clear that he expected some quick action. Hoffman knew that the action had to meet Tomblin's approval. Her position as lodge manager suddenly was precarious.

Several employees had been in the lobby when Tomblin roared through. Hoffman knew that the gossip would spread quickly throughout the lodge. The bellmen were well liked by the other employees, and she knew that they would be concerned about the bellmen's fate. Hoffman called the still shaken George Fletcher into her office and told him to summon the off-duty bellmen for a meeting. After Fletcher left, she attempted to think of alternatives that would satisfy

Tomblin and also maintain the quality of service expected by guests.[49]

## Questions

1. What social influences and norms appear to have played a part in the behaviors of the bellmen?

2. What contextual influence and goals are relevant in this situation to (a) the bellmen, (b) Hoffman, and (c) Tomblin?

3. What should Hoffman do? Why?

# Managing Interpersonal Conflict and Negotiation

## LEARNING OBJECTIVES

When you have finished studying the chapter, you should be able to:

1. State the four basic levels of conflict in organizations.
2. Explain the five sources of interpersonal power that influence conflict management.
3. Name five interpersonal conflict handling styles and describe their use.
4. Identify the basic types of negotiation and explain several negotiation strategies.

# THE DIVIDED SALES FORCE

Leslie Kossoff is the principal owner of Kossoff Management Consulting, headquartered in San Mateo, California. She comments: "Every action salespeople make is somehow tied to remuneration, so there's something concrete to fight for, and it escalates more quickly than in a typical workplace setting."

While Kossoff was working with a West Coast hospital equipment manufacturer on a management problem, she noticed a crippling territory conflict dividing the sales force. She first saw trouble as she sat in on a new-product training session hosted by R&D representatives and attended by salespeople. "About five minutes into it, one of the reps started questioning the R&D person in an unbelievable angry voice, asking who would be making commissions off the new product," she says. Startled by the question, the presenter had no ready answer. Unsatisfied, the disgruntled rep started pointing fingers at the salespeople he thought would "steal" the commissions on this item, naming reps he said were "responsible for undermining the sales force," Kossoff says. "Within fifteen minutes, it had descended into a yelling match. After the vice president of sales stood up and told them to hold their questions until later, the room exploded. The reps were yelling at the VP, saying that he had already promised to address this issue. The sound in the auditorium became so loud that people from other divisions were peering in to see what was going on. Rumors circulated that someone had gone postal and had a gun on site."

The problem, Kossoff soon discovered, was territorial alignment. The vice president of sales had supposedly structured the territories geographically. However, the company's hospital customers had branches that spanned territorial boundaries, which meant that reps were stepping all over each other to make sales. "The clients learned to play the reps against one another," Kossoff says. As a result, salespeople were granting deep discounts in order to protect their customer base from others within their own company. "The vice president finally realized that the company was losing big on sales revenues because of this, "Kossoff says. "The volume was great, but the profit margins stunk."

One of the favorite sayings of the vice president of sales was, "A little bit of fear is a good thing." He had designed his sales territories around that notion, but it blew up in his face. He was nearly fired for his reps' infighting. It took a complete restructuring of the territory system, with clear lines between salespeople's selling areas that the reps themselves collaborated on to determine, to calm the feuding sales force.[1]

*For more information on Kossoff Management Consulting, visit the organization's home page at http://www.kossoff.com.*

The need to manage conflict occurs every day in organizations. **Conflict** refers to a process in which one party (person or group) perceives that its interests are being opposed or negatively affected by another party.[2] This definition implies incompatible concerns among the people involved and includes a variety of conflict issues and events. **Conflict management** consists of diagnostic processes, interpersonal styles, negotiation strategies, and other interventions that are designed to avoid unnecessary conflict and reduce or resolve excessive conflict. The ability to understand and correctly diagnose conflict is essential to managing it.

In this chapter, we examine conflict and negotiation from several viewpoints. First, we present the basic forms of conflict and examine three attitudes about it. Second, we identify four levels of conflict found in organizations. Third, we discuss five interpersonal styles in conflict management and the conditions under which each style may be appropriate. Fourth, we address the types of negotiation, basic negotiation strategies, and some of the complexities involved in negotiations when the parties are from different cultures. We conclude with some highlights of third-party mediation in the negotiation process.

Our attitude is that conflict may sometimes be desirable and at other times destructive. Although some types of conflict can be avoided and reduced, other types of conflict have to be properly managed. The balanced attitude is sensitive to the consequences of conflict, ranging from negative outcomes (loss of skilled employees, sabotage, low quality of work, stress, and even violence) to positive outcomes (creative alternatives, increased motivation and commitment, high quality of work, and personal satisfaction). Leslie Kossoff, in her role as a consultant to the West Coast hospital equipment manufacturer, clearly did a good job in recognizing the conflicting interests among the sales personnel, diagnosing the underlying problem, and helping to develop a constructive conflict resolution approach.

The balanced attitude recognizes that conflict occurs in organizations whenever interests collide. Sometimes, employees will think differently, want to act differently, and seek to pursue different goals. When these differences divide interdependent individuals, they must be managed constructively. How easily or effectively conflict can be managed depends on various factors, such as how important the issue is to the people involved and whether strong leadership is available to address it. Table 9.1 identifies some of the factors that distinguish types of conflict that are difficult to resolve from types of conflict that are easier to resolve.

**Table 9.1**

| Effects of Various Dimensions of Conflict | | |
|---|---|---|
| **DIMENSION** | **DIFFICULT TO RESOLVE** | **EASY TO RESOLVE** |
| The issue itself | A matter of principle | Simply dividing up something |
| Size of the stakes | Large | Small |
| Continuity of interaction | Single transaction | Long-term relationship |
| Characteristics of participants' "groups" | Disorganized, with weak leadership | Cohesive, with strong leadership |
| Involvement of third parties | No neutral third party available | Trusted, prestigious, neutral third party available |

Source: Adapted from Greenhalgh, L. Managing conflict. In R. J. Lewicki, D. M. Saunders, and J. W. Minton (eds.), *Negotiation*, 3rd ed. Boston: Irwin/McGraw-Hill, 1999, 7.

**Learning Objective:**

1. State the four basic levels of conflict in organizations.

# LEVELS OF CONFLICT

Four primary levels of conflict may be present in organizations: intrapersonal (within an individual), interpersonal (between individuals), intragroup (within a group), and intergroup (between groups). Figure 9.1 suggests that these levels are often cumulative and interrelated. For example, an employee struggling with whether to stay on a certain job may show hostility toward coworkers, thus triggering interpersonal conflicts.

## INTRAPERSONAL CONFLICT

**Intrapersonal conflict** occurs within an individual and usually involves some form of goal, cognitive, or affective conflict. It is triggered when a person's behavior will result in outcomes that are mutually exclusive. Inner tensions and frustrations commonly result. For example, a graduating senior may have to decide between jobs that offer different challenges, pay, security, and locations. Trying to make such a decision may create one (or more) of three basic types of intrapersonal goal conflict.

- *Approach–approach conflict* means that an individual must choose between two or more alternatives, each of which is expected to have a positive outcome (e.g., a choice between two jobs that appear to be equally attractive).
- *Avoidance–avoidance conflict* means that an individual must choose between two or more alternatives, each of which is expected to have a negative outcome (e.g., relatively low pay or extensive out-of-town traveling).
- *Approach–avoidance conflict* means that an individual must decide whether to do something that is expected to have both positive and negative outcomes (e.g., accepting an offer of a good job in a bad location).

Many decisions involve the resolution of intrapersonal goal conflict. The intensity of intrapersonal conflict generally increases under one or more of the following conditions: (1) several realistic alternative courses of action are available for handling the conflict, (2) the positive and negative consequences of the alternative courses of action are roughly equal, or (3) the source of conflict is important to the individual.

**Figure 9.1**                    **Levels of Conflict in Organizations**

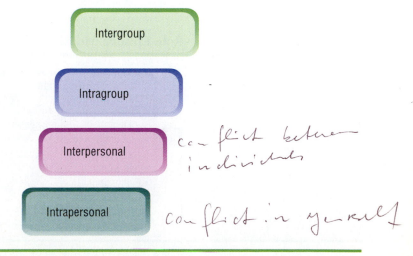

**Workplace Violence.**    Severe unresolved intrapersonal conflict within employees, customers, or others may trigger violent interpersonal conflict. Much violence in the workplace has its source in severe intrapersonal conflict.[3] In Chapter 7 we discussed workplace violence, pointing out that it is a major source of work stress and that the problem is severe. In a recent year, the U.S. National Institute for Organizational Safety and Health reported an average of 13 workplace murders every week and an estimated 1 million nonfatal assaults annually.[4] These grim statistics emphasize the dire consequences of not adequately diagnosing and managing interpersonal conflict and stress in the workplace.

Based on past incidents of workplace violence, indicators of potentially violent employees include

- direct or veiled threats of harm, making inappropriate references to guns, or fascination with weapons;
- intimidating, belligerent, harassing, bullying, or other inappropriate and aggressive behavior;
- numerous conflicts with supervisors and other employees or extreme changes in behavior;
- statements showing fascination with incidents of workplace violence, indicating approval of the use of violence to resolve a problem, or indicating identification with perpetrators of workplace homicides; and
- statements indicating desperation (over family, financial, and other personal problems) to the point of contemplating suicide.[5]

## INTERPERSONAL CONFLICT

**Interpersonal conflict** occurs when two or more individuals perceive that their attitudes, behaviors, or preferred goals are in opposition. As with intrapersonal conflict, much interpersonal conflict is based on some type of role conflict or role ambiguity.

**Role Conflict.**    In the work setting, a **role** is the cluster of tasks and behaviors that others expect a person to perform while doing a job. Figure 9.2 presents a role episode model, which involves role senders and a focal person. Role senders are individuals who have expectations of how the focal person should behave. A role episode begins before a message is sent because role senders have expectations, perceptions, and evaluations of the focal person's behaviors. These, in turn, influence the actual role messages that the senders transmit. The focal person's perceptions of these messages and pressures may then lead to role conflict. **Role conflict** occurs when a focal

**Figure 9.2**                    **Role Episode Model**

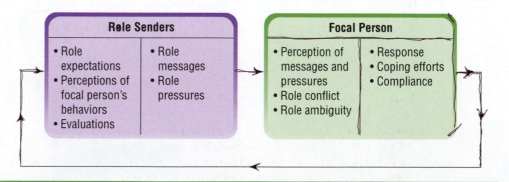

Source: Based on Kahn, R. L., et al. *Organizational Stress: Studies in Role Conflict and Ambiguity.* New York: John Wiley & Sons, 1964, 26.

person responds with behaviors that serve as inputs to the role senders' process. A **role set** is the group of role senders that directly affect the focal person. A role set might include the employee's manager, other team members, close friends, immediate family members, and important clients or customers.

Four types of role conflict may occur as a result of incompatible messages and pressures from the role set.

- *Intrasender role conflict* may occur when different messages and pressures from a single member of the role set are incompatible.
- *Intersender role conflict* may occur when the messages and pressures from one role sender oppose messages and pressures from one or more other senders.
- *Interrole conflict* may occur when role pressures associated with membership in one group are incompatible with pressures stemming from membership in other groups.
- *Person–role conflict* may occur when role requirements are incompatible with the focal person's own attitudes, values, or views of acceptable behavior. Intrapersonal conflict typically accompanies this type of role conflict.[6]

**Role Ambiguity.**   **Role ambiguity** is the uncertainty and lack of clarity surrounding expectations about a single role. Like role conflict, severe role ambiguity causes stress and triggers subsequent coping behaviors. These coping behaviors often include (1) initiating aggressive action (e.g., verbal abuse, theft, and violence) and hostile communication, (2) withdrawing, or (3) approaching the role sender or senders to attempt joint problem solving. Research findings suggest that high levels of role conflict and role ambiguity have numerous dramatic effects, including stress reactions, aggression, hostility, and withdrawal behaviors (turnover and absenteeism).[7] Stress is a common reaction to severe role conflict and role ambiguity (see Chapter 7). However, effective managers and professionals possess the ability to cope with the many ambiguities inherent in their roles.

## INTRAGROUP CONFLICT

**Intragroup conflict** refers to disputes among some or all of a group's members, which often affect a group's dynamics and effectiveness. Family-run businesses can be especially prone to intragroup and other types of conflict. Such conflicts typically become more intense when an owner–founder approaches retirement, actually retires, or dies.

Only 3 in 10 family-run businesses make it to the second generation, and only 1 in 10 survives into the third generation. The biggest obstacles to succession are the relationships among the family members who own the business and bear responsibility for keeping it alive for another generation. What determines whether a family business soars or nosedives? It depends, in larger part, on the respect that family members give each other in the workplace, their willingness to take on roles at work different from those they have at home, and their ability to manage conflict. Randall Carlock, a consultant on family business and founder of the Audio King electronic stores chain, comments, "Families don't express their needs and wants clearly and don't deal with conflict very well. When that moves into their place of business, that spells real trouble. Take the way most parents negotiate with their kids in the business. They basically tell them what they're going to do, or they threaten them, or they tell them, 'You're lucky to have this job.' That's not how you handle an employee, and that's not how you develop a future leader."[8]

Although the consequences of excessive intragroup conflict are typically negative, the balanced view of conflict suggests that some conflict within teams or departments may be useful. For example, Michael Eisner, CEO and chairman of Walt Disney Company, describes the conflict within groups at Disney in positive terms. He credits the existence of "support conflict" with sparking much of the organization's creativity. Eisner states, "This whole business starts with ideas, and we're convinced that ideas come out of an environment of supportive conflict, which is synonymous with appropriate friction. We create a very loose environment where people are not afraid to speak their minds or be irreverent. They say what they think, and they are urged to advocate strongly for ideas. That can be hard and somewhat uncomfortable at times as people say a lot of challenging, provocative things. However, this gets a lot of ideas out there so that we can take a look at them."[9]

### INTERGROUP CONFLICT

**Intergroup conflict** refers to opposition, disagreements, and disputes between groups or teams. It often occurs in union–management relations. Such conflict may be highly intense, drawn out, and costly to those involved. Under high levels of competition and conflict, the parties develop attitudes toward each other that are characterized by distrust, rigidity, a focus only on self-interest, failure to listen, and the like.

**Diversity-Based Conflict.**   In previous chapters we've discussed how serious intergroup conflicts may arise from workforce diversity. The most difficult diversity-based conflicts to resolve in organizations appear to relate to issues of race, gender, ethnicity, and religion. The following Managing Diversity Competency feature presents highlights of the pressures and conflicts experienced by employees in some public accounting firms stemming from gender differences.

## COMPETENCY:   MANAGING DIVERSITY

### WOMEN IN CPA FIRMS

Women working as certified public accountants (CPAs) have long struggled with high levels of conflict. Historically, turnover among such women has been greater than turnover among men. CPA firms had attempted to treat all professionals alike, regardless of gender. Although this approach clearly is appropriate much of the time, it created an unusual circumstance with regard to family. Women who wanted to have children often faced having their careers derailed. As a result, large public CPA firms (e.g., Deloitte & Touche and Ernst & Young) historically have had few women as senior managers and partners.

A series of surveys among CPAs highlighted the higher levels of conflict and stress experienced by women. Further, data gathered from these surveys indicated that many accounting managers assumed that their firms were doing everything possible to further women's careers. Often managers seemed to believe that the high turnover rates for women simply reflected personal choices and preferences and thus were not part of their firms' responsibilities. In addition, many managers indicated that there was little they could do to improve the situation.

Information about high levels of conflict and negative attitudes opened a lot of eyes at CPA firms. Many organizations began to take steps to help women reduce conflict between family and professional career demands. Among the more successful programs have been the use of flexible work arrangements and flexible career paths (reducing the "up or out" syndrome prevalent at many firms). More "personal friendly" policies are emphasized and enforced by higher management at those firms. For example, if job responsibilities permit, many CPA firms now permit employees to work out of their homes 2 or more days a week but often require such employees to be at the office at least 1 day a week. In addition, CPA firms have begun to hire more experienced people, getting away somewhat from the notion that new accountants

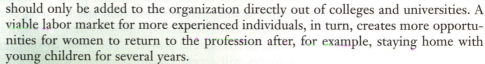

should only be added to the organization directly out of colleges and universities. A viable labor market for more experienced individuals, in turn, creates more opportunities for women to return to the profession after, for example, staying home with young children for several years.

As a result of these types of improvements, the situation in North American CPA firms has improved substantially for women. One indication of this improved environment is that turnover rates among women and men CPAs are now virtually identical.[10]

**Learning Objective:**

2. Explain the five sources of interpersonal power that influence conflict management.

# POWER IN CONFLICT MANAGEMENT

Conflict in organizations often reflects interpersonal sources of power held and used by managers, subordinates, and coworkers. There are five important interpersonal sources of power—reward power, coercive power, legitimate power, expert power, and referent power—that people can use in conflict situations.[11]

## REWARD POWER

**Reward power** is an individual's ability to influence others' behaviors by rewarding them. For example, to the extent that subordinates value rewards that the manager can give—praise, promotions, money, time off, and so on—they may comply with requests and directives. A manager who controls the allocation of merit pay raises in a department has reward power over the employees in that department. Accordingly, employees may comply with some attempts by managers to influence their behaviors because they expect to be rewarded for their compliance.

## COERCIVE POWER

**Coercive power** is an individual's ability to influence others' behaviors by punishing them. For example, subordinates may comply because they expect to be punished for failure to respond favorably to manager's request. Punishment may take the form of reprimands, undesirable work assignments, closer supervision, tighter enforcement of work rules, suspension without pay, and the like. The organization's ultimate punishment is to fire the employee.

Recall, however, that punishment can have undesirable side effects. For example, the employee who receives an official reprimand for shoddy work may find ways to avoid punishment, such as by refusing to perform the task, falsifying performance reports, or being absent frequently.

## LEGITIMATE POWER

**Legitimate power** most often refers to a manager's ability to influence subordinates' behaviors because of the manager's formal position in the organization. Subordinates may respond to such influence because they acknowledge the manager's legitimate right to tell them what to do. Nonmanagerial employees also may possess legitimate power. For example, a safety inspector at Lockheed Martin Vought's plant in Camden, Arkansas, has the legitimate power to shut down production if there is a safety violation, even if the plant manager objects and tries to stop the safety inspector.

Legitimate power is an important organizational concept. Typically, a manager is empowered to make decisions within a specific area of responsibility, such as customer service, quality control, marketing, or accounting. This area of responsibility,

in effect, defines the activities for which the manager (and sometimes other employees) can expect to exercise legitimate power to influence behavior. The farther removed that managers get from their specific areas of responsibility, the weaker their legitimate power becomes. Employees have a zone of indifference with respect to the exercise of managerial power.[12] The **zone of indifference** is an area within which employees will accept certain directives without questioning the manager's power. The manager may have considerable legitimate power to influence subordinates' behavior. Outside that zone, however, legitimate power disappears rapidly. For example, a secretary will type letters, answer the phone, open the mail, and do similar tasks for a manager without question. However, if the manager asks the secretary to go out for a drink after work, the secretary may refuse. The manager's request clearly falls outside the secretary's zone of indifference. The manager has no legitimate right to expect the secretary to comply.

## EXPERT POWER

**Expert power** is an individual's ability to influence others' behaviors because of recognized competencies, talents, or specialized knowledge. To the extent that managers can demonstrate their competencies, they will acquire expert power. However, expert power often is relatively narrow in scope. For example, a team member at Overhead Door Company might carefully follow the advice of her team leader about how to program a numerically controlled lathe, yet ignore advice from the team leader regarding which of three company health plans she should choose. In this instance, the team member is recognizing expertise in one area while resisting influence in another. A lack of expert power often causes problems for new managers and employees. Even though a young accountant might possess a great deal of knowledge about accounting theory and procedures, that expertise must be correctly demonstrated and applied over time to be recognized and accepted.

## REFERENT POWER

**Referent power** is an individual's ability to influence others because he is respected, admired, or liked. For example, subordinates' identification with a manager often forms the basis for referent power. This identification may include the desire of subordinates to be like the manager. (See Chapter 11 for an explanation of how this source of power is related to charismatic leadership.) A young manager may copy the leadership style of an older, admired, and more experienced manager. The older manager thus has some referent power to influence the behavior of the younger manager. Referent power usually is associated with individuals who possess admired personality characteristics, charisma, or a good reputation. It often is associated with political leaders, movie stars, sports figures, or other well-known individuals (hence their use in advertising to influence consumer behavior). However, managers and employees also may have considerable referent power because of the strength of their personalities. Meg Whitman, CEO of eBay, uses her referent power to motivate employees to achieve the organization's goals.

Managers and employees alike possess varying amounts of interpersonal sources of power. Of course, these sources don't operate independently but often serve as the foundation on which various types of conflict are played out. Without power, working through conflict to a person's satisfaction is difficult.[13]

**Learning Objective:**

3. Name five interpersonal conflict handling styles and describe their use.

## INTERPERSONAL CONFLICT HANDLING STYLES

Individuals handle interpersonal conflict in various ways.[14] Figure 9.3 presents a model for understanding and comparing five interpersonal conflict handling styles. The styles are identified by their locations on two dimensions: *concern for self* and *concern for others*. The desire to satisfy your own concerns depends on the extent to which you are *assertive* or *unassertive* in pursuing personal goals. Your desire to satisfy the

**Figure 9.3**                          **Interpersonal Conflict Handling Styles**

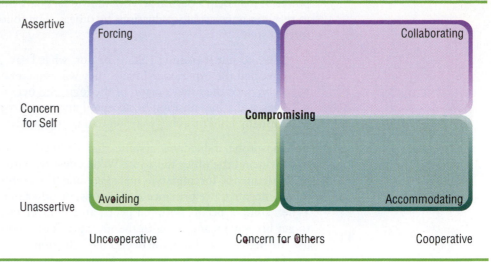

concerns of others depends on the extent to which you are *cooperative* or *uncooperative*. The five interpersonal conflict handling styles thus represent different combinations of assertiveness and cooperativeness. Although you may have a natural tendency toward one or two of the styles, you may use all of them as the situation and people involved change. For example, the style you use in working through a conflict with a good friend may be quite different from the style you use with a stranger after a minor auto accident. The Developing Competencies section at the end of this chapter contains a questionnaire that you can use to assess your own styles for handling conflict. We suggest that you complete this questionnaire now.

### AVOIDING STYLE

The **avoiding style** refers to unassertive and uncooperative behaviors. A person uses this style to stay away from conflict, ignore disagreements, or remain neutral. The avoidance approach reflects an aversion to tension and frustration and may involve a decision to let a conflict work itself out. Because ignoring important issues often frustrates others, the consistent use of the avoidance style usually results in unfavorable evaluations by others. The following statements illustrate the avoiding style.

- If there are rules that apply, I cite them. If there aren't, I leave the other person free to make her own decision.
- I usually don't take positions that will create controversy.
- I shy away from topics that are sources of disputes with my friends.
- That's okay. It wasn't important anyway. Let's leave well enough alone.

When unresolved conflict gets in the way of accomplishing goals, the avoiding style will lead to negative results for the organization. This style may be desirable under some situations, as when (1) the issue is minor or only of passing importance and thus not worth the individual's time or energy to confront the conflict; (2) the individual doesn't have enough information to deal effectively with the conflict at that time; (3) the individual's power is so low relative to the other person's that there's little chance of causing change (e.g., disagreement with a new strategy approved by top management); and (4) others can resolve the conflict more effectively.

### FORCING STYLE

The **forcing style** refers to assertive and uncooperative behaviors and represents a win–lose approach to interpersonal conflict. Those who use the forcing approach try to achieve their own goals without concern for others. This style relies on coercive power. It may help a person achieve individual goals, but like avoidance, forcing tends to result in unfavorable evaluations by others. The following statements illustrate the forcing style.

- I like to put it plainly: Like it or not, what I say goes, and maybe when others have had the experience I have, they will remember this and think better of it.
- I convince the other person of the logic and benefits of my position.
- I insist that my position be accepted during a disagreement.
- I usually hold onto my solution to a problem after the controversy starts.

Forcing-prone individuals assume that conflict resolution means that one person must win and the other must lose. When dealing with conflict between subordinates or departments, forcing-style managers may threaten or actually use demotion, dismissal, negative performance evaluations, or other punishments to gain compliance. When conflict occurs between peers, an employee using the forcing style might try to get his way by appealing to the manager. This approach represents an attempt to use the manager to force the decision on the opposing individual.

Overreliance on forcing by a manager lessens employees' work motivation because their interests haven't been considered. Relevant information and other possible alternatives usually are ignored. In some situations the forcing style may be necessary, as when (1) emergencies require quick action, (2) unpopular courses of action must be taken for long-term organizational effectiveness and survival (e.g., cost-cutting and dismissal of employees for unsatisfactory performance), and (3) the person needs to take action for self-protection and to stop others from taking advantage of her.

The disclosure by current or former organizational members of illegal, immoral, or illegitimate organizational practices in an attempt to change those practices is called **whistle-blowing**. All too often top management believes that whistle-blowers are creating negative rather than positive conflict. As a result, role senders commonly use the forcing style of conflict when dealing with whistle-blowers. The following Managing Ethics Competency feature contains an example of the coercive pressures experienced by one whistle-blower in his effort to be ethical.

## COMPETENCY: MANAGING ETHICS

### RON GARDNER BLOWS THE WHISTLE

The Kentucky Transportation Cabinet (department) allegedly punished Ron Gardner, a resident state engineer, who reported that armed bridge inspectors were soliciting bribes from contractors during a bridge painting project in Louisville, Kentucky. Gardner filed a lawsuit under the state's whistle-blower law, alleging that he was transferred to another job and denied higher-paying positions after alerting his supervisors that inspectors involved in the repainting of the John F. Kennedy Bridge solicited bribes from contractors, padded timesheets, and took kickbacks from suppliers. One inspector pulled a gun on a contractor during an argument, Gardner claims. If victorious, Gardner could be entitled to punitive damages.

The department and its painting contractors already were in conflict when Gardner assumed the post of resident engineer in Bullitt County, overseeing the work. After being ignored by his superiors, he contacted the FBI. The FBI had been tipped off by the contractors and was conducting its own surveillance.

*For more information on Kentucky Transportation Cabinet, visit the organization's home page at http://www.kytc.state. ky.us.*

Federal agents finished gathering evidence and arrested Kevin Earles in connection with an alleged scheme to solicit bribes from the contractors on the bridge project. The FBI had taped a contractor and an undercover FBI agent paying Earles a total of $15,000 in bribes. The transportation cabinet has fired Earles and suspended two other inspectors. The cabinet also terminated the painting contractors after a lengthy dispute.[15]

## ACCOMMODATING STYLE

The **accommodating style** refers to cooperative and unassertive behaviors. Accommodation may represent an unselfish act, a long-term strategy to encourage cooperation by others, or just complying with the wishes of others. Individuals using the accommodating style are typically evaluated favorably by others, but they may also be perceived as weak and submissive. The following statements illustrate the accommodating style.

- Conflict is best managed through the suspension of my personal goals in order to maintain good relationships with others.
- If it makes other people happy, I'm all for it.
- I like to smooth over disagreements by making them appear less important.
- I ease conflict by suggesting that our differences are trivial and then show goodwill by blending my ideas into those of the other person.

When using the accommodating style, an individual may act as though the conflict will go away in time and appeal for cooperation. The person will try to reduce tensions and stress by reassurance and support. This style shows concern about the emotional aspects of conflict but little interest in working on its substantive issues. The accommodating style simply results in the individual covering up or glossing over personal feelings. It is generally ineffective if used consistently. The accommodating style may be effective in the short run when (1) the individual is in a potentially explosive emotional conflict situation, and smoothing is used to defuse it; (2) maintaining harmony and avoiding disruption are especially important in the short run; and (3) the conflicts are based primarily on the personalities of the individuals and cannot be easily resolved.

## COLLABORATING STYLE

The **collaborating style** refers to strong cooperative and assertive behaviors. It is the win–win approach to interpersonal conflict handling. The person using collaboration desires to maximize joint results. An individual who uses this style tends to (1) see conflict as natural, helpful, and leading to a more creative solution if handled properly; (2) exhibit trust in and candor with others; and (3) recognize that when conflict is resolved to the satisfaction of all, commitment to the solution is likely. An individual who uses the collaborating style is often seen as dynamic and evaluated favorably by others. The following statements illustrate the collaborating style.

- I first try to overcome any distrust that might exist between us. Then I try to get at the feelings that we mutually have about the topics. I stress that nothing we decide is cast in stone and suggest that we find a position that we can give a trial run.
- I tell the others my ideas, actively seek out their ideas, and search for a mutually beneficial solution.

- I like to suggest new solutions and build on a variety of viewpoints that may have been expressed.
- I try to dig into an issue to find a solution good for all of us.

With this style, conflict is stated openly and evaluated by all concerned. Sharing, examining, and assessing the reasons for the conflict should lead to development of an alternative that effectively resolves it and is fully acceptable to everyone involved. Collaboration is most practical when (1) a high level of cooperation is needed to justify expending the extra time and energy needed to make working through the conflict worthwhile; (2) sufficient parity in power exists among individuals so that they feel free to interact candidly, regardless of their formal status; (3) the potential exists for mutual benefits, especially over the long run, for resolving the dispute through a win–win process; and (4) sufficient organizational support is given for investing the necessary time and energy in resolving disputes in this manner. The norms, rewards, and punishments of the organization—especially those set by top management—provide the framework for encouraging or discouraging collaboration.

## COMPROMISING STYLE

The **compromising style** refers to behaviors at an intermediate level of cooperation and assertiveness. The individual using this style engages in give-and-take concessions. Compromising is commonly used and widely accepted as a means of resolving conflict. The following statements illustrate the compromising style.

- I want to know how and what others feel. When the timing is right, I explain how I feel and try to show them where they are wrong. Of course, it's often necessary to settle on some middle ground.
- After failing to get my way, I usually find it necessary to seek a fair combination of gains and losses for all of us.
- I give in to others if they are willing to meet me halfway.
- As the old saying goes, half a loaf is better than nothing. Let's split the difference.

An individual who compromises with others tends to be evaluated favorably. Various explanations are suggested for the favorable evaluation of the compromising style, including: (1) it is seen primarily as a cooperative "holding back"; (2) it reflects a pragmatic way of dealing with conflict; and (3) it helps maintain good relations for the future.

The compromising style shouldn't be used early in the conflict resolution process for several reasons. First, the people involved are likely to compromise on the stated issues rather than on the real issues. The first issues raised in a conflict often aren't the real ones, and premature compromise will prevent full diagnosis or exploration of the real issues. For example, students telling professors that their courses are tough and challenging may simply be trying to negotiate an easier grade. Second, accepting an initial position is easier than searching for alternatives that are more acceptable to everyone involved. Third, compromise is inappropriate to all or part of the situation when it isn't the best decision available. That is, further discussion may reveal a better way of resolving the conflict.

Compared to the collaborating style, the compromising style doesn't maximize mutual satisfaction. Compromise achieves moderate, but only partial, satisfaction for each person. This style is likely to be appropriate when (1) agreeing enables each person to be better off, or at least not worse off than if no agreement were reached; (2) achieving a total win–win agreement simply isn't possible; and (3) conflicting goals or opposing interests block agreement on one person's proposal.

## ORGANIZATIONAL USE

Studies conducted on the use of different interpersonal conflict handling styles indicate that collaboration tends to be characteristic of (1) more successful rather than less successful individuals and (2) high-performing rather than medium- and low-performing organizations. People tend to perceive collaboration in terms of the constructive use of conflict. The use of collaboration seems to result in positive feelings in others, as well as favorable self-evaluations of performance and abilities.

In contrast to collaboration, forcing and avoiding often have negative effects. These styles tend to be associated with a less constructive use of conflict, negative feelings from others, and unfavorable evaluations of performance and abilities. The effects of accommodation and compromise appear to be mixed. The use of accommodation sometimes results in positive feelings from others. But these individuals do not form favorable evaluations of the performance and abilities of those using the accommodating style. The use of the compromising style generally is followed by positive feelings from others.[16]

**Learning Objective:**

4. Identify the basic types of negotiation and explain several negotiation strategies.

# NEGOTIATION IN CONFLICT MANAGEMENT

**Negotiation** is a process in which two or more individuals or groups, having both common and conflicting goals, state and discuss proposals for specific terms of a possible agreement. Negotiation includes a combination of compromise, collaboration, and possibly some forcing on vital issues. A negotiation situation is one in which

- two or more individuals must make a decision about their combined goals,
- the individuals are committed to peaceful means for resolving their dispute, and
- there is no clear or established method or procedure for making the decision.[17]

## TYPES OF NEGOTIATION

The four basic types of negotiation are distributive, integrative, attitudinal structuring, and intraorganizational.[18]

**Distributive Negotiations.**    Traditional win–lose, fixed-amount situations—wherein one party's gain is the other party's loss—characterize **distributive negotiations**. They often occur over economic issues, communications are guarded, and expressions of trust are limited. The use of threats, distorted statements, and demands are common. In short, the parties are engaged in intense, emotion-laden conflict. The forcing and compromise conflict handling styles characterize distributive negotiations.

Some individuals and groups still believe in extreme distributive (win–lose) negotiations, and negotiators have to be prepared to counter them. Awareness and understanding probably are the most important means for dealing with win–lose negotiation ploys by the other party. Four of the most common win–lose strategies that you might face as a negotiator are the following.[19]

- *I want it all.* By making an extreme offer and then granting concessions grudgingly, if at all, the other party hopes to wear down your resolve. You will know that you have met such a negotiator when you encounter the following tactics: (1) the other party's first offer is extreme; (2) minor concessions are made grudgingly; (3) you are pressured to make significant concessions; and (4) the other party refuses to reciprocate.
- *Time warp.* Time can be used as a powerful weapon by the win–lose negotiator. When any of the following techniques are used, you should refuse to be forced into an unfavorable position: (1) the offer is valid only for a limited time; (2) you are pressured to accept arbitrary deadlines; (3) the other party stalls or delays the progress of the negotiation; and (4) the other party increases pressure on you to settle quickly.
- *Good cop, bad cop.* Negotiators using this strategy hope to sway you to their side by alternating sympathetic with threatening behavior. You should be on your

guard when you are confronted with the following tactics: (1) the other party becomes irrational or abusive; (2) the other party walks out of a negotiation; and (3) irrational behavior is followed by reasonable, sympathetic behavior.

- *Ultimatums.* This strategy is designed to try to force you to submit to the will of the other party. You should be wary when the other party tries any of the following: (1) you are presented with a take-it-or-leave-it offer; (2) the other party overtly tries to force you to accept its demands; (3) the other party is unwilling to make concessions; and (4) you are expected to make all the concessions.

**Integrative Negotiations.**    Joint problem solving to achieve results benefiting both parties is called **integrative negotiations**. The parties identify mutual problems, identify and assess alternatives, openly express preferences, and jointly reach a mutually acceptable solution. Rarely perceived as equally acceptable, the solution is simply advantageous to both sides. Those involved are strongly motivated to solve problems, exhibit flexibility and trust, and explore new ideas. The collaborative and compromise conflict handling styles are dominant in integrative negotiations.

In the best-seller, *Getting to Yes*, R. Fisher and W. Ury outline four key principles for integrative (win–win) negotiations. These principles provide a foundation for an integrative negotiation strategy.

- *Separate the people from the problem.* The first principle in reaching a mutually agreeable solution is to disentangle the substantive issues of the negotiation from the interpersonal relationship issues between the parties and deal with each set of issues separately. Negotiators should see themselves as working side by side, dealing with the substantive issues or problems instead of attacking each other.
- *Focus on interests, not positions.* People's egos tend to become identified with their negotiating positions. Furthermore, focusing only on stated positions often obscures what the participants really need or want. Rather than focusing only on the positions taken by each negotiator, a much more effective strategy is to focus on the underlying human needs and interests that had caused them to adopt those positions.
- *Invent options for mutual gains.* Designing optimal solutions under pressure in the presence of an adversary tends to narrow people's thinking. Searching for the one right solution inhibits creativity, particularly when the stakes are high. These blinders can be removed by establishing a forum in which various possibilities are generated before decisions are made about which action to take.
- *Insist on using objective criteria.* The parties should discuss the conditions of the negotiation in terms of some fair standard, such as market value, expert opinion, custom, or law. This principle steers the focus away from what the parties are willing or unwilling to do. By using objective criteria, neither party has to give in to the other, and both parties may defer to a fair solution.[20]

Ron Shapiro is a good example of an individual who emphasizes integrative negotiations. Note the emphasis on the importance of the compromise and collaborative approaches in the following Managing Communication Competency feature.

# COMPETENCY:   MANAGING COMMUNICATION

## *RON SHAPIRO ON NEGOTIATING NICE*

Ron Shapiro is coauthor of *The Power of Nice: How to Negotiate So Everyone Wins— Especially You*, and CEO of the Shapiro Negotiations Institute. He has negotiated countless deals—ranging from real estate acquisitions to corporate mergers, from

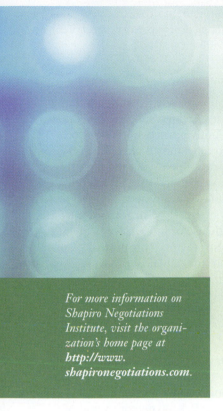

major financial packages to home loans, from settling symphony orchestra and umpire strikes to completing contracts for professional athletes.

Shapiro, at one time, represented Oprah Winfrey before she became really famous. He lost her as a client when another agent lured her away with promises of getting her more money for her TV contract. Against his better judgment, Shapiro's firm ended up suing Oprah because she still owed them some commissions. Shapiro won and got his money, but today recognizes the court victory as a short-term gain that cost him a lot of long-term goodwill. Shapiro says, "My relationship with Oprah is a good example of how not to negotiate. I derived a career-long lesson from that experience: Don't negotiate as if you'll never again do business with the person across the table."

Shapiro now argues that "the power of nice" is the path to successful negotiations. He states: "Forget about winners and losers. Forget about conquerors and victims. Negotiation is not war. It isn't about getting the other side to wave a flag and surrender. Don't think hurt. Think help. Don't demand. Listen. The best way to get most of what you want is to help the other side get some of what it wants. . . . On the surface, negotiation may seem to be about winning and losing. After all, to the victor belong the spoils. Can it be true that only the hardest, toughest and meanest negotiators will be the most successful? . . . These types of negotiators will undoubtedly achieve success in deals, but most will fall short in the long run. I believe that you can be 'nice' and still get what you are after. In fact, you often get better results, achieve more of your goals and build long-term relationships with even greater returns."[21]

*For more information on Shapiro Negotiations Institute, visit the organization's home page at http://www.shapironegotiations.com.*

**Attitudinal Structuring.**    **Attitudinal structuring** is the process by which the parties seek to establish desired attitudes and relationships. Throughout any negotiations, the parties reveal certain attitudes (e.g., hostility or friendliness and competitiveness or cooperativeness) that influence their communications.

At one time, hostile and competitive attitudes prevailed between the major San Francisco hotels and the members of Culinary Local 2. One element in their attitudinal restructuring was the use of La Vonne Ritter as a third-party mediator. She spent several days with union and hotel leadership developing a training program for problem-solving teams composed of hotel management and union representatives. They also created a mission statement for the new working relationships. The following elements of the mission statement focus on attitudinal structuring.

- It shall be the mission of the San Francisco Hotels Multi-Employer Group and the unions to create a new partnership in labor relations.
- We are committed to jointly creating world-class models in the hotel industry demonstrating that union–employer partnerships can achieve a truly successful competitive edge.
- Acknowledging that joint ownership of the process is necessary to ensure success of the parties, we will share all relevant information to foster better communication.
- To accomplish this mission, we commit ourselves to openness, human dignity, courtesy, mutual respect, and an ever increasing level of trust.[22]

**Intraorganizational Negotiations.**    Groups often negotiate through representatives. For example, representatives of OPEC nations set oil prices for the cartel. However, these representatives first have to obtain agreement from the leaders of their respective nations before they can work out an agreement with each other. In **intraorganizational negotiations**, each set of negotiators tries to build consensus for agreement and resolve intragroup conflict before dealing with the other group's negotiators. For example, the members of the federation of San Francisco hotels had to spend a considerable amount of time negotiating among themselves the new concepts, attitudes, and practices that were necessary to reach satisfactory agreement with the members of Culinary Local 2.

## NEGOTIATOR'S DILEMMA

Negotiators increasingly realize the importance of cooperatively creating value by means of integrative negotiations. However, they must also acknowledge the fact that both sides may eventually seek gain through the distributive process. The **negotiator's dilemma** means that the tactics of self-gain tend to repel moves to create greater mutual gain. An optimal solution results when both parties openly discuss the problem, respect each other's substantive and relationship needs, and creatively seek to satisfy each other's interests. However, such behavior doesn't always occur.[23]

Win–win negotiators are vulnerable to the tactics of win–lose negotiators. As a result, negotiators often develop an uneasiness about the use of integrative strategies because they expect the other party to use distributive strategies. This mutual suspicion often causes negotiators to leave joint gains on the table. Moreover, after win–win negotiators have been stung in several encounters with experienced win–lose strategists, they soon "learn" to become win–lose strategists. Finally, if both negotiators use distributive strategies, the probability of achieving great mutual benefits is virtually eliminated. The negotiations will likely result in both parties receiving only minimal benefits.

Graphically, the integrative and distributive negotiation strategies may be placed on vertical and horizontal axes, representing the two negotiating parties. Then, a matrix of possible outcomes emerging from the negotiating process can be developed to illustrate the negotiator's dilemma, as shown in Figure 9.4 for person A and person B.

## NEGOTIATING ACROSS CULTURES

The numerous issues and complexities relevant to all negotiations are increased—sometimes dramatically—when negotiators are from different cultures.[24] Table 9.2 provides examples of some of these differences from a study of more than 300 negotiators in 12 countries. As previously discussed, two fundamental approaches to negotiation are win–win versus win–lose. Note that 100 percent of the respondents from Japan emphasized win–win in their approach to negotiations. In contrast, only

**Figure 9.4**                **Matrix of Negotiated Outcomes**

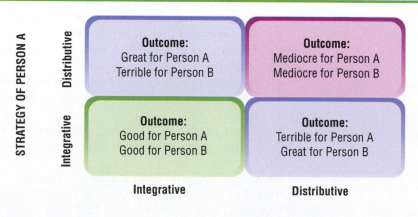

Source: Adapted from Anderson, T. Step into my parlor: A survey of strategies and techniques for effective negotiation. *Business Horizons*, May–June 1992, 75.

**Table 9.2** | **Cultural Effects on Negotiating Style**

### NEGOTIATING ATTITUDE: WIN–WIN OR WIN–LOSE?

| | Japan | China | Argentina | France | India | USA | UK | Mexico | Germany | Nigeria | Brazil | Spain |
|---|---|---|---|---|---|---|---|---|---|---|---|---|
| *Win–Win* (%): | 100 | 82 | 81 | 80 | 78 | 71 | 59 | 50 | 55 | 47 | 44 | 37 |

### PERSONAL STYLE: FORMAL OR INFORMAL?

| | Nigeria | Spain | China | Mexico | UK | Argentina | Germany | Japan | India | Brazil | France | USA |
|---|---|---|---|---|---|---|---|---|---|---|---|---|
| *Formal* (%): | 53 | 47 | 46 | 42 | 35 | 35 | 27 | 27 | 22 | 22 | 20 | 17 |

### COMMUNICATION STYLE: DIRECT OR INDIRECT?

| | Japan | France | China | UK | Brazil | India | Germany | USA | Argentina | Spain | Mexico | Nigeria |
|---|---|---|---|---|---|---|---|---|---|---|---|---|
| *Indirect* (%): | 27 | 20 | 18 | 12 | 11 | 11 | 9 | 5 | 4 | 0 | 0 | 0 |

### AGREEMENT FORM: GENERAL OR SPECIFIC?

| | Japan | Germany | India | France | China | Argentina | Brazil | USA | Nigeria | Mexico | Spain | UK |
|---|---|---|---|---|---|---|---|---|---|---|---|---|
| *General* (%): | 46 | 45 | 44 | 30 | 27 | 27 | 22 | 22 | 20 | 17 | 16 | 11 |

Source: Adapted from Salacuse, J. W. Ten ways that culture affects negotiating style: Some survey results. *Negotiation Journal*, July 1998, 221–240.

37 percent of the Spanish negotiators utilized a win–win approach. The table also compares negotiators from these countries in terms of the degree of formality in their negotiations, whether their communication tends to be direct or indirect, and whether they emphasize attaining general agreement or detailed understandings or contracts.

The degree of formality refers to a negotiator's style. For example, a negotiator from Germany with a very formal style might insist on addressing individuals by their titles, avoid the use of personal stories and anecdotes, and avoid any mention of private or family life. In contrast, a negotiator from the United States with an informal style might use first names as a form of address, strive to develop a personal relationship with other parties, and dress more casually on purpose. The contrast between direct and indirect communications has to do primarily with how straightforward and to the point communication typically is during the negotiations. Indirect communication consists of heavy use of nonverbal communication (see Chapter 12) and many vague statements. German and U.S. negotiators are typically viewed as very direct in their negotiations. French and Japanese negotiators are viewed as more indirect, relying a great deal on nonverbal cues to help understand the negotiations.

The traditional assumptions and generalizations may not always apply to negotiation and conflict resolution between the parties when long-term and insider relationships have been established. This situation applies particularly to negotiations by the Japanese with those whom they view as insiders. Almost by definition, Japanese businesspeople consider Westerners to be outsiders. Thus Westerners often incorrectly assume that the Japanese never use direct or confrontational approaches to conflict resolution and negotiation. In fact, they often are very direct in resolving differences of opinion with *insiders*. They explicitly state the principal differences among group members and state demands, rejections, and counteroffers directly.[25]

The following Managing Across Cultures Competency feature reveals how Levi Strauss negotiated a difficult ethical problem dealing with the use of child labor in Bangladesh.

## COMPETENCY: MANAGING ACROSS CULTURES

### *LEVI STRAUSS IN BANGLADESH*

An operations manager of Levi Strauss became aware that two of the company's contractors in Bangladesh were employing children younger than 14 years of age. Although this was acceptable under Bangladesh law, it violates International Labor Organization standards that bar employment of children under age 14. Further, Levi Strauss has a well-developed code of ethics that explicitly prohibits child labor violations by its contractors. If a violation occurs, the company policy requires the contractor to fire the children younger than age 14 or lose its business. After studying the issue, however, the manager discovered that the underage children were often the sole source of economic support for their families.

In Bangladesh, local norms are tolerant of child labor practices, and the Bangladesh society appears to place a greater value on the basic economic needs of families than the protection of children. Thus the moral significance of the issues in this case was fairly high, even though Levi Strauss managers and Bangladesh suppliers disagreed on which values are most important.

Levi Strauss is a large multinational corporation operating in a developing country. It was in a relatively powerful position, and it could demand that the contractors fire the underage workers or terminate their contracts. Because the contractors' behavior were against International Labor Organization standards and Levi's code of ethics, the company needed to halt this practice as soon as possible. Additionally, media scrutiny of multinational labor practices had been intense and it would be difficult to explain a delay in taking action.

The distributive (forcing) approach would simply mean requiring the contractors to fire all the children under the age of 14, or face termination of the contracts. Interestingly, Levi Strauss negotiated a compromise with the contractors, when it learned that many of the underage children were the sole breadwinners for their families. The company negotiated with the contractors to have the children quit work and go back to school. The contractors continued paying regular wages to the underage children while they attended school and offered each child a job at age 14. Levi Strauss in turn, funded the children's schooling; including books, uniforms, and tuition. The contractors did not employ additional children under the age of 14.[26]

*For more information on Levi Strauss, visit the organization's home page at http://www.levistrauss.com.*

## MEDIATION

**Mediation** is a process by which a third party helps two (or more) other parties resolve one or more conflicts. Most of the actual negotiations occur directly between the involved individuals. But, when the parties appear likely to become locked in win–lose conflict, a mediator, acting as a neutral party, may be able to help them resolve their differences.[27] Recall the actions of Leslie Kossoff in the Preview Case. Part of her intervention as a consultant to the West Coast hospital equipment manufacturer was to serve as a mediator between R&D and sales personnel.

Mediators need special competencies. They must (1) be able to diagnose the conflict, (2) be skilled at breaking deadlocks and facilitating discussions at the right time, (3) show mutual acceptance, and (4) have the ability to provide emotional support and reassurance. In brief, an effective mediator must instill confidence in and acceptance by the parties in conflict.

Key tasks in the mediator's role include the following.

- *Ensure mutual motivation.* Each party should have incentives for resolving the conflict.
- *Achieve a balance in situational power.* If the situational power of the individuals isn't equal, establishing trust and maintaining open lines of communication may be difficult.
- *Coordinate confrontation efforts.* One party's positive moves must be coordinated with the other party's readiness to do likewise. A failure to coordinate positive initiatives and readiness to respond can undermine future efforts to work out differences.
- *Promote openness in dialogue.* The mediator can help establish norms of openness, provide reassurance and support, and decrease the risks associated with openness.
- *Maintain an optimum level of tension.* If the threat and tension are too low, the incentive for change or finding a solution is minimal. However, if the threat and tension are too high, the individuals involved may be unable to process information and envision creative alternatives. They may begin to polarize and take rigid positions.[28]

# CHAPTER SUMMARY

**1.** State the four basic levels of conflict in organizations.

Conflict occurs at four different levels within organizations: intrapersonal, interpersonal, intragroup, and intergroup. Intrapersonal conflict occurs within the individual. Interpersonal conflict occurs when someone's wishes or desires are perceived to be in opposition to another's. Intragroup conflict occurs between or among group members. Intergroup conflict occurs between groups or teams.

**2.** Explain the five sources of interpersonal power that influence conflict management.

Interpersonal sources of power include reward power, coercive power, legitimate power, expert power, and reference power. These power sources may complement or detract from one another in the conflict management process.

**3.** Name five personal conflict handling styles and describe their use.

The five styles for handling interpersonal conflict are avoiding, forcing, accommodating, collaborating, and compromising. An individual may have a natural preference for one or two of these styles but is likely to use all of them over time when dealing with various interpersonal conflict situations. As a reminder, an instrument for measuring your own conflict handling style is presented in the Developing Competencies section at the end of this chapter.

**4.** Identify the basic types of negotiation and explain several negotiation strategies.

Negotiation is a component in conflict management. The four basic types of negotiation are distributive, integrative, attitudinal structuring, and intraorganizational. The two basic approaches to negotiating tactics and behaviors are the win–win (integrative) and win–lose (distributive) processes. Negotiations involving individuals from different cultures are even more complex than negotiations involving only individuals from the same culture. Mediation can be useful when the negotiating parties anticipate or experience difficulties in reaching agreement.

## KEY TERMS AND CONCEPTS

Accommodating style
Attitudinal structuring
Avoiding style
Coercive power
Collaborating style
Compromising style
Conflict
Conflict management
Distributive negotiations
Expert power
Forcing style
Integrative negotiations
Intergroup conflict
Interpersonal conflict
Intragroup conflict

Intraorganizational negotiations
Intrapersonal conflict
Legitimate power
Mediation
Negotiation
Negotiator's dilemma
Referent power
Reward power
Role
Role ambiguity
Role conflict
Role set
Whistle-blowing
Zone of indifference

## DISCUSSION QUESTIONS

1. Reread the Preview Case about the Divided Sales Force. What levels of conflict are apparent in this case? Explain.
2. Reread the Managing Diversity Competency feature about Women in CPA Firms. What levels of conflict are apparent in this feature? Explain.
3. Give personal examples of (a) approach–approach conflict, (b) avoidance–avoidance conflict, and (c) approach–avoidance conflict.
4. Provide examples of (a) intrasender role conflict, (b) intersender role conflict, (c) interrole conflict, and (d) person–role conflict that you have experienced.
5. Think of a current or past relationship with someone who had much more power than you. How would you describe that person's relative use of the five interpersonal conflict management styles? How would you evaluate that person's conflict management effectiveness?

6. Describe your interpersonal sources of power. Do they influence how you handle conflict situations? Explain.
7. Have you been involved in negotiations when the other party used win–lose tactics? Describe the situation. What did you do in response to these tactics? How did you feel? What was the outcome?
8. Based on your personal experiences, describe a situation when an integrative negotiation approach (win–win) seemed to work. Why was it successful?
9. Will integrative negotiations (win–win) always work? Why or why not? Describe some of the difficulties that an individual might encounter while attempting integrative negotiations.

## DEVELOPING COMPETENCIES

### Competency: Managing Self

### Conflict Handling Styles

*Instructions:* Each numbered item contains two statements that describe how people deal with conflict. Distribute 5 points between each pair of statements. The statement that more accurately reflects your likely response should receive the highest number of points. For example, if response (a) strongly describes your behavior, then record

    5   a.
    0   b.

However, if (a) and (b) are both characteristic, but (b) is slightly more characteristic of your behavior than (a), then record

    2   a.
    3   b.

1. _____ a. I am most comfortable letting others take responsibility for solving a problem.
   _____ b. Rather than negotiate differences, I stress those points for which agreement is obvious.

2. _____ a. I pride myself in finding compromise solutions.
   _____ b. I examine all the issues involved in any disagreement.

3. _____ a. I usually persist in pursuing my side of an issue.
   _____ b. I prefer to soothe others' feelings and preserve relationships.

4. _____ a. I pride myself in finding compromise solutions.
   _____ b. I usually sacrifice my wishes for the wishes of a peer.

5. _____ a. I consistently seek a peer's help in finding solutions.
   _____ b. I do whatever is necessary to avoid tension.

6. _____ a. As a rule, I avoid dealing with conflict.
   _____ b. I defend my position and push my view.

7. _____ a. I postpone dealing with conflict until I have had some time to think it over.
   _____ b. I am willing to give up some points if others give up some too.

8. _____ a. I use my influence to have my views accepted.
   _____ b. I attempt to get all concerns and issues immediately out in the open.

9. _____ a. I feel that most differences are not worth worrying about.
   _____ b. I make a strong effort to get my way on issues I care about.

10. _____ a. Occasionally I use my authority or technical knowledge to get my way.
    _____ b. I prefer compromise solutions to problems.

11. _____ a. I believe that a team can reach a better solution than any one person can working independently.
    _____ b. I often defer to the wishes of others.

12. _____ a. I usually avoid taking positions that would create controversy.
    _____ b. I'm willing to give a little if a peer will give a little, too.

13. _____ a. I generally propose the middle ground as a solution.
    _____ b. I consistently press to "sell" my viewpoint.

14. _____ a. I prefer to hear everyone's side of an issue before making judgments.
    _____ b. I demonstrate the logic and benefits of my position.

15. _____ a. I would rather give in than argue about trivialities.
    _____ b. I avoid being "put on the spot."

16. _____ a. I refuse to hurt a peer's feelings.
    _____ b. I will defend my rights as a team member.

17. _____ a. I am usually firm in pursuing my point of view.
    _____ b. I'll walk away from disagreements before someone gets hurt.

18. _____ a. If it makes peers happy, I will agree with them.
    _____ b. I believe that give-and-take is the best way to resolve any disagreements.

19. _____ a. I prefer to have everyone involved in a conflict generate alternatives together.
    _____ b. When the team is discussing a serious problem, I usually keep quiet.

20. _____ a. I would rather openly resolve conflict than conceal differences.
    _____ b. I seek ways to balance gains and losses for equitable solutions.

21. _____ a. In problem solving, I am usually considerate of peers' viewpoints.
    _____ b. I prefer a direct and objective discussion of my disagreement.

22. _____ a. I seek solutions that meet some of everyone's needs.
    _____ b. I will argue as long as necessary to get my position heard.

23. _____ a. I like to assess the problem and identify a mutually agreeable solution.
    _____ b. When people challenge my position, I simply ignore them.

24. _____ a. If peers feel strongly about a position, I defer to it even if I don't agree.
    _____ b. I am willing to settle for a compromise solution.

25. _____ a. I am very persuasive when I have to be to win in a conflict situation.
    _____ b. I believe in the saying, "Kill your enemies with kindness."

26. _____ a. I will bargain with peers in an effort to manage disagreement.
    _____ b. I listen attentively before expressing my views.

27. _____ a. I avoid taking controversial positions.
    _____ b. I'm willing to give up my position for the benefit of the group.

28. _____ a. I enjoy competitive situations and "play" hard to win.
    _____ b. Whenever possible, I seek out knowledgeable peers to help resolve disagreements.

29. _____ a. I will surrender some of my demands, but I have to get something in return.
    _____ b. I don't like to air differences and usually keep my concerns to myself.

30. _____ a. I generally avoid hurting a peer's feelings.
    _____ b. When a peer and I disagree, I prefer to bring the issue out into the open so we can discuss it.

## Scoring

Record your responses (number of points) in the space next to each statement number and then sum the points in each column.

| Column 1 | Column 2 | Column 3 | Column 4 | Column 5 |
|---|---|---|---|---|
| 3 (a) _____ | 2 (a) _____ | 1 (a) _____ | 1 (b) _____ | 2 (b) _____ |
| 6 (b) _____ | 4 (a) _____ | 5 (b) _____ | 3 (b) _____ | 5 (a) _____ |
| 8 (a) _____ | 7 (b) _____ | 6 (a) _____ | 4 (b) _____ | 8 (b) _____ |
| 9 (b) _____ | 10 (b) _____ | 7 (a) _____ | 11 (b) _____ | 11 (a) _____ |
| 10 (a) _____ | 12 (b) _____ | 9 (a) _____ | 15 (a) _____ | 14 (a) _____ |
| 13 (b) _____ | 13 (a) _____ | 12 (a) _____ | 16 (a) _____ | 19 (a) _____ |
| 14 (b) _____ | 18 (b) _____ | 15 (b) _____ | 18 (a) _____ | 20 (a) _____ |
| 16 (b) _____ | 20 (b) _____ | 17 (b) _____ | 21 (a) _____ | 21 (b) _____ |
| 17 (a) _____ | 22 (a) _____ | 19 (b) _____ | 24 (a) _____ | 23 (a) _____ |
| 22 (b) _____ | 24 (b) _____ | 23 (b) _____ | 25 (b) _____ | 26 (b) _____ |
| 25 (a) _____ | 26 (a) _____ | 27 (a) _____ | 27 (b) _____ | 28 (b) _____ |
| 28 (a) _____ | 29 (a) _____ | 29 (b) _____ | 0 (a) _____ | 30 (b) _____ |
| Total _____ | Total _____ | Total _____ | Total _____ | Total _____ |

Next carry over the totals from the column totals and then plot your total scores on the following chart to show the profile of your conflict handling styles. A total score of 36 to 45 for a style may indicate a strong preference and use of that style. A total score of 0 to 18 for a style may indicate little preference and use of that style. A total score of 19 to 35 for a style may indicate a moderate preference and use of that style.

| | Total | 0 | 10 | 20 | 30 | 40 | 50 | 60 |
|---|---|---|---|---|---|---|---|---|
| Column 1 (Forcing) | _____ | • | • | • | • | • | • | • |
| Column 2 (Compromising) | _____ | • | • | • | • | • | • | • |
| Column 3 (Avoiding) | _____ | • | • | • | • | • | • | • |
| Column 4 (Accommodating) | _____ | • | • | • | • | • | • | • |
| Column 5 (Collaborating) | _____ | • | • | • | • | • | • | • |
| | | 0 | 10 | 20 | 30 | 40 | 50 | 60 |

## Interpretation

When used appropriately, each of these styles can be an effective approach to conflict handling. Any one style or a mixture of the five can be used during the course of a dispute. Are you satisfied with this profile? Why or why not? Is this profile truly representative of your natural and primary conflict handling styles?[29]

## Competency: Managing Communication

### Conflict Management Style Incidents

*Instructions:* Your task is to rank the five alternative courses of action in each of the following four incidents. Rank the selection from the most desirable or appropriate way of dealing with the conflict situation to the least desirable. Rank the most desirable course of action "1," the next most desirable "2," and so on, with the least desirable or least appropriate action as "5." Enter your rank for each item in the space next to each choice.

## Incident One

Pedro Ramirez is the lead team operator of a production molding machine. Recently, he has noticed that one of the men from another machine has been coming over to his machine and talking to one of his men (not on break time). The efficiency of Ramirez's operator seems to be falling off, and there have been some rejects because of his inattention. Ramirez thinks that he detects some resentment among the rest of the team. *If you were Pedro Ramirez, you would:*

_____ a. Talk to your man and tell him to limit his conversation during on-the-job time.

_____ b. Ask the supervisor to tell the lead team operator of the other machine to keep his operators in line.

_____ c. Confront both men the next time you see them together (as well as the other lead operator, if necessary), find out what they are up to, and tell them what you expect of your operator.

_____ d. Say nothing now; it would be silly to make something big out of something so insignificant.

_____ e. Try to put the rest of the team at ease; it is important that they all work well together.

## Incident Two

Elena Esquival is the senior quality control (QC) inspector and has been appointed leader of the QC people on her team. On separate occasions, two of her people have come to her with different suggestions for reporting test results to the machine operators. Pablo Cruz wants to send the test results to the supervisor and then to the machine operator because the supervisor is the person ultimately responsible for production output. Jaime Berlanga thinks that the results should go directly to the lead operator on the machine in question because he is the one who must take corrective action as soon as possible. Both ideas seem good, and Esquival can find no ironclad procedures in the department on how to route the reports. *If you were Elena Esquival, you would:*

_____ a. Decide who is right and ask the other person to go along with the decision (perhaps establish it as a written procedure).

_____ b. Wait and see; the best solution will become apparent.

_____ c. Tell both Cruz and Berlanga not go get uptight about their disagreement; if it is not that important.

_____ d. Get Cruz and Berlanga together and examine both of their ideas closely.

_____ e. Send the report to the supervisor with a copy to the lead operator (even though it might mean a little more copy work for QC).

## Incident Three

Rafael Hernandez is a module leader; his module consists of four very complex and expensive machines and five team members. The work is exacting, and inattention or improper procedures could cause a costly mistake or serious injury. Hernandez suspects that one of his men is taking drugs, or at least showing up for work under the influence of drugs. He feels that he has some strong indications, but he knows he doesn't have a "case." *If you were Rafael Hernandez, you would:*

_____ a. Confront the man outright, tell him what you suspect and that you are concerned for him and for the safety of the rest of the crew.

_____ b. Ask that the suspected offender keep his habit off the job; what he does on the job is part of your business.

_____ c. Not confront the individual right now; it might either "turn him off" or drive him underground.

_____ d. Give the man the "facts of life"; tell him it is illegal and unsafe and that if he gets caught, you will do everything you can to see that the man is fired.

_____ e. Keep a close eye on the man to see that he is not endangering others.

## Incident Four

Lois Muñoz is a supervisor of a production unit. From time to time in the past, the product development section has tapped the production units for operators to supplement their own operator personnel to run test products on special machines. In the past, this approach put very little strain on the production units because the demands were small, temporary, and infrequent. Lately, however, the demand seems to have been almost constant for four production operators. The rest of the production unit must fill in for these missing people, usually by working harder and taking shorter breaks. *If you were Lois Muñoz, you would:*

_____ a. Let it go for now; the "crisis" will probably be over soon.

_____ b. Try to smooth things over with your own unit and with the development supervisor; we all have jobs to do and cannot afford a conflict.

_____ c. Let development have two of the four operators they requested.

_____ d. Go to the development supervisor or his manager and talk about how these demands for additional operators could best be met without placing production in a bind.

_____ e. Go to the manager of production (Muñoz's boss) and get her to "call off" the development people.

## Question

What conflict style did you select in each incident? Why?

# CHAPTER

# Leading Effectively: Foundations

## LEARNING OBJECTIVES

When you have finished studying the chapter, you should be able to:

1. Identify and comment on the essentials of leadership.
2. Describe two traditional models of leadership—traits and behavioral.
3. Explain Hersey and Blanchard's situational model of leadership.
4. Discuss the Vroom–Jago time-driven leadership model.

10

## JEFF FEHRMAN OF SUN TRUST SECURITIES

Jeff Fehrman thinks that successful leaders share a key trait: compassion for others. As the head of a four-person Sun Trust Securities office in Augusta, Georgia, he works hard to incorporate that concept into his own leadership style both with coworkers and clients.

"Those looked at as leaders by others have to care about people," he says. "It's not just about money or how many people you manage. The most important thing is knowing that I've done the best I can for my clients. I also want everybody who works on my team to leave at the end of the day with the feeling that I've done what's right for them, that I'm not just in it for me, but for all of us."

His office includes service/operations manager Karen Stewart, database specialist Frances Tindor, and investment associate Lacy Rich, who handles marketing. Not known for his love of detail, he believes in empowering—and rewarding—his staff. He launched what he hopes will be an annual tradition: a brief staff and spouses' trip. At his expense, Fehrman took the group to Asheville, North Carolina, for dinner and an overnight stay at Biltmore Estate, the century-old Blue Ridge Mountain retreat of George Vanderbilt. "The deal I made is, 'When we get to a million bucks, I'll take everybody to the Caribbean. We've had a tough year, but all things being equal, we're still up 17%. Any time you're up, it's not bad, but we're not at a million yet."

His superior, Sam E. Tyson, senior vice president of trust and investment services, comments: "Jeff is a quiet leader, but effective in making complex concepts really simple. And he's always willing to help others as much as he can. He realizes people took time with him and he pays that back."

Payback is a major element of Fehrman's personal philosophy. He contends: "If you help people, it'll come back to you. If you try to short people, that's going to come back to you, too. Maybe not today, maybe not tomorrow. And maybe not always, but I've seen it over and over."

To that end, he focuses on the client first. "You should never take your client for granted," he says. One of his best qualities, he thinks, is his ability to talk to almost anyone. Fehrman comments: "I can relate to different individuals, whether someone is a doctor or is successful in a manufacturing company. Another of my hallmarks is the ability to keep things simple. In our business, people are very guilty of trying to prove to clients that they're smart. I try to build it down to what's important to the client. You have to genuinely care about people if you're going to be good in this business. People see through you—most of the time—if you're not genuine."[1]

*For more information on Sun Trust Securities, visit the organization's home page at http://www.suntrust.com.*

1. Identify and comment on the essentials of leadership.

# INTRODUCTION TO LEADERSHIP

Leadership embraces the seven foundation competencies developed throughout this book, but it also goes beyond them. A team's or organization's success is greatly influenced by the quality of its leadership. Jeff Fehrman clearly demonstrated several leadership qualities. We note various aspects of his leadership style throughout this chapter.

## LEADERSHIP VERSUS MANAGEMENT

**Leadership** is the process of developing ideas and a vision, living by values that support those ideas and that vision, influencing others to embrace them in their own behaviors, and making hard decisions about human and other resources. Noel Tichy, who has studied many outstanding business leaders, describes leadership in these words:

> Leadership is accomplishing something through other people that wouldn't have happened if you weren't there. And in today's world, that's less and less through command and control, and more and more through changing people's mindsets and hence altering the way they behave. Today, leadership is being able to mobilize ideas and values that energize other people.[2]

A **leader** exhibits the key attributes of leadership—ideas, vision, values, influencing others, and making tough decisions. In contrast, a **manager** directs the work of others and is responsible for results. Effective managers bring a degree of order and consistency to the work for their employees.

In this chapter and Chapter 11, you will discover that leadership is like a prism—something new and different appears each time you look at it from another angle. Our purpose is to identify and describe for you diverse leadership issues, ideas, and approaches. In doing so, we present various leadership perspectives and suggest some of their strengths, limitations, and applications. These chapters also are intended to give you personal insights into your own leadership abilities and those that need further development. Our assumption is simple: Leadership can be learned but not taught. Learning leadership means that an individual is actively seeking to make the personal changes required to become a leader.

As suggested in the Preview Case, Jeff Fehrman led by caring for others—both clients and employees—and behaving with integrity. Through example, Fehrman influences his employees to embrace these values as their own. He behaves and supports his subordinates in ways that they ". . . leave at the end of the day with the feeling that I've done what's right for them, that I'm not just in it for me, but for all of us." At the same time, Fehrman recognizes the need to perform and make hard decisions, such as not taking staff and spouses to the Caribbean because the goal of $1 million in sales hadn't been reached. In recognition of the progress made, however, he treated staff and spouses to dinner and an overnight stay at Biltmore Estate in North Carolina.

Table 10.1 provides an overview of the contrasts between the essentials of leadership and management in terms of four major categories: thinking process, typical pattern of direction setting, approach to employee relations, and method of operation. The pairs of attributes within each category are presented as the extremes of a continuum. Most leaders and managers don't function at these extremes. However, patterns that tend toward leadership on the one hand or management on the other hand are likely to emerge as leaders and managers develop and utilize their competencies.

As you review Table 10.1, mark the point on each continuum that reflects the relative emphasis on leadership or management by a person that you have worked for. Individuals may lean more heavily toward either the leadership or the management profile at various times as they face different issues and problems. However, most

| Table 10.1 | Some Comparisons Between Leadership and Management |
|---|---|

| CATEGORY | LEADERSHIP | | MANAGEMENT |
|---|---|---|---|
| **Thinking Process** | • Originates | | • Initiates |
| | • Focuses on people | | • Focuses on things |
| | • Looks outward | | • Looks inward |
| **Direction Setting** | • Vision | | • Operational plans |
| | • Creates the future | | • Improves the present |
| | • Sees forest | | • Sees trees |
| **Employee Relations** | • Empowers | | • Tightly controls |
| | • Associates | | • Subordinates |
| | • Trusts and develops | | • Directs and coordinates |
| **Method of Operation** | • Effectiveness (does the right things) | | • Efficiency (does things right) |
| | • Creates change | | • Manages change |
| | • Serves clients and customers | | • Serves top managers |

Robinson, G. Leadership versus management. *British Journal of Administrative Management*, January/February 1999, 20–21; Parachin, V. M. Ten essential leadership skills. *Supervision*, February 1999, 13–15; Bennis, W., and Goldsmith, J. *Learning to Lead: A Workbook on Becoming a Leader.* Reading, Mass.: Perseus, 1997.

tend to operate primarily in terms of either the leadership or the management profile.[3] Jeff Fehrman clearly fits the leadership profile.

The following Managing Self Competency feature presents various attributes of leadership, as expressed by Bonnie Reitz of Continental Airlines.

## COMPETENCY:   MANAGING SELF

### BONNIE REITZ OF CONTINENTAL AIRLINES

Bonnie Reitz, senior vice president for sales and distribution, was a central figure in the transformation that saved Continental Airlines in 1994. Then, in the aftermath of the September 11, 2001, terrorist acts and further threats to the survival of Continental, she commented: "This is our time to lead. How we respond can set us apart."

She states that she plans to use the same leadership principles employed in the company's turnaround to restore Continental Airlines after the terrorist attacks. Reitz expresses her leadership principles as follows.

- *Listening.* "Listening is the key to knowing if what we're doing is right. Listen to what your customers have to say. All their ideas are good. You may not agree with them all, you may not use them all, but there's always something to be learned."
- *Focus.* "You can't do everything. Focus on what will make the biggest impact. Communicate your goals relentlessly, so that everyone else knows what their own focus should be."

- *Action.* "Think about doing what has to be done. If it's worth doing, do it. We have 2,000 flights every day. All those accolades we got yesterday? Poof! They were yesterday. It's today, and we've got to do it again."
- *Measurement.* "What gets measured gets done. I believe in unshakable facts. Get as many facts as you can. Don't spend forever on it, but if you have enough facts and the gut intuition, you're going to get it right most of the time."
- *No Surprises.* "If something's not going well, tell us so that we can deal with it. That's a core strength of Continental. We're willing to stand up and talk about issues so people can say, 'Well, it's not as bad as I thought.'"
- *Strength.* "My people know that no matter what they do, I will be right there next to them. Stand up. Have strength of character in good times and in bad. If you do those things—and people know that's how you operate—that's how they start to lead."
- *Integrity.* "You have to be able to look yourself in the mirror every day and say, 'I did the best I could.'"[4]

*For more information on Continental Airlines, visit the organization's home page at http://www. continental.com/ corporate/.*

## LEADERS' USE OF POWER

Leaders and managers use many sources of power to influence followers by appealing to one or more of their needs. Effective leadership depends as much on the acceptance of influence by the follower as on the leader's providing it. Power and influence are central to a leader's or manager's role. In Chapter 9, we described the sources of a manager's power as legitimate, reward, coercive, referent, and expert. It's useful to think of a leader's power in the same way. Let's review those sources of power in relation to the roles of leader and follower.

**Legitimate Power.**    Followers may do something because the leader has the right to request them to do it and they have an obligation to comply. This legitimate power comes from the leader's position in the organization. Consider this example of the exercise of legitimate power.

> My boss is Piero Di Matteo at Los Angeles Air Force Base. He believes that if you carry out your assignments on time, there will be no problem. If you get stuck, he's there to guide you.[5]

**Reward Power.**    Followers may do something to get rewards that the leader influences (e.g., promotions, pay raises, bonuses, development opportunities, and the like). Reward power comes from the leader's ability to provide something positively desired by followers in return for their behaviors that the leader expected and wanted. Consider this example of the exercise of reward power.

> Bill Weingart at First Data merchant Services Corporation in Hagerstown, Maryland, realizes the importance of recognizing and rewarding employees when they achieve their goals. Also, he encourages education and self-improvement. He is a mentor to all who have the opportunity to work with or for him. I expect never to encounter anyone like him again in my entire working career.[6]

**Coercive Power.**    Followers may behave in ways to avoid punishments that the leader controls (e.g., demotions, reprimands, no pay raises, and termination). Coercive power is the potential to influence others through the use of sanctions or punishment. Unfortunately, coercive power doesn't necessarily encourage desired behavior, but it may stop or reduce undesirable behaviors. Consider this example of the application of coercive power:

> The boss looked at me and shouted, "I don't care what your [expletive] job title is or what they [expletive] told you when you were hired. You'll do what I [expletive] tell you to do, the [expletive] way I tell you to do it, and if you don't like it, there's the [expletive] door." I had my résumé out the very next day.[7]

At times, leaders do need to exercise coercive power, which is based on their legitimate power. Demoting or dismissing followers for poor performance, unacceptable behavior (e.g., sexual harassment), and lack of integrity (e.g., lying, deceitful conduct, and the like) are examples of the use of coercive power.

**Referent Power.**   Followers may engage in behaviors because they admire the leader, want to be like the leader, and want to receive the leader's approval. Referent power usually is associated with individuals who possess admired personal characteristics, such as humility, integrity, and courage. Consider this example of the use of referent power.

> Rudy Gragnani, a manager of the Coca-Cola Company bottler in Richmond, Virginia, displayed true leadership for me. A customer, an expressive New Yorker, and I were loudly discussing a problem when Rudy walked by. Later, he chewed me out for yelling at my customer. But at the next management meeting, the New Yorker thanked me. Rudy understood that what he saw as an argument was just New York style. He apologized to me for misreading the situation and forwarded the thanks from the accounting area for my efforts.[8]

**Expert Power.**   Followers may engage in behaviors because they believe that the leader has special knowledge and knows what is needed to accomplish a goal or solve a problem. Expert power has a narrow scope: Followers are influenced by a leader only within that leader's area of expertise. Consider this example of the exercise of expert power.

> I went to work for a manager who was one of the sharpest people I had ever worked for. And the applications we worked on were some of the most intelligently constructed, flexible, reusable, modular applications I had ever seen. And it was a fantastic environment for me to learn in.[9]

An effective leader—whether a first-line manager like Jeff Fehrman or top-level executive like Bonnie Reitz—uses all these sources of power. For successful organizations, the pattern in the use of the sources of power is shifting toward greater reliance on reward, referent, and expert power, with less reliance on coercive and legitimate power. This new pattern is influenced by changing technologies, increasing abilities of employees and teams to make decisions, flattening of organizational hierarchies, and changing work and personal life expectations of employees.

## TRADITIONAL LEADERSHIP MODELS

**Learning Objective:**

2. Describe two traditional models of leadership—traits and behavioral.

The traits and behavioral models are probably the most basic, oldest, and most popular of the leadership models. The more recent, more complex leadership models often draw on elements of these two models.

### TRAITS MODEL OF LEADERSHIP

The **traits model of leadership** is based on characteristics of many leaders—both successful and unsuccessful—and is used to predict leadership effectiveness. The resulting lists of traits are then compared to those of potential leaders to assess their likelihood of success or failure. There is support for the notion that successful leaders have interests and abilities and, perhaps, even personality traits that are different from those of less effective leaders.

**Key Traits.**    Some evidence suggests that four traits are shared by most (but not all) successful leaders.

- *Intelligence.* Successful leaders tend to have somewhat higher intelligence than their subordinates.
- *Maturity and breadth.* Successful leaders tend to be emotionally mature and have a broad range of interests.
- *Achievement drive.* Successful leaders are results oriented; when they achieve one goal, they seek another. They do not depend primarily on employees for their motivation to achieve goals.
- *Honesty.* Successful leaders have integrity. When individuals in leadership positions state one set of values but practice another set, followers quickly see them as untrustworthy. Many surveys show that honesty is the most important characteristic when employees are asked to rank and comment on various traits of successful and unsuccessful leaders. Trust is crucial and translates into the degree of willingness by employees to follow leaders. Confusion over the leader's thinking and values creates negative stress, indecision, and personal politics.[10]

**Organizational Use.**    The traits model of leadership is inadequate for successfully predicting actual leadership effectiveness for at least three reasons.[11] First, in terms of personality traits, there are no consistent patterns between specific traits or sets of traits and leadership effectiveness. More than 100 different personality traits of successful leaders in various leadership positions have been identified. For example, the traits pattern of successful leaders of salespeople includes optimism, enthusiasm, and dominance. The traits pattern of successful leaders of production workers usually includes being progressive, introverted, and cooperative. These descriptions are simply generalities. Many successful leaders of salespeople and production workers do not have all, or even some, of these characteristics. There also is often disagreement over which traits are the most important for an effective leader.

The second limitation of the traits model is that it often attempts to relate physical characteristics—such as height, weight, appearance, physique, energy, and health—to effective leadership. Most of these factors are related to situational factors that can have a significant impact on a leader's effectiveness. For example, people in the military or law enforcement must be a particular minimum height and weight in order to perform certain tasks well. Although these characteristics may help an individual rise to a leadership position in such organizations, neither height nor weight correlates highly with effective leadership. In business and other organizations, height and weight generally play no role in performance and thus are not requirements for a leadership position.

The third limitation of the traits model is that leadership itself is complex. A relationship between personality and a person's interest in particular types of jobs could well exist, which a study relating personality and effectiveness might not identify. The traits approach paints a somewhat fatalistic picture, suggesting that some people, by their traits, are more prone to be leaders than others.

## BEHAVIORAL MODEL OF LEADERSHIP

The **behavioral model of leadership** focuses on what leaders actually do and how they do it. There are several versions of this model, but the one presented here suggests that effective leaders help individuals and teams achieve their goals in two ways. First, they build task-centered relations with employees that focus on the quality and quantity of work accomplished. Second, they are considerate and supportive of employees' attempts to achieve personal goals (e.g., work satisfaction, promotions, and recognition) and work hard at settling disputes, keeping people happy, providing encouragement, and giving positive reinforcement.

The greatest number of studies of leader behavior have come from the Ohio State University leadership studies program, which began in the late 1940s. This research was aimed at identifying leader behaviors that are important for attaining team and organizational goals. These efforts resulted in the identification of two main dimensions of leader behavior: consideration and initiating structure.[12] Our review of the behavioral model is based on that leadership studies program.

**Consideration.**   **Consideration** is the extent to which leaders have relationships with subordinates that are characterized by mutual trust, two-way communication, respect for employees' ideas, and empathy for their feelings. Leaders with this style emphasize the satisfaction of employee needs. They typically find time to listen, are willing to make changes, look out for the personal welfare of employees, and are friendly and approachable. A high degree of consideration indicates psychological closeness between leader and subordinates; a low degree shows greater psychological distance and a more impersonal leader.

When is consideration effective? The most positive efforts of leader consideration on productivity and job satisfaction occur when (1) the task is routine and denies employees little, if any, satisfaction from the work itself; (2) followers are predisposed toward participative leadership; (3) team members must learn something new; (4) employees feel that their involvement in the decision-making process is legitimate and affects their job performance; and (5) employees feel that strong status differences should not exist between them and their leader.

**Initiating Structure.**   **Initiating structure** is the extent to which leaders define and prescribe the roles of subordinates in order to set and accomplish goals in their areas of responsibility. Leaders with this style emphasize the direction of team or individual employee activities through planning, communicating, scheduling, assigning tasks, emphasizing deadlines, and giving orders. They maintain definite standards of performance and expect subordinates to achieve them. In short, leaders with a high degree of initiating structure concern themselves with accomplishing tasks by setting performance goals, giving directions, and expecting them to be followed.

When is initiating structure effective? The most positive effects of leader initiating structure on productivity and job satisfaction occur when (1) a high degree of pressure for output is imposed by someone other than the leader; (2) the task satisfies employees; (3) employees depend on the leader for information and direction on how to complete the task; (4) employees are psychologically predisposed toward being instructed in what to do and how to do it; and (5) more than 12 employees report to the leader.

Figure 10.1 suggests that the dimensions of consideration and initiating structure are not necessarily mutually exclusive and, in fact, may be related in various ways. A "leader" may be high, low, or moderate on both consideration and initiating structure, as suggested in Figure 10.1. For example, Jeff Fehrman and Bonnie Reitz appear to be at the high end of both dimensions.

**Organizational Use.**   Some studies suggest that a leader who emphasizes initiating structure generally improves productivity, at least in the short run. However, leaders who rank high on initiating structure and low on consideration generally have large numbers of grievances, absenteeism, and high employee turnover rates. The view now widely accepted is that effective leaders can have high consideration and initiating structure at the same time. Showing consideration is beneficial insofar as it leads to high levels of team morale and low levels of turnover and absenteeism. At the same time, high levels of initiating structures are useful in promoting high levels of efficiency and performance.

Perhaps the main limitation of the behavioral model was the lack of attention it gave to the effects of the situation on effective leadership style. It focused on

**Figure 10.1**                **Behavioral Leadership Grid**

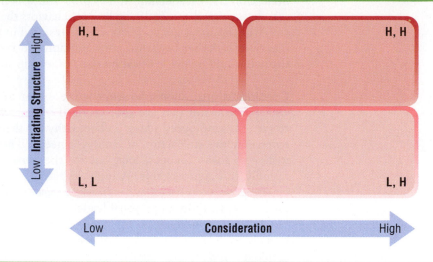

relationships between leaders and employees but gave little consideration to the situation in which the relationships occurred. A better understanding of behavior usually results when both the person and the situation are examined.

Interpersonal communication is the vehicle used by leaders to implement consideration and initiating structure. The following Managing Communication Competency feature conveys how a pattern of high consideration and high initiating structure may be communicated by a leader. This feature relates the actions of Kenneth I. Chenault, CEO of American Express (AmEx) Company, in the aftermath of the terrorist attack on September 11, 2001. Chenault is one of the few African Americans to lead a major corporation.

## COMPETENCY:   MANAGING COMMUNICATION

### KEN CHENAULT OF AMERICAN EXPRESS

Stuck in Salt Lake City on a business trip when the terrorists struck on September 11, 2001, Ken Chenault took command long distance. When the first plane crashed, Chenault was on the phone with a New York colleague from his hotel room. He asked to be transferred to security and instructed them to immediately evacuate the building, which was across the street from the World Trade Towers. Edward P. Gilligan, who heads AmEx's global corporate services unit, recalls that when he arrived home in New Jersey that afternoon, his wife handed him the phone as he walked through the door. It was Chenault, first to check on Gilligan's safety and second to convene a meeting of top execs. "He was there, and he was in the middle of it," says Gilligan.

The hundreds of ad hoc decisions made by Chenault and his team were guided by two overriding concerns: employee safety and customer service. AmEx helped 560,000 stranded cardholders get home, in some cases chartering airplanes and buses to ferry them across the country. It waived millions of dollars in delinquent fees for late-paying cardholders and increased credit limits to cash-starved clients.

Most telling, Chenault gathered 5,000 AmEx employees at the Paramount Theater in New York on September 20, 2001, for a highly emotional "town hall meeting." During the session, Chenault demonstrated poise, compassion, and decisiveness. He

Chapter 10   Leading Effectively:  Foundations

told employees that he had been filled with such despair, sadness, and anger that he had seen a counselor. Twice, he rushed to spontaneously embrace grief-stricken employees. Chenault said he would donate $1 million of the company's profits to AmEx families who had lost loved ones. He stated: "I represent the best company and the best people in the world. In fact, you are my strength, and I love you."

It was a poignant and unscripted moment. Says AmEx board member Charlene Barshefsky, a partner at Wilmer Cutler & Pickering, who viewed a video of the event: "The manner in which he took command, the comfort and the direction he gave to what was obviously an audience in shock . . . was of a caliber one rarely sees." Chenault comments: "The role of the leader is to define reality and to give hope."[13]

*For more information on American Express Company, visit the organization's home page at http://www.americanexpress.com.*

Developers of the traits and behavioral models sought to find characteristics that apply to most leadership situations. In contrast, situational (contingency) leadership models identify variables that permit certain leadership characteristics and behaviors to be effective in given situations. In the next two sections, we present specific situational models of leadership: Hersey and Blanchard's leadership model, and the Vroom–Jago model.

# HERSEY AND BLANCHARD'S SITUATIONAL MODEL

**Learning Objective:**

3. Explain Hersey and Blanchard's situational model of leadership.

**Hersey and Blanchard's situational model** is based on the amount of relationship (supportive) and task (directive) behavior that a leader provides to subordinates in a situation. In turn, the amount of either relationship or task behavior is based on the readiness of the followers to perform needed tasks.[14]

**Task behavior** is the extent to which a leader spells out to subordinates what to do, where to do it, and how to do it. Leaders who use precise directions and tight controls are engaged in close supervision of their subordinates. **Relationship behavior** is the extent to which a leader listens, provides support and encouragement, and involves subordinates in the decision-making process. **Follower readiness** is the subordinates' ability and willingness to perform the tasks. Followers have various degrees of readiness, as shown in Figure 10.2. In R1, the followers are either unable or unwilling to perform the task, whereas in R4, they are able, willing, and confident that they can. In R2, followers are unable but are willing to perform a task and are confident that they can. In R3, followers are able to do the task but aren't confident that they can. According to the situational leadership model, as the readiness level of individuals increases from R1 to R4, a leader should change her style from task to relationship behaviors to increase subordinates' commitment, competence, and performance.

## LEADERSHIP STYLES

Figure 10.2 also shows the association between task and relationship leader behaviors and follower readiness. The appropriate style of leadership is shown by the curve running through the four leadership quadrants, S1–S4.

A **telling style** provides clear and specific instruction. Because followers are either unable or unwilling to perform the task, specific direction and close supervision are needed. That is, the leader tells subordinates what to do and how to perform various tasks.

A **selling style** provides both task and relationship leader behaviors. It is likely to be effective when followers are willing but still unable to carry out their tasks. This style encourages two-way communication between the leader and followers and helps subordinates build confidence in their ability to perform the tasks.

**Figure 10.2**              **Hersey and Blanchard's Situational Leadership Model**

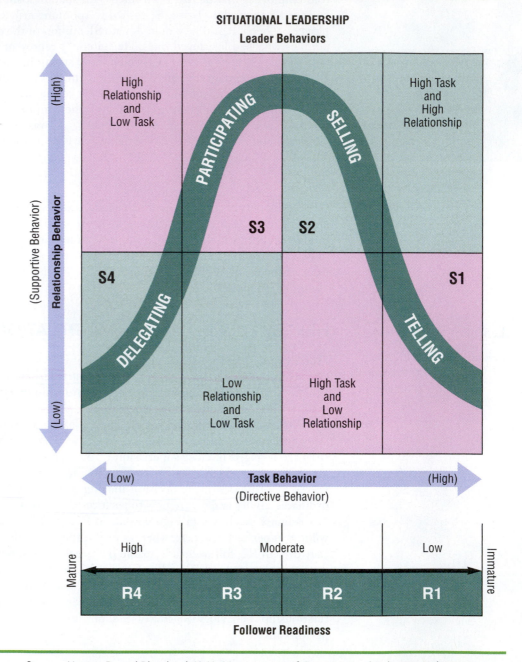

Source: Hersey, P., and Blanchard, K. H. *Management of Organizational Behavior: Utilizing Human Resource*, 5th ed. Englewood Cliffs, N.J.: Prentice-Hall 1988. Used by permission from Ronald Campbell, President, Leadership Studies, Escondido, California.

A **participating style** requires the leader to maintain two-way communication and to support followers in the use of their competencies. It seems to work best when the followers are able but not fully confident of their ability to perform their tasks.

A **delegating style** provides little task or relationship behaviors because subordinates are empowered to make decisions. They decide how and when to perform tasks and also know how to perform them. When followers are able and willing to perform their tasks and confident that they can do so, a delegating style of leader behavior is most appropriate.

## ORGANIZATIONAL USE

Hersey and Blanchard's situational leadership model is simple to understand, and its recommendations are straightforward. In practice, the readiness level of followers must be checked constantly in order for the leader to determine what combination of task and relationship behaviors would be most appropriate in the situation. An inexperienced employee (low readiness) may perform at as high a level as an experienced employee if given direction and close supervision. If a style is appropriate, it should also help followers increase their levels of readiness. Thus, as a leader develops a team and helps its members learn to manage themselves, the leadership style used should be changed to fit the changing situation.

The model has several limitations.[15] First, if each individual has a unique readiness level, how does a leader address those different readiness levels in a team situation? Does the leader assume the average level and choose a leadership style accordingly? Second, the model focuses on one contingency factor—follower readiness. In most situations, many other factors, such as time and work pressures, influence a leader's choice of behavior. A leader should take these other factors into consideration when choosing a leadership style. Third, the model is based on the assumption that a leader can easily adapt his leadership style to fit the situation, which is rarely the case. Fourth, although the model is widely used to help people improve their diagnostic abilities, it isn't strongly supported by scientific research. That is, some studies have supported the model, but others haven't been able to confirm the model's basic premises. For leaders of professionals and managers, we do not believe that the follower readiness dimension, ranging from "immature" to "mature," is very meaningful. Perhaps this concept has more meaning for leaders of nonprofessional employees.

The following Managing Across Cultures Competency feature demonstrates how cultural values and traditions may play a much greater role in the choice of effective leadership style than "follower readiness." This feature is based on perspectives regarding working relationships in Vietnam by Lady Barton, the author of two books on Vietnam.

## COMPETENCY:  MANAGING ACROSS CULTURES

### WORKING RELATIONSHIPS IN VIETNAM

In Vietnamese *xin phep* means "Allow me," "Permit me," or "Be kind enough to listen to me." The phrase invites what can be described as comprehensive consultation. For Westerners, comprehensive consultation implies relinquishing power, yet *xin phep* has little to do with the "yes" and "no" of power and control. For a Vietnamese, *xin phep* shows respect and right relationship; it asks for community input, elicits advice, builds consensus, and develops support to help a project run more smoothly.

A useful phrase is, "If you agree, we thought we might. . . ." The speaker then describes the idea and rationale, giving much more detail than is usual in the West. No one takes the proposed steps until everyone is comfortable with them. *Xin phep* is used with Vietnamese colleagues about anything and everything that affects them. Trust built through consultation about little details makes quick decisions possible for later, larger concerns.

A Western CEO may delegate decision making, but Vietnamese culture does not allow that to the same extent. The slower Vietnamese decision-making process is a cultural tradition that is likely to remain in place for the near future. Relationships count, and listening is more important than talking. As in the West, unofficial relationships affect the agreement process and are often stronger than official relationships. Patience, endurance, and a sense of humor are key ingredients in decision making.

A consensus culture, such as Vietnam's, often seems cumbersome to Westerners. Discussion requires time and effort. But, as in Western organizations, failure to engage in comprehensive consultation may result in reduced effectiveness. In Vietnamese life, everyone discusses details to exhaustion. As one Vietnamese editor says: "We have too much democracy."[16]

**Learning Objective:**

4.  Discuss the Vroom–Jago time-driven leadership model.

# VROOM–JAGO LEADERSHIP MODEL

Victor Vroom and Arthur Jago developed a model that focuses on the leadership role in decision-making situations.[17] Victor Vroom recently revised this model to (1) give greater consideration to ranges that may exist in situational variables; (2) clarify the presentation of the five leadership styles in the earlier model; and (3) further emphasize the time-driven dimension to the choice of leadership style in relation to decision-making situations. The **Vroom–Jago time-driven leadership model** prescribes a leader's choice(s) among five leadership styles based on seven situational factors, recognizing the time requirements and costs associated with each style.[18]

## LEADERSHIP STYLES

There are five core leadership styles that vary in terms of the levels of empowerment and participation available to the leader's subordinates. These styles are summarized in increasing levels of empowerment and participation.

- *Decide style*—You make the decision and either announce or sell it to the team. You may use your expertise and collect information from the team or others who you believe can help solve the problem. The role of your employees is clearly one of providing specific information that you request, rather than generating or evaluating solutions.
- *Consult individually style*—You present the problem to team members individually, getting their ideas and suggestions without bringing them together as a group. Then you make the decision. This decision may or may not reflect their influence.
- *Consult team style*—You present the problem to team members in a meeting, get their suggestions, and then make the decision. It may or may not reflect their influence.
- *Facilitate style*—You present the problem to the team in a meeting. You act as facilitator, defining the problem to be solved and the boundaries within which the decision must be made. Your objective is to get concurrence on a decision. Above all, you take care to ensure that your ideas are not given any greater weight than those of others simply because of your position. Your role is much like that of chairperson, coordinating the discussion, keeping it focused on the problem, and being sure that the essential issues are discussed. You don't try to influence the team to adopt "your" solution. You are willing to accept and implement any solution that has the support of the entire team.
- *Delegate style*—You permit the team to make the decision within prescribed limits. The team undertakes the identification and diagnosis of the problem, developing alternative procedures for solving it and deciding on one or more alternative solutions. You don't enter into the team's deliberations unless explic-

itly asked, but behind the scenes you play an important role, providing needed resources and encouragement. This style represents the highest level of subordinate empowerment.

## SITUATIONAL VARIABLES

The Vroom–Jago time-driven leadership model focuses on seven situational factors (contingency variables) that should be assessed by the leader to determine which leadership style to use. Victor Vroom developed a Windows-based computer program called Expert System that enables the leader to record judgments on a five-point scale as to the extent to which a factor is present in a particular situation. Specifically, 5 = high presence, 3 = moderate presence, and 1 = low presence. Following presentation of the seven situational factors, we demonstrate their use with a simplified "high" or a "low" presence evaluation.

- *Decision significance*—the degree to which the problem is highly important and a quality decision is imperative. In brief, how important is the technical quality of the decision?
- *Importance of commitment*—the degree to which subordinates' personal willingness to support the decision has an impact on the effectiveness of implementation. In brief, how important is subordinate commitment to the decision? Employees are more likely to implement enthusiastically a decision that is consistent with their goals, values, and understanding of the problem.
- *Leader expertise*—the degree to which the leader has relevant information and competencies to understand the problem fully and select the best solution to it. In brief, does the leader believe that she has the ability and information to make a high-quality decision?
- *Likelihood of commitment*—the degree to which subordinates will support the leader's decision if it is made. Followers who have faith and trust in the judgments of their leaders are more likely to commit to a decision, even if the subordinates were not heavily involved in making it. In brief, if the leader were to make the decision, would subordinate(s) likely be committed to it?
- *Team support*—the degree to which subordinates relate to the interests of the organization as a whole or a specific unit in solving the problem. In brief, do subordinates share the goals to be achieved by solving this problem?
- *Team expertise*—the degree to which the subordinates have the relevant information and competencies to understand fully the problem and select the best solution to it. In brief, does the leader think that subordinates have the abilities and information to make a high-quality decision?
- *Team competence*—the degree to which team members have the abilities needed to resolve conflicts over preferred solutions and work together in reaching a high-quality decision. In brief, are team members capable of handling their own decision-making process?

## SOLUTION MATRIX

The solution matrix shown in Table 10.2 represents the main features of the Vroom–Jago time-driven leadership model. This matrix begins on the left where you evaluate the significance of the situation—high (H) or low (L). The column headings denote the situational factors that may or may not be present. You progress across the matrix by selecting high (H) or low (L) for each relevant situation factor. After you determine the significance of the decision, you then evaluate the degree (high or low) to which employee commitment is important to implementation of the decision. As you proceed across the matrix, record a value (H or L) for only those situational factors that call for a judgment, until you reach the recommended leadership style.

**Table 10.2**

## Vroom–Jago Time-Driven Leadership Model

| Problem Statement | Decision Significance | Importance of Commitment | Leader Expertise | Likelihood of Commitment | Team Support | Team Expertise | Team Competence | |
|---|---|---|---|---|---|---|---|---|
| | | | | | | | | Note: Dashed line (—) means not a factor. |
| | H | H | H | H | — | — | — | *Decide* |
| | | | | L | H | H | H | *Delegate* |
| | | | | | | | L | *Consult Group* |
| | | | | | | L | — | |
| | | | | | L | — | — | |
| | | | L | H | H | H | H | *Facilitate* |
| | | | | | | | L | *Consult Individually* |
| | | | | | | L | — | |
| | | | | | L | — | — | |
| | | | | L | H | H | H | *Facilitate* |
| | | | | | | | L | *Consult Group* |
| | | | | | | L | — | |
| | | | | | L | — | — | |
| | | L | H | — | — | — | — | *Decide* |
| | | | L | — | H | H | H | *Facilitate* |
| | | | | | | | L | *Consult Individually* |
| | | | | | | L | — | |
| | | | | | L | — | — | |
| | L | H | — | H | — | — | — | *Decide* |
| | | | | L | — | — | H | *Delegate* |
| | | | | | | | L | *Facilitate* |
| | | L | — | — | — | — | — | *Decide* |

Source: Vroom, V. H. Leadership and decision-making. *Organizational Dynamics*, Spring 2000, 82–94.

**Decision-Time Penalty.**   The **decision-time penalty** is the negative result of decisions not being made when needed. Leaders often must make decisions when time is of the essence. For example, air traffic control supervisors, emergency rescue squad leaders, and nuclear energy plant managers may have little time to get inputs from others before having to make a decision. The time penalty is low when there are no severe pressures on the leader to make a quick decision.

Negative effects on "human capital" occur because the delegate and consult styles (especially the consult-team version) use time and energy, which can be translated into costs even if there are no severe time constraints. Many managers spend almost 70 percent of their time in meetings and that time always has a value, although the precise costs of meetings vary with the reasons for them. For example, while Jonathan Wheeler, vice president of human resources at Centex Homes, is in a meeting, other decisions are being delayed. What's the cost to Centex for these delays? One cost, obviously, is the value of time lost through the use of participative decision making. Benefits gained from employees participating in meetings include being members of a team, strengthening their commitment to the organization's goals, and contributing to the development of their leadership capabilities (mainly as related to managing self and communication competencies). Thus the cost of holding a meeting must be compared to the cost of not holding a meeting.

Although participation can have negative effects on human capital, it can also have positive effects. As we emphasize throughout this book, participative leader behaviors help develop the technical skills and managerial competencies of employees, build teamwork, and foster loyalty and commitment to organizational goals. The Vroom–Jago model considers the trade-offs among four criteria by which a leader's decision-making style can be evaluated: decision quality, employee commitment to implementation, costs, and employee development. The consult and delegate styles are viewed as most supportive of employee development.

We apply this model in the following Managing Change Competency feature. We ask you to assume the role of the executive director and select the leadership style that you would use.

## COMPETENCY:   MANAGING CHANGE

### HOW WOULD YOU LEAD?

You are the executive director of a repertory theater affiliated with a major university. You are responsible for both financial and artistic direction of the theater. You recognize that both sets of responsibilities are important, but you have focused your efforts where your own talents lie—on ensuring the highest level of artistic quality to the theater's productions. Reporting to you is a group of four department heads responsible for production, marketing, development, and administration, along with an assistant dean, who is responsible for the actors who are also students in the university. They are a talented set of individuals, and each is deeply committed to the theater and experienced in working together as a team.

Last week you received a comprehensive report from an independent consulting firm commissioned to examine the financial health of the theater. You were shocked by the major conclusion of the report:

> The expenses of operating the theater have been growing much more rapidly than income, and by year's end the theater will be operating in the red. Unless expenses can be reduced, the surplus will be consumed, and within five years the theater might have to be closed.

You have distributed the report to your staff and are surprised at the variety of reactions that it has produced. Some dispute the report's conclusions, criticizing its assumptions or methods. Others are more shaken, but even they seem divided over steps that should be taken and when. None of them or, in fact, anyone connected with the theater want it to close. It has a long and important tradition both in the university and the surrounding community.

As executive director—and armed with the solution matrix shown in Table 10.2— what leadership style should you choose when making a decision about how to lead? Start with *decision significance* on the left-hand side of the matrix. This first column requires that you make a decision about the importance of the issue. After you make that decision, go to the next column, *importance of commitment*. Again, you must make a decision about the importance of having staff members committed. After you make this decision, you face another decision and then another. As you make each decision, follow the columns across the matrix. Eventually, at the far right-hand side of the matrix, you will arrive at the recommended best style of leadership to use, which is based on your previous seven decisions. We used this method and obtained the results shown in the following table. Based on this analysis, we selected the style of leadership that we recommend for this situation. Do you agree?

| Problem Statements | Answers |
|---|---|
| • Decision significance | High |
| • Importance of commitment | High |
| • Leader expertise | Low |
| • Likelihood of commitment | Low |
| • Team support | High |
| • Team expertise | High |
| • Team competence | High |

We recommend that you use the facilitate style with the teams. A different answer to one or more of these situational factors would probably result in a different recommended leadership style.[19]

## ORGANIZATIONAL USE

The Vroom–Jago time-driven leadership model is consistent with earlier work on group and team behaviors (see Chapter 8). If leaders can diagnose situations correctly, choosing the best leadership style for those situations becomes easier. These choices, in turn, enable them to make high-quality, timely decisions. If the situation requires delegation, the leader must learn how to establish the desired goals and limitations and then let employees determine how best to achieve the goals within those limitations. If the situation calls for the leader alone to make the decision, the leader should be aware of potential positive and negative consequences of not asking others for their input.

The model does have some limitations. First, most subordinates have a strong desire to participate in decisions affecting their jobs, regardless of the model's recommendation of a style for the leader to use. If subordinates aren't involved in the decision, they are more likely to become frustrated and not be committed to the decision. Second, certain competencies of the leader play a key role in determining the relative effectiveness of the model. For example, in situations involving conflict, only leaders skilled in conflict resolution may be able to use the kind of participative decision-making strategy suggested by the model. A leader who hasn't developed such skills may obtain better results with a more directive style, even though this style is different from the style that the model proposes. Third, the model is based on the assumption that decisions involve a single process. Often, decisions go through several cycles and are part of a solution to a bigger problem than the one being addressed at the time.

Choosing the most appropriate leadership style can be difficult. A theme of employee empowerment has begun to prevail in most leading business organizations. Evidence shows that this leadership style can result in productive, healthy organizations. However, participative management is not appropriate for all situations, as contingency theorists note.

## CHAPTER SUMMARY

**1.** Identify and comment on the essentials of leadership.

Leadership includes the seven foundation competencies developed throughout this book—and more. Leadership also includes developing ideas and a vision, expressing and living by values, influencing others, and making hard decisions. Leaders draw on five sources of power to influence the actions of followers: legitimate, reward, coercive, referent, and expert.

**2.** Describe two traditional models of leadership—traits and behavioral.

Two of the traditional leadership models are the traits and behavioral models. The traits model emphasizes the personal qualities of leaders and attributes success to certain abilities, skills, and personality characteristics. However, this model fails to explain why certain people succeed and others fail as leaders. The primary reason is that it ignores how traits interact with other situational variables. The behavioral model emphasizes leaders' actions instead of their personal traits. We focused on two leader behaviors—initiating structure and consideration—and how they affect employee performance and job satisfaction. The behavioral model tends to ignore the situation in which the leader is operating. This omission is the focal point of the two contingency models of leadership that we reviewed. The contingency approach emphasizes the importance of various situations, factors, or contingencies to leaders and on their leadership styles.

**3.** Explain Hersey and Blanchard's situational model of leadership.

Hersey and Blanchard's model states that leaders should choose a style that matches the readiness of their subordinates to follow. If subordinates are not ready to perform a task, a directive leadership style will probably be more effective than a relationship style. As the readiness level of the subordinates increases, the leader's style should become more participative and less directive.

**4.** Discuss the Vroom–Jago time-driven leadership model.

The Vroom–Jago model presents a leader with choices among five leadership styles based on seven situational (contingency) factors. Time requirements and other costs associated with each style are recognized in the model. The leadership styles lie on a continuum from decide (leader makes the decision) to delegate (subordinate or team makes the decision). A solution matrix (Table 10.2) is used to diagnose the situation and arrive at the recommended leadership style.

## KEY TERMS AND CONCEPTS

Behavioral model of leadership
Consideration
Decision-time penalty
Delegating style
Follower readiness
Herscy and Blanchard's situational model
Initiating structure
Leader
Leadership

Manager
Participating style
Relationship behavior
Selling style
Task behavior
Telling style
Traits model of leadership
Vroom–Jago time-driven leadership model

## DISCUSSION QUESTIONS

1. Think of a manager that you have worked for. Was this manager also a leader? Explain your response.
2. Max De Pree, former CEO of Herman Miller, stated, "The first responsibility of a leader is to define reality. The last is to say thank you. In between the leader is a servant." What challenges and dilemmas might you experience in attempting to lead on the basis of this advice?
3. Describe a manager that you have worked for in terms of her use (or lack of use) of the five sources of power: legitimate, reward, coercive, referent, and expert.

4. In terms of your description in Question 3, how effective was this manager in using each of these sources of power?
5. How would you characterize Bonnie Reitz of Continental Airlines, in terms of the behavioral model of leadership? What specific principles presented in the Managing Self Competency feature represent *consideration and initiating structure*?
6. Reread the Managing Communication Competency feature on Ken Chenault. What aspects of Chenault's leadership appear to be consistent with the Vroom–

Jago leadership model? What aspects seem to differ from it?

7. Make a list of the conditions under which you failed to exercise effective leadership in a situation. Make another list of the conditions under which you exercised successful leadership in a situation. What are the differences in the lists?

8. Assume that you have been selected as a team leader for four other classmates. The team's assignment is to develop a 20-page paper on the traits model of leadership and then to present the paper to the class. This project represents 30 percent of the course grade. How might

the Hersey and Blanchard's model be helpful to you as the team leader? What limitations does this model impose on you as team leader?

9. Leslie Sucor, director of process management at Burlington Northern Santa Fe Railway Company, discovered that she could improve the performance of her subordinates through the decide style of leadership rather than the delegate style. According to the Vroom–Jago time-driven model of leadership, under what conditions would this style be effective? What are some drawbacks to this style that she should consider?

# DEVELOPING COMPETENCIES

## Competency:  Managing Self

### What's Your Leadership Style?

The following statements can help you diagnose your leadership style according to the behavioral model of leadership. Read each item carefully. Think about how you usually behave when you are the leader. Then, using the following key, circle the letter that most closely describes your style. Circle only one choice per statement.

A = Always          O = Often          ? = Sometimes          S = Seldom          N = Never

**Column 1**

1. I take time to explain how a job should be carried out.  A O ? S N
2. I explain the part that coworkers are to play in the group.  A O ? S N
3. I make clear the rules and procedures for others to follow in detail.  A O ? S N
4. I organize my own work activities.  A O ? S N
5. I let people know how well they are doing.  A O ? S N
6. I let people know what is expected of them.  A O ? S N
7. I encourage the use of uniform procedures for others to follow in detail.  A O ? S N
8. I make my attitude clear to others.  A O ? S N
9. I assign others to particular tasks.  A O ? S N
10. I make sure that others understand their part in the group.  A O ? S N
11. I schedule the work that I want others to do.  A O ? S N
12. I ask that others follow standard rules and regulations.  A O ? S N

**Column 2**

13. I make working on the job more pleasant.  A O ? S N
14. I go out of my way to be helpful.  A O ? S N
15. I respect others' feelings and opinions.  A O ? S N
16. I am thoughtful and considerate of others.  A O ? S N
17. I maintain a friendly atmosphere in the group.  A O ? S N
18. I do little things to make it more pleasant for others to be a member of my group.  A O ? S N
19 I treat others as equals.  A O ? S N
20. I give others advance notice of change and explain how it will affect them.  A O ? S N
21. I look out for others' personal welfare.  A O ? S N
22. I am approachable and friendly toward others.  A O ? S N

### Scoring

The point values for Always (A), Often (O), Sometimes (?), Seldom (S), and Never (N) are as follows: A=5; O=4; ?=3; S=2; and N=1. Sum the point values for items 1 through 12 in Column 1. Then, sum the point values for items 13 through 22 in Column 2.

**Column 1**

| Item | Points |
|------|--------|
| 1 | _____ |
| 2 | _____ |
| 3 | _____ |
| 4 | _____ |
| 5 | _____ |
| 6 | _____ |
| 7 | _____ |
| 8 | _____ |
| 9 | _____ |
| 10 | _____ |
| 11 | _____ |
| 12 | _____ |

Total [       ]

**Column 2**

| Item | Points |
|------|--------|
| 13 | _____ |
| 14 | _____ |
| 15 | _____ |
| 16 | _____ |
| 17 | _____ |
| 18 | _____ |
| 19 | _____ |
| 20 | _____ |
| 21 | _____ |
| 22 | _____ |

Total [       ]

## Interpretation

The items in Column 1 reflect an initiating structure or task leadership style. A score greater than 47 indicates that you describe your leadership style as high on initiating or task structure. You see yourself as planning, directing, organizing, and controlling the work of others. The items in Column 2 reflect a considerate or relationship style. A score greater than 40 indicates that you see yourself as a considerate leader. A considerate leader is one who is concerned with the comfort, well-being, and personal welfare of her subordinates.

In general, managers rated high on initiating structure and at least moderate on consideration tend to be in charge of more productive teams than those whose leadership styles are low on initiating structure and high consideration.[20]

## Competency:  Managing Teams

### Southwestern Manufacturing Company

Ramona Ortega pulled the trailer into the parking lot of the Loew's Anatole Hotel in Dallas and sighed with relief that her long trip from Santa Fe, New Mexico, was over. The trailer was packed with samples of handmade Native American dolls from her factory. She hoped that she would get many orders for them during the next 3 days at the Southwestern art and furniture shows in Dallas. As she checked into her room, she recalled many of the difficult times she and her husband, Hector Ortega, had overcome during the last 3 years.

First, productivity at the factory had been lower than they thought it should be. They had hired local workers to help them, and her husband had devised a pay system for the workers. He had carefully explained the system to them and had offered them the opportunity to ask questions about how the system worked. Because many of the workers had never made dolls, they didn't ask any questions. Their only request was to be paid a straight hourly wage. Although the Ortegas had thought that an incentive system would encourage workers to be more productive, they finally agreed to pay them on an hourly basis. The manual skills required for assembling the dolls were similar, so all employees were paid at the same rate.

The Ortegas soon found that the work habits of their employees were erratic. They were surprised one day when none of the workers showed up for work. They soon learned that it was the first day of deer hunting season and that many employees in Santa Fe treated it like a holiday. As the workers explained later, it was a tradition to take this day off.

Hector Ortega knew of potential markets for other products handcrafted by Native Americans, so he had held a meeting the previous month with several of the employees to discuss making new products. Because the buying for dolls was seasonal—especially before the holiday season and Mother's Day—he thought that employees could work on other products, such as small drums, at other times. This approach would increase the firm's productivity and overall profitability. The workers listened to his suggestions, but explained that they only knew how to make the dolls. He decided not to pursue the idea until he and his wife could figure out why the workers were unwilling to cooperate. However, the Ortegas knew that competition from other companies eventually would require their workers to learn new skills to produce other products.

Several squabbles among employees had erupted in the plant. Usually this involved some of the Hispanic and Native American women. None of the squabbles were serious or prolonged, but they contributed to an underlying tension among the workers. The previous week, Ramona Ortega had been in the factory when Rosa Gonzalez complained that Carla Lightfoot and Paul Jimenez were making fun of her. When Hector Ortega asked Gonzalez what they had said, she didn't know because they were speaking in Tewa, a language that she didn't understand. He had been in the middle of negotiating a large contract with Toys "R" Us and was unable to drop everything to sort out the situation. Ramona Ortega was uncertain about what to do because she didn't understand Tewa either.

These minor squabbles between workers may have been one of the reasons why the Ortegas' efforts to develop a team leader had failed. Ramona Ortega had attended a week-long seminar in Albuquerque for small business owners that focused on building good working relationships among employees. When she came back to the plant, she and her husband began applying some of these techniques. For example, they began forming workers into teams that consisted of one person from each of the three stages in making dolls. After introducing the concepts to the workers, Hector Ortega asked the teams to discuss ways that they could cooperate with each other to increase their productivity and report back to him or

Judith Ramirez within a week. When they came back the following week, members of all the teams said that they hadn't come up with any ideas on how to cooperate with each other. When he asked more specifically about what they had discussed, he found out that the teams hadn't even met, much less discussed anything.

The Ortegas then decided to appoint a leader for each team. This time they gave the workers a month to meet informally and report back on the teams' progress. At the end of the month, the workers gathered in the office and the results were the same: No one had discussed teamwork and cooperation. The Ortegas decided to drop the team concept temporarily until they could think of a way to gain employee support and help them work together to make the company more successful.[21]

## Questions

1. What are the two most important leadership problems facing the Ortegas?
2. What are your recommendations for resolving or reducing these leadership problems?
3. Based on the Vroom–Jago model, what is your diagnosis of this situation? What leadership style does it suggest for the Ortegas?

# C H A P T E R

# Leading Effectively: Contemporary Developments

## LEARNING OBJECTIVES

When you have finished studying the chapter, you should be able to:

1. State the characteristics of transactional leadership.
2. Describe the features of charismatic leadership.
3. Explain the nature of transformational leadership.
4. Assess the limitations on a leader's impact.

11

# CECILIA CLAUDIO
# OF FARMERS GROUP

Born in Portugal, Cecilia Claudio is senior vice president and chief information officer (CIO) at Farmers Group, Inc., which is headquartered in Los Angeles. Farmers Group provides a variety of insurance policies and services in the United States through its 18,000 employees and independent agents. Claudio reflects on her views of leadership as follows: "The most important thing a CIO can do is create an environment where people can succeed. The people in my IT division are the most important asset I have for my success and the company's success. So they have to feel that they are in control of their destiny, because when they're not, a sense of doom comes upon them."

The information technology (IT) division of Farmers was deeply entrenched in existing systems and functioned mainly in a support role when Claudio came on board in 1998. Her mission, given to her by the company chairman and CEO, was to transform IT into a strategic business partner that could help Farmers become a more customer-responsive company. A key step in achieving the long-range goal was to outsource existing and traditional applications development and support. Claudio's first move was to enlist the support of the employees in her division by focusing on how she could boost their morale. She conducted a confidential employee satisfaction survey. From those responses, she devised a six-point plan leading to a reassignment of employees into more meaningful jobs.

She held a divisionwide meeting and promised, "'Over the next few months, you will see a new IT created,'" she recalls. "Of course, their response was, 'Yeah, we've heard that before. Whatever.'" To gain their confidence and support, Claudio started with small steps. Although Farmers had a formal dress code, she persuaded top management to allow business-casual dress in IT. Next, she guaranteed staff members the time and money to attend training in two new technologies of their choice.

As she delivered on each of the six points of the plan, the staff bought into her vision. When it came to outsourcing the traditional systems, rather than creating anxiety and despair, the announcement generated enthusiasm. Claudio notes: "I said to them, 'The jobs you're doing today aren't keeping you current in the marketplace. I want you to have confidence in your ability to sell yourself to any IT organization, but I want you to choose to stay at Farmers. So I want you to develop a tool kit so you'll have the choice.' And the sign-on was incredible."

Claudio sums up her leadership philosophy this way: "I'm not perfect. I have to remind myself every day that my success depends on the people around me and that I'm also responsible for their success."[1]

*For more information on Farmers Group, Inc., visit the organization's home page at* **http://www.farmers.com.**

By listening, focusing on changes that improved not only IT's impact on the business but also the lives of the employees in the division, and communicating the changes in those terms, Claudio garnered the staff's loyalty. In just under 3 years, turnover in the division dropped from 15 percent to 7 percent. About 15 percent of the 1,500-plus people on her staff have gained new skills and have been placed in new and better jobs.[2]

The models of leadership presented in Chapter 10 provide important insights into Claudio's success as a leader, but they don't provide a complete profile of her leadership or that of other leaders. These models didn't address the full range of questions and issues about effective leadership. Recall our comment from Chapter 10: The topic of leadership is like that of a prism—there is something new and different each time you look at it from a new angle. In this chapter, we present additional lenses for understanding and addressing the range of leadership issues and the pressures on leaders in particular situations. Our focus is on the contemporary perspectives of transactional, charismatic, and transformational leadership. We conclude with a discussion of the conditions under which leaders may not have a major influence on subordinates' behavior. Clearly, the leadership of Cecilia Claudio had a significant influence in transforming the IT division at Farmers Group.

Leadership is future-oriented. It involves influencing people to move from where they are (here) to some new place (there). However, different leaders define or perceive here and there differently. For some, the journey between here and there is relatively routine, like driving a car on a familiar road. Others see the need to chart a new course through unexplored territory. Such leaders perceive fundamental differences between the way things are and the way things can or should be. They recognize the shortcomings of the present situation and offer a sense of passion and excitement to overcome them.

## Learning Objective:

1. State the characteristics of transactional leadership.

# TRANSACTIONAL LEADERSHIP

**Transactional leadership** involves motivating and directing followers primarily through contingent reward-based practices. The transactional leader tends to focus on a carrot (but sometimes a stick) approach, set performance expectations and goals, and provide feedback to followers.

Three primary components of transactional leadership are usually viewed as prompting followers to achieve their performance goals.

- *Contingent rewards*—leader identifies a path that links the achievement of goals to rewards, clarifies expectations, exchanges promises and resources for support, arranges mutually satisfactory agreements, negotiates for resources, exchanges assistance for effort, and provides commendations for successful performance.
- *Active management by exception*—leader monitors followers' performance, takes corrective action if deviations from standards occur, and enforces rules to prevent mistakes.
- *Passive management by exception*—leader intervenes when problems become serious but may wait to take action until mistakes are brought to her attention.[3]

Transactional leadership is best viewed as insufficient, but not bad, in developing maximum leadership potential. One leadership expert makes the following point:

Without the transactional base, expectations are often unclear, direction is ill-defined, and the goals you are working toward are too ambiguous. . . . Transactions clearly in place form the base for more mature interactions.[4]

The following Managing Change Competency feature describes the transactional leadership of Craig Conway, who became CEO of PeopleSoft in 1999. He replaced David Duffield, the company's CEO and founder, after the software firm experienced problems in the marketplace. Conway's transactional leadership style contrasted greatly with Duffield's more charismatic leadership. Duffield had called employees "PeoplePeople" and spoken earnestly of the "PeopleSoft family."[5]

## COMPETENCY:  MANAGING CHANGE

### CRAIG CONWAY OF PEOPLESOFT

Conway's first days on the job as CEO were tense. Less than a month after taking over, he summoned the top dozen or so PeopleSoft executives to a meeting in a company conference room. It lasted more than 14 hours. "He went up to a whiteboard and started outlining his vision, and the room erupted," says Baer Tierkel, a former PeopleSoft executive who left the company but counts himself an admirer of Conway. "There was arguing back and forth. It became clear who on the management team had bought into the future and who hadn't." Several executives in the meeting soon left the company.

Why Conway's whiteboard strategizing had created such an uproar was soon evident. His plan meant the swift demise of some of the most cherished features of Duffield's old PeopleSoft. "David would walk around the hall, in his casual attire, hugging people," says David Thompson, the company's CIO and a 7-year PeopleSoft employee. Conway wears power suits and makes it clear that other executives should too. He doesn't do hugs. When Conway arrived, employees' dogs wandered about the company's headquarters in Pleasanton, California, a reflection of Duffield's passion for pets. Conway banned dogs. Conway also canceled the free breakfasts that were costing the company about $1 million a year.

He also moved quickly to halt the exodus of key employees, which had begun when Duffield announced he was looking for a successor and had sped up when it became clear that Conway was it. Within months of his arrival, half of PeopleSoft's top 12 executives were gone, and scores of software developers had bolted to join Evolve Software, a competing firm. To stem the resignations, Conway cut stock option vesting time and sweetened compensation. Conway states: "The first thing I had to do was stabilize the management team. We didn't have enough players on the field."

When Conway arrived, the average gap between the moment a customer received its bill and when it paid was 103 days. Conway sent out collection letters and leaned on his accounts receivable people; now the time between billing and payment averages only 63 days (the industry average is about 80 days).

Conway added a three-part mantra to the company's mission statement: "Competitiveness. Intensity. Accountability." Asked what has changed since Conway signed on, CIO Thompson states: "There's definitely more intensity, and we're certainly a more competitive company. And I'd say we're a lot more accountable too."

Early on, Conway made the radical decision to halt every ongoing software project and put almost all of PeopleSoft's 2,000 programmers to work rewriting 138 PeopleSoft applications—including programs for human resources, accounting, and supply-chain management—into "pure" Internet form.

In September 2000, PeopleSoft released its Internet-based software, called PeopleSoft 8. It was an instant hit. The success merely drove Conway to push employees harder. He had his executives rank each of the company's programmers and then held a meeting with the top 100 a month after PeopleSoft 8's release. Some of the programmers had been expecting a bonus. Instead, they received a command to rewrite for the Web the company's 20 customer relationship management

*For more information on PeopleSoft, visit the organization's home page at http://www.peoplesoft. com.*

applications. Conway comments: "The look on their faces was incredulous. It had been a mega-marathon, and I was asking them to run another race." By March 2001, the company had a working version, and it unveiled the software for customers in June 2001.[6]

**Learning Objective:**

2. Describe the features of charismatic leadership.

## CHARISMATIC LEADERSHIP

**Charismatic leadership** involves motivating and directing followers primarily by developing in them a strong emotional commitment to a vision and set of shared values. By showing great passion and devotion to the vision and values, such leaders influence followers by appealing to their emotions at a deep level.

### BROAD MODEL

The broad model of charismatic leadership includes the following interrelated attributes, as shown in Figure 11.1.

- *Emphasizes shared vision and values*—leader focuses on creating a mental image of a highly desirable future and their values, linking these values to the organization's mission, goals, and expected behaviors.
- *Promotes shared identity*—leader focuses on creating common bonds among followers and a shared sense of "who we are" and "what we stand for" as an organization.

**Figure 11.1**    **Broad Model of Charismatic Leadership**

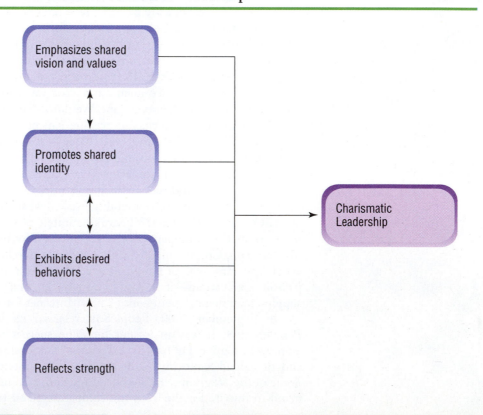

- *Exhibits desired behaviors*—leader displays personal commitment to the values, identity, and goals that he is promoting, engaging in self-sacrifice to show commitment to those values and goals.
- *Reflects strength*—leader displays and creates the impression of self-confidence, social and physical courage, determination, optimism, and innovation.[7]

Charismatic leaders gain power because their followers identify with them. Followers identify with and are inspired by charismatic leaders in the hope (and with the leaders' promises) that they will succeed. Charismatic leaders, such as Herb Kelleher of Southwest Airlines and Oprah Winfrey, have the ability to distill complex ideas into simple messages, communicating with symbols, metaphors, and stories. They relish risk and emotionally put themselves on the line, working on followers' hearts as well as minds.[8]

Charismatic leaders are outstanding in their managing communication competency. The following Managing Communication Competency feature on Sir Richard Branson, chairman of the Virgin Group, provides a few examples of his charismatic leadership. The Virgin Group, headquartered in London, consists of 160 companies in such diverse industries as Virgin Atlantic Airways, Virgin Records, and Virgin Cola.

## COMPETENCY:  MANAGING COMMUNICATION

### RICHARD BRANSON OF THE VIRGIN GROUP

Many chief executives focus on creating shareholder value and devote their attention primarily to customers. Branson believes that the correct pecking order is employees first, customers next, and then shareholders. His logic is this: If your employees are happy, they will do a better job. If they do a better job, the customers will be happy, and thus business will be good and the shareholders will be rewarded. Branson regularly takes entire flight crews out to dinner and parties when he arrives on a Virgin Atlantic flight. He even stays at the crew's hotel rather than in expensive hotels downtown away from the crew. He gives every Virgin employee a Virgin card, which provides big discounts on the airline as well as at Virgin Megastores and other Virgin businesses.

Consider this example. While vacationing on his private Caribbean island, called Necker, he brought 20 employees from various Virgin companies to the island. These were not senior executives, but the rank and file—a housekeeper, a switchboard operator, a reservations clerk, a pilot. They were invited because of excellent performance—a regular perk for Virgin employees. Branson notes: "The idea is to have fun, but by talking to employees, you learn a lot as well." Reminded that it is the rare chief executive who takes employees along on vacation, Branson laughs and says, "I can assure you, it's no sacrifice." He attends as many orientations for new staff as possible in order to set the tone and send the message: "Get out there and have a good time. Really enjoy yourself, because most of your life is spent working, and you ought to have a great time doing it. It's much nicer paying the bills when everybody is having a good time."

He is frequently on the road to visit Virgin businesses, talking with employees and customers. He is known for his ever-present notebook and pen, which he pulls out whenever he chats with employees and customers. Branson insists that talking and writing things down is a crucial element in his role as chairman. His writings create lists of items for immediate action. He reads mail from employees every morning before he does anything else. This habit, which he started in Virgin's early days, influences company–employee dynamics. Employees don't hesitate to air their grievances

*For more information on Virgin Group Ltd., visit the organization's home page at **http://www. virgin.com**.*

directly with him. Branson has proved with his actions that he actively listens. Virgin has more than 35,000 employees around the world, and he gets some 50 e-mail messages or letters each day from nonmanagerial employees. They vary from small ideas to frustrations with middle management to significant proposals. He addresses each concern by answering personally or by initiating some action. Branson states, "Instead of needing a union when they have a problem, they come to me. I will give the employee the benefit of the doubt on most occasions."[9]

## RESTRICTED MODEL

Some leadership experts have a more restricted model of charismatic leadership. As suggested in Figure 11.2, they contend that *charisma* exists only when five elements are present and operate in combination with each other.

- There is a person with extraordinary gifts and qualities.
- There is a social or organizational crisis or desperate situation.

**Figure 11.2**    **Restricted Model of Charismatic Leadership**

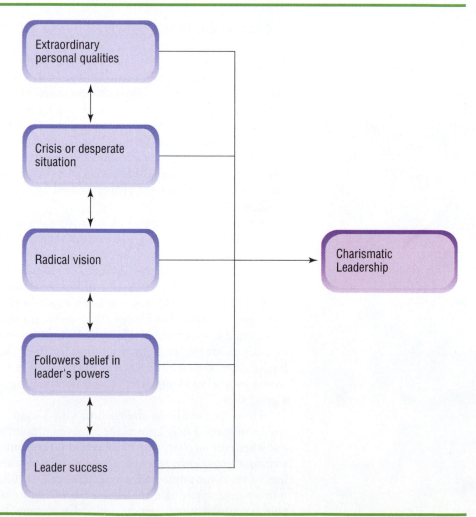

- There is a radical vision or set of ideas promising a solution to the crisis as proposed by the person (potential charismatic leader).
- There is a set of followers who are attracted to the gifted person (leader) and come to believe in the leader's exceptional powers and radical vision.
- There is the realization (validation) of the person's (leader's) extraordinary gifts and radical vision by repeated success in dealing with the perceived crisis.[10]

This restricted model of charismatic leadership has been summed up in this way:

> Charismatic leadership involves more than a set of extraordinary characteristics of a person—it involves a social process that is the product of the complex interactions of all of these elements. Especially important are the triggers provided by a perceived crisis and the radical vision promising a solution to the crisis. Without a radical vision, a person of exceptional qualities may be an inspirational or cultural leader who attracts people, but is unlikely to achieve the kinds of dramatic social change that charisma can produce. . . . Because of the highly emotional . . . basis of the followers' attraction to the leader and to the radical vision, charisma is inherently unstable. It must be transformed into institutional patterns in order to achieve permanence over time.[11]

Martin Luther King's leadership illustrates this model of charisma. The crisis in civil rights, King's extraordinary personal characteristics, his ability to inspire commitment to a radical vision (at the time), followers who were attracted to him and his expressed vision, and a series of successes (breaking down the walls of segregation through nonviolent protest) all came together and resulted in a growing social movement. Recall the vision and values he dramatically expressed in his "I Have a Dream" speech:

> I say to you today, my friends, that in spite of the difficulties and frustrations of the moment, I still have a dream . . . it is a dream deeply rooted in the American dream.
>
> I have a dream that one day this nation will rise up and live out the true meaning of its creed: "We hold these truths to be self-evident: that all men are created equal."
>
> When we let freedom ring, when we let it ring from every village and every hamlet, from every state and every city, we will be able to speed up that day when all of God's children, black men and white men, Jews and Gentiles, Protestants and Catholics, will be able to join hands and sing in the words of the old Negro spiritual, "Free at last! Free at last! Thank God Almighty, we are free at last."[12]

## TRANSFORMATIONAL LEADERSHIP

**Learning Objective:**

3. Explain the nature of transformational leadership.

**Transformational leadership** involves anticipating future trends, inspiring followers to understand and embrace a new vision of possibilities, developing others to be leaders or better leaders, and building the organization or group into a community of challenged and rewarded learners.[13] Transformational leadership may be found at all levels of the organization: teams, departments, divisions, and the organization as a whole.

As suggested in Figure 11.3 and this discussion, the transformational leadership model builds on and extends the features of transactional and charismatic leadership. For a leader, it clearly is the most comprehensive and challenging to implement. The components of transformational leadership that primarily relate to followers include inspirational motivation, intellectual stimulation, idealized influence, and individualized consideration.[14]

**Figure 11.3**                **Model of Transformational Leadership**

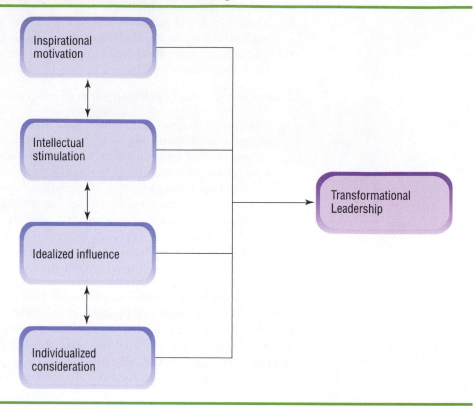

## INSPIRATIONAL MOTIVATION

**Inspirational motivation** involves behaviors and communication that guide followers by providing them with a sense of meaning and challenge. Transformational leaders, such as Gordon Bethune of Continental Airlines, display great enthusiasm and optimism, which carries over into the lives of followers and fosters a sense of team spirit. Such leaders get followers involved in, and eventually committed to, a vision of a future that may be significantly different from the present. Transformational leaders inspire others by what they say and do. Recall that Cecilia Claudio provided inspirational motivation in a number of ways.

A **vision** is a view of a future desired state. Martin Luther King's vision was framed in his "I Have a Dream" speech in these words:

> I have a dream that one day this nation will rise up and live out the true meaning of its creed: "We hold these truths to be self-evident: that all men are created equal."

The framing and inspirational promotion of a consistent vision and set of values is the foundation of transformational leadership. One leadership expert sums it up this way:

> Transformational leaders are shapers of values, creators, interpreters of institutional purpose, exemplars, makers of meanings, pathfinders, and molders of organizational culture. They are persistent and consistent. Their vision is so compelling that they know what they want from every interaction. Their visions don't blind others, but empower them.[15]

When Gordon Bethune joined Continental Airlines as an executive in 1994, it was on the verge of bankruptcy. Soon after, he was appointed CEO. Bethune and the other key executives engaged in transformational leadership. In 1994, the vision of Continental's key leaders was to become the lowest cost airline in the industry. After much discussion and in the midst of great gloom and despair among employees at all levels, a very simple transformation vision was formulated: "Go Forward." This elementary vision and theme was driven by the realization that the company's history was not going to be of help in avoiding bankruptcy. Nothing from the past could create inspiration for the future. The rallying cry of the turnaround was "Do it fast, do it right away, do it all at once."

Four cornerstones of change were encompassed in the "Go Forward" vision.

- *Fly to win*—change the markets served by emphasizing the Houston, Newark, and Cleveland hubs and change the customer mix by appealing to more business travelers.
- *Fund the future*—change the financing strategy to gain cash by selling nonstrategic assets and refinancing the purchase of new planes.
- *Make reliability a reality*—change the customers' experiences regarding service, including better on-time departures and arrivals.
- *Working together*—change the culture to one of fun and action while restoring employees' trust in higher management.

For years, the way to get ahead at Continental had been to torpedo someone and then get her job. As part of the company's transformation, in the span of several months, 50 of the 61 top managers were replaced with 20 individuals. Cutting the bureaucracy and costs facilitated the creation of a new culture. All new managers had to have three core competencies: They had to be bright; they had to be driven to get things done; and they had to be team players. They were expected to treat everyone with dignity, respect, and honesty so as to create a collaborative and fun work environment. When people were let go, the top leaders went out of their way to honor any contracts and let them resign with dignity. The transformational leadership of Bethune and his fellow executives was humane but not soft.[16]

## INTELLECTUAL STIMULATION

**Intellectual stimulation** is the encouragement given to followers to be innovative and creative. Transformational leaders urge followers to question assumptions, explore new ideas and methods, and approach old situations with new perspectives. In addition, such leaders actively seek new ideas and creative solutions from followers. Followers' ideas aren't criticized just because they may differ from those of the leader. Leaders have a relatively high tolerance for mistakes made by conscientious followers, who aren't publicly criticized for those errors. Transformational leaders focus on the "what" in problems rather than "who" to blame for them.

Under transformational leadership, followers feel free to encourage leaders to reevaluate their own perspectives and assumptions. Transformational leaders are willing to abandon systems and practices that are no longer useful even if they developed them in the first place. Nothing is too good, fixed, political, or bureaucratic that it can't be changed or discontinued. The prevailing view is that it is better to question ourselves than to leave all the questioning about us to our competitors. Transformational leaders view risk taking as necessary and desirable for the long-term development and success of the organization.

## IDEALIZED INFLUENCE

**Idealized influence** reflects the behaviors of transformational leaders that followers strive to emulate or mirror. Followers typically admire, respect, and trust such leaders. They identify with these leaders as people, as well as with the vision and values that they are advocating. Positive idealized influence allows followers to feel free to question what is being advocated.

The goals of followers are often personally meaningful and consistent with their self-concepts. They willingly give extra effort because of the intrinsic rewards obtained from performing well, not just because of the potential for receiving greater monetary and other extrinsic rewards. Immediate short-term goals are viewed as a means to the followers' commitments to a greater vision.

To further earn such idealized influence, transformational leaders often consider the needs and interests of followers over their own needs. They may willingly sacrifice personal gain for the sake of others. Such leaders can be trusted and demonstrate high standards of ethical and moral conduct. Followers come to see such leaders as operating according to a pattern of open communication. Thus they can be very direct and challenging to some followers (e.g., poor performers) and highly empathetic and supportive of others (e.g., those with a seriously ill family member).

Although transformational leaders minimize the use of power for personal gain, they will use all the sources of power—expert, legitimate, reward, referent, and coercive—at their disposal to move individuals and teams toward a vision and its related goals. As an example of referent power, followers often describe transformational leaders as individuals who have had a major impact on their own personal and professional development.

William George, chairman and former CEO of Medtronic, Inc., has provided transformational leadership to foster the development, learning, and achievement of meaningful goals by the company's employees. Medtronic is a leading medical technology company with 26,000 employees and is headquartered in Minneapolis, Minnesota. George's leadership is credited with creating an innovative learning culture. He resigned from his position as CEO in 2001 but continues to serve as chairman of the board. Recently, he received the Distinguished Executive of the Year Award at the Academy of Management's Annual Conference. The following Managing Self Competency feature presents a brief excerpt from his keynote address at that conference.

## COMPETENCY:    MANAGING SELF

### WILLIAM GEORGE OF MEDTRONIC

My basic premise is that those companies that devote themselves to maximizing shareholder value as their primary purpose will ultimately fail to do so in the long run. The best path to long-term growth in shareholder value comes from having a well-articulated mission that employees are willing to commit to, a consistent set of values, and a clear business strategy that is adaptable to changing business conditions. Companies that pursue their mission in a consistent and unrelenting manner in the end will create shareholder value far beyond what anyone believes is possible.

Employees today are seeking meaning in their work. They know that they spend more time at work than anywhere else in their lives. Shouldn't their work be meaningful? Don't they have a right to a meaningful job? Everyone wants to be fairly compensated for his or her efforts. But that is not enough for today's employees. Their real motivation comes from believing that their work has a purpose, and they are a part of a larger effort to achieve something truly worthwhile.

Can these very high levels of motivation be sustained over a long period of time? Or just for the short-term push? I have found they will last if the motivation is deeply rooted in the intrinsic purpose of the work. It cannot be applied artificially by management or consultants. That is why so many motivational programs designed and created by consultants ultimately wear off and fail in the end. They are not intrinsic to the purpose of the work. If people embrace the mission of the organization with a passion, it is not only sustainable, it is unstoppable as long as their leaders keep the trust and stay the course.[17]

*For more information on Medtronic, Inc., visit the organization's home page at http://www. medtronic.com.*

## INDIVIDUALIZED CONSIDERATION

**Individualized consideration** is the special attention paid by a transformational leader to each follower's needs for achievement and growth. Transformational leaders may act as coach, mentor, teacher, facilitator, confidant, and counselor. Followers and colleagues are encouraged to develop to successively higher levels of their potential. Individual differences are embraced and rewarded to enhance creativity and innovation. An open dialogue with followers is encouraged and "management by continuous engagement" is standard practice. Listening skills are sharp and reflect this observation: It's not what you tell them, it's what they hear.

Transformational leaders empower followers to make decisions. At the same time, they monitor followers to determine whether they need additional support or direction and to assess progress. With trust in leaders' intentions, followers think: This person is trying to help me by noting mistakes, as opposed to pointing a finger at me in some accusatory way.

Kierstin Higgins is the founder of Accommodations by Apple, Inc., a small business in Lenexa, Kansas, that specializes in corporate relocations to the Kansas City area. She is a firm believer in individual consideration and applies it in working with the firm's customers and employees. Higgins says that, for example, when a client explodes in anger over a perceived shortcoming in the firm's services, "we try to round-table everybody together and discuss what happened to understand why the client reacted that way. The services we provide are very personal for our customers—ranging from airport pickups to the transfer of medical records. The focus on family issues for our customers creates intense demands on our employees." Higgins states that, when problems occur, "It's important to shore up our employees. They are very young and energetic, but they're also very emotional, with major ups and major downs. Trying to help them learn from the challenges they've experienced, as opposed to getting burned out," is, she believes, the essence of being a good leader in her company.[18]

## ORGANIZATIONAL USE

Faced with increasing turbulence in their environments, organizations need transformational leadership more than ever—and at all levels, not just at the top. The need for leaders of vision, confidence, and determination, whether they are leading a small team or an entire organization, is increasing rapidly. Such leaders are needed to motivate others to assert themselves, to join enthusiastically in team efforts, and to have positive feelings about what they're doing. Top managers must come to understand, appreciate, and support as never before employees who are willing to make unpopular decisions, who know when to reject traditional ways of doing something, and who can accept reasonable risks. A "right to fail" must be nurtured and be an integral part of an organization's culture.

Transformational leadership fosters synergy. **Synergy** occurs when people together create new alternatives and solutions that are better than their individual efforts. The greatest chance for achieving synergy is when people don't see things the same way; that is, differences present opportunities. Relationships don't break down because of differences but because people fail to grasp the value of their differences and how to take advantage of them. Synergy is created by people who have learned to think win–win, and listen in order to understand the other person. One of the messages of Martin Luther King's "I Have a Dream" speech was that of synergy. He challenged people to confront their differences and to learn from them. Stereotyping keeps people from appreciating and building on their differences because they limit listening for understanding.

4. Assess the limitations on a leader's impact.

# DO LEADERS MATTER?

The underlying assumption of all the leadership models presented in Chapter 10 and this chapter is that leaders *can* and *do* make a difference. Although some of these models contain different conclusions about which leadership style works best, all are based on the assumption that leaders can make a difference in organizations. However, some experts have questioned this assumption, believing that the varying nature of a situation or type of followers casts some doubt on the relative importance of leaders in organizations. They suggest that leaders sometimes have little impact on the attitudes and behaviors of their followers. In certain situations, no matter what a leader does, employees are satisfied or dissatisfied with their jobs, attain or fail to reach their goals, and perform well or poorly without a leader exerting much influence. The evidence for these assertions isn't conclusive, but they warrant your attention. As outlined in Table 11.1, these claims can be classified as (1) low leader power, and (2) substitutes for leadership.

## LOW LEADER POWER

One perspective is that leaders have little power to influence most organizational outcomes.[19] This view emphasizes that situations are more important determinants of organizational and follower effectiveness than leaders' behaviors. This perspective stresses three points.

First, *factors outside the leader's immediate control* affect profits and other factors of success more than anything a leader might do. Consider the situation facing Lockheed Martin, the largest defense contractor in the United States, several years ago. This giant corporation had been formed by the merger of Martin Marietta, Lockheed Corporation, and Loral Vought, and much of its revenues came from U.S. defense contracts. When the federal government announced that it was cutting defense contracts, Vance Coffman, then CEO, found that he had no choice but to slash millions of dollars from the company's budget to keep the company operating.

Second, *leaders may not unilaterally control the resources needed* to influence others. A leader's power to reward or punish people may be constrained by organizational policies, politics, and/or the power of external stakeholders. Lockheed Martin's shareholders and creditors exerted strong pressures on Coffman and the board to divest noncore businesses to raise cash and improve the firm's financial position.[20]

Third, *the selection process* through which the leaders pass may socialize them in such a way that they tend to act similarly. Therefore the impact of a leader on the organization may be reduced. For example, in presidential election campaigns, it is virtually impossible for some leaders—extremists of the right or left—to be elected. Candidates who eventually win elections are more alike than different.[21] The selection process generally reduces the impact of any change in high-level leadership. In

| Table 11.1 | Potential Limits on a Leader's Impact | |
|---|---|---|
| | **LOW LEADER POWER** | **SAMPLE LEADER SUBSTITUTES** |
| | • Key factors may be beyond leaders' control. | • Group/team norms and cohesiveness |
| | • Leaders have little control of needed resources. | • Formal rewards beyond leaders' control |
| | • Selection process limits leaders' ability to stand out. | • Organizational rules and regulations |

some organizations, leaders tend to be longtime employees who have paid their dues while climbing the organizational ladder. In doing so, they have followed proven career paths that their predecessors used. For example, when W. R. Howell, long-time CEO of JC Penney, retired, James Oesterreicher was appointed CEO. Oesterreicher had been a lifetime Penney employee and was steeped in a culture that was limiting Penney's growth and profitability. He was appointed because he followed the career steps and moves required to get ahead. However, it was during his tenure that Penney's stock fell from $74 per share to less than $10 per share. Only then did the Penney board reluctantly ask him to step down.

## SUBSTITUTES FOR LEADERSHIP

A **leadership substitute** is something that acts in place of a formal leader and makes leadership unnecessary or less important.[22] According to this view, the success of a particular leader depends on the characteristics of the followers, team, situation, and/or organization. Each can act as a substitute for a particular leader behavior. Consider the case of Robert Kennedy, an ophthalmologist at the University of Texas Southwestern Medical Center. The tasks that his staff perform are intrinsically challenging and meaningful. Hence the leadership substitutes view suggests that leader consideration (see Chapter 10) would have little impact on his followers because the tasks that they are performing give them considerable intrinsic motivation and job satisfaction. Therefore Kennedy has little need generally to engage in considerate behaviors to influence his followers. The model further suggests, though, that Kennedy should direct his considerate behavior toward followers who perform routine tasks that provide little job challenge and satisfaction. In essence, substitutes can free a leader's time to concentrate on other activities that need attention.

The research on leadership substitutes provides some support for this view.[23] Leadership substitutes, such as employee maturity, organizational rules, governmental regulations, group norms and cohesiveness, team performance, design of jobs, and professional recognition, affect subordinates' behaviors. Of course, leaders' actions still influence the substitutes through employee selection, task design, team assignments, and the design of reward systems. Part of being an effective leader is knowing when to use substitutes—indirect and more subtle means—to influence others. For example, a charismatic leader who is in charge of a highly effective team may need to provide less active leadership than a transactional leader in the same situation. Leadership substitutes may be important in some instances but do not eliminate the role of the leader. Still, we contend that leaders typically make or can make a substantial difference in organizations.

# CHAPTER SUMMARY

**1.** State the characteristics of transactional leadership.

Transactional leadership involves influencing followers primarily through contingent reward-based exchanges. Leaders attempt to identify clear goals for followers, the specific paths for achieving the goals, and the rewards that will be forthcoming for achieving them. A follower's performance is monitored and corrective actions are taken if he strays from the expected path. The emphasis is on exchanging units of work for units of rewards (salary, bonuses, size of office, etc.).

**2.** Describe the features of charismatic leadership.

Charismatic leadership involves influencing followers primarily through developing their emotional commitment to a vision and set of shared values. The leader relies on referent and reward power in contrast to the transactional leader's reliance on reward, legitimate, and expert power. There are two models of charismatic leadership: broad and restricted. The broad model suggests that charismatic leadership emphasizes a shared vision and values, promotes a shared identity, exhibits desired behaviors, and reflects strength. The restricted model suggests that charismatic leadership can occur only when there is a crisis, the leader proposes a radical vision or set of ideas, and the followers are emotionally attracted to the vision and leader.

**3.** Explain the nature of transformational leadership.

Transformational leadership involves influencing followers through a complex and interrelated set of behaviors and abilities. Some of these include anticipating the future, inspiring relevant stakeholders (especially followers) to embrace a new vision or set of ideas, developing followers to be leaders or better leaders, and guiding the organization or group into a community of challenged and rewarded learners. This model extends and incorporates features of transactional and charismatic leadership. The components of transformational leadership that primarily relate to followers include inspirational motivation, intellectual stimulation, idealized influence, and individualized consideration. Transformational leaders are both challenging and empathetic—and are people of integrity.

**4.** Assess the limitations on a leader's impact.

The question, Does leadership matter?, focuses attention on situations in which leaders are constrained and their behaviors may have minimal impact on their followers. The issue of leader irrelevance relates to the characteristics of situations that make it difficult for the leader to influence followers effectively. Examples of leadership substitutes include rules and regulations and group or team peer pressure. Our position is clear: Leaders typically make a significant difference.

## KEY TERMS AND CONCEPTS

Charismatic leadership
Idealized influence
Individualized consideration
Inspirational motivation
Intellectual stimulation

Leadership substitute
Synergy
Transactional leadership
Transformational leadership
Vision

## DISCUSSION QUESTIONS

1. Based on Cecilia Claudio's leadership style, as described in the Preview Case, identify those aspects of her behavior that are consistent with one or more features of transformational leadership.
2. Based on Craig Conway's leadership style, as indicated in the Managing Change Competency feature, what aspects of his behavior illustrate one or more of the components of transactional leadership?
3. Assume that you have just taken a job at a large manufacturing facility. What insights provided in this chapter can help you be an effective "follower" in this situation?
4. In what three ways did a manager you have worked for use transactional leadership?
5. Based on the manager identified in Question 4, in what ways did that person exhibit one or more characteristics

of the charismatic leadership model? If none, explain your conclusion.
6. Think of a person that you know who exhibits or comes closest to exhibiting the broad model of charismatic leadership. Describe three behaviors of this person that are consistent with being a charismatic leader.
7. Review the Managing Self Competency feature concerning William George. Identify three of his statements that reflect transformational leadership.
8. What are the three competencies that you need to develop most in order to become a transformational leader?
9. Based on your work experiences to date, how would you answer the question, "Does leadership matter?" Explain.

# DEVELOPING COMPETENCIES

## Competency:  Managing Self

### Transformational Leadership

*Instructions:* The following statements refer to the possible ways in which you might prefer to behave toward others when you are in a leadership role. Please read each statement carefully and decide to what extent it applies to your preferred or actual behaviors. Then circle the appropriate number.

| | |
|---|---|
| To a Very Great Extent | 5 |
| To a Considerable Extent | 4 |
| To a Moderate Extent | 3 |
| To a Slight Extent | 2 |
| To Little or No Extent | 1 |

Your preference is to . . .

1. pay close attention to what others say when they are talking.   5  4  3  2  1
2. communicate clearly.   5  4  3  2  1
3. be trustworthy.   5  4  3  2  1
4. care about other people.   5  4  3  2  1
5. not put excessive energy into avoiding failure.   5  4  3  2  1
6. make the work of others more meaningful.   5  4  3  2  1
7. seem to focus on the key issues in a situation.   5  4  3  2  1
8. get across your meaning effectively, often in unusual ways.   5  4  3  2  1
9. be relied on to follow through on commitments.   5  4  3  2  1
10. have a great deal of self-respect.   5  4  3  2  1
11. enjoy taking carefully calculated risks.   5  4  3  2  1
12. help others feel more competent in what they do.   5  4  3  2  1
13. have a clear set of priorities.   5  4  3  2  1
14. keep in touch with how others feel.   5  4  3  2  1
15. rarely change once you have taken a clear position.   5  4  3  2  1
16. focus on strengths, of yourself and of others.   5  4  3  2  1
17. seem most alive when deeply involved in some project.   5  4  3  2  1
18. show others that they are all part of the same group.   5  4  3  2  1
19. get others to focus on the issues you see as important.   5  4  3  2  1
20. communicate feelings as well as ideas.   5  4  3  2  1
21. let others know where you stand.   5  4  3  2  1
22. know just how you "fit" into a group.   5  4  3  2  1
23. learn from mistakes; do not treat errors as disasters, but as learning.   5  4  3  2  1
24. be fun to be around.   5  4  3  2  1

### Interpretation

The survey measures your preferences on each of six basic leader behavior patterns, as well as a set of emotional responses, usually associated with transformational leaders. Your score can range from 4 to 20 on each leader behavior pattern. Each statement reflects the extent to which you prefer or actually engage in a particular behavior. The higher you score, the more you prefer or actually demonstrate transformational leader behaviors. Scores of 16 to 20 on a behavioral pattern are consistent with transformational leadership on that dimension.

**Management of Attention (Add numbers for items 1, 7, 13, 19.) Your score _____**
This dimension focuses on paying attention to people with whom you are communicating. You prefer to "focus in" on the key issues under discussion and help others to see clearly these key points. You have clear ideas about the relative importance or priorities of different issues under discussion.

**Management of Meaning (Add numbers for items 2, 8, 14, 20.) Your score _____**
This dimension centers on your communication competencies, specifically your ability to get the meaning of a message across, even if this means devising an innovative approach.

**Management of Trust (Add numbers for items 3, 9, 15, 21.) Your score _____**
This dimension focuses on your perceived trustworthiness as shown by your willingness to follow through on promises, avoidance of "flip-flop" shifts in position, and preference to take clear positions.

**Management of Self (Add numbers for items 4, 10, 16, 22.) Your score _____**
This dimension concerns your general attitudes toward yourself and others, that is, your overall concern for others and their feelings, as well as for "taking care of" feelings about yourself in a positive sense (e.g., self-regard).

**Management of Risk (Add numbers for items 5, 11, 17, 23.) Your score _____**
This dimension focuses on effective transformational leaders being deeply involved in what they do. They do not spend excessive amounts of time or energy on plans to "protect" themselves against failure or blame. These leaders are willing to take risks, not on a hit-or-miss basis, but after careful assessment of the odds of success or failure.

**Management of Feelings (Add numbers for items 6, 12, 18, 24.) Your score _____**
Transformational leaders seem to consistently generate a set of feelings in others. Others feel that their work be-

comes more meaningful and that they are the "masters" of their own behavior; that is, they feel competent. They feel a sense of community, a "we-ness" with their colleagues and coworkers.[24]

## Competency:  Managing Change

### Meg Whitman of eBay

Founded in September 1995 and headquartered in San Jose, California, eBay is the leading online marketplace for the sale of goods and services by a diverse community of individuals and businesses. Today, eBay has more than 42 million registered users and is the most popular shopping site on the Internet.

eBay's mission is to help anyone trade practically anything on earth, locally, nationally, and internationally. It features a variety of international sites, specialty sites, categories, and services that aim to provide users with the necessary tools for efficient online trading in both auction-style and fixed-price formats. On any given day, millions of items are listed on eBay in thousands of categories.

Meg Whitman joined eBay as its CEO in 1998. She works in an open cubicle, reflecting eBay's casual setup. Her cubicle with low walls and no view—and surfaces piled with paper—is wedged between two other cubicles. When Whitman needs to talk with technology chief Maynard Webb, she calls out through the partition; when she wants to show him something, she simply walks around the partition to his cubicle. When she sits down to speak as CEO of eBay, however, there is nothing casual about her style. She is all about profit margins, sales growth, and managing her 2,400 employees.

Whitman is many things—a mom, wealthy, a Wall Street darling, and maybe even, as some say, the best CEO in America. One thing she isn't is the stereotype of a new-economy executive. A onetime Procter & Gamble brand manager, Bain consultant, and Hasbro division manager, Whitman is a person with experience and discipline. The casual trappings, the cubicle and the like, only go so far in explaining her leadership style.

This company looks like a dot-com, but its approach is corporate. Whitman's executives handle categories (e.g., toys, cars, and collectibles) like brand managers at P&G handle Bounty or Tide. They dwell on data, following every transaction and customer nuance just as executives do at Wal-Mart. Whitman is one of eBay's greatest strengths. She is considered the reason it's the only startup among all its once promising peers that isn't dead or under the gun. Four years after Whitman came to run this online market, eBay is thriving.

When Whitman arrived at eBay, she promised to transform the company from an online auction house into a much bigger, general-purpose shopping destination—the first place people turn when they want to buy anything. Analysts, who applaud this strategy and are reassured by Whitman's record, see eBay as the one company that really taps into the boundless potential of the Internet. eBay owns no inventory or warehouses, which helps make it highly profitable. It has clev-

erly used e-mail, message boards, and the natural watchfulness of its virtual community to forge bonds with customers and to police the behavior of its buyers and sellers. Its Web site enables small sellers to participate in a vast marketplace—and lets eBay collect fees on even the tiniest of transactions.

The superficially casual, fundamentally businesslike quality permeates eBay. Employees are cheerful and informal. Their no-nonsense cubicles are littered with sports souvenirs, Godzilla figurines, and Beanie Babies. There are free sodas in the break rooms. But when you talk to eBay people, you don't hear much about fun and games. You hear about plans, systems, numbers, and results.

Whitman has a craving for statistics and, more specifically, for bottom-line results. Asked what it is like reporting to Whitman, one manager says, "I have numbers. I know them. They're very clear. And the expectations are high." Another manager comments: "Two years ago we were a secondary collectibles marketplace. Now we're a trading platform." In plain English, that means eBay is diversifying, offering not just old ceramic plates and baseball cards but a wide array of products from bigger brand-name stores, including new items at set prices. "We want people to think of eBay first when they're in shopping mode, the way they might think of Wal-Mart," says a marketing executive.

In response to a question about eBay being an Internet survivor, Whitman states: "People are really pleased to have a survivor—a thriver. They're enthusiastic that eBay has done well because it bodes well for other companies. eBay will not be the only great company that comes out of the Internet, but it's proof that this wasn't just two years (e.g., 2000 and 2001) where nothing happened."

In a series of interviews, Whitman has provided a number of insights and perspectives on her strategic thinking and leadership. "One of the reasons I believe eBay has been so successful is that we have stuck to our business plan from inception. At eBay, we do one thing: We work every day to be the world's most compelling commerce platform on the Internet. Despite the turmoil in the financial markets, we have stayed focused on our goals. Those goals include attracting more customers, expanding the goods traded on the site, spreading eBay to more global markets, and making the user experience more fun, exciting, and easier.

"We believe there are a number of reasons why eBay will continue to prosper. First, our company continues to execute—as demonstrated by our solid performance record to date. Second, despite the shakeout in the industry, the Internet continues to thrive according to all the key measurements of growth. Finally, eBay is well positioned to experience continued growth because the size of our potential markets is huge—nearly $1.7 trillion in collectibles, practical items, computers, used autos, and international markets. There were 77 million Internet users in 1997. Today there are more than 300 million. It is estimated that there will be about 510 million users by 2004. And people are spending more time on the Web. They are finding greater reasons to use it—whether it's sending an e-mail, shopping, or managing their finances. The Internet is in the very early stages of its evolution, and its future is very bright.

"We're very confident of eBay's strong future growth. The size of our potential market, which is about $1.7 trillion today, will increase substantially by 2005. Based on this and our strong performance we have demonstrated to date, we are targeting a revenue goal of $3 billion in 2005, which implies revenue growth rates approaching 50 percent per year. Obviously, we are very confident about the future of the Internet and the future of eBay."[25]

## Questions

1. What aspects of Meg Whitman's leadership reflect transactional leadership? Explain.
2. What aspects of Meg Whitman's leadership reflect transformational leadership? Explain.

# Fostering Interpersonal Communication

**LEARNING OBJECTIVES**

When you have finished studying the chapter, you should be able to:

1. Describe the basic elements of interpersonal communication.
2. Discuss how interpersonal communication networks affect relationships among employees.
3. Explain the fabric of abilities that foster dialogue.
4. Describe how nonverbal communication affects dialogue.

## NEAL PATTERSON'S SCATHING E-MAIL MESSAGE

Neal L. Patterson is chairman of the board, CEO, and cofounder of Cerner Corporation. Formed in 1979 and headquartered in Kansas City, Missouri, this firm is a major provider of information and financial management systems and software designed to improve health care. Cerner has 3,400 employees in offices worldwide, 2,100 of whom are located in Kansas City.

On March 13, 2001, Patterson sent an e-mail message originally intended for 400 of Cerner's managers concerning the work ethic in the company. The e-mail message was leaked and posted on Yahoo!. Its belligerent tone surprised thousands of readers, including analysts and investors. In the stock market, the valuation of the company, which was $1.5 billion on March 20, 2001, plummeted by 22 percent in 3 days. The stock has since recovered.

Patterson is variously described by people who know him as "arrogant," "candid," and "passionate." Patterson says he wishes that he had never hit the send button. "I was trying to start a fire. I lit a match, and I started a firestorm."

Patterson's message stated, in part: "We are getting less than 40 hours of work from a large number of our K.C.-based EMPLOYEES. The parking lot is sparsely used at 8 A.M.; likewise at 5 P.M. As managers, you either do not know what your EMPLOYEES are doing; or you do not CARE. You have created expectations on the work effort which allowed this to happen inside Cerner, creating a very unhealthy environment. In either case, you have a problem and you will fix it or I will replace you. NEVER in my career have I allowed a team which worked for me to think they had a 40-hour job. I have allowed YOU to create a culture, which is permitting this. NO LONGER."

Patterson went on to list six potential punishments, including laying off 5 percent of the staff in Kansas City. "Hell will freeze over," he vowed, before he would dole out more employee benefits. The parking lot would be his yardstick of success, he said; it should be "substantially full" at 7:30 A.M. and 6:30 P.M. on weekdays and half-full on Saturdays. "You have two weeks," he said. "Tick, tock."

Patterson claims that the e-mail message was taken out of context, and that most employees at Cerner understood that he was exaggerating to make a point. He said he was not carrying out any of the punishments listed. Instead, Patterson claims that he wanted to promote discussion.

Patterson acknowledges that his memo "added noise" to what was already out there. At the end of the week, as the company's share price fell, Patterson sent another e-mail message to his managers. Unlike the first memo, it was not called a Management Directive, but rather a Neal Note. It was both an apology to those he offended and a restatement of the work-ethic issue within the company.[1]

*For more information on Cerner Corporation, visit the organization's home page at http:///www.cerner.com.*

Clearly, Neal Patterson's communication was both ineffective and counterproductive. His message created an atmosphere of fear without specifying what, if anything, was actually going wrong at the company. Moreover, it established a simplistic gauge of success—measuring worker productivity by counting the number of cars in the parking lot. This method is like judging a book by its word count. Patterson made the classic mistake of overusing and misusing e-mail. As we show in this chapter, e-mail is not useful for fostering dialogue and problem solving with respect to issues that have significant emotional content.

In Chapter 1, we discussed communication as one of the seven foundation managerial competencies. Interpersonal communication is the focus of this chapter. We begin by discussing the process, types, and patterns of verbal, nonverbal, and other forms of communication used by employees on the job. We then present ways to foster effective dialogue in organizations. Finally, we examine the nature and importance of nonverbal communication.

**Interpersonal communication** is the transmission and reception of thoughts, facts, beliefs (values), attitudes, and feelings—through one or more media—that produce a response.[2] Neal Patterson sent a set of aggressive, demanding, and threatening thoughts, attitudes, and feelings in the e-mail message that was intended only for Cerner's managers. Unfortunately, it became a public document. His e-mail produced many responses, including the need to send another e-mail message to apologize to those he had offended and to restate his perceived concerns over the "work ethic" at company headquarters without the list of six potential punishments.

## ELEMENTS OF INTERPERSONAL COMMUNICATION

**Learning Objective:**

1. Describe the basic elements of interpersonal communication.

For accurate interpersonal communication to take place, the thoughts, facts, beliefs, attitudes, or feelings that the sender intended to send must be the same as those understood and interpreted by the receiver. Recall Patterson's statement that his e-mail message was taken out of context and that most employees at Cerner understood he was exaggerating to make a point. However, he appears to acknowledge that a significant minority of employees did not interpret his e-mail message as mere exaggeration and that there was no way for others to interpret the "context" as he supposedly intended. His initial claim of wanting to "promote discussion" through the e-mail message is impossible for others to interpret, especially given his high degree of power relative to the intended recipients. Fortunately, he issued an apology.

Figure 12.1 presents the elements of interpersonal communication involving only two people; the process is not easy, and by looking at its components, you can readily see that it becomes increasingly complex as more people participate.

### SENDER AND RECEIVER

Exchanges between people are an element of interpersonal communication. Thus labeling one person as the sender and the other as the receiver is arbitrary. These roles shift back and forth, depending on where the individuals are in the process. Thus when the receiver responds to the sender, the original receiver becomes the sender and the initiating sender becomes the receiver.

Consider the comment of a manager at CIBC Oppenheimer about dealing with a stockbroker who made a mistake in a client's statement but failed to notify the client:

> I was facing a tough decision about whether to fire this broker or just reprimand him for knowingly violating our policy. I wrestled with it in my head for almost a week and pretty much made up my mind about what I was going to do. But I gave his former boss a call and talked it through with her. She was really sympathetic and knew that I was struggling. She made me talk out my decision and asked me hard questions along the way. We looked at the problem from several perspectives: mine, my boss's, the broker's and the client's.[3]

**Figure 12.1**                         **Elements of Interpersonal Communication**

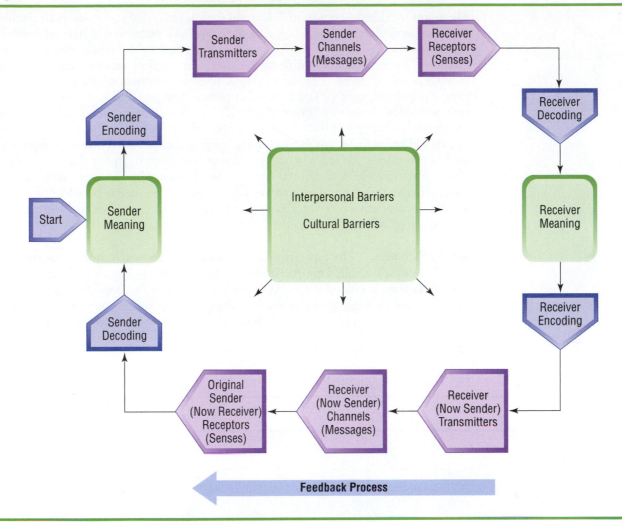

The manager's statement suggests that the goals of the sender and receiver substantially influence the communication process. For example, the sender may have certain intentions in communicating, such as adding to or changing the thoughts, beliefs, attitudes, and/or behaviors of the receiver or changing the sender's relationship with the receiver. These intentions may be presented openly (the manager wanted a new broker) or developed deceptively. If the receiver doesn't agree with them, the probability of distortion and misunderstanding can be quite high (the manager concluded that the broker was immature and too embarrassed to call the client). The fewer the differences in goals, attitudes, and beliefs, the greater is the probability that accurate communication will occur.

## TRANSMITTERS AND RECEPTORS

**Transmitters** (used by the sender) and **receptors** (used by the receiver) are the means (media) available for sending and receiving messages. They usually involve one or more of the senses: seeing, hearing, touching, smelling, and tasting. Transmission can take place both verbally and nonverbally. Once transmission begins, the communication process moves beyond the direct control of the sender. A message that has been transmitted cannot be brought back. How many times have you thought to yourself: I wish I hadn't said that? In the Preview Case, it is clear that Neal Patterson wishes he hadn't said what he did in his e-mail message, which became public.

## MESSAGES AND CHANNELS

**Messages** include the transmitted data and the coded (verbal and nonverbal) symbols that give particular meaning to the data. By using both verbal and nonverbal symbols, the sender tries to ensure that messages are interpreted by the receiver as the sender intended. To understand the difference between an original meaning and a received message, think about an occasion when you tried to convey inner thoughts and feelings of happiness, rage, or fear to another person. Did you find it difficult or impossible to transmit your true "inner meaning"? The greater the difference between the interpreted meaning and the original message, the poorer will be the communication. Words and nonverbal symbols have no meaning by themselves. Their meaning is created by the sender, the receiver, and the situation or context. In our discussion of potential interpersonal and cultural barriers, we explain why messages aren't always interpreted as they were meant to be. **Channels** are the means by which messages travel from sender to receiver. Examples of channels would be the "air" during face-to-face conversation, e-mail via the Internet, and the telephone.

**Media Richness.**    The capacity of a communication approach to transmit cues and provide feedback is called **media richness**.[4] As suggested in Figure 12.2, the richness of each medium is a blend of several factors. One factor is the *speed of personalized feedback* provided through the medium. It is shown on the vertical axis as varying from slow to fast. A second factor is the *variety of cues and language* provided through the

**Figure 12.2**                    **Examples of Media Richness**

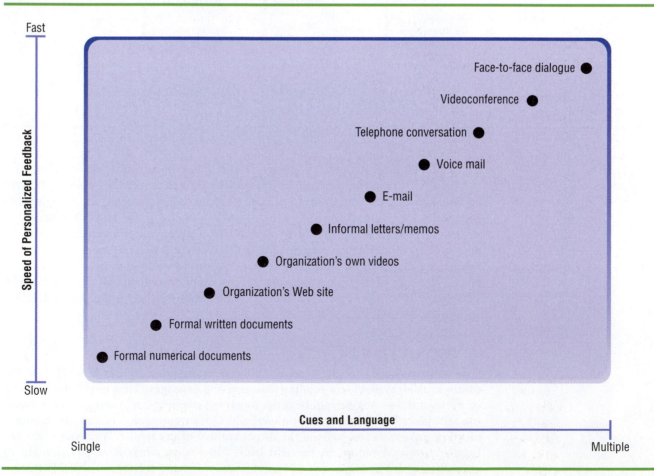

medium. It is shown on the horizontal axis as varying from simple to multiple. A **cue** is a stimulus, either consciously or unconsciously perceived, that results in a response by the receiver. Figure 12.2 relates 10 different media to the combination of these two factors. Because these two factors are continual, a medium may vary somewhat in richness, depending on its use by sender and receiver. For example, electronic mail (e-mail) may be associated with slower or quicker feedback than indicated in Figure 12.2. The speed depends on accessibility to e-mail messages and the receiver's tendency to reply immediately or later. Messages that require a long time to digest or that can't overcome biases are low in richness. Neal Patterson's e-mail message resulted in quick and unanticipated feedback, including the 22 percent drop in Cerner Corporation's value within 3 days of his e-mail message becoming public. No other negative event or news had become known about Cerner during these 3 days.

**Data** are the output of communication. The various forms of data include words spoken face-to-face and in telephone calls; words written in e-mail messages, letters, and memos; and words compiled in computer printouts. They become information when they reinforce or change the receivers' understanding of their thoughts, feelings, attitudes, or beliefs. The use of groupware (various information technologies) may help such information exchange but can't always substitute for face-to-face dialogue. The reason is that, as suggested in Figure 12.2, face-to-face dialogue is the richest medium. It provides immediate feedback so that receivers can check the accuracy of their understanding and ask for clarification if they need to. It also allows sender and receiver simultaneously to observe body language, tone of voice, and facial expression. These observations add meaning to the spoken words. Finally, it enables sender and receiver quickly to identify symbols and use language that is natural and personal. Because of these characteristics, solving important and tough problems—especially those involving uncertainty and emotional content—almost always requires face-to-face dialogue.

## MEANING AND FEEDBACK

The sender's message is transmitted through channels to the receiver's five senses. As Figure 12.1 suggests, received messages are changed from their symbolic form (e.g., spoken words) to a form that has meaning. **Meaning** represents a person's thoughts, feelings, beliefs, and attitudes.

**Encoding** gives personal meaning to messages that are to be sent. Vocabulary and knowledge play an important role in the sender's ability to encode. Unfortunately, some professionals have difficulty communicating with people in general. They often encode meaning in a form that only other professionals in the same field can understand. Lawyers often encode (write) contracts that directly affect consumers but use language that only other lawyers can decode. Consumer groups have pressed to have such contracts written in language that almost everyone can understand. As a result, many banks, credit card firms, and other organizations have simplified the language in their contracts.

**Decoding** gives personal, interpreted meaning to messages that are received. Through a shared language, people can decode many messages so that the meanings received are reasonably close to the meanings transmitted. Decoding messages accurately is often a major challenge in communicating.[5]

Interpersonal communication accuracy should be evaluated in relation to the ideal state, which occurs when the sender's intended meaning and the receiver's interpretation of it are the same. The transmission of factual data of a nonthreatening nature approximates the ideal state. For example, the sharing of the time, place, and procedures for a high school or college commencement ceremony generally results in easy and accurate interpersonal communication. The communication between a manager and a subordinate during a performance review session is another, more complex, matter.

The receiver's response to the message is **feedback**. It lets the sender know whether the message was received as intended. Interpersonal communication becomes a dynamic, two-way process, through feedback, rather than just an event. In the Preview Case, Neal Patterson received much unanticipated feedback from his e-mail message.

## INTERPERSONAL BARRIERS

Barriers to interpersonal communication are numerous. Some of them we have discussed in previous chapters. Let's review briefly the more important barriers that stem from individual differences in personality and perceptions.

Individual personality traits that serve as barriers include low adjustment (nervous, self-doubting, and moody), low sociability (shy, unassertive, and withdrawn), low conscientiousness (impulsive, careless, and irresponsible), low agreeableness (independent, cold, and rude), and low intellectual openness (dull, unimaginative, and literal-minded). Introverts are more likely to be quiet and emotionally inexpressive (see Chapter 2).

Individual perceptual errors include perceptual defense (protecting oneself against ideas, objects, or situations that are threatening), stereotyping (assigning attributions to someone solely on the basis of a category in which the person has been placed), halo effect (evaluating another person based solely on one impression, either favorable or unfavorable), projection (tendency for people to see their own traits in others), and high expectancy effect (prior expectations serving to bias how events, objects, and people are actually perceived). Individuals who make the fundamental attribution error (underestimating the impact of situational or external causes of behavior and overestimating the impact of personal causes of behavior when they seek to understand why people behave the way they do) are less likely to communicate effectively. This error too readily results in communicating blame or credit to individuals for outcomes. A related attribution error is the self-serving bias (communicating personal responsibility for good performance but denying responsibility for poor performance). (See Chapter 3.)

In addition to these underlying interpersonal communication barriers, there also are some direct barriers.

**Noise.**   Any interference with the intended message in the channel represents **noise**. A radio playing loud music while someone is trying to talk to someone else is an example of noise. Noise sometimes can be overcome by repeating the message or increasing the intensity (e.g., the volume) of the message.

**Semantics.**   The special meaning assigned to words is called **semantics**. However, the same words may mean different things to different people. Consider this comment by a manager to a subordinate: How about the report for production planning? I think that they want it soon! The manager could have intended one of several meanings in her comment.

> *Directing:* You should get the report to me now. That's an order.
> *Suggesting:* I suggest that we consider getting the report out now.
> *Requesting:* Can you do the report for me now? Let me know if you can't.
> *Informing:* The report is needed soon by production planning.
> *Questioning:* Does production planning want the report soon?

Consider the semantics for five words in American (U.S.) English versus British English vocabularies.

- *Pavement:* American—a hard road surface; British—footpath, sidewalk.
- *Table* (verb): American—to remove from discussion; British—to bring to discussion.

- *Tick off* (verb): American—to anger; British—to rebuke.
- *Canceled check:* American—a check paid by the bank; British—a check that is stopped or voided.
- *Ship:* American—to convey by boat, train, plane, truck or other means; British— to convey only by boat.[6]

**Language Routines.**    A person's verbal and nonverbal communication patterns that have become habits are known as **language routines**. They can be observed by watching the ways people greet one another. In many instances, language routines are quite useful because they reduce the amount of thinking time needed to produce common messages. They also provide predictability in terms of being able to anticipate what is going to be said and how it is going to be said. The culture of Wal-Mart and its image is reinforced through language, including its slogan: "Always Low Prices, Always Wal-Mart."

Conversely, language routines sometimes cause discomfort, offend, and alienate when they put down or discriminate against others. Many demeaning stereotypes of individuals and groups are perpetuated through language routines. For example, several years ago a manager at Texaco (now ChevronTexaco) made tapes of conversations available to the public. These tapes contained demeaning comments made by board members and managers about minorities within the company, including blacks, Jews, other minorities, and women. Public outrage led to boycotts of Texaco, which ended up settling a racial discrimination case out of court for $176 million. After the lawsuit was settled, boycotts were called off, criticism trickled off, and Texaco's sales rebounded.[7]

**Lying and Distortion.**    In the extreme form of deception, **lying**, the sender states what is believed to be false in order to seriously mislead one or more receivers. The intention to deceive implies a belief that the receiver will accept the lie as a fact. In contrast, honesty means that the sender abides by consistent and rational ethical principles to respect the truth. Everyday social flattery in conversations may not be completely honest, but it is normally considered acceptable and rarely regarded as dishonest (lying). **Distortion** represents a wide range of messages that a sender may use between the extremes of lying and complete honesty. Of course, the use of vague, ambiguous, or indirect language doesn't necessarily indicate the sender's intent to mislead. This form of language may be viewed as acceptable political behavior. Silence may also be a form of distortion, if not dishonesty. Not wanting to look incompetent or take on a manager in a departmental meeting, a subordinate may remain quiet instead of expressing an opinion or asking a question.

Personal distortion in interpersonal communications may occur through **impression management**, or the process by which a sender knowingly attempts to influence the perceptions that the receivers form (see Chapter 3).[8] Three impression management strategies—ingratiation, self-promotion, and face-saving—are commonly used.

- *Ingratiation* involves using flattery, supporting others' opinions, doing favors, laughing excessively at others' jokes, and so on.
- *Self-promotion* involves describing the sender's personal attributes to others in a highly positive and exaggerated way.
- *Face-saving* involves using various tactics, such as (1) apologizing in a way to convince others that the bad outcome isn't a fair indication of what the sender is really like as a person; (2) making excuses to others by admitting that the sender's behavior in some way caused a negative outcome, but strongly suggesting that the person isn't really as much to blame as it seems (because the outcome wasn't intentional or there were extenuating circumstances); or (3) presenting justifications to others by appearing to accept responsibility for an outcome, but denying that the outcome actually led to problems.

Impression management strategies can range from relatively harmless minor forms of distortion (being courteous to another person even if you don't like the individual) to messages that use extreme ingratiation and self-promotion to obtain a better raise or promotion than others. The personal ethics, self-awareness of the sender, and the political climate of the individual's organization combine to influence the degree to which distortion tactics are used. In brief, the greater the frequency of distortion tactics and the more they approach the lying end of the distortion continuum, the more they will serve as a hurdle to interpersonal communication.

The following Managing Ethics Competency feature is adapted from a column written by Timothy McMahon, a professor of management at the University of Houston. It highlights the use of distortion and what some suggest as outright lying by the top leadership of the Enron Corporation. The patterns of distortion and deception in communications by Enron's top executives and its auditing firm (Arthur Andersen) and the loss of trust by people in the reliability of data from them led to Enron's bankruptcy in 2001. If statements and reports by Enron's top executives and auditors had been valid, the company's stock would not have risen as rapidly as it did and there could have been early market corrections in the price of its shares. In Chapter 15, we add to this account in a Managing Ethics Competency feature that focuses on Sherron Watkins, an executive at Enron, who challenged the use of deceptive accounting and communication practices.

## COMPETENCY:   MANAGING ETHICS

### ENRON'S DECEPTIVE LEADERS

Enron's leaders often chided the uninitiated that they didn't get "it"—unconstrained deregulation and the Enron method of operation. Well, obviously, Ken Lay, Jeffrey Skilling, Andrew Fastow, et al., are the ones who didn't get the most important "it."

What happened, and its causes, really is quite simple, in spite of the swirling details. Much of what was done was "wrong." A CBS poll of average citizens denounced Enron's actions 20 to 1. But some legal eagles, aggressive accountants, finance wizards, and other business experts continue to tell us that, well, you know, many of the "wrong" actions are technically okay because they aren't illegal.

There is no legal statute, government regulation, or agency rule that tells us that we should return a lost wallet when we find it. Does that mean it is right to keep it? Of course not. Despite all the complexities, this is how simple the Enron fiasco is. The behaviors were wrong. It has to do with ethics.

Although no one has owned up to it, responsibility for the Enron tragedy rests at the feet of the leadership—top management and the board of directors. This fact is inescapable. What was done was wrong and technical loopholes carry no weight here. It is really that clear. Leadership, and its reflection in organization culture and processes, is the cause of the disaster. Yet again we are reminded that the "soft stuff" (culture) really is the hard core. And it will be this soft stuff that will be the strongest deterrent to future Enrons.

The arrogance of Enron's top leaders is well known and well demonstrated. Out-of-control arrogant leaders are poor listeners and often overreact to what they perceive as criticism. Warnings of questionable practices were repeatedly ignored by Enron leadership. Several stock analysts experienced the rash reactions of Skilling to their simple requests for information.

Arrogant leaders also are not very good learners, as they much prefer to convert others to their way of thinking. *The Economist* documented an occasion when Lay was singing the praises of Drexel Burnham Lambert and its star, Michael Milken, who, he claimed, was simply "innovative and aggressive." But the arrogant Drexel collapsed and Milken ended up in jail. It appears that an important lesson was missed.

The good news here is that leaders can learn to get their egos under control. It is possible for all leaders to learn to be better listeners, better learners, and more empathetic; in short, it is possible to develop more emotional intelligence, the stuff of true success.[9]

## CULTURAL BARRIERS

Recall that *culture* refers to the distinctive ways that different populations, societies, or smaller groups organize their lives or activities. **Intercultural communication** occurs whenever a message sent by a member of one culture is received and understood by a member of another culture.[10] The effects of cultural differences on barriers to interpersonal communication can be wide ranging. They depend on the degrees of difference (or similarity) between people in terms of language, religious beliefs, economic beliefs, social values, physical characteristics, use of nonverbal cues, and the like. The greater the differences, the greater are the barriers to achieving intercultural communication.

**Cultural Context.**   The conditions that surround and influence the life of an individual, group, or organization is its **cultural context**.[11] Differences in cultural context may represent a hurdle to intercultural communication. Nations' cultures vary on a continuum from low context to high context. Figure 12.3 shows the approximate placement of various countries along this continuum.

In a **high-context culture**, interpersonal communication is characterized by (1) the establishment of social trust before engaging in work-related discussions, (2) the high value placed on personal relationships and goodwill, and (3) the importance of the surrounding circumstances during an interaction. In a high-context culture people rely on paraphrasing, tone of voice, gesture, posture, social status, history, and social setting to interpret spoken words, all of which requires time. Factors such as trust, relationships among friends and family members, personal needs and difficulties,

**Figure 12.3**              **Examples of Cultures on the Cultural Context Continuum**

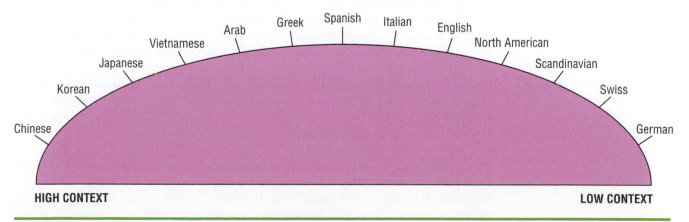

HIGH CONTEXT                                                                    LOW CONTEXT

Source: Based on Hall, E. *Understanding Cultural Differences.* Yarmouth, ME.: Intercultural Press, 1989; Munter, M. *Guide to Managerial Communication: Effective Business Writing and Speaking,* 5th ed. Englewood Cliffs, N.J.: Prentice-Hall, 1999.

weather, and holidays must be taken into consideration. For example, Japanese executives—when meeting foreign executives for the first time—do not immediately "get down to business." They engage in a period of building trust and getting to know each other that foreign executives often are impatient with but must conform to.

In contrast, a **low-context culture** is characterized by (1) directly and immediately addressing the tasks, issues, or problems at hand; (2) the high value placed on personal expertise and performance; and (3) the importance of clear, precise, and speedy interactions. The use of behavioral modification techniques and other reinforcement approaches discussed in Chapter 5 are based on low-context communication. There we described how a manager can motivate employees with statements focusing on positive or corrective feedback and goal setting. In a heterogeneous country, such as the United States, multiple subcultures have their own unique characteristics. In contrast, the cultural context of a homogeneous country, such as Japan, reflects the more uniform characteristics of its people.

Let's now consider three of the challenges in cross-cultural nonverbal communication—body language, ethnocentrism, and personal space around an individual. While considering them, we give some tips for successful nonverbal communication across cultures.

### Body Language.
Posture, gestures, eye contact, facial expression, touching, voice pitch and volume, and speaking rate differ from one culture to another.[12] As a simple, but potentially disastrous example, nodding the head up and down in Bulgaria means "no," not "yes." You must avoid using any gestures considered rude or insulting. For instance, in Buddhist cultures, the head is considered sacred, so you must never touch anyone's head. In Muslim cultures, the left hand is considered unclean, so never touch, pass, or receive with the left hand. Pointing with the index finger is rude in cultures ranging from the Sudan to Venezuela to Sri Lanka. The American circular "A-OK" gesture carries a vulgar meaning in Brazil, Paraguay, Singapore, and Russia. Crossing your ankle over your knee is rude in Indonesia, Thailand, and Syria. Pointing your index finger toward yourself insults the other person in Germany, the Netherlands, and Switzerland. Avoid placing an open hand over a closed fist in France, saying "tsk tsk" in Kenya, and whistling in India.

Prepare yourself to recognize gestures that have meaning only in the other culture. Chinese stick out their tongues to show surprise and scratch their ears and cheeks to show happiness. Japanese suck in air, hissing through their teeth to indicate embarrassment or "no." Greeks puff air after they receive a compliment. Hondurans touch a finger to the face below the eye to indicate caution or disbelief.

Finally, resist applying your own culture's nonverbal meanings to other cultures. Vietnamese may look at the ground with their heads down to show respect, not to be "shifty." Russians may exhibit less facial expression and Scandinavians fewer gestures than Americans are accustomed to, but that doesn't mean that they aren't enthusiastic. The British may prefer more distant personal and social space and might consider it rude if you move too close. Closely related is the concept of touch. Anglos usually avoid touching each other very much. In studies of touching behaviors, researchers observed people seated in outdoor cafes in each of four countries and counted the number of touches during an hour of conversation. The results were: San Juan, Puerto Rico, 180 touches per hour; Paris, 110 per hour; Gainesville, Florida, 1 per hour; and London, 0 per hour.[13]

### Ethnocentrism.
The greatest barrier to intercultural communication occurs when a person believes that only his culture makes sense, espouses the "right" values, and represents the "right" and logical way to behave.[14] This type of thinking is called **ethnocentrism**. When two ethnocentric people from different cultures interact, there is little chance that they will achieve a common understanding. Ethnocentric reactions to strongly differing views are anger, shock, or even amusement. In ethno-

centric organizations, such as Enron, executives, managers, and employees came to believe that their way was the best way to organize and work. Such people view all others as inferior and may recognize cultural and other forms of diversity, but only as a source of problems. Their strategy is to minimize the sources and impacts of cultural diversity. Ethnocentric executives and managers ignore or deny that cultural diversity can lead to advantages.

The following Managing Across Cultures Competency feature presents various aspects of interpersonal communication for the vast majority of the black South African population.

## COMPETENCY:   MANAGING ACROSS CULTURES

### UBUNTU IN SOUTH AFRICA

*Ubuntu* means humaneness—a pervasive spirit of caring and community, harmony and hospitality, and respect and responsiveness—that individuals and groups display toward one another. *Ubuntu* is the foundation for basic values that reveal themselves in the ways that South African blacks think about and behave toward each other and everyone else they encounter.

In the South African milieu, black children are socialized from birth to listen to the context and nuances of language in conversation. The importance of language in establishing a sense of community, belonging, shared heritage, and common welfare is emphasized. The pervasive wisdom is that to talk and to name is to create experience, to construct reality. Until the middle of the nineteenth century, it was through oral tradition that black African folk proverbs, ballads, legends, and mythology were sustained and kept alive, rather than through written history. These intergenerationally transmitted stories formed the bedrock of reason, wisdom, and morality. A mastery of the art and skill of oratory is still a prerequisite for black leadership. It becomes even more so during celebrations when skillful orators take center stage with their poetry and praise singing.

In the *ubuntu* context, the social effect of conversation is emphasized, with primacy given to establishing and reinforcing relationships. Unity and understanding among affected group members is valued above efficiency and accuracy of language. A premium is placed on personal rapport (i.e., the general sense of what is being said), which can easily get lost in translation.

Under *ubuntu*, the decision-making process is a circular, inclusive one, proceeding at a deliberate speed, and often given to deviations in order to delve into other matters, however remotely related to the issue at hand. Those who look at issues from different angles are seen as interesting and as providing valuable insights. Diversity of view is not only permitted, but it also is protected and encouraged. Before closure, considerable time is allowed to ensure that all voices have been heard, and that a consensus has been reached.[15]

## INTERPERSONAL NETWORKS

**Learning Objective:**

2. Discuss how interpersonal communication networks affect relationships among employees.

An **interpersonal communication network** is the pattern of communication flows, relationships, and understandings developed over time among people, rather than focusing on the individual and whether a specific message is received as intended by the sender. Networks involve the ongoing flow of verbal, written, and nonverbal messages (data) between two people or between one person and all other network members simultaneously. Communication networks can influence the likelihood of a match between messages as sent and as actually received and interpreted. The more accurately the message moves through the channel, the more clearly the receiver will understand it.

## TYPES OF NETWORKS

Recall that the elements of interpersonal communication shown in Figure 12.1 are based on a network of only two people. Obviously, communication often takes place among many individuals and larger groups. Claudia Gonzales, a telecommunications manager for Abaco Grupo Financiero in Mexico, normally has ongoing links with many people both inside and outside her organization. Her communication network extends laterally, vertically, and externally. Vertical networks typically include her immediate superior and subordinates and the superior's superiors and the subordinates' subordinates. Lateral networks include people in the same department at the same level (peers) and people in different departments at the same level. External networks include customers, suppliers, regulatory agencies, pressure groups, professional peers, and friends. Thus a person's communication network can be quite involved.

Size limits the possible communication networks within a team or informal group. In principle, as the size of a team increases arithmetically, the number of possible communication interrelationships increases exponentially. Accordingly, communication networks are much more varied and complex in a 12-person team than in a 5-person team. Although every team member (theoretically) may be able to communicate with all the others, the direction and number of communication channels often are somewhat limited. In committee meetings, for example, varying levels of formality influence who may speak, what may be discussed, and in what order. The relative status or ranking of team members also may differ. Members having higher status probably will dominate communications more than those with lower status. Even when an open network is encouraged, team members may actually use a limited network arrangement.

To provide a sense of the potential and powerful effects of communication networks, let's consider a single team of five members. In this example, we don't address the complicating effects of multiple teams and different team sizes. A five-person team has about 60 possible communication networks but only 5 basic networks—the star (sometimes called the wheel), the Y, the chain, the circle, and the all-channel network—as illustrated in Figure 12.4. Each line between each pair of names represents two-way communication. The degree of restriction on members in communicating with each other differentiates the networks. At one extreme, the star network is the most restricted: All communication between members must flow through Jane. At the other extreme, the all-channel network is the least restricted and most open: Each member communicates with all other members directly.

## ORGANIZATIONAL USE

Communication networks can affect the selection of team leaders, the ease and speed of team learning, the effectiveness and efficiency of the team, and member satisfaction with the team's progress.[16] Table 12.1 provides a brief comparison of the five basic communication networks in terms of four assessment criteria. The first criterion, *degree of centralization*, is the extent to which some team members have access to more communication possibilities than do other members. The star network is the most centralized because all communication flows from and to only one member. The all-channel network is the least centralized because any member can communicate with all other members. The second criterion, *leadership predictability*, indicates the ability to anticipate which team member is likely to emerge as the leader. In Figure 12.4, the following individuals are likely to emerge as leaders: Jane in the star

**Figure 12.4**            **Five Alternative Communication Networks for a Five-Person Team**

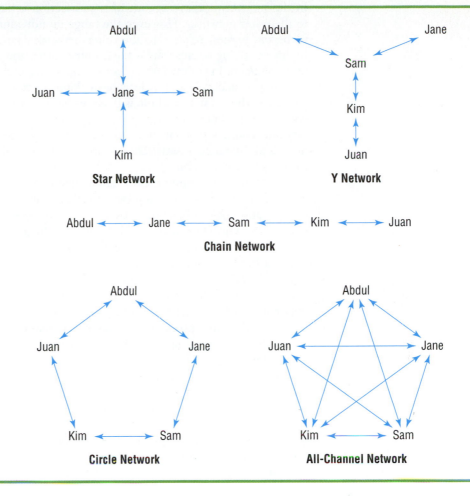

network, Sam in the Y network, and possibly Sam in the chain network. In each of these networks, the anticipated leaders have more information and greater control over its dissemination than the other members.

The third and fourth assessment criteria in Table 12.1, *average group satisfaction* and *range in individual member satisfaction*, reflect the levels and range of satisfaction

**Table 12.1**

**Effects of Five Communication Networks**

| | TYPE OF COMMUNICATION NETWORK | | | | |
|---|---|---|---|---|---|
| FACTOR | Star | Y | Chain | Circle | All-Channel |
| Degree of centralization | Very high | High | Moderate | Low | Very low |
| Leadership predictability | Very high | High | Moderate | Low | Very low |
| Average group satisfaction | Low | Low | Moderate | Moderate | High |
| Range in individual member satisfaction | High | High | Moderate | Low | Very low |

of team members. Several interesting relationships exist between these two criteria. In the star network, average member satisfaction is likely to be the lowest compared to the other networks. However, the range in individual member satisfaction is likely to be the highest relative to the other networks. Jane might find the star network highly satisfying because she is the center of attention and has considerable influence over the team. In contrast, the other members are highly dependent on Jane and may well play a small role in the decision-making process. Accordingly, the average satisfaction of the team as a whole is likely to be relatively low. The all-channel network creates the potential for greater participation by all members in terms of their interests and abilities to contribute to the team. Average satisfaction may be relatively high, and the range of satisfaction scores for individuals probably will be smaller than for the other networks.

Networks are important for day-to-day communication in organizations. First, no single network is likely to prove effective in all situations for a team with a variety of tasks and goals. The apparently efficient, low-cost, and simple method of a superior instructing subordinates is likely to be ineffective if used exclusively. Dissatisfaction may become so great that members will leave the team or lose their motivation to contribute. Second, teams that face complex problems requiring a lot of coordination may deal with them ineffectively because of inadequate sharing of information, consideration of alternatives, and the like. Third, a team must consider trade-offs or opportunity costs. A team committed to the use of the all-channel network may deal poorly with simple problems and tasks that require little member coordination. In such cases, members also may become bored and dissatisfied with team meetings. They often simply come to feel that their time is being wasted. Another trade-off with the all-channel network is higher labor costs. That is, team members must spend more time on a problem and its solution in meetings with the all-channel network than with a star network. Hence a team should use the type of network that is most appropriate to its goals and tasks.

Teams are increasingly networked—both within and across organizations—through the use of computer-based collaboration technologies. One example of this development is presented in the following Managing Teams Competency feature.

## COMPETENCY:   MANAGING TEAMS

### LOCKHEED'S TEAM COLLABORATION TECHNOLOGIES

Lockheed Martin Aeronautics Company, a major defense contractor with headquarters in Fort Worth, Texas, was awarded in 2001 the first piece of the largest manufacturing contract ever—$200 billion to build a new family of supersonic stealth fighter planes for the U.S. Defense Department. It also marks the kickoff of a new technology era, one that could transform the basic workings of many major corporations.

Lockheed's contract will require intricate communication among numerous teams and organizations. More than 80 suppliers will be working at 187 locations to design and build components of the Joint Strike Fighter. It's up to the 75-member tech group at Lockheed's aeronautics division to link and enable the U.S. Air Force, Navy, and Marines, Britain's Defense Ministry, and eight other U.S. allies to track progress and make changes midstream if necessary.

All told, teams using more than 40,000 computers will be collaborating with each other to get the first plane in the air in just 4 years—the same amount of time it took to get the much simpler F-16 from contract to delivery in the 1970s. A project this enormous requires special computer technology to keep all its teams and organizations moving in sync. Lockheed and its partners will be using a system of 90 Web software tools to share designs, track the exchange of documents, and keep an eye on progress against goals. "We're getting the best people, applying the best designs, from wherever we need them," says Mark Peden, vice president for information systems at Lockheed Martin Aeronautics. "It's the true virtual connection." Instead of simply sending data from PC to PC, the Web tools being used let individuals and teams separated by distance interact with one another as if there were not even a wall between them. They can talk via their computers while looking at shared documents, carry on e-mail chats, and use electronic white boards—where two or more people can draw pictures or charts, in real time, as others watch and respond.[17]

*For more information on Lockheed Martin Aeronautics Company, visit the organization's home page at* **http://www. lmaeronautics.com.**

**Learning Objective:**

3.  Explain the fabric of abilities that foster dialogue.

## FOSTERING DIALOGUE

**Dialogue** is a process whereby people suspend their defensiveness to enable a free flow of inquiry into their own and others' assumptions and beliefs. As a result, dialogue can build mutual trust and common ground. A necessary condition for dialogue is assertive communication. **Assertive communication** means confidently expressing what you think, feel, and believe while respecting the right of others to hold different views. True dialogue requires that interacting individuals demonstrate multiple abilities and behaviors. Figure 12.5 illustrates the idea that dialogue is characterized by a specific group of interrelated abilities and behaviors. They include communication openness, constructive feedback, appropriate self-disclosure, active listening, and supportive nonverbal cues.

**Figure 12.5**    **Interrelated Abilities and Behaviors That Foster Dialogue**

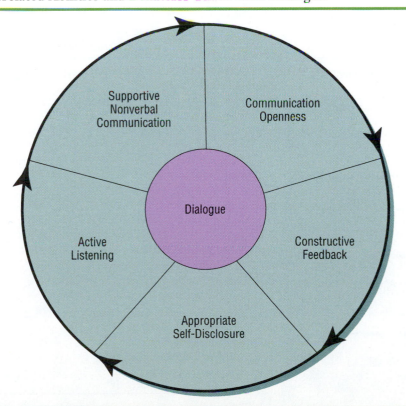

## COMMUNICATION OPENNESS

Communication openness may be viewed as a continuum ranging from closed, guarded, and defensive to open, candid, and nondefensive. Figure 12.6 shows that, at the extreme left-hand side of the continuum, every message (regardless of the medium of transmission) is weighed, analyzed, and scrutinized. Communication occurs on two levels: direct and meta-communication. **Meta-communication** brings out the (hidden) assumptions, inferences, and interpretations of the parties that form the basis of open messages. In closed communication, senders and receivers consciously and purposely hide their real agendas and "messages," and game playing is rampant. Meta-communication focuses on inferences such as (1) what I think you think about what I said; (2) what I think you really mean; (3) what I really mean but hope you don't realize what I mean; (4) what you're saying but what I think you really mean; and (5) what I think you're trying to tell me but aren't directly telling me because . . . (you're afraid of hurting my feelings, you think being totally open could hurt your chances of promotion, and so on). At the extreme right-hand side of the continuum, the communication is totally open, candid, and supportive. The words and nonverbal cues sent convey an authentic message that the sender chose without a hidden agenda. The purpose of communication is to reveal intent, not conceal it. The individuals express what they mean and mean what they convey. Breakdowns in communication at this end of the continuum are due primarily to honest errors (e.g., the different meanings that people assign to words such as *soon* or *immediately*). Communication openness usually is a matter of degree rather than an absolute. The nature of language, linguistics, and different situations (coworker to coworker, subordinate to superior, friend to friend, or spouse to spouse) create the situational forces that allow for degrees of shading, coloring, amplification, and deflection in the use of words and nonverbal cues as symbols of meaning.

**Organizational Use.**    The degree of openness must be considered in relation to the context associated with such openness. (We address contextual factors at length in

**Figure 12.6**    **Elements in Communication Openness**

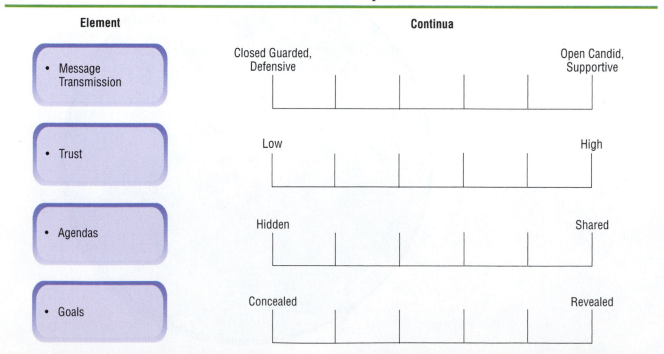

Chapter 9 in terms of conflict and negotiation, and in Chapter 15 in terms of organizational culture.) We note several of these factors here briefly. First, the history of the relationship is perhaps the most significant factor affecting trust and risk taking in communication. Has the other person violated your or others' trust in the past? Has the other person provided cues (verbal and/or nonverbal) soliciting or reinforcing your attempts to be open and candid? Or has the other person provided cues to the contrary? Has the history of the relationship created a level of such comfort that both you and the other person can focus on direct communication, rather than meta-communication?

Second, if the communication is likely to be partly adversarial or the other person is committed to damaging or weakening your position or gaining at your expense, engaging in guarded communication is rational. Conversely, if the communication is likely to be friendly and the other person is trying to please you, strengthen your position, or enhance your esteem, guarded communication may be viewed as irrational.

Third, when you communicate with someone of higher status and power, you are communicating with someone who has some control over your future. That person may be responsible for appraising your performance, judging your promotability, and determining the amount of your merit pay increase. The tendency is to project a favorable image and to encode negative messages with qualifiers, which is understandable and certainly may be rational. This perception is especially valid if past encounters with that person reinforce your use of some distortion over completely honest disclosures. Clearly, the pattern of behaviors by Enron's top leaders did not encourage or support communication openness. In fact, it did quite the opposite.

## CONSTRUCTIVE FEEDBACK

In giving feedback, people share their thoughts and feelings about others with them. Feedback may involve personal feelings or reactions to others' ideas or proposals. The emotional impact of feedback varies according to how personally it is focused. When you attempt to achieve dialogue, feedback should be supportive (reinforcing ongoing behavior) or corrective (indicating that a change in behavior is appropriate). The following are principles of constructive feedback that can foster dialogue.

- Constructive feedback is based on a foundation of trust between sender and receiver. When an organization is characterized by extreme personal competitiveness, the emphasis is on the use of power to punish and control, rigid superior–subordinate relationships, and a lack of trust for constructive feedback.
- Constructive feedback is specific rather than general. It uses clear and recent examples. Saying, "You are a dominating person," isn't as useful as saying, "Just now when we were deciding the issue, you did not listen to what others said. I felt I had to accept your argument or face attack from you."
- Constructive feedback is given at a time when the receiver appears to be ready to accept it. When a person is angry, upset, or defensive, that probably isn't the time to bring up other issues.
- Constructive feedback is checked with the receiver to determine whether it seems valid. The sender can ask the receiver to rephrase and restate the feedback to test whether it matches what the sender intended.
- Constructive feedback covers behaviors that the receiver may be capable of doing something about.
- Constructive feedback doesn't include more than the receiver can handle at any particular time. For example, the receiver may become threatened and defensive if the feedback includes everything the receiver does that annoys the sender.[18]

**Organizational Use.**    Individuals, teams, and organizations all depend on relevant feedback to improve the way they develop and perform. One approach to obtaining such feedback is through the collection and tabulation of perceptions from multiple individuals about the behaviors and performance of a single individual. For example, **360-degree feedback** is a questionnaire-based process that gathers structured feedback from a number of sources about the competencies and behaviors of an individual or team. For a manager, questionnaires on observed behaviors might be completed by herself, subordinates, peers, superiors, and customers with whom she interacts. The results are compiled in a feedback report, with data from each source presented separately. These data and results are provided to the individual who then plans how to build on strengths and improve personal performance. Normally, this discussion would take place with the person's superior.

In this book, we have presented various instruments that create opportunities for giving yourself feedback based on your self-perceptions. Some of these instruments could be easily adapted to solicit feedback from those with whom you interact regularly. For example, most of the specific abilities presented in the Professional Competencies Self-Assessment Inventory in the Developing Competencies section at the end of Chapter 1 could be incorporated in a 360-degree feedback questionnaire that solicits perceptions about you from others. However, there is controversy over the use and application of 360-degree feedback. Clearly, there needs to be an environment of trust and communication openness before the implementation of a formal 360-degree feedback process. It doesn't work in a highly political or top–down organization. In general, 360-degree feedback appears to work best if it is used for coaching and professional development purposes. It may not work as well when the feedback is used in a person's performance review process unless specific abilities and behaviors can be linked to specific performance goals. A number of other issues and recommendations with respect to the 360-degree feedback process are beyond our scope here.[19]

## APPROPRIATE SELF-DISCLOSURE

**Self-disclosure** is any information that individuals communicate (verbally or nonverbally) about themselves to others. People often unconsciously disclose much about themselves by what they say and how they present themselves to others. The ability to express yourself to others usually is basic to personal growth and development. Nondisclosing individuals may repress their real feelings because to reveal them is threatening. Conversely, total-disclosure individuals, who expose a great deal about themselves to anyone they meet, actually may be unable to communicate with others because they are too self-centered. The presence of appropriate self-disclosure, say, between superior and subordinate or team members and customers, can facilitate dialogue and sharing of work-related problems.

**Organizational Use.**   A person's level in an organization often complicates self-disclosure. An individual is likely to minimize self-disclosure to those having greater formal power because of their ability to reward or punish. Even when a subordinate is able and willing to engage in "appropriate" forms of self-disclosure at work, a perception of the superior's trustworthiness in not using the revealed information to punish, intimidate, or ridicule is likely to influence the amount and form of self-disclosure.

## ACTIVE LISTENING

Active listening is necessary to encourage maximum levels of feedback and openness. **Listening** is a process that integrates physical, emotional, and intellectual inputs in a search for meaning and understanding. Listening is effective when the receiver understands the sender's message as intended.

As much as 40 percent of an 8-hour workday for many employees is devoted to listening. However, tests of listening comprehension suggest that people often listen at only 25 percent efficiency. Listening skills influence the quality of peer, manager–subordinate, and employee–customer relationships. Employees who dislike a manager may find it extremely difficult to listen attentively to the manager's comments during performance review sessions. The following guidelines are suggested for increasing active listening skills to foster dialogue.

- Having a reason or purpose for listening. Good listeners tend to search for value and meaning in what is being said, even if they are not predisposed to be interested in the particular issue or topic. Poor listeners tend to rationalize any or all inattention on the basis of a lack of initial interest.
- Suspending judgment, at least initially. Good listening requires concentrating on the sender's whole message, rather than forming evaluations on the basis of the first few ideas presented.
- Resisting distractions, such as noises, sights, and other people, and focusing on the sender.
- Pausing before responding to the sender.
- Rephrasing in your own words the content and feeling of what the sender seems to be saying, especially when the message is emotional or unclear.
- Seeking out the sender's important themes in terms of the overall content and feeling of the message.
- Using the time differential between the rate of thought (400 or 500 words per minute) and the rate of speech (100 to 150 words per minute) to reflect on content and search for meaning.[20]

**Organizational Use.**   Most of these active listening skills are interrelated. That is, you can't practice one without improving the others. Unfortunately, like the guidelines for improving feedback, the guidelines for improving active listening are much easier to understand than to develop and practice. The more you practice active listening skills, the more likely you will be able to enter into effective dialogue.

The following Managing Self Competency feature reports on a stressful conversation between David Jones and Jeremy Fine and the failure to engage in effective dialogue. The conversation and situation is real, the names are fictitious. As you will see, both parties needed to do a better job in fostering dialogue.

# COMPETENCY:   MANAGING SELF

## *THE STRESSFUL CONVERSATION*

David Jones was the director of a nonprofit institution. He was in the uncomfortable position of needing to talk with an ambitious researcher, Jeremy Fine, who had a much higher opinion of his job performance than did others in the organization. The complication for Jones was that, in the past, Fine had received artificially high evaluations. There were several reasons for this situation. One had to do with the organization's culture: The nonprofit wasn't a confrontational "in-your-face" kind of place. Additionally, Fine had tremendous confidence in both his own abilities and the quality of his academic background. Together with his defensive response to even the mildest criticism, this led others—including Jones—to let slide discussions of issues that were interfering with Fine's ability to deliver high-quality work. For instance, Fine had a cutting sense of humor, which had offended people inside and outside his unit. No one had ever said anything to him directly. As time passed, more and more people were reluctant to work with him. Because Fine had received almost no concrete criticism over the years, his biting style was entrenched and the staff was restive.

In an effort to ease into the conversation with the opening of "How about those Red Sox?", Fine got the wrong idea about where Jones was heading. He remained his usual cocky, superior self. Sensing this, Jones felt that he had to take off the velvet gloves. The conversation quickly became brutally blunt. Jones did almost all the talking. When the monologue was over, Fine stared icily at the floor. He got up in stiff silence and left. Jones was relieved. From his point of view, the interaction had been painful but swift. There wasn't too much blood on the floor, he observed wryly. But 2 days later, Fine handed in his resignation, taking a lot of institutional memory—and talent—with him.

Given Fine's history, Jones's conversational game plan—easing in and then, when that didn't work, the painful-but-quick bombshell—was doomed. A better approach would have been for Jones to split the conversation into two parts. In a first meeting, he could have raised the central issues of Fine's biting humor and disappointing performance. A second meeting could have been set up for the discussion itself. Handling the situation incrementally would have allowed time for both Jones and Fine to prepare for a two-way conversation instead of one of them delivering a monologue.

When Jones gave negative feedback to Fine, it would have been helpful if he had begun with an admission of regret and some responsibility for his contribution to their shared problem. "Jeremy," he might have said, "the quality of your work has been undercut—in part by the reluctance of your colleagues to risk the edge of your humor by talking problems through with you. I share responsibility for this because I have been reluctant to speak openly about these difficulties with you, whom I like and respect and with whom I have worked a long time." This approach effectively sets the tone for Jones's discussion with Fine. It recognizes the problems, it recognizes Fine, it recognizes their relationship, and it recognizes Jones's responsibility.[21]

# NONVERBAL COMMUNICATION

**Nonverbal communication** includes nonlanguage human responses (e.g., body motions and personal physical attributes) and environmental effects (e.g., a large or small office).[22] Nonverbal cues may contain many hidden messages and can influence the process and outcome of face-to-face communication. Even a person who is silent or inactive in the presence of others may be sending a message, which may or may not be the intended message (including boredom, fear, anger, or depression).

## TYPES OF NONNVERBAL CUES

The basic types of nonverbal cues are presented in Table 12.2, along with the numerous ways people can and do communicate without saying or writing a word. Nonverbal communication is important to verbal communication in that neither is adequate by itself for effective dialogue. Verbal and nonverbal cues can be related by

- repeating, as when verbal directions to some location are accompanied by pointing;
- contradicting, as in the case of the person who says, What, me nervous? while fidgeting and perspiring anxiously before taking a test—a good example of how the nonverbal message might be more believable when verbal and nonverbal signals conflict;
- substituting nonverbal for verbal cues, as when an employee returns to the office with a stressful expression that says, I've just had a horrible meeting with my manager—without a word being spoken; and

| Table 12.2 | Basic Types of Nonverbal Cues | |
|---|---|---|
| **TYPE OF CUE** | **EXPLANATION AND EXAMPLES** | |
| Body motion | Gestures, facial expressions, eye behavior, touching, and any other movement of the limbs and body | |
| Personal physical characteristics | Body shape, physique, posture, body or breath odors, height, weight, hair color, and skin color | |
| Paralanguage | Voice qualities, volume, speech rate, pitch, nonfluencies (saying "ah," "um," or "uh"), laughing, yawning, and so on | |
| Use of space | Ways people use and perceive space, including seating arrangements, conversational distance, and the "territorial" tendency of humans to stake out a personal space | |
| Physical environment | Building and room design, furniture and other objects, interior decorating, cleanliness, lighting, and noise | |
| Time | Being late or early, keeping others waiting, cultural differences in time perception, and the relationship between time and status | |

- complementing the verbal cue through nonverbal "underlining," as when a person pounds the table, places a hand on the shoulder of a coworker, uses a tone of voice indicating the great importance attached to the message, or presents a gift as a way of reinforcing an expression of gratitude or respect.

Nonverbal cues have been linked to a wide variety of concepts and issues. We briefly consider two: (1) cultural differences and (2) status differences, in terms of the relative ranking of individuals and groups.

## CULTURAL DIFFERENCES

Throughout this book, we have mentioned the impact of culture on communication. Because of the many differences in nonverbal expression, people from different cultures often misunderstand each other, which is a significant barrier to cross-cultural communication.[23] Earlier in this chapter, we examined how three forms of nonverbal communication—body language, personal space, and ethnocentrism—affect cross-cultural communication. Let's now examine two additional forms of nonverbal communication: chromatics and chronemics.

**Chromatics.**  **Chromatics** is communication through the use of color. Colors of clothing, products, packaging, or gifts send intended or unintended messages when people communicate cross-culturally. For example, in Hong Kong red signifies happiness or good luck. The traditional bridal dress is red, and at Chinese New Year luck money is distributed in *hong bao*, or red envelopes. Men in Hong Kong avoid green because of the Cantonese expression, "He's wearing a green hat," which means "His wife is cheating on him." In Chile, a gift of yellow roses conveys the message, "I don't like you," whereas in the Czech Republic giving red roses indicates a romantic interest.

**Chronemics.**  **Chronemics** reflects the use of time in a culture.[24] Before reading any further, please complete the instrument in Table 12.3 to determine how you use your personal time. In a culture with a **monochronic time schedule**, things are done linearly, or one activity at a time. Time is seen as something that can be controlled or wasted by people. This time schedule is followed in individualistic cultures, such as those in Northern Europe, Germany, and the United States. Being a few minutes late

## Table 12.3

| The Polychronic Attitude Index | | | | | |
| --- | --- | --- | --- | --- | --- |

Please consider how you feel about the following statements. Circle your choice on the scale provided: strongly agree, agree, neutral, disagree, or strongly disagree.

| | STRONGLY DISAGREE | DISAGREE | NEUTRAL | AGREE | STRONGLY AGREE |
| --- | --- | --- | --- | --- | --- |
| I do not like to juggle several activities at the same time. | 5 | 4 | 3 | 2 | 1 |
| People should not try to do many things at once. | 5 | 4 | 3 | 2 | 1 |
| When I sit down at my desk, I work on one project at a time. | 5 | 4 | 3 | 2 | 1 |
| I am comfortable doing several things at the same time. | 1 | 2 | 3 | 4 | 5 |

***Add up your points, and divide the total by 4. Then plot your score on the scale.***

| 1.0 | 1.5 | 2.0 | 2.5 | 3.0 | 3.5 | 4.0 | 4.5 | 5.0 |
| --- | --- | --- | --- | --- | --- | --- | --- | --- |
| Monochronic | | | | | | | | Polychronic |

The lower the score (below 3.0), the more monochronic your organization or department is; the higher the score (above 3.0), the more polychronic it is.

Source: Adapted from Bluedorn, A. C., Kaufman, C. F., and Lane, P. M. How many things do you like to do at once? An introduction to monochronic and polychronic time. *Academy of Management Executive*, 1992, 6(4), 17–26. Used with permission of Bluedorn, A. C., 1999.

for a business appointment is an insult, so punctuality is extremely important. Keith Hughes, the former CEO of The Associates First Capital Corporation, used to lock the doors when a meeting was supposed to start and didn't unlock them until the meeting was over.

With a **polychronic time schedule**, people tend to do several things at the same time. Many people may like to drive and conduct business at the same time (cars and cellular phones) or watch the news and a ball game at the same time (picture-in-picture TV). Schedules are less important than personal involvement and the completion of business. In Latin America and the Middle East, time schedules are less important than personal involvement. In Ecuador, businesspeople come to a meeting 15 or 20 minutes late and still consider that they're on time.

## STATUS DIFFERENCES

The following are only three of the many relationships between nonverbal cues and organizational status.

- Employees of higher status typically have better offices than do employees of lower status. For example, executive offices at EDS are more spacious, located on the top floors of the building, and have finer carpets and furniture than those of first-line managers. Most senior offices at EDS are at the corners, so they have windows on two sides.
- The offices of higher status employees are better "protected" than those of lower status employees. Here, *protected* means how much more difficult it would be for you to arrange to visit the governor of your state than for the governor to arrange to visit you. Top executive areas are typically least accessible and are often sealed off from others by several doors and assistants. Having an office with a door and

a secretary who answers the telephone protects even lower level managers and many staff personnel.

- The higher the employee's status, the easier that employee finds it to invade the territory of lower status employees. A superior typically feels free to walk right in on subordinates, whereas subordinates are more careful to ask permission or make an appointment before visiting a superior.[25]

Carried to excess, these and other nonverbal status cues are likely to create barriers to dialogue, especially from the perspective of the employees with lower formal status. However, effective managers often use supportive nonverbal cues when meeting with subordinates, such as (1) lightly touching subordinates on the arm when they arrive and shaking hands, (2) smiling appropriately, (3) nodding to affirm what was said, (4) slightly pulling their chairs closer to subordinates and maintaining an open posture, and (5) engaging in eye contact to further demonstrate listening and interest.

## ORGANIZATIONAL USE

You need to be cautious in assuming that there are hard and fast rules for quickly interpreting a particular nonverbal cue. In this section, we present three brief incidents to illustrate stereotypic and simple interpretations of nonverbal cues, which are then followed by the facts.

You're a sales rep presenting your organization's latest planning software to a senior-management prospect. Midway through your presentation, the potential customer leans back in her chair, looks briefly away and crosses her arms in front of her. You read this body language as unspoken resistance to your price or benefits and immediately shift gears. It turns out that she liked your software but was simply chilled by the cold temperature in the conference room.

A presenter stands fixed behind a lectern, exhibiting little noticeable body language. The content of his presentation features real-world illustrations, stories, and supporting visual aids. He throws in some self-deprecating humor for good measure. Aside from solid eye contact and periodic head movements, he could be a mannequin. For the audience, this noticeable lack of body energy likely has an effect equivalent to passing out sleeping pills. In fact, the speaker scores high on audience evaluations for authenticity, pragmatic content, and storytelling.

You're being introduced to the sponsors of an important presentation that you're giving next week. To create a good first impression, you arrive full of energy. You talk fast, and shake hands firmly and quickly. Your gestures are sharp and energetic. You walk away convinced that your hosts were impressed by your enthusiasm and credibility. In fact, to establish a credible first impression, it's often best to talk and move less, with fewer gestures, and to use a slower, lower manner of speaking. People subconsciously associate self-confidence and empathy with a more controlled body style. Your hosts likely thought you were either trying too hard to impress or were wired on too much coffee.[26]

## CHAPTER SUMMARY

**1.** Describe the basic elements of interpersonal communication.

The basic elements in the communication process—senders, receivers, transmitters, receptors, messages, channels, noise, meaning, encoding, decoding, and feedback—are interrelated.

Face-to-face interpersonal communication has the highest degree of information richness. An information-rich medium is especially important for performing complex tasks and resolving social and emotional issues that involve considerable uncertainty and ambiguity. Important issues usually contain significant amounts of uncertainty, ambiguity, and people-related (especially social and emotional) problems.

There are many potential challenges to effective interpersonal communication. We briefly reviewed the underlying interpersonal barriers discussed in previous chapters. Direct barriers include aggressive communication approaches, noise, semantics, demeaning language, and lying and distortion. The barriers stemming from cultural differences always are present. They may be especially high when the interaction takes place between individuals from high-context and low-context cultures.

**2.** Discuss how interpersonal communication networks affect relationships among employees.

Through their many communication networks, individuals repeat the interpersonal communication process dozens of times each day. We identified five types of communication networks: the star, Y, chain, circle, and all-channel. These networks operate both vertically and laterally in organizations. They can range from closed and centralized to open and decentralized and may hinder or support organizational diversity.

**3.** Explain the fabric of abilities that foster dialogue.

The communication process involves a number of complex factors and barriers that require many interwoven abilities to overcome. The abilities and behaviors that foster dialogue include communication openness, constructive feedback, active listening, appropriate self-disclosure, and supportive nonverbal verbal communication. They require both sender and receiver to play a dynamic role in the communication process. In open communication sender and receiver are able to discuss, disagree, and search for understanding without resorting to personal attacks or hidden agendas. Feedback received from others provides motivation for a person to learn and change his behavior. By being an active listener, the receiver hears the whole message without interpretation or judgment. How much someone is willing to share with others depends on the person's ability to disclose information.

**4.** Describe how nonverbal communication affects dialogue.

Nonverbal cues play a powerful role in supporting dialogue. Throughout this chapter, we described how cultural barriers can impede communication effectiveness. We examined specifically how certain nonverbal messages—the use of gestures, color, and time—can affect cross-cultural communication. Formal organizational position is often tied to status. Status symbols, such as office size, the floor on which the office is located, number of windows, location of a secretary, and access to senior-level employees, all influence communication patterns. We concluded with some cautionary comments on the need to avoid simplistic stereotypes as to the meaning of nonverbal cues employed by an individual.

# KEY TERMS AND CONCEPTS

Assertive communication
Channels
Chromatics
Chronemics
Cue
Cultural context
Data
Decoding
Dialogue
Distortion
Encoding
Ethnocentrism

Feedback
High-context culture
Impression management
Intercultural communication
Interpersonal communication
Interpersonal communication network
Language routines
Listening
Low-context culture
Lying
Meaning
Media richness

Messages
Meta-communication
Monochronic time schedule
Noise
Nonverbal communication
Polychronic time schedule

Receptors
Self-disclosure
Semantics
360-degree feedback
Transmitters

## DISCUSSION QUESTIONS

1. Recall Neal Patterson's scathing e-mail message in the Preview Case. What types and forms of communication should he undertake to reduce or eliminate the damage that he has done?
2. Describe some problems that an individual from a low-context culture and an individual from a high-context culture could have in trying to lead a meeting.
3. Describe your communication network at work or in school. Is it effective? Would you like to make any changes in it? Why or why not?
4. The Internet and e-mail are making it easier to communicate with people from different cultures. Do you agree or disagree with that statement? Explain.

5. Think of a team of which you are a member. How would you assess the members' self-awareness?
6. Why is media richness important in communication?
7. According to Ken Blanchard, author of the *One-Minute Manager*, feedback is the "breakfast of champions." What are some of the barriers that managers need to overcome when giving others feedback?
8. Describe the common nonverbal cues used by someone you have worked for. Are they usually consistent or inconsistent with that person's verbal expressions? Explain.
9. If your job transfers you to a foreign culture, what nonverbal communication practices must you be sensitive to?

## DEVELOPING COMPETENCIES

### Competency:  Managing Self

#### Interpersonal Communication Practices

*Instructions:* This survey is designed to assess your interpersonal communication practices. For each item in the survey, indicate which of the alternative reactions best represents how you would handle the situation described. Some alternatives may be equally characteristic or equally uncharacteristic of your reaction. Although that is a possibility, choose the alternative that is relatively more characteristic of your reaction. For each item, distribute five points between the alternatives in any of the following combinations.

|    | A | B |
|----|---|---|
| 1. | 5 | 0 |
| 2. | 4 | 1 |
| 3. | 3 | 2 |
| 4. | 2 | 3 |
| 5. | 1 | 4 |
| 6. | 0 | 5 |

Thus, there are six possible combinations for responding to the pair of alternatives presented to you with each survey item. Be sure that the numbers you assign to each pair sum to 5. To the extent possible, please relate each situation in the survey to your own personal experience. In this survey, we alternate the words he and she and him and her to balance use of the feminine and masculine genders.

1. If a friend of mine had a personality conflict with a mutual acquaintance of ours with whom it was important for her to get along, I would
   _____ A. tell my friend that I felt she was partially responsible for any problems with this other person and try to let her know who the person being affected by her is.
   _____ B. not get involved because I wouldn't be able to continue to get along with both of them once I had entered into the conflict.
2. If one of one of my friends and I had a heated argument in the past and I realized that he will be ill at ease around me from that time on, I would
   _____ A. avoid making things worse by discussing his behavior and just let the whole thing drop.
   _____ B. bring up his behavior and ask him how he felt the argument had affected our relationship.
3. If a friend began to avoid me and act in an aloof and withdrawn manner, I would
   _____ A. tell here about her behavior and suggest she tell me what was on her mind.
   _____ B. follow her lead and keep our contacts brief and aloof because that seems to be what she wants.
4. If two of my friends and I were talking and one of my friends slipped and brought up a personal problem of

mine that involved the other friend, and of which he was not yet aware, I would

_____ A. change the subject and signal my friend to do the same.

_____ B. fill in my uninformed friend on what the other friend was talking about and suggest that we go into it later.

5. If a friend were to tell me that, in her opinion, I was doing things that made me less effective than I might be in social situations, I would

_____ A. ask her to spell out or describe what she has observed and suggest changes I might make.

_____ B. resent the criticism and let her know why I behave the way I do.

6. If one of my friends aspired to an office in our student organization for which I felt he was unqualified and if he had been tentatively assigned to that position by the president of the student organization, I would

_____ A. not mention my misgivings to either my friend or the president and let them handle it in their own way.

_____ B. tell my friend and the president of my misgivings and then leave the final decision up to them.

7. If I felt that one of my friends was being unfair to me and her other friends, but none of them had mentioned anything about it, I would

_____ A. ask several of those people how they perceived the situation to see if they felt that she was being unfair.

_____ B. not ask the others how they perceived our friend but wait for them to bring it up to me.

8. If I were preoccupied with some personal matters and a friend told me that I had become irritated with him and others and that I was jumping on him for unimportant things, I would

_____ A. tell him I was preoccupied and would probably be on edge a while and would prefer not to be bothered.

_____ B. listen to his complaints but not try to explain my actions to him.

9. If I had heard some friends discussing an ugly rumor about a friend of mine that I knew could hurt her and she asked me what I knew about it, if anything, I would

_____ A. say that I didn't know anything about it and tell her no one would believe a rumor like that anyway.

_____ B. tell her exactly what I had heard, when I had heard it, and from whom I had heard it.

10. If a friend pointed out the fact that I had a personality conflict with another friend with whom it was important for me to get along, I would

_____ A. consider his comments out of line and tell him I didn't want to discuss the matter any further.

_____ B. talk about it openly with him to find out how my behavior was being affected by this.

11. If my relationship with a friend has been damaged by repeated arguments on an issue of importance to us both, I would

_____ A. be cautious in my conversations with her so that the issue wouldn't come up again to worsen our relationship.

_____ B. point to the problems that the controversy was causing in our relationship and suggest that we discuss it until we had resolved it.

12. If in a personal discussion with a friend about his problems and behavior, he suddenly suggested we discuss my problems and behavior as well as his own, I would

_____ A. try to keep the discussion away from me by suggesting that other, closer friends often talked to me bout such matters.

_____ B. welcome the opportunity to hear what he felt about me and encourage his comments.

13. If a friend of mine began to tell me about her hostile feelings about another friend who she felt was being unkind to others (and I wholeheartedly agreed), I would

_____ A. listen and also express my own feelings to her so she would know where I stood.

_____ B. listen but not express my own negative views and opinions because she might repeat what I said to her in confidence.

14. If I thought an ugly rumor was being spread about me and suspected that one of my friends had quite likely heard it, I would

_____ A. avoid mentioning the issue and leave it to him to tell me about it if he wanted to.

_____ B. risk putting him on the spot by asking him directly what he knew about the whole thing.

15. If I had observed a friend in social situations and thought that she was doing a number of things that hurt her relationships, I would

_____ A. risk being seen as a busybody and tell her what I had observed and my reactions to it.

_____ B. keep my opinions to myself, rather than be seen as interfering in things that are none of my business.

16. If two friends and I were talking and one of them inadvertently mentioned a personal problem that involved me but of which I knew nothing, I would

_____ A. press them for information about the problem and their opinions about it.

_____ B. leave it up to my friends to tell me or not tell me, letting them change the subject if they wished.

17. If a friend seemed to be preoccupied and began to jump on me for seemingly unimportant things and to become irritated with me and others without real cause, I would

_____ A. treat him with kid gloves for a while on the assumption that he was having some temporary personal problems that were none of my business.

_____ B. try to talk to him about it and point out to him how his behavior was affecting people.

18. If I had begun to dislike certain habits of a friend to the point that it was interfering with my enjoying her company, I would

_____ A. say nothing to her directly but let her know my feelings by ignoring her whenever her annoying habits were obvious.

_____ B. get my feelings out in the open and clear the air so that we could continue our friendship comfortably and enjoyably.
19. In discussing social behavior with one of my more sensitive friends, I would
  _____ A. avoid mentioning his flaws and weaknesses so as not to hurt his feelings.
  _____ B. focus on his flaws and weaknesses so he could improve his interpersonal skills.
20. If I knew that I might be assigned to an important position in our group and my friends' attitudes toward me had become rather negative, I would
  _____ A. discuss my shortcomings with my friends so I could see where to improve.
  _____ B. try to figure out my own shortcomings by myself so I could improve.

## Scoring Key

In this survey 10 of the items deal with your receptivity to feedback and 10 are concerned with your willingness to disclose yourself. Transfer your scores from each item to this scoring key. Add the scores in each column. Now, transfer these scores to Figure 12.7 by drawing a vertical line through the feedback score and a horizontal line through the self-disclosure line.

| Receptivity to Feedback | Willingness to Self-Disclose |
|---|---|
| 2.  B _____ | 1.  A _____ |
| 3.  A _____ | 4.  B _____ |
| 5.  A _____ | 6.  B _____ |
| 7.  A _____ | 9.  B _____ |
| 8.  B _____ | 11. B _____ |
| 10. B _____ | 13. A _____ |
| 12. B _____ | 15. A _____ |
| 14. B _____ | 17. B _____ |
| 16. A _____ | 18. B _____ |
| 20. A _____ | 19. B _____ |
| Total: _____ | Total: _____ |

As Figure 12.7 suggests, higher scores in receptivity to feedback and willingness to disclose yourself indicate a greater willingness to engage in open interpersonal communication. Of course, you need to be mindful of the situational factors that may influence your natural personal preference to be relatively more open or closed in interpersonal communication.[27]

## Question

1. Based on your scores, what communication abilities do you need to develop?

**Figure 12.7**    **Personal Openness in Interpersonal Communication**

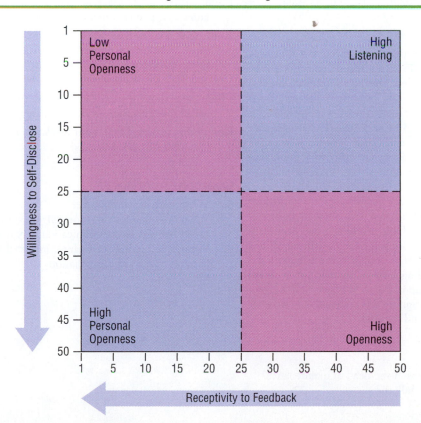

## Competency:  Managing Communication

### Xographics

#### Part A

Xographics is a division of a large telecommunications company. Ellen Bohn, the new production superintendent, had recently moved to Xographics from Rolm Communications where she had been a manager of a large office staff. The three managers reporting to Bohn all had 20 or more years' experience with Xographics. They had seen it go from a productive company to one that was badly troubled with problem workers and poor performance.

In talking with one of the supervisors, Bohn learned that many of them were upset because they had to report any machine breakdown to the production manager or one of his assistants within 15 minutes of the breakdown. They felt that this didn't give the workers the opportunity to repair the machine themselves. The breakdown report was forwarded to the production superintendent's office. The assistant told Bohn that the word was that once a worker got five reports, he or she was taken off the machine and given a lower paying job.

#### Questions

1. What should Bohn do?
2. What other problems (unidentified by Bohn) might be present?
3. What additional steps might the supervisors take?

#### Part B

One of the major problems that Bohn faced was that only about 40 percent of the jobs listed for scheduled maintenance shutdowns were ever performed. During an informal conversation with Ken Viet, Xographics personnel director, Bohn learned that the maintenance department was operating at about 30 percent efficiency. Viet said that the maintenance workers had recently staged a slowdown in order to force the company to increase their wages. Viet also told Bohn that maintenance workers usually quit about an hour early in order to wash up.

The head of the maintenance department had worked his way up through the ranks. He started with Xographics immediately after graduation from high school and had been with the company 25 years. His reason for the "inefficiency" was the lack of qualified maintenance people in the area, with the personnel department sending him individuals not qualified to maintain the mill's machines. He didn't have time to train each newly hired worker, assigning this responsibility to other workers who had been around for a while.

#### Questions (continued)

4. How might Bohn approach the head of maintenance?
5. Who else should Bohn talk to?

#### Part C

Two months after Bohn joined Xographics, the company held its annual picnic at a local park. Most of the employees and their families were there. Bohn saw Viet at the picnic and handed him a beer. The following conversation then took place.

**Ken:**  Hey, Ellen, got a minute?

**Ellen:**  Sure. What's up?

**Ken:**  Well, I was talking with one of your supervisors that I know pretty well. You know, an off-the-record chat about the company.

**Ellen:**  Yeah?

**Ken:**  He told me that the company's management style is the mushroom style: Keep them in the dark and feed 'em a lot of manure. He said that nobody knew you were hired until you showed up at the plant. We heard that the guard didn't even know who you were.

**Ellen:**  Yeah, I guess that's so.

**Ken:**  This supervisor said that he has been doing his job for ten years and has never received any performance appraisal. His raises are just added into his check. No one has pointed out his strong and weak points.

**Ellen:**  Yeah, I guess that's so. But, I'm not totally sure. You know that I've been here only a few months myself.

**Ken:**  Yeah, I know that, but listen to this. Tom Kerr, the new head of industrial engineering, hasn't talked to or even been introduced to anybody in the paper-machine area, and Tom has been on the job for three months.

**Ellen:**  Ken, how widespread do you think this feeling is about the mushroom style of management?

**Ken:**  I don't know, Ellen, but I think you ought to find out if you want this place to produce.

#### Questions (continued)

6. What steps can Bohn take?
7. What does this conversation tell you about the company? What barriers to communication may exist?
8. What role has the company's informal communication network played in this situation?

# The Organization

# CHAPTER

# Making Decisions in Organizations

## LEARNING OBJECTIVES

When you have finished studying the chapter, you should be able to:

1. Explain the basic concepts for making ethical decisions.
2. Describe the attributes of three models of managerial decision making.
3. Explain two methods for stimulating organizational creativity.

13

## PAMELA LOPKER OF QAD

Pamela Lopker is the chairman and president of QAD, Inc., which is headquartered in Carpintera, California. Cofounded by Lopker in 1979, QAD now has 1,300 employees. It offers enterprise resource planning (ERP) and supply chain software to firms in various industries. We introduce the decision-making process by offering several of Lopker's comments for consideration.

"I make bad decisions all the time. But I've been successful because I've developed a process for identifying and changing those decisions quickly. I approach every decision with an eye to the long-term outcome. That's a hard method to adopt in a fast-paced business environment. But it's the only way to create sustainable value on either a professional or a personal level. The quick-fix method that I see so many companies rely on is just that—a quick fix. There's a big difference between investing heavily in marketing the product that you have today—with no sense of what it takes to survive tomorrow—and investing heavily in R&D today so that you can have tomorrow's product.

"Even in my personal life, I looked at decisions from the perspective of what's going to be better for me over the long term. When I was in college, I needed to decide on a career path. While most of my peers were concerned with following their passion, with doing what they "loved" to do, I was looking for a career that would support me financially over the long run. Sometimes making important decisions is just a matter of asking some basic questions: What are my skills? Where is a certain industry going? What should I be doing now to get to where I want to be later? Because I was always strong in math and in analytical thinking, I figured that I would do statistical or actuarial work. Then I realized that statistics wasn't a booming industry. Computer science seemed like a better long-term bet, so I changed my major.

"As a leader, I try not to make decisions for others. Sure, being a dictator is often the fastest way to get things done. But it's not a process that allows an organization to sustain growth. I want the people in my organization to learn the lessons that come with making decisions: that everything is a compromise, that nothing is ever completely logical, but that you can deal with things through a logical decision-making process."[1]

*For more information on QAD, Inc., visit the organization's home page at http://www.qad.com.*

Key decisions in organizations frequently involve pressures from various groups, such as shareholders, competitors, governmental agencies, suppliers, employees, and managers. These pressures often result in the need to modify the way decisions are being made or to change decisions that have previously been made. Pamela Lopker reflects this perspective in her comments.

We presented concepts and issues related to making managerial, team, and individual decisions in several previous chapters. In this chapter, we expand on them. First, we discuss several issues that are fundamental to ethical decision making. Next, we review the features of three main decision-making models. Then, we conclude with a presentation of two approaches for stimulating creativity in decision making.

1. Explain the basic concepts for making ethical decisions.

# MAKING ETHICAL DECISIONS

Decisions and behaviors in organizations have an underlying foundation of ethical concepts, principles, and rules.[2] Because of the importance of ethics in management, we recognize it throughout this book in the Managing Ethics Competency features, as well as in relation to a number of topics, such as leadership and organizational change.

**Ethics** has to do with the rightness or wrongness of the decisions and behaviors of individuals and the organizations of which they are members. Ethical issues in organizations are more common and complex than generally recognized. In fact, ethical issues influence the decisions that employees make daily. Some ethical issues involve factors that blur the distinction between "right" and "wrong." As a result, employees may experience ethical dilemmas. A survey of randomly selected employees in the United States identified five main types of unethical behaviors that they had engaged in during the past year: (1) cutting corners on quality, (2) covering up errors, (3) abusing or lying about sick days, (4) lying to or deceiving customers about the quality of their products, and (5) putting inappropriate pressure on others. Fifty-six percent of the respondents indicated that they felt some pressure to act unethically or illegally.[3]

There are no simple rules for making ethical decisions. Our goal here is to help you develop your competency in applying ethical concepts to decision making. Your assessment of alternatives will be improved by examining five key components that comprise the foundation of ethical decision making: ethical intensity, decision-making principles and decision rules, affected individuals, benefits and costs, and determination of rights. As suggested in Figure 13.1, these components are interrelated and need to be considered as a whole in order to make ethical decisions.

## ETHICAL INTENSITY

**Ethical intensity** is the degree of moral importance given to an issue.[4] It is determined by the combined impact of six factors, which are shown in Figure 13.2 and described as follows.

- **Magnitude of consequences** is the harm or benefits accruing to individuals affected by a decision or behavior. An action that causes 1,000 people to suffer a particular injury has greater consequences than an action that causes 10 people to suffer the same injury. A decision that causes the death of a human being is of greater consequence than one that causes a sprained ankle.
- **Probability of effect** is the likelihood that a decision will be implemented and that it will lead to the harm or benefit predicted. The production of an automobile that would be dangerous to occupants during normal driving has greater probability of harm than the production of a NASCAR race car that endangers the driver when curves are taken at high speed. The sale of a gun to a known

**Figure 13.1**                    **Components of the Foundation for Making Ethical Decisions**

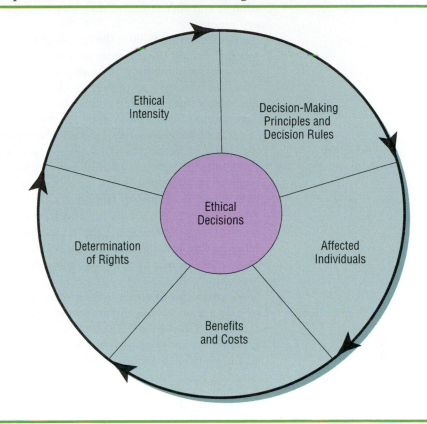

armed robber has a greater probability of harm than the sale of a gun to a law-abiding hunter.

- **Social consensus** is the amount of public agreement that a proposed decision is bad or good. Actively discriminating against minority job candidates is worse than not actively seeking out minority job candidates. Bribing a customs official in Canada evokes greater public condemnation than bribing a customs official in a country such as the Philippines where such behavior is generally accepted as a

**Figure 13.2**                    **Determinants of Ethical Intensity**

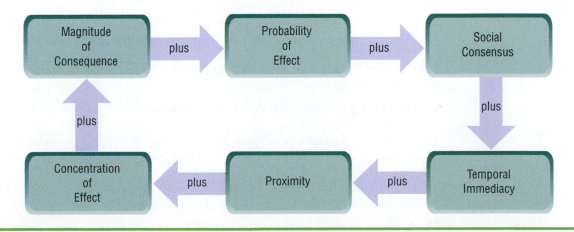

way of doing business. Managers and employees will have difficulty deciding what is and isn't ethical if they aren't guided by a reasonable amount of public agreement.

- **Temporal immediacy** is the length of time that elapses from making a decision to experiencing the consequences of that decision. A shorter length of time implies greater immediacy. Releasing a drug that will cause 1 percent of the people who take it to have acute nervous reactions within 1 month has greater temporal immediacy than releasing a drug that will cause 1 percent of those who take it to develop nervous disorders after 30 years of use. The reduction in the retirement benefits of current retirees has greater temporal immediacy than the reduction in the future retirement benefits of employees who are currently 22 years of age.
- **Proximity** is the sense of closeness (social, cultural, psychological, or physical) that the decision maker has for victims or beneficiaries of the decision. When Don Ritter at Mobil was laid off as a result of the Exxon/Mobil merger, it had a greater impact on his work team because the members knew and liked Ritter better than they did those laid off in another division of Mobil. For North Americans, the sale of dangerous pesticides in Canadian, U.S., and Mexican markets has greater ethical proximity (social, cultural, and physical) than does the sale of such pesticides in Russia.
- **Concentration of effect** is the inverse function of the number of people affected by a decision. A change in a warranty policy denying coverage to 20 people with claims of $20,000 each has a more concentrated effect than a change denying coverage to 2,000 people with claims of $200 each. Cheating an individual or small group of individuals out of $5,000 has a more concentrated effect than cheating an organization, such as the IRS, out of the same sum.

**Organizational Use.**   The six factors of ethical intensity potentially are influenced by the characteristics of the decision issue itself. Ethical intensity rises with increases in one or more of its factors and declines with reductions in one or more of these factors, assuming that all other conditions remain constant. However, different individuals may rate the ethical intensity of the same decision differently because they place different values on the principles and rules of ethics in decision making. Table 13.1 provides a questionnaire for you to use in rating the ethical intensity of 10 different behaviors.

## ETHICAL PRINCIPLES AND RULES

There are no universally accepted principles and rules for resolving all the ethical issues in complex decision-making situations. In addition, individuals and groups differ over what influences both ethical and unethical behaviors and decisions. Numerous principles and rules have been suggested to provide an *ethical justification* for a person's decisions and behaviors.[5] They range from those that justify self-serving decisions to those that require careful consideration of others' rights and costs.

**Self-Serving Principles.**   The following three ethical principles are used to justify self-serving decisions and behaviors.

- **Hedonist principle:** You do whatever is in your own self-interest but do nothing that is clearly illegal.
- **Might-equals-right principle:** You do whatever you are powerful enough to impose on others without respect to socially acceptable behaviors but do nothing that is clearly illegal.
- **Organization interests principle:** You act on the basis of what is good for the organization but do nothing that is clearly illegal.

All three of these self-serving principles appeared to be present in the following incident. Several years ago, the American Society of Composers, Authors and

| **Table 13.1** | **Ethical Intensity of Selected Behaviors** |
|---|---|

*Instructions*

Evaluate each of the 10 behaviors shown in this questionnaire in terms of its ethical intensity. The overall scale of ethical intensity varies from −5, which indicates highly unethical behavior, to +5, which indicates a highly acceptable and ethical behavior. Write down the number on each scale at or near the point that reflects your assessment. What factors were most important in arriving at your rating of the ethical intensity for each behavior?

**BEHAVIORS**                                         **ETHICAL INTENSITY**

| | Unethical/ Negative | Neutral | Ethical/ Positive |
|---|---|---|---|
| 1. Covering up mistakes by coworkers | −5 | 0 | +5 |
| 2. Giving a favor to a client out of friendship. | −5 | 0 | +5 |
| 3. Giving a favor to a client for a bribe. | −5 | 0 | +5 |
| 4. Discriminating against an employee on the basis of race. | −5 | 0 | +5 |
| 5. Presenting misleading information to a customer. | −5 | 0 | +5 |
| 6. Presenting only positive features of your organization's products to a customer. | −5 | 0 | +5 |
| 7. Manipulating performance data and indicators to give the appearance of reaching your goals. | −5 | 0 | +5 |
| 8. Rewarding people differently based on differences in performance. | −5 | 0 | +5 |
| 9. Bending the rules to help the organization. | −5 | 0 | +5 |
| 10. Using an office PC for personal use. | −5 | 0 | +5 |

Publishers (ASCAP) sent a letter to summer camps warning them to pay up if they wanted to sing copyrighted songs such as *Edelweiss* and *This Land Is Your Land*. As a result, several cash-strapped camps stopped singing the songs. After television talk shows and newspapers reported the story, ASCAP took out full-page ads saying that it "never sought, nor was it ever its intention to license Girl Scouts singing around the campfire." The credibility of this letter wilted in light of ASCAP's admission that it would reimburse 16 Girl Scout councils that had already paid fees ranging from $77 to $256.[6]

**Balancing Interests Principles.**    The following three ethical principles are used to justify decisions intended to balance the interests of multiple individuals or groups.[7]

- **Means–end principle:** You act on the basis of whether some overall good justifies a moral transgression but do nothing that is clearly illegal.
- **Utilitarian principle:** You act on the basis of whether the harm from the decision is outweighed by the good in it—that is, the greatest good for the greatest number—but do nothing that is clearly illegal.
- **Professional standards principle:** You act on the basis of whether the decision can be explained before a group of your peers but do nothing that is clearly illegal.

These principles provide the ethical foundation for many decisions in organizations. They create the basis for helping to resolve ethical dilemmas—for example, Nortel was able to justify employee layoffs but recognized certain responsibilities for providing career counseling and severance packages for the employees affected.

As a result of the Internet and related information technologies, privacy issues have become major concerns in the attempt to balance the interests of individuals, organizations, and the public at large. A report, entitled *Nothing Sacred: The Politics of Privacy*, issued by the Center for Public Integrity concluded that the privacy of Americans is being compromised.[8] The growing perception is that employees and consumers have lost too much of their privacy to employers, marketers, and governmental agencies. In a recent survey of adults, 82 percent complained that they had lost all control over how their personal information is used by companies. With regard to employees, an increasing number of firms are exercising their legal authority to monitor employee e-mail messages, use of the Internet, behaviors (by the use of security cameras), and conversations at work.[9]

Privacy issues have become ethical dilemmas in terms of (1) distribution and use of employee data from computer-based human resource information systems; (2) increasing use of paper-and-pencil honesty tests, resulting from polygraph testing being declared illegal in most situations; (3) procedures and bases for substance abuse and AIDS testing; and (4) genetic testing. The ethical dilemmas in each of these areas revolve around balancing the rights of the individual, the needs and rights of the employer, and the interests of the community at large.

**Concern for Others Principle.**    The following are three ethical principles that focus on the need to consider decisions and behaviors from the perspective of those affected and the public as a whole.

- **Disclosure principle:** You act on the basis of how the general public would likely respond to the disclosure of the rationale and facts related to the decision but do nothing that is clearly illegal.
- **Distributive justice principle:** You act on the basis of treating an individual or group equitably rather than on arbitrarily defined characteristics but do nothing that is clearly illegal.
- **Golden rule principle:** You act on the basis of placing yourself in the position of someone affected by the decision and try to determine how that person would feel but do nothing that is clearly illegal.

These three ethical principles are often *imposed* on certain categories of decisions and behaviors through laws, regulations, and court rulings. In effect, governments impose ethical principles and rules that organizations are expected to comply with in certain situations. For example, U.S. civil rights laws forbid organizations from considering personal characteristics, such as race, gender, religion, or national origin, in decisions to recruit, hire, promote, or fire employees. These laws are based on the ethical principle of distributive justice, which requires the same treatment of individuals regardless of age, race, gender, and the like. For example, employees who are similar in relevant respects should be treated similarly and employees who differ in relevant respects should be treated differently in proportion to the differences between them. On this basis, the U.S. Equal Pay Act of 1963 asserts that paying women and men different wages is illegal when their jobs in the same organization require equal skills, effort, responsibility, and working conditions.[10]

Table 13.2 lets you assess a significant course of action that you're considering in relation to the nine ethical principles just described.

**Organizational Use.**    As suggested previously, no single factor influences the degree to which decisions and behaviors are likely to be ethical or unethical. However, the following actions can help integrate ethical decision making into the day-to-day life of an organization.

- Top managers must demonstrate their commitment to ethical behaviors and decisions to other managers and employees.
- A clear code of ethics should be promulgated and followed.
- A whistle-blowing and/or ethical concerns procedure should be established and followed.
- Managers and employees alike should be involved in the identification of ethical problems to arrive at a shared understanding of them and to help solve them.
- The performance appraisal process should include consideration of ethical issues.
- The organizational priorities and efforts related to ethical issues should be widely publicized.[11]

## CONCERN FOR OTHERS

The highest form of ethical decision making involves a careful determination of who will receive benefits or incur costs as the consequence of a decision. For major decisions, this assessment may include a variety of stakeholders—shareholders, customers, lenders, suppliers, employees, and governmental agencies, among others. The more specific an individual or group can be about who may benefit and who may incur costs from a particular decision, the more likely it is that ethical implications will be fully considered. As discussed in the Preview Case, Pamela Lopker reflects a concern for others in describing her approach to making decisions. Recall her comments: "I want the people in my organization to learn the lessons that come from making decisions. . . ."

The ethical interpretation of the effects of decisions on specific individuals or groups can change over time. For example, **employment at will** means that the parties in an employment situation do not have equal bargaining power. Under this doctrine, the right of a manager to fire an employee is absolute and generally is viewed as creating little cost to either party. The presumption is that the organization can easily recruit and train (if necessary) another employee and that the fired employee can easily find another job.

The employment-at-will doctrine increasingly has been challenged successfully in wrongful termination cases in the courts. These challenges are based on the distributive justice principle and the golden rule principle. Before 1980, companies in the United States were free to fire most nonunion employees "at will." Employees

**Table 13.2**

## Ethical Assessment of a Decision

### Incident

The manager of a department in a medium-sized public company with a good profit record is 55 and has worked in the company for 20 years. He is married and has two children in college. His life is his work. However, he is becoming less effective, and has lost the ability to lead the people working for him. Several of the brightest young people in his department have left as a result of the situation. If you were president of the company, which of the following alternatives would you be likely to select: (1) declare him ineffective and dismiss him with severance compensation; (2) retire him early on part pension; (3) retire him early on full pension; (4) transfer him to a staff support advisory position; (5) attempt to take corrective action and leave him on the job; (6) transfer him to a new line management position at the same pay until age 60; (7) or do nothing? Select one of these alternatives for further assessment.

### Instructions

How would you evaluate the ethics of the chosen alternative with respect to the degree to which it is based on each of the ethical principles shown?

| ETHICAL PRINCIPLE | HIGH DEGREE 5 | 4 | UNCERTAIN/ UNDECIDED 3 | 2 | LOW DEGREE (NONE) 1 |
|---|---|---|---|---|---|
| *To what degree is the action based on this ethical principle:* | | | | | |
| 1. Hedonist | 5 | 4 | 3 | 2 | 1 |
| 2. Might-equals-right | 5 | 4 | 3 | 2 | 1 |
| 3. Organization interests | 5 | 4 | 3 | 2 | 1 |
| 4. Means–end | 5 | 4 | 3 | 2 | 1 |
| 5. Utilitarian | 5 | 4 | 3 | 2 | 1 |
| 6. Professional standards | 5 | 4 | 3 | 2 | 1 |
| 7. Disclosure | 5 | 4 | 3 | 2 | 1 |
| 8. Distributive justice | 5 | 4 | 3 | 2 | 1 |
| 9. Golden rule | 5 | 4 | 3 | 2 | 1 |

### Further Review

Do you want to implement the alternative tentatively selected? Explain. Do you want to assess one or more of the other alternatives? Explain. Which alternative appears to be the worse in terms of the 9 ethical principles? Explain.

Source: Incident only adapted from *Questionnaires*. Institute of Business Ethics, The Open University. Available online at http://www.open.ac.uk/business-ethics; accessed March 12, 2002.

were fired for any reason without explanation and rarely went to court to challenge a termination. The vast majority who did had their suits dismissed. However, the courts have recently ruled in favor of exceptions to the employment-at-will doctrine, especially if questionable termination procedures were followed.[12]

## BENEFITS AND COSTS

An assessment of the benefits and costs of a decision requires a determination of the interests and values of those affected. **Values** are the relatively permanent and deeply held desires of individuals. A global values survey by the Institute for Global Ethics asked respondents to reply to the following: "Please look at the list of 15 values carefully and check the five values that are most important to you in your daily life." The most frequent choice was truth, followed by compassion, responsibility, freedom, and reverence for life. The five values chosen least—starting with the very least—were respect for elders, devotion, honor, social harmony, and humility.[13]

Care must be taken to guard against assuming that others attach the same importance to these values that you do or that people in different cultures hold the same values. Conflicting values can lead to different interpretations of ethical responsibilities. For example, Greenpeace and other environmental groups have "preservation of nature" as one of their top values. In the survey just cited, it was ranked as eighth in importance and selected as most important by only 2 percent of the respondents. Active members of Greenpeace contend that most managers are irresponsible and unethical in not showing more concern about air and water pollution, land use, protection of endangered species, and the like.

**Organizational Use.**   The utilitarian principle is a common approach to the balancing or weighing of benefits and costs in organizations. Utilitarianism emphasizes the provision of the greatest good for the greatest number in judging the ethics of a decision. A manager who is guided by utilitarianism considers the potential effect of alternative actions on employees who will be affected and then selects the alternative benefiting the greatest number of employees. The manager accepts the fact that this alternative may harm others. However, so long as potentially positive results outweigh potentially negative results, the manager considers the decision to be both good and ethical.

According to some critics, utilitarianism has been misused by U.S. organizations. They suggest that there is too much short-run maximizing of personal advantage and too much discounting of the long-run costs of disregarding ethics. Those costs include rapidly widening gaps in income between rich and poor, creation of a permanent underclass with its hopelessness, and harm done to the environment. These critics believe that too many people and institutions are acquiring wealth for the purposes of personal consumption and power and that the end of acquiring wealth justifies any means of doing so. As a result, these critics suggest that trust of leaders and institutions, both public and private, has declined.[14]

## DETERMINATION OF RIGHTS

The notion of rights also is complex and continually changing. One dimension of rights focuses on who is entitled to benefits or participation in decisions to change the mix of benefits and costs. Union–management negotiations frequently involve conflicts and dilemmas over management's rights to hire, promote, fire, and reassign union employees, as well as to move work to other countries or to outsource work. Slavery, racism, gender and age discrimination, and invasion of privacy often have been challenged by appeals to values based on concepts of fundamental rights.

**Organizational Use.**   As suggested previously, issues of responsibilities and rights in the workplace are numerous and vary greatly. A few examples include unfair and reverse discrimination, sexual harassment, employee rights to continued employment, employer rights to terminate employment "at will," employee and corporate free speech, due process, and the right to test for substance abuse and acquired immune deficiency syndrome (AIDS). Some experts believe that workplace rights and the establishment of trust with employees is the most crucial internal issue facing organizations today.[15]

The following Managing Ethics Competency feature reports an actual incident, but the names and places have been disguised. It reflects a variety of ethical principles and issues discussed in this section, including Andrea Stevenson's right to report the incident without punishment.

## COMPETENCY:   MANAGING ETHICS

### ANDREA STEVENSON'S DILEMMA

This new project was exciting for Grantville's city government. The rapidly growing city planned to construct a bike path through the scenic part of town, hoping that carefully landscaped green areas would attract another kind of green: tourist dollars. Andrea Stevenson, a Grantville purchasing agent, received a phone message meant for City Supervisor Mike McDonald regarding the new bike path, and she wanted to leave it with his project files. He was out of the office for the afternoon, which was just as well. As a new employee, Stevenson found McDonald a bit intimidating. She headed into his deserted office and began searching his files.

"What are you dong?" came the voice from behind. Startled, she dropped the files and looked up to see McDonald in his doorway. "I . . . I got a phone message for you that I thought should go with the bike path project files."

"Those files are confidential," he said. "Clean up this mess and leave my files alone." He stormed out and Stevenson knelt down to pick up the files. As she reached for a piece of paper under the desk, she saw that it was the bidder's list. Glancing at it, she saw that Grantville Group, a local engineering firm, had been scratched off the top of the list. Another name, Baxter Brothers Engineering, had been written in. "That's funny," Stevenson, thought. "I know that name. Isn't that one of McDonald's golfing buddies?"

The next day, McDonald stopped at Stevenson's desk and smiled. "Look, I'm sorry I flew off the handle yesterday," he said. "Can I buy you lunch?" Stevenson wondered whether she could swallow this change of tone, let alone lunch. She had a sinking feeling, and it wasn't just at the prospect of lunch with the boss. As a single mom, Stevenson needed her job and didn't want to make waves. But something seemed a bit off.

*Questions:*   Before reading on, what would you do if you were Andrea Stevenson? Why?

*What happened:*   Andrea Stevenson politely, but firmly, declined the offer of lunch and later decided to become a whistle-blower. It took the help of several others, but eventually widespread corruption in bidding was uncovered. Contracts had routinely been awarded to family members and friends. The driving forces behind the investigations were the local newspaper and TV station. In the end, the city revised its code of ethics and now trains employees in the new code. A Board of Ethics was set up to handle inquiries. Three employees were charged with crimes. Other perpetrators were transferred to other departments—one at a higher salary.

Andrea Stevenson didn't suffer any repercussions for whistle-blowing and is still at the same job. Mike McDonald resigned and stated that he was looking at another job.[16]

---

**Learning Objective:**

2. Describe the attributes of three models of managerial decision making.

## MODELS OF MANAGERIAL DECISION MAKING

In previous chapters, we introduced a number of concepts and models that are important to understanding individual, team, and managerial decision making. In this section, we describe the main features of three managerial decision-making models: rational, bounded rationality, and political. In doing so, we introduce you to the different ways in which managerial decision making is viewed. Each model is useful for gaining insights into the complex array of managerial decision-making situations in an organization.

## RATIONAL MODEL

The **rational model** involves a process for choosing among alternatives to maximize benefits to an organization. It includes comprehensive problem definition, thorough data collection and analysis, and a careful assessment of alternatives. The criteria for evaluating alternatives are well-known and agreed upon. The generation and exchange of information among individuals presumably is unbiased and accurate. Individual preferences and organizational choices are a function of the best alternative for the entire organization.[17] Thus the rational model of decision making is based on the explicit assumptions that:

1. all available information concerning alternatives has been obtained,
2. these alternatives can be ranked according to explicit criteria, and
3. the alternative selected will provide the maximum gain possible for the organization (or decision makers).

An implicit assumption is that ethical dilemmas do not exist in the decision-making process and that the means–end and utilitarian principles will dominate the consideration of ethical issues.

**Xerox's Six-Step Process.**   Xerox developed the companywide six-step rational process for guiding decision making presented in Table 13.3. Column 1 shows the six steps, column 2 identifies the key question to be answered in each step, and column 3 indicates what's needed to proceed to the next step. Managers and employees receive extensive training in the use of various decision-making tools to help them work through these steps.[18]

**Table 13.3** — **Portion of Xerox's Rational Decision-Making Process**

| STEP | QUESTION TO BE ANSWERED | WHAT'S NEEDED TO GO TO THE NEXT STEP |
|---|---|---|
| 1. Identify and select problem | What do we want to change? | Identification of the gap; "desired state" described in observable terms |
| 2. Analyze problem | What's preventing us from reaching the "desired state"? | Key cause(s) documented and ranked |
| 3. Generate potential solutions | How could we make the change? | Solution list |
| 4. Select and plan the solution | What's the best way to do it? | Plan for making and monitoring the change; measurement criteria to evaluate solution effectiveness |
| 5. Implement the solution | Are we following the plan? | Solution in place |
| 6. Evaluate the solution | How well did it work? | Verification that the problem is solved, or agreement to address continuing problems |

Source: Adapted from Garvin, D. A. Building a learning organization. *Harvard Business Review*, July–August 1993, 78–91; Brown, J. S., and Walton, E. Reenacting the corporation: Organizational change and restructuring of Xerox. *Planning Review*, September/October 1993, 5–8.

In terms of the individual, the rational model puts a premium on logical thinking.[19] Recall one of Pam Lopker's comments in the Preview Case: "I want people in my organization to learn the lessons that come with making decisions: that everything is a compromise, that nothing is ever completely logical, but that you can deal with things through a logical decision-making process." Her comments suggest both the merits and limits of attempting to use the rational model, such as Xerox's six-step process. Clearly, a good feature of this model is that it helps keep people from jumping to premature conclusions about the nature of the problem and course of action to take. It encourages more deliberation, including the search for critical pieces of information.

**Organizational Use.**   One obvious limitation of the rational model is that its full use can take a considerable amount of time. The use of human resources may exceed any benefit. This approach requires considerable data and information, which may be hard to obtain. Moreover, if the situation keeps changing, the decisions selected from a drawn out process may quickly become obsolete. Another limitation is that managers may have to act when goals are vague or conflicting. Even when the rational process is used, decision makers may simply change the stated goals, criteria, or weights if a favored alternative doesn't come out on top. In brief, we suggest using the rational model to the extent feasible but don't expect it to be the sole or even primary guide in making many managerial decisions.[20]

The following Managing Change Competency feature tells how Richard H. Brown, chairman of the board and CEO of Electronic Data Systems (EDS), used elements of the rational model and other decision-making processes. Headquartered in Plano, Texas, EDS is a large information technology services company with about 140,000 employees in 58 countries.

# COMPETENCY:   MANAGING CHANGE

## RICHARD BROWN OF EDS

When Richard Brown arrived at Electronic Data Systems (EDS) in early 1999, he resolved to create a culture that did more than pay lip service to the ideals of collaboration, openness, and decisiveness. The company was known for its bright, aggressive people, but employees had a reputation for competing against one another at least as often as they pulled together—a culture of lone heroes. Individual operating units had little or no incentive to share information or cooperate with one another to win and retain business. There were few sanctions for "lone" behaviors and for failure to meet performance goals. Indecision was common. As one company veteran put it, "Meetings, meetings, and more meetings. People couldn't make decisions, wouldn't make decisions. They didn't have to. No accountability." EDS was losing business, revenue was flat, earnings were declining, and the price of the company's stock was down sharply.

During his first year at EDS, Brown installed six operating mechanisms that signaled he would not put up with the old culture of rampant individualism and information hoarding. One mechanism was the "performance call," as it is known throughout the company. Once a month, the top 100 or so EDS executives worldwide take part in a conference call during which the past month's numbers and crucial activities are reviewed in detail. Openness and information sharing are the rules; information hoarding isn't tolerated. Everyone knows who is on target, who is ahead of projections, and who is behind for the year. Those who are behind must explain the shortfall—and how they plan to get back on track. It's not enough for a manager to say that she's assessing, reviewing, or analyzing a problem. To do so in front of

*For more information on Electronic Data Systems (EDS), visit the organization's home page at http://www.eds.com.*

Brown is to invite two questions in response: When you've finished your analysis, what are you going to do? and How soon are you going to do it? The only way that EDS's managers can answer those questions satisfactorily is to make a decision and execute it.

Brown encourages people to bring conflict to the surface. He views conflict as a sign of organizational health and an opportunity to demonstrate openness and full exploration of an issue. He tries to create a safe environment for disagreement by reminding employees that the conflict isn't personal. Conflict in any global organization is built in. And, Brown believes, it's essential if everyone is going to think in terms of the entire organization, not just one little corner of it. Instead of seeking the solution favorable to their units, managers and employees will look for the solution that's best for EDS and its shareholders.[21]

## BOUNDED RATIONALITY MODEL

The **bounded rationality model** describes the limitations of rationality and emphasizes the decision-making processes often used by individuals or teams. This model helps explain why different individuals or teams may make different decisions when they have exactly the same information. This model also recognizes the reality that complete information—concerning available alternatives or the outcome of some course of action—may be impossible for an individual or team to obtain, regardless of the amount of time and resources applied to the task. As portrayed in Figure 13.3, the bounded rationality model reflects the individual's or team's tendencies to:

1.  select less than the best goal or alternative solution (that is, to satisfice),
2.  undertake a limited search for alternative solutions, and
3.  cope with inadequate information and control of external and internal environmental forces influencing the outcomes of decisions.[22]

**Satisficing.**    **Satisficing** is the tendency to select an acceptable, rather than an optimal, goal or decision. In this case, *acceptable* might mean easier to identify and achieve, less controversial, or otherwise safer than the best alternative. For example, profit goals are often stated as a percentage, such as a 12 percent rate of return on investment or a 6 percent increase in profits over the previous year. These goals may

**Figure 13.3**    **Bounded Rationality Model**

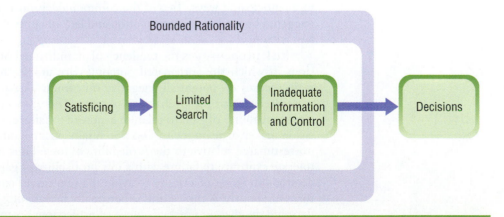

not be the optimal attainable. They may, in fact, reflect little more than top management's view of reasonable goals that are challenging but not impossible to achieve. Herbert Simon, who introduced the bounded rationality model, comments:

> Satisficing doesn't necessarily mean that managers have to be satisfied with what alternative pops up first in their minds or in their computers and let it go at that. The level of satisficing can be raised—by personal determination, setting higher individual or organizational standards, and by the use of an increasing range of sophisticated management science and computer-based decision-making and problem-solving techniques.
>
> As time goes on, you obtain more information about what's feasible and what you can aim at. Not only do you get more information, but in many, if not most, companies there are procedures for setting targets, including procedures for trying to raise individuals' aspiration levels [goals]. This is a major responsibility of top management.[23]

**Limited Search.**    Individuals and teams often make a limited search for possible goals or solutions to a problem, considering alternatives only until they find one that seems adequate. For example, in choosing the "best" job, as a college graduate you won't be able to evaluate every available job in your particular field. You might hit retirement age before obtaining all the information needed for a decision! Even the rational decision-making model recognizes that identifying and assessing alternatives cost time, energy, and money. In the bounded rationality model, an individual or team stops searching for alternatives as soon as an acceptable goal or solution is discovered.

One form of limited search is **escalating commitment**—a process of continuing or increasing the allocation of resources to a course of action even though a substantial amount of feedback indicates that the choice made is wrong. One of the explanations for escalating commitment is that individuals feel responsible for negative consequences, which motivates them to justify previous choices. In addition, individuals may become committed to a choice simply because they believe that consistency in action is a desirable form of behavior. Several years ago, there was an escalating commitment to a single, integrated bag handling system for all airlines at the Denver International Airport. Although numerous problems with the integrated system continued after repeated and expensive failed efforts to resolve them, the key decision makers continued for more than a year to increase their commitment to making it work. They refused to recognize that the problem was the system itself. Finally, as a result of increased pressures from various stakeholders to open the new airport, the integrated bag handling system was scrapped.

**Inadequate Information and Control.**    Decision makers often have inadequate information about problems and face environmental forces that they can't control. These conditions typically have an impact on the process and results of their decisions in unanticipated ways. Two of the common decision-making biases that are partially triggered by inadequate information and lack of control are risk propensity and problem framing.

**Risk propensity** is the tendency of an individual or team to make or avoid decisions in which the anticipated outcomes are unknown. A risk-averse individual or team focuses on potentially negative outcomes. The probability of loss is overestimated relative to the probability of gain. Therefore the decision maker requires a high probability of gain to tolerate exposure to failure. Conversely, a risk-seeking decision maker or team focuses on potentially positive outcomes. Probability of gain is overestimated relative to the probability of loss. Thus risk seekers may be willing to tolerate exposure to failure with a low probability of gain. Some decisions can be understood in terms of a desire to avoid the unpleasant consequences of a decision that turns out poorly. A choice can be personally threatening because a poor result can undermine the decision maker's sense of professional competence, create problems for the organization, and even get the decision maker demoted or fired. Most individuals have a low propensity for risk. They purchase many types of insurance to avoid the risk of large but improbable losses. They invest in savings accounts, CDs, and money market funds to avoid the risk of extreme fluctuations in stocks and bonds. Generally, they prefer decisions that produce satisfactory results more than risky decisions that have the same or higher expected outcomes.[24]

**Problem framing** is the tendency to interpret issues in either positive or negative terms. Individuals or teams in favorable circumstances tend to be risk averse because they think that they have more to lose. In contrast, individuals or teams in unfavorable situations tend to think that they have little to lose and therefore may be risk seeking. Focusing on potential losses increases the importance of risk. In contrast, focusing on potential gains lessens the importance of risk. Thus a positively framed situation fosters risk taking by drawing managerial attention to opportunities rather than the possibility of failure. An example of positive versus negative framing is that of the certainty of wining $6,000 or the 80 percent probability of winning $10,000. Most people prefer the certain gain to the uncertain chance of larger gain. Which would you choose? Although risk aversion commonly is assumed to hold for most decisions, many exceptions have been documented. People prefer to take risks when making a choice between a certain loss and a risky loss. For example, what happens when individuals are asked to choose between the certainty of losing $8,000 and the 80 percent probability of losing $10,000? In this case, most people prefer the risky alternative.[25] Which would you choose?

### Organizational Use.
Decision rules are a part of the bounded rationality model. They provide quick and easy ways for managers to reach a decision without a detailed analysis and search. They are written down and easily applied. A general rule used by organizations—as well as by individuals—is the **dictionary rule**. It involves ranking items the same way a dictionary does: one criterion (analogous to one letter) at a time. The dictionary rule gives great importance to the first criterion. It is valid in decision making only if this first criterion is known to be of overriding importance.[26]

Consider what can happen when management too hastily uses the dictionary rule. The director and his staff at the Ohio Department of Claims experienced a growing backlog of social benefit appeals. They implemented a change in handling procedures. Their brief analysis led to a pooling idea that grouped similar claims for mass handling. However, the analysis failed to focus on the reason for the growing number of claims. After the backlog grew to the point that claims took a year to process, the director discovered a loophole in the legislation that had inadvertently eased eligibility requirements. The director made the legislature aware of the oversight and the loophole was closed. In the meantime, the agency was subjected to constant criticism and legal action for its slow, error-prone claims management. As the incident suggests, managers often want to find out quickly what is wrong and fix it immediately. The all too common result is poor problem definition and a choice of criteria that proves to be misleading. Symptoms are analyzed while more important concerns may be ignored.[27]

Recall one of the comments by Herbert Simon in the previous quote: "The level of satisficing can be raised—by personal determination, setting higher individual or organizational standards, and by the use of an increasing range of sophisticated management science and computer-based decision-making and problem-solving techniques." Knowledge management is an emerging focus for doing so.

**Knowledge management** is the art of adding or creating value by systematically capitalizing on the know-how, experience, and judgment found both within and outside an organization. Knowledge management is a means of raising the level of satisficing.[28] Knowledge is different from data and information. *Data* represent observations or facts having no context and are not immediately or directly useful. *Information* results from placing data within some meaningful context, often in the form of a message. *Knowledge* is that which a person comes to believe and value on the basis of the systematic organized accumulation of information through experience, communication, and inference. Knowledge can be viewed both as a *thing* to be stored and manipulated and as *process* of applying expertise.

Knowledge can be either tacit or explicit. **Tacit knowledge** is developed from direct experience and usually is shared through conversation and storytelling. The campus food director at the University of Washington telling a new manager how to handle abusive students or a sales manager at the Four Seasons Hotel telling a catering person about the habits of a particular client are examples of conveying tacit knowledge. In contrast, **explicit knowledge** is more precise and formally expressed, such as a computer database and software program that creates information and analyses on customer purchasing habits or a training manual describing how to close a sale.

## POLITICAL MODEL

The **political model** describes decision making by individuals to satisfy their own interests. Preferences based on personal self-interest goals seldom change as new information is learned. Problem definition, data search and collection, information exchange, and evaluation criteria are merely methods used to tilt (bias) the outcome in the decision maker's favor.[29]

The distribution of power in an organization and the effectiveness of the tactics used by managers and employees determine the impact of the decisions. The political model doesn't explicitly recognize ethical dilemmas. However, it often draws on two of the self-serving ethical principles discussed previously: (1) the hedonistic principle—do whatever you find to be in your own self-interest; and (2) the might-equals-right principle—you are strong enough to take advantage without respect to ordinary social conventions.

The political model is prevalent in organizations throughout the world. For example, French culture values relatively high power distance. That is, relationships between superiors and subordinates are unequal, with different levels of status and privilege. The political model in French organizations is based on various underlying assumptions and expected behaviors, three of which are as follows.

- Power, once attained, should not be shared except with the inside group of senior managers. Some are born to lead and others to follow; it is difficult for people to change. Secretaries are there to follow orders. Middle managers need to consult with their bosses as well as many others in the organization before making a decision.
- If individuals have been recognized as being top-management material, it does not matter if they are put in a job where they have no experience. Being of superior ability, they should be able to learn how to do their jobs with experience.
- It is harmful to reveal information unnecessarily because then the decision-making process cannot be controlled. When, where, and how to communicate information is a delicate question that often only the upper echelons can decide.[30]

**Organizational Use.**  The political model is most vividly expressed in organizations through the use of various **influence methods**—the means by which individuals or groups attempt to exert power or influence others' behaviors. The influence methods presented in Table 13.4—rational persuasion, inspirational appeal, and consultation—often are the most effective in many workplace situations. The least effective methods seem to be pressure, coalition, and legitimating. However, to assume that certain methods will always work or that others will always fail is a mistake. Differences in effectiveness occur when attempts to influence are downward rather than upward in the organizational hierarchy. Likewise, differences in effectiveness appear when various methods are used in combination rather than independently. This

| Table 13.4 | **Influence Strategies** |
| --- | --- |

| INFLUENCE STRATEGY | DEFINITION |
| --- | --- |
| Rational persuasion | Use logical arguments and factual evidence. |
| Inspirational appeal | Appeal to values, ideals, or aspirations to arouse enthusiasm. |
| Consultation | Seek participation in planning a strategy, activity, or change. |
| Ingratiation | Attempt to create a favorable mood before making request. |
| Exchange | Offer an exchange of favors, share of benefits, or promise to reciprocate at later time. |
| Personal appeal | Appeal to feelings of loyalty or friendship. |
| Coalition | Seek aid or support of others for some initiative or activity. |
| Legitimating | Seek to establish legitimacy of a request by claiming authority or by verifying consistency with policies, practices, or traditions. |
| Pressure | Use demands, threats, or persistent reminders. |

Source: Adapted from Yukl, G., Guinan, P. J., and Sottolano, D. Influence tactics used for different objectives with subordinates, peers, and superiors. *Group & Organization Management*, 1995, 20, 275; Buchanan, D., and Badham, R. *Power, Politics and Organizational Change*. London: Sage, 1999, 64.

process is complex, and to understand fully the effectiveness of various influence strategies requires an understanding of the power sources available, the direction of attempts to influence (i.e., upward, downward, or laterally), and the goals being sought.

Having the *capacity* (power) to influence the behaviors of others and effectively using it aren't the same thing. Managers who believe that they can always effectively influence the behaviors of others by acquiring enough power simply to order other people around generally are ineffective. The ineffective use of power has many negative implications, both for the individual and the organization. For example, the consequences of an overreliance on the pressure method are often negative. Managers who are aggressive and persistent with others—characterized by a refusal to take *no* for an answer, reliance on repeated reminders, frequent use of face-to-face confrontations, and the like—usually suffer negative consequences. Compared to other managers, the managers who rely heavily on the pressure method typically (1) receive the lowest performance evaluations, (2) earn less money, and (3) experience the highest levels of job tension and stress.[31]

The following Managing Self Competency feature reveals the ineffective and incorrect use of influence methods by Douglas Ivester, who was encouraged to resign as the CEO of Coca-Cola in 2000, just 2 years after he was appointed. Most observers attribute much of his downfall to his inability to use politically based influence methods effectively.

## COMPETENCY: MANAGING SELF

### DOUGLAS IVESTER'S BLUNDERS

It doesn't pay to ignore complaints of racial discrimination in promotions, as former Coca-Cola CEO Doug Ivester apparently did. His refusal to confront the issue was part of the reason he lost his job—and why the company ended up in a historic legal settlement, which included an internal race task force with unprecedented power.

Cyrus Mehri was one of the lead attorneys in the racial discrimination lawsuit against the company. He comments: "Ivester was on notice of [racial discrimination] problems as early as 1995 when the leading African-American in the company went to him and said—there is a problem here, there are glass walls, glass ceilings. Ivester apparently took a detailed report, stuck it in his drawer and didn't do anything. In 1997, the U.S. Department of Labor came in and charged that the company had a serious problem. Ivester stuck that report in the drawer and didn't do anything. Then our clients came along in 1998 and confronted the company through internal channels, and the company ignored them. Litigation was the last resort. In November 1999, Ivester demoted Carl Ware, the most senior African American in the corporation and head of its Africa division. In December, Ivester was encouraged to resign [by the board] and replaced with Douglas Daft, who is far-sighted, enlightened. He is going to embrace the settlement."

The class action case—filed in April 1999—was settled with final agreement reached in November 2000. Among its allegations, Mehri said, were that 36 percent of low-level administrative positions at the company are filled by African Americans but that only 7 percent of professional positions and just 1.5 percent of management positions are. A glass ceiling was apparently in place at a company known for its generous contributions to the African American community and for which one in four customers were African American.

Ironically, Carl Ware, the African American who Ivester demoted, had been a lead person in dealing with the employee racial discrimination lawsuit. Through the back-and-forth of the well-publicized suit, Ware had stood at Ivester's side, agreeing to be cohead of a companywide diversity committee. Ware, former president of Atlanta's city council, was the face of Coca-Cola to much of the city and was a symbol of how African Americans could advance at Atlanta's most famous company. Called one of the "12 most powerful blacks in corporate America" by Ebony magazine, Ware was also one of a dozen executives to join President Clinton on a trip to Africa in 1998. "This is a guy you light candles around," said a person close to the board.

So how did Ivester break the demotion news to Ware? By a telephone call to Ware, who was in Europe, say several people. Soon thereafter Ware announced his retirement, to be effective at the end of 2000. To board members and some current and former executives, Ivester's handling of the matter was ham-handed. "Ware was a big blunder," stated a person close to the company.[32]

*For more information on Coca-Cola, visit the organization's home page at http://www.coca-cola.com.*

## STIMULATING ORGANIZATIONAL CREATIVITY

**Learning Objective:**

3. Explain two methods for stimulating organizational creativity.

**Organizational creativity** is the generation of unique and useful ideas by an individual or team in an organization. Innovation builds on unique and useful ideas.[33] Creativity helps employees uncover problems, identify opportunities, and make novel choices in solving problems. In Chapter 8, we presented two approaches for stimulating creativity in organizations—namely, the nominal group technique and brainstorming. In addition, we have discussed various ways of reducing obstructions to creativity and innovation. As suggested in Figure 13.4, three broad categories of obstructions include perceptual, cultural, and emotional blocks.

1. *Perceptual blocks* include such factors as the failure to use all the senses in observing, failure to investigate the obvious, difficulty in seeing remote relationships, and failure to distinguish between cause and effect.

**Figure 13.4**     **Obstructions to Creativity and Innovation**

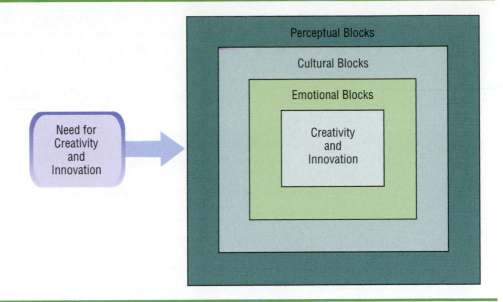

2. *Cultural blocks* include a desire to conform to established norms, overemphasis on competition or conflict avoidance and smoothing, the drive to be practical and narrowly economical above all else, and a belief that indulging in fantasy or other forms of open-ended exploration is a waste of time.

3. *Emotional blocks* include the fear of making a mistake, fear and distrust of others, grabbing the first idea that comes along, and the like.[34] For many organizations, fostering creativity and innovation are essential to their ability to offer high-quality products and services. Two methods, in particular, may be used to foster creativity with any individual or team: the lateral thinking and devil's advocate methods.

## LATERAL THINKING METHOD

The **lateral thinking method** is a deliberate process and set of techniques for generating new ideas by changing an individual's or team's way of perceiving and interpreting information. We can best explain this method by contrasting it with the **vertical thinking method**, which is a logical step-by-step process of developing ideas by proceeding continuously from one bit of information to the next. Table 13.5 presents the primary differences between lateral thinking and vertical thinking. Edward de Bono, the British physician and psychologist who developed the lateral thinking method, stated that the two processes are complementary, not at odds with each other.

Lateral thinking fosters the generation of unique ideas and approaches, and vertical thinking is useful for assessing them. Lateral thinking enhances the effectiveness of vertical thinking by offering it more to select from. Vertical thinking improves the impact of lateral thinking by making good use of the ideas generated. You probably use vertical thinking most of the time, but when you need to use lateral thinking, vertical thinking capabilities won't suffice.[35]

The lateral thinking method includes several techniques for (1) developing an awareness of current ideas and practices, (2) stimulating alternative ways of looking at a problem, and (3) aiding in the development of new ideas. Here, we consider only three of the techniques for fostering the development of new ideas: reversal, analogy, and cross-fertilization.

**Table 13.5**

## Characteristics of Lateral Versus Vertical Thinking

| LATERAL THINKING | VERTICAL THINKING |
|---|---|
| 1. Tries to find new ways for looking at things; is concerned with change and movement. | 1. Tries to find absolutes for judging relationships; is concerned with stability. |
| 2. Avoids looking for what is "right" or "wrong." Tries to find what is different. | 2. Seeks a "yes" or "no" justification for each step. Tries to find what is "right." |
| 3. Analyzes ideas to determine how they might be used to generate new ideas. | 3. Analyzes ideas to determine why they do not work and need to be rejected. |
| 4. Attempts to introduce discontinuity by making "illogical" (free association) jumps from one step to another. | 4. Seeks continuity by logically proceeding from one step to another. |
| 5. Welcomes chance intrusions of information to use in generating new ideas; considers the irrelevant. | 5. Selectively chooses what to consider for generating ideas; rejects information not considered to be relevant. |
| 6. Progresses by avoiding the obvious. | 6. Progresses using established patterns; considers the obvious. |

Source: Based on de Bono, E. *Lateral Thinking: Creativity Step by Step.* New York: Harper & Row, 1970; de Bono, E. *Six Thinking Hats.* Boston: Little, Brown, 1985.

**Reversal Technique.**   The **reversal technique** involves examining a problem by turning it completely around, inside out, or upside down. Engineers at Conoco asked, "What's good about toxic waste?" By so doing, they discovered a substance in refinery waste that they now are turning into both a synthetic lubricant and—they hope—a promising new market. Ronald Barbaro, president of Prudential Insurance, considered the idea, "You die before you die," and came up with "living benefit" life insurance. It pays death benefits to people suffering from terminal illnesses before they die. Prudential has sold more than a million such policies.[36]

**Analogy Technique.**   The **analogy technique** involves developing a statement about similarities among objects, persons, and situations. Some examples of analogies are: This organization operates like a beehive or This organization operates like a fine Swiss watch. The technique involves translating the problem into an analogy, refining and developing the analogy, and then retranslating the problem to judge the suitability of the analogy. If an analogy is too similar to the problem, little will be gained. Concrete and specific analogies should be selected over more abstract ones. Analogies should describe a specific, well-known issue or process in the organization. For an organization that is ignoring increased environmental change, an analogy might be: We are like a flock of ostriches with our heads buried in the sand.

**Cross-Fertilization Technique.**   The **cross-fertilization technique** involves asking experts from other fields to view the problem and suggest methods for solving it from their own areas of expertise. For the technique to be effective, these outsiders should be from fields entirely removed from the problem. An attempt can then be made to apply new methods to the problem. Each year, Hallmark Cards brings to its Kansas City headquarters 50 or more speakers who might provide fresh ideas to the firm's more than 700 artists, designers, writers, editors, and photographers. Also, Hallmark staffers often go from Hallmark's midtown headquarters to a downtown loft, where teams of writers and artists get away from phones to exchange ideas. They also may spend days in retreat at a farm in nearby Kearney, Missouri, taking part in fun exercises, such as building birdhouses.[37]

The following Managing Teams Competency feature describes how the Rich Products Corporation stimulates lateral thinking and attempts to reduce perceptual, cultural, and emotional blocks to innovation and creativity. Rich Products, headquartered in Buffalo, New York, is a family-owned food company that makes more than 2,000 products. The firm has more than 7,000 associates (employees) and sales exceeding $1.4 billion in 75 countries.

## COMPETENCY:    MANAGING TEAMS

### STIMULATING CREATIVITY AT RICH'S

Rich's can claim many product firsts. The world's first frozen nondairy whipped topping. The first frozen bakery product. The first sheeted pizza dough. The list goes on and on. Each new product formulated has solved a problem, met a need, or offered an advantage to customers they'd never had before. Thousands of solutions later, that resolve still holds. The creation of diverse offerings range from toppings and icings to desserts; from breads and rolls to pizza crusts; from sweet baked goods such as cinnamon rolls, cookies, and donuts, to barbecue meat products.

Mindy Rich, the company's executive vice president for innovation comments: "This company was founded on an innovative product. When you grow to 7,000 people, you want those people thinking innovatively and creatively about how they do their jobs. We want to have a company that embraces change and thrives on change. . . . The theory is you have to be willing to try new things. You have to be willing to fail. That's what innovation is all about. We call it fail forward."

Mary Beth Debus, the manager for training and development notes: "Mindy Rich has always said that we use creativity to lead us to innovation and the practical definition of that is making money. Creativity in our organization is strategic. Each department and team has its own scorecard tied to performance appraisals and bonuses and one of the measures is meeting a target for innovation. Last year, for example, each business team was held accountable for implementing four ideas outside its scope, and the company as a whole exceeded that measurement by 600 percent."

Rich's leadership emphasizes that part of creating the right culture and fostering creativity involves putting goals in place around innovation. This encourages managers to capitalize on their teams' innate ingenuity. Individuals and teams on the front lines are seen as having the potential and abilities to be creative, not simply because of who they are, but because of where they are—dealing directly with customers, suppliers, and others. Rich's management sees an important part of its role as channeling creativity in a way that contributes to the firm's long term effectiveness and profitability.[38]

*For more information on Rich Products Corporation, visit the organization's home page at http://www.richs.com.*

### DEVIL'S ADVOCATE METHOD

In the **devil's advocate method**, a person or team—the devil's advocate—develops a systematic critique of a recommended course of action. This critique points out weaknesses in the assumptions underlying the proposal, internal inconsistencies in it, and problems that could lead to failure if it were followed. The devil's advocate acts like a good trial lawyer by presenting arguments against the majority position as convincingly as possible. Figure 13.5 illustrates the basic decision-making process when this method is utilized. Individuals assigned to the devil's advocate role should be rotated

**Figure 13.5**                    **Decision Making with a Devil's Advocate**

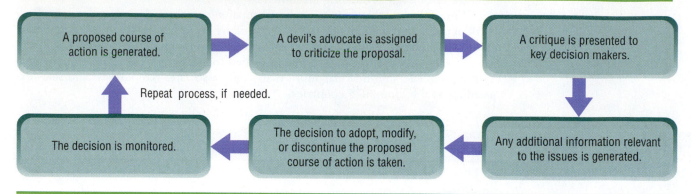

Source: Adapted from Cosier, R. A., and Schrivenk, C. R. Agreement and thinking alike: Ingredients for poor decisions. *Academy of Management*, February 1991, 71.

to avoid any one person or team being identified as a critic on all issues. However, playing this role, even for a short time, may be advantageous for a person and the organization.

Steve Huse, chairperson and CEO of Huse Food Group, indicates that the devil's advocate role is an opportunity for employees to demonstrate their presentation and debating skills. How well someone understands and researches issues is apparent when that person presents a critique. The organization avoids costly mistakes by hearing viewpoints that identify potential pitfalls. In addition, the use of the devil's advocate approach can increase the probability of creative solutions to the problems and reduce the likelihood of groupthink.[39] Recall that groupthink in decision making is caused by excessive consensus and similarity of views in groups—a sure way to kill organizational creativity (see Chapter 8).

The devil's advocate method is effective in helping bring to the surface and challenge assumptions on which a proposed course of action is based—an essential element in fostering creativity. The devil's advocate method shouldn't be overused, and it is best applied to especially important and complex issues.

## CHAPTER SUMMARY

**1.** Explain the basic concepts for making ethical decisions.

Individuals often experience ethical dilemmas when making decisions. We addressed five important issues, which can be stated as questions, in ethical decision making: What is the ethical intensity? What are the principles and rules? Who is affected? What are the benefits and costs? Who has rights?

**2.** Describe the attributes of three models of managerial decision making.

The rational, bounded rationality, and political models are commonly used to explain managerial decision making. Each model explains some aspects of managerial decision-making situations and processes. All three models are needed to grasp the complexity and entire range of decision making.

**3.** Explain two methods for stimulating organizational creativity.

Creativity is needed in changing, complex, and uncertain environments. This situation often results in ambiguity and disagreement over both the goals to be achieved and the best course of action to pursue. Organizational creativity and innovation are crucial to the discovery and implementation of unique and useful ideas. Two approaches for stimulating organizational creativity are the lateral thinking method and the devil's advocate method.

## KEY TERMS AND CONCEPTS

Analogy technique
Bounded rationality model ✓
Concentration of effect
Cross-fertilization technique
Devil's advocate method ✓
Dictionary rule ✓
Disclosure principle ✓
Distributive justice principle ✓
Employment at will
Escalating commitment ✓  *consulting*
Ethical intensity ✓
Ethics
Explicit knowledge
Golden rule principle
Hedonist principle
Influence methods
Knowledge management
Lateral thinking method
Magnitude of consequences

Means–end principle
Might-equals-right principle
Organization interests principle
Organizational creativity
Political model ✓
Probability of effect
Problem framing
Professional standards principle
Proximity
Rational model ✓
Reversal technique
Risk propensity
Satisficing ✓
Social consensus
Tacit knowledge
Temporal immediacy
Utilitarian principle
Values
Vertical thinking method

## DISCUSSION QUESTIONS

1.  Evaluate the ethical intensity of the grading system and practices used by an instructor in a course that you have completed. Your evaluation should include an assessment of each of the six components of ethical intensity.
2.  Review the comments by Pamela Lopker, chairman and president of QAD, Inc., in the Preview Case. Which of these comments are consistent with the attributes of the rational model? With the political model?
3.  What are the differences between the organization interests principle and the utilitarian principle?
4.  What are the differences between the professional standards principle and the distributive justice principle?
5.  Arrange the ethical principles presented in Table 13.2 in rank order from your most preferred to least preferred.

What does this ranking tell you about how you are likely to interpret situations involving ethical dilemmas?
6.  Think of an organization or group in which you are an active member. Describe a choice that seemed to be based on the political model. Why do you think the choice followed the political model?
7.  Think of an important choice you have made within the past year. How did you come to recognize the problem that prompted the stages of decision making and your eventual choice? Was it a good or bad choice? Explain.
8.  Describe a specific problem that you have experienced that was probably affected by the problem framing bias.
9.  What are two differences between the lateral thinking method and the devil's advocate method?

## DEVELOPING COMPETENCIES

### Competency:  Managing Self

### Ethical Dilemmas

#### Susan Johnson's Situation

Susan Johnson is a first-line manager. One of her employees, Meg O'Brien, has been in her department for 8 months. Despite Johnson's repeated efforts at training and coaching, O'Brien is performing below an acceptable level, but the supervisors of three other departments gave her "average" ratings. Johnson talked to these supervisors and discovered that they did so in order to avoid hassles resulting from the employee's likely reaction; they explained that O'Brien files grievances and Equal Employment Opportunity (EEO) complaints regularly. Johnson's supervisor, Barbara Lopez, has told Johnson to give O'Brien an excellent rating and a glowing recommendation for a vacant position in another division to get rid of her.

1. What ethical conflict(s) does Johnson face?
2. In addition to Johnson, O'Brien, and Lopez, who might be affected by Johnson's decision?
3. What actions are open to Johnson?
4. Which of these actions best meets ethical considerations while resolving the situation as positively as possible for the people involved/affected? What ethical principles serve as the basis for your actions?
5. How would you evaluate the ethical intensity of this situation?

### Frank Epps's Situation

Frank Epps is a manager reviewing applications for an open position in his department. One of the company's standard procedures for the hiring process is a background check. Epps's friend, Michael Kee, is one of the applicants and is well qualified for the position. Kee recently told Epps that 12 years ago he embezzled $4,000 from his employer. The employer pressed charges, and Kee was ultimately sentenced to 1 year of probation. According to organizational policy, this incident would disqualify Kee as a candidate for the position. Kee has convinced Epps that the embezzlement was a one-time error in judgment that will never happen again. He has asked Epps not to do the formal background check.[40]

1. What ethical conflict(s) does Epps face?
2. In addition to Epps and Kee, who might be affected by Epps's decision?
3. What actions are open to Epps?
4. Which of these actions best meets ethical considerations while resolving the situation as positively as possible for the people involved/affected? On what ethical principles did you base your response?
5. What level of ethical intensity would you assign to this situation?

## Competency: Managing Change

### Nestlé's CEO on Managing Change

Peter Brabeck-Letmathe is the chief executive officer of Nestlé. Headquartered in Switzerland this firm is the largest food company in the world with some 225,000 employees. The following are brief excerpts from his comments on the preferred decision-making process for managing change.

"Big, dramatic change is fine for a crisis. If you come in as CEO and a turnaround is necessary, then fine, have a revolution. In that situation, change is relatively easy because the whole organization understands that, just to survive, you need to do things differently. They are prepared for change. They understand when you say, The cancer is here, where do I cut?

"But not every company in the world is in crisis all the time. Many companies are like us—not as big, of course—but they are performing well. Growing, innovating, and so forth—good and fit. Why should we manufacture dramatic change? Just for change's sake? To follow some sort of fad without logical thinking behind it? We are very skeptical of any kind of fad and of the self-appointed gurus you hear from all the time, making pronouncements. It is easy to be dogmatic when you don't actually have to run a business. When you run a business, you must be pragmatic. Big, disruptive change programs are anything but that. You cannot underestimate the traumatic impact of abrupt change, the distraction it causes in running the business, the fear it provokes in people, the demands it makes on management's time.

"And frankly, you could make the case that any kind of onetime change program is actually a very worrisome warning—it's a bad sign that a company's leaders have had to make such an intervention. Think of medicine again. If you take preventive care of your health, and you've taken the time for check-ups, you won't wake up one day to find you have to cut off your leg. That is why we see adapting, improving, and restructuring as a continuous process. We put on our books restructuring charges of up to $300 million, before operating profit, as operating expenses, year after year. Most of our competitors—most companies, in fact—would account for these as extraordinary charges. Very different philosophies, no?

"You know, all this talk about reinvention in business reminds me of 1968, when a whole generation thought you couldn't have social change without a revolution. Or of the beginning of the century, with the Marxists, when some people felt they needed to kill millions of people because of some great philosophical idea. I hope we're past that now because it doesn't make sense. Not for society, not for business. Evolution can happen if you believe in it. You can have slow and steady change, and that is nothing to be ashamed of. Our growth has happened without frenzy, without bloodshed. Just constantly challenging people to be better, day by day, bit by bit."[41]

### Questions

1. Which of Brabeck-Letmathe's comments are consistent with the rational model? Explain.
2. Which of his comments are consistent with the bounded rationality model? Explain.

# C H A P T E R

# Designing Organizations

## LEARNING OBJECTIVES

When you have finished studying the chapter, you should be able to:

1. Explain how environmental, strategic, and technological factors affect the design of organizations.
2. State the differences between mechanistic and organic organizations.
3. Describe four traditional organization designs—functional, place, product, and multidivisional.
4. Describe three contemporary organization designs—multinational, network, and virtual.

14

# YUM! BRANDS INC.

Increasing competition and slow sales in the fast-food segment of the restaurant industry made it increasingly difficult for PepsiCo to compete effectively. The benefits that PepsiCo could once bring to the restaurant industry in terms of marketing, low-cost source of beverages, shared advertising expenses, and management became difficult to sustain when PepsiCo's beverage business started to lose significant market share to Coca-Cola, especially in markets outside the United States. In 1997, after disappointing sales from its restaurants, PepsiCo sold off its three restaurants—Pizza Hut, KFC, and Taco Bell—to Yum! Brands. The executives at PepsiCo believed that, if the company could refocus on its core beverage business, its performance would improve—and Yum! Brands believed that performance of the three restaurants would also improve. Since the spinoff, Yum! Brands has purchased the Long John Silver's and A&W restaurants. Its margins have improved almost 4 points (11.6 percent to just over 15 percent) and revenues and profits have grown steadily. Today, Yum! Brands has more than 32,000 restaurants in more than 100 countries and annual sales that exceed $23 billion.

Yum! Brands' managers are aware that two major trends affect competition in the fast-food industry. First, most people are becoming health-conscious and are selective about how they eat. Newer menus that focus on balanced nutrition and good taste are a key to gaining and maintaining market share. Second, the average U.S. family eats about 50 percent of its meals outside the home each week. In 1970, collectively they spent about $6 billion on fast food; in 2002, they spent more than $110 billion, or more on fast food than on higher education, PCs, or new cars.

How have these two trends affected Yum! Brands? Each of its restaurant chains faces a different set of competitors. KFC faces tough competition from Chick-Fil-A, Boston Market, Church's, Popeye's, and other smaller restaurants featuring chicken menus. It serves the conventional fast-food population, along with health-conscious people who buy its rotisserie-cooked chicken. Taco Bell appeals to the fast growing Tex–Mex fast-food segment. It competes with Taco Bueno, and numerous mom-and-pop restaurants. Pizza Hut has traditionally offered sit-down pizza meals, and competes against Pizza Inn, Ceci's, and many local pizzerias. In the home delivery segment, it competes against Domino's, Little Caesar's, Papa John's, and many local mom-and-pop restaurants.

Yum! Brands is committed to global growth and doesn't open international restaurants based on U.S. customer tastes. In Japan, KFC sells tempura crispy strips. In northern England, KFC sells gravy and potatoes, and in Thailand it offers fresh rice with soy or sweet chili sauce. In Holland, KFC makes a potato-and-onion croquette, and in France it sells pastries alongside chicken. Yum! Brands' executives know that local franchise operators need to have flexibility in menus while maintaining quality control and a central marketing standard. For example, in China KFC is the most recognized brand, ahead of Coke and McDonald's. By the end of 2003, Yum! Brands will have more than 590 KFCs and 111 Pizza Huts in 130 cities there, even though the cost of a KFC value meal is equivalent to about 6 hours of the average person's salary in China.

How has Yum! Brands designed its organization to compete in this industry? First, it has invested heavily in technology by designing a management support system for the more than 24,000 local store managers that covers everything from labor and inventory management to product cost analysis and financial reporting. The system is accessed over the Internet and can prompt kitchen staff to make more pepperoni pizzas or automatically order stock when supplies run low. A video on the computer screen can prompt staff to ask, "Would you like fries with that?" All five restaurant chains use the system, saving the need for large-scale investment for each.

*For more information on Yum! Brands Inc., visit the organization's home page at* **http://www.yum.com.**

Second, managers in various regions of the world have autonomy to make decisions for their own regions. For example, in China, there are no governmental laws on franchising, but there are hundreds of laws that influence KFC's operations, which are often enforced at the whim of a governmental official. KFC had to stop serving mashed potatoes temporarily after a government official realized that it didn't have a standard for dried potato-powder imports and stopped all shipments. Sam Su, who heads up Yum! Brands' China operation, immediately contacted government officials and got a standard passed that allowed KFC to continue making mashed potatoes. Much of the cost of doing business in China is based on developing relationship with officials and doing business with the government as a partner. In China,

KFC is run as 18 different companies, many of which are joint ventures with rotating government-appointed chief executives. To help government officials maintain relationships with their constituents, Su regularly hosts small groups of low-income senior citizens for a program of culture and food. After the speech by a local politician and a traditional dance performance celebrating, for example, a good harvest, KFC provides these people with free food. Su also hosts special kids' meal programs and builds playgrounds for children to enjoy. A local actor dressed in a chicken costume, "Chicky," entertains the children. Su also had to inform Yum! Brands employees not to wear "logo" clothes identifying them as Yum! Brands employees when the United States and China are having major international disputes.[1]

How is Yum! Brands organized to compete in the global fast-food industry? The basis for any successful organization is for people to work together and understand how their actions interrelate with the actions of others to support the organization's strategy. Yet talented people in even the best-managed organizations are sometimes left groping to understand how their own activities contribute to their organization's success. An organization's design is crucial in clarifying the roles of managers and employees that hold the organization together. **Organization design** is the process of selecting a structure of tasks, responsibilities, and authority relationships within organizations.[2] The connections among various divisions or departments in an organization can be represented in the form of an organization chart. An **organization chart** is a representation of an organization's internal structure, indicating how various tasks or functions are interrelated. Figure 14.1 shows an abridged Yum! Brands organization chart. Each box represents a specific job, and the lines connecting them reflect the formal lines of communication between individuals performing those jobs.

Organization design decisions often involve the diagnosis of multiple factors, including an organization's culture, power and political behaviors, and job design. Organization design represents the outcomes of a decision-making process that includes environmental factors, strategic choices, and technological factors. Specifically, organization design should:

- ease the flow of information and decision making in meeting the demands of customers, suppliers, and regulatory agencies;
- clearly define the authority and responsibility for jobs, teams, departments, and divisions; and
- create the desired balance of integration (coordination) among jobs, teams, departments, and divisions, with built-in procedures for fast response to changes in the environment.

We frequently refer to departments and divisions as we discuss organization design. The term *department* typically is used to identify a specialized function within an organization, such as human resource, production, accounting, and purchasing. In contrast, the term *division* typically is used to identify a broader, often autonomous part of an organization that performs many, if not all, the functions of the parent organization with respect to a product or large geographic area. Figure 14.1 shows that Pizza Hut is responsible for all the functions involved in developing, producing, and marketing pizzas. Similarly, Taco Bell is responsible for marketing its own Tex–Mex products, as is KFC for its chicken products.

**Figure 14.1**                    **Organization Chart: Yum! Brands Inc.**

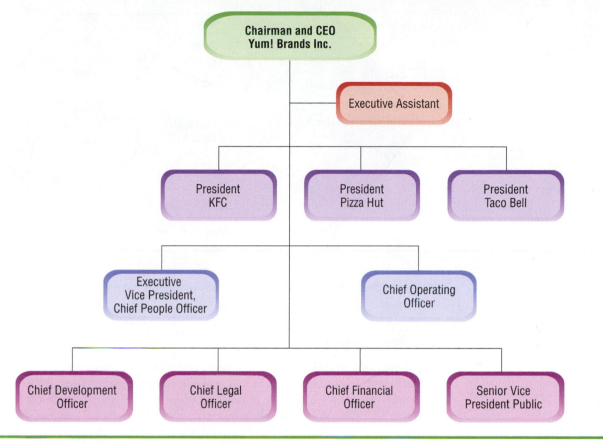

Source: Adapted from personal conversation with Barry Mike, director of internal communications, Pizza Hut, Inc., January 2002; see also http://www.triconglobal.com (January 2002), and http://www.yum.com (September 2002).

In this chapter, we first note how environmental factors, strategic choices, and technological factors can influence the design of an organization.[3] Then, we present an overview of the restaurant industry and how Yum! Brands' design enables it to compete effectively in this industry. Then, we introduce and compare mechanistic and organic organizations and show how each type reflects a basic design decision. Strategic choice by top managers also influences the structure of the organization. Next, we describe the functional, place, product, and multidivisional bases of design and the requirements for their integration. Finally, we describe three emerging approaches to organization design—multinational, network, and virtual organizations. These designs are intended to overcome the limitations of the others in the face of complex, diverse, and changing environments, technologies, and business strategies.

## KEY FACTORS IN ORGANIZATION DESIGN

**Learning Objective:**

1.  Explain how environmental, strategic, and technological factors affect the design of organizations.

Every organization design decision (e.g., greater decentralization and empowerment of employees) solves one set of problems but creates others. At Yum! Brands, giving Su authority to cater to the local Chinese market's tastes and customs increases sales at KFC, but violates Yum! Brands' need to have a consistent set of practices in all stores. Because every organization design has some drawbacks, the key is to select one that minimizes them. Figure 14.2 identifies several variables for each of the three primary factors—environmental, strategic, and technological—that affect organization design decisions. Other factors (e.g., suppliers, customers, and new competitors)

**Figure 14.2**                    **Key Factors in Organization Design**

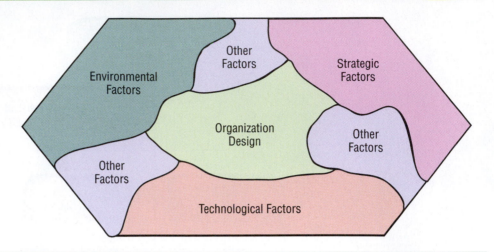

can also affect the design of an organization, but we have chosen these three as most important.

## ENVIRONMENTAL FACTORS

The environmental factors that managers and employees need to be aware of are (1) the characteristics of the present and possible future environments and (2) how they affect the organization's ability to function effectively. Hypercompetition in some industries, including consumer electronics, airlines, and personal computers, is requiring managers to adopt new ways of thinking about their environments. As markets become global and competition escalates, the quest for productivity, quality, and speed has spawned a remarkable number of new organization designs. Yet, many organizations have been frustrated by their inability to redesign themselves quickly enough to stay ahead of their rivals.

Perhaps the best way to understand the impact of the environment on organization design is to look at the various factors that comprise the environment. Every organization exists in an environment and, although specific environmental factors vary from industry to industry, a few broad ones exert an impact on the strategies of most organizations. We chose the four that we believe to be most important.[4] As shown in Figure 14.3, they are suppliers, distributors, competitors, and customers.

**Suppliers.**   To obtain required materials, an organization must develop and manage relationships with its suppliers. Yum! Brands' goal is to secure high-quality materials at reasonable prices. To accomplish this goal, it has established long-term contracts with many suppliers in which it agrees to purchase from them certain quantities of flour, pepperoni, sausage, cheese, beef, vegetables, and the like. Yum! Brands buys 85 percent of its ingredients locally. As chicken is a major ingredient for KFC, Yum! Brands has entered into long-term contracts with Pilgrim's Pride, Purdue, and other chicken raisers to supply its KFC restaurants. Similarly, McDonald's also has a long-term contract with J.R. Simplot to supply it with potatoes. To supply McDonald's, Simplot has contracts with more than 1,000 potato growers throughout the world. Such long-term contracts by both Yum! Brands and McDonald's ensure product uniformity, cost stability, and delivery reliability. Customers are drawn to familiar brands and expect reasonable cost and product consistency.

Another supplier in this industry is the worker. In the United States there are roughly 3.5 million fast-food workers, by far the largest group of minimum wage earners. The automation of the restaurant kitchen has enabled fast-food chains to rely

**Figure 14.3**                    **Forces in an Organization's Environment**

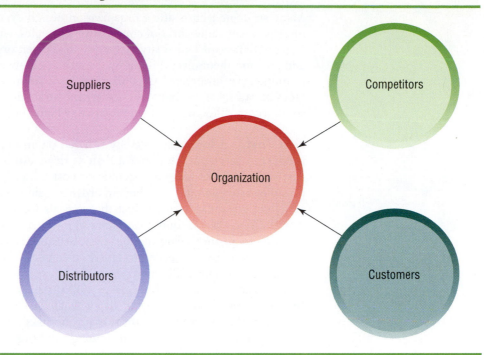

on low-paid and unskilled workers. Turnover is over 150 percent a year in many restaurants.

**Distributors.**   An organization must establish channels of distribution that give it access to customers. Distributors are the various organizations that help another organization deliver and sell its products. Yum! Brands distributes its products through franchisees and company owned stores. Store managers can develop personalized relationships with customers and devise ways to offer them good quality in both sales and service. Bill Heinecke brought the franchise rights for Pizza Hut in Thailand in 1980 for $5,000. At that time, pizza wasn't sold in Thailand, and cheese wasn't a popular part of a person's diet. Through aggressive advertising, he was able to introduce Pizza Hut's fast-food restaurants in Thailand. Today, he has a chain of more than 114 restaurants, which have made him a multimillionaire.

**Competitors.**   Competitors can also influence the design of an organization. As mentioned in the Preview Case, Yum! Brands' five restaurant chains face a large number of competitors, including McDonald's, Wendy's, Burger King, Pizza Inn, and Papa John's, in addition to millions of local mom-and-pop restaurants. In this industry, organizations compete on price and value. To be inexpensive requires organization designs that are simple and easy to manage. Cost savings must be gained at every step of the process, including labor, raw materials, acquisition of land, and construction.

**Customers.**   Relationships with customers are vital. Customers can easily evaluate the costs of various products and easily switch buying habits with minimal inconvenience. Yum! Brands tries to manage customer relationships in several ways. On a global level, the company engages in massive countrywide advertising campaigns to create product awareness in customers. In the United States, Yum! Brands has combined its five product lines into one outlet offering multiple products. These outlets usually are tied in with gas stations and are located primarily along interstate highways. Internationally, permitting regional managers to fine-tune their marketing campaigns to fit local customs is important.

## STRATEGIC FACTORS

Many strategic factors affect organization design decisions. We focus on one of the most popular frameworks of competitive strategies, which was developed by Michael Porter of Harvard University. According to Porter, organizations need to distinguish and position themselves differently from their competitors in order build and sustain a competitive advantage.[5] Organizations have attempted to build competitive advantages in various ways, but three underlying strategies appear to be essential in doing so: low cost, differentiation, and focused, which are illustrated in Figure 14.4.

**Low Cost.** A **low-cost strategy** is based on an organization's ability to provide a product or service at a lower cost than its rivals. An organization that chooses a low-cost strategy seeks to gain a significant cost advantage over other competitors and pass the savings on to consumers in order to gain market share. Such a strategy aims at selling a standardized product that appeals to an "average" customer in a broad market. The organization must attain significant economies of scale in key business activities (e.g., purchasing and logistics). Because the environment is stable, few product modifications are needed to satisfy customers. The organization's design is functional, with accountability and responsibility clearly assigned to various departments.

Organizations that have successfully used a low-cost strategy include Yum! Brands in fast-food restaurants, Black & Decker in power tools, BIC in ballpoint pens, and Wal-Mart in discount stores. The risks involved in following this strategy are (1) getting "locked in" to a technology and organization design that is expensive to change, (2) the ability of competitors to copy the strategy (e.g., Target copying Wal-Mart), or, most important, (3) management not paying attention to shifts in the environment (e.g., customer demand for different types of products and/or services and losing market share, as happened at Kmart).

The low-cost strategy is based on locating and taking advantage of opportunities for an organization to seek cost-based advantages in all its activities. One firm that has succeeded in implementing this strategy is 7-Eleven. It didn't arrive at this strategy without problems. In the mid 1980s, it expanded rapidly into various businesses, including a dairy, gasoline refining, and office rental space. It even constructed a

**Figure 14.4**         **Strategies Model**

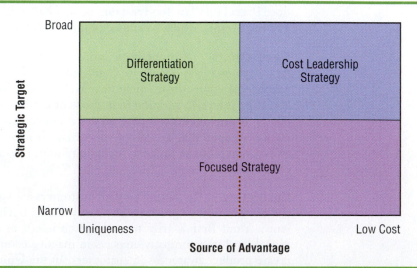

Source: Adapted with the permission of The Free Press, a division of Simon & Schuster, from *Competitive Strategy: Techniques for Analyzing Industries and Competitors* (p. 39) by Michael E. Porter. Copyright © 1980 by The Free Press.

46-floor office tower in Dallas and leased office space to organizations in the Dallas area. Unfortunately, the recession of 1989–1990, the rise of numerous nontraditional competitors (e.g., Shell, Exxon/Mobil, and ChevronTexaco) in the convenience store industry, and the collapse of the Dallas real estate market brought the firm into bankruptcy. Ito-Yokado purchased the company in 1990 and immediately sold off all businesses not directly related to the convenience stores and adopted a low-cost business strategy.  The following Managing Change Competency feature illustrates some of the ways that 7-Eleven achieves its low-cost advantage.

## COMPETENCY:   MANAGING CHANGE

### 7-ELEVEN

7-Eleven uses sophisticated computer systems to manage its inventory. Each 7-Eleven store is equipped with a personal computer network that records every purchase made. These data are fed directly from the cash register into the store's computer. The information generated by each store enables the store manager to make such decisions about which items to add and drop, when to reorder, and what the proper inventory level for different items should be. This system permits fast recording of products directly from manufacturers such as Coca-Cola, PepsiCo, and Frito-Lay. It also enables the manufacturers to improve their forecasts of product demand.

To further reduce costs, 7-Eleven consolidated a number of its delivery operations for regional markets into combined mega-distribution centers. For example, the distribution system in Irving, Texas, serves North Texas 7-Elevens. PepsiCo, Coca-Cola, American Brands, and Interstate Bakeries, among others, ship their goods to this centralized site rather than to each store. 7-Eleven then delivers everything a store needs in one shipment each day. This system enables the company to offer a variety of fresh food, such as deli-style sandwiches and fresh fruit, two major growth product lines for 7-Eleven, and minimizes distribution costs.

7-Eleven uses one advertising agency for its promotion and marketing. This exclusive contract eases the coordination, design, and implementation of nationwide advertising campaigns. Its ads reflect low price, fast replacement of fresh food, and quality name brands.

7-Eleven locates its stores in high-traffic areas, such as strip shopping centers or busy street corners in large cities. The rental cost per square foot is considerably cheaper in these locations than in shopping malls. These locations also permit shoppers to drive or walk directly to the stores. And because these stores are smaller than the typical grocery store, shoppers have less difficulty locating merchandise and need to spend less time in the store (the typical shopper buys less than five items at a time). Most 7-Eleven stores are open 24 hours a day,  spreading the cost of operating the stores over 24 hours. Finally, employees are paid slightly above the minimum wage. The turnover rate is 180 percent per year. Employees receive some training in how to use the systems that manage the stores, but this training period is short.[6]

*For more information on 7-Eleven, visit the organization's home page at http://www. 7-eleven.com.*

**Differentiation.**   A **differentiation strategy** is based on providing customers with something unique and makes the organization's product or service distinctive from its competition. An organization that chooses a differentiation strategy typically uses a product organization design whereby each product has its own manufacturing, marketing, and research and development (R&D) departments. The key managerial assumption behind this strategy is that customers are willing to pay a higher price for a product that is distinctive in some way. Superior value is achieved through higher quality, technical superiority, or some special appeal. Toyota's strategy with Lexus is based on exceptional manufacturing quality, the use of genuine wood paneling, advanced sound systems, high engine performance, and comparatively high fuel economy (for luxury cars).

Other organizations that have successfully used a differentiation strategy include Procter & Gamble in a variety of product lines, American Express in credit cards, Nordstrom in department stores, and Krups in coffeemakers and espresso makers. The biggest disadvantage that these organizations face is maintaining a price premium as the product becomes more familiar to customers. Price is especially an issue when a product or service becomes mature. Organizations may also overdo product differentiation, which places a burden on their R&D departments, as well as a drain on their financial and human resources. Nissan faced this issue during the 1990s. The carmaker had created so many different models of automobiles that customers became confused and production costs soared. Nissan scaled back the number of models, but it still lags behind its competitors in styling.

**Focused.**    A **focused strategy** is designed to help an organization target a specific niche in an industry, unlike both the low-cost and the differentiation strategies, which are designed to target industrywide markets. An organization that chooses a focused strategy may utilize any of a variety of organization designs, ranging from functional to product to network, to satisfy its customers' preferences. The choice of organization design reflects the niche of a particular buyer group, a regional market, or customers that have special tastes, preferences, or requirements. The basic idea is to specialize in ways that other organizations can't match effectively.

Organizations that have successfully used a focused strategy include Karsten Manufacturing, Southwest Airlines, and Chaparral Steel. Karsten Manufacturing has implemented its focused strategy by designing and producing a line of golf clubs under the Ping label. It was able to carve out a defensible niche in the hotly contested golf equipment business. Karsten uses ultrasophisticated manufacturing equipment and composite materials to make golf clubs almost on a customized basis. Southwest Airlines is among the most profitable airlines in the industry. It achieved its success by focusing on short-haul routes, flying into airports located close to or within cities, not serving meals, not transferring baggage, and offering no reserved seating.

The greatest disadvantage that an organization faces in using a focused strategy is the risk that its underlying market niche may gradually shift toward a broader market. Distinctive customer tastes may "blur" over time, thus reducing the defensibility of the niche. For example, when Calloway Golf introduced its own line of golf equipment, it targeted the same customers that Karsten had targeted. In an attempt to differentiate Ping from Calloway, Karsten introduced a broader line of clubs that would appeal to the wider golfing public, thus losing its distinctive niche in the market place.

## TECHNOLOGICAL FACTORS

**Technology** is a process by which an organization changes inputs into outputs. Although there are literally hundreds of technologies, we focus on how in general technology influences the design of an organization. The coordination of teams and departments, the delegation of authority and responsibility, and the need for formal integrating mechanisms are all influenced by the degree to which units must communicate with each other to accomplish their goals. At Yum! Brands, each global product division is a profit center and responsible for its own restaurants, R&D, human resources, and marketing. As we noted earlier, some of its information management support systems cross the five product lines. When the company uses a product organization design, responsibility for coordinating products is in the hands of product managers, not regional managers. Therefore one of the primary differences between the geographic design and the product design is the degree to which local managers responsible for various products share information and resources.

**Task Interdependence.**   **Task interdependence** refers to the extent to which work performed by one person or department affects what other members do.[7] Three types of task interdependence have been identified—pooled, sequential, and reciprocal—and are shown in Figure 14.5.

- *Pooled interdependence* occurs when departments or teams are relatively autonomous and make an identifiable contribution to the organization. For example, the many sales and services offices of State Farm Insurance don't engage in day-to-day decision making, coordination, and communication with each other. The local State Farm agents operate their offices without much interaction with other agents. Managers in regional offices coordinate, set policies, and solve problems for agents in their territories. The performance of each agent and regional office is readily identifiable. Pooled interdependence exists when the performance of one person has no direct impact on that of another. Golf and tennis teams rely on pooled interdependence. The scores of the players on each team are added at the end of the match to arrive at the team's total, even though the players on each team may not see or talk with their teammates during play.
- *Sequential interdependence* occurs when one team or department must complete certain tasks before one or more other teams or departments can perform their tasks. Football teams use sequential interdependence. When the offense is on the field, the defense is resting, waiting to return to the field.  British Petroleum uses sequential interdependence to deliver gasoline and other products to a variety of

**Figure 14.5**              **Types of Task Interdependence in Organization Design**

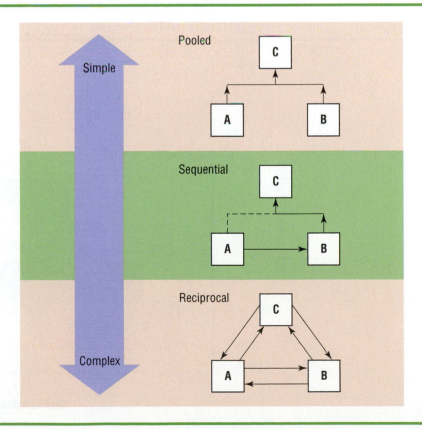

consumers. This process starts with exploration (the search for crude oil and natural gas), production (drilling of wells for retrieval of gas and oil), supply (transport of the raw material via ship and/or pipeline to refineries), refining (the breakdown of hydrocarbons into various byproducts), distribution (transportation of product by pipeline, truck, or rail), and marketing (the sale of products to the customer). The flow of materials is always the same. A predetermined order or flow of activities defines sequential interdependence.

- *Reciprocal interdependence* occurs when the outputs from one team or department become the inputs for another team or department and vice versa. Basketball, soccer, hockey, and volleyball teams rely on reciprocal interdependence. Essentially, reciprocal interdependence exists when all units within an organization depend on one another to produce an output. Figure 14.5 shows that reciprocal interdependence is the most complex type and that pooled interdependence is the simplest type of technological interdependence. The greater the interdependence among teams or departments, the greater is the need for coordination. Placing reciprocally interdependent teams or departments under one executive often improves integration and minimizes information processing costs within a unit. For example, in Yum! Brands' Pizza Hut division, the marketing research, advertising, and sales departments all report to the vice president of marketing for that product line. Employees in these departments must communicate and coordinate more with each other than, for example, with employees in the Taco Bell division.

## INTEGRATIVE FRAMEWORK

Figure 14.6 illustrates seven commonly used approaches to organization design. These approaches, and the conditions under which they are most likely to be effec-

**Figure 14.6**    **Organization Design Options**

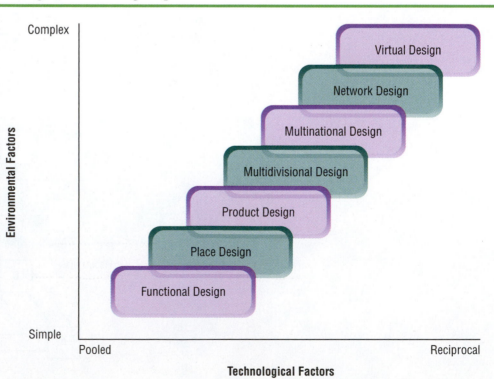

tive, are contrasted in terms of the key factors in organization design. Environmental forces comprise a continuum on the vertical axis, ranging from simple to complex. Technological interdependence comprises a continuum on the horizontal axis, ranging from pooled to reciprocal. At one end of the continuum is a cluster of choices that reflect uniformity in customers, technologies, and geographic markets, represented by firms such as Avis Rent-a-Car, Allstate Insurance Company, and Motel 6. At the other end of the continuum are organization design choices that reflect diversity in customers, technologies, and geographic markets, represented by firms such as Procter & Gamble, DuPont, and General Electric.

The comparative framework broadly portrays how the design of an organization may differ and change as a result of various patterns of environmental and technological factors. The simplest environment (lower left) implies that some version of the functional organization design is likely to be appropriate. The most complex environment (upper right) implies that some form of the network or virtual organization design is likely to be appropriate. In general, designs become more complex as an organization moves from a functional design to a network design. Moreover, the designs require more coordination among people and activities as they become increasingly complex.

**Learning Objective:**

2.  State the differences between mechanistic and organic organizations.

# MECHANISTIC AND ORGANIC ORGANIZATIONS

A **mechanistic organization** is designed so that individuals and functions will behave in predictable ways. A reliance on formal rules and regulations, centralization of decision making, narrowly defined job responsibilities, and a rigid hierarchy of authority characterize this organization.[8] The emphasis is on following procedures and rules. If you've ever worked at McDonald's, you probably know how highly standardized each step of the most basic operations must be. For example, boxes of fries are stored two inches from the wall and one inch apart. The operations are the same, whether in Tokyo or Dallas.

In contrast, an **organic organization** is characterized by low to moderate use of formal rules and regulations, decentralized and shared decision making, broadly defined job responsibilities, and a flexible authority structure with fewer levels in the hierarchy. The degree of job specialization is low; instead, a broad knowledge of many different jobs is required. Self-control is expected and there is an emphasis on coordination among employees. Recently, more organizations are moving toward an organic management approach to promote managerial efficiency and to improve employee satisfaction. Many employees heavily involved in R&D at Intel Corporation, Philips Electronics, and Hewlett-Packard, among others, are likely to enjoy decision-making autonomy.

Top management typically makes decisions that determine the extent to which an organization will operate mechanistically or organically. At Yum! Brands, the five groups of restaurants operated throughout the world with relative autonomy (pooled interdependence) until top management decided to merge some of these operations into one at major self-service gas stations in the United States. This move created the need for vastly more coordination of operations.

A mechanistic organization is essentially a bureaucracy. Max Weber, a German sociologist and economist in the early 1900s, defined a bureaucracy as an organization having the following characteristics.

*   The organization operates according to a body of rules or laws that are intended to tightly control the behavior of employees.
*   All employees must carefully follow extensive impersonal rules and procedures in making decisions.

- Each employee's job involves a specified area of expertise, with strictly defined obligations, authority, and powers to compel obedience.
- The organization follows the principle of hierarchy; that is, each lower position is under the tight control and direction of a higher one.
- Candidates for jobs are selected on the basis of "technical" qualifications. They are appointed, not elected.
- The organization has a career ladder. Promotion is by seniority or achievement and depends on the judgment of superiors.[9]

The word **bureaucracy** often brings to mind rigidity, incompetence, red tape, inefficiency, and ridiculous rules. In principle, though, the basic characteristics of a mechanistic system may make a bureaucratic organization design feasible or even desirable in some situations. Any discussion of a mechanistic organization must distinguish between the way it should ideally function and the way some large-scale organizations actually operate.

The degrees to which organizations emphasize a mechanistic or an organic system can vary substantially, as suggested in Figure 14.7. Radio Shack and Target have relatively mechanistic organizations in terms of the selected dimensions. They are represented by organization B. Cisco Systems, Ernst & Young, and Microsoft place more emphasis on the dimensions that represent an organic system. They are represented by organization A. The organic system emphasizes employee competence, rather than the employee's formal position in the hierarchy, as a basis for rewards, including promotion. This type of organization has a flexible hierarchy and empowers employees to make decisions.

**Figure 14.7**  **Organic and Mechanistic Design Features**

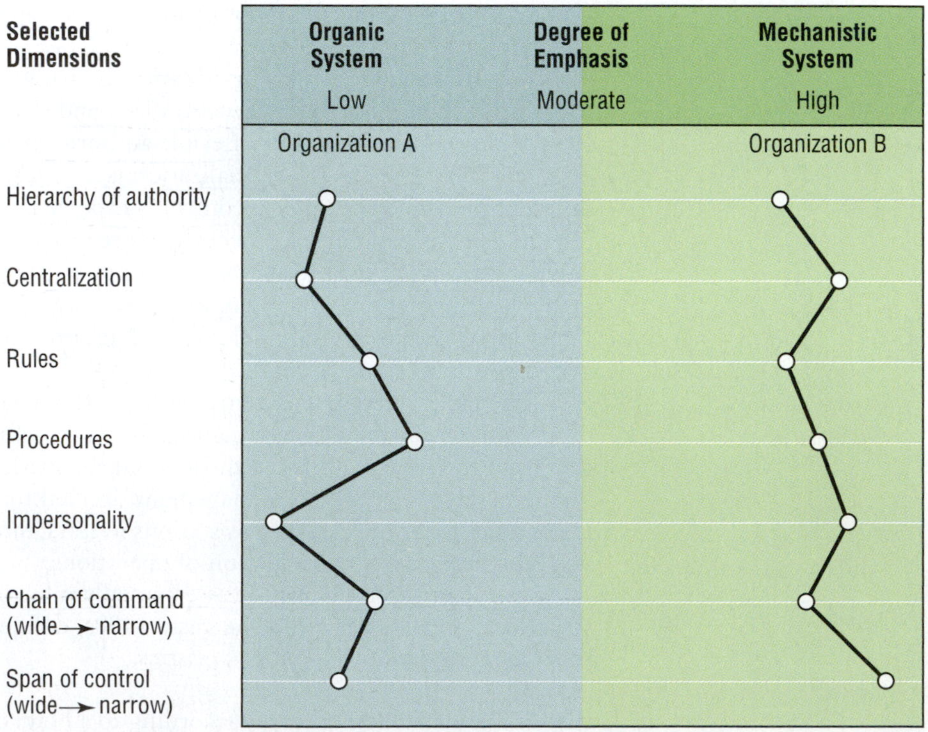

## HIERARCHY OF AUTHORITY

**Hierarchy of authority** indicates who reports to whom. For example, Yum! Brands' organization chart (see Figure 14.1) shows that the chief financial officer reports to the chairman and CEO of Yum! Brands. In a mechanistic system, higher level departments set or approve goals and detailed budgets for lower level departments and issue directives to them. A mechanistic organization has as many levels in its hierarchy as necessary to achieve tight control. An organic organization has few levels in its hierarchy, which makes coordination and communication easier and fosters innovation.

The hierarchy of authority is closely related to centralization. **Centralization** means that all major, and oftentimes many minor, decisions are made only at the top levels of the organization. Centralization is common in mechanistic organizations, whereas decentralization and shared decision making between and across levels are common in organic organizations. At Jiffy Lube, Wendy's, and Pier I Imports, top executives make nearly all decisions affecting store operations, including hours of operation, dress codes for employees, starting salaries, advertising, location, and the like. Rules and regulations are sent from headquarters to each store, and detailed reports (e.g., sales, employee attendance, etc.) from the stores are sent up the hierarchy.

## DIVISION OF LABOR

**Division of labor** refers to the various ways of dividing up tasks and labor to achieve goals. A mechanistic organization typically has a high division of labor. In theory, the fewer the tasks a person performs, the better he may be expected to perform them. However, a continued increase in the division of labor may eventually become counterproductive. Employees who perform only very routine and simple jobs that require few skills may become bored and frustrated. The results may be low quality and productivity, high turnover, and high absenteeism. This situation developed in numerous U.S. industries (e.g., automobile, consumer electronics, and steel). Excessive division of labor was compounded by rigid union work rules, which eventually compromised these companies' ability to respond to new technologies and customer needs. In addition, the managerial costs (volume of reports, more managers, and more controls to administer) of integrating highly specialized functions usually are high. Many companies in the fast-food industry, including McDonald's, Wendy's, and Burger King, report that employee turnover exceeds 150 percent a year. To cope with such high turnover, most processes are automated and can be quickly learned.

In contrast, the organic organization tends to reduce the costs of high turnover by delegating decision making to lower levels. Delegation encourages employees and teams to take responsibility for achieving their tasks and linking them to those of others in the organization. The organic organization takes advantage of the benefits from the division of labor, but it is sensitive to the negative results of carrying the division of labor too far.

## RULES AND PROCEDURES

**Rules** are formal statements specifying acceptable and unacceptable behaviors and decisions by employees. One of the paradoxes of rules that attempt to reduce individual autonomy is that someone must still decide which rules apply to specific situations. Rules are an integral part of both mechanistic and organic organizations. In a mechanistic organization, the tendency is to create detailed uniform rules to cover tasks and decisions whenever possible. United Parcel Service (UPS) has rules that cover all aspects of delivering a package to a customer, including which arm to carry the clipboard under (right arm) for the person to sign and which arm to carry the package with (left arm). In a mechanistic organization, the tendency is to accept the need for extensive rules and to formulate new rules in response to new situations. In an organic system, the tendency is to create rules only when necessary (e.g., safety rules to protect life and property).

**Procedures** refer to preset sequences of steps that managers and employees must follow in performing tasks and dealing with problems. Procedures often comprise rules that are to be used in a particular sequence. For example, to obtain reimbursement for travel expenses in most organizations, employees must follow specific reporting procedures, including submission of receipts. Procedures have many of the same positive and negative features that characterize rules, and they often proliferate in a mechanistic organization. Managers in organic systems usually know that rules and procedures can make the organization too rigid and thus dampen employee motivation, stymie innovation, and inhibit creativity. Employee input is likely to be sought on changes in current rules and procedures or on proposed rules and procedures when they are absolutely necessary. Employees at all levels are expected to question, evaluate, and make suggestions about such proposals, with an emphasis on collaboration and communication. In a mechanistic system, rules and procedures tend to be developed at the top and issued via memoranda. Such memos may convey the expectation of strict compliance and the adverse consequences of not complying.

## IMPERSONALITY

**Impersonality** is the extent to which organizations treat their employees, customers, and others according to objective, detached, and rigid characteristics. Managers in a highly mechanistic organization are likely to emphasize matter-of-fact indicators (college degrees, certificates earned, test scores, training programs completed, length of service, and the like) when making hiring, salary, and promotion decisions. Although managers may consider these factors in an organic organization, the emphasis is likely to be on the actual achievements and professional judgments of individuals rather than on rigid quantitative indicators.

Deloitte Consulting is a leading business consulting company that operates as an organic organization. A college graduate applying for a job at Deloitte Consulting goes through an extensive interview process. It may involve several managers, many (if not all) of the employees with whom the applicant would work, and even a casual and informal "interview" by a team of employees. The person responsible for filling the open position solicits opinions and reactions from these employees before making a decision. In most instances, the manager calls a meeting of the employees and other managers who participated in the interview process to discuss a candidate.

## CHAIN OF COMMAND

Early writers on organization design stressed two basic ideas about who reports to whom and who has what authority and responsibility.[10] First, the **chain of command** refers to the hierarchical arrangement of authority and responsibility. They flow in a clear, unbroken vertical line from the highest executive to the lowest employee. Clarity of direction is the basis for the chain. Second, the **unity of command** holds that no subordinate should receive direction from more than one superior. Although some organizations don't rigidly follow unity of command in their designs, overlapping lines of authority and responsibility can make both managing and production tasks more difficult than they should be. Without unity of command, who may direct whom to do what becomes cloudy and confusing. Recall that, in the Preview Case, Yum! Brands' country managers have the authority to make decisions about advertising and slight changes to the menu. Managers in various countries report to the presidents of their product lines. Issues surrounding chain of command and unity of control must be addressed in all organization designs.

## SPAN OF CONTROL

**Span of control** reflects the number of employees reporting directly to one manager. When the span of control is broad, relatively few levels exist between the top and bottom of the organization, as in many R&D labs. At Yum! Brands, the chairman and CEO has a span of control of 10 (see Figure 14.1). Conversely, in a military unit, the span of control is narrower because officers and noncoms need tight control over subordinates in order to get them to respond quickly and precisely. Although there is no "correct" number of subordinates that a manager can supervise effectively, the competencies of both the manager and employees, the similarity of tasks being supervised, and the extent of rules and operating standards all influence a manager's span of control.

In tomorrow's global environment many firms will find that, in order to stay competitive, they must change how they manage. Management blunders by AT&T, Eastman Kodak, and Ford Motor Company have occurred because of their inability to adapt to the speed and turbulence of a changing environment. In some cases, even after massive high-tech investments, management is only beginning to make the organizational changes needed to transform their organizations.

## TRADITIONAL ORGANIZATION DESIGNS

Now that we have examined the various factors that affect managers' choices of an organization design, let's consider some of the design choices available. As we discuss them, we refer to the factors that influence a particular choice of design.

### FUNCTIONAL DESIGN

**Functional design** involves the creation of positions, teams, and departments on the basis of specialized activities. Functional grouping of employees is the most widely used and accepted form of departmentalization. Although the functions vary widely, depending on the organization (e.g., Christ United Methodist Church does not have a production department, nor does Wells Fargo Bank), grouping tasks and employees by function can be both efficient and economical.

**Key Features.**   Departments of a typical manufacturing firm with a single product line often are grouped by function—engineering, human resource, manufacturing, shipping, purchasing, sales, and finance. Tasks also are usually divided functionally by the process used—receiving, stamping, plating, assembly, painting, and inspection (sequential interdependence). Figure 14.8 shows how Pizza Hut uses this organization design.[11] A common theme of functional design is the desirability of standardizing repetitive tasks and automating them whenever possible. This approach helps reduce errors and lowers costs. Management then concentrates on exceptions to eliminate gaps or overlaps.

**Organizational Uses.**   A functional design has both advantages and disadvantages. On the positive side, it permits clear identification and assignment of responsibilities, and employees easily understand it. People doing similar tasks and facing similar problems work together, thus increasing the opportunities for interaction and mutual support. A disadvantage is that a functional design fosters a limited point of view that focuses on a narrow set of tasks. Employees tend to lose sight of the organization as a whole. Coordination across functional departments often becomes difficult as the organization increases the number of geographic areas served and the range of goods or services provided. With the exception of marketing, most employees in a functionally designed organization have no direct contact with customers and often lose touch with the need to meet or exceed customer expectations.

**Figure 14.8**                          **Organization Chart: Pizza Hut**

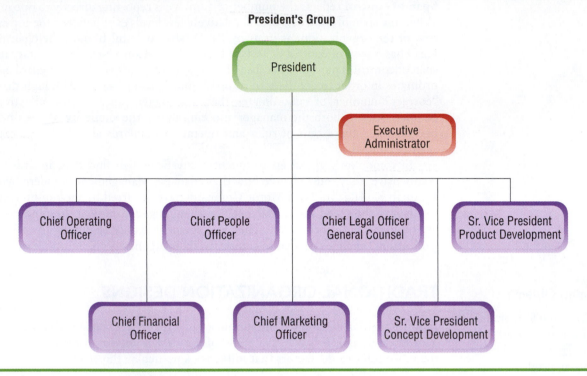

Source: Adapted from personal conversation with Barry Mike, director of internal communications, Pizza Hut, Inc., January 2002; see also http://www.triconglobal.com (January 2002), and http://www.yum.com (September 2002).

A functional design may be effective when an organization has a narrow product line, competes in a uniform environment, pursues a low-cost or focused business strategy, and doesn't have to respond to the pressures of serving different types of customers. The addition of staff departments, such as legal or quality assurance, to a functional design may enable an organization to deal effectively with changes in the organization's environment. As shown in Figure 14.8, functional design is the most elementary type of organization design and often represents a base from which other types of designs evolve.

## PLACE DESIGN

**Place design** involves establishing an organization's primary units geographically while retaining significant aspects of functional design. All functional groups for one geographic area are in one location. Starbucks uses a place design, with the United States divided into six regions. The regions are managed by regional vice presidents who are accountable for the operations and profitability of stores in their areas. Many companies that are marketing-intensive and need to respond to local market conditions or customer needs typically use place designs.

**Key Features.**    Many of the functions required to serve a geographic territory are placed under one manager, rather than assigning different functions to different managers or consolidating many of the functions in a central office. Many international firms use place design to address cultural and legal differences in various countries and the lack of uniformity among customers in different geographic markets.[12] For example, Kendall Healthcare Products Company established a German subsidiary to manufacture locally and market a broad line of products developed in the United

States for German consumption. In this case, localized manufacturing makes sense because health-care product standards vary considerably from country to country. Moreover, the German health-care system has long been a major consumer of Kendall's products.[13]

**Organizational Uses.**    Place design has several potential advantages. Each department or division is in direct contact with customers in its locale and can adapt more readily to their demands. Fast response is a major asset for organizations using place designs. For Celanese Chemical Corporation, it means locating plants near raw materials or suppliers. Potential gains may include lower costs for materials, freight rates, and (perhaps) labor costs. In 1998, Hoechst opened a new plant in Singapore to serve the growing demand for its products in the Far East. It saved millions of dollars in shipping costs (from the United States) and was able to deliver products to customers in Hong Kong, Malaysia, and Laos much faster than before.[14] For marketing, locating near customers might mean lower costs and/or better service. Salespeople can spend more time selling and less time traveling. Being closer to the customer may help them pinpoint the marketing tactic most likely to succeed in that particular region.

Organizing by place clearly increases control and coordination problems. If regional units have different personnel, purchasing, and distribution procedures, management may have difficulty achieving coordination. Further, regional and district managers may want to control their own internal activities to satisfy local customers. Employees may begin to emphasize their own geographically based unit's goals and needs more than those of the organization as a whole. To help ensure uniformity and coordination, organizations such as the IRS, Sheraton Hotels, and the U.S. Postal Service make extensive use of rules that apply in all locations.

## PRODUCT DESIGN

**Product design** involves the establishment of self-contained units, each capable of developing, producing, marketing, and distributing its own goods or services. The Preview Case related how Yum! Brands used this type of design to manage its five product lines. Figure 14.9 shows the product organizational structure of United Technologies, an organization that provides high-tech products to the aerospace, building systems, and automotive industries throughout the world.

**Key Features.**    Elisha Graves Otis, who invented the elevator in 1853, provided the foundation for what today is United Technologies.[15] Throughout its existence, various companies having widely different product lines, as illustrated in Figure 14.9, were added and deleted. Today, it is a $26.2 billion company organized around five distinct product lines. Note that, although these five product lines are all involved in technology, there is little overlap among them in terms of customers, distribution channels, and technology. That is, customers such as Boeing buy Pratt & Whitney jet engines but do no business with UT Automotive products. Each product line faces a different set of competitors and has crafted its business strategy to compete in its particular business environment. Pratt & Whitney has developed a *focused business strategy* to compete in its market. For its Flight Systems product line, customers for its Sikorsky helicopters include the major oil companies that use helicopters to shuttle crews to and from offshore oil platforms, hospitals that use them to move accident victims and the critically ill to their facilities, and the armed forces of the United States that use them for troop movement. Managers handling this product line have little need to communicate with those manufacturing elevators as part of the Otis product line.

**Organizational Uses.**    Most organizations that produce multiple goods or services, such as Morgan Stanley, United Technologies, and American Brands, utilize a

**Figure 14.9**            **United Technologies**

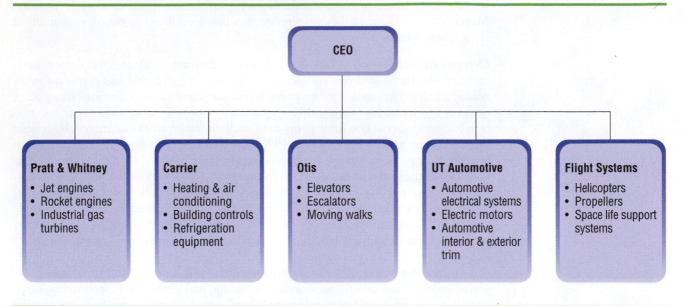

Source: http://www.utc.com

product design. It reduces the information overload that managers face in a purely functional organization design. Under that type of design, the vice president of marketing at United Technologies would have to be able to market a wide variety of products, understand the competitive forces in many industries, and focus on crafting a business strategy to compete in each industry. When the diversity of goods or services and types of customers reach a certain point, the creation of multiple marketing vice presidents (one vice president for each product line) to handle the complexity of the business can be the most effective approach. Each division is then evaluated on its own performance. Moreover, a product design is an attractive alternative to a functional design when environmental and technological factors for each product line are different.

Organizations with a product design usually begin with a functional design and then add some place design features as they begin to serve new geographic markets. Eventually, serving multiple customers creates management problems that can't be effectively dealt with by a functional or place design alone. The addition of new product lines, diverse customers, and technological advances also increases the complexity and uncertainty of the organization's business environment. When changing to a product design, however, companies usually don't completely discard functional or place designs. Instead, the product design may incorporate features of functional and place designs into the organization of each product division. For example, Otis Elevator has functional departments of advertising, finance, manufacturing, and distribution at each of its international plant locations in Russia, Japan, and Korea.

## MULTIDIVISIONAL DESIGN

A variation of the product design is the multidivisional design, sometimes referred to as the M-form.[16] In **multidivisional design**, tasks are organized by division on the basis of the product or geographic markets in which the goods or services are sold.

**Key Features.**    Divisional managers are primarily responsible for day-to-day operating decisions within their units. Freed from these day-to-day operating responsibilities, top-level corporate managers can concentrate on strategic issues, such as allocating resources to the various divisions, assessing new businesses to acquire and divisions to sell off, and communicating with shareholders and others. These top-level managers often are supported by elaborate accounting and control systems and specialized staff. Top-level corporate management may also delegate to product divisions the authority to develop their own strategic plans.

In the Preview Case, we indicated that both KFC and Pizza Hut have restaurants in China. Both restaurant chains face similar problems, including unpaved roads in poor condition that require various types of trucks to traverse them, increase delivery times, and raise transportation costs; and the lack of modern distribution facilities, including an established network of domestic suppliers. Importing foodstuffs is too costly, so Yum! Brands is working with a limited number of suppliers and has been investing resources in them since 1999 to improve quality and increase size. It has relatively large suppliers of chickens, shortening, and flour but relies on local suppliers for all other staples. The following Managing Across Cultures Competency feature highlights some of the problems facing KFC in China.

## COMPETENCY: MANAGING ACROSS CULTURES

### KFC IN CHINA

Samuel Su, president of Yum! Brands' Inc. operations in China, faces numerous problems operating in China besides those already mentioned in the Preview Case. When Yum! Brands Inc. initially went to China in 1987, it faced some startling conditions because it was the first company to introduce Western fast food to the Chinese. First, Chinese government officials had no idea of what franchising meant. Intellectual property and franchise laws were weak, which permitted local officials to interpret the laws as they saw fit. Second, there were no known foreign brand names. Brands are unique symbols or product names that set them apart from the competition and provide the recognition factor that products need to succeed. KFC didn't want franchisees to buy the brand and then be able to sell whatever they wanted to with no legal recourse. Third, foreign multidivisional organizations learned quickly that they couldn't do business in China without government involvement. There are many hierarchical levels in local governments, and each bureaucrat wants "a piece of the action." As a result, KFC has 50 registered companies in China to help it move paperwork through the maze of bureaucratic procedures involved in opening a restaurant.

Another problem is developing a marketing program that will attract Chinese to KFC instead of McDonald's. Su knows that kids don't come alone but bring with them their friends. To attract kids, he needed to tailor the menus (e.g., combo meals) and provide entertainment. Combo meals not only attract kids, but also simplify communication and choice. At KFCs, kids have a corner reserved for them. The corner is staffed with a professional hostess whose job is to talk with the kids. To ensure that they are having a good time, the hostess will sing and dance with them. The average KFC also hosts more than 430 birthday parties annually.

To compete in the fast-food industry, Su must differentiate his company's product not only from McDonald's, but also from millions of mom-and-pop restaurants. Therefore he needed to pay considerable attention to Chinese values. First, when a restaurant opens, it is celebrated with a traditional "Lion Dance" to bring good luck and attended by local politicians. Second, even though traditional Chinese fast-food restaurants have a lot of choice on their menus and are cheap, controlling the standard of their cooking is difficult. KFCs pride themselves on the consistency of their offerings. Employees are trained to prepare food consistently by following rules and procedures spelled out in the operating manual. Third, the menu at KFC provides an important intangible: social freedom. In Chinese restaurants, what you order has social and status implications (e.g., I can afford this). The wrong order can cause the person to loose "face" with her friends. A standard and restricted menu with a limited price range frees the diner from this concern. Fourth, China has a strong desire to catch up with the rest of the world. Dining at an American restaurant enables Chinese people to feel connected to the rest of the world. Su notes: "That for younger Beijing people who have higher incomes and wish to be 'connected' more closely to the outside world, eating at McDonald's or KFC or Pizza Hut is an integral part of their new lifestyle." Fifth, there is a shortage of management talent throughout China. Through its use of standardized recipes, cooking methods, and other practices, KFC is looked upon by the Chinese people as a company that practices scientific management. This acknowledgement attracts consumers anxious to participate in the "modern" world. Last is appearance of the KFC restaurant itself. The cleanliness of the bathrooms, the no smoking policy, the kids corner (no parents allowed), good service, and lack of noise are all attractions that distinguish KFC from other fast-food restaurants.[17]

*For more information on Yum! Brands' Inc. China operation, visit the organization's home page at http://www.yum.com.*

**Organizational Uses.**     A multidivisional design eases problems of coordination by focusing expertise and knowledge on specific goods or services.  A department or division thoroughly familiar with a product line and its set of customers can best handle that line. Such a design clearly meets the needs of a company such as Yum! Brands, which provides diverse products to diverse customers in geographic locations throughout the world.

One disadvantage of the multidivisional design is that a firm must have a large number of managerial personnel to oversee all the product lines.[18] Another disadvantage is the higher cost that results from the duplication of various functions by the divisions. Again refer to Yum! Brands' organization chart in Figure 14.1 All the basic functions (e.g., human resource management, purchasing, finance, etc.) must be performed by all three of the divisions shown—KFC, Pizza Hut, and Taco Bell.

Adoption of a multidivisional design often reduces the environmental complexity facing any one team, department, or division. Employees in a product-based unit can focus on one product line, rather than be overextended across multiple product lines. As with a functional design, an organization with a multidivisional design can deal with complex environments by adding horizontal mechanisms, such as linking roles, task forces, integrating roles, and cross-functional teams.

**Learning Objective:**

4.  Describe three contemporary organization designs— multinational, network, and virtual.

# CONTEMPORARY ORGANIZATION DESIGNS

For organizations to function effectively, their designs must not be static; designs have to change to reflect new environmental challenges, threats, and opportunities. The best design for an organization depends on the nature of the environment, the strategy chosen by top managers, and the degree of  technological interdependence needed by various parts of the organization. During the past decade, several new forms of organization design have been introduced and used by organizations. In particular, three types of organization design—multinational, network, and virtual—have emerged in response to certain deficiencies in traditional organization designs and to rapid changes in the environment.

## MULTINATIONAL DESIGN

Large multibusiness firms, such as General Motors, Toyota, Sanyo, and British Petroleum, operate in various countries, each of which has its own set of customers, governmental officials, and the like. On the one hand, local managers face pressures to be "local insiders"; that is, to design organizations that follow rules and regulations accepted as legitimate by locals. Recall how Su handled problems for KFC in China. The saying, "When in Rome, do as the Romans do," applies. On the other hand, managers face pressures to be "company insiders"; that is, to design organizations to minimize coordination problems with company units in other countries, to manage a diverse set of customers, and to adhere to rules and regulations viewed as appropriate by the company. The problem of operating companies in many countries presents enormous challenges for managers.

**Key Features.**    These multibusiness firms are called **multinational organizations** because they produce and sell products and/or services in two or more countries. A **multinational design** attempts to maintain coordination among products, functions, and geographic areas.[19] Meeting the need for extensive three-way cooperation is especially difficult because operating divisions are separated by distance and time. A further complication is that managers often are separated by culture and language. A "perfect" balance, if such were possible, would require a complex design. Hence most multinational designs focus on the relative emphases that should be given to place and product organization design.

According to a recent United Nations report, there are more than 45,000 multinational organizations. The largest 500 accounted for 80 percent of the world's direct foreign investment. Of these 500, 443 were headquartered in the United States, the European Union, and Japan. Collectively, they have annual revenues in excess of $12.3 trillion and employ more than 37 million people. In addition, direct foreign investment in China alone should grow by about 4 percent a year from a base of more than $1 trillion. Multinational organizations produce a wide range of products, including automobiles, chemicals, computers, industrial equipment, and steel. Clearly, these organizations have a significant impact on the global business world, and being employed by one of them will present ever greater challenges in the coming decades.[20]

A company can be global without necessarily being multinational. Boeing, for example, produces planes in the United States only, but it works with a worldwide network of suppliers and subcontractors and sells planes all over the world. Companies can become multinational by setting up their own subsidiaries in other countries, by establishing joint ventures in other countries with local partners, or by acquiring companies in other countries. IBM, for example, has built up its worldwide network of subsidiaries by setting up wholly owned companies in a large number of countries. To become fully established in the U.S. auto market, Toyota entered into a joint venture with General Motors in California and then set up a wholly owned subsidiary 3 years later in the United States. It now produces cars and trucks at several U.S. locations.

**Basic Options.**    Figure 14.10 suggests the various combinations from which a multinational design might be selected. It also shows the likely effects of choosing a design based primarily on place or product. At Campbell Soup, strong delegation of authority by place gives country or regional managers the ability to respond and adapt to local food preferences. In contrast, product-line managers with worldwide authority may focus on achieving global efficiencies (integration) in production and universal (standard) products.

**Organizational Uses.**    The forces generating global integration in many industries include (1) the growing presence and importance of global competitors and

**Figure 14.10**    **Basic Options in Multinational Design**

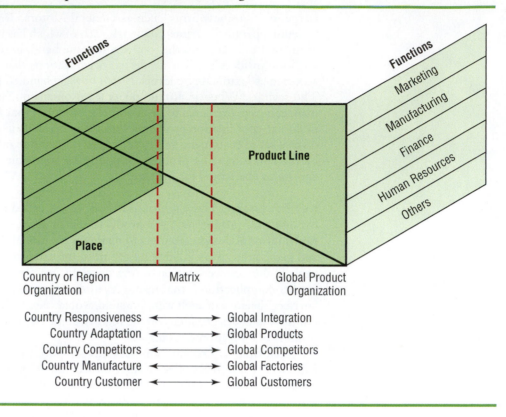

Country Responsiveness ←——————→ Global Integration
Country Adaptation ←——————→ Global Products
Country Competitors ←——————→ Global Competitors
Country Manufacture ←——————→ Global Factories
Country Customer ←——————→ Global Customers

customers, (2) the global rise in market demand for products, (3) new information technologies, and (4) efficient factories that can manufacture goods for customers throughout the world. Worldwide product divisions in firms dealing with such forces are likely to dominate decisions, overpowering the interests of geographically based divisions. Pressures from national governments and local markets also may be strong, often requiring multinational corporations to market full product lines in all the principal countries they serve. Marketing opportunities, however, may not be open to companies unless they negotiate terms with host governments. Therefore a worldwide product-line division may not be as effective at opening new markets as a geographically organized division because, under the latter type of organization, local managers can respond more effectively to local governments' concerns. A division operating under a place design often can establish relations with host governments, invest in distribution channels, develop brand recognition, and build competencies that no single product-line division could afford. Thus valid reasons still exist for country or regional (Europe, North America, Latin America, Central Asia, the Pacific Rim, and the Middle East) organization.

The following Managing Communications Competency feature illustrates how Electrolux uses a multinational design that emphasizes global operations. It also reveals some of the tensions inherent in multinational design when top management tries to balance place, function, and product-line considerations. Originally founded in 1912, this Swedish company is best known for its vacuum cleaners. By the early 1960s, Electrolux was in serious financial difficulty, primarily because of its limited product line, dated technology, and its product organization design. In the mid 1960s, Electrolux was bought by the Wallenbergs, a Swedish family that also had major holdings in other businesses, including Ericsson (telecommunications), Saab (automobiles), and Astra (pharmaceuticals). The Wallenbergs infused capital into Electrolux, but a slowdown in the European economy during the 1970s, forced it to sell

## ELECTROLUX

Until the 1970s, the appliance industry in Europe had been segmented by national markets: differences in customer tastes and income levels, distribution channels, high transportation costs, and governmental regulations and tariffs all played a part in ensuring that local markets were served by local producers. By the late 1970s, several European countries had formed the Common Market and the appliance industry started to go multinational. In response, Electrolux decided to redesign itself to become a multinational corporation, which required several significant changes.

First, the company needed to centralize its planning process so that products could be produced and introduced in several countries simultaneously. Local plants needed to be coordinated and share resources to achieve a common goal. Second, integration of management philosophy was needed. For example, when Electrolux acquired Zanussi, an Italian appliance maker, it needed to change Zanussi's hierarchical top-down mechanistic system to be more consistent with Electrolux's team-based, organic system. At Electrolux, managers were known by their first names throughout the organization, whereas at Zanussi, managers were addressed by their titles. Third, inefficiencies were rampant. Because of tailor-made specifications for different markets (e.g., Spain, Italy, and France), product development centers in Europe weren't being used efficiently. At one point, these centers were producing hundreds of different motors for vacuum cleaners and refrigerators, even though market research had revealed that the firm needed fewer than 10. Plant utilization was quite low, employment levels were high, and output per employee was unacceptably low. Similarly, Zanussi had too many staff people in relation to its production workers, and staff reductions were needed.

To gain some efficiency from being a multinational corporation, Electrolux tried to match staffing requirements with sales and limited the number of motors it was going to market worldwide. Standardizing motors allowed Electrolux to develop a global product strategy, letting it change certain features for local market tastes but retaining a product's essential features. For example, when Electrolux introduced its new "Jet-System" washing machine that allowed people to use less detergent and reduced water consumption by one-third, it was able to introduce that product throughout Europe. Because nearly 70 percent of the company's production costs are in raw materials and components from external suppliers, Electrolux began to negotiate rates with a few suppliers for all product lines, thus achieving considerable standardization and lowering costs by 17 percent. It also required all suppliers to make a commitment to quality and to use just-in-time (JIT) delivery systems for inventory. Currently, Electrolux organizes its businesses around product lines. These product lines (e.g., vacuum cleaners) have common distribution channels, technologies, customers, competitors, and geographic markets. Managers are responsible for all functions, including manufacturing, advertising, and sales, for their product lines.[21]

*For more information on Electrolux, visit the organization's home page at http://www.electrolux.com.*

off Electrolux's North American vacuum cleaner business. Since then, Electrolux has acquired more than 40 different companies throughout Europe.

## NETWORK DESIGN

Many of today's organizations outsource noncore functions to other companies while retaining control over their core functions. Such companies may be thought of as having a hub surrounded by outside companies that can be added or deleted as needed. You undoubtedly recognize the Nike and Reebok brand names. What you probably don't know is that Nike has limited production facilities of its own and that Reebok doesn't own any of its plants. Both organizations contract their manufacturing to companies located in South Korea and Taiwan where labor is plentiful and cheap. Doing so saves these companies from having to make major investments in plants and equipment and permits them to do what they do best—change designs with changes in customer tastes. Similarly, Dell and Gateway buy computer components made by other companies and perform only the final assembly themselves, putting together customized PCs.

**Key Features.**    The type of organization we just described is one type of network design. A **network design** focuses on sharing authority, responsibility, and resources among people, departments, and/or other organizations that must cooperate and communicate frequently to achieve common goals.[22] Various designs (functional, product, or place) must be applied in a network organization as tasks and goals change.

A network design is sometimes called a *modular organization*. It resembles a mosaic of mutually interdependent departments and organizations. This mosaic can't be woven from typical organization charts that show authority and reporting relationships. A network organization exists only when most of the following factors operate in support of one another.

- *Distinctive competence.* The organization maintains superiority through innovation and adaptation by combining resources in novel ways. Often these resources come from different parts of the organization or other organizations.
- *Responsibility.* People who must collaborate to perform their tasks share responsibility. The organization's design includes extensive use of cross-functional, special-purpose, and self-managed teams.
- *Goal setting.* Common goals linked to satisfying the needs of one or more important external groups (e.g., customers or clients, suppliers, shareholders, lenders, and governments) are formulated. Performance is less internally driven and more dependent on satisfying customer needs or speeding up product development.
- *Communication.* The primary focus is on lateral rather than vertical communication. The information necessary to make decisions is widely shared and distributed, and open communication is the norm.
- *Information technology.* Many information technologies (including groupware) assist employees in networking internally (with others in the organization who may even be separated geographically by great distances) or externally (with customers, suppliers, regulatory agencies, and others). Typical information technologies and related groupware include e-mail, special PC software decision aids, voice mail, mobile phones, fax, telecommuting, teleconferencing, local and wide-area computer networks, and the like.
- *Organization design.* The design has a bias toward an organic system with as few organizational levels as possible. This design supports individual initiative and collaboration among individuals in teams.
- *Balanced view.* Individuals, teams, departments, and divisions do not view themselves as isolated islands having only their unique goals and ways of doing things. They view themselves in relation to others with common goals and rewards. Forms of cooperation and trust evolve over time, based on a history of past performance. The basic assumption of trust is that each person, team, or department depends on resources controlled by others and that mutual gains are obtained by pooling resources and finding win–win solutions for all.

**Organizational Uses.**    A network design is particularly effective in creating alliances of flexible partnerships.[23] Partners in an alliance could be customers, suppli-

ers, and firms that would be defined as competitors under different circumstances. Corning, Inc., uses its 23 joint ventures with foreign partners such as Siemens (Germany), Samsung (South Korea), and CIBA-GEIGY (Switzerland), to compete in a growing number of related high-tech markets. The flexibility with which Corning approaches its partnerships—letting the form be determined by the goals and letting the ventures evolve over time—is one reason for its success. But even more important is the time and effort expended by Corning executives to create the conditions for long-lasting, mutually beneficial relationships.

A network design is intended to create successful external relationships by having "six I's" in place: importance, investment, interdependence, integration, information, and institutionalization. Because the relationships are important, they get adequate resources, management attention, and sponsorship. Agreement to provide long-term investment tends to help equalize benefits and costs over time. The participants are interdependent, which helps maintain a balance of power. The participants are integrated in order to maintain essential points of contact and communication. Each partner is informed about the plans and directions of the others. Finally, when a network design is working well, it has strong employee social ties and shared values, which help solidify trust.

## VIRTUAL ORGANIZATION

The need for fast response to customer needs has led some firms to become even more specialized and focused in their activities. The principal developments in information technologies over the past 10 years have both pushed and enabled organizations to move toward a variation of the networked organization called a virtual organization.

**Key Features.**    A **virtual organization** seeks to coordinate and link people from many different locations to communicate and make decisions on a real-time basis.[24] Such an organization is composed of continually evolving networks of organizations (e.g., suppliers and distributors) that are linked electronically to share costs, skills, access to markets, and expertise. In a virtual organization, users of sophisticated personal computers can easily tap company databases and work together as if they were in the same room. The PCs have videoconferencing capability, electronic blackboards, scanners, faxes, and groupware. These PCs are also connected to the company's intranet, which contains home pages for various functions and sources of information.

The production of movies in the entertainment industry by DreamWorks, Lucasfilms, Universal, and Castle Rock rely on virtual organizations. Filmmakers, directors, producers, actors, agents, make-up artists, costume specialists, special-effects artists, technicians, and lawyers all come together from different companies to produce a film. They must be closely coordinated to produce a film with exacting specifications. After the film is complete, these independent contributors disband and then regroup with different people to produce another film with a different set of actors, producers, directors, and so on. Thus this industry consists of many different specialized firms, each of which is highly dependent on the people, knowledge, and inputs of other firms to create films that are beyond the scope and capability of any one filmmaker.

Four advances in information technology have enabled organizations to utilize a virtual form of organization design: open systems, distributed computing, real time, and global networking.

- *Open systems.* Portable software and compatible technology now exist and are widely used. These capabilities extend to the external network of suppliers, consumers, regulatory agencies, and even competitors to create an open system. The shift is away from departments or divisions with their own unique computing capabilities to a network of linked business processes. In addition, organizations can be in close touch with their customers, suppliers, and others, enabling people to act not only in their own self-interests, but with a shared vision and commitment. Open systems also mean that teams are free to work with other teams to pursue a common task.

- *Distributed computing.* Access and use have shifted from centralized computing in mechanistic organizations where access was limited to a few people or departments to distributed computing whereby information is available to the primary users of that information. In virtual organizations, planning, information processing, and knowledge are distributed throughout the organization by empowered individuals and teams.

- *Real time.* The new information technologies also capture information online and update databanks in real time. These capabilities provide an instantaneous, accurate picture of many processes, such as sales, production, and cash flow. At Frito-Lay, a real-time network allows the company's manufacturing plants to adjust continuously to changing market conditions. Just-in-time receipt of raw materials from suppliers and delivery of products to customers minimizes the need for warehousing and has permitted Frito-Lay to shift from mass production to custom online production. Customer orders arriving electronically can be processed instantly. Corresponding invoices are sent electronically and databases automatically updated.

- *Global networking.* Information networks are the backbone of virtual organization design. Global networking permits both real-time communication and access of electronically stored information at will from anywhere in the world. For global organizations, such as British Petroleum, Texas Instruments, Ford, Samsung, and NEC, a virtual organization design redefines time and space for employees, suppliers, customers, and competitors alike. At Ford, for example, the company is using the Web as a way for suppliers to work more closely with designers in the lab or at test sites. In a virtual design, any individual, team, or department can quickly communicate and share information with any other individual, team, or department. Work can be performed at a variety of locations, including employees' homes, with the office becoming part of a network rather than a place.

**Organizational Uses.**    Virtual design is the latest type of organization design that managers are using to satisfy customer demand. A virtual design permits managers to change an organization's structure quickly to meet changing conditions and situations. Internal departments, job responsibilities, and lines of authority are shifted as needed. Boundaries between an organization and its customers and suppliers are blurred; indeed, some customers and suppliers begin to spend more time in the organization than some of its own employees. General Electric's thrust during the 1990s was to become boundaryless, both internally and externally with customers and suppliers. That is, it moved to eliminate, insofar as posible, chains of command and rigid departmental lines and to substitute for them teams empowered to make decisions.

In addition to constantly recreating organizational structures, a virtual organization has several other important charactertistics.

- Its employees continually master new manufacturing and information technologies, speeding the production process and the flow of information throughout the organization.
- Its employees respond quickly to changing customer demands with customized products and services avaliable at any time and place.
- Its emloyees are reciprocally interdependent. The entire workforce must be capable of mastering all the competencies needed to serve clients effectively.

- Its managers delegate authority and responsibility to employees while providing them with a clear vision of the organization's purpose and goals.

The following Managing Teams Competency feature illustrates how British Petroleum (BP) has used a virtual design to create problem-solving teams. British Petroleum employs more than 107,000 people, operates in 60 countries around the world, and has annual sales that exceed $174 billion. It explores for gas and oil reserves in the Gulf of Mexico, South America, western Africa, the Caspian Sea, the Middle East, and the Atlantic Ocean west of the Shetland Islands. Its exploration and development costs are among the lowest in the industry.

## COMPETENCY:  MANAGING TEAMS

### BRITISH PETROLEUM'S VIRTUAL ORGANIZATION

When John Browne, BP's CEO, took over for David Simon in 1995, he knew that for BP to be successful, he had to develop an organization that learns and gets all employees involved in solving problems. He believed that the people closest to BP's assets and customers should make decisions.

To implement his strategy, he created virtual teams. These teams enable people separated by time, distance, and geography to share their knowledge. If it is easy for people to communicate, connect, and share knowledge, Browne believes that they will. To make doing so easier, BP produces videos that can be viewed on its intranet, has created electronic yellow pages that can be searched in a variety of ways, and encourages people to list interests, expertise, and experiences that they are willing to share with anyone who wants to contact them. BP's virtual organization relies on a growing system of sophisticated PCs that permit users to tap into the company's databases. All its PCs are connected to BP's intranet, which contains more than 40,000 home pages. These home pages are sites on which functional experts offer guidance based on the experience they've gained in dealing with a multitude of issues and problems. There are sites for sharing technical data on the muds used as drilling lubricants and for sharing information about processes that are available to reduce the amount of pipe that gets stuck in wells. There is a site where people can raise questions and exchange information. Brown's idea was to create an organization that would enable the best minds to solve a problem, even if it meant scouring the world for these people.

British Petroleum used the virtual team design to learn and pass on lessons from its exploration and development of the Andrew oil field in the North Sea to contractors and suppliers. People who had encountered similar exploration problems in the Gulf of Mexico shared information quickly with those in the Andrew field. Using virtual teams, BP and its contractors and suppliers were able to figure out radical ways to cut developmental costs and time. By fully utilizing the expertise of its own people and working closely with contractors and suppliers, BP saved an estimated $30 million or more in the Andrew field's first year of operation. But this estimate, according to Browne, doesn't take into account benefits that are harder to measure, such as the ability to see the expression in someone's eyes during a videoconference when that person makes a commitment. Each member of Browne's staff and each general manager of a business unit is a member of at least one virtual team. These teams allow people to share information with each other continuously. Browne recently participated in a management conference that connected people in Johannesburg with others in Singapore.[25]

*For more information on British Petroleum, visit the organization's home page at **http://www.bp.com.***

# CHAPTER SUMMARY

**1.** Explain how environmental, strategic, and technological factors affect the design of organizations.

The environment facing an organization consists of external stakeholders. We indicated that four groups in particular—suppliers, distributors, competitors, and customers—can affect how an organization operates. Strategic factors and the choice of business strategy—low cost, focused, differentiation—have a direct impact on an organization's design. Organizations pursuing a low-cost strategy usually seek designs that emphasize functional departments (e.g., accounting, finance, marketing). Focused strategies are intended to help an organization target a specific niche within an industry. Organizations pursuing this strategy are typically organized by product. Differentiation strategies are based on the organization's ability to provide customers with a unique product or service. These organizations are typically organized along product lines. Technological factors determine the degree of coordination needed among individuals, teams, and departments to reach the organization's goals. Three types of interdependence—pooled, sequential, and reciprocal—were identified and discussed.

**2.** State the differences between mechanistic and organic organizations.

If top management supports tight, centralized control of day-to-day decisions, a mechanistic organization is more likely to be used than an organic one. Mechanistic organizations are bureaucratic and function effectively when the environment is stable. Organic organizations have fewer rules and regulations and function effectively in rapidly changing environments and ambiguous situations. People gain influence by contributing to the resolution of issues and solution of problems.

**3.** Desribe four traditional organization designs—functional, place, product, and mutlidivisional.

A functional design separates the organization along various departmental lines, such as marketing, finance, and human resource, and top managers may integrate departments as needed. In place departmentalization, the different geographical areas served by the organization present different environmental conditions. All functions are usually performed at each place. A product design emphasizes the nature of the organization's products and/or services. Each product is unique and requires special attention by top management. A multidivisonal form (M-form) is a product design that is useful to organizations that offer a wide array of products in geographically dispersed markets.

**4.** Describe three contemporary organization designs—multinational, network, and virtual.

A multinational design attempts to maintain three-way organizational capabilities among products, functions, and geographic areas. Production in several countries presents enormous coordinating problems for managers who must adhere to headquarters policies and local customs at the same time. A network design emphasizes horizontal coordination for managing complex task interdependencies. This type of design also features the use of various information technologies that enable the organization to process vast amounts of data. A virtual design is based on the concept that people do not need to work face-to-face but may function well when connected electronically. Mainly used in high-tech and filmmaking organizations, this type of design cannot be effectively implemented without adequate electronic capabilities.

# KEY TERMS AND CONCEPTS

Bureaucracy
Centralization
Chain of command
Differentiation strategy
Division of labor

Focused strategy
Functional design
Hierarchy of authority
Impersonality
Low-cost strategy

Mechanistic organization ✓
Multidivisional design
Multinational design
Multinational organizations
Network design
Organic organization ✓
Organization chart
Organization design
Place design

Procedures
Product design
Rules
Span of control ✓   *Span of mgmt*
Task interdependence
Technology
Unity of command ✓
Virtual organization

## DISCUSSION QUESTIONS

1. What are the three most important managerial competencies that Yum! Brands' leaders need to develop to maintain and increase its global market share in the fast-food industry?
2. Is the business strategy of KFC similar to that of 7-Eleven? Explain.
3. What impact does the choice of strategy by KFC have on how this organization is designed?
4. How does technological interdependence affect the design of British Pertroleum's virtual organization design?
5. What do you see as the major strengths of Electrolux's organization design? Its major weaknesses?
6. The following are some reasons for organizational ineffectiveness.

   • Lack of goal clarity—strategic goals are not clear or linked to particular aspects of the organization's design.
   • Lack of internal alignment—the design of the organization is internally inconsistent.
   • Ineffective links to customers—the design does not effectively integrate the demands of customers.

   • Lack of external fit—the design does not fit the needs of the environment.

   Identify and describe briefly one organization (e.g., Kmart, Enron, or Sunbeam, among others) whose ineffectiveness you believe reflects these reasons.

7. Global managers must be capable of balancing the often-contradictory pulls of being locally responsive and globally efficient. How did Pizza Hut address these contradictory pulls?
8. ARAMARK Corporation, a global provider of managed services, is organized by product line, including campus dining, business dining, uniform rentals, corrections (feeding prisoners), and sports and recreation (managing concessions at various sports arenas). The sports and recreation division, for example, in 2002 served more than 60,000 meals each day at the Olympic Village in Salt Lake City, Utah. What are some likely organization design problems that Joe Neubauer, ARAMARK'S CEO, faces?
9. What practices typically found in a functional organization design have to be changed when top management chooses a virtual design?

## DEVELOPING COMPETENCIES

### Competency: Managing Self

### Inventory of Effective Design

*Instructions:* Listed are statements describing an effective organization design. Indicate the extent to which you agree or disagree with each statement as a description of an organization you currently work for or have worked for in the past. Write the appropriate number next to the statement.

1. Strongly disagree
2. Disagree
3. Somewhat disagree
4. Uncertain
5. Somewhat agree
6. Agree
7. Strongly agree

_____ 1. Employees who try to change things are usually recognized and supported.

_____ 2. The organization makes it easy to get the skills needed to progress.

_____ 3. Employees almost always know how their work turns out, whether it is good or bad.

_____ 4. Employees have flexibility over the pace of their work.

_____ 5. Managers facilitate discussion at meetings to encourage participation by subordinates.

_____ 6. Few policies, rules, and regulations restrict innovation in this organization.

_____ 7. Boundaries between teams, departments, and divisions rarely interfere with solving joint problems.

_____ 8. There are few hierarchical levels in this organization.

_____ 9. Everyone knows how their work will affect the work of the next person or team and the quality of the final product or service.

_____ 10. The organization is well informed about technological developments relevant to its processes, goods, or services.

_____ 11. The organization is constantly trying to determine what the customer wants and how to meet customer needs better.

_____ 12. The organization can adapt to most changes because its policies, organization design, and employees are flexible.

_____ 13. Different parts of the organization work together; when conflict arises, it often leads to constructive outcomes.

_____ 14. Everyone can state the values of the organization and how they are used to make decisions.

_____ 15. A great deal of information is shared openly, as appropriate.

## Scoring and Interpretation

Sum the points given to statements 1–15. A score of 75–105 suggests an effective organization design. A score of 70–89 suggests a mediocre design that probably varies greatly in terms of how specific aspects of the organization work for or against the design's effectiveness. A score of 50–69 suggests a great deal of ambiguity about the organization and how it operates. A score of 15–49 suggests that the design is contributing to serious problems.[26]

## Questions

1. What specific design features in your organization led you to rate it as you did?
2. What three managerial competencies were most important in that organization?
3. Is the organization a success? Explain.

## Competency:  Managing Change

### Cisco Systems

Cisco Systems is one of the world's leading technology companies. It is a leader in developing computer routers, switches, networking gear, and leading-edge telecommunications equipment that are at the heart of the Internet. When the company first went public in early 1990, few people had ever heard of it, and even fewer knew about the products that it designed and sold. In fact, most people hardly ever see an actual product developed by Cisco Systems because routers and switches usually are found in computer and telecommunication servers and networks that move and direct the flow of data to desktop computers in businesses and other organizations. Without networking products made by Cisco Systems, the Internet wouldn't be nearly as advanced, fast, and versatile as it is today. By the late 1990s, many people had come to view Cisco Systems as synonymous with the Internet.

By the end of 2000, Cisco had become a $430 billion dollar company, and many of its competitors envied and imitated its organization design. In fact, until the economic downturn of the U.S. economy and the September 11 terrorism attack in 2001, Cisco Systems had continuously grown at rates exceeding 20 and even 30 percent a year. Its computer networking gear is considered to be among the most advanced. Cisco competitors, Lucent Technologies, Nortel Networks, and Ciena Corporation, also sell cutting-edge technologies to telecommunications organizations.

Cisco's rise over the past decade is due in part to the company's leading-edge technologies and its ability to innovate rapidly. Equally important, Cisco Systems, from its earliest days, has relied on a different organization design that allowed it to become flexible and yet pursue a focused business strategy. On the one hand, the company has become extremely profitable because it did not have the same degree of fixed costs in manufacturing plants that saddled many of its competitors, including Alcatel, Lucent Technologies, and Nortel Networks. Moreover, Cisco believes that it has to be able to respond quickly to its customers' changing needs, especially in the telecommunications industry where technological change moves fast. On the other hand, the company was able to increase its revenue by acquiring dozens of companies each year to fill out its product line. As Cisco does comparatively little internal R&D on its own, the company depends heavily on its newly acquired employees to sustain its high rate of product innovation and market growth. This strategy enabled Cisco to take advantage of promising technology after someone else had borne the development cost and risk. Some of the most defining characteristics of Cisco's approach to organizing its people and activities are the following.

### Reliance on Suppliers and Partners

One of the most important hallmarks of Cisco's organization design is its almost total reliance on its suppliers and manufacturing partners to build, assemble, test, and even deliver Cisco's entire line of products. Most of the high-tech components and chips that go into Cisco's products are manufactured by companies that specialize in a particular network component or assembly of the final product. These chips and components are then assembled to create Cisco's end products. Over the past decade, Cisco established strong working relationships with these manufacturers who became an integral part of Cisco's web of suppliers. These suppliers include such companies as Solectron, Flextronics, and Sanmina, who are able to produce vast quantities of key components for Cisco's networking gear at low cost. Cisco relies so heavily on its manufacturing partners that it even teaches them how to control quality to meet Cisco's high standards. Cisco delegates to its manufacturing partners highly intricate, customized product designs that fit each customer's unique specifications. As Cisco's manufacturing partners become more sophisticated in their capabilities, they are also better able to help Cisco in responding to fast-changing technologies. By 2000, these manufacturers had become so important to Cisco that they now build more than 60 percent of Cisco's products and will even ship them directly to customers' locations. These relationships help Cisco manage its inventory and reduce the costs required to produce complex products. Equally important, Cisco has been able to shrink delivery times to customers from 10 weeks to 3 weeks in most cases.

## Fast Product Design

Another important characteristic of Cisco's organization design is the company's capability to design new generations of networking equipment faster than its rivals can. To ensure that it can build the right products for its customers, the company actively encourages its customers to work directly with Cisco's designers and engineers to test new product designs. Cisco asks its customers for ideas, suggestions, criticisms, and other inputs to sharpen its product development skills. Cisco CEO John Chambers regularly visits customers and treats them as long-standing partners. In fact, Cisco's management truly believes that much of the company's product development activity should be performed in conjunction with its customers because they can provide unique and yet realistic insights into how products should perform. Cisco asks its customers what kinds of products and technologies they think they'll need in future years. More important, Cisco wants to use customers' input as the basis for exceeding their expectations with next generation products that are specifically made for each customer's needs. Customers can work with Cisco's engineers in person or over the Internet. Cisco even allows its customers to design and order products through Cisco's Web site, where customers can check on the status of their orders through a real-time, continuously updated database tied to Cisco's manufacturing partners. By encouraging customers to use the Internet, Cisco can also listen directly to customers' complaints and suggestions on how best it can improve future networking gear to make it easier to use and less costly to install.

## Retention of People

CEO John Chambers also believes that, for Cisco to remain on the cutting-edge of technology, the company should seek new ideas and technologies from wherever they may be developed. This belief has led Cisco on a massive buying spree of many leading-edge companies that possess creative design and engineering employees. It tells its soon-to-be acquired employees that Cisco will make them leaders in its field. Cisco has grown so successfully through its acquisitions that comparatively few of its products are "home-grown." Many executives believe that Cisco is one of the few companies that have been successful in retaining the people that it acquired through buyouts of other companies. Cisco makes sure that, when it buys companies, they share some important characteristics: (1) ambitious and talented engineers, (2) products or technologies that complement Cisco's own offerings, (3) managers who will stay and become important team leaders within Cisco after the buyout is completed.

Cisco has been especially successful in retaining people after making an acquisition because it not only offers generous compensation, but it also encourages newly acquired employees to become project leaders within Cisco. Chambers sets up a direct reporting relationship so that newly acquired managers can oversee many of the same employees they worked with before the acquisition. Cisco wants to use these engineers to develop important technology products, helping Cisco improve its own knowledge and skill base over time. As these project leaders become important contributors to Cisco's growth and innovation, they also can rise quickly to senior management levels. Over time, as newly acquired employees become more familiar with Cisco's way of doing business, they in turn are able to manage entire Cisco departments or business units to develop new opportunities for the future.[27]

## Questions

1. What type of organization design does Cisco use? Has it been effective? Explain.

2. What are some potential pitfalls in Cisco's current organization design?

3. Evaluate Cisco's practices for retaining people after making an acquisition.

# CHAPTER

## Cultivating Organizational Culture

15

# TDINDUSTRIES

Many organizations say that people are their most important assets, but TDIndustries lives it. Over the past 50 years, this organization has developed management practices that have enabled it to become one of America's most admired corporations, currently ranking fourth on *Fortune* magazine's top 100 companies to work for. TDIndustries has developed into more than a $200 million mechanical/electrical/plumbing company that employs some 1,500 people, many of whom have been with the company for more than 10 years. CEO Jack Lowe believes that TDI's success can be related to its strong corporate culture.

For TDI, creating a culture that promotes high performance and longevity is based on the concept of servant leadership. The servant leader philosophy for TDI means that managers (servants) cultivate employees (leaders) by serving and meeting the needs of others. In his servant role, Lowe answers his own phone, has no reserved parking space, and works in an 8 × 11–foot cubicle just like everybody else. Keys to the servant philosophy include the following.

- People should work together to build a company. They are partners. Employees ranging from foremen to sheet metal hangers to safety directors hold TDI stock.
- Managers have to earn the recognition and respect of employees.
- Managers assume that their followers are working with them and must see things through their eyes.

- Managers are people builders, who don't hold people down but lift them up.
- Managers can be led. They are not interested in having their own way, but finding the best way.

To keep servant leadership central to TDI's corporate culture, new employees are assigned to servant leadership discussion groups, which meet weekly for 6 weeks to discuss various aspects of servant leadership, such as sharing power, listening, and trusting others—and how they can apply these concepts to their particular jobs. TDI has also started a mentoring program designed to give all new hires a positive start at the company. A mentor adopts a new employee for the first 6 months, and the relationship continues so long as both employees work together on the same job site. If the new hire changes job sites, a different mentor is assigned.

At the same time they are enrolled in the servant leadership classes, recruits enter the first phase of a 2- or 3–week field assignment designed to acquaint them with jobs and working conditions at a construction site. The second phase is an intensive 4-week trade-specific classroom and laboratory training program. The final phase consists of 6 weeks of mentored on-the-job training during which the recruits must earn certification in a variety of skills. Upon successful completion of the program, employees are given a $1 per hour raise and are expected to enroll in the next available trade class.[1]

*For more information on TDIndustries, visit the organization's home page at http://www.tdindustries.com.*

The competencies and values of employees and managers play a large role in determining the effectiveness and success of an organization. As illustrated by the Preview Case, certain styles, character, and ways of doing things are powerful guidelines for behavior. To understand the soul of an organization requires plunging below the charts, financial numbers, machines, and buildings into the world of organizational culture.[2]

In this chapter, we examine the concept of organizational culture and how such cultures are formed, maintained, and changed. We also explore some possible relationships between organizational culture and performance; the relationship between organizational culture and ethical behavior; the challenge of managing a culturally diverse workforce; and, finally, how organizations socialize individuals into their particular cultures. We begin with a brief overview of what organizational culture is and how organizational cultures are formed, maintained, and changed.

**Learning Objective:**

1. Explain how organizational cultures are formed, sustained, and changed.

# THE DYNAMICS OF ORGANIZATIONAL CULTURE

**Organizational culture** represents a complex pattern of beliefs, expectations, ideas, values, attitudes, and behaviors shared by the members of an organization that evolve over time.[3]  More specifically, organizational culture includes:

- routine ways of communicating, such as organizational rituals and ceremonies and the language commonly used;
- the norms shared by individuals and teams throughout the organization, such as no reserved parking spaces;
- the dominant values held by the organization, such as product quality or price leadership;
- the philosophy that guides management's policies and decision making;
- the rules of the game for getting along in the organization, or the "ropes" that a newcomer must learn in order to become an accepted member; and
- the feeling or climate conveyed in an organization by the physical layout and the way in which managers and employees interact with customers, suppliers, and other outsiders.[4]

None of these components individually represents the culture of the organization. Taken together, however, they reflect and give meaning to the concept of organizational culture. Using these six attributes, how would you describe the culture of TDIndustries? These descriptions should give you some insight into why TDI has been rated by *Fortune* magazine as one of the 100 best companies to work for.

As indicated in Figure 15.1, organizational culture exists on several levels, which differ in terms of visibility and resistance to change. Just like peeling an onion, the least visible, or deepest, level of organizational culture is that of shared *assumptions and philosophy*, which represent basic beliefs about reality, human nature, and the way things should be done. For example, at TDI key assumptions are that all managers and employees are partners and that the success of the company depends on their working together. Managers and employees alike are committed to a philosophy of trust and the importance of listening to others' thoughts and ideas.

The next level is that of **cultural values**, which represent collective beliefs, assumptions, and feelings about what things are good, normal, rational, and valuable.[5] Cultural values can be quite different from organization to organization; in some, employees may care deeply about money, but in others they may care more about technological innovation or employee well-being. These values tend to persist over time, even when organizational membership changes. At TDI, cultural values are represented by the servant leadership concept.

The next level is that of **shared behaviors**, including norms (see Chapter 8), which are more visible and somewhat easier to change than values. The servant lead-

**Figure 15.1**                    **Layers of Organizational Culture**

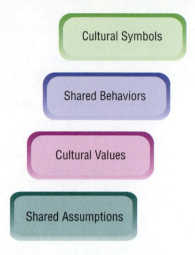

ership program for all new hires at TDI focuses on mentoring and sharing TDI's expectations of behaviors with them.

The most superficial level of organizational culture consists of symbols. **Cultural symbols** are words (jargon or slang), gestures, and pictures or other physical objects that carry a particular meaning within a culture.[6] Someone entering a New York City Police Department precinct station encounters symbols of authority and spartan surroundings, including physical barriers between officers and civilians; the attire of the duty officer; emblems of authority, such as the American flag, seals, certificates, photos of various city leaders, and signs prohibiting certain behaviors; and hard straight chairs, vending machines, and instructions. In contrast, someone entering the lobby of OxyChem encounters warmth, including comfortable chairs and soft couches, decorative pictures, plants and flowers, and reading materials. Bill Arnold, president of Centennial Medical Center, symbolized his commitment to an open door communication policy by ripping his door from its hinges and suspending it from the ceiling where everyone could see it.

The cultural symbols of McDonald's also convey a standard meaning. McDonald's restaurants are typically located in rectangular buildings with large windows to let the sun in and with neatly kept surroundings. Parking lots are large and paved; there is rarely any visible litter. A drive-in window indicates that speedy service is available. The most prominent symbol is the golden arch sign that towers over the building, where zoning laws permit. Inside, bright colors and plants create a homey atmosphere. Glistening stainless steel appliances behind the counter provide an up-to-date, efficient, and sanitary appearance. Above all, everything is *clean*. Cleanliness is achieved by endless sweeping and mopping of floors, rapid removal of garbage, instant collecting of dirty trays and cleaning of spills, washing of windows to remove smudges and fingerprints, cleaning of unoccupied tables, and constant wiping of the counter. Both the interior and exterior convey cultural symbols of predictability, efficiency, speed, courtesy, friendliness, and cleanliness.

Organization culture is important for employees and managers alike. Achieving a good match between the values of the organization and those of the employee first requires that a potential employee figure out what an organization values and second that she find an organization that shares her personal values. You can address the first task by making a list of the 8 values that are most characteristic of your ideal workplace and the 8 that are least characteristic of it from the 54 values shown in Table 15.1. Then return to the Preview Case: What are TDI's values? Would you like to work for this organization?

**Table 15.1**

## What Do You Value at Work?

The 54 items listed below cover the full range of values you'd likely encounter at an organization. Please divide it into two groups—the 27 that would be most characteristic of your ideal workplace and the 27 that would be the least characteristic. Keep halving the group until you have a rank ordering, then fill in your top and bottom eight choices. Please be sure that you choose four values from the **YOU ARE** list and four values from the **YOUR COMPANY OFFERS** list. Test your fit at a firm by seeing whether the company's values match your top and bottom eight.

*Top Eight Choices*

|  |  |  |  |  |  |  |  |
|--|--|--|--|--|--|--|--|
|  |  |  |  |  |  |  |  |

*Bottom Eight Choices*

|  |  |  |  |  |  |  |  |
|--|--|--|--|--|--|--|--|
|  |  |  |  |  |  |  |  |

*The Choice Menu*
**YOU ARE:** 1. Flexible 2. Adaptable 3. Innovative 4. Able to seize opportunities 5. Willing to experiment 6. Risk-taking 7. Careful 8. Autonomy-seeking 9. Comfortable with rules 10. Analytical 11. Attentive to detail 12. Precise 13. Team-oriented 14. Ready to share information 15. People-oriented 16. Easygoing 17. Calm 18. Supportive 19. Aggressive 20. Decisive 21. Action-oriented 22. Eager to take initiative 23. Reflective 24. Achievement-oriented 25. Demanding 26. Comfortable with individual responsibility 27. Comfortable with conflict 28. Competitive 29. Highly organized 30. Results-oriented 31. Interested in making friends at work 32. Collaborative 33. Eager to fit in with colleagues 34. Enthusiastic about the job
**YOUR COMPANY OFFERS:** 35. Stability 36. Predictability 37. High expectations of performance 38. Opportunities for professional growth 39. High pay for good performance 40. Job security 41. Praise for good performance 42. A clear guiding philosophy 43. A low level of conflict 44. An emphasis on quality 45. A good reputation 46. Respect for the individual's rights 47. Tolerance 48. Informality 49. Fairness 50. A unitary culture throughout the organization 51. A sense of social responsibility 52. Long hours 53. Relative freedom from rules 54. The opportunity to be distinctive, or different from others

Source: Adapted from Siegel, M. The perils of culture conflict. *Fortune*, November 9, 1998, 259; Chatman, J. A. and Jehn, K. A. Assessing the relationship between industry characteristics and organizational culture: How different can they be? *Academy of Management Journal*, 1994, 37, 522–553.

## FORMING A CULTURE

An organizational culture forms in response to two major challenges that confront every organization: (1) external adaptation and survival and (2) internal integration.[7]

**External adaptation and survival** has to do with how the organization will find a niche in and cope with its constantly changing external environment. External adaptation and survival involves addressing the following issues.

- *Mission and strategy:* Identifying the primary purpose of the organization and selecting strategies to pursue this mission.
- *Goals:* Setting specific targets to achieve.
- *Means:* Determining how to pursue the goals, including selecting an organizational structure and reward system.
- *Measurement:* Establishing criteria to determine how well individuals, teams, and departments are accomplishing their goals.

**Internal integration** has to do with the establishment and maintenance of effective working relationships among the members of an organization. Internal integration involves addressing the following issues.

- *Language and concepts:* Identifying methods of communication and developing a shared meaning for important concepts.
- *Group and team boundaries:* Establishing criteria for membership in groups and teams.
- *Power and status:* Determining rules for acquiring, maintaining, and losing power and status.
- *Rewards and punishments:* Developing systems for encouraging desirable behaviors and discouraging undesirable behaviors.[8]

An organizational culture emerges when members share knowledge and assumptions as they discover or develop ways of coping with issues of external adaptation and internal integration. Figure 15.2 shows a common pattern in the emergence of organizational cultures. In relatively new organizations, such as Dell Computers, eBay, and Microsoft, the founder or a few key individuals may largely influence the organization's culture. Later in the life of the organization, its culture will reflect a complex mixture of the assumptions, values, and ideas of the founder or other early top managers and the subsequent experiences of managers and employees.

The national culture, customs, and societal norms of a country also shape the cultures of organizations operating in it. The dominant values of a national culture may be reflected in the constraints imposed on organizations by others. For example, a country's form of government may have a dramatic impact on how an organization does business. In addition, the members of the organization have been raised in a particular society and thus bring the dominant values of the society into the firm. For example, in the United States individuals learn values such as freedom of speech and respect for individual privacy from the nation's cultural values. Thus the presence or absence of these and other values within the larger society has implications for organizational behavior. Finally, increased global operations have forced awareness that differences in national cultures may have a significant impact on organizational effectiveness. Multinational corporations have discovered that organizational structures and cultures that might be effective in one part of the world may be ineffective in another. The following Managing Across Cultures Competency feature illustrates the impact of both U.S. and German cultures on the behavior of managers at Daimler-Chrysler.

One perspective is that societal-level cultural differences created the conflicts within DaimlerChrysler. But some of the new organization's employees argued that different management philosophies and values were the root of the problem. Most likely, both explanations have some merit. Ultimately, DaimlerChrysler will develop its own unique culture—one that blends elements of both the U.S. and German ways of doing business. The sooner that happens, the easier it will be for everyone in the organization to work together productively.

**Figure 15.2**                    **How Cultures Emerge**

## COMPETENCY:   MANAGING ACROSS CULTURES

### DAIMLERCHRYSLER'S DIVERSE CULTURES

In a windowless conference room 15 stories below the executive suite, seven German and U.S. employees of DaimlerChrysler are debating the newly merged automaker's future. At the heart of the debate is the fact that, after the formal merger of the two organizations, it remains essentially two separate companies, one German and one U.S. Why?

If DaimlerChrysler is to become a global organization, it must convince employees at all levels that moving to various parts of the world is important. Dozens of teams are now shuttling between the company's dual headquarters in Stuttgart, Germany, and Auburn Hills, Michigan. Recently, the company wanted to move 60 employees between Germany and the United States on jobs lasting between 2 and 5 years. There were few takers. Part of the problem has to do with personal concerns: Most Americans don't speak German and don't want to leave their spacious U.S. homes for apartments or smaller houses in Stuttgart, where real estate is far more expensive. Resistance is strong even though DaimlerChrysler is providing **expatriates** (those who live in a foreign country while maintaining permanent residence or citizenship in their home country) the equivalent of 3 months' salary to cover all moving expenses, including hotels and meals and the costs of arranging for housing in the new location, plus a bonus if the cost of living in the new country is higher than in the United States.

The crux of the integration problem lies in the differences in the corporate cultures of the two companies. Chrysler managers want to operate by using a low-cost business strategy. They want advertisements for new cars to be placed on the Internet, reducing the need for elaborate four-color brochures that focus on reliability, efficiency, and an easy-going lifestyle. Daimler managers want glossy four-color brochures that emphasize distinctiveness, wealth, and demanding engineering. During the debate over the brochure, both groups did agree on the colors of blue and yellow for it. Ms. Vahdiek, the Daimler lawyer, noted that those were also the colors of Lufthansa, the German Airline. Mr. Wilhelm, Chrysler's human resource representative, noted that these were the colors of the University of Michigan.

In Germany, meetings would last all day and then all the managers would go out to dinner. In Stuttgart, the group usually dined at Dopo, an Italian restaurant with a good wine list. Over dinner, the real issues surfaced. The U.S. managers wanted to use video-conferencing or conference calls in an effort to reduce the 14 hours of travel time between their locations in the United States and Stuttgart and the expense involved. They pictured their German counterparts as "running around with steel helmets and always saying 'Yes, General.'" The Germans pictured their American counterparts as "cowboys—always shooting from the hip."

Another difference is that the U.S. and German managers had different notions of what is valued. In the old Chrysler organization, "empowerment" was practiced. Employees had access to senior managers and addressed them by first name. At Daimler, employees focused on social justice. Titles, office location, and other perks were important status symbols that dictated power and authority relationships among employees. The differences in these corporate values created stumbling blocks for the development of effective cross-cultural teams. The Daimler managers perceived that the Chrysler managers only wanted to see results and were not detail-oriented. Conversely, the Chrysler managers believed that the Daimler managers were more process-oriented, too slow in accomplishing their goals, and very detail-oriented. Finally, Chrysler was not as much a global company as Daimler, so it placed less value

*For more information on
DaimlerChrysler, visit the
organization's home page
at **http://www.
daimlerchrysler.com**.*

on international assignments as stepping stones for its managers. Most Daimler managers, however, had lived outside Germany at some point in their careers. Taking an international assignment was a necessary step in their professional development to broaden their managing across cultures and managing self competencies.[9]

## SUSTAINING A CULTURE

The ways in which an organization functions and is managed may have both intended and unintended consequences for maintaining and changing organizational culture. Figure 15.3 illustrates one basic method of maintaining an organization's culture: The organization hires individuals who seem to fit its culture; the organization then maintains its culture by removing employees who consistently or markedly deviate from accepted behaviors and activities.

Specific methods of maintaining organizational culture, however, are a great deal more complicated than just hiring the right people and firing those who don't work out. The most powerful indicators of the organization's culture are (1) what managers and teams pay attention to, measure, and control; (2) the ways that managers (particularly top managers) react to critical incidents and organizational crises; (3) managerial and team role modeling, teaching, and coaching; (4) criteria for allocating rewards and status; (5) criteria for recruitment, selection, promotion, and removal from the organization; and (6) organizational rites, ceremonies, and stories.[10]

**What Managers and Teams Pay Attention to.**   One of the more powerful methods of maintaining organizational culture involves the processes and behaviors that managers, individual employees, and teams pay attention to—that is, the events that get noticed and commented on. Dealing with events systematically sends strong signals to employees about what is important and expected of them. For example, Tom Salonek, president of Go-e-biz.com, an E-business consulting firm, holds a 15-minute meeting every morning at 7:25 A.M. sharp with his salespeople, who use cell phones to call in from the road. They share their challenges and results from the

**Figure 15.3**                **Methods of Maintaining Organizational Culture**

previous day. Salonek closely monitors sales contacts they have made, giving them an extra $20 a day for making their daily contact goal quotas.

**Reactions to Incidents and Crises.**    When an organization faces a crisis, such as the September 11, 2001, terrorism attacks or loss of a major customer, the handling of that crisis by managers and employees reveals a great deal about its culture. The manner in which the crisis is dealt with can either reinforce the existing culture or bring out new values and norms that change the culture in some way. For example, an organization facing a dramatic reduction in demand for its product might react by laying off or firing employees. Or it might reduce employee hours or rates of pay with no workforce reduction. The alternative chosen indicates the value placed on human resources and can reinforce and maintain the current culture or indicate a major change in the culture. Such a situation occurred at Lincoln Electric after the firm formalized a guaranteed continuous employment policy in 1958. Every worker with more than 2 years' service with the company has been guaranteed at least 30 hours per week, 49 weeks per year. The company responded to declining demand for its arc welding products and electrical motors during the recession of the 1980s by cutting back all employee hours from 40 to 30. Many employees were reassigned and the total workforce was reduced slightly through normal retirement and restricted hiring. Year-end incentive bonuses were still paid.[11]

**Role Modeling, Teaching, and Coaching.**    Aspects of an organization's culture are communicated to employees by the way managers treat them. As the Preview Case indicates, TDIndustries' managers relate to employees according to the principles of the servant leadership concept. All new hires at TDI attend its formal training program and mentors reveal TDI's culture through day-to-day coaching on the job. At the Four Seasons Hotels and Resorts, all new trainees are shown films that emphasize customer service. Managers also demonstrate good customer or client service practices in their interactions with customers. The repeated emphasis on good customer relations in both training and day-to-day behavior helps create and maintain a customer-oriented culture throughout the Four Seasons organization.[12]

**Allocation of Rewards and Status.**    Employees also learn about an organization's culture through its reward system. The rewards and punishments attached to various behaviors convey to employees the priorities and values of both individual managers and the organization. At TDIndustries, employees are eligible for a 401(k) plan after just 90 days and can earn up to $7,000 for referring a new hire to the company. All employees are cross-trained to perform a variety of tasks to reduce production bottlenecks and status differences among the plumbing, electrical, mechanical, and other trades. At Sara Lee, programs encourage managers at different levels to own stock in the company. The rationale is that managers should have a stake in the financial health of the firm, based on its overall performance.

Similarly, in many organizations the status system maintains certain aspects of its culture. The distribution of perks (a corner office on an upper floor, executive dining room, carpeting, a private secretary, or a private parking space) demonstrates which roles and behaviors are most valued by an organization. At Chase Manhattan Bank in New York City, Jim Donaldson was promoted to vice president for global trusts. His new office was well furnished with most of the symbols of relatively high status. But before he was allowed to move in, his boss ordered the maintenance department to cut a 12-inch strip from the entire perimeter of the carpet. At Chase Manhattan, wall-to-wall carpeting is a status symbol given to senior vice presidents and above.

However, an organization may use rewards and status symbols ineffectively and inconsistently. If it does, it misses a great opportunity to influence its culture because an organization's reward practices and its culture appear to be strongly linked in the minds of its members. In fact, some authorities believe that the most effective method of influencing organizational culture may be through the reward system.[13]

**Recruitment, Selection, Promotion, and Removal.**   As Figure 15.3 suggests, one of the fundamental ways that organizations maintain a culture is through the recruitment process. In addition, the criteria used to determine who is assigned to specific jobs or positions, who gets raises and promotions and why, who is removed from the organization by firing or early retirement, and so on reinforce and demonstrate basic aspects of an organization's culture. These criteria become known throughout the organization and can maintain or change an existing culture.

**Rites and Ceremonies.**   **Organizational rites and ceremonies** are planned activities or rituals that have important cultural meaning. Certain managerial or employee activities can become rituals that are interpreted as part of the organizational culture. Rites and ceremonies that sustain organizational culture include rites of passage, degradation, enhancement, and integration. Table 15.2 contains examples of each of these four types of rites and identifies some of their desirable consequences.

A ceremony used at Mary Kay Cosmetics Company provides a good example of rites of enhancement. During elaborate awards ceremonies, gold and diamond pins, fur stoles, and the use of pink Cadillacs are presented to salespeople who achieve their sales quotas. Music tends to arouse and express emotions, and all the participants know the Mary Kay Song: "I've Got that Mary Kay Enthusiasm," which was written by a member of the organization to the tune of the hymn "I've Got that Old Time Religion." This song is a direct expression of the Mary Kay culture and is fervently sung during the awards ceremonies. The ceremonies are reminiscent of a Miss America pageant, with all the participants dressed in glamorous evening clothes. The setting is typically an auditorium with a stage in front of a large, cheering audience. The ceremonies clearly are intended to increase the identity and status of high-performing employees and emphasize the company's rewards for excellence.[14]

**Organization Stories.**   Many of the underlying beliefs and values of an organization's culture are expressed as stories that become part of its folklore. These stories transmit the existing culture from old to new employees and emphasize important aspects of that culture—and some may persist for a long time. Southwest Airlines has a unique culture. Herb Kelleher, its founder and now chairman of the board, made the development and maintenance of culture one of his primary duties. Kelleher's style can be described as a combination of Sam Walton's thriftiness (e.g., no company cars or club memberships and executives stay in the same hotels as flight crews) and Robin Williams's wackiness. He has shown up at Southwest parties as Elvis, a drag queen, and in other "fun uniforms." He arm-wrestled the president of a North Carolina

**Table 15.2**

| **Organizational Rites and Ceremonies** | | |
| --- | --- | --- |
| **TYPE** | **EXAMPLE** | **POSSIBLE CONSEQUENCES** |
| Rites of passage | Basic training, U.S. Army | Facilitate transition into new roles; minimize differences in way roles are carried out |
| Rites of degradation | Firing a manager | Reduce power and identity; reaffirm proper behavior |
| Rites of enhancement | Mary Kay Cosmetics Company ceremonies | Enhance power and identity; emphasize value of proper behavior |
| Rites of integration | Office party | Encourage common feelings that bind members together |

Source: Adapted from Trice, H. M., and Beyer, J. M. *The Cultures of Work Organizations.* Englewood Cliffs, N.J.: Prentice-Hall, 1993, 111.

aviation firm over the right to use the slogan "Just Plane Smart." (Kelleher lost, saying he had suffered a wrist fracture diving in front of a bus to save a small child.) He also lost a H-O-R-S-E game at Hobby Airport to Houston Rockets Coach Rudy Thomjanovich. He wrote a column for the company's newsletter entitled "So, What Was Herb Doing All This Time?" In one column, he recalls the time when a customer service representative volunteered to stay with an elderly passenger who was afraid to stay alone when her flight was grounded due to fog. The agent "knew" that was what Herb would have done.[15]

## CHANGING A CULTURE

The same basic methods used to maintain an organization's culture may be used to modify it. That is, culture might be modified by changing (1) what managers and teams pay attention to, (2) how crises are handled, (3) criteria for recruiting new members, (4) criteria for promotion within the organization, (5) criteria for allocating rewards, and (6) organizational rites and ceremonies.[16]

Changing organizational culture can be tricky, and at least two concerns suggest caution. First, some people question whether the deeply held, core values of organizational culture are amenable to change. In their view, focusing managerial efforts on changing ineffective behaviors and procedures is more meaningful than attempting to change organizational culture. Some managers further argue that changing behavior will work only if it can be based on the existing culture.

Second, accurately assessing organizational culture in itself is difficult. Most large, complex organizations actually have more than one culture. The Gainesville, Florida, Police Department, for example, has distinctly different cultures based on the shifts to which officers are assigned and their rank. Sometimes these multiple cultures are called **subcultures**. Every organization may have at least three cultures—an operating culture (line employees), an engineering culture (technical and professional people), and an executive culture (top management). Each culture stems from very different views typically held by these groups of individuals.[17] Faced with a variety of subcultures, management may have difficulty (1) accurately assessing them and (2) effecting needed changes.

Despite these concerns, we believe that changing organizational cultures is both feasible and, in the case of failing organizations or significant shifts in an organization's external environment, essential. Successfully changing organizational culture requires:

- understanding the old culture first because a new culture can't be developed unless managers and employees understand where they're starting from;
- providing support for employees and teams who have ideas for a better culture and are willing to act on those ideas;
- finding the most effective subculture in the organization and using it as an example from which employees can learn;
- not attacking culture head-on but finding ways to help employees and teams do their jobs more effectively;
- treating the vision of a new culture as a guiding principle for change, not as a miracle cure;
- recognizing that significant organizationwide cultural change takes 5 to 10 years; and
- living the new culture because actions speak louder than words.

The transformation of Harley-Davidson is one example of how a company changed its culture.[18] When Richard Teerlink took over as president of Harley-Davidson in 1987, the differences in quality between Harley-Davidson and its competitors were striking. For example, only 5 percent of Honda's motorcycles failed to pass inspection; over 50 percent of Harleys failed the same test. Honda's value added per employee was three times that of Harley's. Harley's relations with its dealers were poor because they were forced to provide customers with free service because of factory defects. So what did Teerlink do? He set out to change the culture of Harley-Davidson, which he accomplished before retiring in 1999.

First, he began emphasizing organizational and individual learning at all levels through a Leadership Institute. The institute was designed to introduce new workers to Harley's goals and culture while providing current workers with a better understanding of the organization's design and effects of competition on Harley's performance. Managers prepared a series of nontechnical explanations of how cash flow and flexible production affect financial success. Line workers were taught how products, sales, and productivity affect profitability. Substantial changes in employee job descriptions, responsibilities, and production processes were undertaken in an effort to increase job enrichment and worker empowerment. These efforts were implemented through cross training and expansion of job responsibilities. Teerlink eliminated the positions of vice president in marketing and operations because these jobs didn't add value to the product. Teams of employees, such as a "create-demand team" that is in charge of producing products and a "product-support team," now make these decisions. Employees formed quality circles that became a source of bottom-up ideas for improving quality. Employees created a peer review system to evaluate each other's performance instead of relying solely on first-line supervisors' evaluations. These evaluations help determine employees' pay.

Second, to recapture the Harley mystique, Teerlink revitalized the Harley Hogs, a customer group formed to get people more actively involved in motorcycling. To attract women riders, The Ladies of Harley group was formed to increase ridership and interest among young women motorcyclists. Teerlink and his staff regularly attended road rallies and helped clubs sponsor various charitable events. Harley also issued a credit card to thousands of riders and encouraged them to use the card for the purchase of a motorcycle, service, and accessories. The sale of merchandise, including T-shirts, clothing, jewelry, small-leather goods, and numerous other products, permits customers to identify with the company. As Teerlink noted, "There are very few products that are so exciting that people will tattoo your logo on their body."

We cover planned organizational change extensively in Chapter 16. Many of the specific techniques and methods for changing organizational behaviors presented in that chapter also may be used to change organizational culture. Indeed, any comprehensive program of organizational change, in some sense, is an attempt to change the culture of the organization.

We can't overemphasize how difficult deliberately changing organizational cultures may be. In fact, the incompatibility of organizational cultures and their resistance to change has been one of the most significant barriers to successful corporate mergers, as illustrated by the DaimlerChrysler case. For a merger to be effective, at least one (and sometimes both) of the merging organizations may need to change its culture.

**Learning Objective:**

2. Describe four types of organizational culture.

## TYPES OF ORGANIZATIONAL CULTURE

Cultural elements and their relationships create a pattern that is distinct to an organization (e.g., the culture of Southwest Airlines versus that of American Airlines). However, organizational cultures do have some common characteristics.[19] One proposed framework is presented in Figure 15.4. The vertical axis reflects the relative control orientation of an organization, ranging from stable to flexible. The horizontal axis reflects the relative focus of attention of an organization, ranging from internal functioning to external functioning. The extreme corners of the four quadrants represent

**Figure 15.4**      **Framework of Types of Cultures**

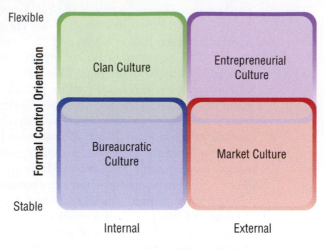

Source: Adapted from Hooijberg, R., and Petrock, F. On cultural change: Using the competing values framework to help leaders execute a transformational strategy. *Human Resource Management*, 1993, 32, 29–50; Quinn, R. E., *Beyond Rational Management: Mastering the Paradoxes and Competing Demands of High Performance*. San Francisco: Jossey-Bass, 1988.

four pure types of organizational culture: bureaucratic, clan, entrepreneurial, and market. In a culturally homogeneous organization such as Southwest Airlines, one of these basic types of culture will be predominant. At the Dallas Police Department, Bank of America, Microsoft, and other culturally fragmented organizations, multiple cultures are likely not only to exist, but also to compete for superiority.

As is true of organization designs, different organizational cultures may be appropriate under different conditions, with no one type of culture being ideal for every situation. However, some employees may prefer one culture to others. As you read about each type of culture, consider which best fits your preferences. Employees who work in an organization with a culture that fits their own view of an ideal culture tend to be committed to the organization and optimistic about its future.

## BUREAUCRATIC CULTURE

An organization that values formality, rules, standard operating procedures, and hierarchical coordination has a **bureaucratic culture**. Recall that the long-term concerns of a bureaucracy are predictability, efficiency, and stability. Its members highly value standardized goods and customer service. Behavioral norms support formality over informality. Managers view their roles as being good coordinators, organizers, and enforcers of written rules and standards. Tasks, responsibilities, and authority for all employees are clearly defined. The organization's many rules and processes are spelled out in thick manuals, and employees believe that their duty is to "go by the book" and follow legalistic procedures.

Most local, state, and federal governments have bureaucratic cultures, which can impede their effectiveness. The federal personnel manual, which spells out the rules for hiring and firing, runs to thousands of pages. Hundreds of pages are needed just to explain how to fill out some of the forms. The approval process for ordering a computer can take months, during which time the equipment ordered could be a generation old by the time it is installed.

## CLAN CULTURE

Tradition, loyalty, personal commitment, extensive socialization, teamwork, self-management, and social influence are attributes of a **clan culture**.[20] Its members recognize an obligation beyond the simple exchange of labor for a salary. They understand that contributions to the organization (e.g., hours worked per week) may exceed any contractual agreements. The individual's long-term commitment to the organization (loyalty) is exchanged for the organization's long-term commitment to the individual (security). Because individuals believe that the organization will treat them fairly in terms of salary increases, promotions, and other forms of recognition, they hold themselves accountable to the organization for their actions.

A clan culture achieves unity by means of a long and thorough socialization process. Long-time clan members serve as mentors and role models for newer members. The clan is aware of its unique history and often documents its origins and celebrates its traditions in various rites. Members have a shared image of the organization's style and manner of conduct. Public statements and events reinforce its values.

In a clan culture, members share feelings of pride in membership. They have a strong sense of identification and recognize their common fate in the organization. The up-through-the-ranks career pattern results in an extensive network of colleagues whose paths have crossed and who have shared similar experiences. Shared goals, perceptions, and behavioral tendencies foster communication, coordination, and integration. A clan culture generates feelings of personal ownership of a business, a product, or an idea. In addition, peer pressure to adhere to important norms is strong. The richness of the culture creates an environment in which few areas are left totally free from normative pressures. Depending on the types of its norms, the culture may or may not generate risk-taking behavior or innovation. Success is assumed to depend substantially on sensitivity to customers and concern for people. Teamwork, participation, and consensus decision-making are believed to lead to this success.

The following Managing Communication Competency feature highlights how Synovus Financial Corporation, a 113-year-old Columbus, Georgia, firm, communicates its culture to its employees and customers. Synovus is a $16 billion organization that employs more than 11,000 people in the southeastern United States. Bill Turner, Synovus's current CEO, has written a book, *The Learning of Love—A Journey Toward Servant Leadership*, that describes his life experiences and the values that form his organization's culture. The organization's name was deliberately chosen because it is the combination of the words synergy and novus—synergy, meaning that the interaction of separate parts yields a result that is greater than the sum of the parts, and novus, meaning superior quality and different from others in the same category.[21]

## COMPETENCY:  MANAGING COMMUNICATION

### SYNOVUS

Synovus spends more than $10 million annually to train and develop its team members (employees) at its own Center for People Development. According to the center's director, Genei Mize, the center wants to look at the whole person and in doing so, believes that people will produce at a high level that benefits not only themselves but also the organization. At the Center, team members are steeped in Synovus's culture through lectures, role-playing, participation in simulations, and leadership training exercises. All programs are aimed at maximizing the growth opportunity (personal and organizational development) and interpersonal capabilities of team members. Managers from various parts of the organization share their experiences with team members so that they can learn more about the people within the company. They discuss information collected from other programs and from the company's on-line résumé builder, which allows team members to "tell their own stories." Bill Johnson, current president of Synovus, tells a story that his grandfather told him about a woman mill worker who had sewn her life savings into the hem of her dress and was injured when the dress was caught in a piece of machinery. The mill's secretary offered to keep her money safe and pay her monthly interest while she recovered from her injuries. The secretary soon offered the same service to all the mill workers. This act of kindness inspired the establishment of a savings bank that later became Synovus. More than a century has passed since that torn dress, but the spirit conveyed by the story keeps Synovus alive.

To retain team members, Synovus contributes up to 21 percent of team members' salaries to a retirement plan (the national average is 7 percent). Entitled a Wealth Building/Retirement Plan, it is based on the entire company's annual performance. Synovus also has an extensive benefits package, Right Choice, which serves to remind employees why they joined the organization initially. Benefits include health insurance, adoption assistance, flexible work hours, job sharing, flexible spending accounts, tuition assistance, prescription drug programs, and many more. It also matches 50 cents for every dollar that a team member spends to buy shares in Synovus stock. More than 80 percent of eligible team members participate in that program. The organization also sponsors team appreciation weeks, tree lightings, breakfasts with Santa, weekend retreats, Easter egg hunts, bass fishing tournaments, and other events to encourage team members and their families to have some fun.

*For more information on Synovus, visit the organization's home page at http://www.synovus.com.*

## ENTREPRENEURIAL CULTURE

High levels of risk taking, dynamism, and creativity characterize an **entrepreneurial culture**. There is a commitment to experimentation, innovation, and being on the leading edge. This culture doesn't just quickly react to changes in the environment—it creates change. Effectiveness means providing new and unique products and rapid growth. Individual initiative, flexibility, and freedom foster growth and are encouraged and well rewarded. In late 2000 and throughout much of 2001, many of the dot-com companies failed because their leaders lacked the management competencies to build the companies and manage external relationships with financial backers.

Entrepreneurial cultures usually are associated with small to mid-sized companies that are still run by a founder, such as Microsoft, Dell, and many Silicon Valley start-ups. Innovation and entrepreneurship are values held by the founder(s). Jeff Bezos started Amazon.com in his two-bedroom home in Seattle. Later, he and his friends converted his garage to an office and ran extension cords from every outlet to power three computers. To save money, Bezos went to Home Depot and bought wooden doors. Using angle brackets and 2 × 4s, he converted the doors into desks that cost $60 each. Today, the firm's desks are still made the same way. Initially, money is tight for most start-ups, and the entrepreneur's ability to raise seed money often is crucial to its survival.

## MARKET CULTURE

The achievement of measurable and demanding goals, especially those that are financial and market-based (e.g., sales growth, profitability, and market share) characterize a **market culture**. Hard-driving competitiveness and a profit orientation prevail throughout the organization. CEO Christos Cotsakos describes the market culture of E*Trade this way: "At E*Trade we're an attacker. We're predatory. We believe in the God-given right to market share."  Richard Causey, chief accounting officer at Enron, stated that Kenneth Lay, CEO of Enron, laid the foundation for a market culture by encouraging a ruthless, winner-take-all culture. Enron recruited a band of cocky, inexperienced MBAs and left them alone to do whatever it took to structure a deal, regardless of the consequences. "Pushing the limits was what you were told to do, and you were given the resources to do it," says Causey. Tyco and Gulf & Western, among others, are organizations that have created market cultures.

In a market culture, the relationship between individual and organization is contractual. That is, the obligations of each party are agreed upon in advance. In this sense, the control orientation is formal and quite stable. The individual is responsible for some level of performance, and the organization promises a specified level of rewards in return. Increased levels of performance are exchanged for increased rewards, as outlined in an agreed upon schedule. Neither party recognizes the right of the other to demand more than was originally specified. The organization doesn't promise (or imply) security, and the individual doesn't promise (or imply) loyalty. The contract, renewed annually if each party adequately performs its obligations, is utilitarian because each party uses the other to further its own goals. Rather than promoting a feeling of membership in a social system, the market culture values independence and individuality and encourages members to pursue their own financial goals. For example, the store manager at Pizza Hut who increases sales will make more money, and the firm will earn more profits through the greater sales volume generated.

A market culture doesn't exert much social pressure on an organization's members, but when it does, members are expected to conform. At Enron, employees (in theory) were permitted to book their business travel themselves with any agency. However, Sharon Lay, Ken Lay's sister, owned a Houston travel agency that received $6.8 million in commissions from Enron for travel. Employees who didn't book their travel through her agency did so only once. Memos from Ken Lay's office reminded them that they should use her travel agency.

In market cultures superiors' interactions with subordinates largely consist of negotiating performance–reward agreements and/or evaluating requests for resource allocations. Managers aren't formally judged on their effectiveness as role models or mentors. The absence of a long-term commitment by both parties results in a weak socialization process. Social relations among coworkers aren't emphasized, and few economic incentives are tied directly to cooperating with peers. Managers are expected to cooperate with managers in other departments only to the extent necessary to achieve their performance goals. As a result, they may not develop an extensive network of colleagues within the organization. The market culture often is tied to monthly, quarterly, and annual performance goals based on profits.

## ORGANIZATIONAL USES

Organizational culture has the potential to enhance organizational performance, individual satisfaction, the sense of certainty about how problems are to be handled, and so on. However, if an organizational culture gets out of step with the changing expectations of internal and/or external stakeholders, the organization's effectiveness can decline. Organizational culture and performance clearly are related, although the evidence regarding the exact nature of this relationship is mixed. Studies showing that the relationship between many cultural attributes (featured in the popular press as being important for performance) and high performance hasn't been consistent over time. Based on what we know about culture–performance relationships, a contingency approach seems to be a good one for managers and organizations to take.

Further investigations of this issue are unlikely to discover one "best" organizational culture (either in terms of strength or type).

We do know the following about the relationships between culture and performance.

- Organizational culture can have a significant impact on a firm's long-term economic performance.
- Organizational culture will probably be an even more important factor in determining the success or failure of firms during the next decade.
- Organizational cultures that inhibit strong long-term financial performance are not rare; they develop easily, even in firms that are filled with reasonable and intelligent people.
- Although tough to change, organizational cultures can be made more performance enhancing if managers understand what sustains a culture.[22]

We can summarize the effects of organizational culture on employee behavior and performance with four key ideas. First, knowing the culture of an organization allows employees to understand both the firm's history and current methods of operation. This knowledge provides guidance about expected future behaviors. Second, organizational culture can foster commitment to corporate philosophy and values. This commitment generates shared feelings of working toward common goals. Third, organizational culture, through its norms, serves as a control mechanism to channel behaviors toward desired behaviors and away from undesired behaviors. Finally, certain types of organizational cultures may be related directly to greater effectiveness and productivity than others.

The need to determine which attributes of an organization's culture should be preserved and which should be modified is constant. In the United States during the 1980s, many organizations began changing their cultures to be more responsive to customers' expectations of product quality and service. During the late 1990s, many organizations began to reassess how well their cultures fit the expectations of the workforce. Since World War II, the U.S. workforce has changed demographically, becoming more diverse. More and more employees have begun to feel that organizational cultures established decades ago are out of step with contemporary values. We address the challenge of adjusting established organizational cultures to meet the expectations of a demographically diverse workforce in the remainder of this chapter.

**Learning Objective:**

3. Discuss how organizational culture can influence ethical behaviors of managers and employees.

# ETHICAL BEHAVIOR AND ORGANIZATIONAL CULTURE

Ethical problems in organizations continue to concern managers and employees greatly. The Enron bankruptcy and scandal is the most prominent recent example of a failure to promote ethical behavior among an organization's managers, employees, and contractors. Arthur Andersen's CEO Joseph Berardino admitted before a congressional hearing looking into the Enron bankruptcy that "America harbors a cottage industry of accountants and bankers devoted to circumventing audit rules." KPMG Peat Marwick, a Big Five accounting firm, recently formed a new unit designed to help its clients create a "moral organization." The firm maintains that the application of auditing ethics can promote good business practices and benefit its corporate culture.

## IMPACT OF CULTURE

Managers and researchers are beginning to explore the potential impact that organizational culture can have on ethical behavior. Organizational culture involves a complex interplay of formal and informal systems that may support either ethical or unethical behavior. Formal systems include leadership, structure, policies, reward systems, orientation and training programs, and decision-making processes. Informal systems include norms, heroes, rituals, language, myths, sagas, and stories.

Organizational culture appears to affect ethical behavior in several ways. For example, a culture emphasizing ethical norms provides support for ethical behavior. In addition, top management plays a key role in fostering ethical behavior by exhibiting the correct behavior. If lower level managers observe top-level managers sexually harassing others, falsifying expense reports, diverting shipments to preferred customers, misrepresenting the organization's financial position, and other forms of unethical behavior, they assume that these behaviors are acceptable and will be rewarded in the future. Thus the presence or absence of ethical behavior in managerial actions both influences and reflects the culture. The organizational culture may promote taking responsibility for the consequences of actions, thereby increasing the probability that individuals will behave ethically. Alternatively, the culture may diffuse responsibility for the consequences of unethical behavior, thereby making such behavior more likely. In short, ethical business practices stem from ethical organizational cultures.

An important concept linking organizational culture to ethical behavior is **principled organizational dissent**, by which individuals in an organization protest, on ethical grounds, some practice or policy. Some cultures permit and even encourage principled organizational dissent; other cultures punish such behavior.

An employee might use various strategies in attempting to change unethical behavior, including:

- secretly or publicly reporting unethical actions to a higher level within the organization;
- secretly or publicly reporting unethical actions to someone outside the organization;
- secretly or publicly threatening an offender or a responsible manager with reporting unethical actions; or
- quietly or publicly refusing to implement an unethical order or policy.

### WHISTLE-BLOWING

As a form of principled organizational dissent, **whistle-blowing** is the disclosure by current or former employees of illegal, immoral, or illegitimate organizational practices to people or organizations that may be able to change the practice. The whistle-blower lacks the power to change the undesirable practice directly and so appeals to others either inside or outside the organization.

The collapse of Enron started when Sherron Watkins sat down at her computer on August 14, 2001, and began typing a questioning and now famous memo to her boss, Kenneth Lay. "I am incredibly nervous that we will implode in a wave of accounting scandals," she wrote. Watkins's seven-page memo has become the smoking gun in an unfolding investigation of alleged financial misdealing at Enron and Arthur Andersen. The following Managing Ethics Competency feature highlights some of these issues.

## COMPETENCY:   MANAGING ETHICS

### SHERRON WATKINS AT ENRON

The public knew of Sherron Watkins's memo on January 14, 2002, only after Enron had declared bankruptcy (on December 2, 2001). In her memo, Watkins presents evidence that Kenneth Lay and other Enron executives knew about Enron's shaky finances well before the public and other employees. In the summer of 2001 after the resignation of then CEO Jeff Skilling, Lay invited employees to forward any concerns to him. Watkins sent him the memo detailing her uneasiness about "funny" accounting practices to hide company losses, stating that "Enron has become a risky place to work." Accountants at Arthur Andersen were advised of her concerns, but no action was taken at the time.

The shredding of documents by Enron and Arthur Andersen employees reflects a culture that was rewarded at Enron. In the spring of 2001, former Enron executive Cliff Baxter warned then CEO Skilling about dubious financial practices that could eventually be Enron's downfall. By speaking out, he lost any chance to become company president. The culture at Enron encouraged and rewarded managers to take high-flying risks. Skilling had installed few internal controls and encouraged managers to push financial practices to the limit. With a lack of financial controls, questionable accounting and financial transactions were ignored. Former Enron employees said that Skilling created and embodied the in-your-face Enron culture, where risk-taking, deal-making, and "thinking outside the box" were richly rewarded. Skilling believed all that mattered was money: You buy loyalty with money. Arthur Andersen, providing both auditing and consulting services, ignored questionable practices because it was being paid $52 million annually for its services.

Top managers were looking at the numbers and punished those who didn't produce. Increasing revenues were rewarded with huge raises. Bonuses and rave performance reviews were based on doing deals—the more the bigger and better. Unfortunately, the estimated profits attached to the deals often bore little resemblance to the profits generated by them. Baxter, who was in charge of Enron North American, himself negotiated and sold big energy deals off the books to Enron's partnerships, or Joint Energy Development investments, such as JEDI II. Resulting billion dollar losses weren't recorded. Similarly, Michael Kopper, finance manager, and Andrew Fastow, chief financial officer, reportedly created a partnership for $125,000 to shift Enron losses off the company's books and then sold the partnership back to Enron for $10.5 million. Management and the board of director's committees that were supposed to watch over the firm's financial practices, along with the external auditors, had been hand picked by the CEO and were loyal to him.[23]

These types of whistle-blowing activities aren't without risk. Watkins says that life at Enron has been extremely painful since her disclosure. Her computer was confiscated and her office was moved away from others in the accounting department. When he told his superiors about Fastow's deals, Jeff McMahon, Enron's treasurer, was immediately reassigned to another job away from the "action." Cliff Baxter committed suicide, knowing that the finances of Enron were shady at best and fraud at worst. Individuals engaging in principled organizational dissent risk dismissal, demotion, isolation, ostracism, and threats of harm and even death to self and family. Often millions or even billions of dollars are at stake. Moreover, the whistle-blower could be wrong about individual or organizational actions. Thus misguided attempts to stop apparently unethical behavior might unnecessarily harm employees or organizations.

The following actions can help create an organizational culture that encourages ethical behavior.

- Be realistic in setting values and goals regarding employment relationships. Do not promise what the organization cannot deliver.
- Encourage input from throughout the organization regarding appropriate values and practices for implementing the culture. Choose values that represent the views of both employees and managers.

- Opt for a *strong* culture that encourages and rewards diversity and principled dissent, such as grievance or complaint mechanisms or other internal review procedures.
- Provide training programs for managers and teams on adopting and implementing the organization's values. These programs should stress the underlying ethical and legal principles and cover the practical aspects of carrying out procedural guidelines.[24]

An effective organizational culture should encourage ethical behavior and discourage unethical behavior. Admittedly, ethical behavior may "cost" the organization and individuals. A global firm that refuses to pay a bribe to secure business in a particular country may lose sales. An individual may lose financially by not accepting a kickback. Similarly, an organization or individual might seem to gain from unethical actions. An organization may flout U.S. law by quietly paying bribes to officials in order to gain entry to a new market. A purchasing agent for a large corporation might take kickbacks for purchasing all needed office supplies from a particular supplier. However, such gains are often short term.

In the long run, an organization can't successfully operate if its prevailing culture and values aren't similar to those of society. That is as true as the observation that, in the long run, an organization cannot survive unless it provides high-quality goods and services that society wants and needs. An organizational culture that promotes ethical behavior is not only compatible with prevailing cultural values in the United States, but it also makes good business sense.

<table>
<tr><td>Learning Objective:</td></tr>
<tr><td>4. Explain why fostering cultural diversity is important.</td></tr>
</table>

# FOSTERING CULTURAL DIVERSITY

In Chapter 1, we emphasized that organizations are becoming increasingly diverse in terms of gender, race, ethnicity, and nationality. More than half the U.S. workforce consists of women, minorities, and recent immigrants. The growing diversity of employees in many organizations can bring substantial benefits, such as more successful marketing strategies for different types of customers, improved decision making, and greater creativity and innovation. The U.S. Department of Labor's statistics for Workforce 2000 suggest that 80 percent of all new employees entering the U.S. workforce during the next decade will be women or people of color. Whether motivated by economic necessity or choice, organizations will be competing in this marketplace for talent. At DuPont, a group of African-American workers recently opened promising new markets for the firm by focusing on black farmers. A multicultural team gained the company about $45 million in new business by changing the way DuPont designs and markets decorating materials (e.g., countertops) in order to appeal more to overseas customers.

## CHALLENGES

Along with its benefits, cultural diversity brings costs and concerns, including communication difficulties, intraorganizational conflict, and turnover. Effectively fostering cultural diversity promises to continue to be a significant challenge for organizations for a long time. To succeed, organizations have to work hard to resolve these issues. In the following Managing Self Competency feature, Linda Glick, chief information officer for Levi Strauss and Company, describes both the benefits and the challenges stemming from a multicultural workforce.

## ORGANIZATIONAL USES

There are no easy answers to the challenges of fostering a culturally diverse workforce. However, research has revealed some common characteristics that are present

### LINDA GLICK AT LEVI STRAUSS

Linda Glick started her career at Levi Strauss as a programmer. Soon managers at Strauss recognized her as a person with excellent communication, across culture, and team competencies. Her ability to speak two foreign languages was a major plus for a company that views its products as having global appeal. Her initial assignment in the international group proved especially valuable because it was a small group where titles and other symbols of Levi's culture were not important. Levi's team members yelled and screamed at each other over business issues, but still went out together for beer later. This assignment gave Glick an opportunity to understand Levi's entire business operations across all product lines. During that early assignment, she learned that effective leaders at Strauss were those who listened, understood others' concerns, and used creative thinking to solve problems—and let others make decisions.

Later, as a manager working overseas, she also faced unique challenges. When she went to Japan, she lacked the ability to speak Japanese. In her first meeting with a supplier of zippers, she encountered gender prejudice. The Japanese managers thought that she was a translator and treated her as such. She was expected to sit quietly, not ask questions, stand up when men left the room, serve tea, and the like. The meeting was conducted entirely in Japanese. When she asked questions in English, the Japanese replied in Japanese. Although Japanese suppliers saw her as a wonderful person, they had a difficult time accepting her as a line manager with responsibility. However, because she understood Levi Strauss's business thoroughly and took a high-energy approach to business (e.g., serious negotiations, on-time meetings, and organized meeting agendas), she eventually was accepted.

Her experience in Mexico required different behaviors. Meetings were chaotic, leaders lost control of conversations, and meetings that were scheduled to start at 9:00 A.M. usually didn't begin until much later. She had a hard time understanding the macho attitudes that were shown toward women. It wasn't her personality to be aggressive, to fight to be heard, but she found that if she didn't speak up, she would be ignored and undervalued.

Glick's philosophy is: "Change is painful and hard. We all gravitate toward the comfortable, familiar and cozy. We don't know if we have the stamina and resilience to take on change and see it through successfully." To be an effective manager in a multicultural corporation such as Levi Strauss, the person needs to stay focused, have a belief in her own abilities, and a belief that others can make good decisions.[25]

*For more information on Levi Strauss's culture, visit the organization's home page at http://www.levistrauss.com.*

in organizations having effective diversity management programs. These characteristics have been distilled into the following helpful guidelines.

- Managers and employees must understand that a diverse workforce will embody different perspectives and approaches to work and must truly value variety of opinion and insight.
- Managers must recognize both the learning opportunities and the challenges that the expression of different perspectives presents for the organization.
- The organizational culture must create an expectation of high standards of performance and ethics from everyone.
- The organizational culture must stimulate personal development.
- The organizational culture must encourage openness.
- The organizational culture must make workers feel valued.
- The organization must have a clearly stated and widely understood mission.

Table 15.3 contains a questionnaire that you can use to examine your awareness of diversity issues. Take a moment to complete it now. What did you learn about yourself?

<table>
<tr><td>**Learning Objective:**</td><td></td></tr>
</table>

**Learning Objective:**

5. Describe the process of organizational socialization and its affect on culture.

# SOCIALIZATION OF NEW EMPLOYEES

The general meaning of the term **socialization** is the process by which older members of a society transmit to younger members the social skills and knowledge needed to function effectively in that society. Similarly, **organizational socialization** is the systematic process by which an organization brings new employees into its culture.[26] In other words, it involves the transmission of organizational culture from managers and senior employees to new employees, providing the social knowledge and skills needed to perform organizational roles and tasks successfully.

Organizational socialization provides the means by which new employees learn the ropes to skip and those to know. It includes learning work group, departmental, and organizational values, rules, procedures, and norms; developing social and working relationships; and developing the skills needed to perform a job. Interestingly, the stages that an employee goes through during organizational socialization resemble, in many respects, the five stages of group development discussed in Chapter 8.

## STEPS IN SOCIALIZATION

Figure 15.5 presents an example of an organizational socialization process. It doesn't represent the socialization process of every organization. However, many firms with strong cultures—such as Disney, TDIndustries, and Southwest Airlines—frequently follow at least some of these steps in socializing new employees.

**Table 15.3**

| **Diversity Questionnaire** |
|---|
| *Directions*<br>Indicate your views by placing a T (true) or F (false) next to each of these nine statements.<br><br>1. I know about the rules and customs of several different cultures. _____<br>2. I know that I hold stereotypes about other groups. _____<br>3. I feel comfortable with people of different backgrounds from my own. _____<br>4. I associate with people who are different from me. _____<br>5. I find working on a multicultural team satisfying. _____<br>6. I find change stimulating and exciting. _____<br>7. I enjoy learning about other cultures. _____<br>8. When dealing with someone whose English is limited, I show patience and understanding. _____<br>9. I find that spending time building relationships with others is useful because more gets done. _____<br><br>*Interpretation*<br>The more true responses you have, the more adaptable and open you are to diversity. If you have five or more true responses, you probably are someone who finds value in cross-cultural experiences.<br><br>If you have less than five true responses, you may be resistant to interacting with people who are different from you. If that is the case, you may find that your interactions with others are sometimes blocked. |

Source: Adapted from Gardenswartz, L., and Rowe, A. What's your diversity quotient? *Managing Diversity Newsletter*, Jamestown, New York (undated).

**Figure 15.5**      **Steps in Socialization**   intervention for big culture

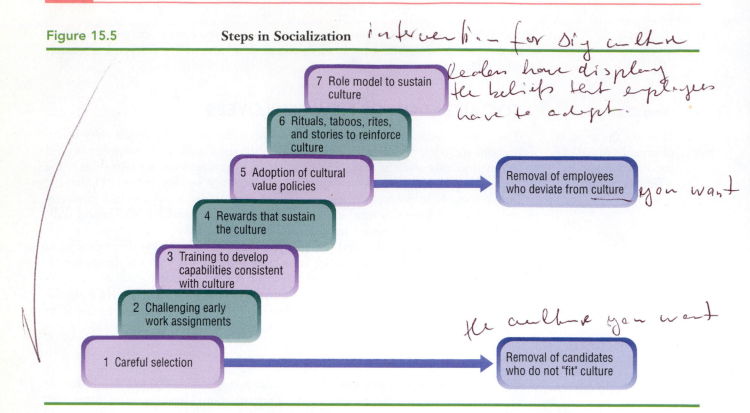

leaders have display
the beliefs that employees
have to adopt.

you want

the culture you want

*Step One.* Entry-level candidates are selected carefully. Trained recruiters use standardized procedures and seek specific capabilities that are related to the success of the business.

*Step Two.* Humility-inducing experiences in the first months on the job cause employees to question their prior behaviors, beliefs, and values. At the U.S. Naval Academy, this indoctrination includes saluting all upper classmen, standing at attention while being spoken to by upper classmen, and memorizing trivial facts about the Academy (e.g., its date of founding, number and names of buildings, the score of last year's football game against West Point, and the like). Self-questioning promotes openness to acceptance of the organization's norms and values.

*Step Three.* Tough on-the-job training leads to mastery of one of the core disciplines of the business. Promotion is then tied to a proven track record.

*Step Four.* Careful attention is given to measuring results and rewarding performance. Reward systems are true indicators of the values that underlie an organization's culture. If the reward system rewards individual managers and employees for results, effective use of teams isn't likely because there is no reward (recognition) for helping others succeed in their tasks.

*Step Five.* Adherence to the organization's values is emphasized. Identification with common values allows employees to justify personal sacrifices caused by their membership in the organization.

*Step Six.* Reinforcing folklore provides legends and interpretations of important events in the organization's history that validate its culture and goals. Folklore reinforces a code of conduct for "how we do things around here."

*Step Seven.* Consistent role models and consistent traits are associated with those recognized as being on the fast track to promotion and success.

Disney World has an effective socialization process that uses some of these seven steps to help ensure that 30,000 visitors a day will have fun.[27] Disney annually hires more than 2,000 people and employs more than 25,000 at Disney World. Pay starts between $6.35 and $6.45 an hour and those who cannot afford housing are housed in a separate Disney gated complex. Disney carefully screens all potential members (Step One). After recruits complete their applications, they are screened for criminal records. Those who have a record are dropped from consideration. All workers at Disney World must strictly follow Disney rules (e.g., no mustaches, visible tattoos, dangling body piercing items, and no hair color outside of the "normal" colors) and norms (such as always taking the extra step to make sure guests have a good experience) and behave in a certain way. To learn these rules, norms, and behaviors, new cast members (recruits) receive formal training at Disney University in groups of 45 and follow a rigid program. During the Tradition I program, which lasts a day and a half, new cast members learn the Disney language and the four Disney values: safety, courtesy, show or entertainment, and efficiency. They also receive training in how to answer guests' questions no matter how simple or difficult the question (Step Five). About 40 percent of new cast members complete Tradition I training. Many simply quit when they understand what their jobs and the rules will entail. Once the cast members have completed the Tradition I phase, they move on to further socialization in the attraction areas (Adventureland, Fantasyland, and so on) that they will join. This session, which can last as long as a day and a half, covers rules for each area. Last but not least is on-the-job training by experienced cast members who actually work in an attraction. This part of the socialization process can take up to $2\frac{1}{2}$ weeks to complete during which the new cast members wear a costume, learn to sing a song (where appropriate), and begin to relate effectively with other cast members and guests (Step Three).

## ORGANIZATIONAL USES

All organizations and groups socialize new members in some way, but the steps can vary greatly in terms of how explicit, comprehensive, and lengthy they are. Generally, rapid socialization is advantageous. For the individual, it quickly reduces the uncertainty and anxiety surrounding a new job. For the organization, it helps the new employee become productive quickly. Organizations with strong cultures may be particularly skillful at socializing individuals. If the culture is effective, socialization will contribute to organizational success. However, if the culture needs changing, strong socialization reduces the prospects for making needed changes.

Socialization creates some additional dilemmas. For example, GE, Xerox, Disney, and other organizations use executive development programs to socialize new hires. How strong should the socialization be? Does the organization want its hires to think alike, at least in terms of a certain level of logic and intelligent analysis? To have the same business values and sense of professionalism? In some sense, the answer to these questions has to be yes. Yet, oversocialization runs the risk of creating rigid, narrow-minded corporate men and women. The goal of most organizations' socialization processes is to develop independent thinkers committed to what they believe to be right while at the same time helping them become collaborative team players who have good interpersonal skills. This goal poses a challenge for socialization, which, to be effective, must balance these two demands.

The socialization process may affect employee and organizational success in a variety of ways.[28] Table 15.4 lists some possible socialization outcomes. These outcomes aren't determined solely by an organization's socialization process. For example, job satisfaction is a function of many things, including the nature of the task, the individual's personality and needs, the nature of supervision, opportunities to succeed and be rewarded, and the like (see Chapter 2). Rather, successful socialization may contribute to job satisfaction, whereas unsuccessful socialization may contribute to job dissatisfaction.

**Table 15.4**

| Possible Outcomes of Socialization Process | |
|---|---|
| **SUCCESSFUL SOCIALIZATION IS REFLECTED IN** | **UNSUCCESSFUL SOCIALIZATION IS REFLECTED IN** |
| • Job satisfaction | • Job dissatisfaction |
| • Role clarity | • Role ambiguity and conflict |
| • High work motivation | • Low work motivation |
| • Understanding of culture, perceived control | • Misunderstanding, tension, perceived lack of control |
| • High job involvement | • Low job involvement |
| • Commitment to organization | • Lack of commitment to organization |
| • Tenure | • Absenteeism, turnover |
| • High performance | • Low performance |
| • Internalized values | • Rejection of values |

# CHAPTER SUMMARY

**1.** Explain how organizational cultures are developed, sustained, and changed.

Organizational culture is the pattern of beliefs and expectations shared by members of an organization. It includes a common philosophy, norms, and values. In other words, it expresses the "rules of the game" for getting along and getting things done and ways of interacting with outsiders, such as suppliers and customers. Some aspects of organizational culture are cultural symbols, heroes, rites, and ceremonies. Organizational culture develops as a response to the challenges of external adaptation and survival and of internal integration. The formation of an organization's culture also is influenced by the culture of the larger society within which the organization must function.

The primary methods for both sustaining and changing organizational culture include (1) identifying what managers and teams pay attention to, measure, and control; (2) recognizing the ways that managers and employees react to crises; (3) using role modeling, teaching, and coaching; (4) developing and applying fairly criteria for allocating rewards; (5) utilizing consistent criteria for recruitment, selection, and promotion within the organization and removal from it; and (6) emphasizing organizational rites, ceremonies, and stories.

**2.** Describe four types of organizational culture.

Although all organizational cultures are unique, four general types were identified and discussed: bureaucratic, clan, entrepreneurial, and market. They are characterized by differences in the extent of formal controls and focus of attention.

**3.** Discuss how organizational culture can influence ethical behaviors of managers and employees.

Organizational culture also can have a strong effect on ethical behavior by managers and employees alike. One concept linking culture to ethical behavior is principled organizational dissent. Cultures that encourage dissent and permit whistle-blowing provide guidelines for ethical behaviors.

**4.** Explain why fostering cultural diversity is important.

Fostering cultural diversity is expected to be one of the principal challenges facing organizations for years to come. How they respond to this challenge will determine the effectiveness of culturally diverse teams, an organization's communication process, and employees' personal development.

**5.** Describe the steps of organizational socialization and its affect on culture.

Socialization is the steps by which new members are brought into an organization's culture. At firms having a strong culture, socialization steps are well developed and the focus of careful attention. All organizations socialize new members, but depending on how it is done, the outcomes could be either positive or negative in terms of job performance, satisfaction, and commitment to the organization. We presented a seven-step process for socializing new employees.

## KEY TERMS AND CONCEPTS

Bureaucratic culture
Clan culture
Cultural symbols
Cultural values
Entrepreneurial culture
Expatriates
External adaptation and survival
Internal integration
Market culture

Organizational culture
Organizational rites and ceremonies
Organizational socialization
Principled organizational dissent
Shared behaviors
Socialization
Subcultures
Whistle-blowing

*figure 15.5 + table 15.4*

## DISCUSSION QUESTIONS

1. Provide two examples of how organizational culture is expressed at your college or university.
2. Describe how that culture affects your behavior.
3. Describe the culture at TDIndustries. What organizational behaviors led you to describe its culture in this way?
4. What are the primary methods that Richard Teerlink used to change the culture of Harley-Davidson?
5. Can Teerlink's methods be used in other organizations? Explain.
6. Use the words in Table 15.1 to describe the culture of Starbucks (visit its Web site at http://www.starbucks.com), Dell Computer (visit its Web site at http://www.dell.com), or another organization with which you

are familiar.  How does its organizational culture affect the type of employee who chooses to work there?
7. What role does its reward system play in maintaining the culture at TDIndustries?
8. How might an organization use its culture to increase the probability of ethical behavior and decrease the probability of unethical behavior by its managers and employees?
9. What type of organizational culture would you prefer to work in? Why? Table 15.1 can help you understand your own values.
10. Describe the steps used in socializing new employees by an organization with which you are familiar. How successful is this process?

## DEVELOPING COMPETENCIES

### Competency:  Managing Ethics

### Assessing Behaviors in an Organization

*Instructions:* Think of an organization that you currently work for or used to work for. Indicate how you feel about each behavior that someone in the organization might have exhibited. Use the following scale and place one number after each behavior to indicate how you feel about that behavior. There are no right or wrong answers.

1. Very acceptable
2. Acceptable
3. Somewhat acceptable
4. Uncertain
5. Somewhat unacceptable

6. Unacceptable
7. Very unacceptable

1. _____ Taking home a few supplies (e.g., paper clips, pencils, and pens).
2. _____ Calling in sick when some personal time (e.g., play golf or take in a movie) is needed.
3. _____ Using a company telephone, fax, or computer for personal business.
4. _____ Making personal copies on a company copy machine.
5. _____ Using a company car to make a personal trip.

6. _____ Eating at a very expensive restaurant on a company business trip.
7. _____ Charging wine and cocktails as well as food on a company business trip.
8. _____ Taking a significant other along on a company business trip at the company's expense.
9. _____ Staying at an expensive hotel on a company business trip.
10. _____ On a company business trip, charging a $7 cab ride to your expense account when you actually walked.

### Interpretation of Results

More than 200 managers responded to this survey. Compare your responses to theirs.

1. 50 percent thought that taking home a few office supplies was acceptable.
2. 70 percent reported that calling in sick to take personal time was unacceptable.
3. 74.7 percent reported that making personal calls on the telephone, using a fax, or computer was unacceptable.
4. 54.6 percent indicated that making personal copies on a copy machine was acceptable.
5. 70.6 percent thought that using a company car for a personal trip was unacceptable.
6. 59.1 percent reported that eating at a very expensive restaurant was acceptable.
7. 50 percent believed that charging wine and cocktails was acceptable.
8. 85 percent thought that taking a significant other along on a business trip at the company's expense was unacceptable.
9. 55 percent indicated that staying at an expensive hotel on a company business trip was acceptable.
10. 41 percent indicated that charging $7 for a cab ride when they walked was very unacceptable.[29]

### Questions

1. Would you expect these results to vary by type of culture (e.g., bureaucratic, clan, entrepreneurial, or market)? Explain.
2. Choose several items about which you and the managerial respondents disagree. How do their behaviors differ from your own values (see Table 15.1)? Would you recommend that they change theirs? If so, how?

## Competency: Managing Teams

### Southwest Airlines' Team Culture

San Antonio lawyer Herb Kelleher founded Southwest Airlines in 1966 with one of his clients, Rollin King, at a bar in San Antonio. King came up with the idea of starting a low-fare airline and Kelleher liked it. They doodled a plan on a cocktail napkin and Kelleher put up $10,000 of his own money to get it started. (His stake is now worth more than $200 million.)

He fought competitors in the courts to get the airline started and likened these fights to being in the French Foreign Legion. Texas International, Braniff, and Continental tried to stop Kelleher, but he was determined to show them that Southwest could become a reality and survive. On June 18, 1971, Kelleher told Lamar Muse, then CEO of Southwest Airlines, to go ahead with scheduled flights no matter what the courts decided. Lamar said: "Gee, Herb, what do I do. Suppose the sheriff shows up and tries to prevent the flights?" "So what!" said Kelleher. "Leave tire tracks on his shirt. We're going, come hell or high water." This same spirit also led to at least one fistfight with personnel of another airline. One time, some Braniff people went up to the roof of the terminal building at Hobby Field in Houston and hung a sign over Southwest's to advertise Braniff's service to Dallas. The Southwest station manager went up there and tried to cut it down with a knife. He ended up getting into a fistfight on the top of the terminal building.

According to Kelleher, people are the airline's most important asset, and they provide legendary service. No one has ever been laid off, not even after the terrorists' attacks on September 11, 2001. Kelleher believes that people want to work for a "winner." He also believes that you want to show your

people that you value them and that you are not going to hurt them just to get some more money in the short term. Laying people off breeds a lack of trust, a sense of insecurity, and a lack of loyalty. As a result, Southwest can hire and hold the very best people. At Southwest Airlines the human resource function is called the People Department, which is crucial to Southwest's success. According to the department's mission statement, "recognizing that our people are the competitive advantage, we deliver resources and services to prepare our people to be winners, to support the growth and profitability of the company, while preserving the values and special culture of Southwest Airlines." Elizabeth Sartain, executive vice president of the People Department, comments that Southwest can change a person's skill levels through training, but it can't change attitudes, so people are hired for their attitudes, not for their technical skills. In fact, the airline rejects about 100,000 applicants a year, and the turnover rate is less than half (e.g., about 7 percent) that of most other airlines. Because its organizational culture is crucial for developing dedication to excellence, a new hire's first 6 months at Southwest are a period of indoctrination and mentoring. This time is also used to weed out anyone who doesn't fit the culture.

All new hires attend Southwest's University for People. During classes, all are told that they have a responsibility for self-improvement and training. Once a year, all employees, including senior management, are required to participate in a program designed to reinforce shared values. Except for flight training, which is regulated by the FAA, all training is done on the employee's own time. The university operates at capacity, 7 days a week. The fun and spirit of Southwest emerges in graduates very early. Humor and service are significant aspects of the culture. Employees are taught that, if they want customers to have fun, they must create a fun-loving environment. That means that employees must be self-confident enough to reach out and share their sense of humor and fun. They must be willing to play and expend the extra energy it takes to create a fun experience for their customers. For example, Southwest's "positively outrageous service" stresses friendliness, caring, warmth, and company spirit. Gate attendants are taught how to play games with customers, such as guess the weight of the gate agent, name three things to do in Tulsa, and who has the most holes in his sock to pass the time if a plane is delayed. The games are never in poor taste and provide the winners with a free dinner or a Southwest "fun" hat. Recently, a class of new pilots stumbled into Kelleher's office wearing dark sunglasses and holding white canes.

Another characteristic of the strong culture is employee commitment and motivation, which leads to cooperative relationships among employee teams. That is, the majority of employees share the same goals and basically agree on how to pursue them. For example, gate agents and flight crews clean planes along with members of the maintenance department. All share the goal of a 15-minute turnaround, or about one-third of the time needed by competitors. Because of these team-oriented values, the company has few of the rigid work rules that characterize most of its competitors. At Southwest everybody pitches in regardless of the task. Just before he retired, Kelleher wrote to all employees and asked them to save $5 a day by cutting nonfuel costs. Employees responded by cutting costs 5.6 percent, or more than $10 a day. Although 85 percent of Southwest's pilots are unionized, they identify more with the airline than with their union. As a result, there have been few strikes since Southwest was formed in 1971.

Since being diagnosed with prostate cancer a few years ago, Kelleher had been thinking of stepping down. For him, cancer was never an issue. It was just something that he had to get through, and he has tried to keep a sense of humor about it. For example, one day he walked into an exam room with a lighted cigarette. The doctors went berserk. Told to put it out, he said: "I don't have anywhere to put it out. If you want smokers to put out cigarettes, you ought to have ashtrays."

In 2001, he reached the age of 70 and decided to retire. His biggest concern was that he wanted a successor who would respect Southwest's culture and who was altruistic. He picked two people, Jim Parker and Colleen Barrett, for the job. Parker is CEO and Barrett is president and chief operating officer. Since Kelleher is a legend for his smoking and drinking, he says that Barrett can do the smoking and Parker can do the drinking.[30]

## Questions

1. Use the words in Table 15.1 to describe the organizational culture of Southwest Airlines.
2. Why haven't other organizations, including other airlines, been able to copy Southwest's culture?
3. What role does socialization play at Southwest Airlines?
4. Access Southwest Airlines Web site at http://www.iflyswa.com. What symbols does Southwest use on its Web site to convey its culture?

# Guiding Organizational Change

**LEARNING OBJECTIVES**

When you have finished studying the chapter, you should be able to:
1. Identify pressures for change, two types of change programs, and how to perform an organizational diagnosis.
2. Diagnose reasons for individual and organizational resistance to change and describe methods for overcoming it.
3. Discuss methods for promoting change.
4. Describe ethical issues posed by organizational change.

16

# CIGNA

From 1993 until 2002, Tom Valerio was in charge of changing the way in which CIGNA did business. He likened his task to trying to parallel-park an aircraft carrier. Because he lacked both a staff and budget, he had to rely on his managing change, communication, and team managerial competencies to move 6,500 people to a vision that Gerald Isom, the organization's president, wanted. That vision was to transform CIGNA from an unprofitable insurer into a top-performing casualty insurance company.

In 1993, CIGNA was performing poorly. Battered by poor decisions and natural disasters, such as hurricanes Hugo and Andrew, it lost more than $275 million. For every dollar in premiums that came in, the company paid out $1.40 in claims and expenses. Valerio felt that, although the numbers were miserable, there were deeper problems. To uncover them, he invited more than a thousand employees to a series of brown-bag lunches at company headquarters in Philadelphia. He gave each employee a packet of Post-it-Notes and told them to write down which parts of the organization were working, which weren't, and why. He learned that CIGNA had poor relationships with customers and agents and that CIGNA's technology was outdated and couldn't provide information that employees needed in order to do their jobs. Under the guise of reengineering, massive layoffs had occurred and, as a result, employees didn't trust management to tell them the truth.

To start the transformation process, Isom and Valerio linked the goal of change to profitability. They believed that people wanted to be a part of something that was profitable. Second, they directed agents to go after customers in carefully targeted markets where CIGNA knew the risks and could make profits. Next, he created a scorecard that tracked answers to four questions: How do customers see us? What must we excel at? How can we continue to learn and improve? and How do we look to shareholders? All executives had an electronic version of the scorecard on their desktop computers so that they could tell whether their employees were meeting their goals—and also follow every other unit's performance. If the scorecard flashed green, the department was on target; yellow indicated flagging performance, and red warned that the department was in trouble. The scorecard didn't permit managers to hide bad performance. If Isom noticed a red light, he immediately started asking questions. The scorecard forced people to focus on goals in all four areas. It also created a culture in which people were willing to step up and announce that they were in trouble. People grew to trust Isom after he stopped punishing people for admitting they needed help.

Valerio also realized that employees needed to do a much better job communicating among units. For example, a good decision for inland marine insurance might be a poor decision for workers' compensation insurance. To help managers keep the big picture in focus, Valerio created a transformation map—a one-page document that laid out intermediate milestones and ultimate goals.

Did the changes matter? Just look at the numbers. After losing $275 million in 1993, CIGNA recorded a profit of $989 million in 2001.[1]

*For more information on CIGNA, visit the organization's home page at* **http://www.cigna.com**.

Understanding and managing organizational change presents complex challenges. Planned change may not work, or it may have consequences far different from those intended. In many instances, organizations must have the capacity to adapt quickly and effectively in order to survive. Often the speed and complexity of change severely test the capabilities of managers and employees to adapt rapidly enough. However, when organizations fail to change, the costs of that failure may be quite high. Hence managers and employees must understand the nature of the change needed and the likely effects of alternative approaches to bring about that change.

Because organizations exist in changing environments, bureaucratic organizations are increasingly ineffective. Organizations with rigid hierarchies, high degrees of functional specialization, narrow and limited job descriptions, inflexible rules and procedures, and impersonal, autocratic management can't respond adequately to demands for change. As we pointed out in Chapter 14, organizations need designs that are flexible and adaptive. Organizations also need reward systems and cultures that allow greater participation in decisions by employees and managers alike.

In this chapter, we examine the pressures on organizations to change, type of change programs, and why accurate diagnosis of organizational problems is crucial. We explore the difficult issue of resistance to change at both the individual and organizational levels and examine ways to cope with that inevitable resistance. In addition, we identify three methods for making organizational and behavioral changes. Finally, we explore some ethical issues associated with organizational change.

<table>
<tr><td>Learning Objective:</td></tr>
<tr><td>1. Identify pressures for change, two types of change programs, and how to perform an organizational diagnosis.</td></tr>
</table>

# CHALLENGES OF CHANGE

Organizational change can be difficult and takes time, as we pointed out in the Preview case. Despite the challenges, many organizations successfully make needed changes, but at the same time, failure also is common. There is considerable evidence that adaptive, flexible organizations have a competitive advantage over rigid, static organizations.[2] As a result, managing change has become a central focus of effective organizations.

## PRESSURES FOR CHANGE

Most organizations around the world have tried to change themselves—some more than once—over the past decade. Yet for every successful change, there is an equally prominent failure. General Electric's dramatic performance improvement stands in stark contrast to a string of disappointments that have plagued Westinghouse. The rise of Asea Brown Boveri (ABB) to global leadership in the power equipment industry only emphasizes Hitachi's inability to reverse its declining market share in that area.

Organizations that are well positioned to change will prosper, but those that ignore them will founder. For example, Sycamore Networks, a maker of hardware and software for optical networks that interface with existing Internet and computer systems, is in a position to exploit the phenomenal growth of the World Wide Web and its use. Genentech and other large biotechnology firms should thrive in the emerging global economy. ABB, which owns power generation facilities in 16 countries, is well positioned to take advantage of deregulation in the electric power industry as governments around the world seek to reduce government regulation and red tape.[3]

There is an almost infinite variety of **pressures for change**. In this section, we examine three of the most significant ones: (1) globalization of markets, (2) spread of information technology and computer networks, and (3) changes in the nature of the workforce employed by organizations.

**Globalization.**    Organizations face global competition on an unprecedented scale. **Globalization** means that the main players in the world's economy are now international or multinational corporations.[4] Their emergence creates pressures on domestic corporations to internationalize and redesign their operations. Global markets now exist for most products, but to compete effectively in them, firms often must transform their cultures, structures, and operations.

Historically, the primary forces at work in globalization have included:

• the economic recoveries of Germany and Japan after their defeat in World War II;
• the emergence of new "industrial" countries, such as South Korea, Taiwan, Singapore, and Spain;
• the dramatic shift from planned economies to market economies that has occurred in Eastern Europe, Russia and other republics of the former Soviet Union, and to a certain extent in the People's Republic of China; and
• the emergence of new "power blocks" of international traders, stemming from the economic unification of Europe and the "yen block" of Japan and its Pacific Rim trading partners.

These and other powerful globalization forces are pushing domestic firms around the world to abandon "business as usual" in order to remain competitive. In some industries, global strategies are replacing country-by-country approaches. For example, consider Gillette's shift to world products. As was typical for consumer goods companies, Gillette traditionally developed new products one market at a time, with gradual rollouts around the world. Starting with its Sensor razor, however, Gillette created a global product with a global launch—the same improved product was advertised and available everywhere in the world at roughly the same time. Although globalization strategies aren't easy to implement, many organizations have effectively moved outside their domestic markets. Ford, Merck & Company, and IBM have strong, profitable operations in Europe. McDonald's, Walt Disney, DuPont, and Amway have highly successful Asian operations. Amway sells more than $500 million worth of housewares door to door in Japan each year. Procter & Gamble has recently reorganized to ensure that its marketing efforts proceed simultaneously worldwide. The company has eliminated regional business units and put profit responsibility in the hands of seven executives who are responsible for global product units.

**Information Technology.**    Coping with international competition requires a flexibility that many organizations often do not possess. Fortunately, the revolution in information technology permits organizations to develop the needed flexibility. **Information technology** (IT) comprises networks of computers (many of them complex), telecommunications systems, and remote-controlled devices.[5] As discussed throughout this book, IT is having a profound impact on individual employees, teams, and organizations. For example, experts who have studied its impact on organizations have observed that IT:

• changes almost everything about a company—its structure, its products, its markets, and its processes;
• increases the value of invisible assets, such as knowledge, competencies, and training;
• democratizes a company because employees have more information and can talk to anyone in the company;
• increases the flexibility of work by allowing more people to work at home, on the road, or at hours that suit them; and
• allows companies to unify their global operations and to work a 24-hour day spanning the world.

However, the potential effects of IT aren't uniformly positive. Organizations that rely on sophisticated information technologies are more vulnerable to sabotage, espionage, and vandalism. Moreover, IT can create new social divisions (e.g., the computer literate versus the nonuser and the educated versus the uneducated) even as it brings people together. If the full potential of IT is to be realized, employees must be better educated, better trained, and better motivated than at any time in history. However, wisdom and intuition remain essential for good management, and having more information, faster, cannot replace good judgment and common sense.

Still, despite these cautions, the impact of IT is dramatic. For example, Adaptec is a Silicon Valley producer of computer hardware. Just a short time ago, the company had to wait 105 days after placing an order to receive computer boards from its Singapore assembly plant. By using more sophisticated computer software and the Internet, Adaptec has reduced its production cycle to 55 days. Not only do its customers now get their orders filled in half the time, but the company also has cut its work-in-process inventory by half, with a positive impact on profits.[6] The Internet makes it possible for a design, a fashion, or an idea to be known instantaneously around the world. A New York apparel manufacturer put his spring line on the Internet and had five orders from Beijing in the People's Republic of China within hours. Information technology permits an IBM engineer to ask colleagues in virtually any country for help when confronted with a difficult problem. General Electric operates its own private global phone network, allowing employees to communicate directly with each other from anywhere in the world by using just seven digits. Information technology allows CRSS, a large architectural firm, to exchange drawings with 3M, one of its largest clients, almost instantaneously.[7]

The globalization phenomenon and information technologies are linked in interesting ways. Highly decentralized organizations, with operating units scattered throughout the world, face some significant challenges in terms of coordination and cooperation. However, advanced computer and telecommunication technologies provide mechanisms to link employees in ways only imagined in the past. For example, many multinational corporations rely on the use of virtual teams to accomplish their work. *Virtual teams* are groups of geographically and/or organizationally dispersed coworkers who are assembled via a combination of telecommunications and information technologies to accomplish organizational tasks.[8] Such teams rarely meet or work together face-to-face. Virtual teams may be set up on a temporary basis and used to accomplish a specific task, or they may be relatively permanent and used to address ongoing strategic planning issues. The membership of virtual teams may be quite fluid, with members changing according to task demands even for those teams with an ongoing assignment.

Sun Microsystems used virtual teams to introduce a new product after it acquired a small firm in the United Kingdom that made fault-tolerant computers for the telecommunications industry. Its leaders saw an opportunity to expand Sun's presence in the networking industry but needed to act quickly. Virtual teams were formed to take feedback from customers, marketing, engineering, and manufacturing to create the new product. The teams adopted the motto "We've got to find a way to do this" and the team name Netra. Time was tight: The teams were trying to complete their work in half the time usually allowed for such projects. By using knowledge gained from other teams around the world, these teams created the new product in time.[9]

**Changing Nature of the Workforce.**    In addition to coping with the challenges presented by globalization and rapid changes in information technology, organizations must attract employees from a changing labor market. For this reason among others, we have explored the challenges of managing cultural diversity throughout this book.

As discussed in Chapter 1, the labor market continues to grow more diverse in terms of gender and ethnicity. Thus equal opportunity pressures on hiring, promotion, and layoff practices will persist for some time to come. Other trends add to the challenge for organizations. For example, the dual-career family has become the norm, rather than the exception, in most industrialized societies. Further, the number of temporary workers continues to grow as a percentage of all workers. The contingent workforce includes part-time employees, freelancers, subcontractors, and independent professionals hired by companies to cope with unexpected or temporary challenges. By some accounts, about 25 percent of U.S. workers now fall into these categories. This percentage is expected to continue to grow as companies find that they can operate efficiently and effectively with a smaller core of permanent employees supplemented by a changing cast of temporary help—and save money by not having to provide employee benefits. The U.S. Bureau of Labor Statistics expects the number of temporary workers to increase by another 50 percent by 2006.[10] Temporary-employment agencies, such as Manpower and Kelly Services, are among the fastest growing organizations in the United States. The largest of the agencies—Manpower, Inc.—has more employees than General Motors or IBM. Among the challenges facing organizations are those of motivating and rewarding temporary and part-time employees whose morale and loyalties may be quite different from those of permanent employees.

The workforce is increasingly better educated, less unionized, and characterized by changing values and aspirations. Although these changes won't lessen the motivation to work, they continue to affect the rewards that people seek from work and the balance that they seek between work and other aspects of their lives. The quality of work life (QWL) represents the degree to which people are able to satisfy important personal needs through their work.[11] Achieving a high QWL is an important goal for many working women and men. Typically, employees desire pleasant working conditions, participation in decisions that affect their jobs, and valuable support facilities such as day-care centers for their children. These and other employee expectations put additional pressures on organizations and affect their ability to compete effectively in the labor market.

Of course, changes in globalization, information technology, and the workforce represent only some of the challenges facing organizations. The following Managing Across Cultures Competency feature highlights Corning's entry and success in China and identifies the pressures for change that challenge China as it develops nationwide communication and transportation systems. Ten years ago, China's supply of cheap labor produced numerous toy and textile products (often shoddy). Today, the Pudong industrial zone outside Shanghai houses organizations such as Intel, Matsushita, Krupp, and Alcatel. These organizations make everything from digital switching equipment to videoconferencing equipment to high-end chips. The emergence of China as a reliable, stable producer of high-value, technologically sophisticated products is affecting many global organizations.

## COMPETENCY:   MANAGING ACROSS CULTURES

### CORNING

A few years ago, Corning manufacturing in China was done in just one plant. However, Corning soon found that China's labor force was not only vast and cheap but that it also was highly educated and disciplined. In the Pudong area, for example, Corning found a pool of talented engineers. Few industries are more capital intensive and technologically sophisticated than the semiconductor industry. Making the tiniest silicon wafers requires expensive equipment, costing about US$1.5 billion per new plant. Owing in part to Chinese government incentives designed to attract global organizations, Corning has expanded its operations to nine plants, manufacturing fiber-optic cable, liquid crystal display screens, and catalytic converters. China will soon be the world's second largest market for telecom equipment, behind the United States, so Corning bought two plants formerly owned by Lucent to manufacture equipment for that industry.

*For more information on Corning, visit the organization's home page at http://www.corning.com.*

Corning has also built plants for manufacturing pollution-control devices for cars. A few years ago, China began to implement new pollution-control guidelines, including requirements that new cars manufactured there have catalytic converters. Corning makes ceramic casings that go into those pollution-control devices. The recently opened Shanghai casings plant supplies devices not only for local carmakers, but it also exports them to customers in South Korea and Japan. The fact that Lexus and Toyota, among others, purchase Chinese-made casings attests to their quality. According to Simon MacKinnon, Corning's greater-China president, "Our quality is as good, if not better than our casings plants in Germany, South America, and the U.S."[12]

## TYPES OF CHANGE APPROACHES

Distinguishing between change that inevitably happens to all organizations and change that is deliberately planned by members of an organization is important. Our focus is primarily on intentional, goal-oriented organizational change. **Planned organizational change** represents a deliberate attempt by managers and employees to improve the functioning of teams, departments, divisions, or an entire organization in some important way.[13]

There are two radically different approaches to achieve organizational change: economic and organizational development.[14] Each approach is guided by a different set of assumptions about the purpose and means for change. We have illustrated these differences in Table 16.1.

**Economic Approach.**    In 1994, Al Dunlap became CEO of financially troubled Scott Paper. When Dunlap took over, he immediately laid off 11,000 employees. He based his goals on financial returns. "I have a goal of $176 million this year and there is no time to involve others or develop people," Dunlap stated. He believed that this single goal focused all employees' attention. He didn't involve other managers and made it clear that he was commander-in-chief. He also fired many members of the top-management team and recruited new people who believed in his purpose: to restore shareholder wealth. Dunlap attracted them to the organization by promising financial incentives, mainly stock options, if the company returned to profitability. They were instructed simply to follow his commands. Not long after taking these steps, Dunlap sold off several businesses, retaining the core consumer products businesses. He sold Scott Paper's paper division to Scott's long-time competitor Kimberly-Clark. He moved Scott's headquarters from Philadelphia to a much smaller location near his home in Florida. Within 15 months, Dunlap managed to return Scott to profitability, making himself and many of the company's top managers rich.

**Table 16.1**

| Approaches to Change | | |
| --- | --- | --- |
| **MEANS** | **ECONOMIC** | **ORGANIZATIONAL DEVELOPMENT** |
| Purpose | Profit | Develop employees' competencies |
| Leadership | Top-down | Participative |
| Focus | Structure and strategy | Culture |
| Motivation | Incentives lead performance | Incentives lag performance |

Virtually all of Dunlap's change efforts focused on changing the company's strategy and structure. Dunlap resigned immediately after collecting his bonus and left Scott Paper struggling without his leadership to compete in the businesses to which he had committed the firm.[15]

**Organizational Development Approach.**   The opposite of the economic approach is the organizational development approach. When Andrew Sigler took over as CEO of Champion International (a global paper and forest products company) in the late 1970s, he gathered his top executives and many employees to help develop a new vision for the company. Called the Champion Way, the key values in that vision included involvement of all employees in improving the company, fair treatment of all employees, support for the community in the vicinity of its plants, and openness and truthfulness in the company. The emphasis on values is intended to create an emotional attachment to the firm, which is essential to commitment. If employees are committed to the organization, top-down control systems will be unnecessary. The purpose of this approach is to develop the competencies of employees so that they can become problem-solvers. This approach to change emphasizes asking employees to examine why the existing structure and systems aren't meeting the challenges facing the organization. Sigler believed that employees are motivated by the way management involves them in managing the firm. At Champion, skilled-based pay systems (see Chapter 6) were used to support high involvement and teamwork. He resigned shortly before the company merged with International Paper in 2000 for $6.7 billion. During Sigler's tenure at Champion, the changes he introduced enabled Champion to be sold for 1.5 times its 1981 market value, when he launched the program.[16]

**Sequencing the Approaches.**   Jack Welch, former CEO of General Electric, used the economic approach first and then followed it with the organizational development approach with great success. In 1981, Welch demanded that every GE business had to achieve a number one or two position in its industry. Businesses that didn't meet this objective had to be fixed, sold, or closed. Labeled "Neutron Jack" by employees, after the neutron bomb that kills people but causes relatively little damage to buildings and other structures, employment dropped by more than 120,000 between 1981 and 1985 while sales increased 20 percent and profits increased 38 percent. The number of management levels dropped from nine to six. Corporate staff was reduced by 60 percent. He followed this economic approach with an organizational development approach in the early 1990s. He declared that the organization had to become "boundaryless." He initiated Workout, an open-forum process in which executives from each business unit (e.g., plastics, jet engines, and medical diagnostics) learned about barriers to organizational effectiveness. The purpose of Workout was to break down hierarchy and to promote feedback and open communication. Welch also articulated a set of values and made promotions and other rewards contingent on behaving consistently with these values. John Reed at Citigroup and Archie Norman at Asda PLC, a large British supermarket chain, used similar sequencing to achieve successful changes in their organizations.[17]

## ORGANIZATIONAL USE

We believe that managers that face major changes need to think through the long-term consequences of using either the economic approach or the organizational development approach. Moreover, finding managers with the managerial competencies needed to sequence change properly is difficult. In many small dot-com start-up organizations, the primary goal of the founder and managers is to prepare their organization for the initial public offering (IPO). Maximizing market value prior to the sale of shares is their sole purpose, so they emphasize shaping the organization's strategy, structure, and systems to build quickly its presence in the marketplace.

Transactional leaders with a strong top-down style usually lead such firms. They attract others by using high-powered incentives, such as stock options and various perks. The lure is getting rich quickly. In contrast to the economic approach, change agents who want to build an institution are driven more by the organizational development approach. The focus of these managers often is to build an organization based on a deeply held set of values and a strong culture, such as Southwest Airlines, Dell Computers, and Microsoft. Such leaders attract others who share their passion about the vision and strategies they are pursuing to make their organizations stand out in their industries and contribute to their communities, as well as profitable.

**Success Indicators.**    All successful change approaches share some common characteristics. For example, effective change programs may involve:

- motivating change by creating a readiness for the change among managers and employees and attempting to overcome resistance to change (which we discuss in detail shortly);
- creating a shared vision of the desired future state of the organization;
- developing political support for the needed changes;
- managing the transition from the current state to the desired future state; and
- sustaining momentum for change so that it will be carried to completion.

The initiatives required to address each of these aspects of a change program are summarized in Figure 16.1.

Similarly, the conditions necessary for successfully carrying out effective change programs include the following.

- The organization's members must be the key source of energy for change, not some party external to the team or organization.
- Key members of the organization must recognize the need for change and be attracted by the potentially positive outcomes of the change program.
- A willingness to change norms and procedures must exist.

These programs and the conditions necessary for them are similar in certain respects. Change must come from within the organization. People must be aware of the need for change, believe in the potential value of the changes proposed, and be willing to change their behaviors in order to make the team, department, or organization more effective. Absent these beliefs and behaviors, effective organizational change is problematic. Managers must be open to trying different approaches at different times, as Jack Welch did at GE.

## ORGANIZATIONAL DIAGNOSIS

**Organizational diagnosis** is the process of assessing the functioning of the organization, department, team, or job to discover the sources of problems and areas for improvement. It involves collecting data about current operations, analyzing those data, and drawing conclusions for potential change and improvement. An accurate diagnosis of organizational problems and functioning is absolutely essential as a starting point for planned organizational change.

Information needed to diagnose organizational problems may be gathered by questionnaires, interviews, or observation—and from the organization's records. Typically, some combination of these data gathering methods is used. An advantage of the information collecting process is that it increases awareness of the need for change. Even with widespread agreement on the need for change, people may have different ideas about the approach to be used and when, where, and how it should be implemented.

To diagnose an organization, managers need to have an idea about what information to collect and analyze. Choices on what to look for invariably depend on man-

**Figure 16.1**                    **Initiatives Contributing to Effective Change Management**

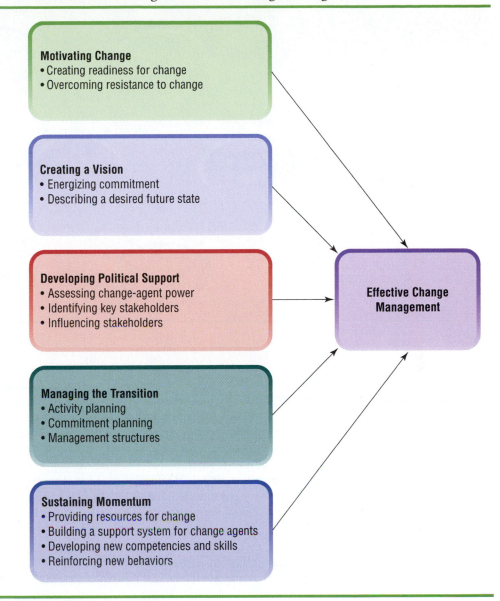

Source: Reprinted with permission from Cummings, J. G., and Worley, C. G. *Organization Development and Change*, 6th ed. Cincinnati: South-Western, 1997, 154.

agers' perceptions, the leadership practices used, how the organization is structured, its culture, and the like. Potential diagnostic models provide information about how and why certain organizational characteristics are interrelated. We illustrate one such model in Figure 16.2. Based on concepts presented throughout this book, this model illustrates how a change in one element usually affects others. For example, a change in an organization's reward system from one based on individual performance to a team-based system will affect the type of individuals joining the organization. Their decision will reflect the needs they want to satisfy on the job and their evaluation of the type and effectiveness of teams, how leaders make decisions, the type of decisions that teams can make, the structure of the department or division, and the culture of the organization. Based on this model, what changes did Tom Valerio at CIGNA use to make his organization more effective? How were the changes he initiated interrelated?

**Figure 16.2**          **Diagnostic Model of Change**

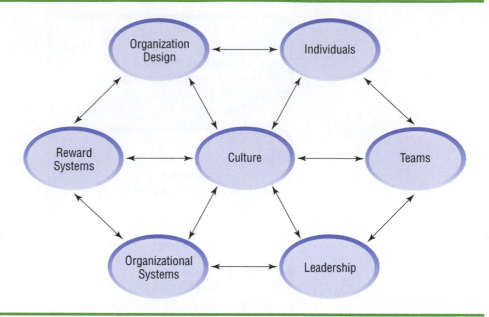

Any planned change program also requires a careful assessment of individual and organizational capacity for change. Two important aspects of individual readiness for change are the degree of employee satisfaction with the status quo and the perceived personal risk involved in changing it. Figure 16.3 shows the possible combinations of these concerns. When employees are dissatisfied with the current situation and perceive little personal risk from change, their readiness for change probably would be high. In contrast, when employees are satisfied with the status quo and perceive high personal risk in change, their readiness for change probably be low.

With regard to individual readiness for change, another important aspect is employee expectations regarding the change effort because expectations play a crucial

**Figure 16.3**          **Employee Readiness for Change**

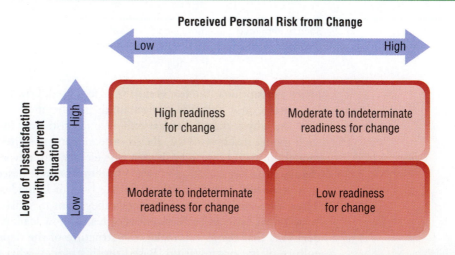

Source: Adapted from Zeira, Y., and Avedisian, J. Organizational planned change: Assessing the chances for success. *Organizational Dynamics*, Spring 1989, 37.

role in behavior. If people expect that nothing of significance will change, regardless of the amount of time and effort they might devote to making it happen, this belief can become a self-fulfilling prophecy. And when employee expectations for improvement are unrealistically high, unfulfilled expectations can make matters worse. Ideally, expectations regarding change should be positive yet realistic.

In addition, the organization's capacity for change must be accurately assessed. Approaches that require a massive commitment of personal energy and organizational resources probably will fail if the organization has few resources and its members don't have the time or opportunity to implement the needed changes. Under such circumstances, the organization may benefit most from starting with a modest effort. Then, as the organization develops the necessary resources and employee commitment, it can increase the depth and breadth of the change.

When managers and employees conduct an organizational diagnosis, they should recognize two additional important factors. First, organizational behavior is the product of many things. Therefore what is observed or diagnosed—employee behaviors, issues and problems, and the current state of the organization—has multiple causes. Trying to isolate single causes for complex problems can lead to simplistic and ineffective change strategies. Second, much of the information gathered about an organization during a diagnosis will represent symptoms rather than causes of problems. Obviously, change strategies that focus on symptoms won't solve underlying problems. For example, at one Marriott Hotel, an awards program that recognized perfect attendance failed to reduce absenteeism because it didn't deal with the causes of the problem. Careful diagnosis revealed that employees were absent from work because of poor bus service, lack of child care, and family pressures. The awards offered weren't sufficient to change employee behaviors and, more important, didn't address the employees' real problems.

Potential resistance to change represents another important aspect of readiness and motivation for change. Both individual and organizational resistance to change must be diagnosed.

<table>
<tr><td>

**Learning Objective:**

2. Diagnose reasons for individual and organizational resistance to change and describe methods for overcoming it.

</td><td>

# RESISTANCE TO CHANGE

Change involves moving from the known to the unknown. Because the future is uncertain and may negatively affect people's careers, salary, and competencies, organization members generally do not support change unless compelling reasons convince them to do so. **Resistance to change** often is baffling because it can take so many forms. Overt resistance may be expressed through strikes, reduced productivity, shoddy work, and even sabotage. Covert resistance may be expressed by increased tardiness and absenteeism, requests for transfers, resignations, loss of motivation, lower morale, and higher accident or error rates. One of the most damaging forms of resistance is passive resistance by employees—a lack of participation in formulating change proposals and ultimately a lack of commitment to the proposals, even when they have had an opportunity to participate in making such decisions.

As Figure 16.4 shows, resistance to change occurs for a variety of reasons. Some are traceable to individuals, but others involve the nature and structure of organizations.[18] The combination of these two sources of resistance can be devastating to change efforts. Managers and employees need to understand the reasons for resistance to change and its sources.

## INDIVIDUAL RESISTANCE

The six reasons for individual resistance to change shown in Figure 16.4 aren't the only reasons why individuals might resist workplace change, but they are common and frequently are important.

</td></tr>
</table>

**Figure 16.4**                 **Sources of Resistance to Change**

**Perceptions.**   In Chapter 3, we discussed the notion of perceptual defense—a perceptual error whereby people tend to perceive selectively those things that fit most comfortably with their current view of the world. Once individuals have established an understanding of reality, they may resist changing it. Among other things, people may resist the possible impact of change on their lives by (1) reading or listening only to what they agree with, (2) conveniently forgetting any knowledge that could lead to other viewpoints, and (3) misunderstanding communication that, if correctly understood, wouldn't fit their existing attitudes and values. For example, managers enrolled in management training programs at Lockheed Martin are exposed to different managerial philosophies and techniques. In the classroom, they may competently discuss and answer questions about these new ideas, yet carefully segregate in their minds the approaches that they believe wouldn't work from those that they believe would work or that they already practice.

**Personality.**    Some aspects of an individual's personality may predispose that person to resist change. In Chapter 2, we indicated that self-esteem is an important personality characteristic that determines how a person behaves in an organization. People with low self-esteem are more likely to resist change than those with high self-esteem because low self-esteem people are more likely to perceive the negative aspects of change than the positive aspects. Low self-esteem people are not as likely as high self-esteem people to work hard to make change succeed. Another personality characteristic is adjustment. People who are nervous, self-doubting, and moody typically have a difficult time changing their behaviors. They may resist change until those that they depend on endorse it. These employees are highly dependent on their supervisors for performance feedback. They probably won't accept any new techniques or methods for doing their jobs unless their supervisors personally support the changes and indicate how these changes will improve performance and/or otherwise benefit the employees.

Managers must be careful to avoid overemphasizing the role played by personality in resistance to change because they can easily make the fundamental attribution error (see Chapter 3). There is a tendency to "blame" resistance to change in the workplace on individual personalities. Although personality may play a role (as we have just discussed), it seldom is the only important factor in a situation involving change.

**Habit.**    Unless a situation changes dramatically, individuals may continue to respond to stimuli in their usual ways. A habit can be a source of comfort, security, and satisfaction for individuals because it allows them to adjust to the world and cope with it. Whether a habit becomes a primary source of resistance to change depends, to a certain extent, on whether individuals perceive advantages from changing their behaviors. For example, if an organization suddenly announced that all employees would immediately receive a 10 percent pay raise, few would object even though the pay raise might result in changes in behavior as employees could pursue a more expensive lifestyle. However, if the organization announced that all employees could receive a 10 percent pay raise only if they switched from working during the normal workday to working evenings and nights, many might object. Employees would have to change many personal habits about when they slept, ate, talked with family members, and so on.

**Threats to Power and Influence.**    Some people in organizations may view change as a threat to their power or influence. The control of something needed by others, such as information or resources, is a source of power in organizations. Once a power position has been established, individuals or teams often resist changes that they perceive as reducing their ability to influence others. For example, programs such as those to improve the quality of work life at Ford, General Motors, and Gaines Pet Food tend to focus on nonmanagerial employees and are often perceived as increasing their power at the expense of that of managers. Generally, though, **Quality of work life programs** (QWL programs) involve joint participation by employees and managers concerning the design of employees' jobs and the introduction of self-managed teams.[19] Participation of managers along with employees can lessen resistance to such programs. Novel ideas or a new use for resources also can disrupt the power relationships among individuals and departments in an organization and therefore are often resisted.

**Fear of the Unknown.**    Confronting the unknown makes most people anxious. Each major change in a work situation carries with it an element of uncertainty. People starting a new job may be concerned about their ability to perform adequately. Women starting a second career after raising a family may be anxious about how they will fit in with other employees after a long absence from the workplace. An employee may wonder what might happen if he relocates to company headquarters in another state. Will my family like it? Will I be able to find friends? What will top managers think of me if I refuse to relocate? Consequences of these types of decisions cannot be known in advance, so people are typically anxious about making them. Individuals may be so anxious and threatened by change that they refuse promotions that require moving to a new location or significant shifts in job duties and responsibilities.

**Economic Reasons.**    Money weighs heavily in people's considerations, and they certainly can be expected to resist changes that might lower their incomes. In a very real sense, employees have invested in the status quo in their jobs. That is, they have learned how to perform their work well, how to get good performance evaluations, and how to interact effectively with others. Changes in established work routines or job duties may threaten their economic security. Employees may fear that, after changes are made, they won't be able to perform as well and thus may not be as valuable to the organization, their supervisors, or their coworkers.

Sometimes the problems and dissatisfaction in a company are so serious that a general readiness for change exists. At Enron, Arthur Anderson, Kmart, and other organizations, employees knew that some kind of change was necessary for their organizations to survive. However, the real trick is for managers to create a sense of readiness to change while things seem to be going well. The following Managing Self Competency feature can help you assess your readiness for change. If your

## COMPETENCY: MANAGING SELF

### ARE YOU READY TO CHANGE?

**Instructions**

Read each of the following statements and then use the scale shown to reflect your opinion. Record your answer in the blank at the left of the question's number.

| 1 | 2 | 3 | 4 | 5 | 6 | 7 |
|---|---|---|---|---|---|---|
| Completely disagree | | | Neither agree nor disagree | | | Completely agree |

_____ 1. I believe that an expert who doesn't come up with a definitive answer probably doesn't know too much.

_____ 2. I think it would be fun to live in a foreign country for a period of time.

_____ 3. The sooner we all agree on some common values and ideals, the better.

_____ 4. A good teacher is one who makes you wonder about your way of looking at things.

_____ 5. I enjoy parties where I know most of the people more than ones where all or most of the people are strangers.

_____ 6. Supervisors who hand out vague assignments give me a chance to show initiative and originality.

_____ 7. People who lead even, regular lives—in which few surprises or unexpected events arise—really have a lot to be grateful for.

_____ 8. Many of our most important decisions are actually based on insufficient information.

_____ 9. There is really no such thing as a problem that can't be solved.

_____ 10. People who fit their lives to a schedule probably miss most of the joy of living.

_____ 11. A good job is one in which what is to be done and how it is to be done are always clear.

_____ 12. It is more fun to tackle a complicated problem than to solve a simple one.

_____ 13. In the long run, it is possible to get more done by tackling small, simple problems than large and complicated ones.

_____ 14. Often the most interesting and stimulating people are those who don't mind being different or original.

_____ 15. What we are used to is always preferable to what is unfamiliar.

_____ 16. People who insist on a "yes" or "no" answer just don't know how complicated things really are.

**Interpretation**

To get your total score, you need to do several things. First, sum your responses to the *odd*-numbered items and write your score here_____. Second, add 64 points to that score to create the first subtotal and record it here_____. Third, sum your responses to the *even*-numbered items and write your score here_____. Then subtract that number from the subtotal for the odd-numbered items to determine your overall score.

Your overall score is_____. Your score should be somewhere between 16 and 112. The lower your overall score, the more willing you may be to deal with uncertainty and ambiguity that typically go with change. Higher scores suggest a preference for more predictable and structured situations and indicate that you don't respond as well to change. Research data show that the range of scores for a group is usually between 20 and 80, with a mean of 45. How does your score compare to these norms?[20]

readiness score is low, what competencies do you need to develop to increase your readiness for change?

## ORGANIZATIONAL RESISTANCE

To a certain extent, the nature of organizations is to resist change. Organizations often are most efficient at doing routine tasks and tend to perform more poorly, at least initially, at doing something for the first time. Thus, to ensure operational efficiency and effectiveness, some organizations may create strong defenses against change. Moreover, change often opposes vested interests and violates certain territorial rights or decision-making prerogatives that departments, teams, and informal groups have established and accepted over time. Again, Figure 16.4 shows several of the more significant reasons for organizational resistance to change.

**Organization Design.**   Organizations need stability and continuity in order to function effectively. Indeed, the term *organization* implies that the individual, team, and department have a certain structure. Individuals have assigned roles, established procedures for getting the job done, consistent ways of getting needed information, and the like. However, this legitimate need for structure also may lead to resistance to change. Organizations may have narrowly defined jobs, clearly identified lines of authority and responsibility, and limited flows of information from top to bottom. The use of a rigid design and an emphasis on the authority hierarchy may cause employees to use only certain specific channels of communication and to focus narrowly on their own duties and responsibilities. Typically, the more mechanistic the organization, the more numerous are the levels through which an idea must travel (see Chapter 14). This type of design, then, increases the probability that any new idea will be screened out because it threatens the status quo. More adaptive and flexible organizations are designed to reduce the resistance to change created by rigid organizational structures.

**Organizational Culture.**   Organizational culture plays a key role in change. Cultures are not easy to modify and may become a major source of resistance to needed changes (see Chapter 15). One aspect of an effective organizational culture is whether it has the flexibility to take advantage of opportunities to change. An ineffective organizational culture (in terms of organizational change) is one that rigidly socializes employees into the old culture even in the face of evidence that it no longer works.

Walt Disney's death in 1966 was a major blow to Disney Corporation. His image and reputation were almost "alive" at the company's studios in Burbank, California. Managers became overly cautious about making changes, oftentimes asking, "What would Walt have done?" Disney's performance began to slide as these "hero worshipers" continued to produce films that were out of date in terms of moviegoer preferences. When Michael Eisner joined Disney as CEO, he reassigned and replaced many managers. As a result, many of the new managers, most of whom had never met Disney, began to create a culture that was more risk-taking and ambitious.

**Resource Limitations.**   Some organizations want to maintain the status quo, but others would change if they had the resources to do so. Change requires capital, time, and individuals with a lot of competencies. At any particular time, an organization's managers and employees may have identified changes that could or should be made, but they may have had to defer or abandon some of the desired changes because of resource limitations. Continental Lite, formerly a division of Continental Airlines, quickly learned that it didn't have the resources (planes, ground crews, and terminals) to compete effectively against Southwest Airlines for the budget-conscious traveler. Without these resources, Continental was unable to change quickly and had to abandon its attempt to compete directly with Southwest in certain air commuter markets.

**Fixed Investments.**   Resource limitations aren't confined to organizations with insufficient assets. Capital-intensive organizations, such as Exxon/Mobil, Lockheed Martin, and Duke Power, may be unable to change because of fixed capital investments in assets that they can't easily alter (equipment, buildings, and land). The plight of the central business districts in many cities illustrates this resistance to change. Most large cities developed before the automobile and can't begin to accommodate today's traffic volumes and parking demands. The fixed investments in buildings, streets, transit systems, and utilities are enormous and usually prevent rapid and substantial change. Therefore many older central urban areas are unable to meet the competition of suburban shopping centers.

Fixed investments aren't limited to physical assets; they also may be expressed in terms of people. For example, consider employees who no longer are making a significant contribution to an organization but have enough seniority to maintain their jobs. Unless they can be motivated to perform better or retrained for other positions, their salaries and fringe benefits represent, from the organization's perspective, fixed investments that can't easily be changed.

**Interorganizational Agreements.**   Agreements between organizations usually impose obligations on them that can restrain their actions. Labor negotiations and contracts provide some examples. Nike's relationship with colleges and various NFL teams precludes Adidas and other sporting apparel manufacturers from negotiating with them until the current contract expires. Ways of doing things that once were considered the rights of management (the right to hire and fire, assign tasks, promote and demote, and the like) may become subject to negotiation and fixed in a union–management contract. Other types of contracts also may constrain organizations. For example, proponents of change may face delay because of arrangements with competitors, commitments to suppliers and other contractors, and pledges to public officials in return for licenses, permits, financing, or tax abatement.

## OVERCOMING RESISTANCE

Realistically, resistance to change will never cease completely. Managers and employees, however, can learn to identify and minimize resistance and thus become more effective change agents. People often have difficulty with clearly understanding situations that involve change. Part of the reason is that even analyzing a change problem may be quite complex when a large number of variables must be considered.

Kurt Lewin, a pioneering social psychologist, developed a way of looking at change that has been highly useful for managers and employees when faced with the challenge of change.[21] Lewin viewed change not as an event but rather as a dynamic balance of forces working in opposite directions. His approach, called **force field analysis**, suggests that any situation can be considered to be in a state of equilibrium resulting from a balance of forces constantly pushing against each other. Certain forces in the situation—various types of resistance to change—tend to maintain the status quo. At the same time, various pressures for change are acting opposite to these forces. The combined effect of these two sets of forces is illustrated in Figure 16.5. When Durk Jager took over as CEO of Procter & Gamble (P&G) in 1999, he restructured the company along seven global product lines—baby care, beauty care, and so on—instead of four geographical regions—North America, Asia, Europe, and Latin America. Product line managers now were responsible and had the authority to make decisions that extended across geographic boundaries. The establishment of global products caused P&G's geographical managers to lose power. Initially, the driving forces were overcoming the resisting forces. One year later, however, Jager was forced to leave P&G because of poor financial results. The resisting forces had emerged in strength, which spelled his doom and that of the change program.[22]

**Figure 16.5**                    **Force Field Analysis**

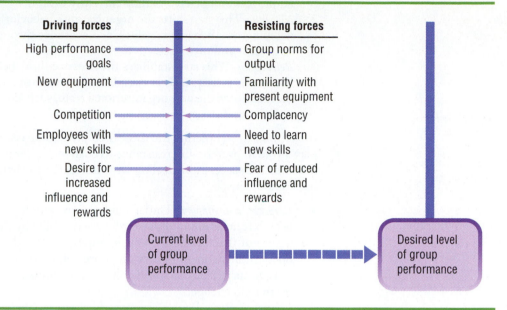

Source: Adapted from Zand, D. E. Force field analysis. In N. Nicholson (ed.), *Blackwell Encyclopedic Dictionary of Organizational Behavior*. Oxford, England: Blackwell, 1995, 181.

To initiate change, an organization must take one or more of three actions to modify the current equilibrium of forces:

• increasing the strength of pressure for change;
• reducing the strength of the resisting forces or removing them completely from the situation; and/or
• changing the direction of a force—for example, by changing a resistance into a pressure for change.

Using force field analysis to understand the processes of change has two primary benefits. First, managers and employees are required to analyze the current situation. By becoming competent at diagnosing the forces pressing for and resisting change, individuals should be able to understand better the relevant aspects of a change situation. Second, force field analysis highlights the factors that can be changed and those that can't be changed. People typically waste time considering actions related to forces over which they have little, if any, control. When individuals and teams focus on the forces over which they do have some control, they increase the likelihood of being able to change the situation.

Of course, careful analysis of a situation doesn't guarantee successful change. For example, people in control have a natural tendency to increase the pressure for change to produce the change they desire. Increasing such pressure may result in short-run changes, but it also may have a high cost: Strong pressure on individuals and teams may create conflicts that disrupt the organization. Often the most effective way to make needed changes is to identify existing resistance to change and focus efforts on removing resistance or reducing it as much as possible.

An important part of Lewin's approach to changing behaviors consists of carefully managing and guiding change through a three-step process.

1. *Unfreezing.* This step usually involves reducing those forces maintaining the organization's behavior at its present level. Unfreezing is sometimes accomplished

by introducing information to show discrepancies between behaviors desired by employees and behaviors they currently exhibit.

2. *Moving.* This step shifts the organization's behavior to a new level. It involves developing new behaviors, values, and attitudes through changes in organizational structures and processes.

3. *Refreezing.* This step stabilizes the organization's behavior at a new state of equilibrium. It is frequently accomplished through the use of supporting mechanisms that reinforce the new organizational state, such as organizational culture, norms, policies, and structures.

In addition to completing the three-step process successfully, other important factors play a role in overcoming resistance to change. For example, studies have shown that methods for successfully dealing with resistance to change often include the following components.

- *Empathy and support.* Understanding how employees are experiencing change is useful. It helps identify those who are troubled by the change and understand the nature of their concerns. When employees feel that those managing change are open to their concerns, they are more willing to provide information. This openness, in turn, helps establish collaborative problem solving, which may overcome barriers to change.

- *Communication.* People are more likely to resist change when they are uncertain about its consequences. Effective communication can reduce gossip, rumors, and unfounded fears. Adequate information helps employees prepare for change.

- *Participation and involvement.* Perhaps the single most effective strategy for overcoming resistance to change is to involve employees directly in planning and implementing change. Involved employees are more committed to implementing the planned changes and more likely to ensure that they work than are employees who have not been involved.

The following Managing Change Competency feature demonstrates the effects of participation and involvement in overcoming resistance to change at Royal Dutch/Shell. The company is the world's tenth largest corporation with operations in more than 135 countries. It operates more than 46,000 gas stations worldwide, has annual sales that exceed $135 billion, and employs more than 90,000 people. Faced with a consolidating industry, Shell tried to restructure itself to stay more competitive. When the effort stalled, Steve Miller, one of Shell's managing directors, stepped in to restart and manage it.

## COMPETENCY: MANAGING CHANGE

### SHELL'S CHANGE PROCESS

Two years after Shell started a change program several years ago that was designed to restore its competitiveness, Steve Miller concluded that change was happening too slowly. The company had downsized and reorganized, and all senior managers had attended workshops that dealt with the changes needed and the reasons for them. Performance had improved a bit, but morale was low. The company's leaders agreed that Shell had to move aggressively into the Internet Age, but couldn't agree on how to implement the idea and so the change effort stalled.

Miller believed that, once the folks at the refineries understood the problems, were empowered, and started to make changes, top-level managers would have to change their behaviors. To get this message across, Miller set aside half this time to work with employees who needed to respond to competitive threats on a daily basis. Week in and week out, he met with Shell employees in 25 countries.

One of the challenges facing Shell was figuring out how better to use its 49,000 gas stations to boost retail sales of all company products. To begin tackling that problem, Miller set up a 5-day "retailing boot camp." Cross-functional teams (e.g., a trucker, a gas station manager, and a marketing employee) went to "camp" and then went home to develop a new business plan. Later they returned to camp and received feedback on their plans from other Shell employees. After another cycle of revising their plans and getting more feedback, they went home to put their plans into action. After 2 more months, they returned to camp for a follow-up session that focused on what had worked, what had failed, and what they had learned. These employees got to design a new Shell and participate in a culture that changed from one where following the rules was rewarded to one where being entrepreneurial was rewarded. These workers taught top-level managers that change could happen.

Miller admits that most of the people in the boot camps found the process to be "scary as hell." Top management had convinced itself that change was essential to Shell's survival, but it didn't believe that lower level employees had the ability to solve "real" problems. Similarly, lower level employees didn't have the polished communication skills to make presentations before top managers and answer strategic questions. Miller soon found out that, as people move up the corporate ladder, they get farther from the real work of Shell and tend to devalue it. Top-level people get caught up in broad strategy issues, such as whether Shell should buy Pennzoil-Quaker State, but what really drives the business is increasing sales at the retail gas station.[23]

*For more information on Shell, visit the organization's home page at http://www.shell.com.*

## PROMOTING CHANGE

The main objective of planned organizational change is to alter the behavior of individuals within the organization. In the final analysis, organizations survive, grow, prosper, decline, or fail because of the things that employees do or fail to do. Behavior therefore should be a primary target of planned organizational change. In other words, to be successful, change programs must have an impact on employee roles, responsibilities, and working relationships.

At some fundamental level, all organizational change depends on changes in behavior. Of course, managing effective change also depends on identifying specific aspects of the organization that will be the initial target of change efforts. We use Figure 16.2 as an organizing framework to explore three methods for promoting change.

### INTERPERSONAL METHODS

Change programs focused on behavior (the *individual* variable in Figure 16.2) tend to rely on active involvement and participation by many employees. Successfully changing behaviors can improve individual and team processes in decision making, problem identification, problem solving, communication, working relationships, and the like. One popular approach to focus on people who are having problems fitting in with others or dealing with change is to use survey feedback.

**Survey Feedback.**   In **survey feedback** information is (1) collected (usually by questionnaire) from members of an organization, department, or team; (2) organized into an understandable and useful form; and (3) fed back to the employees who provided it.[24] In Chapter 12, we discussed how 360 degree feedback is used by managers to improve the performance of employees; 360 degree feedback is just one form of survey feedback.[25] It leads to a comprehensive assessment of an employee's performance and usually leads to change methods that increase the likelihood that the person's competencies will be taken into account. This information provides the basis for planning actions to deal with specific issues and problems. The primary objective of all interpersonal methods is to improve the relationships among team members through the discussion of common problems, rather than to introduce a specific change, such as a new computer system. Survey feedback also is frequently used as a diagnostic tool to identify team, department, and organizational problems. Because of its value in organizational diagnosis, survey feedback often is utilized as part of large-scale, long-term change programs in combination with other approaches and techniques.

## TEAM METHODS

As the name suggests, the purpose of team methods is to get a handle on team performance problems. As illustrated in Figure 16.6, team performance is influenced by the competencies of its members, organizational structure, the organization's reward system, organizational culture, and other factors. Team methods are designed to improve relations among team members and their team's performance.

**Figure 16.6**    **The Team Performance Curve**

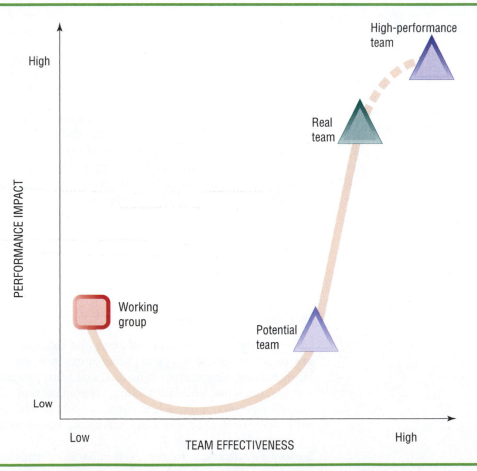

Source: Adapted from Katzenbach, J. R., and Smith, D. K. *The Wisdom of Teams.* Boston: Harvard Business School Press, 1993, 84.

**Team Building.**    In **team building** team members diagnose how they work together and plan changes to improve their effectiveness.[26] Many different teams comprise an organization, and much of its success depends on how effectively those teams and the people in them can work together. We explored how to improve team functioning in Chapter 8 and urge you to reread that chapter.

Team building begins when members recognize a problem. An effective team can recognize barriers to its own effectiveness and design and take actions to remove them. During team building, members of the team contribute information concerning their perceptions of issues, problems, and working relationships. Steve Miller at Dutch Royal/Shell used this technique. Usually information is gathered during team meetings or prior to meetings, using interviews or questionnaires. Managers then analyze the information and diagnose work-related problems. Using problem diagnosis as the starting point, team members plan specific actions and assign individuals to implement them. At some later stage, team members evaluate their plans and progress to determine whether their actions solved the problems identified. As team effectiveness grows, the potential impact on organizational performance increases. Another good way to define team building is that it consists of the activities designed to move the team up the performance curve shown in Figure 16.6.

The goal of many team-building methods is to change the culture of the organization. In Chapter 15 we explored changing organizational culture and pointed out just how difficult such changes can be. Among other issues and problems, just assessing accurately the organization's culture before any plans for changes can be developed may be a daunting task. In addition, some aspects of culture (e.g., the deepest core values shared by employees) may be almost impossible to change. Despite these challenges, some organizations have successfully changed their cultures. How did they do it? A detailed examination of successful cultural change suggests that the odds for success can be increased by giving attention to seven main issues.

1.  *Capitalize on dramatic opportunities.*  The organization needs to take advantage of the moment when obvious problems or challenges that are not being met "open the door" to needed change. When Ford acquired Jaguar, obvious quality problems with the Jaguar automobile made justifying needed changes easier.
2.  *Combine caution with optimism.*  Managers and employees need to be optimistic with regard to the advantages of cultural change; otherwise they will be unwilling to make the attempt. Yet, because cultural change can have negative impacts, the organization needs to proceed with caution. Expectations for improvement must be positive, yet realistic.
3.  *Understand resistance to cultural change.*  Resistance to change needs to be diagnosed. Identifying and reducing sources of resistance is valuable in cultural change as well as in other change programs.
4.  *Change many elements but maintain some continuity.*  "Don't throw the baby out with the bathwater" is a common saying that sums up the importance of recognizing what is of value and retaining it. Southwest Airlines, a firm that we have examined in several places in this book, has grown and prospered since its founding in the early 1970s, yet it managed to retain a core of cultural ideas and beliefs that Herb Kelleher instilled when he founded the organization.
5.  *Recognize the importance of implementation.*  A survey indicated that over 90 percent of planned changes in strategy and culture were never fully implemented. A large percentage of failed change programs are failures of implementation rather than failures of ideas. Management needs to recognize that having a vision and a plan, although important, is only part of the battle. Planned changes must be carried through.
6.  *Modify socialization tactics.*  Socialization is the primary way that people learn about a culture (see Chapter 14). Thus changing socialization processes can be an effective approach to cultural change.[27]

7. *Find and cultivate innovative leadership.* Cultural change must begin at the top of the organization, and good leadership is crucial. What has happened at Ford since 1999 has truly been amazing. In 1999, Ford was named one of the world's best-run automakers and reported a profit of $7.2 billion. The Firestone tire problem, closing five plants, laying off 35,000 people, and eliminating four car lines, including Mercury Cougar and Lincoln Continental, contributed to a loss of $5.5 billion in 2001. Jacques Nasser was forced out as CEO in October 2001 and Nick Scheele replaced him. Scheele, who now shares responsibility for the company with Bill Ford, is articulate, approachable, and popular with subordinates. He leaves operational details to others while he concentrates on relations with the board of directors, the government, and the press, with whom he communicates candidly. Besides having to negotiate plant closings and layoffs with the United Auto Workers in 2003, he must keep sales moving at a time when Ford will have few new models. Ford plans to replace 17 percent of its sales volume in 2004 with new products, compared to 35 percent at GM and 56 percent with its Japanese counterparts.[28]

## ORGANIZATIONAL METHODS

Organizationwide change programs frequently are aimed at changing an organization's design, reward systems, culture, and organizational systems, as shown in Figure 16.2. Approaches to change that focus on organizational methods involve redefining positions or roles and relationships among positions and redesigning departmental, divisional, and/or organizational structure. Unfortunately, implementing design or structural change has sometimes been used as an excuse for organizations simply to downsize their workforces without identifying and exploring the reasons for inefficiency and poor performance.

Issues of strategic change need to be addressed in organizational methods of change. At its most basic level, a strategy is a *plan*—an intended course of action to attain organizational goals. Dick Clark Productions provides a good example of a firm that has constantly reassessed its options and developed new strategies and lines of business over the years. The company is a diverse entertainment enterprise that operates three core businesses: television productions, corporate productions (trade shows, special event marketing, etc.), and theme restaurants that draw on the names of Dick Clark and American Bandstand. The corporate production and theme restaurants segments of the business represent successful strategic reorientations that the firm has undertaken. Dick Clark Productions maintains an active, effective planning and strategy formulation process that constantly assesses performance and looks for new opportunities.

Kmart began as Kresge's, opening its first store more than 100 years ago in downtown Detroit. Since then, the U.S. retail scene has changed dramatically. Some old-line retailers, such as J. C. Penney and Sears, have remained competitive by adapting to these changes, whereas Montgomery Ward has disappeared from the scene and Kmart is in serious trouble. What has changed? First, shoppers now demand low prices, convenient superstores, and a wide assortment of quality, brand name merchandise. Wal-Mart, Sams' Club, and Target, the leading low-cost mass merchandisers, have met these changes in the way people shop and what they want, but Kmart hasn't. Second, shoppers are attracted to shopping malls and plazas rather than stand-alone stores, and they want to shop in up-to-date, pleasant, and comfortable surroundings. However, many of Kmart's stores are in stand-alone locations and need updating. Third, Home Depot and Lowe's have attracted many traditional Kmart garden and home improvement shoppers with their aggressive marketing, wide variety of merchandise, and low costs. Fourth, the Internet has radically changed the way many people shop, drawing customers from many walk-in retailers, including Kmart, which belatedly introduced a Web shopping site. The following Managing Change Competency feature illustrates some of the organizational methods that Kmart is using in an attempt to survive.

# COMPETENCY:  MANAGING CHANGE

## CAN KMART SURVIVE?

When Kmart declared bankruptcy on January 22, 2002, it hired James Adamson, a turnaround specialist, to develop a new strategy for the company. With Wal-Mart and Target stealing its customers, Kmart's top leaders needed to move quickly. While focusing on fixing finances and store operations, management needed to develop a strategy for giving customers a reason to shop at Kmart.

Adamson used an economic approach to save cash quickly. He secured $2 billion in financing from the bankruptcy court, closed 284 stores, and laid off 22,000 employees. According to Adamson, "The decision to close these under-performing stores, which do not meet our financial requirements going forward, is an integral part of the Company's reorganization effort." Even after these closings and layoffs, Kmart will be a $37 billion organization with more than 1,900 Kmart and Kmart Super Center retail outlets and its e-commerce shopping site, http://www.blue-light.com. These moves are intended to improve cash flow by $550 million and improve profits by $31 million annually. He must avoid the quick-fix mistakes of prior CEOs whose aggressive price-cutting strategy touched off an unwinnable price war with Wal-Mart.

If Kmart is to survive, it must address group and organizational level issues. First, the company needs to create an urban merchandising strategy that will appeal to African Americans and Hispanics. To do so, store managers will need the authority to stock merchandise that suits their customers' varying tastes. Kmart also needs to add fashion lines named after popular black or Hispanic icons and let local store managers promote them. Second, Kmart needs to beef up its new brands such as Sesame Street, Joe Boxer, and Disney. By strengthing its private brands, Kmart will connect with young mothers, its core customer. Third, Charles Conway, former Kmart CEO, hoped that by adding groceries, shoppers would visit Kmart more. Unfortunately, none of the firm's top managers were experienced in the grocery business. Adamson hired Julian Day because of his experience at Safeway. Selling groceries adds a level of complexity to Kmart's already overburdened distribution system. Adamson and Day need to set specific profitability goals for food sales, and if they aren't met, to get out of the business.[29]

*For more information on Kmart, visit the organization's home page at http://www.kmart.com.*

## Learning Objective:

4. Describe ethical issues posed by organizational change.

# ETHICAL ISSUES IN ORGANIZATIONAL CHANGE

Serious ethical issues may arise in any organizational change program, no matter how carefully thought out and well managed it might be. Managers and employees need to be aware of potential ethical issues in four main areas: change approach selection, change target selection, managerial responsibilities, and manipulation.[30]

When choosing the change approach or combination of approaches deemed best for the situation, managers and employees should recognize the ethical issues involved in selecting the criteria to be used. Does the manager or change agent have a vested interest in using a particular technique so that other alternatives might not receive fair consideration? Do individuals involved in the organizational diagnosis have biases that might predetermine the problems identified and thus influence the change approach chosen?

Selection of the change target raises ethical concerns about participation in the change program. What is to be the target of change? Which individuals, teams, or departments of the organization will the change effort focus on? Which members of the organization will participate in diagnosing, planning, and implementing the change and to what degree? Who will make this determination? Issues of power and political behavior raise serious ethical concerns when managers attempt to make inappropriate changes or choices concerning what is to be changed that overstep the boundaries of their legitimate roles. To what extent can managers make choices about changing the behaviors of employees, and where should the line be drawn in this regard?

A major ethical concern in the area of managerial responsibility involves whose goals and values are to guide the change effort. The reason is that organizational change is never value-free. The value systems of managers and employees always underlie assumptions about what the organization should be doing. Ethical concerns arise if managers involved in the change process fail to recognize the potential problems associated with incompatible goals and values held by the organization's members. Whose vision guides the change? Whose values influence the adoption of goals and methods chosen to accomplish them?

Finally, the reality of power differences raises the possibility of manipulation in the change process. Making changes in organizations without some employees feeling manipulated in some way is difficult. Often the organization needs to make changes that do, in fact, result in some individuals or groups being worse off after the change than they were before. Ethical issues concern the degree of openness surrounding planned changes. To what extent should the organization disclose all aspects of the change in advance? To what degree do employees have the right to participate in, or at least be aware of, changes that affect them, even indirectly?

These questions are not easily addressed, and we have no simple answers to them. As a starting point, managers and employees need some basis for recognizing the potential ethical concerns involved in organizational change so that fair and informed choices can be made. Organizations must be sensitive to the probability that ethical problems will emerge during planned change programs.

## CHAPTER SUMMARY

**1.** Identify pressures for change, two types of change programs, and how to perform an organizational diagnosis.

A rapidly changing environment places many demands on managers and employees, including the need to plan for and manage organizational change effectively. Pressures for change stem from globalization, the increasingly heavy use of computers and other sophisticated information technology, and the changing nature of the workforce.

The two main types of change approaches are economic and organizational development. The economic approach focuses on changing the organization's structure and decision-making authority relationships, and its goal is to improve the financial well being of the organization. The organizational development approach focuses on developing employees' competencies and commitment to the organization. An accurate, valid diagnosis of current organizational functioning, activities, and problems is an essential foundation for effective organizational change. The readiness for change, availability of resources for change, and possible resistance to change are among the factors that should be accurately diagnosed.

**2.** Diagnose reasons for individual and organizational resistance to change and describe methods for overcoming it.

Individuals may resist change because of their perceptions or personalities. In addition, habits, fear of the unknown, economic insecurities, and threats to established power and influence relationships may generate further resistance to change. Organizational resistance to change may be caused by organizational structure and culture, resource limitations, fixed investments not easily altered, and interorganizational agreements. Force field analysis can help managers and employees diagnose and overcome resistance to change. Resistance can also be reduced through open communication and high levels of employee participation in the change process.

**3.** Discuss methods for promoting change.

Three methods are available for promoting organizational change: interpersonal, team, and organizational. The interpersonal method focuses on changing employees' behaviors so that they can become more effective performers and usually involves some use of survey feedback. As the name suggests, the team method focuses on ways to improve the performance of entire teams, and team-building activities are its foundation. The organizational method is aimed at changing the organization's structure, reward system, level at which decisions are made, and the like.

**4.** Describe ethical issues posed by organizational change.

Managers and employees need to be aware of and knowledgeable about potential ethical issues that can arise during organizational change. Ethical issues may emerge during selection of the change approach, selection of the change targets, determination of managerial responsibilities for the goals selected, and potential manipulation of employees.

## KEY TERMS AND CONCEPTS

Contingent workforce
Force field analysis ✓
Globalization
Information technology
Organizational diagnosis
Planned organizational change ✓

Pressures for change
Quality of work life
Quality of work life programs
Resistance to change ✓
Survey feedback
Team building

## DISCUSSION QUESTIONS

1. What are some of the pressures for change and resistance to change facing Tom Valerio at CIGNA? Explain.
2. From Table 16.1 what change approach did Tom Valerio at CIGNA use? Explain.
3. Why is organizational diagnosis essential to the success of any change effort?
4. Think of a situation in which someone asked you to change your behavior. Did you change? If so, why? If not, why not?
5. What competencies do you need to develop, based upon your answers to the Managing Self Competency feature? How do you plan to do so?
6. Rosabeth Kanter, a leading authority on change, stated that trying to change an organization is like trying to

teach elephants to dance. Why is changing an organization's direction so difficult?
7. Based on the force field analysis, why is it hard for people to lose weight?
8. From your own experience, describe a team, department, or organization that needed to change. Which of the change approaches presented was used? Was it successful?
9. Identify and describe an ethical dilemma or issue created by some organizational change effort with which you are familiar. How was the ethical problem handled? What, if anything, would you do differently?

## DEVELOPING COMPETENCIES

### Competency:  Managing Self

### Measuring Support for Change

*Instructions:* This questionnaire is designed to help you understand the level of support or opposition to change within an organization. Please respond to each item according to

how true it is in terms of an organization with which you are familiar. Circle the appropriate number on the scale that follows the item.

| Not True | Usually Not True | Somewhat Untrue | Neutral | Somewhat True | Usually True | True |
|----------|------------------|-----------------|---------|---------------|--------------|------|
| 1 | 2 | 3 | 4 | 5 | 6 | 7 |

## Values and Visions

1. Do people throughout the organization share values or visions?

    1     2     3     4     5     6     7

## History of Change

2. Does the organization have a good track record in implementing change smoothly?

    1     2     3     4     5     6     7

## Cooperation and Trust

3. Is there a lot of cooperation and trust throughout the organization (as opposed to animosity)?

    1     2     3     4     5     6     7

## Culture

4. Does the organization's culture support risk taking (as opposed to being highly bureaucratic and rule bound)?

    1     2     3     4     5     6     7

## Resilience

5. Are people able to handle change (as opposed to being worn out from recent, unsettling changes)?

    1     2     3     4     5     6     7

## Punishments and Rewards

6. Does the organization reward people who take part in change efforts (as opposed to punishing those who try but fail)?

    1     2     3     4     5     6     7

## Respect and Status

7. Will people be able to maintain respect and status when the change is implemented (as opposed to losing them as a result of the change)?

    1     2     3     4     5     6     7

## Status Quo

8. Will the change be mild (and not cause a major disruption of the status quo)?

    1     2     3     4     5     6     7

## Interpretation

Scores 1, 2, and 3 are low; 4 and 5 are mid-range; and 6 and 7 are high. However, these are just numbers, and one person's 5 may be another person's 3. The value of the scores lies in understanding the meanings that people attach to them.

Generally, low to mid-range scores should be cause for concern. Lower scores indicate possible areas of resistance to change.

## Values and Visions

Low scores may indicate that values may be in conflict and that individuals and groups may not perceive any common ground. This situation is serious and almost guarantees that any major change will be resisted unless people learn how to build a shared set of values. In contrast, low scores may indicate a communication problem. In some organizations, values and visions remain secret, with people not knowing where the organization is headed. Although this communication problem needs to be solved, it may not indicate deeper potential resistance.

## History of Change

Low scores indicate a strong likelihood that a change will be resisted forcefully. Those who want the change will need to demonstrate repeatedly that they are serious this time. People are likely to be very skeptical, so persistence will be crucial.

## Cooperation and Trust

Low scores should be taken seriously. Building support for any major change without some degree of trust is difficult, if not impossible. The opposite of trust is fear, so a low score indicates not just the absence of trust but also the presence of fear.

## Culture

Mid-range to low scores indicate that people may have difficulty carrying out changes even though they support the changes. They are saying that the reward systems and procedures followed in the organization hinder change. The change agents must be willing to examine these issues in depth to determine their causes.

## Resilience

Low scores probably indicate that people are burned out. Even though they may see the need for change, they may have little strength to give to the effort. Two important questions should be asked:

- Is this change really necessary at this time?
- If it is, how can the organizations support people so that the change causes minimal disruption?

## Punishments and Rewards

Low scores indicate strong potential resistance. Who in their right minds would support something that they knew would harm them? If employees' perceptions are accurate, the change agents must find a way to move forward with the change *and find ways to make it rewarding for others*. Low scores indicate a misunderstanding about the scope and reasons for change. The change agents must let people know why they are misinformed. This message will likely need to be communicated repeatedly (especially if trust also is low).

## Respect and Status

Low scores indicate that change agents must find ways to make this a win–win situation.

## Status Quo

Low scores indicate that people regard the potential change as very disruptive and stressful. The more involved people are in the change process, the less resistance they are likely to experience. Most often, people resist change when they feel out of control.[31]

## Competency: Managing Change

### How Allen Questrom Saved J. C. Penney

In September 2000, when Allen Questrom began his first day as J. C. Penney's new CEO, things didn't look good. The company's valuation was down to about $3 billion, from a peak of $20 billion; its stock stood at $13 per share, down from the $70s range in 1997. By October 2000, the share price would dip into single digits for the first time in decades.

The one-time retailing icon of Middle America—which celebrated its 100th anniversary in April 2002—was in dire financial difficulty. When times were good, customers upgraded to stores such as Kohl's and Old Navy. When times were economically tight, shoppers sought better value. Customers buying in bulk at "big box" stores Wal-Mart and Target were undercutting Penney's prices and leading customers out of the malls, which were themselves suffering. To make matters worse, Eckerd, the drugstore chain that J. C. Penney owns and operates, was turning in one disappointing quarter after another.

To turn Penney around, in the summer of 2000 Penney's board borrowed a page out of a typical Hollywood script: It brought the reluctant old pro out of retirement. Actually, the 61-year-old Questrom was enjoying his second retirement. He was the celebrated CEO who ran Neiman Marcus in the late 1980s, revived Barney's in the late 1990s, and, in between, steered Federated from bankruptcy to being the largest department store chain in the country, thanks in part to a Questrom-orchestrated $4 billion takeover of its main rival, the May Company.

But J. C. Penney presented a host of organizational problems. How could Questrom—with his background in high-end merchandising, his outsider status in an insular culture, and his arrival in the midst of a bad market—bring the once-proud retailer back to profitability?

His first move was to get the red ink off the balance sheet so that, when the stores started making money again, the company could turn a profit. Penney sold off inventory and shrank long-term debt. By selling off the company's direct-insurance service unit to Aegon for $1.3 billion, Penney was able to cover $900 million of corporate debt and still have money for increased marketing efforts. Penney closed 44 unprofitable stores, and laid off 5,000 staff. And, as he told financial analysts, he "put a renewed focus on expense control."

Hiring Questrom was actually Penney's second bold gesture that eventually paid off. The first—centralization of merchandising—was already underway by the time he came on board. For the first 97 years of the company's existence, managers at each of the 1,140 stores had almost complete control over what they put on their shelves. For instance, the jeans selection at the J. C. Penney outlet in the Tri-County Mall in Cincinnati, Ohio, was entirely different from that offered at the Boise, Idaho, Town Square store. This approach was expensive and ineffective because there are no economies of scale.

The decentralized organization clearly was one of the reasons for low productivity and unprofitability. Now that J. C. Penney has a centralized purchasing system, it can take a centralized approach to marketing. National television ads can feature clothing lines that the shopper can find at the local J. C. Penney store, whether in Pittsburgh, Pennsylvania, or Peoria, Illinois.

Vanessa Castagna, who came to J. C. Penney from Wal-Mart in 1999 as COO, centralized the buying process in 2000. According to most people, the move was about 45 years too late. "When people came back from the war and they wanted to move to the suburbs, all the malls were created," Questrom told analysts and investors. "And now we had national chains that we competed with. We didn't change our systems because we had been living with that for 55 years."

Another thing that Questrom did with J. C. Penney is actually more notable for what he didn't do. He didn't get rid of the Eckerd drugstore chain. Penney got into the drugstore business in the 1960s, with a regional chain called Thrift Drug. In the 1990s, the company acquired Kerr's, Fay's, some Rite-Aid stores, some Revco outlets, the Genovese chain, and Eckerd. With 2,600 locations, Eckerd is now the fourth largest drugstore chain in the country. But when Questrom took over, financial analysts expected him to sell off the Eckerd stores. They believed that J. C. Penney had no business being in the drugstore business.

Questrom saw pharmaceuticals as a growth industry. People are living longer, and when they do, they typically need more prescription and over-the-counter drugs. Questrom also recognized that drugstores were no longer merely drugstores but were like supermarkets, where grandparents could get their arthritis medications and, on the way out of the store, spend money on toys for their grandkids.

Questrom hired J. Wayne Harris, another outsider, to be chairman and CEO of Eckerd. Together, they restructured the management of the stores and the stores themselves (you may have noticed a more circuitous route from the pharmacy area to the exit door). They redesigned Eckerd as a convenience store that happened to fill and refill prescriptions—rather than a drugstore that happened to sell greeting cards.

However, Merrill Lynch analysts say that a spin-off of Eckerd could happen as early as spring 2003.

The catalog division of J. C. Penney, which shipped its first goods some 40 years ago, is the nation's largest. In 2000, revenues topped $3.8 billion. That same year, Penney's Web site was the largest online retailer of apparel and home furnishings. The site had 1.3 million unique visitors a month and an industry-high 18 percent of those visitors bought something.

Dot-com start-ups had catchy names and cheap prices but ran into hurdles when it came to filling orders. With its experience in the catalog business, though, J. C. Penney has the organizational systems to handle high volumes. The company's gift fulfillment centers across the country process orders from both the old-school catalog and the new Internet catalog. The 45-acre distribution center in Lenexa, Kansas, can ship 8 million items in 2 to 3 days.

Even though Penney's Web site was popular, it wasn't profitable. "It's a very costly way to do business," Questrom has said, noting that the company lost $40 million on it in 2000. Because the catalog and the Web site operations are two sides of the same coin, Questrom combined them. And because no one in the company had the kind of experience he thought was needed to run the division, he brought in two managers he'd worked with before who had financial, operations, marketing, and merchandising backgrounds.

J. C. Penney is in the process of renovating its existing stores across the country with wider aisles, fewer walls, and new floors, paint, and lighting. New stores, like the one at Stonebriar Center in Frisco, Texas, feature televisions and electronic kiosks. The new look has already impressed the investment houses.

Questrom has said that getting J. C. Penney back on its feet would take 2 to 5 years. "One should not assume, because we're going to have a few good months of sales, that we've made the turn," he cautioned. If he stays true to form, Questrom will leave J. C. Penney once he's convinced the ship has been righted. He'll probably take a little well-deserved rest—until the next board of directors comes calling, looking to lure the old pro out of retirement.[32]

## Questions

1. What change approach did Allen Questrom use to change J. C. Penney?
2. What methods did he use to achieve specific changes?
3. What competencies did Questrom use to make these changes?
4. What are some forms of resistance to change from store managers has Questrom likely had to overcome?

# INTEGRATING CASES

## A DAY IN THE LIFE OF YOLANDA VALDEZ

Yolanda Valdez, senior vice-president for marketing of ClearVision Optical Group, arrived at her office at 7:25 A.M. Settling in at her desk, she began to think about the problems she should handle in the course of the day.

ClearVision Optical Group is a specialty retailer operating under the name of ClearVue with annual sales of over $20 million. The optical group owns 750 stores in forty states, Canada, Mexico, Puerto Rico, The Netherlands, and England. It is the United States' largest provider of eye care products and services, and it seeks to expand its market share in other free world countries. ClearVision is one group of S. G. Davis, an Illinois-based company that also has pharmaceutical and medical product groups. The optical group is planning to expand into other broadly based health care markets, and in 1980 it began experimenting with small shops that sell only sunglasses. ClearVision is a marketing-oriented company that bases its strategy on understanding customer needs and developing and delivering distinctive characteristics that appeal to customers. An example of this is ClearVue's in-store labs that cut lenses for eyeglass frames on a "while-you-wait" basis, often getting the customer's prescription filled within an hour. This service differentiates ClearVue from its competitors, who typically do not offer such speedy service.

Valdez' duties as senior vice-president for marketing broadly include determination and evaluation of the strategic and operational directions for the company. Her specific responsibilities include marketing research, advertising programs, the eyeglass frame line, contact lenses, and in-store merchandising-display programs.

A high-priority item on Valdez' list of things to accomplish today was to construct a questionnaire to survey customer attitudes about the firm's line of frames. This was to be circulated to each of ClearVue's retail store managers to determine whether the current frame styles were preferred by customers and if the selection of frames was adequate at each price level. Valdez realized that she would have a greater likelihood of uninterrupted work before most of the other employees came at 8:30, so she began working on the questionnaire at 7:45. She had scarcely begun clarifying her definition of the problem and stating her objectives when her secretary, Linda Brown, came in with a list of activities planned for the day.

A meeting with the research analysis group working on contact lenses was scheduled for 9:15. There was another meeting set for 10:15 with the group working on fall displays for use in the stores. Valdez was scheduled to lunch with a representative of a prospective advertising agency at 12:00, and she had an appointment with the president at 3:00 to discuss progress on an evaluation of the firm's frame suppliers. She told her secretary she needed some letters typed and put in the mail before the afternoon and a summary of the supplier evaluation typed before her meeting with the president. Her secretary reminded Valdez that the vice-president for finance wanted to see her that day to discuss the details of financing for the new sunglass stores.

When Linda left, Valdez settled back to work on the questionnaire. She outlined what she hoped to accomplish and wrote down a list of specific pieces of information she wanted to get from the store managers. At 8:20 the senior vice-president for operations in the western division called and asked Valdez if she could get a cup of coffee with him and discuss some new ideas he had for marketing children's eyewear. Yolanda agreed to meet him in five minutes. They discussed the plans she was currently considering and how the new suggestions would modify those plans. As she was walking back to her office at 8:45, a woman who worked in the optical lab on the premises asked her if she could give her some advice. Yolanda said she could spare a moment. The woman questioned her on career opportunities in marketing, both in the company and in the entire field. She confessed that she had wanted to get more training and go into marketing, but had never taken the opportunity. Yolanda told her about her experiences in the field and advised her about the best route to take to get into the company's marketing department. After she left, Valdez called the president and asked for his opinion of a major new advertising and display campaign for children's eyewear based on the suggestions she had received. They discussed various ways in which the advertising budget could be reallocated to finance such a campaign. They decided that some funds could be taken from fashion eyewear programs, and some additional money could be trimmed from other elements of the budget and allocated to this campaign. The president mentioned that he would like to see the ideas Valdez had for this campaign before they were sent to an advertising agency.

As Valdez hung up, she realized it was time for the meeting with the contact lens group. She walked into the conference room and sat down at the head of the table. She chatted informally with a few of the people in the group before they got down to business. Valdez listened to their presentation, and after they were finished, she stated some new ideas on the situation and thanked them for the results. She set some goals for the contact lens group that she wanted accomplished before the next meeting. This meeting was over at 10:15, and the group working on fall store displays came in for their meeting. Valdez told them about the children's eyewear. The meeting ended at 11:20.

As Valdez walked out of the conference room, she was stopped by a man from the display group. He talked to Valdez for a few moments about some ideas he had for different types of displays for the sunglass stores. Then he hesitated for a moment and asked Valdez if he could speak to her about a situation that had been troubling him. Valdez said she would like to help with the problem if possible. The man told her that he had been experiencing conflict with his team leader in the display group: he felt she had not been allowing free expression of ideas, and "had it in" for him. The man admitted that he did not know how to cope with the situation and had been considering looking for another job. Valdez promised to look into the matter further.

When she returned to her office and found a stack of phone messages waiting for her, she first returned the call of the vice-president for finance and arranged to meet with him at 1:30. She also returned the call of the vice-president for manufacturing. He needed to talk to her about manufacturing problems with one of the new specialty lenses, so they set up a time to discuss the problem at 2:00. Leaving the rest of the messages on her desk, Valdez left for her lunch appointment with the ad agency representative. At lunch, she discussed plans for network TV advertising and asked for ideas and strategies for effective new messages and the most effective timing for ads. All the time, she was attempting to evaluate whether or not ClearVision should hire this new agency for its next campaign. Since this would be ClearVision's first use of network TV advertising, it was a particularly important decision. After lunch, they drove to the agency's offices and discussed in detail the creative and media scheduling aspects of the campaign.

Valdez was back in her office at 1:15. She made some routine calls to subordinates to check on their progress on certain projects until 1:30. Then the vice-

president for finance came in to discuss the acquisition of an existing chain of sunglass stores. They talked about integrating these stores into ClearVision Optical Group's strategic plan until Keisha Jackson, the vice-president for personnel, knocked on the door. The vice-president for finance stayed to hear what Jackson had to say, and the three discussed possible solutions to the new company employee benefits program.

They left at 2:30. Valdez collected her phone messages and began returning calls. She had just finished talking with a frame supplier representative in New York and an ad agency reporting the completion of a print ad campaign for the next quarter when she had to leave for her meeting with the president. Valdez talked with him for half an hour about expansion strategy and another half-hour about her evaluation of the frame suppliers the firm was currently using.

At 4:00 Valdez went back to her office and found a report on her desk about an inventory control model that gave appropriate purchase quantities and intervals for the current frame line. One of her subordinates in the frame management group had researched the matter and felt that frame purchasing could be more efficient. Valdez recalled that she had told the man to come up with a better method if he could, and this report gave his findings on the matter. Valdez read the report carefully and thought about its implications. She called the man in and asked him to explain some aspects of the model more clearly. They discussed how the model would work in practice and the dollar savings that would result from it. The man left Valdez' office at 4:45, and Valdez began working on the frame line questionnaire again. Five minutes later, Linda Brown came in with some letters for her to sign and some personnel evaluations the head of personnel had sent over to be filled out. She decided to forget about the questionnaire and work on it at home, where she was less likely to be interrupted. She worked on the performance evaluations until 5:45, when she packed her papers in her briefcase and headed for home.

## Questions

1. What competencies are illustrated by Valdez?
2. Is she a good leader?

# BOB KNOWLTON

Bob Knowlton was sitting alone in the conference room of the laboratory. The rest of the group had gone. One of the secretaries had stopped and talked for a while about her husband's coming induction in the

Army, and had finally left. Knowlton, alone in the laboratory, slid a little further down in his chair, looking with satisfaction at the results of the first test run of the new photon unit.

He liked to stay after the others had gone. His appointment as project head was still new enough to give him a deep sense of pleasure. His eyes were on the graphs before him, but in his mind he could hear Dr. Jerrold, the head of the laboratory, saying again, "There's one thing about this place that you can bank on. The sky is the limit for a person who can produce." Knowlton felt again the tingle of happiness and embarrassment. Well, dammit, he said to himself, he had produced. He had come to Simmons Laboratories two years ago. During a routine testing of some rejected Clanson components he had stumbled on the idea of the photon correlator, and the rest just happened. Jerrold had been enthusiastic; a separate project had been set up for further research and development of the device, and he had gotten the job of running it. The whole sequence of events still seemed a little miraculous to Knowlton.

He had shrugged off his reverie and bent determinedly over the sheets when he heard someone come into the room behind him. He looked up expectantly. Jerrold often stayed late himself, and now and then dropped in for a chat. This always made his day's end especially pleasant. But it wasn't Jerrold. The man who had come in was a stranger. He was tall, thin, and rather dark. He wore steel-rimmed glasses and had on a very wide leather belt with a large brass buckle. The stranger smiled and introduced himself. "I'm Simon Fester. Are you Bob Knowlton?" Bob said "yes," and they shook hands. "Doctor Jerrold said I might find you in. We were talking about your work, and I'm very much interested in what you're doing." Knowlton waved him to a chair. Fester didn't seem to belong in any of the standard categories of visitors: customers, visiting firemen, shareholders. Bob pointed to the sheets on the table. "These are the preliminary results of a test we're running. We've got a new gadget by the tail and we're trying to understand it. It's not finished, but I can show you the section that we're testing." He stood up, but Fester was deeply engrossed in the graphs. After a moment he looked up with an odd grin. "These look like plots of a Jennings surface. I've been playing around with some autocorrelation functions of surfaces—you know that stuff." Knowlton, who had no idea what Fester was referring to, grinned back and nodded, and immediately felt uncomfortable. "Let me show you the monster," he said, and led the way to the workroom.

After Fester left, Knowlton slowly put the graphs away, feeling vaguely annoyed. Then, as if he had made a decision, he quickly locked up and took the long way out so that he would pass Jerrold's office. But the office was locked. Knowlton wondered whether Jerrold and Fester had left together.

The next morning Knowlton dropped into Jerrold's office, mentioned that he had talked with Fester, and asked who he was.

"Sit down for a minute," Jerrold said. "I want to talk to you about him. What do you think of him?" Knowlton replied truthfully that he thought Fester was very bright and probably very competent. Jerrold looked pleased.

"We're taking him on," he said. "He has a very good background at a number of laboratories, and he seems to have ideas about the problems we're tackling here." Knowlton nodded in agreement, instantly wishing that Fester not be placed with him.

"I don't know yet where he will finally land," Jerrold continued, "but he seems interested in what you're doing. I thought he might spend a little time with you by way of getting started." Knowlton nodded thoughtfully. "If his interest in your work continues, you can add him to your group."

"Well, he seemed to have some good ideas even without knowing exactly what we are doing," Knowlton answered. "I hope he stays; I'd be glad to have him."

Knowlton walked back to the lab with mixed feelings. He told himself that Fester would be good for the group. He was no dunce; he'd produce. Knowlton thought again of Jerrold's promise when he had promoted him: "The person who produces gets ahead in this outfit." The words now seemed to him to carry the overtones of a threat.

The next day, Fester didn't appear until midafternoon. He explained that he had had a long lunch with Jerrold, discussing his place in the lab. "Yes," said Knowlton. "I talked with him this morning about it, and we both thought that you might work with my group for a while."

Fester smiled in the same knowing way that he had smiled when he mentioned the Jennings surfaces. "I'd like to," he said.

Knowlton introduced Fester to the other members of the lab. Fester and John Link, the mathematician of the group, hit it off well together. They spent the rest of the afternoon discussing a method of analysis of patterns that Link had been worrying over for the last month.

It was 6:30 when Knowlton finally left the lab that night. He had waited almost eagerly for the end of the day to come—when all the lab personnel would all be gone and he could sit in the quiet room, relax, and think it over. "Think what over?" he asked himself. He didn't know. Shortly after 5:00 they had all gone except Fester, and what followed was almost a duel. Knowlton was annoyed that he was being cheated out of his quiet period, and finally resentful, determined that Fester should leave first.

Fester was sitting at the conference table reading, and Knowlton was sitting at his desk in the little glass-enclosed office that he used during the day when he needed to be undisturbed. Fester had gotten last year's progress reports out and was studying them carefully.

Time dragged. Knowlton doodled on a pad, the tension growing inside him. What the hell did Fester think he was going to find in the reports?

Knowlton finally gave up, and they left the lab together. Fester took several of the reports with him to study that evening. Knowlton asked him if he thought the reports gave a clear picture of the lab's activities.

"They're excellent," Fester answered with obvious sincerity. "They're not only good reports; what they report is damn good too!" Knowlton was surprised at the relief he felt, and grew almost jovial as he said goodnight.

Driving home, Knowlton felt more optimistic about Fester's presence in the lab. He had never fully understood the analysis that Link was attempting. If there was anything wrong with Link's approach, Fester would probably spot it.

And if I'm any judge, he thought, he won't be especially diplomatic about it.

He described Fester to his wife, Lucy, who was amused by the broad leather belt and the brass buckle.

"It's the kind of belt the Pilgrims must have worn," she laughed.

"I'm not worried about how he holds his pants up," Knowlton laughed with her. "I'm afraid that he's the kind that just has to make like a genius twice each day. And that can be pretty rough on the group."

Knowlton had been asleep for several hours when he was jarred awake by the telephone. He realized it had rung several times. He swung off the bed, muttering about damn fools and telephones. It was Fester. Without any excuses, apparently oblivious of the time, he plunged into an excited recital of how Link's patterning problem could be solved.

Knowlton covered the mouthpiece to answer his wife's stage whisper, "Who is it?"

"It's the genius."

Fester, completely ignoring the fact that it was 2:00 in the morning, proceeded excitedly to explain a completely new approach to certain of the photon lab problems that he had stumbled onto while analyzing some past experiments. Knowlton managed to put some enthusiasm in his own voice and stood there, still half-dazed and very uncomfortable, listening to Fester talk endlessly, it seemed, about what he had discovered. He said that he not only had a new approach but also an analysis that showed how inherently weak the previous experiment was. He finally concluded by saying that further experimentation along that earlier line certainly would have been inconclusive.

The following morning Knowlton spent the entire morning with Fester and Link, the usual morning group meeting having been called off so that Fester's work of the previous night could be gone over intensively. Fester was very anxious that this be done, and

Knowlton wasn't too unhappy to call the meeting off for reasons of his own.

For the next several days Fester sat in the back office that had been turned over to him and did nothing but read the progress reports of the work that had been done in the last six months. Knowlton caught himself feeling apprehensive about the reaction that Fester might have to some of his work. He was a little surprised at his own feelings. He had always been proud—although he had put on a convincingly modest face—of the way his team had broken new ground in the study of photon measuring devices. Now he wasn't sure. It seemed to him that Fester might easily show that the line of research they had been following was unsound or even unimaginative.

The next morning, as was customary, the members of Knowlton's group, including the secretaries, sat around the table in the conference room for a group meeting. He had always prided himself on the fact that the team as a whole guided and evaluated its work. He was fond of repeating that it was not a waste of time to include secretaries in such meetings. He would point out that, often what started out as a boring recital of fundamental assumptions to a naïve listener, uncovered new ways of regarding these assumptions that wouldn't have occurred to the lab member who had long ago accepted them as a necessary basis for the research he was doing. These group meetings also served another purpose. He admitted to himself that he would have felt far less secure if he had had to direct the work completely on his own. Team meetings, as a principle of leadership, justified the exploration of blind alleys because of the general educative effect of the team. Fester and Link were there, as were Lucy Martin and Martha Ybarra. Link sat next to Fester, the two of them continuing their conversation concerning Link's mathematical study from yesterday. The other group members, Bob Davenport, George Thurlow, and Arthur Oliver, sat there waiting quietly.

Knowlton, for reasons that he didn't quite understand, brought up a problem that all of them had previously spent a great deal of time discussing. The team had come to an implicit conclusion that a solution was impossible and that there was no feasible way of treating it experimentally. Davenport remarked that there was hardly any use of going over it again. He was satisfied that there was no way of approaching the problem with the equipment and the physical capacities of the lab.

This statement had the effect of a shot of adrenaline on Fester. He said he would like to know in detail what the problem was, and walking to the blackboard, began both discussing the problem and simultaneously listing the reasons why it had been abandoned. Very early in the description of the problem it became evident that Fester was going to disagree about the impossibility of solving it. The group realized this and finally the descriptive materials and their recounting of the reasoning that had led to its abandonment dwindled away. Fester began his analysis, which as it proceeded might have well been prepared the previous night although Knowlton knew that to be impossible. He couldn't help being impressed with the organized and logical way that Fester was presenting ideas that must have occurred to him only a few minutes before.

However, Fester said some things that left Knowlton with a mixture of annoyance, irritation and, at the same time, a rather smug feeling of superiority in at least one area. Fester was of the opinion that the way that the problem had been analyzed was typical of what happened when such thinking was attempted by a team, and with an air of sophistication that made it difficult for a listener to dissent, he proceeded to make general comments on the American emphasis on team ideas, satirically describing the ways in which they led to a "high level of mediocrity."

Knowlton observed that Link stared studiously at the floor and was conscious of George Thurlow's and Bob Davenport's glances at him at several points of Fester's little speech. Inwardly, Knowlton couldn't help feeling that this was one point at least in which Fester was off on the wrong foot. The whole lab, following Dr. Jerrold's lead, talked, if not actually practiced, the theory of small research teams as the basic organization for effective research. Fester insisted that the problem could be solved and that he would like to study it for awhile himself.

Knowlton ended the session by remarking that the meetings would continue and that the very fact that a supposedly unsolvable experimental problem was now going to get another look was yet another indication of the value of such meetings. Fester immediately remarked that he was not at all averse to meetings for the purpose of informing the group of the progress of its members. He went on to say that the point he wanted to make was that creative advances were seldom accomplished in such meetings, that they were made by the individual "living with" the problem closely and continuously, forming a sort of personal relationship with it. Knowlton responded by saying that he was glad Fester had raised these points and that he was sure the team would profit by reexamining the basis on which they had been operating. Knowlton agreed that individual effort was probably the basis for making major advances but that he considered the group meetings useful primarily because of the effect they had on keeping the team together and on helping the weaker members of the team keep up with the advances of the ones who were able to move more easily and quickly when analyzing problems.

As days went by and the meetings continued, Fester came to enjoy them because of the direction the meetings soon took. Typically, Fester would hold forth on some subject, and it became clear that he was, without question, more brilliant and better prepared on the topics germane to the problems being studied. He probably was more capable of going ahead on his own than anyone there, and Knowlton grew increasingly disturbed as he realized that his leadership of the team had been, in fact, taken over. In Knowlton's occasional meetings with Dr. Jerrold, whenever Fester was mentioned, he would comment only on Fester's ability and obvious capacity for work, somehow never quite feeling that he could mention his own discomforts. He felt that they revealed a weakness on his own part. Moreover, Dr. Jerrold was greatly impressed with Fester's work and with the contacts he had with Fester outside the photon laboratory.

Knowlton began to feel that the intellectual advantages that Fester had brought to the team might not quite compensate for evidences of a breakdown in the cooperative spirit that had been evident in the group before Fester's coming. More and more of the morning meetings were skipped. Fester's opinion concerning the abilities of others of the team, with the exception of Link's, was obviously low. At times during morning meetings or in smaller discussions he had been rude, refusing at certain times to pursue an argument when he claimed that it was based on the other person's ignorance of the facts involved. His impatience with the others also led him to make remarks of this kind to Dr. Jerrold. This Knowlton inferred from a conversation he had had with Jerrold. The head of the lab had asked whether Davenport and Oliver were going to be retained, but he hadn't mentioned Link. This conversation led Knowlton to believe that Fester had had private conversations with Jerrold.

Knowlton had little difficulty making a convincing case regarding whether Fester's brilliance actually was sufficient recompense for the beginning of his team's breaking up. He spoke privately with Davenport and Oliver. Both clearly were uncomfortable with Fester's presence. Knowlton didn't press the discussion beyond hearing them in one way or another say that they sometimes felt awkward around Fester. They said that sometimes they had difficulty understanding the arguments he advanced. In fact, they often felt too embarrassed to ask Fester to state the grounds on which he based such arguments. Knowlton didn't talk to Link in this manner.

About six months after Fester's coming to the photon lab, meetings were scheduled at which the sponsors of much of the ongoing research were coming to get some idea of its progress. At special meetings, project heads customarily presented the research being conducted by their groups. The other members of the laboratory groups were invited to other, more general meetings later in the day and open to all. The special meetings usually were restricted to project heads, the head of the laboratory, and the sponsors. As the time for his special meeting approached, Knowlton felt that he must avoid the presentation at all costs. He felt that he couldn't present the ideas that Fester had advanced—and on which some work had been done—in sufficient detail and answer questions about them. However, he didn't feel that he could ignore these newer lines of work and present only the work that had been started or completed before Fester's arrival (which he felt perfectly competent to do). It seemed clear that keeping Fester from attending the meeting wouldn't be easy in spite of the fact that he wasn't on the administrative level that had been invited. Knowlton also felt that it wouldn't be beyond Fester, in his blunt and undiplomatic way, if he was present at the meeting, to comment on Knowlton's presentation and reveal the inadequacy that he felt.

Knowlton found an opportunity to speak to Jerrold and raised the question. He remarked to Jerrold that, of course, with the interest in the work and Fester's contributions he probably would like to come to these meetings. Knowlton said that he was concerned about the feelings of the others in the group if Fester were invited. Jerrold brushed this concern aside by saying that he felt the group would understand Fester's rather different position. He thought that, by all means, Fester should be invited. Knowlton then immediately said that he had thought so too and further that Fester should make the presentation because much of it was work that he had done. As Knowlton put it, this would be a nice way to recognize Fester's contributions and to reward him because he was eager to be recognized as a productive member of the lab. Jerrold agreed, and so the matter was decided.

Fester's presentation was very successful and in some ways, dominated the meeting. He held the interest and attention of those attending, and following his presentation the questions persisted for a long period. Later that evening at the banquet, to which the entire laboratory was invited, a circle of people formed about Fester during the cocktail period before the dinner. Jerrold was part of the circle and the discussion concerned the application of the theory Fester was proposing. Although this attention disturbed Knowlton, he reacted and behaved characteristically. He joined the circle, praised Fester to Jerrold and the others, and remarked how able and brilliant some of his work was.

Knowlton, without consulting anyone, began to consider the possibility of a job elsewhere. After a few weeks he found that a new laboratory of considerable size was being organized in a nearby city. His training and experience would enable him to get a project-head job equivalent to the one he had at the lab, with slightly more money.

He immediately accepted it and notified Jerrold by letter, which he mailed on a Friday night to Jerrold's home. The letter was brief, and Jerrold was stunned. The letter merely said that Knowlton had found a better position; that there were personal reasons why he didn't want to appear at the lab any more; that he would be glad to come back later (he would be only forty miles away), to assist if there were any problems with the past work; that he felt sure that Fester could, however, supply any leadership that was required for the group; and that his decision to leave so suddenly was based on some personal problems (he hinted at family health problems involving his mother and father, which were fictitious). Dr. Jerrold took it at face value but still felt that Knowlton's behavior was very strange and quite unaccountable. Jerrold had always felt that his relationship with Knowlton had been warm; that Knowlton was satisfied and, as a matter of fact, quite happy and productive.

Jerrold was considerably disturbed because he had already decided to place Fester in charge of another project that was going to be set up soon. He had been wondering how to explain this decision to Knowlton in view of the obvious help, assistance, and value Knowlton had been getting from Fester and the high regard in which Knowlton held him. In fact, Jerrold had considered letting Knowlton add to his staff another person with Fester's background and training, which apparently had proved so valuable.

Jerrold did not make any attempt to contact Knowlton. In a way he felt aggrieved about the whole thing. Fester, too, was surprised at the suddenness of Knowlton's departure and when Jerrold, in talking to him, asked him whether he preferred to stay with the photon group rather than to head the Air Force project that was being organized, he chose the Air Force project and moved into that job the following week. The photon lab was hit hard. The leadership of the photon group was given to Link, with the understanding that it would be temporary until someone else could be brought in to take over.

## Questions

1. What attributions did Bob Knowlton make?
2. What team norms seemed to be operating in Knowlton's team?
3. What leadership style did Knowlton *need* from Dr. Jerrold after Fester arrived? Explain.
4. What leadership style did Knowlton seem to get from Dr. Jerrold *before* and *after* Fester arrived?

5. What leadership style did Knowlton use with his subordinates?

6. What leadership style did Knowlton use with Fester? Was it effective? Explain.

7. What would you have done with Fester if you were Knowlton?

8. What would you have done to influence Dr. Jerrold if you were Knowlton?

Source: This case was developed by Dr. Alex Bavelas. Edited for *Organizational Behavior*, 10th edition, and used with permission.

# ROBERT PRINCETON AT FALLS VIDEO

In May of 1987, Robert Princeton, age 24, graduated from Middlebury College with a Bachelor's degree in Theatre. In October of 1987, he accepted a job as the Assistant Manager of Falls Video, a rapidly growing chain of video rental outlets located in northeastern New York State.

## BACKGROUND ON FALLS VIDEO

Falls Video had been founded by "Momma and Poppa" Valencia in 1983. The operation began as a video rental business in a corner of their Glens Falls grocery store. They experienced immediate success, and expanded the operation to include four new video rental outlets by 1985. At the same time that the video business was expanding, so was the grocery business, with three new stores established in surrounding towns. Momma Valencia was the mastermind behind this growth. Poppa Valencia was content to remain in the Glens Falls office and keep the books for the growing business. One of the decisions that Momma had made was to separate the grocery and video stores. As she expanded the number of grocery and video outlets, it became apparent that she needed management assistance. In June of 1985, she split the management duties of the organization. Momma continued to manage the grocery stores. She brought in her son, Mario, to run the video business.

Mario, age 28 in 1987, had been working in the grocery stores since he was 18. In May of 1985, after several years of part-time study and evening classes, Mario had graduated with his Associate's degree in Accounting from a nearby community college. He was eager to take charge of the rapidly growing video business. Mario was put in charge of hiring, firing, loss prevention, video buying, and the day to day management of all video stores, including the supervision of personnel.

By the summer of 1987, Falls Video had eight rental outlets within a twenty-five mile radius of Glens Falls. However, problems had begun to arise. Losses due to stolen or misplaced videotapes were up. There were inadequate supplies of newly released films to satisfy customer demand. Turnover, absenteeism, and tardiness were way up among the 35 full- and part-time employees of the chain. Momma Valencia was particularly puzzled by the personnel problems. She was experiencing no such difficulties with her grocery staff. When she asked Mario about it, he replied that she had only four stores to manage, and he had eight! Besides, he insisted, it was hard to attract competent workers at the low wages that they had to pay to remain profitable.

## PRINCETON JOINS THE TEAM

In the early fall of 1987, Momma Valencia decided to hire Robert Princeton as the Assistant Manager of Falls Video in order to help Mario out. While the average starting salary for a liberal arts graduate in 1987 was around $16,000, Robert was hired at an annual salary of $21,500 because Momma Valencia believed that he had a lot of potential. Robert had convinced Momma that he was very interested in working in business. He had taken a course in Organizational Behavior as well as several courses in Industrial Psychology while in college.

Princeton began his work with enthusiasm. He made it a point to visit each store at least twice a week, and, over time, got to know every staff member personally. Robert found that by taking a staff member out to lunch or dinner he could really get them to open up about their perceptions of the organization. Princeton found this contact with the staff very gratifying. However, he quickly encountered some misunderstandings with his boss, Mario. On one occasion, he allowed a part-time employee to take the weekend off in order to attend an out-of-state funeral. When Mario found out, he was furious that the store was understaffed during the critical weekend period. He informed Princeton that all future schedule changes would have to have his personal approval. Feeling somewhat embarrassed, Princeton sheepishly agreed. On another occasion, Princeton offered to train the staff in the basics of film appreciation, since he felt that this would help them to better assess and satisfy customer needs. Mario said that it was a foolish idea, and told Princeton not to waste any company time on it. Although Princeton felt that this was indeed a good idea, he did not pursue it any further. At one point, Princeton mentioned to Mario that many of the full-time employees wanted the company to institute an employee health insurance program. Mario's casual response was that they could not afford the expense, and that Princeton should be channeling his efforts into saving money rather than spending it. Even though Princeton was convinced that such a program would boost morale and reduce turnover, he let the matter drop.

In spite of all of these frustrations, Princeton kept up his efforts. Although he was troubled by the lack of guidance that he received from Mario, he felt that he could demonstrate his value to the organization. After all, when he had approached Momma Valencia with his concerns about his working relationship with Mario, she had said: "Mario is a good and capable boy, and so are you. Work hard and you will be successful." This discussion motivated Princeton to take a more strategic perspective in his efforts.

Princeton immediately initiated a survey of customer preferences in movies to develop recommendations for new titles to purchase. He initiated exit interviews with employees who quit. As a result of this, Princeton did an informal survey of staff members' perceptions of Falls Video management. Finally, he developed a proposal to track video rentals and customer creditworthiness on a microcomputer system.

## THE FINAL DAYS

In early January of 1988, Robert Princeton scheduled a meeting with Mario to discuss his accomplishments of the previous three months. Mario was silent and looked sullen as Princeton presented the results of his work. Princeton provided detailed recommendations for the purchase and resale of new titles. He suggested a variety of changes in personnel policy and management practice designed to boost morale and reduce absenteeism and turnover. He explained how the computer tracking system could reduce losses of videos and improve customer service. Princeton was taken aback by Mario's sudden response:

"Who the _____ do you think you are?" (followed by a long pause. . .),

"Strategic management is *my* job! *Your* job is to supervise the workers. I tell *you* what to do, and you tell *them* what to do! It's as simple as that. Any questions?"

"Well, yes . . . but . . . I thought . . ." stammered Princeton.

"You're not paid to think—you're paid to do what you're told," shouted Mario.

"Poppa showed me your expense account yesterday. The poor old guy almost had a coronary when he tallied it. It's off the wall! Your travel and entertainment expenses in one week are more than mine in a whole month! We give you an office and a telephone here in Glens Falls. I expect you to use them! We hardly ever see you around this office. We're not rich like your family and that snobby private school they sent you to. We have to run this operation on a shoestring. As I've told you before, *that's* where I need your help. Now get to work on making a *real* contribution to this organization's bottom line."

Princeton was flabbergasted! He was proud of his accomplishments, and thought that they proved his value to the organization. Rather than get into a heated argument on the spot, Princeton felt that he had better sleep on it.

The next morning when Princeton arrived for work he found a sealed envelope on his desk with his name on it, marked "Personal and Confidential." At first he assumed that it must be an apology from Mario. He was surprised to find that it was a letter of reprimand for abuse of his expense account and insubordination, signed by both Poppa and Mario Valencia. It concluded with the statement: "If you wish to continue your employment with Falls Video, you must learn to become more cost conscious!"

Princeton spent the rest of the morning in his office with the door closed, thinking.

At 11:30, he asked Momma Valencia to have lunch with him. After some hesitation, she agreed. During lunch, Princeton complained that he was not being allowed to have a strategic impact on the organization. Momma's response had been: "Roberto, I hired you as an assistant manager to Mario. Your job is to work for Mario. Mario's job is strategic planning. I still believe that you have a lot of potential. But you must understand the ways of the family. Poppa and Mario run the business. You must cooperate with them. Without cooperation, we cannot run a successful family business."

At 1:30 P.M., Robert Princeton submitted his resignation. He had no job prospects, and wasn't sure what his next move would be. His parents had offered to pay for him to enroll in an MBA program. His immediate plan was to explore this possibility.

## Questions

1. Which of the core competencies does Mario Valencia possess?  Robert Princeton?
2. Describe possible sources of personality differences between Princeton and Valencia.

3. How could Valencia have used the guidelines for applying the expectancy model of motivation to manage Princeton better?

4. How might Falls Video management have benefited from implementing the self-managing team model of decision making?

5. Characterize the interpersonal conflict handling styles used by Valencia and Princeton.

# THE ROAD TO HELL

John Baker, chief engineer of the Caribbean Bauxite Company Limited of Barracania in the West Indies, was making his final preparations to leave the island. His promotion to production manager of Keso Mining Corporation near Winnipeg—one of Continental Ore's fast-expanding Canadian enterprises—had been announced a month before, and now everything had been attended to except the last vital interview with his successor, the able young Barracanian Matthew Rennalls. It was vital that his interview be a success and that Rennalls leave Baker's office uplifted and encouraged to face the challenge of his new job. A touch on the bell would have brought Rennalls walking into the room, but Baker delayed the moment and gazed thoughtfully through the window, considering just exactly what he was going to say and, more particularly, how he was going to say it.

Baker, an English expatriate, was forty-five years old and had served his twenty-three years with Continental Ore in many different places: the Far East; several countries of Africa; Europe; and for the last two years, the West Indies. He had not cared much for his previous assignment in Hamburg and was delighted when the West Indian appointment came through. Climate was not the only attraction. Baker had always preferred working overseas in what were called the "developing countries" because he felt he had an innate knack—more than most other expatriates working for Continental Ore—of knowing just how to get on with regional staff. After only twenty-four hours in Barracania, however, he realized that he would need all of his innate knack if he were to deal effectively with the problems in this field that now awaited him.

At his first interview with Glenda Hutchins, the production manager, the whole problem of Rennalls and his future was discussed. Then and there, it was made quite clear to Baker that one of his important tasks would be the grooming of Rennalls as his successor. Hutchins had pointed out that not only was Rennalls one of the brightest Barracanian prospects on the staff of Caribbean Bauxite—at London University, he had taken first-class honors in the B.Sc. engineering degree—but, being the son of the minister of finance and economic planning, he also had political pull.

Caribbean Bauxite had been particularly pleased when Rennalls decided to work for them, rather than for the government in which his father had such a prominent post. The company ascribed his action to the effect of their vigorous and liberal regionalization program that, since World War II, had produced eighteen Barracanians at the middle management level and had given Caribbean Bauxite a good lead in this respect over all other international concerns operating in Barracania. The success of this timely regionalization policy had led to excellent relations with the government—a relationship that gained added importance when Barracania, three years later, became independent, an occasion that encouraged a critical and challenging attitude toward the role foreign interests would play in the new Barracania. Hutchins, therefore, had little difficulty convincing Baker that the successful career development of Rennalls was of prime importance.

The interview with Hutchins was now two years in the past, and Baker, leaning back in his office chair, reviewed just how successful he had been in the grooming of Rennalls. What aspects of the latter's character had helped, and what had hindered? What about his own personality? How had that helped or hindered? The first item to go on the credit side, without question, would be the ability of Rennalls to master the technical aspects of his job. From the start, he had shown keenness and enthusiasm, and he had often impressed Baker with his ability in tackling new assignments and the constructive comments he invariably made in departmental discussions. He was popular with all ranks of Barracanian staff and had an ease of manner that stood him in good stead when dealing with his expatriate seniors.

Those were all assets, but what about the debit side? First and foremost was his racial consciousness. His four years at London University had accentuated this feeling and made him sensitive to any sign of condescension on the part of expatriates. Perhaps to give expression to this sentiment, as soon as he returned home from London, he threw himself into politics on behalf of the United Action Party, which was later to win the preindependence elections and provide the country with its first prime minister.

The ambitions of Rennalls—and he certainly was ambitious—did not, however, lie in politics. Staunch nationalist that he was, he saw that he could serve himself and his country best—was not Bauxite responsible for nearly half the value of Barracania's export trade?—by putting his engineering talent to the best use possible. On this account, Hutchins found that she had an unexpectedly easy task in persuading Rennalls to give up his political work before entering the production department as an assistant engineer.

It was, Baker knew, Rennall's well-repressed sense of racial consciousness that had prevented their relationship from being as close as it should have been. On the surface, they could not have seemed more agreeable. Formality between the two was minimal. Baker was delighted to find that his assistant shared his own peculiar "shaggy dog" sense of humor, so jokes were continually being exchanged. They entertained one another at their houses and often played tennis together—and yet the barrier remained invisible, indefinable, but ever present. The existence of this screen between them was a constant source of frustration to Baker, since it indicated a weakness that he was loath to accept. If successful with people of all other nationalities, why not with Rennalls?

At least he had managed to break through to Rennalls more successfully than had any other expatriate. In fact, it was the young Barracanian's attitude—sometimes overbearing, sometimes cynical—toward other company expatriates that had been one of the subjects Baker raised last year when he discussed Rennalls' staff report with him. Baker knew, too, that he would have to raise the same subject again in the forthcoming interview, because Martha Jackson, the senior person in charge of drafting, had complained only yesterday about the rudeness of Rennalls. With this thought in mind, Baker leaned forward and spoke into the intercom: "Would you come in, Matt, please? I'd like a word with you." Rennalls came in, and Baker held out a box and said, "Do sit down. Have a cigarette."

He paused while he held out his lighter and then went on. "As you know, Matt, I'll be off to Canada in a few days' time, and before I go, I thought it would be useful if we could have a final chat together. It is indeed with some deference that I suggest I can be of help. You will shortly be sitting in this chair doing the job I am now doing, but I, on the other hand, am ten years older, so perhaps you can accept the idea that I may be able to give you the benefit of my longer experience."

Baker saw Rennalls stiffen slightly in his chair as he made this point, so he added in explanation, "You and I have attended enough company courses to remember those repeated requests by the human resources manager to tell people how they are getting on as often as the convenient moment arises, and not just the auto-

matic once a year when, by regulation, staff reports have to be discussed."

Rennalls nodded his agreement, so Baker went on, "I shall always remember the last job performance discussion I had with my previous boss back in Germany. She used what she called the 'plus and minus technique.' She firmly believed that when managers seek to improve the work performance of their staff by discussion, their prime objective should be to make sure the latter leave the interview encouraged and inspired to improve. Any criticism, therefore, must be constructive and helpful. She said that one very good way to encourage a person—and I fully agree with her—is to discuss good points, the plus factors, as well as weak ones, the minus factors. So I thought, Matt, it would be a good idea to run our discussion along these lines."

Rennalls offered no comment, so Baker continued, "Let me say, therefore, right away, that as far as your own work performance is concerned, the pluses far outweigh the minuses. I have, for instance, been most impressed with the way you have adapted your considerable theoretical knowledge to master the practical techniques of your job—that ingenious method you used to get air down to the fifth shaft level is a sufficient case in point. At departmental meetings, I have invariably found your comments well taken and helpful. In fact, you will be interested to know that only last week I reported to Ms. Hutchins that, from the technical point of view, she could not wish for a more able person to succeed to the position of chief engineer."

"That's very good indeed of you, John," cut in Rennalls with a smile of thanks. "My only worry now is how to live up to such a high recommendation."

"Of that I am quite sure," returned Baker, "especially if you can overcome the minus factor which I would like now to discuss with you. It is one that I have talked about before, so I'll come straight to the point. I have noticed that you are more friendly and get on better with your fellow Barracanians than you do with Europeans. In point of fact, I had a complaint only yesterday from Ms. Jackson, who said you had been rude to her—and not for the first time, either.

"There is, Matt, I am sure, no need for me to tell you how necessary it will be for you to get on well with expatriates, because until the company has trained sufficient personnel of your caliber, Europeans are bound to occupy senior positions here in Barracania. All this is vital to your future interests, so can I help you in any way?"

While Baker was speaking on this theme, Rennalls sat tensed in his chair, and it was some seconds before he replied. "It is quite extraordinary, isn't it, how one can convey an impression to others so at variance with what one intends? I can only assure you once again that my disputes with Jackson—and you may remember also

Godson—have had nothing at all to do with the color of their skins. I promise you that if a Barracanian had behaved in an equally peremptory manner, I would have reacted in precisely the same way. And again, if I may say it within these four walls, I am sure I am not the only one who has found Jackson and Godson difficult. I could mention the names of several expatriates who have felt the same. However, I am really sorry to have created this impression of not being able to get on with Europeans—it is an entirely false one—and I quite realize that I must do all I can to correct it as quickly as possible. On your last point, regarding Europeans holding senior positions in the company for some time to come, I quite accept the situation. I know that Caribbean Bauxite—as it has been doing for many years now—will promote Barracanians as soon as their experience warrants it. And, finally, I would like to assure you, John—and my father thinks the same, too—that I am very happy in my work here and hope to stay with the company for many years to come."

Rennalls had spoken earnestly, and Baker, although not convinced by what he had heard, did not think he could pursue the matter further except to say, "All right, Matt, my impression may be wrong, but I would like to remind you about the truth of that old saying 'What is important is not what is true, but what is believed.' Let it rest at that."

But suddenly Baker knew that he did not want to "let it rest at that." He was disappointed once again at not being able to break through to Rennalls and at having again to listen to his bland denial that there was any racial prejudice in his makeup.

Baker, who had intended to end the interview at this point, decided to try another tack. "To return for a moment to the plus and minus technique I was telling you about just now, there is another plus factor I forgot to mention. I would like to congratulate you not only on the caliber of your work but also on the ability you have shown in overcoming a challenge that I, as a European, have never had to meet.

"Continental Ore is, as you know, a typical commercial enterprise—admittedly a big one—that is a product of the economic and social environment of the United States and Western Europe. My ancestors have all been brought up in this environment for the past two or three hundred years, and I have, therefore, been able to live in a world in which commerce (as we know it today) has been part and parcel of my being. It has not been something revolutionary and new that has suddenly entered my life. In your case," went on Baker, "the situation is different, because you and your forebears have only had some fifty and not two or three hundred years. Again, Matt, let me congratulate you—and people like you—on having so successfully overcome this particular hurdle. It is for this very reason

that I think the outlook for Barracania—and particularly Caribbean Bauxite—is so bright."

Rennalls had listened intently, and when Baker finished, he replied, "Well, once again, John, I have to thank you for what you have said, and, for my part, I can only say that it is gratifying to know that my own personal effort has been so much appreciated. I hope that more people will soon come to think as you do."

There was a pause, and, for a moment, Baker thought hopefully that he was about to achieve his long-awaited breakthrough. But Rennalls merely smiled back. The barrier remained unbreached. There were some five minutes' cheerful conversation about the contrast between the Caribbean and Canadian climates and whether the West Indies had any hope of beating England in a soccer game before Baker drew the interview to a close. Although he was as far as ever from knowing the real Rennalls, he was nevertheless glad that the interview had run along in this friendly manner and, particularly, that it had ended on such a cheerful note.

This feeling, however, lasted only until the following morning. Baker had some farewells to make, so he arrived at the office considerably later than usual. He had no sooner sat down at his desk than his secretary walked into the room with a worried frown on her face. Her words came fast. "When I arrived this morning, I found Mr. Rennalls already waiting at my door. He seemed very angry and told me that he had a vital letter to dictate that must be sent off without any delay. He was so worked up that he couldn't keep still and kept pacing about the room, which is most unlike him. He wouldn't even wait to read what he had dictated. Just signed the page where he thought the letter would end. It has been distributed, and your copy is in your tray."

Puzzled and feeling vaguely uneasy, Baker opened the envelope marked "confidential" and read the following letter:

14 August 1990

FROM:     Assistant Engineer
TO:          Chief Engineer Caribbean Bauxite Limited
SUBJECT: Assessment of Interview between Messrs.
              Baker and Rennalls

It has always been my practice to respect the advice given to me by seniors, so after our interview, I decided to give careful thought once again to its main points and to make sure that I had understood all that had been said. As I promised you at the time, I had every intention of putting your advice to the best effect.

It was not, therefore, until I had sat down quietly in my home yesterday evening to consider the interview objectively that its main purpose became clear. Only then did the full enormity of what you said dawn on me.

The more I thought about it, the more convinced I was that I had hit upon the real truth—and the more furious I became. With a facility in the English language which I—a poor Barracanian—cannot hope to match, you had the audacity to insult me (and through me every Barracanian worth his salt) by claiming that our knowledge of modern living is only a paltry fifty years old, while yours goes back two hundred to three hundred years. As if your materialistic commercial environment could possibly be compared with the spiritual values of our culture! I'll have you know that if much of what I saw in London is representative of your most boasted culture, I hope fervently that it will never come to Barracania. By what right do you have the effrontery to condescend to us? After all, you Europeans think us barbarians, or, as you say amongst yourselves, we are "just down from the trees."

Far into the night I discussed this matter with my father, and he is as disgusted as I. He agrees with me that any company whose senior staff think as you do is no place for any Barracanian proud of his culture and race. So much for all the company claptrap and specious propaganda about regionalization and Barracania for the Barracanians.

I feel ashamed and betrayed. Please accept this letter as my resignation, which I wish to become effective immediately.

cc:  Production Manager
    Managing Director

## Questions

1.  What were Baker's intentions in the conversation with Rennalls? Were they fulfilled or not, and why?
2.  Was Baker alert to nonverbal signals? What did both Baker and Rennalls communicate to one another by nonverbal means?
3.  How did Baker's view of himself affect the impression he formed of Rennalls?
4.  What kind of interpersonal relationship had existed between Baker and Rennalls prior to the conversation described in the case? Was the conversation consistent or inconsistent with that relationship?
5.  What, if anything, could Baker or Rennalls have done before, during, or after the conversation to improve the situation?
6.  How would you characterize the personality attributes of Baker and Rennalls?
7.  What perceptual errors and attributions are evident?

Source: Prepared and adapted with permission from G. Evans, late of Shell International Petroleum Co. Ltd., London, for Shell-BP Petroleum Development Company of Nigeria, Limited.

# AIRLINE FLIGHT CREDIT—YOURS OR MINE? AN ETHICAL QUESTION

Steve Robbins had just received a real "feather" for his professional cap. The university at which Steve was on the faculty was developing an educational exchange program with a university in Sweden. The exchange was to be negotiated and finalized at a meeting in conjunction with an international conference in Copenhagen, Denmark. Steve had been chosen as one of the four faculty members to attend the conference. Such a selection was a coveted position, and Steve was definitely pleased to have received the honor. Needless to say, he was looking forward to the trip, as well as the responsibility the university had placed upon him.

Steve, who had taught at Middleton State University for ten years, was a highly respected, tenured, full professor of business management. He had held several college- and university-wide committee positions, including being elected Faculty Senate president. Many felt the honor of being chosen to attend the Copenhagen conference was a well-deserved one.

As the time grew nearer to the departure date, Steve began making his travel plans. At this time, Steve was informed by his administration that, if he chose, he could take along his spouse, at his own expense. This new development pleased Wendy, Steve's wife, and Steve was glad he could share this experience with her. Anticipation and excitement was running high at the Robbins household.

On the date of departure for Denmark, several of the faculty members and spouses drove together to the International Airport at Kansas City, from where their United Airlines flight was to depart. Flight 503 was to leave Kansas City at 8:10 A.M. and arrive at O'Hare Airport in Chicago at 9:00 A.M. The party boarded the flight, and all went according to schedule.

After the two-hour layover in Chicago, the Middleton State University party heard the boarding call for Flight 125, their nonstop flight to Copenhagen. When it was their turn, the group boarded the DC-10 that would take them to the international conference. Steve and Wendy had noticed there was a rather large number of passengers waiting for the flight, and they speculated as to just how full the flight was booked. Their answer was quick in coming.

The airline attendant came into their section of the plane and announced that the flight was overbooked. The attendant went on to say that any passenger willing to get off the flight and take a later flight to Copenhagen would be compensated for his or her inconvenience. The later flight was scheduled to arrive in Copenhagen six hours after Flight 125. To compensate those passengers willing to take the later flight, United would "pay" each ticket holder the equivalent of flying credit worth one thousand dollars, which could be used for any destination to which United flew.

Steve and Wendy were very impressed with the generous offer. If they both got off Flight 125 and took the later flight, they could receive flying credit worth two thousand dollars. That was certainly enough to get them to Hawaii and back, which had been a long-standing item on their wish list! However, there were some catches.

The first catch simply involved timing. Steve was scheduled to register for the international conference between 1:00 P.M. and 4:00 P.M., with the dinner and conference sessions beginning at 4:30 P.M. The later flight, Flight 350, would not arrive in Copenhagen until 4:00 P.M., which would not allow for Steve to have time to pick up baggage and reach the conference center before the dinner was to begin.

A second factor to consider was an ethical issue. The couple had paid for Wendy's ticket, so if any benefits were to be gained from it, they undeniably belonged to Steve and Wendy. However, Middleton State University had purchased Steve's ticket. So, if Steve were to receive flying credit worth one thousand dollars because he got off the flight, would that flying credit belong to him or to Middleton State University? Steve and Wendy decided to stay on Flight 125 as planned. However, two of the other faculty members and spouses from Middleton State University decided to get

off Flight 125, take the later flight, and receive the flying credit worth two thousand dollars. They tried to convince Steve and Wendy that being late was "not that big of a deal, and anyway, who would know?" But Steve and Wendy stayed with their decision to remain on Flight 125.

## Questions

1. What factors should an employee in Robbins' position consider when faced with such a situation?
2. Did the Robbins make the correct decision by staying on Flight 125? Why or why not?
3. If the Robbins had decided to take the later flight and receive the flying credit, does the flying credit from his ticket belong to him or to Middleton State? Why do you feel this way?
4. If he could have taken the later flight and still arrived at the international conference on time, would it have been a different situation?
5. If you were the president of Middleton State University, what would you say to Robbins if he had opted to take the later flight and was therefore late to the conference that he had been sent to attend? What would you say to him, had the later flight not caused him to be late for the conference and he had opted to take it?
6. If Robbins had been faced with the described situation on a return flight, rather than the flight to the conference, would a decision to take the later flight and receive the flight credit have been an ethical one?

Source: This case was prepared by Ron Stephens of Central Missouri State University and Melody Waller LaPreze of University of Missouri-Columbia and is intended to be used as a basis for class discussion, rather than to illustrate either effective or ineffective handling of the situation. The names of the institution, individuals, and locations have been disguised to preserve anonymity. All rights reserved to the authors. © 1990 by Ron Stephens and Melody Waller LaPreze. Presented and accepted by the refereed Midwest Society for Case Research. See R. A. Cook (ed.) Annual Advances in Business Cases 1990. South Bend, Ind.: Midwest Society for Case Research, 1990, 58–60. Used with permission.

# IT'S MY BIKE

Debbie Martin was overjoyed when she was selected the new Supplier Quality Manager for the commercial product division of Cold Air Corporation. In this role, she was responsible for monitoring the quality of component parts for twelve production lines scattered throughout the large manufacturing plant. When she started the new position, Debbie knew she would be faced with many opportunities and conflicts. Her im-

mediate supervisor, the manager of shipping and receiving, was not known as an easy person to work for. He expected his subordinates to have a take charge attitude and to avoid bothering him with trivial issues. What Debbie had not envisioned was just how trivial and non-productive some of the conflicts in her new position would be. She certainly had not expected to be on the verge of a fistfight.

Debbie was just starting her shift when she received a telephone call from Ronnie, one of her subordinates. Ronnie was a purchasing parts inspector, and was responsible for inspecting certain incoming parts for all production lines in the plant. He was complaining that the Airhandler Quality team had borrowed "the bike" for a special project and would not return it. He reminded Debbie of his current project and how covering the entire 15-acre plant on foot would only delay completion of the project. Debbie rolled her eyes as she thought about the logistics of inspecting component parts in the plant's three separate buildings. She also realized that Ronnie had a tendency to get excited over little things. He was a very conscientious, detail-oriented worker, but was easily upset when things did not go according to his plans. Debbie asked him to work on another project while she checked into the problem with the bike.

The bike, actually an adult size tricycle with a basket, had a colorful history at Cold Air. The bike had been acquired by Debbie's predecessor to aid in transporting testing materials and small samples from one end of the plant to another. Given the size of the plant, it was often necessary to travel one-fourth of a mile or more to test parts delivered to some of the more distant lines. Debbie knew of three other bikes in use in the plant, but hers seemed to have the most problems. In the six months Debbie had been supervisor, she had experienced numerous problems with the bike.

First, it had been taken and painted by people in the metal works department. The bike had been missing for over two weeks when Ronnie spied a bike with a new paint job. Since Ronnie had etched "Receiving Inspection" on the bottom of the bike's frame, they were able to identify and retrieve it. After getting the bike back, Debbie had assumed the problems were over. Being a new manager, she also did not want to raise a stink over the bike being taken. Also, the ill will would not be worth the inconvenience and the possibility of creating an enemy in another department.

The second episode began more innocently than the first. The Airhandler Quality group was being pushed to quickly implement the transfer of new production processes from a plant in Illinois. The Illinois plant was being closed and operations transferred to the local plant. It was necessary to get the new equipment into place and operating quickly. Because portions of the new production lines were at one end of the main plant and the Airhandler office was at the other, there was a lot of walking involved. Steve Gregg, Airhandler Quality Engineer, approached Debbie about borrowing the bike to expedite Airhandler's project. Debbie agreed to accommodate on the condition that the bike would be returned when her department needed it. Steve agreed to the arrangement.

Approximately one week later the company changed suppliers for one of its components. There were a few problems in integrating the slightly different components into production. This required Ronnie to make more frequent inspections. Ronnie needed the bike to more efficiently complete his assignment. Ronnie called Frank Jones, Steve's assistant, and told him that he needed the bike and that he would be by later in the morning to pick it up. That afternoon Steve called Debbie to find out why Ronnie had come and taken the bike. She promptly reminded him of their agreement. Steve said he understood the arrangement and asked to borrow the bike again once Ronnie was finished with it. Wanting to be cooperative, Debbie agreed to loan the bike one more time.

The second time that the Airhandler Quality team borrowed the bike brings us back to the situation at hand. Debbie could not believe what Ronnie was telling her. How could Steve refuse to return something that he had just recently borrowed? Debbie was heading out the door to see Steve when the phone rang again. It was Ronnie. He had just met Steve and had requested that he return the bike immediately. Steve stated that the request would have to come from Debbie. He further stated that he would not return the bike to Ronnie without an official request from Debbie.

Ronnie was angry. He told Debbie that if she wanted the bike he would be happy to get it. He was not afraid to confront Steve and take the bike by force if necessary. He just wanted Debbie's approval. Debbie told him again to be patient while she addressed the issue with Steve. Debbie hung up the phone and marveled at the amount of time being consumed by the $250 tricycle!

After taking two "productive" telephone calls, Debbie was again headed out the door to find Steve when the phone rang. It was Ronnie again, but this time he had Frank with him. He asked Debbie to tell Frank to give him the bike. She told him to put Frank on the telephone and she would talk to him. After talking with Debbie, Frank agreed to return the bike. Even though the situation was resolved for the moment, Debbie knew she still needed to speak to Steve.

Steve was headed out of his office when Debbie first saw him. She stopped and asked him if he had a minute to discuss the bike. He said he didn't at the moment as he was late for a meeting. Plus, he didn't see what the big deal was about the bike. His group needed it more than her department, so she could just give him the bike and buy a new one. As he was heading down the hall, he reminded her that the product transition was the most important project in the plant and that she should not mind helping his department succeed.

Steve's comments struck a nerve with Debbie. Was this the type of thanks she got for helping someone?

She realized the product transition was an important project. That was why she let Airhandler Quality group borrow the bike in the first place. She knew that she could no longer tolerate the situation. She could talk to her superior and get him to talk to Steve's superior or go to their common manager, the Production Manager. But, she wondered, were there other options that she did not see? What were the consequences?

## Questions

1. Are conflicts such as this unusual in organizations?
2. Why is the $250 bike a source of conflict?

3. What are the causes of the conflict?
4. What options are available to Debbie to resolve the conflict?

This case was prepared by Joe Thomas and Bill Gash, Middle Tennessee State University and is intended to be used as a basis for class discussion. The views represented are those of the case authors and do not necessarily reflect the views of the Society for Case Research. The authors' views are based on their own professional judgments. The names of the organization and individuals have been disguised to preserve the identity of individuals for purpose of anonymity. Presented to and accepted by the Society for Case Research. All rights reserved to the authors and SCR. Copyright © 1998 by Joe Thomas and Bill Gash. Used with permission.

# WHAT DO WE DO WITH HOWARD?

Agrigreen, Inc., manufactures various agricultural fertilizers in several plants in the western United States and Canada. Tad Pierson, appointed three months ago as a project engineer at one of the Agrigreen plants, had been told last week by Burt Jacobs, the new manager of engineering to whom he reports, that he was to take on the added responsibility of supervising the plant surveying group. Having worked with members of this group in the past, Pierson was aware of some performance problems and conflicts that existed within the group. Contemplating what action, if any, he should take as their new supervisor, he reviewed the history of the surveying group with others in the company (see Figure 1) and then talked with each group member individually to arrive at the following picture of the situation.

## HOWARD LINEBERRY, LEAD SURVEYOR

After receiving his surveyor's certificate from the local civil technologies college, Howard Lineberry had gone to work for the State Highway Department as a chainman. The job hadn't paid very well, and he always felt that the lead surveyor didn't like him and often had him doing work that was better suited for a rodman, a position of lower status than chainman on a survey crew.

So, when a job for a lead surveyor had opened up at Agrigreen eighteen years ago, Lineberry had been glad to get it. He told Pierson how excited he had been to be hired into the newly created position. Previously, survey work at Agrigreen had been handled on a part-time basis by drafting personnel or project engineers, mainly Frank Silverton (see Figure 2). Because of significant growth during the preceding three years, survey work had begun to eat up nearly all of Silverton's working

hours. As a project engineer, his salary was too high to justify using him for survey activities, so management had decided to hire someone with an education in surveying and some experience to support the work of Silverton and the five other project engineers.

Jerry Givens, manager of the engineering staff at the time, and since retired, was the man who had hired and first supervised Lineberry. Since being hired, he has worked for four different supervisors. He remembered Givens as a "cantankerous, hard-headed boss who had very specific things that he wanted done and definite ideas on how they should be accomplished." He often lost his temper and openly criticized Lineberry or anyone else doing something he didn't like. Nevertheless, Lineberry felt that he got along well with Givens. He usually had Lineberry's daily work scheduled by the time Lineberry arrived in the morning and explained what needed to be done and how it should be done. Only occasionally would Givens have to stop by during the day to change the focus of activities.

After Givens retired, Lineberry reported to Paul Jackson, the new manager of engineering. Unlike Givens, Jackson expected Lineberry to plan his day based on the work that needed to be done and to go ahead and do it. About that time, Lineberry had been thinking that he could do a better job supporting the project engineers, who were increasingly busy on more and larger projects, if he worked with them more directly. The increased pace of work often resulted in last minute requests for Lineberry to provide information and fieldwork. He felt that he had handled fairly well what had become frequent daily changes in his work schedule.

Then one day Jackson accused Lineberry, in front of a couple of the engineers, of being "disorganized and possibly lazy." Later, maybe as a result of thinking about

**Figure 1**

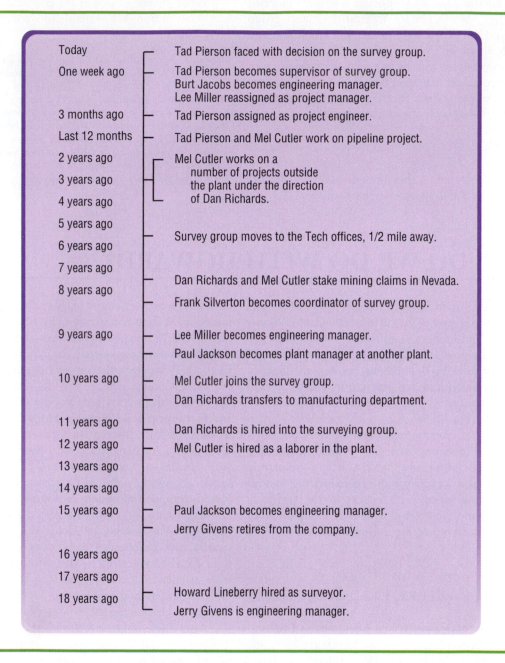

| | |
|---|---|
| Today | Tad Pierson faced with decision on the survey group. |
| One week ago | Tad Pierson becomes supervisor of survey group. Burt Jacobs becomes engineering manager. Lee Miller reassigned as project manager. |
| 3 months ago | Tad Pierson assigned as project engineer. |
| Last 12 months | Tad Pierson and Mel Cutler work on pipeline project. |
| 2 years ago | Mel Cutler works on a number of projects outside the plant under the direction of Dan Richards. |
| 3 years ago | |
| 4 years ago | |
| 5 years ago | |
| 6 years ago | Survey group moves to the Tech offices, 1/2 mile away. |
| 7 years ago | |
| 8 years ago | Dan Richards and Mel Cutler stake mining claims in Nevada. Frank Silverton becomes coordinator of survey group. |
| 9 years ago | Lee Miller becomes engineering manager. Paul Jackson becomes plant manager at another plant. |
| 10 years ago | Mel Cutler joins the survey group. Dan Richards transfers to manufacturing department. |
| 11 years ago | Dan Richards is hired into the surveying group. |
| 12 years ago | Mel Cutler is hired as a laborer in the plant. |
| 13 years ago | |
| 14 years ago | |
| 15 years ago | Paul Jackson becomes engineering manager. Jerry Givens retires from the company. |
| 16 years ago | |
| 17 years ago | |
| 18 years ago | Howard Lineberry hired as surveyor. Jerry Givens is engineering manager. |

what Paul had said, or maybe as a result of just bad luck, according to Lineberry, he made an error fixing the location of a building foundation. The error wasn't noticed until it was time to erect the new mill. What followed, Linebery remembered, was "pure hell as the foundation was demolished and replaced at considerable cost in time and money." After that, people stopped talking when he walked up, and he often overheard "little biting comments" about him. Lineberry had "considered quitting, but good jobs were hard to get."

After the foundation incident, Jackson became increasingly critical and finally decided that Lineberry needed someone to assist him and double check his "error prone" work. At the same time, Agrigreen was planning to build a new wastewater holding pond, and the project would require extra surveying help. Jackson hired Dan Richards to assist Lineberry. Richards was a bright, hard-working young man who had the same training as Lineberry and who was also pursuing a degree in engineering. As the project proceeded, Richards had openly expressed his feelings that his leader, Howard Lineberry, was slow and stupid. Lineberry felt relieved a year and half later when Richards was transferred to the manufacturing department.

**Figure 2**

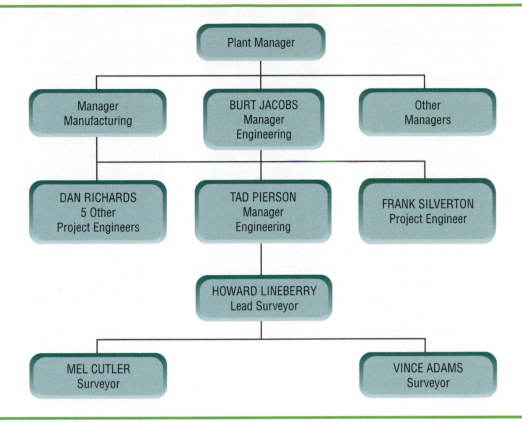

Mel Cutler, who had been employed in the plant for two years as a laborer, replaced Richards. He had previously worked for another employer as a draftsman and had also gained considerable experience in surveying. Lineberry immediately liked Cutler, something he had never felt for Dan Richards. Cutler was willing to work with Lineberry on how to do the jobs and often caught small errors before they became problems.

Ten years have passed since Cutler first joined Lineberry, who now felt a "slight pang" as he wished things were still the same between them. But, during the past five years, relations between them had become increasingly tense. Recently, the only verbal exchanges between them had been terse and directly concerned with the job. Much of the enjoyment of his job is gone, and Lineberry often dreaded coming to work.

A few months after Cutler had been hired, another supervisory change occurred. Lee Miller, a former project engineer, took the manager's job when Paul Jackson was promoted to plant manager at another Agrigreen plant. Miller had been very successful as an engineer but as a supervisor was somewhat indecisive.

Meanwhile, increasing workloads had resulted in the hiring of additional draftsmen, and office space was getting tight. Miller corrected the situation by remodeling some space in the basement of the Tech offices located about a half-mile from the plant, and Lineberry and Cutler moved there. Nobody bothered either of them much in the new location. Lineberry felt good about the change because he now had space for the survey equipment and he was away from the mainstream of the operation. He needed to see the engineers only when he felt like it and wasn't bothered as often by hearing their derogatory comments.

Four years ago, Miller had told Lineberry and the other surveyors that he would like them to coordinate their job assignments and schedules through Frank Silverton, indicating that Silverton had much more surveying experience than he did and would know better what the needs were. Lineberry remembered feeling uncomfortable about this arrangement because Silverton wasn't really his boss, and he still had to have Miller sign his time cards and approve his vacation.

During the past four years, Cutler had occasionally worked on small projects outside the plant, most frequently for Dan Richards, who always specified which individual he wanted when requesting help.

Recently, the company had constructed a fifty-mile pipeline to deliver raw material to the plant, and Cutler was chosen to work under Tad Pierson on that project. Pierson was a recent engineering graduate charged with overseeing the pipeline survey and construction, which had lasted from April through December the previous year. Lineberry still felt angry about Cutler's assignment to the project because he has had "more experience than Mel at surveying and could have used the overtime money." The only benefit to Lineberry resulting from Cutler's outside work was that Miller had hired Vince Adams to help Lineberry during the summer months. Lineberry and Adams thought much the same way about many things, and Lineberry had a genuine affection for this "just-out-of-high-school" young man.

Following completion of the pipeline project, Tad Pierson had been made a project engineer, and because of the lack of space in the plant offices, was given space in the Tech offices near Lineberry, Adams, and Cutler. Pierson was openly friendly with Cutler, but Lineberry felt that Pierson "acted coolly" toward him and Adams. They seemed to having nothing in common, and each time Lineberry had tried to talk to Pierson, Pierson seemed to cut the discussion short and make an excuse to leave.

A week ago, Lee Miller had stepped down as manager of engineering and resumed duties as one of the project engineers. Burt Jacobs, a big, loud, direct person (in Lineberry's opinion), who had been the manager of purchasing and stores (plant supplies) replaced him as manager. Jacobs was an engineer about half Miller's age and several years younger than Lineberry. Only this morning, Jacobs had called the engineering department together to say that change was needed because of the friction between engineering and the other departments in the plant. He also said that the surveyors were now to report to Pierson (which made Lineberry very uneasy) and that anyone needing surveying services must now schedule it through Pierson.

## Mel Cutler, Surveyor's Helper

Mel Cutler arrived in town without a job and was a "happy man" when he got the call from Agrigreen. The company needed a plant laborer, and he needed a job. He remembered the job for the next two years as "the most exhausting and filthy job I have ever worked." Finally, ten years ago a surveyor's helper position had opened up, and with his background in surveying and drafting he was able to get the job.

Cutler was assigned to Howard Lineberry. For the first few years, they worked well together. Both men had young families, and they shared many of the same outside interests. Cutler had been willing to go along with the way Lineberry had always done things until about five years ago when he noticed that they "experienced continual problems due to the way Howard kept his notes." Cutler tried to show Lineberry the way he

had been trained to keep notes, but "Howard would have nothing to do with it." The debate continued for several weeks.

Soon, Lineberry started keeping the work schedule to himself, and Cutler often had no idea what they were going to do next until Lineberry stopped the truck and started unloading equipment. In addition, Lineberry's frequent snack breaks were starting to bother Cutler. He began losing respect for Lineberry and thought that Lineberry was "growing less concerned about his job." No amount of criticism from Frank Silverton, their boss, seemed to have any effect on Lineberry or the number of errors he committed.

Moving the surveyors out of the plant had been wrong in Cutler's opinion. He said, "Howard started taking advantage of the situation almost immediately by coming in late and leaving early a couple of times each week." Lately, Lineberry had been taking naps after lunch, justifying it by saying that he often worked late and was just making up the time. For the past year or so, he had been far more likely to be late for work than to be on time. Whenever Silverton mentioned it, Lineberry always had an excuse. Silverton gave up trying to get him to work on time and settled for just getting some good work done.

Years ago, Dan Richards had first called to see if Cutler wanted to help him stake Agrigreen mining claims in Nevada, and Cutler had jumped at the chance. This turned out to be the first of many surveying expeditions that the two men made together. Looking back, Cutler could see how they had developed a "lot of respect and trust in each other's work." They often joked about Lineberry's laziness and what an idiot they thought he was.

Cutler had been extremely happy when he became part of the pipeline survey crew. He had met Tad Pierson, the pipeline field engineer, at a party that Richards had given and had immediately liked him. Shortly into the project, Pierson, on Richard's recommendation, put Cutler in charge of the pipeline survey crew and made him responsible for inspections for the eastern half of the pipeline.

Cutler felt good about the assignment and vowed that he would be "the best worker Tad had ever seen." The hours were long—he had averaged more than thirty-five hours overtime a week for fifteen weeks straight and had never once complained. Pierson was also working long days, and Cutler felt that they had developed an unspoken respect for each other as solid, hard workers. Pierson had backed him without question when Cutler had ordered the contractor to dig up a quarter mile of pipeline that had been buried rather hastily while he had been gone from the work site. Cutler had felt, and later proved, that the contractor buried the pipe to prevent proper inspection.

Cutler had talked with Pierson about Lineberry, indicating he didn't look forward to working for him again when the pipeline is completed. Later, after Pierson had been reassigned to the plant, Cutler regularly stopped by to talk with him, often pointing out some of the things that Lineberry and Adams were doing; Cutler and Pierson laughed and shook their heads.

Cutler had been excited to hear at this morning's meeting that Tad Pierson was now in charge of the surveyors. He wondered how long it would take Pierson to fire Howard.

## TAD PIERSON, PROJECT ENGINEER

In reviewing his own career with Agrigreen, Tad Pierson had the following thoughts.

I don't know; I guess I've known Dan Richards since I was about fourteen or so. We used to pal around in high school and have always been close. Dan told me he had wanted out of this area so badly because of Howard. He really hates the guy, and I guess I don't have much respect for him either. It's really ironic that now I'm Howard's boss.

Yeah, it was Dan that talked me into going back to school. When I was ready to give up as I'd done before, he told me, "You can always quit." He knew it'd make me mad enough to stay. I guess I owe him for that. That, and his pulling the strings that got me on here. When I called him yesterday, to let him know about the change, he almost fell off his chair laughing. Then he stopped and said that he wished he was me so he could fire Howard. He was serious; he really hates him.

I don't know what I'm going to do. I think the company would be money ahead to fire Howard. But, I went through the firing thing with a guy on the pipeline crew last summer. With all the letters and documentation and stuff you have to go through, it'd take two years to get rid of him. When I think of how long he's been here and his family and all, I get kind of squeamish. I guess I just don't know what to do. I'm going to think on it some.

When Burt asked me if I'd take the surveyors I told him I would, but not like Frank had. If I wanted to fire Howard, I wanted to be able to do it. He told me, "They'd be yours; just document it. I'm going to have

my hands full trying to fix other messes without trying to handle that problem too." I almost get the feeling that both of us are in up to our ears.

With regard to Howard, about a month ago I went over to see Mel for a minute. There was Howard, with his head down on the drafting table, sound asleep. He didn't even hear me come or go. Vince wasn't any better; he was sitting there holding his hard hat and staring into it, dazed. I don't know if he knew I was there or not either. What a pair!

The pipeline was different. You knew it was just a summer thing, so we could put up with a lot of stuff. Mel's a good man. He's pretty sour on the company though. He doesn't think Howard should get paid more than he does and "still get away with the crap he does." He's already told me I should fire both Howard and Vince.

I just don't know what to do. I talked with some of the engineers. Half of them don't trust the work they get from Howard—they'd rather go out and do it themselves, and they do. I sometimes wonder what the heck we even have the surveyors for. I wonder what I should do?

## Questions

1. What is the problem in this case?
2. What is your view of Howard Lineberry's performance? Discuss how motivational models can be applied to explain his behavior.
3. How would you describe the behaviors of Richards and Cutler? What was the nature of their relationships with Lineberry?
4. What problems, if any, were created with the placement of the surveying group within the structure of the organization?
5. What responsibility, if any, should management bear for the problems that developed?
6. What should Pierson do to resolve the situation involving Lineberry?

Source: This case was prepared by William E. Stratton of Idaho State University, Pocatello, Idaho, and J. Dale Reavis. It was presented to and accepted by the refereed Society for Case Research. All rights reserved to the authors and the SCR. Copyright © 1995 by William E. Stratton and J. Dale Reavis. It was edited for *Organizational Behavior*, 10th edition, and used with permission.

# CHAD REYNOLDS' DILEMMA

Park Plaza Hotel was a chain of twelve full-service upscale suburban hotels located in large cities throughout the Midwest and Southeast. Each hotel offered complete food and beverage service, including restaurants, bars, and banquet facilities catering to the needs of the traveling public, conventions, and the local community.

Each hotel in the chain was operated as a free-standing unit but received support through functional departments headed by vice-presidents at the corporate level. The smallest hotel in the chain had 300 rooms, and the largest had 500 rooms. Figure 1 shows organization charts of key corporate positions and a typical hotel.

Hotel management has traditionally experienced high levels of turnover. Rapid growth in the industry created many new job opportunities, and burnout caused by the demanding nature of the work and long hours opened others. To meet the need for developing managerial talent, most hotel companies operate management trainee and/or internship programs. Employees who successfully complete these programs are then placed on well-defined career paths. They are given special assignments or projects and supervisory assignments in all functional areas of hotel operations, in-

cluding rooms, food and beverage, accounting, personnel, and maintenance.

Chad Reynolds had been recruited directly out of college. After completing Park Plaza's management trainee program, he was initially assigned to the Atlanta hotel. After rotating through various departmental assignments and accepting several promotions and two transfers, Reynolds felt ready to prove himself as an executive assistant manager. This position would be the final step in preparation for becoming the general manager in one of the chain's hotels.

When the executive assistant manager's position became open in Atlanta, Reynolds accepted it immediately. It would be like old home week. The promotion and transfer to Atlanta would give him a chance to work with several people who had helped him establish his career. In addition, the corporate personnel director

**Figure 1**

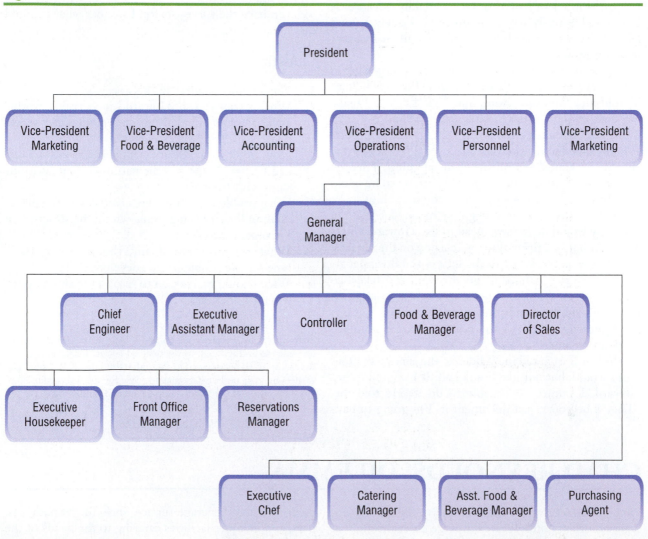

assured Reynolds that he would be considered for the general manager's position at the new Orlando hotel when he had successfully completed this assignment. With his ultimate objective of being a general manager in sight, all the long hours and six- to seven-day work weeks finally seemed to have been worth the effort.

Reynolds's homecoming was better than he had expected. He quickly renewed many acquaintances and rekindled friendships he had previously made in the hotel and community. However, the excitement of settling into his new position was quickly dampened by the following conversation he had with Nancy Benson, the hotel's controller.

**Benson:** Chad, do you have time for a cup of coffee and a few questions?

**Reynolds:** Sure, let's go down to the coffee shop.

**Benson:** No, I've got the coffee pot on in my office, and I want to talk to you in private anyway.

**Reynolds:** By your tone of voice, this sounds serious.

**Benson:** Chad, you and I have known each other for almost six years, and I need to talk to someone I can trust. I'm not sure, but I think we may have a problem in our food and beverage department.

**Reynolds:** I'm all ears.

**Benson:** For the past six months, our food and beverage costs have been anywhere from 1 to 2 percent over budget.

**Reynolds:** That sounds a little off, but not too bad.

**Benson:** Not too bad? This could be serious, and it's my responsibility to spot potential problems! On our combined annual food and beverage budgets of $2.7 million, this could amount to over $50,000 a year.

**Reynolds:** Okay, I get your point. Have you talked with Mike Schwerzek (food and beverage director) about your concerns?

**Benson:** Yes, on several occasions. He assures me that all control procedures are being adhered to, and the only problem is that the catering sales staff is cutting too many special deals with banquet customers, forcing up the costs.

**Reynolds:** I'm sure you've checked into this. Does his reasoning make any sense?

**Benson:** No, it doesn't. I've been working with Ryan Haase (accounts payable clerk) to determine the ingredient costs for all our menu items. Based on established menu prices in the restaurants and selling prices of last month's banquet menus, we should have been well below budget on our food costs.

**Reynolds:** Have you shared any of your concerns with John Anderson (general manager)?

**Benson:** Yes.

**Reynolds:** Well, don't keep me in suspense. What did he say?

**Benson:** Not much then, but he called me in a couple of days later and repeated most of the same things Mike had told me earlier. On top of that, he told me I was spending too much time counting pennies, and I shouldn't worry as long as we remained profitable and our percentage costs held steady.

**Reynolds:** Let me talk with John, and I'll get back to you as soon as possible.

**Benson:** I'd appreciate it if you'd keep my name out of this. Mike has been accusing me of being out to get him. If I'm wrong, I don't want to create any more hard feelings because Mike seems to be well liked by his staff.

**Reynolds:** No problem. I'll do a little checking on my own and try to bring the subject up for discussion at the right time.

As the executive assistant manager and member of the hotel's executive committee, Reynolds had access to all the information about the operation, but his primary responsibility was for operation of the rooms department. He and Mike Schwerzek had the same reporting relations to the general manager (see Figure 1), but in the general manager's absence, the executive assistant manager was officially in charge of all hotel operations. However, in practice, the executive assistant manager was expected to devote only limited time and attention to food and beverage operations.

Normally, food and beverage operations, as well as other operational issues in the hotel, were discussed during budget deliberations and at executive committee meetings. The executive committee was composed of the general manager, the executive assistant manager, food and beverage manager, director of sales, controller, and chief engineer. Under the direction of the general manager, this committee was responsible for the oversight and coordination of all hotel operations.

The opportunity to discuss food and beverage costs came up sooner than Reynolds had expected. John Anderson had asked him if he wanted to include any items on the agenda at the biweekly executive committee meeting. In addition to normal operating issues, Reynolds mentioned that he would be interested in discussing food and beverage costs because they were the only cost categories continually over budget. Reynolds was surprised when Anderson said that Nancy Benson must have been bending his ear. Reynolds admitted that she had but that he had also been doing some checking on his own to satisfy his curiosity.

Reynolds was surprised and troubled when Anderson cut the conversation short by saying that he had complete confidence in Mike Schwerzek and didn't want the subject brought up again. Reynolds definitely felt that he was between a rock and a hard place. Anderson had been the general manager when Reynolds entered the management training program and had become his mentor, but he also valued Nancy Benson's ability to spot potential trouble.

Although he could have walked away from the issue, Reynolds decided not to do so. Besides wanting to satisfy his own curiosity, he knew that a better understanding of food and beverage operations would be to his benefit when he finally became a general manager. He adjusted his schedule so that he could spend more time observing purchasing, receiving, food preparation, and service activities in the food and beverage department. Mike Schwerzek must have sensed Reynolds's increased presence because he openly complained at the next executive committee meeting that Reynolds was spending too much time in the food and beverage areas. Although Schwerzek continued to protest, John Anderson encouraged Reynolds to learn as much about the food and beverage areas as possible in order to prepare himself for his planned promotion to a general manager's position.

Two months passed before Reynolds brought up the subject of food and beverage costs again with Anderson. On a quiet Saturday morning, Reynolds stepped into Anderson's office, carrying a legal pad full of notes.

**Reynolds:** John, you and I have been with this company for a long time. I'm concerned about a potential problem and I need to share these concerns with you.

**Anderson:** Okay, have a seat and take your time.

**Reynolds:** It's about our food and beverage department. I think Nancy was right; there seems to be something that's just not quite right in those areas. I'm still not sure I can put my finger on it, but I've come up with some very interesting information. I think the problem may be bigger than just a cost issue. Let me tell you some of the things that I've picked up over the past two months. First, I don't know whether you're aware of it, but Mike Schwerzek, Jeff Randall (executive chef), and Anna Ellingson (purchasing agent) all worked together before coming here. In fact, Jeff and Anna were hired based on Mike's recommendations.

Second, four months ago, Mike hired his brother, Larry Schwerzek, as a relief cook to work on weekends and to help out on extremely busy nights. The fact that they are related and working

in the same department is a violation of company policy. When I mentioned the policy to Mike, he told me that the way he interpreted it, is that it doesn't apply to temporary help. Disregarding the questions of company policy, Larry has no previous culinary experience. In fact, right now, he is working as a maintenance helper for an apartment complex. Mike said that it's a good arrangement because he only works when needed, and he can depend on him to come in on short notice.

Third, eight months ago, we stopped purchasing from Southeastern Meats here in town and began purchasing all of our fresh fish, poultry, and meat and some frozen products from Carver Meats in Chattanooga. Mike and Jeff say we are getting the same quality product and service at a better price. I've reviewed the old invoices, and the quality (grade) specified and delivered on the invoice is the same, but the prices are a few pennies higher per pound or item. Although it's only a rumor around town, it's probably worth noting that some food and beverage people feel that Carver Meats sometimes substitutes lower grades of meats in its shipments, and there is some suspicion that it has given kickbacks to purchasing agents or chefs.

Fourth, Wendell Johnson (storeroom clerk) tells me that the night cooks are concerned because on several occasions Larry Schwerzek has used the chef's keys to get supplies from the storeroom and hasn't completed the required requisitions. They're afraid to say anything to Mike or Jeff because they know they are friends, but they're also afraid of being blamed if anything comes up missing.

Finally, last night, I was working late to assist with the end of the month inventories and to spot check the different departments. When I went to the kitchen, Anna Ellingson and Larry Schwerzek were taking inventory. When I asked Anna where the chef or the executive sous chef was, she told me they were both busy, so she had asked Larry to help her. This procedure seemed odd to me because it's company policy for either the chef or executive sous chef to supervise and participate in the inventory procedure. I decided to stick around and spend some time with the night audit crew. After the kitchen and all food and beverage outlets were shut down, I went back and reinventoried the meat cooler. The counts and weights I got and recorded on these inventory sheets were different and several pounds less than those reported on the inventory sheets.

**Anderson:** Mike told me you had been snooping around.

**Reynolds:** Hey, maybe if he thinks I'm snooping, he has something to hide.

**Anderson:** It sounds like all of the things you've found are just judgment calls. Maybe Mike is right. He feels you two have a personality clash and you are envious of the strong support he gets from his staff.

**Reynolds:** Come off it, John! You know better than that. If you're not sure about my concerns, call in Victor Herche (vice-president of food and beverage) and let him or someone on his staff take a look into the situation.

**Anderson:** Cool down. Let me think about what you've said, and I'll get back to you.

Monday afternoon Anderson's secretary called Reynolds and asked him to come to Anderson's office. When he arrived, Anderson and Schwerzek were discussing food costs. Much to Reynolds's surprise, Anderson asked him to summarize the facts he had presented Saturday morning. Schwerzek comfortably defended his position on all the points raised. Even when pressed on the question of inventory procedures and company policy, he dodged the issue by saying that it had been a very busy period and that he was confident in Larry and Anna's abilities to do the job. As for the differences in meat counts and weights, he said that mistakes are possible when you're counting and weighing hundreds of items and working in several coolers and freezers. At the end of a fairly heated discussion, Schwerzek told Anderson to keep Reynolds out of his hair because his continual questioning and snooping were becoming disruptive. Anderson supported Schwerzek and told Reynolds to limit his future involvement in the food and beverage areas.

Feeling a bit let down and perhaps even betrayed after this meeting, Reynolds decided to vent his frustrations to Nancy Benson. He had visited with her many times during his investigation to ask her questions and get accounting information. However, this was the first time he'd had a detailed discussion with her about what he had observed. After recounting the events of the past few weeks, they agreed that there was a problem but that they weren't sure what to do next.

## Questions

1. If you were Chad Reynolds, what courses of action could you take?
2. Identify and discuss the roles of potential change agents.
3. What are the potential causes of and possible approaches to dealing with the apparent conflict between the parties involved?
4. What sources of power are being used by the key players in this case?
5. Should Reynolds bypass the chain of command and contact the corporate office? What are the implications of this decision?
6. What ethical considerations should Reynolds consider in his decision of what to do next?

Source: This case was prepared by Roy A. Cook of Fort Lewis College, Durango, Colorado, and Jeryl L. Nelson of Wayne State College, Wayne, Nebraska. It was presented to and accepted by the refereed Society for Case Research. All rights reserved to the authors and the SCR. Copyright © 1994 by Roy A. Cook and Jeryl L. Nelson. Edited for *Organizational Behavior*, 10th edition, and used with permission.

# CONFLICT RESOLUTION AT GENERAL HOSPITAL

General Hospital was founded in 1968 as a nonprofit community hospital in the Northeast. In 1981, the facility was expanded from 175 beds to 275 beds, and the emergency room was upgraded. Also, in 1981, General Hospital signed an agreement with a nearby medical center for patient services that it wasn't equipped to provide.

During the 1980s, approximately 90 percent of General Hospital's beds were occupied. However, in 1994, the nearby medical center underwent renovations and obtained state-of-the-art equipment. As a result, General Hospital's patient occupancy rate had dropped to 65 percent by the end of 1996. It had to eliminate services in areas in which it couldn't compete. General Hospital also had a 35 percent increase in Medicare and Medicaid patients from 1993 to 1996. These government health insurance plans generated significantly less revenue than many private health insurance plans.

General Hospital's CEO Mike Hammer realized that his hospital was in a nosedive and that a long-term, high-speed fix was in order. Without it, the hospital would soon begin to face survivability issues and possibly lose its accreditation. An experienced health-care executive, Hammer knew that he had to cut costs and increase revenues so that promising current services could be expanded and new services added in areas in which General Hospital could successfully compete against the medical center. Hammer felt that under his leadership the current management team could get the job done with one exception: cost control.

In Mike Hammer's experience, physicians were a major factor in the inability of hospitals to regulate costs. He believed that physicians in the main didn't understand, nor were they interested in, the role of costs in determining the viability of hospitals. He felt that this lack of concern stemmed from the physicians' strong allegiance to their profession as opposed to the hospitals in which they had patient privileges.

In the past, Hammer had tried two approaches to controlling physician-driven costs, each of which had failed. Early in his tenure as General Hospital's CEO, he had tried to convince Director of Medicine Dr. Mark Williams to get the staff physicians to become cost sensitive in their decision making. Even when Hammer spotted a wasteful practice, physicians defended their actions as "the practice of good medicine." He rarely won any of these battles. Also, in 1993, he hired a consultant who studied the situation and recommended a formal comprehensive cost containment program. However, the hospital's board of trustees failed to support the program because the director of medicine vehemently opposed it. Even private meetings with Dr. Williams could not get him to change his mind or even to use the proposed program as a focus for constructive change. Dr. Williams felt that Hammer was asking for a cultural change that was impossible.

Forcing them to adhere to the plan would make it significantly more difficult to attract and keep talented physicians. Therefore the plan was not implemented.

The failure to achieve comprehensive cost control led Hammer to believe that physician-controlled costs had to be addressed on a step-by-step basis, one physician at a time. He theorized that, once a series of cost containment steps had been taken and reductions accrued, the culture would begin to change and more ambitious attempts at cost control would stand a better chance of success. Hammer had just hired a new hospital administrator, Marge Harding, who was effectively the hospital's chief operating officer (COO). He thought that perhaps the time had arrived to test his theory and see if cost control could begin to become a reality.

## The Meeting

Hammer met with Harding and suggested a course of action.

**Hammer:** As I mentioned last week, we have to get aggressive in the cost area. Here's what I want you to do. Select something that the physicians are doing that can be done at less cost and implement the change. And remember, as COO you have the unilateral authority to place contracts and fire employees who are in an at-will employment status. In fact, don't tell me what you're doing. That will allow us more time and help us play good cop-bad cop with the doctors.

**Harding:** I'll get right on it. I'm sure that I can get some good results.

**Hammer:** Good, Marge! That's all I have for now.

Harding was delighted that Hammer had given her a cost-reduction assignment. In her ten years in the health-care field, she had seen many financial abuses but until now never had the authority to do anything about them. She judged that her registered nurse experience, a three-year stint as assistant hospital administrator at another hospital, her baccalaureate degree in finance, and her masters degree in health-care administration would serve her well in a cost-cutting role. Also, her dad and one of her brothers were physicians, so she wasn't awed by medical doctors. In fact, she rather enjoyed challenging them, as she considered many of them to be one-dimensional. She felt that physicians knew the scientific elements of medicine well but lacked the sensitivity, knowledge, and skill needed to deliver patient care in a cost-effective manner. Harding also knew that health-care reform was a hot item and that, if she could improve the cost of operating General Hospital significantly, she would have a good chance of getting a CEO position, perhaps within the next five years, before she reached forty.

## The Change

That night in the solitude of her condo while listening to a CD, Marge reviewed in her mind the orientation tour that she had gone through two weeks earlier at General Hospital. As she identified candidates for cost cutting, she listed the pros and cons of each. Next, she telephoned her friend, Joel Cohen, a 4.0 GPA MBA graduate of a prestigious business school. She got him to help her identify more clearly some cost-cutting alternatives, to formulate additional advantages and disadvantages, and to finalize her first choice: to computerize the interpretation of EKG readings.

All EKG readings at General Hospital were interpreted by Dr. James Boyer, an attending cardiologist. Dr. Boyer had been approved by both the board of trustees and the hospital medical staff to interpret EKGs. Furthermore, he was held in high esteem by his colleagues for accurate and timely reports. He had hardly ever missed a day of work in fifteen years and had always arranged for a suitable replacement when he went on vacation. Dr. Boyer was particularly valuable at dovetailing his services with the many other hospital activities involved in elective admissions.

Marge Harding knew that computerized EKG interpretations were the norm today. Furthermore, she determined that replacing Dr. Boyer with a computerized EKG interpretation service would save General

Hospital at least $100,000 per year for the next three years and provide nearly instantaneous results.

She signed a one-year contract on behalf of General Hospital with Health Diagnostics. The equipment was installed and the hospital's EKG technicians were trained. Finally, the computerized EKG interpretation system was put online and Harding issued two directives, one to the EKG department to use the system and another to her assistant, John Will. She was taking a week's vacation and was instructing Will to provide liaison between the contractor and the hospital and to introduce the system and its benefits to the medical and nursing staffs. Finally, just prior to catching a plane to her vacation paradise, Harding sent a letter to Dr. Boyer notifying him that his services were no longer needed and that he was involuntarily separated from General Hospital unless he successfully competed for a vacant position within the next thirty days.

## EARLY PROBLEMS

During the first week of computerized operations, many EKG problems emerged. Some EKG interpretations came back on time, others were a few hours late, and still others never arrived at General Hospital. At times, reports were returned inadvertently with a different patients' EKG analyses on them. Such mix-ups resulted in misfilings and at times confused physicians and even caused a few misdiagnoses. At other times, the patients were actually at other hospitals! The overwhelming problem was incorrect EKG interpretations in 25 percent of the reports.

The physicians were furious. They did not recognize the physicians who had certified the EKG reports. "What happened to Dr. Boyer?" became an echo. When they discovered that Dr. Boyer had been fired, they vehemently complained to Dr. Williams. Dr. Boyer's colleagues felt strongly that, as Dr. Boyer was part of the medical staff, a review of his termination was in order. Dr. Williams worried about the potential for legal liabilities resulting from inaccurate readings, as well as EKG reports signed by physicians not certified by General Hospital's certification committee. The nursing director, Nancy Ames, was unaware of the extent of the change and the ensuing problems.

The overall result was that the hospital's operation was quickly becoming seriously jeopardized. John Will was powerless to discontinue the computerized EKG service because he had no legitimate authority to do so.

## THE FOLLOWING MONDAY

At 10:00 A.M. the following Monday, the medical staff convened to discuss the problem. Dr. Williams strongly urged Harding to come to the meeting, but she didn't attend. Instead she sent John Will with a message: "General Hospital needs to stay abreast of ongoing technological developments in science and medicine, especially when costs are reduced. The computerized EKG system stays." This incensed the medical staff. Dr. Williams sent Will back to Harding with a rebuttal message: "Either speak to us today and resolve this problem, or we will admit all new patients to other hospitals." Dr. Williams was totally frustrated. He had brought the matter up with Mike Hammer that morning but felt that he had been brushed off. Hammer said that he was very busy and that, hopefully the problem would get resolved by those directly involved.

### Questions

1. Were the communications between the parties equally effective?
2. How would you characterize Hammer's leadership style relative to the attempted change?
3. How successful was Harding in carrying out Hammer's directive to select and implement a cost-saving idea?
4. Should Harding meet with Dr. Williams? If so, what should be her position and how should the meeting be structured?

Source: This case was prepared by James W. Lawson and Charles Connant of St. Peter's College, Jersey City, New Jersey. It was presented to and accepted by the refereed Society for Case Research. All rights reserved to the authors and the SCR. Copyright © 1994 by James W. Lawson and Charles Connant. It was edited for *Organizational Behavior*, 10th edition, and used with permission.

# NURSE ROSS

The following situation was reported by Miss Jackson, who had known Miss Evelyn Ross for several years and also had worked in some of the same hospitals as Miss Ross on different occasions. Miss Ross, a registered nurse, began working at Benton Hospital when she was 31 years old. This hospital was an industrial hospital in Orange County, just south of Los Angeles. The bed capacity of the hospital was about 150, and 50 to

100 patients received treatment daily through the hospital's clinic facilities. The hospital was built and operated by a large shipbuilding concern. All the employees of the company's shipyards and their dependents could receive medical care through the company's hospitalization plan.

The nursing staff was headed by a director of nurses who had two assistants. One was in charge of nursing services in the hospital, and the other was in charge of the clinic nursing services. However, the two departments operated as a coordinated unit, and personnel were exchanged between them in the event the work load became too heavy in either place.

The medical director of the hospital, Dr. Peake, was energetic and his manner was usually quite brusque. Although he was a stickler for discipline and efficiency, he was fair in his treatment of the staff and they respected him and cooperated well. Dr. Peake had many progressive ideas and had helped to build the hospital up from 75 to 150 beds. The new ideas he had were discussed in staff conferences. Any persons or heads of departments who might be affected by proposed changes participated in these conferences.

Miss Ross worked as a head nurse, both in the hospital and in the clinic, during her employment there. (Miss Jackson at that time was employed as assistant head nurse in the clinic.) Miss Ross resigned her position to enter the Army Nurse Corps as a first lieutenant. She served in the Army for two-and-a-half years, most of which was duty in the South Pacific. During the time she was overseas, she was promoted to captain. She was transferred to reserve status upon leaving the corps. Shortly after this she took a three-month course in operating room supervision.

In the meantime, Miss Jackson had moved to the East Coast and was employed at Hughes Hospital, a large industrial hospital in Manchester, Vermont. They had corresponded during this time and Miss Jackson wrote that the position of operating room supervisor would soon be open at the hospital and thought Miss Ross had a good chance of getting the position if she wanted to move to the East Coast. Miss Ross applied to the director of nursing at the hospital and was accepted for the position. She began working soon thereafter at Hughes.

Hughes Hospital was set up much like Benton Hospital. It took care of the medical needs of most of the community in addition to serving the employees of the Hughes Steel Company, the city's principal employer. It had clinic facilities for emergency and outpatient care. The bed capacity was 250 and the clinic staff treated well over 100 patients daily, although often a complete record of the number of patients was not kept.

The organization of the nursing department was quite similar to that of Benton Hospital with one important exception: the hospital department and the clinic department were operated as two completely separate units. The clinic was in a building separate from the hospital building; thus, the problem of moving a stretcher case from the clinic to the hospital was an extreme ordeal. Besides the lack of proper equipment for moving patients, there was a shortage of male orderlies, and nurses' aides had to be utilized for this arduous task. This shortage of personnel and equipment was especially acute when emergency cases and accident victims came into the clinic and had to be moved to the hospital with a minimum loss of time and disturbance.

The director of nurses, Miss Mahaffey, was about 45 years old; she had been at the hospital three years. Miss Linden had been the hospital supervisor for six months, and Miss Hartman had been employed as clinic supervisor for over a year. There were 24 graduate nurses employed in the hospital wards, 30 aides, and 10 maids. The staff under Miss Hartman in the clinic consisted of 5 graduate nurses, 4 aides, and 2 maids. The orderly personnel numbered only six for all three shifts. One was utilized throughout the hospital on the evening shift, one on the night shift, and during the day shift one worked in the clinic, one in the operating room (OR), and one for each of the two men's wards in the hospital. Miss Ross, as supervisor of the OR, had a staff of four nurses, three aides, and the one orderly. The nurses in the OR rotated turns, being "on call" each night for any emergency surgery cases.

Miss Ross found that the work was quite strenuous and often entailed long hours, but she was deeply interested in it and never seemed to object. She frequently stayed to help in emergency surgery cases, as a number of rather serious accidents occurred from time to time in the steel plants that the hospital served. Miss Mahaffey praised her highly for increasing the efficiency and cleanliness of the operating rooms.

Dr. McMillan, the medical director of the hospital, was nearly 65 years old. He had been employed as a company doctor for the Hughes Steel Company for over 20 years. Dr. McMillan would usually arrive at his offices in the hospital about nine in the morning, would dictate answers to his correspondence, make sporadic rounds of some of the hospital wards (very rarely did he put in an appearance at the clinic), leave for lunch promptly at noon, and, only two or three times a week, return to the hospital for a few hours after lunch. On his occasional ward rounds, he would stop at the floor nurse's desk, inquire if everything was going all right, then say, "Fine! Fine!" and go on his way.

When Dr. McMillan suffered a heart attack severe enough to prevent him from retaining his position at the hospital, a new medical director had to be found. The president of the steel company was familiar with the shipbuilding concern and knew Dr. Peake had been at Benton. He contacted Dr. Peake to see if he would be interested in the position as the hospital medical director. Dr. Peake accepted. He entered the new situation with his usual brusque and energetic manner and made complete daily rounds in the clinic and hospital. He often spent considerable time talking to patients, nurses, aides, and the staff physicians.

After nearly a month of concentrated observation of the clinic and hospital routines, Dr. Peake had a conference with Miss Mahaffey and the nursing supervisors. He criticized the "unprofessional attitude" of several of the nurses, and said he had had complaints from many of the patients about the care they were receiving. He asked why so many of the nurses seemed to be away from their wards when he made morning rounds. Miss Mahaffey said the nurses were permitted to leave the wards at intervals between nine and eleven to have coffee in the hospital dining room. The time for this was not rigidly enforced. Dr. Peake also talked to Dr. Albright, the staff physician in charge of the clinic, and to the clinic nurses to ascertain why patients often had to wait so long to see a doctor in the clinic. (The gist of these conferences was given by Miss Jackson, who was assistant supervisor of the clinic.) The clinic staff agreed that there was definitely a "bottle-neck" in the clinic, but they felt that it was due primarily to a shortage of personnel when needed most, the inconvenience of having to transport the patients the distance to the hospital, and the lack of satisfactory laboratory facilities in the clinic itself. Dr. Peake told the staff that the new additions being built onto the hospital were going to be utilized for clinic facilities. In the meantime, he said he would try to help them find some way to ease the situation.

During the second week of August of that year, Miss Mahaffey asked Miss Ross to come into her office.

**Miss Mahaffey:** Miss Ross, Dr. Peake tells me that you worked with him at Benton Hospital. I knew that he had been at Benton at one time, but didn't realize that it was during the same time you were there. He said that you are familiar with the clinic-hospital arrangement there and told me to relieve you of your present position so that you may help to coordinate the clinic and hospital units here.

**Miss Ross:** I'm sorry to hear that. I have been very happy with my present position. Will I be working in the clinic or in the hospital?

**Miss Mahaffey:** Both. I want you to know that I consider Miss Linden a very capable supervisor and I don't want her to be hurt in this new arrangement. Also, I want to know everything that is going on down there. I expect you to report to me at least once a day. I don't know what Dr. Peake expects you to do that hasn't already been done. He should

hire more people if he expects to make this a model hospital. He comes in here and all he does is criticize.

**Miss Ross:** I'll do the best I can. I am familiar with the setup that Dr. Peake had at Benton. Maybe I can help put it into operation here.

A few hours later Dr. Peake entered Miss Ross's office in the OR unit.

**Dr. Peake:** Hello, Rossie, I have a new job for you.

**Miss Ross:** Miss Mahaffey has told me about it.

**Dr. Peake:** You know how things were at Benton. I want the units to be set up in exactly that way here. During the past few months I have arranged for another physician to help out in the clinic during their busy hours and we've hired a couple more aides, but there doesn't seem to be too much improvement. Maybe you can help me find out what the trouble is there. Our new building program has been started and when it is finished I want the two units to be operating as one integrated unit. I don't like to take you away from the surgery—you've been doing a fine job here—but I feel you can help me get the clinic and hospital units functioning better together.

**Miss Ross:** I can try, Dr. Peake.

**Dr. Peake:** Good! Now I don't want you to go through anybody—if you have any problems, come right to me!

Miss Ross—knowing the strained relationship between Dr. Peake and Miss Mahaffey—was especially dubious about bypassing her immediate supervisor, the director of nurses. She decided at that time it would be best to observe the regular channels of communications.

Miss Ross reported for her new job and discussed Dr. Peake's plans and ideas for integrating the two units with both Miss Linden and Miss Hartman. She also told them that the reason he picked her for the job was because she had worked at Benton under him. They had known that both she and Miss Jackson had worked at Benton for a time while Dr. Peake was there. Neither of the supervisors seemed very surprised. Miss Linden remarked that it sounded like another of Dr. Peake's "wild ideas." Both Miss Linden and Miss Hartman seemed concerned over the shortage of an adequate staff and said that any changes that would improve the situation would be welcomed.

Personnel problems were especially acute in the hospital at that time. Several staff members were off duty because of illness and there were more patients than usual. The clinic was open Saturday and Sunday for emergencies only. One nurse and two aides were on duty weekends but were not too busy. Miss Ross arranged to transfer the two aides to the hospital for the weekends. Miss Linden was elated with the additional help. On the following Wednesday, the clinic was far behind in its work because of an emergency that had arisen. Miss Ross went to Miss Linden to see if someone could go over for the afternoon to help. The following conversation ensued:

**Miss Ross:** Miss Hartman is swamped. She had an emergency to take care of and the other patients are not being seen. Have you anyone you can send to help?

**Miss Linden:** I am not going to send anyone to that clinic. They have enough help! We are too short here.

Miss Ross went over to one of the wards and found two of the aides in the ward kitchen drinking coffee. She asked if they were slack right then.

One of them said, "Oh, sure. We haven't had very much to do all afternoon."

Miss Ross returned to Miss Linden and told her of the episode. She asked that one of them be sent to help out in the clinic. Miss Linden complied reluctantly.

Shortly after this Miss Linden went on a vacation for two weeks. Miss Mahaffey asked Miss Ross to take charge of the hospital unit until her return. Thus Miss Ross was faced with the problem of making out time schedules for all the nurses, aides, orderlies, and maids employed in the hospital unit. Dr. Peake had also asked her to initiate a study to determine the personnel needs in the various hospital wards and the clinic departments, and to help with the plans for the layout of new equipment in the building additions. During the two weeks of Miss Linden's absence, Miss Ross found that (1) one ward had more nurses than another one, although the work loads were the same, and (2) maids were not doing the cleaning assigned to them and some were not even aware of what their duties were. With the cooperation of Miss Hartman and the approval and permission of Miss Mahaffey, Miss Ross arranged to reallocate the nursing personnel so that all wards would have equal coverage in relation to their work loads.[1] She made out schedules to provide available clinic help as relief in the hospital on weekends and instructed the maids as to their duties.

There seemed to be a gradual improvement in the amount and quality of patient care and most of the employees seemed to be more satisfied when they were placed in jobs where they were kept busy and understood their duties. Patients commented on the improved care they received after the changes had been made. Dr. Peake praised Miss Ross and Miss Mahaffey for the success of the new program.

Two days after Miss Linden returned from her vacation Miss Ross was called to the office of the director of nurses.

**Miss Mahaffey:** Miss Ross, Miss Linden has requested a transfer to the operating room, because she doesn't think you and she will get along. She is doing a good job in the hospital and I don't want to lose her. Hereafter, you will not interfere with the operation of the hospital unit and its personnel. Miss Linden will take care of everything over there.

**Miss Ross:** I don't understand, Miss Mahaffey. Do you mean that my job is finished?

**Miss Mahaffey:** No. You are to continue working in the clinic and help set up new departments there as the building program continues. I really don't know what made Dr. Peake think you would be able to do anything to improve the situation. He will just have to realize that we haven't sufficient personnel.

Miss Ross left the interview feeling very confused as to her exact status because she knew Dr. Peake would expect her to continue to try to coordinate the two units.

## Questions:

1. What are the types and sources of conflicts?
2. If you were a consultant to Hughes Hospital, what changes might you recommend?
3. What are the critical problems and issues facing Nurse Ross?
4. How should Nurse Ross deal with these critical problems and issues?

Source: Fox, W. M. Nurse Ross. *Journal of Management Case Studies*, 1985, 1, 85–89. Used with permission. ©Robert Randall, 320 Riverside Drive, NY, NY 10025.

# REFERENCES

## Chapter 1

1. Adapted from Yokoyama, J., and Bergquist, J. The world famous Pike Place Fish story: A breakthrough for managers. *Retailing Issues Newsletter*. College Station, Texas: Center for Retailing Studies, Texas A&M University, November 2001, 1–7; Welcome to Pike Place Fish at http://www.pikeplacefish.com/about/, accessed February 28, 2002; Ramsey, R.D. Fun at work: Lessons from the fish market. *Supervision*, April 2001, 7–8.

2. Wood, R. *Competency-Based Recruitment and Selection*. West Sussex, England: John Wiley & Sons, 1998; Morgan, G. *Riding the Waves of Change: Developing Managerial Competencies for a Turbulent World*. San Francisco: Jossey-Bass, 1998.

3. Weisinger, H. *Emotional Intelligence at Work*. San Francisco: Jossey-Bass, 1998; Whetten, D.A., and Cameron, K.S. *Developing Management Skills*, 5th ed. Upper Saddle River, N.J.: Pearson Education, 2002.

4. Luthans, F. Positive organizational behavior: Developing and managing psychological strengths for performance improvement. *Academy of Management Executive*, 16(1), 57–75.

5. Hall, D.T. *Careers in and Out of Organizations*. Thousand Oaks, Calif.: Sage, 2002.

6. Adapted from JnJ Careers home page at http://www.jnj.com/careers/, accessed February 27, 2002; Fulmer, R.M. Johnson & Johnson: Frameworks for leadership. *Organizational Dynamics*, 2001, 29, 211–220.

7. This section draws from Ellinor, L., and Gerard, G. *Dialogue: Rediscover the Transforming Power of Conversations*. New York: John Wiley & Sons, 1998; F.M. Jablin and L.L. Putnam (eds.), *The New Handbook of Organizational Communication*. Thousand Oaks, Calif.: Sage, 2001; Yankelovich, D. *The Magic of Dialogue: Transforming Conflict into Cooperation*. New York: Simon & Schuster, 1999.

8. Yokoyama and Bergquist, 2.

9. Adapted from Weeks, H. Taking the stress out of stressful conversations. *Harvard Business Review*, July–August 2001, 112–119.

10. This section draws from Williams, M.A., Williams, M.W., and Clifton, D.O. *The 10 Lenses: Your Guide to Living and Working in a Multicultural World*. Washington, D.C.: Capital Books, 2001; Cox, T., Jr., O'Neil, P.H., and Quinn, R.E. *Creating the Multicultural Organization: A Strategy for Capturing the Power of Diversity*. New York: John Wiley & Sons, 2001.

11. Wheeler, M.L., Capitalizing on diversity: Navigating the sea of the multicultural workforce and workplace. *Business Week*, December 14, 1998. Unpaginated insert.

12. Jackson, S.E., and Ruderman, M.N. *Diversity in Work Teams*. Washington, D.C.: American Psychological Asso-ciation, 1996; Lau, D.C., and Murnighan, J.K. Demographic diversity and faultlines: The compositional dynamics of organizational groups. *Academy of Management Review*, 1998, 23, 325–340.

13. Hammonds, K.H. You've come a short way, baby. *Business Week*, November 23, 1998, 82–83.

14. Diversity—Part I: Building a competitive workforce. *Forbes*, May 13, 1999. Special insert, 1–31.

15. Catalyst. *Advancing Women in Business: The Catalyst Guide*. San Francisco: Jossey-Bass, 1998.

16. McDevitt, D., and Rowe, P.M. *The United States in International Context: 2000*. Washington, D.C.: U.S. Bureau of the Census, 2002.

17. McDevitt and Rowe.

18. Adapted from *Diversity Works at Fannie Mae*. Washington, D.C.: Office of Diversity, Fannie Mae, 2002.

19. This section draws from T. Donaldson, and P. Werhane, (eds.), *Ethical Issues in Business: A Philosophical Approach*. Old Tappan, N.J.: Prentice Hall 1999; Ferrell, O.C., Fraedrich, J., and Ferrell, L. *Business Ethics: Ethical Decision Making and Cases*, 5th ed. Boston: Houghton Mifflin, 2002.

20. Velasquez, M.G. *Business Ethics: Concepts and Cases*. Old Tappan, N.J.: Prentice Hall, 2002.

21. McNamara, C. *Complete Guide to Ethics Management: An Ethics Toolkit for Managers*. Guide available at http://www.mapnp.org/library/ethics/ethxde.htm, accessed February 26, 2002.

22. Our Credo, from Johnson & Johnson home page at http://www.jnj.com, accessed February 27, 2002.

23. Harris, P.R., and Moran, R.T. *Managing Cultural Differences*, 5th ed. Woburn, Mass.: Butterworth-Heineman, 2001; M. Gannon and K. Newman (eds.). *The Blackwell Handbook of Cross-Cultural Management*. Malden, Mass.: Blackwell, 2001.

24. Adler, N.J. *International Dimensions of Organizational Behavior*, 4th ed. Cincinnati: South-Western, 2002.

25. Hofstede, G. *Culture's Consequences: Comparing Values, Behaviors, Institutions, and Organizations Across Nations*, 2nd ed. Thousand Oaks: Calif.: Sage, 2001.

26. Kirkman, B.L., Gibson, C.B., and Shapiro, D.L. "Exporting" teams: Enhancing the implementation and effectiveness of work teams in global affiliates. *Organizational Dynamics*, 2001, 30, 12–29.

27. Javidan, M., and House, R.J. Cultural acumen for the global manager: Lessons from project GLOBE. *Organizational Dynamics*, 2001, 29, 289–305.

28. Adapted from Osland, J.S., and Bird, A. Beyond sophisticated stereotyping: Cultural sensemaking in context. *Academy of Management Executive*, 2000, 14(1), 65–76.

29. Adapted from Delano, J. Executive commentary. *Academy of Management Executive*, 2000, 14(1), 77–79.

30. This section draws from Rees, F. *How to Lead Work Teams: Facilitation Skills*, 2nd ed. New York: John Wiley & Sons,

2001; Earley, P.C., and Gibson, C.B. *Multinational Work Teams: A New Perspective.* Mahwah, N.J.: Laurence Erlbaum Associates, 2002; LaFasto, F.M.J., and Larson, C.E. *When Teams Work Best: 6000 Team Members and Leaders Tell What It Takes to Succeed.* Thousand Oaks, Calif.: Sage, 2001.

31. Adapted from Ludin, S. Go fish. *T+D*, August 2001, 70–72.

32. Adapted from Gregerson, J. A league of their own. *Food Engineering*, November 2001, 36–42.

33. Muczyk, J.P., and Steel, R.P. Leadership style and the turnaround executive. *Business Horizons*, March–April 1998, 39–46.

34. Davis, S., and Meyer, C. *Blur: The Speed of Change in the Connected Economy.* Reading, Mass.: Addison-Wesley, 1998, 5.

35. Adapted from Buss, D.D. Embracing speed. *Nation's Business*, June 1999, 12–17.

## Chapter 2

1. Adapted from Hawn, C. Oracle on the edge. *Forbes*, August 20, 2001, 83–88; Oracle down another exec. *Client Server News*, September 3, 2001; Ellison, L. The Oracle speaks. *Business Week*, February 26, 2001, 96ff.

2. Pervin, L.A., and John, O.P. *Handbook of Personality*, 2nd ed. New York: Guilford, 1999.

3. Janada, L. *The Psychologists Book of Personality Tests.* New York: John Wiley & Sons, 2001; Judge, T.A., Bono, J.A., and Locke, E.A. Personality and job satisfaction: The mediating role of job characteristics. *Journal of Applied Psychology*, 2000, 85, 237–249.

4. Turkheimer, E. Heritability and biological explanation. *Psychological Review*, 1998, 105, 782–791; Plomin, R., and Caspi, A. Behavioral genetics and personality. In L.A. Pervin and O.P. John (eds.). *Handbook of Personality*, 2nd ed. New York: Guilford, 1999, 251–276.

5. Cross, S.E., and Markus, H.R. The cultural constitution of personality. In L.A. Pervin and O.P. John (eds.). *Handbook of Personality*, 2nd ed. New York: Guilford, 1999, 378–396; Miller, J.G. Cultural psychology: Implications for basic psychological theory. *Psychological Science*, 1999, 10, 85–91.

6. Pervin, L.A. *Personality: Theory and Research*, 4th ed. New York: John Wiley & Sons, 1984, 10.

7. McCrae, R.R., and Costa, P.T. A five-factor theory of personality. In L.A. Pervin and O.P. John (eds.). *Handbook of Personality*, 2nd ed. New York: Guilford, 1999, 139–153; Barrick, M.R., and Mount, M.K. The big five personality dimensions and job performance: A meta-analysis. *Personnel Psychology*, 1991, 44, 1–26; Seibert, S.E., Crant, J.M., and Kraimer, M.L. Proactive personality and career success. *Journal of Applied Psychology*, 1999, 84, 416–427.

8. Duffy, M.K., Shaw, J.D., and Stark, E.M. Performance and satisfaction in conflicted interdependent groups: When and how does self-esteem make a difference? *Academy of Management Journal*, 2000, 43, 772–784; Leary, M.R. Making sense of self-esteem. *Current Directions in Psychological Science*, 1999, 8, 32–35.

9. Adapted from Hilb, M. Computex Corporation. In G. Oddou and M. Mendenhall (eds.). *Cases in International Organizational Behavior*. Oxford: Blackwell, 1999, 55–57.

10. Judge, T.A., and Bono, J.E. Relationship of core self-evaluations—self-esteem, generalized self-efficacy, locus of control, and emotional stability—with job satisfaction and job performance: A meta-analysis. *Journal of Applied Psychology*, 2001, 86, 80–93.

11. Mueller, S.L., and Thomas, A.S. Culture and entrepreneurial potential: A nine country study of locus of control and innovativeness. *Journal of Business Venturing*, 2001, 16(1), 51–54; Moyle, P. The effects of transition stress: A relocation study. *Journal of Organizational Behavior*, 1999, 20, 625–627.

12. Dweck, C.S. *Self-theories: Their Role in Motivation, Personality and Development.* Philadelphia: Psychology Press, 1999; VandeWalle, D., Cron, Wm. L., and Slocum, J.W., Jr. The role of goal orientation following performance feedback. *Journal of Applied Psychology*, 2001, 86, 629–640.

13. VandeWalle, D., Brown, S.P., Cron, W.L., and Slocum, J.W., Jr. The influence of goal orientation and self-regulation tactics on sales performance: A longitudinal field test. *Journal of Applied Psychology*, 1999, 84, 249–259.

14. Flynn, F.J., Chatman, J.A., and Spataro, S.E. Getting to know you: The influence of personality on impressions and performance of demographically different people in organizations. *Administrative Science Quarterly*, 2001, 46, 414–442.

15. Adapted from Caminti, S. What team leaders need to know. *Fortune*, February 20, 1995, 94, 98.

16. Petty, R.E., Wegener, D.T., and Fabrigar, L.R. Attitudes and attitude change. *Annual Review of Psychology*, 1997, 48, 609–647.

17. Cote, S. Affect and performance in organizational settings. *Current Directions in Psychological Science*, 1999, 8, 65–68.

18. Snyder, C.R., LaPointe, A.B., Crowson, J.J., and Early, S. Preferences of high- and low-hope people for self-referential input. *Cognition and Emotion*, 1998, 12, 807–823; Luthans, F. Positive organizational behavior. *Academy of Management Executive*, 2002, 16(1), 57–72.

19. Box, T. The little dealership that could. *Dallas Morning News*, August 23, 2001, D-1ff.

20. Dormann, C., and Zapf, D. Job satisfaction: A meta-analysis of stabilities. *Journal of Organizational Behavior*, 2001, 22, 483–505; Trevor, C.O. Interactions among actual ease-of-movement determinants and job satisfaction in the prediction of voluntary turnover. *Academy of Management Journal*, 2001, 44, 621–638.

21. Kirkman, B.L., and Shapiro, D.L. The impact of cultural values on job satisfaction and organizational commitment in self-managing work teams: The mediating role of employee resistance. *Academy of Management Journal*, 2001, 44, 557–570.

22. Adapted from Delahoussaye, M., Dobbs, K., and Kline, L. *Training*, April 2001, 36ff; Dobbs, K. Knowing how to keep your best and brightest. *Workforce*, April 2001, 57–66; Kline, L. The secret of their success. *D Magazine*, July 2001, 32–35.

23. Cable, M., and Parsons, C.K. Socialization tactics and person–organization fit. *Personnel Psychology*, 2001, 54, 1–30.

24. Mowday, R.T., Porter, L.W., and Steers, R.M. *Employee–Organization Linkages: The Psychology of Commitment, Absenteeism, and Turnover*. New York: Academic Press, 1982; Brown, S.P. A meta-analysis and review of organizational research on job involvement. *Psychological Bulletin*, 1996, 120, 235–255; Dessler, G. How to earn your employees' commitment. *Academy of Management Executive*, May 1999, 58–67.

25. Adapted from Shellenbarger, S. An employer's support in nanny-abuse case wins mother's loyalty. *Wall Street Journal*, September 30, 1998, B1.

26. Trevino, L.K., and Youngblood, S.A. Bad apples in bad barrels: A causal analysis of ethical decision making behavior. *Journal of Applied Psychology*, 1990, 75, 378–385.

27. The following examples are from Carroll, A.B. In search of the moral manager. *Business Horizons*, March/April, 1987, 2–6; see also, Mitroff, I.I. On the fundamental importance of ethical management. *Journal of Management Inquiry*, 1998, 7, 68–79.

28. Adapted from Drago, M. Don't care now? You may when telephone bill arrives. *Bryan–College Station* (Texas) *Eagle*, July 12, 1996, A1, A5.

29. Masterson, S.S., Lewis, K., Goldman, B.M., and Taylor, M.S. Integrating justice and social exchange: The differing effect of fair procedures and treatment on work relationships. *Academy of Management Journal*, 2000, 43, 738–748.

30. Reprinted with permission from Howard, P.J., Medina, P.L., and Howard, J.M. The big five locator: A quick assessment tool for consultants and trainers. In J.W. Pfeiffer (ed.). *The 1996 Annual: Volume 1, Training*. San Diego, Pfeiffer & Company, 1996, 119–122. Copyright © 1996 Pfeiffer, an imprint of John Wiley & Sons, Inc. All rights reserved.

31. Goleman, D. *Working with Emotional Intelligence*. New York: Bantum Press, 1998; Goleman. D. What makes a leader? *Harvard Business Review*, November–December, 1998, 93–102.

32. Adapted from Schutte, N.S., Malouff, J.M., Hall, L.E., Haggerty, D.J., Cooper, J.T., Golden, C.J., and Dornheim, L. Development and validation of a measure of emotional intelligence. *Personality and Individual Differences*, 1998, 25, 167–177.

## Chapter 3

1. Adapted from Wells, E.O. Options, equity, & rancor. *Inc*, July 2001, 51–60; Changes in financial strength ratings. *Value Line Investment Survey* (Part 2—Selection & Opinion), August 2001, 4077–4078; Perry, H.R. Internet industry. *Value Line Investment Survey* (Part 3—Ratings and Report), August 2001, 2216–2241.

2. Goldstone, R.L. Perceptual learning. *Annual Review of Psychology*, 1998, 49, 585–612.

3. Adapted from Sunoo, B.P. Redesign for a better work environment. *Workforce*, February 2000, 39–46; see also Ayling, P. Citibank looks at feng shui for comfort. *Australian Banking & Finance*, March 12, 2001, 28ff.

4. Henderson, J.M., and Hollingworth, A. High-level scene perception. *Annual Review of Psychology*, 1999, 50, 243–271.

5. Farah, M.J., Wilson, K.D., Drain, M., and Tanaka, J.N. What is "special" about face perception? *Psychological Review*, 1998, 105, 482–498.

6. Weiner, B., and Graham, S. Attribution in personality psychology. In L.A. Pervin and O.P. John (eds.). *Handbook of Personality*, 2nd ed. New York: Guilford, 1999, 605–628.

7. Chattopadhyau, P., Glick, W.H., Miller, C.C., and Huber, G.P. Determinants of executive beliefs: Comparing functional conditioning and social influence. *Strategic Management Journal*, 1999, 20, 763–788.

8. Adler, N.J. *International Dimensions of Organizational Behavior*, 4th ed. Cincinnati: South-Western, 2002.

9. Axtrell, R.E. *Gestures: The Do's and Taboos of Body Language Around the World*. New York: John Wiley & Sons. Copyright 1991. This material is used with permission of John Wiley & Sons.

10. VandeWalle, D. Implicit theories of personality: A review. Paper presented at the Academy of Management, Washington, D.C., August 2001.

11. Zaidman, N. Stereotypes of international managers: Content and impact on business interactions. *Group & Organization Management*, 2000, 25(March), 45–65.

12. Cady, S.H., and Fandt, P.M. Managing impressions with information: A field study. *Journal of Applied Behavioral Science*, 2001, 37(2), 80–105; Turnley, W.H. Achieving desired images while avoiding undesired images: Exploring of self-monitoring in impression management. *Journal of Applied Psychology*, 2001, 86, 351ff; Bolino, M.C. Citizenship and impression management: Good soldiers or good actors? *Academy of Management Review*, 1999, 24, 82–98.

13. Adapted from Lancaster, H. Making the switch from a Mr. fix-it to a problem-solver. *Wall Street Journal*, March 23, 1999, B1.

14. Funder, D.C. On the accuracy of personality judgment: A realistic approach. *Psychological Review*, 1995, 102, 652–670.

15. Frazer, R.A., and Wiersma, U.J. Prejudice versus discrimination in the employment interview: We may hire equally, but our memories harbour prejudice. *Human Relations*, 2001, 54(2), 173–193.

16. Karakowsky, L., and McBey, K. Do my contributions matter? The influence of expertise on member involvement and self-evaluations in the work group. *Group & Organization Management*, 2001, 26(March), 70–93.

17. Conlin, M. The new workforce. *Business Week*, March 20, 2000, 64–68; see also Stone, D.L., and Colella, A. A model of factors affecting the treatment of disabled individuals in organizations. *Academy of Management Review*, 1996, 21, 352–401.

18. Smith. D.M. *Women at Work*. Upper Saddle River, N.J.: Prentice-Hall, 2000; see also Varma, A., Stroh, L.K., and Schmitt, L.B. Women and international assignments. *Journal of World Business*, 2001, 36, 380–389.

19. Daniels, C. To hire a lumber expert, click here. *Fortune*, April 3, 2000, 267–270.

20. Snyder, M., and Stukas, A.A. Interpersonal processes: The interplay of cognitive, motivational, and behavioral activities in social interaction. *Annual Review of Psychology*, 1999, 50, 273–303.

21. Davidson, O.B. and Eden, D. Remedial self-fulfilling prophecy: Two field experiments to prevent Golem effects among disadvantaged women. *Journal of Applied Psychology*, 2000, 85, 386–398.

22. Kierein, N.M. Pygmalion in work organizations: A meta-analysis. *Journal of Organizational Behavior*, 2000, 21(8), 913–914; McNatt, D.B. Ancient Pygmalion joins contemporary management: A meta-analysis result. *Journal of Applied Psychology*, 2000, 75, 314–322.

23. Brelis, M. Continental Airlines CEO sparks stunning turnaround with empowered workforce. *Knight-Ridder/Tribune Business News*, June 3, 2001; Frank, A. Continental's new president won't alter flight plan. *The (Newark) Star-Ledger*, May 16, 2001.

24. Kasof, J. Attribution and creativity. In M.A. Runco and S.R. Pritzker (eds.). *Encyclopedia of Creativity*, vol. 1. San Diego: Academic Press, 1999, 147.

25. Elkins, T.J., and Phillips, J.S. Evaluating sex discrimination claims: The mediating role of attributions. *Journal of Applied Psychology*, 1999, 84, 186–199.

26. Hinton, P.R. *The Psychology of Interpersonal Perception*. London: Routledge, 1993.

27. Barsoux, J.L. The set-up-to-fail syndrome. *Harvard Business Review*, March–April 1998, 101–113.

28. Bartel, C.A. Social comparison in boundary-spanning work: Effects of community outreach on members' organizational identity and identification. *Administrative Science Quarterly*, 2001, 379–413.

29. Westman, M., Etzion, D., and Danon, E. Job insecurity and crossover of burnout in married couples. *Journal of Organizational Behavior*, 2001, 22, 467–484; Wiesenfeld, B.M., Brockner, J., and Thibault, V. Procedural fairness, manager's self-esteem, and managerial behaviors after a layoff. *Organizational Behavior and Human Decision Processes*, 2000, 83, 1–32.

30. Adapted from Yost, E.B., and Herbert, T.T. Attitudes toward women as managers. In L.D. Goodstein and J.W. Pfeiffer (eds.). *The 1985 Annual: Developing Human Resources*. San Diego: University Associates, 1985, 117–127. Reprinted with permission.

31. Adapted from Wallace, D. Fudge the numbers or leave. *Business Ethics*, May/June 1996, 58–59.

## Chapter 4

1. Adapted from Stebens, M. Employee incentive programs: A winning deal all around. *Rural Telecommunications*, July/August 2001, 48ff.

2. Weiss, H.M. Learning theory and industrial and organizational psychology. In M.D. Dunnette and L.M. Hough (eds.). *Handbook of Industrial & Organizational Psychology*, 2nd ed. Palo Alto, Calif.: Consulting Psychologist Press, 1990, 170–221.

3. Kanfer, R. Motivation theory and industrial and organizational psychology. In M.D. Dunnette and L.M. Hough (eds.), *Handbook of Industrial & Organizational Psychology*, 2nd ed. Palo Alto, Calif.: Consulting Psychologist Press, 1990, 75–169.

4. Ambrose, M.L., and Kulik, C.T. Old friends, new faces: Motivation research in the 1990s. *Journal of Management*, 1999, 24, 231–292.

5. Skinner, B.F. *About Behaviorism*. New York: Knopf, 1974; Dragoi, V., and Staddon, J.E.R. The dynamics of operant conditioning. *Psychological Review*, 1999, 106, 20–24.

6. Latham, G.P., and Huber, V.L. Schedules of reinforcement: Lessons from the past and issues for the future. *Journal of Organizational Behavior Management*, 1992, 12, 125–149; Komaki, J.L. *Leadership from an Operant Perspective*. New York: Routledge, 1998.

7. Adler, N.J. *International Dimensions of Organizational Behavior*, 4th ed. Cincinnati: South-Western, 2002; Javidan, M., and House, R.J. Cultural acumen for the global manager: Lessons from the GLOBE project. *Organizational Dynamics*, 2001, 29(4), 289–305.

8. Rousseau, D.M. The idiosyncratic deal: Flexibility versus fairness. *Organizational Dynamics*, 2001, 29(4), 260–273; Kerr, S. Organizational rewards: Practical, cost-neutral alternatives that you may know, but don't practice. *Organizational Dynamics*, 1999(1), 61–70.

9. Adapted from Markowich, M.M., and Eckberg, S. Get control of the absentee-minded. *Personnel Journal*, 1996, 75(3), 15–21.

10. Leivo, A.K. A field study of the effects of gradually terminated public feedback on housekeeping performance. *Journal of Applied Social Psychology*, 2001, 31, 1184–1203.

11. Besser, T.L. Rewards and organizational goal achievement: A case study of Toyota Motor manufacturing in Kentucky. *Journal of Management Studies*, 1995, 32, 383–401.

12. Zhou, J., and George, J.M. When job dissatisfaction leads to creativity: Encouraging the expression of voice. *Academy of Management Journal*, 2001, 44, 682–696.

13. Mazur, J.E. *Learning and Behavior*. Upper Saddle River, N.J.: Prentice-Hall, 2002.

14. Grote, D.F. Discipline without punishment. *Across the Board*, September/October 2001, 52–57; see also Butterfield, K.D., Trevino, L.K., and Ball, G.A. Punishment from the manager's perspective: A grounded investigation and inductive model. *Academy of Management Journal*, 1996, 39, 479–512; Dunegan, K.J. Fines, frames, and images: Examining formulation effects on punishment decisions. *Organizational Behavior & Human Decision Processes*, 1996, 68, 58–68.

15. Stajkovic, A.D., and Luthans, F. A meta-analysis of the effects of organizational behavior modification on task performance. *Academy of Management Journal*, 1997, 40, 1122–1149.

16. Reed, P. Human response rates and causality judgments on schedules of reinforcement. *Learning and Motivation*, 2001, 32, 332–348.

17. Latham, G.P., and Huber, V.L. Schedules of reinforcement: Lessons from the past and issues for the future.

*Journal of Organizational Behavior Management*, 1992, 12, 125–150.

18. Bandura, A. *Social Learning Theory*. Upper Saddle River, N.J.: Prentice-Hall, 1977; Bandura, A. *Self-efficacy: The exercise of self-control*. New York: W. H. Freeman, 1997.

19. Vancouver, J.B., Thompson, C.M., and Williams, A.A. The changing signs in the relationships among self-efficacy, personal and performance. *Journal of Applied Psychology*, 2001, 48, 605–620; Brown, S.P., Ganesan, S., and Challagalla, G. Self-efficacy as a moderator of information-seeking effectiveness. *Journal of Applied Psychology*, 2001, 86, 1041–1051.

20. Adapted from Kinni, T.B. *America's Best: Industry Week's Guide to World-Class Manufacturing Plants*. New York: John Wiley & Sons, 1996, 313–314.

21. Judge, T.A., and Bono, J.E. Relationship of core self-evaluations traits—self-esteem, generalized self-efficacy, locus of control, and emotional stability—with job satisfaction and job performance: A meta-analysis. *Journal of Applied Psychology*, 2001, 86, 80–93; Stajkovic, A.D., and Luthans, F. Social cognitive theory and work-related performance: A meta-analysis. *Psychological Bulletin*, 1998, 124, 240–261.

22. Rachlin, H. *The Science of Self-Control*. Cambridge, Mass.: Harvard University Press, 2000.

23. Manz, C.C., and Sims, H.P., Jr. *The New Super Leadership*. San Francisco, Calif.: Berrett-Koehler, 2001.

24. Lee, C., and Bobko, P. Self-efficacy beliefs: Comparison of five measures. *Journal of Applied Psychology*, 1994, 79, 364–370; Maurer, T.J., and Pierce, H.R. A comparison of Likert scale and traditional measures of self-efficacy. *Journal of Applied Psychology*, 1998, 83, 324–330.

25. Adapted from Peterson, M. 2 Drug makers to pay $875 million to settle fraud case. *New York Times*, October 4, 2001, p. C1.

## Chapter 5

1. Adapted from Chen, A. Coming: The e-wallet wars: Why you need Microsoft to buy Starbucks. *Time*, August 6, 2001; Schultz, H., and Jones-Yang, D. *Pour Your Heart Into It: How Starbucks Built a Company One Cup at a Time*. Westport, Conn.: Hyperion Press, 1997; http://www.starbucks.com, December 2001.

2. For additional information, visit the company's home page at http://www.starbucks.com.

3. Kanfer, R., Wanberg, C.R., and Kantrowitz, T.M. Job search and employment: A personality-motivational analysis and analytic review. *Journal of Applied Psychology*, 2001, 86, 837–855.

4. Personal communication with M. Denkowski, recruiting supervisor, Sante Fe International, December 2001.

5. Personal communication with P. Ginn, manager, wireless products, Nortel Networks, December 2001.

6. Maslow, A.H. *Motivation and Personality*. New York: Harper & Row, 1970. For an excellent overview of motivation models, see Ambrose, M.L., and Kulik, C.T. Old friends, new faces: Motivation research in the 1990s. *Journal of Management*, 1999, 25, 231–237.

7. Adler, N.J. *International Dimensions of Organizational Behavior*, 4th ed. Cincinnati: South-Western, 2002, 174–177.

8. Maslow, A.H., and Kaplan, A.R. *Maslow on Management*. New York: John Wiley & Sons, 1998; Landy, F.J., and Becker, W.S. Motivation model reconsidered. In L.L. Cummings and B.M. Staw (eds.), *Research in Organizational Behavior*, vol. 9. Greenwich, Conn.: JAI Press, 1987, 1–38.

9. McClelland, D.C. *Motivational Trends in Society*. Morristown, N.J.: General Learning Press, 1971.

10. Adapted from DeVoe, D., and Prencipe, L.W. Mastering motivation—In the midst of economic and emotional volatility, managers can take action to boost staff morale. *InfoWorld*, November 19, 2001, 42ff.

11. McClelland, D.C., and Burnham, D. Power is the great motivator. *Harvard Business Review*, March–April 1976, 100–111; Payne, D.K. *Training Resources Group*. Boston: McBer & Company, 1998; Sagie, A., Elizur, D., and Yamauchi, H. The structure and strength of achievement motivation: A cross-cultural comparison. *Journal of Organizational Behavior*, 1996, 17, 431–445.

12. Personal conversation with Patty Scheibmeir, director, research & development, Pizza Hut, Dallas, Texas, December 2001; http://www.papajohns.com, December 2001.

13. Herzberg, F.I., Mausner, B., and Snyderman, B.B. *The Motivation to Work*. New York: John Wiley & Sons, 1959.

14. Robertson, C.J., Al-Khatib, J.A., Al-Habib, M., and Lanoue, D. Beliefs about work in the Middle East and convergence versus divergence of values. *Journal of World Business*, 2001, 36, 223–244; Scullion, H., and Brewster, C. The management of expatriates: Messages from Europe. *Journal of World Business*, 2001, 36, 346–365.

15. Schuler, R.S., Jackson, S.E., Jackofsky, E.F., and Slocum, J.W., Jr. Managing human resources in Mexico: A cultural understanding. *Business Horizons*, May–June 1996, 55–61; Greer, C.R., and Stephens, G.K. Employee relations issues for U.S. companies in Mexico. *California Management Review*, 1996, 38(3), 121–145.

16. Adapted from Kriska, P. Motivating employees in Romania. Unpublished manuscript, Cox School of Business, Southern Methodist University, Dallas, Texas, December 2001.

17. Villanova, P. Predictive validity of situational constraints in general versus specific performance domains. *Journal of Applied Psychology*, 1996, 81, 532–548.

18. Vroom, V.H. *Work and Motivation*. New York: John Wiley & Sons, 1964.

19. Smith, L.F. Difficulty, consequence and effort in academic task performance. *Psychological Reports*, 1999, 85, 869–880.

20. Varma, A., Stroh, L.K., Schmitt, L.B. Women and international assignments: The impact of supervisor–subordinate relationships. *Journal of World Business*, 2001, 36, 380–388.

21. Allen, R.E., Lucero, M.A., and Van Norman, K.L. An examination of the individual's decision to participate in an employee involvement program. *Group & Organization*

*Management*, 1997, 22, 117–144; Fudge, R.S., and Schlacter, J.L. Motivating employees to act ethically: An expectancy theory approach. *Journal of Business Ethics*, 1999, 18, 295–296.

22. Pehanich, M. The Dean dairy lets workers run the show. *Food Processing*, October 2001, 36ff.

23. Adams, J.S. Toward an understanding of inequity. *Journal of Abnormal and Social Psychology*, 1963, 67, 422–436.

24. Colella, A. Coworkers distributive fairness judgments on the workplace accommodation of employees with disabilities. *Academy of Management Review*, 2001, 26, 100–116; Korsgaad, M.A., Roberson, L., and Rymph, R.D. What motivates fairness? The role of subordinate assertive behavior on managers' interactional fairness. *Journal of Applied Psychology*, 1998, 83, 731–744.

25. Adapted from Kurlantzick, J. Those sticky fingers. *U.S. News & World Report*, June 4, 2001, 44ff; Fishman, N.H. Signs of fraud. *The CPA Journal*, 2000, 70(12), 60–65.

26. Brockner, J. Making sense of procedural fairness: How high procedural fairness can reduce or heighten the influence of outcome favorability. *Academy of Management Review*, 2002, 27, 58–76; Masters, S.S. A trickle-down model of organizational justice: Relating employees' and customers' perceptions of and reactions to fairness. *Journal of Applied Psychology*, 2001, 86, 594–604.

27. Koys, D.J. The effects of employee satisfaction, organization citizenship behavior and turnover on organizational effectiveness: A unit-level, longitudinal study. *Personnel Psychology*, 2001, 54(1), 101–125; Bolino, M.C. Citizenship and impression management: Good soldiers or good actors? *Academy of Management Review*, 1999, 24, 82–98.

28. Colquitt, J.A., Conlon, D.E., Wesson, M.J., Porter, C.O., and Ng, K.Y. Justice at the millennium: A meta-analytic review of 25 years of organizational justice research. *Journal of Applied Psychology*, 2001, 86, 425–445; Rioux, S.M., and Penner, L.A. The causes of organizational citizenship behavior: A motivational analysis. *Journal of Applied Psychology*, 2001, 86, 1306–1314; Bachrach, D.G., Bendoly, E., and Podsakoff, P.M. Attribution of the "causes" of group performance as an alternative explanation of the relationship between organizational citizenship behavior and organizational performance. *Journal of Applied Psychology*, 2001, 86, 1285–1293.

29. Tepper, B.J., and Hoobler, D.J. Justice, citizenship, and role definition effects. *Journal of Applied Psychology*, 2001, 86, 789–796; Lambert, S.J. Added benefits: The link between work-life benefits and organizational citizenship behavior. *Academy of Management Journal*, 2000, 43, 801–815.

30. Personal communication with R. Sorrentino, partner, Deloitte Consulting, Dallas, Texas, December 2001.

31. Adapted from a survey of employees conducted by Seglin, J.L. The happiest workers in the world. *Inc.*, May 1996, 62–76.

32. Adapted from http://www.alberto.com, December 2001; www.suntimes.com/output/tech/cst-fin-cent04.html,

December 2001; Bernick, C.L. When your culture needs a makeover. *Harvard Business Review*, June 2001, 53–61.

## Chapter 6

1. Adapted from Kroll, L. Hard drive. *Forbes*, November 26, 2001, 160ff; Rosen, C. Enterprise moves to the Web to communicate with auto-repair shops and car-rental customers. *Information Week*, July 30, 2001, 67ff; Cole, W. Suddenly loyalty is back in business. *Time*, December 10, 2001, Y13–16; Berry, L.L. *Discovering the Soul of Service*. New York: Free Press, 1999.

2. Scherreik, S. Your performance review: Make it perform. *Business Week*, December 17, 2001, 139–140.

3. Locke, E.A., and Latham, G.P. *A Theory of Goal Setting & Task Performance*. Englewood Cliffs, N.J.: Prentice-Hall, 1990, 7.

4. Latham, G.P. The importance of understanding and changing employee outcome expectancies for gaining commitment to an organizational goal. *Personnel Psychology*, 2001, 54, 707–716.

5. Locke and Latham, 252–257.

6. Adapted from Waxler, C. The million-dollar suggestion box. *Forbes*, September 7, 1998, 171–172.

7. Erez, A., and Judge, T.A. Relationship to core self-evaluations to goal setting, motivation and performance. *Journal of Applied Psychology*, 2001, 86, 1270–1279; Stajkovic, A.D., and Luthans, F. Social cognitive theory and self-efficacy. *Organizational Dynamics*, Spring 1998, 62–75.

8. Adapted from Salter, C. Life in the fast lane. *Fast Company*, October 1998, 172–178.

9. VandeWalle, D., Cron, Wm. L., and Slocum, J.W., Jr. The role of goal orientation following performance feedback. *Journal of Applied Psychology*, 2001, 86, 629–640.

10. Wright, P.M., O'Leary-Kelly, A.M., Cortina, J.M., Klein, H.J., and Hollenbeck, J.R. On the meaning and measurement of goal commitment. *Journal of Applied Psychology*, 1994, 79, 795–808.

11. Adapted from Marchetti, M. Helping reps count every penny. *Sales & Marketing*, July 1998, 77.

12. VandeWalle, D. A goal orientation model of feedback seeking behavior. *Human Resource Management* (in press).

13. Fenn, D. Healthful habits pay off. *Inc.*, April 1996, 111.

14. Kaptein, M., and Wempe, J. Twelve Gordian knots when developing an organizational code of ethics. *Journal of Business Ethics*, 1998, 19, 853–870.

15. Adapted from Cohen, A. Worker watchers: Want to know what your employees are doing online? *Fortune/Cnet Technology Review*, Summer 2001, 70–80; Cohen, A. No web for you! The Internet is the office's biggest time and money waster since the coffee break. *Fortune*, October 30, 2000, 208ff; Fickenscher, L. The side effects of surfing on the job. *New York Times*, May 21, 2000, B12.

16. Borton, L. Working in a Vietnamese voice. *Academy of Management Executive*, 2000, 14(4), 20–31; Smith, E.D., Jr., and Pham, C. Doing business in Vietnam: A cultural guide. *Business Horizons*, May–June 1996, 47–51.

17. Adapted from Cummings, T.G., and Worley, C.G. *Organization Development and Change*, 7th ed. Cincinnati: South-Western, 2001, 387.

18. Sheldon, K.M., and Kasser, T. Goals, congruence, and positive well-being: New empirical support for human theories. *Journal of Humanistic Psychology*, 2001, 41, 30–51; Hollensbe, E.C., and Guthrie, J. Group pay-for-performance plans: The role of spontaneous goal setting. *Academy of Management Review*, 2000, 25, 864–872.

19. Adapted from Dess, G.P., and Picken, J.C. *Beyond Productivity*. New York: American Management Association, 1999, 164–167.

20. Cappelli, P. *Employment Practices and Business Strategy*. Oxford: Oxford University Press, 1999; Colvin, A.J.S., and Katz, H.C. How high performance organizations and workforce unionization affect company performance. *Personnel Psychology*, 2001, 54, 903–934; Clampitt, P.G., DeKock, R., and Cashman, T. A strategy for communicating about uncertainty. *Academy of Management Executive*, 2000, 14(4), 41–57.

21. Arthur, J.B., and Aiman-Smith, L. Gainsharing and organizational learning. *Academy of Management Journal*, 2001, 44, 737–755; Gomez-Majia, L.H., Welbourne, T.M., and Wiseman, R.M. The role of risk sharing under gainsharing. *Academy of Management Review*, 2000, 35, 492–508; Rewarding experiences. *Journal of Business Strategy*, 1999, 20(6), 3.

22. Schuler, R.S., and Jackson, S.E. *Human Resource Management*, 6th ed. Cincinnati: South-Western, 2000; Tyler, L.S., and Fisher, B. The Scanlon concept: A philosophy as much as a system. *Personnel Administrator*, July 1983, 33–37.

23. Fox, J., and Lawson, B. Gainsharing program lifts Baltimore employees' morale. *American City and County*, September 1997, 112(10), 93–94.

24. McCartney, S. Back on course. *Wall Street Journal*, May 15, 1996, A1.

25. Personal conversation with Steve Watson, Managing Director, Stanton Chase, Dallas, Texas, December, 2001; see also Long, R. Employee profit-sharing: Consequences and moderators. *Industrial Relations* (Canadian), 2000, 55, 477–505.

26. Lee, C., Law, K.S., and Bobko, P. The importance of justice perceptions on pay effectiveness: A two-year study of a skilled-base pay plan. *Journal of Management*, 1999, 25, 851–873.

27. Lawler, E.E. III., and Lefford, G. Skill-based pay: A concept that is catching on. *Management Review*, February 1987, 46–52; see also Murray, B., and Gerhart, B. An empirical analysis of a skilled-based pay program and plant performance outcomes. *Academy of Management Journal*, 1998, 41, 68–79.

28. Personal conversation with David Norwood, president, Denwood Corporation, Dallas, Texas, February 2002.

29. Schuler, R.S., and Rogovsky, N. Understanding compensation practice variations across firms: The impact of national culture. *Journal of International Business Studies*, 1998, 21, 159–177; Dawson, C. Japan: Work-sharing will prolong the pain. *Business Week*, December 24, 2001, 46.

30. Adapted from Locke and Latham, 355–358.

31. Adapted from Wagel, W.H. At Sola Ophthalmics, paying for job skills pays off! *Personnel*, March 1989, 66(3), 20–24. For more information on Sola Optical, visit the organization's home page at http://www.sola.com.

## Chapter 7

1. Adapted from National Institute for Occupational Safety and Health (NIOSH). *Stress*. Cincinnati: NIOSH, 99–101, 1999, 1–2.

2. NIOSH, 2–3; Wojcik, J. Cutting costs of stress. *Business Insurance*, March 26, 2001, 1, 22.

3. Jex, S.M. *Stress and Job Performance*. Thousand Oaks, Calif.: Sage, 1998, 1–8.

4. Bryant, R.A., and Harvey, A.G. *Acute Stress Disorder: A Handbook of Theory, Assessment, and Treatment*. Washington, D.C.: American Psychological Association, 2000.

5. Selye, H. History of the stress concept. In L. Goldberger and S. Breznitz (eds.), *Handbook of Stress*, 2nd ed. New York: Free Press, 1993, 7–20; Selye, H. *The Stress of Life*, 2nd ed. New York: McGraw-Hill, 1978, 1.

6. McGuigan, F.J. *Encyclopedia of Stress*. Old Tappan, N.J.: Prentice-Hall, 1999.

7. Jex, S.M., and Bliese, P.D. Efficacy beliefs as a moderator of the impact of work-related stressors: A multilevel study. *Journal of Applied Psychology*, 1999, 84, 349–361.

8. C.R. Snyder, (ed.), *Coping with Stress: Effective People and Processes*. New York: Oxford University Press, 2001.

9. Friedman, M., and Rosenman, R. *Type A Behavior and Your Heart*. New York: Knopf, 1974.

10. Lee, C., Jamieson, L.F., and Earley, P.C. Beliefs and fears and Type A behavior: Implications for academic performance and psychiatric health disorder symptoms. *Journal of Organizational Behavior*, 1996, 17, 151–168.

11. Adapted from Perrewé, P.L., Ferris, G.R., Frink, D.D., and Anthony, W.P. Political skill: An antidote for workplace stressors. *Academy of Management Executive*, August 2000, 115–123.

12. Baron, R.A., and Byrne, D. *Social Psychology: Understanding Human Interaction*, 6th ed. Boston: Allyn & Bacon, 1991, 606.

13. Turnipseed, D.L. An exploratory study of the hardy personality at work in the health care industry. *Psychological Reports*, 1999, 85, 1199–1218.

14. Shellenbarger, S. Are saner workloads the unexpected key to more productivity? *Wall Street Journal*, March 10, 1999, B1.

15. Melamed, S., Ben-Avi, I., Luz, J., and Green, M.S. Objective and subjective work monotony: Effects on job satisfaction, psychological distress, and absenteeism in blue-collar workers. *Journal of Applied Psychology*, 1995, 80, 29–42.

16. Shellenbarger, S. Technology affords this trader freedom, but also adds binds. *Wall Street Journal*, September 9, 1998, B1.

17. Pearson, C.M., Andersson, L.M., and Porath, C.L. Assessing and attacking workplace incivility. *Organizational Dynamics*, 2000, 29(2), 123–137.

18. Atkinson, W. Keeping violent employees out of the workplace. *Risk Management*, March 2001, 12–21.

19. Chappell, D., and DiMartino, V. *Violence at Work*. Geneva: International Labour Office, 2000.

20. Mink, G. *Hostile Environment: The Political Betrayal of Sexually Harassed Women*. Ithaca, NY: Cornell University Press, 2000.

21. L. Lemoncheck, and J.P. Serba, (eds.), *Sexual Harassment: Issues and Answers*. New York: Oxford University Press, 2001.

22. Kossek, E.E., and Ozeki, C. Work–family conflict, policies, and the job–life satisfaction relationship: A review and directions for organizational behavior—human resources research. *Journal of Applied Psychology*, 1998, 83, 139–149.

23. Holmes, T.H., and Rahe, R.H. The social readjustment rating scale. *Journal of Psychosomatic Medicine*, 1967, 11, 213–218.

24. Adler, J. Stress. *Newsweek*, June 14, 1999, 56–63.

25. DeFrank, R.S., and Ivancevich, J.M. Stress on the job: An executive update. *Academy of Management Executive*, August 1998, 55–66.

26. Jex.

27. Solomon, M. Rage in the workplace. *Computerworld*, July 30, 2001, 30–33.

28. Lee, R.T., and Ashforth, B.E. A meta-analytic examination of the correlates of the three dimensions of job burnout. *Journal of Applied Psychology*, 1996, 81, 123–133.

29. Moore, J.E. Why is this happening? A causal attribution approach to work exhaustion consequences. *Academy of Management Review*, 2000, 25, 335–349.

30. Etzion, D., Eden, D., and Lapidot, Y. Relief from job stressors and burnout: Reserve service as a respite. *Journal of Applied Psychology*, 1998, 83, 577–585.

31. Shellenbarger, S. Three myths that make managers push staff to the edge of burnout. *Wall Street Journal*, March 17, 1999, B1.

32. Brehm, B.A. *Stress Management: Increasing Your Stress Resistance*. Reading, Mass.: Addison-Wesley, 1999.

33. McGhee, P. The key to stress management, retention & profitability? More workplace fun. *HR Focus*, September 2000, 5–6; see also the *Stress Less* Web site at http://www.stressless.com, accessed January 3, 2002.

34. Peeke, P. Weathering life's stress storms. *Prevention*, August 2001, 97–100.

35. Delbecq, A.L., and Friedlander, F. Strategies for personal and family renewal: How a high-survivor group of executives cope with stress and avoid burnout. *Journal of Management Inquiry*, 1995, 4, 262–269.

36. Aitken, S., and Cherwitz, N. Getting a new perspective. *Workspan*, October 2001, 40–43.

37. Adapted from Shellenbarger, S. Employees who value time as much as money now get their reward. *Wall Street Journal*, September 22, 1999, B1.

38. Health Net, Inc. Wellness programs at http://wws2. healthnet.com, accessed January 3, 2002.

39. For this and other extensive information on wellness programs, go to the Web site for the Wellness Council of America at http://www.welcoa.com, accessed January 3, 2002.

40. Adapted from Hunnicutt, D. Discover the power of wellness. *Business and Health*, March 2001, 40–45.

41. Adapted from Milligan, A. Wellness programs could be the cure. *Business Insurance*, January 24, 2000, 3–5.

42. Adapted from a questionnaire developed by Sheldon Cohen contained in Adler, J. Stress. *Newsweek*, June 14, 1999, 63.

43. Adapted from Muchinsky, P.M. *Psychology Applied to Work*, 3rd ed. Pacific Grove, Calif.: Brooks/Cole, 1990, 556–557.

## Chapter 8

1. Adapted from Anders, G. Roche's new scientific method. *Fast Company*, January 2002, 60–66.

2. Homans, G.C. *The Human Group*. New York: Harcourt, Brace and World, 1959, 2.

3. Levi, D. *Group Dynamics for Teams*. Thousand Oaks, Calif.: Sage, 2001.

4. Ackroyd. S., and Thompson, P. *Organizational Misbehavior*. Thousand Oaks, Calif.: Sage, 1999.

5. Turniansky, B., and Hare, A.P. *Individuals and Groups in Organizations*. Thousand Oaks, Calif.: Sage, 1999.

6. Adapted from Lancaster, H. Black managers often must emphasize building relationships. *Wall Street Journal*, March 4, 1997, B1; Mehra, A., Kilduff, M., and Brass, D.J. At the margins: A distinctiveness approach to the social identity and social networks of underrepresented groups. *Academy of Management Journal*, 1998, 41, 441–452.

7. Yarbrough, B.T. *Leading Groups and Teams*. Mason, Ohio: South-Western/Thomson Learning, 2002.

8. LaFasto, F., and Larson, C.E. *When Teams Work Best*. Thousand Oaks, Calif.: Sage, 2001.

9. Adapted from New system keeps the goods flowing. *Chain Store Age*, September 1996, 42–48; Munk, N. Shopping at Macy's. *Forbes*, February 12, 1996, 37–38.

10. W.J. Michalski, and D.G. King, (eds.), *40 Tools for Cross-Functional Teams: Building Synergy for Breakthrough Creativity*. Portland, Ore.: Productivity Press, 1998.

11. Adapted from Beirne, M. Nestlé streamlines confection connections. *Brandweek*, January 10, 2000, 7–8.

12. Kirkman, B.L., and Rosen, B. Beyond self-management: Antecedents and consequences of team empowerment. *Academy of Management Journal*, 1999, 42, 58–74.

13. Purser, R., and Cabana, S. *The Self-Managing Organization: How Leading Companies are Transforming the Work of Teams for Real Impact*. New York: Free Press, 1999.

14. Kraft, R. *Utilizing Self-Managing Teams: Effective Behavior of Team Leaders*. Hamden, Conn.: Garland, 1999.

15. Kirkman, B.L., and Rosen, B. Powering up teams. *Organizational Dynamics*, Winter 2000, 48–65; Osborn, J.D., and Moran, L. *The New Self-Directed Work Teams: Mastering the Challenge*, 2nd ed. Blacklick, Ohio: McGraw-Hill, 2000.

16. Hinds, P., and Kiesler, S. *Distributed Work*. Cambridge, Mass.: MIT Press, 2002.

17. Adapted from Fishman, C. Whole Foods is all teams. *Fast Company*, April 1996, 103–106; About Whole Foods Market, www.wholefoodsmarket.com/company, accessed January 3, 2002.

18. Lurey, J.S., and Raisingham, M.S. An empirical study of best practices in virtual teams. *Information & Management*, 2001, 38, 523–544.

19. This presentation is based primarily on Townsend, D.M., DeMarie, S.M., and Hendrickson, A.R. Virtual teams: Technology and the workplace of the future. *Academy of Management Executive*, 1998, 12(3), 17–29.

20. Suchan, J., and Hayzak, G. The communication characteristics of virtual teams: A case study. *IEEE Transactions on Professional Communication*, 2001, 44, 174–186.

21. Adapted from Alexander, S. Virtual teams going global. *InfoWorld*, November 13, 2000, 55–59.

22. Tuckman, B.W. Development sequence in small groups. *Psychological Bulletin*, 1965, 62, 384–399; Tuckman, B.W., and Jensen, M.A.C. Stages of small group development revisited. *Group & Organization Studies*, 1977, 2, 419–427; Obert, S.L. Developmental patterns of organizational task groups: A preliminary study. *Human Relations*, 1983, 36, 37–52.

23. Richards, T., and Moger, S. Creative leadership processes in project team development: An alternative to Tuckman's stage model. *British Journal of Management*, 2000, 4, 273–283.

24. Caouette, M., and O'Connor, B. The impact of group support systems on corporate teams' stages of development. *Journal of Organizational Computing and Electronic Commerce*, 1998, 8, 57–81.

25. King, R.T., Jr. Levi's factory workers are assigned to teams, and morale takes a hit. *Wall Street Journal*, May 20, 1998, A1, A6.

26. Lancaster, H. Learning some ways to make meetings less stressful. *Wall Street Journal*, May 26, 1998, B1.

27. Denton, D.K. How a team can grow. *Quality Progress*, June 1999, 53–58.

28. Lencioni, P. *The Five Dysfunctions of a Team: A Leadership Fable*. San Francisco: Jossey-Bass, 2002.

29. Bales, R.E. *Personality and Interpersonal Behavior*. New York: Holt, Rinehart and Winston, 1970; Lustig, M.W. Bales' interpersonal rating forms: Reliability and dimensionality. *Small Group Behavior*, 1987, 18, 99–107.

30. Chatman, J.A., and Flynn, F.J. The influence of demographic heterogeneity on the emergence and consequences of cooperative norms in work groups. *Academy of Management Journal*, 2001, 44, 956–974.

31. Triandis, H.C., Kurowski, L.L., and Gelfand, M.J. Workplace diversity. In H.C. Triandis, M.D. Dunnette, and L.M. Hough (eds.), *Handbook of Industrial and Organizational Psychology*, vol. 4, 2nd ed. Palo Alto, Calif.: Consulting Psychologists Press, 1994, 796–827.

32. Feldman, D.C. The development and enforcement of group norms. *Academy of Management Review*, 1984, 9, 47–53.

33. Besser, T.L. *Team Toyota*. Ithaca: State University of New York Press, 1996.

34. Lipman-Blumen, J., and Leavitt, H.J. *Hot Groups: Seeding Them, Feeding Them, and Using Them to Ignite Your Organization*. New York: Oxford University Press, 1999.

35. Janis, L.L. *Groupthink*, 2nd ed. Boston: Houghton Mifflin, 1982; Whyte, G. Groupthink reconsidered. *Academy of Management Review*, 1989, 14, 40–56.

36. Hambrick, D.C. Fragmentation and the other problems CEOs have with their top management teams. *California Management Review*, Spring 1995, 110–127.

37. Adapted from Whole Foods Market: Our core values, at http://www.wholefoodsmarket.com/company/, accessed January 3, 2002.

38. La Barre, P. Weird ideas that work. *Fast Company*, January 2002, 68–73; see also Sutton, R.I. *Weird Ideas That Work: 11 1/2 Practices for Promoting, Managing, and Sustaining Innovation*. New York: Free Press, 2001.

39. Major portions of this discussion for the nominal group technique were excerpted from Woodman, R.W. Use of the nominal group technique for idea generation and decision making. *Texas Business Executive*, Spring 1981, 50–53.

40. Dowling, K.L., and Lewis, R.D. A synchronous implantation of the nominal group technique: Is it effective. *Decision Support Systems*, 2000, 29, 229–248.

41. Kramer, T.J., Fleming, G.P., and Mannis, S.C. Improving face-to-face brainstorming through modeling and facilitation. *Small Group Research*, 2001, 32, 533–558; Osborn, A.F. *Applied Imagination*, rev. ed. New York: Scribner, 1957.

42. Mullen, B., Johnson, C., and Salas, E. Productivity loss in brainstorming groups: A meta-analytical integration. *Basic and Applied Social Psychology*, 1991, 12, 3–23.

43. Play, about us, at http://www.lookatmorestuff.com, accessed January 4, 2002; see also Leonard, D, and Swap, W. *When Sparks Fly: Igniting Creativity in Groups*. Boston: Harvard Business School Publishing, 1999.

44. Adapted from Dahle, C. Mind games. *Fast Company*, January–February 2000, 169–180.

45. For a description of the wide array of collaborative software products and services offered by the Ventana Corporation, visit this company's home page at http://www.ventana.com, accessed January 4, 2002.

46. Barki, H., and Pinsonneault, A. Small group brainstorming and idea generation. *Small Group Research*, 2001, 32, 158–206.

47. Blitt, B. The seven sins of deadly meetings. *In Handbook of the Business Revolution*. Boston: Fast Company, 1997, 27–31.

48. Adapted from *The Student Audit Instrument*. Developed by Jon M. Werner, a faculty member in the Department of Management at the University of Wisconsin-Whitewater; Edmondson, A. Psychological safety and learning behavior in work teams. *Administrative Science Quarterly*, 1999, 44, 350–383.

49. Prepared by and adapted with permission of Barnes, F.C., professor, University of North Carolina at Charlotte (presented at Southern Case Research Association).

## Chapter 9

1. Adapted from McMaster, M. Fight club. *Sales and Marketing Management*, April 2001, 44–50.

2. Rahim, M.A. Managing *Conflict in Organizations*, 3rd ed. Westport, Conn.: Quorum Books, 2001.

3. Denenberg, R.V., and Braverman, M. *The Violence-Prone Workplace*. Ithaca, N.Y.: Cornell University Press, 2000.

4. Piturro, M. Workplace violence. *Strategic Finance*, May 2001, 35–38.

5. Mandellblit, B.D. Workplace violence: Alert for the security profession, *Security*, July 2001, 58–60.

6. Polzer, J.T. Role conflict. In C.L. Cooper and C. Argyris (eds.), *The Concise Blackwell Encyclopedia of Management*. Oxford: Blackwell, 1998, 575–576.

7. Polzer, J.T. Role ambiguity. In C.L. Cooper and C. Argyris (eds.), *The Concise Blackwell Encyclopedia of Management*. Oxford: Blackwell, 1998, 574.

8. Kahn, A. Taking on a family business can call for greater expertise. *Bryan–College Station* (Texas) *Eagle*, March 20, 1994, C6; Lenzner, R., and Upbin, B. Brother vs. brother vs. mother vs. cousin. *Forbes*, June 17, 1996, 44–46.

9. Wetlaufer, S. Common sense and conflict: An interview with Disney's Michael Eisner. *Harvard Business Review*, January–February 2000, 116.

10. Adapted from Doucet, M.S., and Hooks, K.L. Toward an equal future. *Journal of Accountancy*, June 1999, 71–80.

11. French, J.R.P., and Raven, B. The bases of social power. In D. Cartwright (ed.), *Studies in Social Power*. Ann Arbor: University of Michigan Institute for Social Research, 1959, 150–167.

12. See, for example, the classic work by Barnard, C.I. *The Functions of the Executive*. Cambridge, Mass.: Harvard University Press, 1938, 110.

13. Mayer, B. *The Dynamics of Conflict Resolution*. San Francisco: Jossey-Bass, 2000.

14. Thomas, K.W. Conflict and negotiation processes in organizations. In M.D. Dunnette and L.M. Hough (eds.), *Handbook of Industrial and Organizational Psychology*, 2nd ed., vol. 3, Palo Alto, Calif.: Consulting Psychologists Press, 1992, 651–717.

15. Adapted from Korman, R. Lawsuit claims engineer demoted for reporting bribes. *ENR*, December 24, 2001, 14–15.

16. Gross, M.A., and Guerrero, L.K. Managing conflict appropriately and effectively: An application of the competence model to Rahim's organizational conflict styles. *International Journal of Conflict Management*, 2000, 11, 200–226; Barki, H., and Hartwick, J. Interpersonal Conflict and its management in information system development. *MIS Quarterly*, 2001, 25, 195–228.

17. R.J. Lewicki, D.M. Saunders, and J.W. Minton, (eds.), *Negotiation*, 3rd ed. Boston: Irwin/McGraw-Hill, 1999, 1.

18. Walton, R.E., and McKersie, R.B. *A Behavioral Theory of Labor Negotiations*, 2nd ed. Ithaca, NY: ILR Press, 1991; Kolb, D.M., and Williams, J. Breakthrough bargaining. *Harvard Business Review*, February 2001, 89–97.

19. Fisher, R., and Ury, W. *Getting to Yes: Negotiating Agreement Without Giving In*, 2nd ed. New York: Penguin Books, 1991.

20. Fisher and Ury.

21. Adapted from Powers of persuasion. *Fortune*, October 12, 1998, 160–164; Shapiro, R. Spotlight on credit congress. *Business Credit*, April 2000, 52–54. Shapiro, R., and Jankowski, M. *The Power of Nice: How to Negotiate So Everyone Wins—Especially You*. New York: John Wiley & Sons, 1998.

22. Korshak, S.R. Negotiating trust in the San Francisco hotel industry. *California Management Review*, Fall 1995, 117–137.

23. Friedman, R.A. *Front Stage Backstage: The Dynamic Structure of Labor Negotiations*. Cambridge, Mass.: MIT Press, 1994.

24. Li, J., and Labig, C.E., Jr. Negotiating with China: Exploratory study of relationship-building. *Journal of Managerial Issues*, 2001, 13, 345–359; Ghauri, P.N., and Usunier, J.C. *International Business Negotiations*. New York: Elsevier Science, 1996; Salacuse, J.W. Ten ways that culture affects negotiating style: Some survey results. *Negotiation Journal*, 1998, 14, 221–240.

25. Paik, Y., and Tung, R.L. Negotiating with East Asians: How to attain "win–win" outcomes. *Management International Review*, 1999, 37, 103–122; Brett, J.M., and Ukumura, T. Inter- and intracultural negotiation: U.S. and Japanese negotiators. *Academy of Management Journal*, 1998, 41, 495–510.

26. Adapted from Buller, P.F., Kohls, J.J., and Anderson, K.S. Managing conflicts across cultures. *Organizational Dynamics*, Spring 2000, 52–66.

27. Noll, D.E. A theory of mediation. *Dispute Resolution Journal*, May–July 2001, 78–84.

28. Herman, M.S., Hollett, N., Gale, J., and Foster, M. Defining mediator knowledge and skills. *Negotiation Journal*, 2001, 17, 139–153.

29. Adapted from Baskerville, D.M. How do you manage conflict? *Black Enterprise*, May 1993, 63–66; Thomas, K.W., and Kilmann, R.H. *The Thomas–Kilmann Conflict Mode Instrument*. Tuxedo, N.Y.: Xicom, 1974; Rahim, M.A. A measure of styles of handling interpersonal conflict. *Academy of Management Journal*, 1983, 26, 368–376.

## Chapter 10

1. Adapted from Fehrman, J. A focus on leadership, a penchant for passion. *Business Investment Marketing*, December 1, 2001, 24–26.

2. Tichy, N.M. The teachable point of view. *Journal of Business Strategy*, January/February 1998, 29–33.

3. Hiebert, M., and Klatt, B. *The Encyclopedia of Leadership: A Practical Guide to Popular Leadership Theories and Techniques*. Blacklick, Ohio: McGraw-Hill, 2001.

4. Adapted from Hammonds, K.H. Continental's turnaround pilot. *Fast Company*, December 2001, 96–101.

5. Fryer, B. Bosses from heaven—and hell! *Computerworld*, August 9, 1999, 46–47.

6. Fryer.

7. Fryer.

8. Fryer; see also VanDerWall, S. *The Courageous Follower: Standing Up To and For Our Leaders*. San Francisco: Berret-Koehler, 1998.

9. Fryer.

10. Northouse, P.G. *Leadership: Theory and Practice*, 2nd ed. Thousand Oaks, Calif.: Sage, 2000.

11. Bass, B.M. *Bass and Stogdill's Handbook of Leadership*, 3rd ed. New York: Free Press, 1990.

12. Fleishman, E.A., and Harris, E.E. Patterns of leadership behavior related to employee grievances and turnover:

Some post hoc reflections. *Personnel Psychology*, 1998, 51, 825–834; Fleishman, E.A. Consideration and structure: Another look at their role in leadership research. In F. Damserau and F.J. Yammarino (eds.), *Leadership: The Multi-Level Approaches*. Greenwich, Conn.: JAI Press, 1998, 285–302.

13. Adapted from Byrne, J.A., and Timmons, H. Tough times for a new CEO. *Business Week*, October 31, 2001, 64–70.

14. Hersey, P., Blanchard, K.H., and Johnson, D.E. *Leading Management of Organizational Behavior: Human Resources*, 8th ed. Englewood Cliffs, N.J.: Prentice-Hall, 2001.

15. Fernandez, C.F., and Vecchio, R.P. Situational leadership theory revisited: A test of an across-jobs perspective. *Leadership Quarterly*, 1997, 8, 67–85.

16. Adapted from Barton, L. Working in a Vietnamese voice. *Academy of Management Executive*, November 2000, 14(4), 20–31.

17. Vroom, V.H., and Jago, A.G. *The New Leadership*. Englewood Cliffs, N.J.: Prentice-Hall, 1988.

18. The discussion of the revised model is based on Vroom, V.H. New developments in leadership and decision making. *OB News*. Briarcliff Manor, N.Y.: Organizational Behavior Division of the Academy of Management, headquartered at Pace University, Spring 1999, 4–5; Vroom, V.H. Leadership and the decision-making process. *Organizational Dynamics*, Spring 2000, 82–93.

19. Vroom, 90.

20. Schriesheim, C. *Leadership Instrument*. Used by permission, University of Miami, Miami, Florida, 2002.

21. Reproduced with permission from Caitlin, L., and White, T. "Case Study: Southwestern Manufacturing Company," *International Business: Cultural Sourcebook and Case Studies* with the permission of South-Western College Publishing. © 1993 by South-Western College Publishing. All rights reserved.

## Chapter 11

1. Adapted from Goff, L.J. Finding your inner leader. *Computerworld*, March 26, 2001, 7–10.

2. Goff, 10.

3. Bass, B.M. Does the transactional-transformational leadership paradigm transcend organizational and national boundaries? *American Psychologist*, 1997, 52, 130–139.

4. Avolio, B.J. *Full Leadership Development: Building the Vital Forces in Organizations*. Thousand Oaks, Calif.: Sage, 1999, 15.

5. Conger, J.A., and Kanungo, R.N. *Charismatic Leadership in Organizations*. Thousand Oaks, Calif.: Sage, 1998; Waldman, D.A., and Yammarino, F.J. CEO charismatic leadership: Levels-of-management and levels-of-analysis effects. *Academy of Management Review*, 1999, 24, 266–285.

6. Adapted from Mount, I. Underlings: That's Mister Conway to you. And I am not a people person. *Business 2.0*, February 2002, 53–58.

7. Jacobsen, C., and House, R.J. Dynamics of Charismatic leadership: A process theory, simulation models, and tests. *Leadership Quarterly*, 2001, 12, 75–112; Gardner, W.L., and Avolio, B.J. The charismatic relationship: A dramaturgical perspective. *Academy of Management Review*, 1998, 23, 14–31.

8. Conger, J.A. Charismatic and transformational leadership in organizations: An insider's perspective on these developing streams of research. In J.A. Conger and J.G. Hunt (eds.), *Leadership Quarterly*, Special Issue: Part 1, 1999, 10, 145–180; Waldman, D.A., Ramirez, G.G., House, R.J., and Puranam, P. Does leadership matter? CEO leadership attributes and profitability under conditions of perceived environmental uncertainty. *Academy of Management Journal*, 2001, 44, 134–143.

9. Adapted from Rifkin, G. How Richard Branson works magic. *Strategy & Business*, 1998, 13(4), 44–52; Kets de Vries, M.F.R. *The New Global Leaders: Richard Branson, Percy Barnevik, and David Simon*. San Francisco: Jossey-Bass, 1999; Wells, M. Red barron. *Forbes*, July 3, 2000, 151–160.

10. Beyer, J.M. Taming and promoting charisma to change organizations. In J.A. Conger and J.G. Hunt (eds.), *Leadership Quarterly*, Special Issue: Part 1, 1999, 10, 307–330.

11. Beyer, J.M., and Browning, L.D. Transforming an industry in crisis: Charisma, routinization, and supportive cultural leadership. Working paper, University of Texas at Austin, 2000, 8.

12. J.M. Washington, and M.L. King, Jr., (eds.), *A Testament of Hope: the Essential Speeches and Writings of Martin Luther King, Jr.* San Francisco: Harper, 1990.

13. Anderson, T.D. *Transforming Leadership: Equipping Yourself and Challenging Others to Build the Leadership Organization*, 2nd ed. Boca Raton, Fla.: CRC Press, 1998.

14. This section draws from Avolio, *Full Leadership Development*, 43–49; Bass, B.M. *Transformational Leadership: Industry, Military, and Educational Impact*. Mahwah, N.J.: Lawrence Erlbaum, 1998; Alimo-Metcalfe, B., and Alban-Metcalfe, R.J. The development of a new transformational leadership questionnaire. *Journal of Occupational and Organizational Psychology*, 2001, 74, 1–27.

15. Egan, G. *Change Agent Skills*. Monterey, Calif.: Brooks/Cole, 1985, 204.

16. Adapted from Brenneman, G. Right away and all at once: How we saved Continental. *Harvard Business Review*, September–October 1999, 162–179; Puffer, S.M. Continental Airlines' CEO Gordon Bethune on teams and new product development. *Academy of Management Executive*, 1999, 13(3), 29–35.

17. Adapted from George, W.W. Medtronic's chairman, William George on how mission-driven companies create long-term shareholder value. *Academy of Management Executive*, 2001, 15(4), 39–47.

18. Adapted from Barrier, M. Leadership skills employees respect. *Nation's Business*, January 1999, 28–30; Accommodations by Apple, Inc., Web site at http://www.kcaccommodations.com, accessed February 14, 2002.

19. Pfeffer, J. Why do smart organizations occasionally do dumb things? *Organizational Dynamics*, Summer 1996, 33–44.

20. Zunitch, V.M. Lockheed Martin now concentrates on slashing debt. *Wall Street Journal*, April 26, 1996, A7.

21. Barone, M. Great men need not apply: We are living in a time of lesser dangers and lesser leaders. *U.S. News & World Report*, February 19, 1996, 40–41.

22. Kerr, S., and Jermier, J.M. Substitutes for leadership: Their meaning and measurement. *Organizational Behavior and Human Performance*, 1978, 22, 374–403.

23. Podsakoff, P.M., MacKenzie, S.B., and Bommer, W.H. Meta-analysis of the relationships between Kerr and Jermier's substitutes for leadership and employee job attitudes, role perceptions, and performance. *Journal of Applied Psychology*, 1996, 81, 380–399; Manz, C.C., and Sims, H.P., Jr. *The New Super Leadership: Leading Others to Lead Themselves.* San Francisco: Berrett Koehler, 2001.

24. Sashkin, M. *Visionary Leadership.* Washington, D.C.: George Washington University, 1997. Used with permission.

25. Adapted from Brown, E. How can a dot-com be this hot? *Fortune*, January 21, 2002, 78–84; Bannan, K. Sole survivor. *Sales and Marketing Management*, July 2001, 36–41; Fishman, C. Facetime: Meg Whitman. *Fast Company*, May 2001, 79–82; Rogers, A. CRN interview, Meg Whitman. *CRN*, November 12, 2001, 20–22; Schonfeld, E. eBay's secret ingredient. *Business 2.0*, March 2002, 52–58. For more information on eBay, visit the organization's home page at http://www.ebay.com/aboutebay.

## Chapter 12

1. Adapted from Wong, E. E-mail warning implodes. *New York Times*, April 5, 2001, Final edition, C1; see also the About Cerner Corporation Web site at http://www.cerner.com, accessed March 5, 2002; Gillespie, M.H. CEO's weaknesses displayed. *Boston Globe*, April 8, 2001, J15; Burton, T.M., and Emma, R. Lots of empty spaces in Cerner parking lot get CEO riled up. *Wall Street Journal*, March 30, 2001, B3.

2. Harris, T.E. *Applied Organizational Communication: Principles and Pragmatics for Future Practice.* Mahwah, N.J.: Lawrence Erlbaum Associates, 2002.

3. Personal interview with D. Bitterman, director—investments, CIBC Oppenheimer, Dallas, Texas, 2002.

4. Russ, G.S., Daft, R.L., and Lengel, R.H. Media selection and managerial characteristics in organizational communications. *Management Communication Quarterly*, 1990, 4, 151–175; Ngwenyama, O.K., and Lee, A.S. Communication richness in electronic mail: Critical social theory and the contextuality of meaning. *MIS Quarterly*, 1997, 21, 145–167; Carlson, J.R., and Zmud, R.W. Channel expansion theory and the experiential nature of media richness perceptions. *Academy of Management Journal*, 1999, 42, 153–170.

5. Mortensen, C.D., and Ayres, C.M. *Miscommunication.* Thousand Oaks, Calif.: Sage, 1997.

6. Scott, J.C. Differences in American and British vocabulary: Implications for international business. *Business Communication Quarterly*, December 2000, 27–39.

7. Brinson, S.L., and Benoit, W.L. The tarnishing Star. *Management Communication Quarterly*, 1999, 12,

483–510; Labich, K. No more crude at Texaco. *Fortune*, September 6, 1999, 205–212.

8. Bolino, M. Citizenship and impression management: Good soldiers or good actors? *Academy of Management Review*, 1999, 24, 82–83; Cady, S.H., and Fandt, P.M. Managing impressions with information: A field study of organizational realities. *Journal of Applied Behavioral Science*, 2001, 37, 180–204.

9. Adapted from McMahan, J.T. The issue is ethics and they showed none. *Houston Chronicle*, February 3, 2002, C1, C4.

10. Francesco, A.M., and Gold, B.A. *International Organizational Behavior.* Englewood Cliffs, N.J.: Prentice-Hall, 1998, 8.

11. Hofstede, G. The universal and the specific in 21st century management. *Organizational Dynamics*, Summer 1999, 34–44; M. Gannon, and K. Newman, (eds.), *The Blackwell Handbook of Cross-Cultural Management.* Maldin; Mass.: Blackwell, 2001.

12. Ting-Toomey, S. *Communicating Across Cultures.* New York: Guilford Press, 1999.

13. Latane, B., Liu, J.H., Nowak, A., Bonevento, M., and Zheng, L. Distance matters: Physical space and social impact. *Personality and Social Psychology Bulletin*, 1995, 21, 795–805.

14. Taylor, L. I'm not insensitive to other cultures—As long as they don't keep bragging about it. *New Statesman*, January 29, 1999, 55–56.

15. Adapted from Mangaliso, M.P. Building competitive advantage from Ubuntu: Management lessons from South Africa. *Academy of Management Executive*, 2001, 15(3), 23–34.

16. L.R. Frey, D.S. Gouran, and M.S. Poole, (eds.), *The Handbook of Group Communication Theory and Research.* Thousand Oaks, Calif.: Sage, 1999.

17. Adapted from Keenan, F., and Ante, S.E. The new teamwork. *Business Week: E.biz.* February 18, 2002, 3–6.

18. Pillutla, M.M., and Chen, X. Social norms and cooperation in social dilemmas: The effects of context and feedback. *Organizational Behavior & Human Decision Processes*, 1999, 78(2), 81–93.

19. DeNisi, A.S., and Kluger, A.N. Feedback effectiveness: Can 360-degree appraisals be improved? *Academy of Management Executive*, 2000, 14(1), 129–139; Bracken, D.W., Timmreck, C.W., Fleenor, J.W., and Summers, L. 360 feedback from another angle. *Human Resource Management*, 2001, 40, 3–20; Peiperl, M.A. Getting 360-degree feedback right. *Harvard Business Review*, January 2001, 142–147.

20. Nichols, M.P. *The Lost Art of Listening.* New York: Guilford, 1995.

21. Adapted from Weeks, H. Taking the stress out of stressful communications. *Harvard Business Review*, July–August 2001, 112–119.

22. Fulfer, M. Nonverbal communication. *Journal of Organizational Excellence*, 2001, 20(2), 19–27; Poyatos, F. *Nonverbal Communication Across Disciplines.* Philadelphia: John Benjamins, 2002; Andersen, P.A. *Nonverbal Communication: Forms and Functions.* Mountain View, Calif.: Mayfield, 1999.

23. Hickson, M.L., Stacks, D.W., Moore, N. *Nonverbal Communication: Studies and Applications*. Los Angeles: Roxbury, 2002; Jandt, F.E. *Intercultural Communication*, 3rd ed. Thousand Oaks, Calif.: Sage, 2001.

24. Bluedorn, A.C., Kaufman, C.F., and Lane, P.M. How many things do you like to do at once? An introduction to monochronic and polychronic time. *Academy of Management Executive*, 1992, 6(4), 17–26.

25. Aquino, K., Brover, S.L., Bradfield, M., and Allen, D.G. The effects of negative affectivity, hierarchical status, and self-determination on workplace victimization. *Academy of Management Journal*, 1999, 42, 260–272.

26. Adapted from Zielinski, D. *Presentations*, April 2001, 36–42.

27. Adapted from Douglas Roberts, formerly manager of training, LTV Missiles and Electronics Group, Grand Prairie, Texas. Used with permission.

## Chapter 13

1. Adapted from Muoio, A. Decisions, decisions. *Fast Company*, October 1998, 93–97; Bylinsky, G. The queen of elegant software. *Fortune*, March 19, 2001, 4–8.

2. Ferrell, O.C., Fraedrich, J., and Ferrell, L. *Business Ethics: Ethical Decision Making and Cases*. Boston: Houghton Mifflin, 2002; Carroll, A.B., and Buchholtz, A.K. *Business and Society: Ethics and Stakeholder Management*. Cincinnati: South-Western, 2002.

3. Jones, D. Doing the wrong thing. *USA Today*, April 4–6, 1997, 1A, 2A.

4. The framework for this section is based primarily on James, T.M. Ethical decision making by individuals in organizations: An issue-contingent model. *Academy of Management Review*, 1991, 16, 366–395; May, D.R., and Paul, K.P. The role of moral intensity in ethical decision making. *Business and Society*, 2002, 41, 84–118.

5. N. Bowie, (ed.), *The Blackwell Guide to Business Ethics*. Malden, Mass.: Blackwell, 2002.

6. Adapted from Hassel, G. Memorable PR missteps of '96. *Houston Chronicle*, January 15, 1997, C1.

7. Weiss, J.W. *Business Ethics: A Stakeholder and Issues Management Approach*, 3rd. ed. Cincinnati: South-Western, 2002.

8. Center for Public Integrity. *Nothing Sacred: The Politics of Privacy*. Washington, D.C.: 1998.

9. Kovach, K.A., Jordan, J., Tansey, K., and Framinan, E. The balance between employee privacy and employer interests. *Business and Society Review*, 2000, 105, 289–298.

10. Jennings, M.M. *Business: Its Legal, Ethical and Global Environment*, 6th ed. Cincinnati: South-Western, 2003.

11. Roussouw, D. *Business Ethics*, 2nd ed. New York: Oxford University Press, 2002.

12. Coleman, F.T. *Ending the Employment Relationship Without Ending Up in Court*. Alexandria, Va.: Society for Human Resource Management, 2002.

13. Institute for Global Ethics. *Global Values, Moral Boundaries: A Pilot Survey*. Camden, Mass.: Institute for Global Ethics, 1997.

14. Swanson, D.L. Toward an integrative theory of business and society: A research strategy for corporate social performance. *Academy of Management Review*, 1999, 24, 506–521.

15. Rowan, J.R. The foundation of moral rights. *Journal of Business Ethics*, 2000, 24, 355–361.

16. Adapted from Evans, J. The case of the puzzled purchasing agent. *Business Ethics*, November/December 2001, 20–22.

17. Harrison, E.F. *The Managerial Decision-Making Process*, 5th ed. Boston: Houghton Mifflin, 1999.

18. Garvin, D.A. Building a learning organization. *Harvard Business Review*, July–August 1993, 78–91.

19. Hammond, J.S., Keeney, R.L., and Raiffa, H. *Smart Choices: A Practical Guide to Making Better Decisions*. Boston: Harvard Business School Press, 1999.

20. Klein, G., and Weick, K.E. Decisions. *Across the Board*, June 2000, 16–23; Garvin, D.A., and Roberto, M.A. What you don't know about making decisions. *Harvard Business Review*, September 2001, 129–136.

21. Adapted from Charan, R. Capturing a culture of indecision. *Harvard Business Review*, April 2001, 74–86.

22. Simon, H.A. *Administrative Behavior: A Study of Decision-Making Processes in Administrative Organizations*, 4th ed. New York: Free Press, 1997.

23. Roach, J.M. Simon says: Decision making is "satisficing" experience. *Management Review*, January 1979, 8–9; Dequech, D. Bounded rationality, institutions, and uncertainty. *Journal of Economic Issues*, 2001, 35, 911–930.

24. Bernstein, P.L. *Against the Gods: The Remarkable Story of Risk*. Somerset, N.J.: John Wiley & Sons, 1997.

25. Kahneman, D., and Tversky, A. *Choices, Values and Frames*. New York: Cambridge University Press, 2000.

26. Schoemaker, P.J.H., and Russo, J.E. A pyramid of decision approaches. *California Management Review*, Fall 1993, 9–31.

27. Adapted from Nutt, P.C. Surprising but true: Half the decisions in organizations fail. *Academy of Management Executive*, November 1999, 75–90.

28. Mack, M.H. Managing codified knowledge. *Sloan Management Review*, Summer 1999, 45–58.

29. Pfeffer, J. *Managing with Power: Politics and Influence in Organizations*. Boston: Harvard Business School Press, 1992; R.M. Kramer, and M.A. Neale, (eds.), *Power and Influence in Organizations*. Thousand Oaks, Calif.: Sage, 1998.

30. Funk, S. Risky business. *Across the Board*, July–August 1999, 10–12.

31. Dulebohn, J.H., and Ferris, G.R. The role of influence tactics in perceptions of performance evaluations' fairness. *Academy of Management Journal*, 1999, 42, 288–303; R.M. Kramer, and M.A. Neale, (eds.), *Power and Influence in Organizations*. Thousand Oaks, Calif.: Sage, 1998.

32. Adapted from Mehri, C. The perils of ignoring racial issues. *Business Ethics*, January/February 2001, 7–8; McKay, B., Deogun, N., and Lublin, J. Tone deaf: Ivester had all skills of a CEO but one: Ear for political nuance. *Wall Street Journal*, December 17, 1999, A1, A6.

33. Hamel, G., Gould, S.J., and Weick, K.E. *On Creativity, Innovation and Renewal*. San Francisco: Jossey-Bass, 2002.

34. Sutton, R.I. *Weird Ideas That Work: 11 1/2 Practices for*

*Promoting, Managing, and Sustaining Innovation.* New York: Free Press, 2002.

35. De Bono, E. *Serious Creativity: Using the Power of Lateral Thinking to Create New Ideas.* New York: HarperCollins, 1992; Fisher, J.R., Jr. The need for lateral thinking in the new century. *National Productivity Review*, Spring 2000, 1–12.

36. Amabile, T.M. How to kill creativity. *Harvard Business Review*, September–October 1998, 77–87.

37. Gryskiewicz, S.S., and Epstein, R. Cashing in on creativity at work. *Psychology Today*, September/October 2000, 62–67.

38. Adapted from Simpson, L. Fostering creativity. *Training*, December 2001, 54–57; Bridger, C. Thinking innovatively. *Buffalo News*, March 1, 2002, 3–4.

39. Cosier, R.A., and Schwenk, C.R. Agreement and thinking alike: Ingredients for poor decisions. *Academy of Management Executive*, February 1990, 69–74.

40. Adapted from Duran, G.J., Gomar, E.E., Stiles, M., Vele, C.A., and Vogt, J.F. Living ethics: Meeting challenges in decision making. In *The 1997b Annual: Volume 1, Training.* Copyright © 1997 by Pfeiffer, An Imprint of Jossey-Bass, Inc., Publishers, San Francisco, Calif.: 127–135. Used with permission.

41. Adapted from Wellaufer, S. Nestlé's Peter Brabeck: The business case against revolution. *Harvard Business Review*, February 2001, 112–121. For more information on Nestlé, visit the organization's home page at http://www.nestle.com.

## Chapter 14

1. Adapted from Ward, H. The ASP model hits the hut. *Computer Weekly*, November 2, 2000, 18; O'Keefe, B. What do KFC and Pizza Hut conjecture up abroad? Are they American symbols? Or have they become global brands. Tricon, the company that owns them both, is betting on the latter. *Fortune*, November 26, 2001, 102ff; personal conversations with Barry Mike, director of internal communications, Pizza Hut, March 2002, Dallas, Texas.

2. Pitts, R.A., and Lei, D. *Strategic Management*, 3rd ed. Cincinnati: South-Western, 2003.

3. Lawrence, T.B., and Jennings, P.D. The temporal dynamics of institutionalization. *Academy of Management Review*, 2001, 26, 624–644; Levitt, R.E., Thompson, J.D., Christiansen, T.R., Kunz, J.C., and Nass, Y.C. Simulating project work processes and organizations: Toward a micro organization theory of organization design. *Management Science*, 1999, 45, 1479–1493.

4. Personal conversation with J. Birch, director of operations, Pizaa Hut, Dallas, Texas, January 2002.

5. Porter, M.E. *Competitive Strategy.* New York: Free Press, 1980; see also Kraatz, M.S., and Zajac, E.J. How organizational resources affect strategic change and performance in turbulent environment. *Organization Science*, 2001, 12, 632–657.

6. Adapted from Pitts, R.A., and Lei, D. *Strategic Management: Building and Sustaining Competitive Advantage.*

Cincinnati: South-Western, 2000, 92–94; Vinzant, C. How do you say "labor shortage"? *Fortune*, September 18, 2000, 342ff; Slurpee and sushi. *Restaurants & Institutions*, September 15, 2000, 18ff.

7. Thompson, J.D. *Organizations in Action.* New York: McGraw-Hill, 1967; Katz, N. Sport teams as a model for workplace teams: Lessons and liabilities. *Academy of Management Executive*, 2001, 15(3), 56–69.

8. Burns, T, and Stalker, G. *The Management of Innovation.* London: Social Science Paperbacks, 1961, 96–125.

9. Adapted from Weber, M. *The Theory of Social and Economic Organization* (trans. Parsons, T.). New York: Oxford University Press, 1947, 329–334.

10. Hellriegel, D., Jackson, S.J., and Slocum, J.W., Jr. *Management: A Competency Based Approach*, 9th ed. Cincinnati: South-Western, 2002, 281.

11. Barry Mike.

12. Carpenter, M.A., Sanders, Wm.G., and Gregersen, H.B. Building human capital with organizational context: The impact of international assignment experience on multinational firm performance and CEO pay. *Academy of Management Journal*, 2001, 44, 493–512; Kostova, K., and Zaheer, S. Organizational legitimacy under conditions of complexity: The case of the multinational enterprise. *Academy of Management Review*, 1999, 24, 64–81.

13. See www.kendallhq.com (January 2002); Morrison, A.J., Ricks, D.A., and Roth, K. Globization versus regionalization: Which way for the multinational? *Organizational Dynamics*, Winter 1991, 17–29.

14. Personal conversation with M. Bohn, director of business systems, Celanese Chemical Corporation, Dallas, Texas, January 2002.

15. See www.utc.com (January 2002).

16. Pitts and Lei, *Strategic Management.*

17. Adapted from Ransom, S., Mike, B., Lonsdale, J., Gordon, S., and Cones, J. International business: Quick service restaurant industry in China. Unpublished manuscript, Cox School of Business, May 2000.

18. Reagans, R., and Zuckerman, E.W. Networks, diversity and productivity: The social capital of corporate R & D teams. *Organization Science*, 2001, 12, 501–517; Galbraith, J.R. *Competing with Flexible Lateral Organizations.* Reading, Mass.: Addison-Wesley, 1996.

19. Gupta, A.K., and Govindarajan, V. Converting global presence into global competitive advantage. *Academy of Management Executive*, 2001, 15(2), 45–58.

20. See www.unctad.org, accessed October 1, 2001; after opening this Web site, search for *Global economic trends and prospects.*

21. Ancona, D., Kochan, T.A., Sully, M., Van Maanen, J., and Westney, D.E. *Organizational Behavior & Processes.* Cincinnati: South-Western, 1999, 9–20.

22. Sparrowe, R.T., Liden, R.C., Wayne, S.J., and Kraimer, M.L. Social networks and performance of individuals and groups. *Academy of Management Journal*, 2001, 44, 316–325; Miles, R.E., and Snow, C.C. The new network firm. *Organizational Dynamics*, Spring 1995, 5–18.

23. Lichenstein, B.B. Self-organized transitions: A pattern amidst the chaos of transformative change. *Academy of*

*Management Executive*, 2000, 14(4), 128–141; Alvarez, S.A., and Barney, J.B. How entrepreneurial firms can benefit from alliances with large partners. *Academy of Management Executive*, 2001, 15(1), 139–148.

24. Markus, M.L., Manville, B., and Agres, C.E. What makes a virtual organization work? *Sloan Management Review*, 2000, 42(1), 13–27; Maznevski, M.L., and Chudoba, K.M. Bridging space over time: Global virtual team dynamics and effectiveness for virtual organizations. *Organization Science*, 2000, 11, 473–492.

25. Adapted from Prokeach, S.E. Unleashing the power of learning: An interview with British Petroleum's John Browne. *Harvard Business Review*, September–October 1997, 147–168.

26. Adapted from Pasmore, W.A. *Designing Effective Organizations: The Sociotechnical Systems Perspective*. New York: John Wiley & Sons, 1988, 157–186.

27. Adapted from Byrne, J.A., and Elgin, B. Cisco behind the hype. *Business Week*, January 21, 2002, 55–61; Pitts and Lei, *Strategic Management*, 2003; Lei, D., and Slocum, J.W., Jr., Organization design to renew competitor advantage. *Organizational Dynamics*, 2002, 31, 1–18.

## Chapter 15

1. Adapted from McLaughlin, C. A strong foundation. *Training*, 2001, 38(3), 80ff; see also http://www.tdindustries.com (March 2002).

2. Meyer, D.E. Radical change, the quiet way (changing corporate culture). *Harvard Business Review*, October 2001, 92–104.

3. Trice, H.M., and Beyer, J.M. *The Cultures of Work Organizations*. Englewood Cliffs, N.J.: Prentice-Hall, 1993, 1–8.

4. Martin, J. *Cultures in Organizations*. New York: Oxford University Press, 1992.

5. Gibson, C.B., and Zellmer-Bruhn, M.E. Metaphors and meaning: An intercultural analysis of the concept of teamwork. *Administrative Science Quarterly*, 2001, 46, 274–298.

6. Higgins, J.M., and McAllaster, C. Want innovations? Then use cultural artifacts that support it. *Organizational Dynamics*, 2002, 31, 74–84.

7. Schein, E.H. How culture forms, develops, and changes. In R.H. Kilmann, M.I. Saxton, and R. Serpa (eds.), *Gaining Control of the Corporate Culture*. San Francisco: Jossey-Bass, 1985, 15–43; Schein, E.H. *Organizational Culture and Leadership*, 49–84.

8. Schein, E.H. Organizational culture. *American Psychologist*, 1990, 45, 109–119.

9. Adapted from Ball, J. Your career matters: Daimler-Chrysler's transfer woes. *Wall Street Journal*, August 24, 1999, B1ff; Bradsher, K. Management by two cultures may be a growing source of strain for DaimlerChrysler. *New York Times*, March 24, 1999, C2.

10. Chatman, J.A., Polzer, J.T., Barsade, S.G., and Neale, M.A. Being different yet feeling similar: The influence of demographic composition and organizational culture on

work process and outcomes. *Administrative Science Quarterly*, 1998, 43, 749–779; Kahnweiler, W.M. Executive managers: Cultural expectations through stories about work. *Journal of Applied Management Studies*, 1997, 6(2), 117–139.

11. Buller, P.F., and Schuler, R.S. *Managing Organizations and People*. Cincinnati: South-Western, 2000, 280–301.

12. Trice and Beyer, 115–116.

13. Personal conversation with James Donaldson, vice president, Global Trust, Chase Manhattan Private Bank, New York, February 2002.

14. Personal conversation with Christi Clinger, operations manager, Mary Kay Cosmetics, Dallas, Texas, February 2002.

15. Freiberg, J., and Freiberg, K. *NUTS! Southwest Airlines' Crazy Recipe for Business and Personal Success*. Austin, Texas: Bard, 1996.

16. Schein, *American Psychologist*, 109–119.

17. Jermier, J, Slocum, J.W., Jr., Fry, L., and Gaines, J. Organizational subculture in a soft bureaucracy: Resistance behind the myth and façade of an official culture. *Organization Science*, 1991, 2, 170–194.

18. Adapted from Shellenbarger, S. From Harley factories to gold mines, more bosses get it. *Wall Street Journal*, July 21, 1999, B1ff; Teerlink, R., and Ozley, L. *More Than a Motorcycle: The Leadership Journey at Harley-Davidson*. Boston: Harvard Business School Press, 2000.

19. Hellriegel, D., Jackson, S.E., and Slocum, J.W., Jr. *Management: A Competency Based Approach*, 9th ed. Cincinnati: South-Western, 2002, 489–493.

20. Kerr, J., and Slocum, J.W., Jr. Managing corporate cultures through reward systems. *Academy of Management Executive*, 1987, 1(2), 99–108.

21. Adapted from the Synovus Web site at http://www.synovus.com, accessed March 2002.

22. DeLong, D.W., and Fahey, L. Diagnosing cultural barriers to knowledge management. *Academy of Management Executive*, 2000, 14(4), 113–127.

23. Adapted from Duffy, M., and Dickerson, J.F. Enron spoils the party. *Time*, February 4, 2002, 20–25; Landers, J. Enron panel says many share blame. *Dallas Morning News*, February 3, 2002, A1ff; Oldham, C. Diary of deception. *Dallas Morning News*, February 3, 2002, 3H–4H; Miller, S. To tell the truth. *People Weekly*, February 4, 2002, 63ff; Greider, Wm. Crimes in the suites. *The Nation*, February 4, 2002, 11ff; Eisenberg, D. Ignorant & poor? *Time*, February 11, 2002, 37–39; Eichenwald, K., and Henriques, D.B. Enron's many strands: The Company unravels; Enron buffed image to a shine even as it rotted from within. *New York Times*, February 10, 2002, A1ff.

24. Pruzan, P. The question of organizational consciousness: Can organizations have virtues and visions? *Journal of Business Ethics*, 2001, 29, 271–280.

25. Adapted from Smith, D.M. *Women at Work*. Upper Saddle River, N.J.: Prentice-Hall, 2000, 139–143.

26. O'Reilly, C.A., and Chatman, J.A. Culture as social control: Corporations, cults, and commitment. In B.M. Staw and L.L. Cummings (eds.), *Research in*

*Organizational Behavior*, vol. 18. Greenwich, Conn: JAI Press, 1996, 157–200.

27. See the Walt Disney Company Web site at http://www. disney.com (March 2002).

28. Young, D.W. The six levers for managing organizational culture. *Business Horizons*, 2000, 43(5), 19–29; Sparrowe, R.T., Liden, R.C., Wayne, S.J., and Kraimer, M.L. Social networks and the performance of individuals and groups. *Academy of Management Journal*, 2001, 44, 316–325.

29. Adapted from Reiss, M.C., and Mitra, K. The effects of individual differences factors on the acceptability of ethical or unethical workplace behaviors. *Journal of Business Ethics*, 1998, 17, 1581–1593.

30. Adapted from Freiberg and Freiberg; Buller and Schuler, 261–279; Brooker, K. The chairman of the board looks back. *Fortune*, May 28, 2001, 62ff; see also the Southwest Airlines Web site at www.southwest.com/about_swa/press/factsheet.html (March 2002).

# Chapter 16

1. Adapted from Breen, B., and Dahle, C. 20/20 Change agent. *Fast Company*, December 1999, 402ff.

2. Weick, K.E., and Sutcliffe, K.M. *Managing the Unexpected*. San Francisco: Jossey-Bass, 2001.

3. Cummings, T.G., and Worley, C.G. *Organizational Development and Change*, 7th ed. Cincinnati: South-Western, 2001, 359–362.

4. Gupta, A.K., and Govindarajan, V. Converting global presence into global competitive advantage. *Academy of Management Executive*, 2001, 15(2), 45–58.

5. Pearlson, K.E., and Saunders, C.S. There's no place like home: Managing telecommuting paradoxes. *Academy of Management Executive*, 2001, 15(2), 117–128.

6. Siehman, P. How a tighter supply chain extends the enterprise. *Fortune*, November 8, 1999, 272A–272B.

7. Kanter, R.M. Managing the extended enterprise in a globally connected world. *Organizational Dynamics*, Summer 1999, 7–23.

8. Maznevski, M.L., and Chudoba, K.M. Bridging space over time: Global virtual team dynamics and effectiveness. *Organization Science*, 2000, 11, 473–492.

9. Kanter, R.M. Strategy as improvisational theater: Companies that want to outpace the competition throw out the script and improve their way to new strategies. *Sloan Management Review*, 2002, 43(2), 76–82.

10. Kador, J. The end of work as we know it: They're mobile, they're in demand, and armed with skills. Today's contingent workforce. *InfoWorld*, August 21, 2000, 63ff.

11. Chang, S.G.C., and Ledford, G.E. A hierarchical construct of self-management leadership and its relations to quality of work life and perceived work group effectiveness. *Personnel Psychology*, 1997, 50, 275–309.

12. Adapted from http://www.corning.com, accessed April 12, 2002; Corning to build plant in China. *New York Times*, May 8, 1998, C6(N).

13. Quy, N.H. Time, temporal capability, and planned change. *Academy of Management Review*, 2001, 26, 601–625.

14. Beer, M. How to develop an organization capable of sustained high-performance: Embrace the drive for results–capability development paradox. *Organizational Dynamics*, 2001, 29, 233–247.

15. Beer, M., and Nohria, N. Resolving the tension between theories E and O of change. In M. Beer and N. Nohria (eds.), *Breaking the Code of Change*. Boston: Harvard Business School Press, 2000, 1–34.

16. Weber, J. *Champion International*. Boston: Harvard Business School Publishing, 2000, Case # 9-499-019.

17. Collingswood, H., and Coutu, D.L. Jack on Jack: The HBR Interview. *Harvard Business Review*, 2002, 80(2), 88–94; Welch, J.F., Jr. *Jack: Straight From the Gut*. New York: Warner Business Books, 2001.

18. Dent, E.B., and Goldberg, S.G. Challenging "resistance to change." *Journal of Applied Behavioral Science*, 1999, 35, 25–41; Kraatz, M.S., and Moore, J.H. Executive migration and institutional change. *Academy of Management Journal*, 2002, 45, 120–143.

19. Cummings and Worley, 10–11.

20. Adapted from Nutt, P.C. *The Tolerance for Ambiguity and Decision Making*. Columbus, Ohio: Fisher School of Business, 2002. Used with permission.

21. Lewin, K. *Field Theory in Social Science*. New York: Harper & Row, 1951; Lewin, K. Frontiers in group dynamics. *Human Relations*, 1947, 1, 5–41; Zand, D.E. Force field analysis. In N. Nicholson (ed.), *Blackwell Encyclopedic Dictionary of Organizational Behavior*. Oxford, England: Blackwell, 1995, 160–161.

22. Blood in the boardroom: More CEOs are being sacked than ever before by antsy investors and impatient directors. *Time*, November 6, 2000, 98ff; Kemp, G. How can P&G rebuild its sliding reputation? *Marketing*, June 15, 2000, 17.

23. Adapted from Maxwell, R. How do we break out of the box we're stuck in? *Fast Company*, November 2000, 260ff.

24. Cummings and Worley, 134–140; Born, D., and Mathieu, J.E. Differential effects of survey-guided feedback: The rich get richer and the poor get poorer. *Group & Organization Development*, 1996, 21, 388–404.

25. Collins, M.L. *360 Feedback: A Manager's Guide*. Plano, Tex.: Thin Book Services, 2000.

26. Voight, M., and Callaghan, J. A team building intervention program: Application and evaluation with two university soccer teams. *Journal of Sport Behavior*, 2001, 24, 420–431.

27. Meyerson, D.E. Radical change, the quiet way. *Harvard Business Review*, 2001, 79(9), 92–101.

28. Taylor, A. III. The fiasco at Ford. *Fortune*, February 4, 2002, 111–112.

29. Adapted from http://www.kmart.com, accessed April 12, 2002; Muller, J. Kmart's shopping list for survival. *Business Week*, March 25, 2002, 38.

30. R.L. Lowman, (ed.), *The Ethical Practice of Psychology in Organizations*. Washington, D.C.: American Psychological Association, 1998.

31. Adapted from Maurer, R. Working with resistance to change: The support for change questionnaire. In J.W. Pfeiffer (ed.), *The 1996 Annual—Volume 2 Consulting*. San Diego: Pfeiffer & Company, 1996, 161–174.

32. Adapted from McGill, A. How Allen Questrom saved JCPenney. *D Magazine*, April, 2002, 33–35. Used with permission.

## Integrating Cases

1. The hospital budget stipulated how many persons in each category could be employed, so this interchange of personnel among the units seemed to be the best answer to solving the problem of emergency needs and excessive patient loads in any one department.

# AUTHOR INDEX

Note: In the entry Ackroyd, S., R-8n.4 (195), R-8 refers to page R-8 in the References section at the end of the book; n.4 represents note 4 on page R-8; (195) refers to the text page where that endnote appears.

# SUBJECT AND ORGANIZATIONAL INDEX

Subject and Organizational Index

Ratio schedule, 104
Rational model
    defined, 329
    Xerox six-step process, 329
Receptors, 291
Referent power, 253
    defined, 232
Reinforcement, 96
Relationship behavior, 257
Relations-oriented role, 209
Rennalls, Matthew, 441–444
Resistance to change, 415
Restricted model of charismatic
    leadership, 276–277
Reversal technique, 338
Reward, 96
Reward power, 252
    defined, 231
Reward systems
    cafeteria-style benefit plans, 160
    countries, 162
    deciding among, 161
    flexible benefit plans, 160
    gain-sharing programs, 157–159
    high-performance work system,
      156
    profit-sharing programs, 159
    skill-based pay, 159
Rewards
    cafeteria-style benefit plans, 160
    Fleet Financial Group, 159
    flexible benefit plans, 160
    gain-sharing programs, 157
    Marshall Industries, 156
    profit-sharing programs, 159
    Scanlon plan, 158
    skill-based pay, 159
Reynolds, Chad, 451–455
Rich Products Corporation, 339
Risk propensity, 332
Risk taking, 24
Roche Company, 193
Rockford Memorial Hospital, 97
Role, 228
Role ambiguity, 175, 229
Role conflict, 175, 228
Role overload, 173
Role set, 229
Ruhl, Johnnie, 91
Rules, 357

## S

Santin Engineering, 25–26
Satisficing, 331
Scanlon plan, 158
Schedules of reinforcement, 103–106
Schnatter, John, 125
Secondary reinforcer, 96

Second-level outcomes, 130
Security needs, 120
Selective screening, 67
Self-actualization needs, 120
Self competency, see Managing self
    competency
Self-control, 107
Self-disclosure, 306
Self-efficacy questionnaire, 112
Self-esteem, 42
Self-fulfilling prophecy, 78
Self-managed teams, 199
Self-oriented role, 209
Self-serving bias, 83
Selling style of leadership, 257
Selye, Hans, 169
Semantics, 294
Sexual harassment, 176
Sexual orientation, 11
Shapiro Negotiations Institute, 238–239
Shared behaviors, 378
Shell, 422–423
Simmons Laboratories, 435
Skill-based pay, 159
Sociability, 41
Social consensus, 321
Social learning theory
    defined, 106
    forethought, 107
    organizational uses, 109–110
    self-control, 107
    self-efficacy, 108
    symbolizing, 106
    vicarious learning, 107
Socialization, 397
Sola Optical, 164–165
Southwest Airlines, 402–403
Span of control, 359
Speed, 25
Starbucks, 115–116, 160
Steelcase, 108
Stereotypes, avoiding, 20–21
Stereotyping, 76
Storming stage of team development,
    204–205
Stress
    aggressive behavior, 176–177
    behavioral effects, 179
    career development, 175
    communication technology, 175
    defined, 168
    depersonalization, 181
    effects, 178–182
    emotional effects, 179
    fight-or-flight response, 168
    hardy personality, 172–173
    impacts on health, 179
    impacts on performance, 179–180
    incivility, 176
    individual differences, 170

interpersonal relations, 175–176
    job burnout, 180
    job conditions, 174
    life stressors, 177–178
    managing, 182–186
    nature, 168–170
    organizational sources, 173–177
    past experience, 169
    perception, 169
    personality and, 170–173
    physiological effects, 179
    post-traumatic stress disorder, 179
    role ambiguity, 175
    role conflict, 175
    role overload, 173
    sexual harassment, 176
    social support, 170
    sources of, 173–178
    technology workers, 175
    Type A personality, 170–172
    Type B personality, 172
    workload, 173–174
    workplace violence, 176
Stress management
    defined, 182–183
    individual initiatives, 183–184
    modifying behaviors, 185
    organizational initiatives, 184–186
    perception, 183
    personal vision, 183
    reducing work stressors, 184–185
    stress response, 183
    stress trigger, 183
    wellness programs, 185–186
Stressors, 168
Subcultures, 386
Success attributions, 83
Sun Trust Securities, 249
Superordinate goals, 207
Suppliers, 348
Survey feedback, 423
Synergy, 281
Synovus Financial Corporation,
    389–390

## T

Tacit knowledge, 334
Task behavior, 257
Task group, 194
Task interdependence, 353
Task-oriented role, 209
TDIndustries, 377
Team building, 425
Team effectiveness, 206–214
Team empowerment, 199
Team empowerment questionnaire, 200
Team goals, 207
Team size, 208–209